Relational Database
Writings
1991–1994

C. J. Date

ADDISON-WESLEY PUBLISHING COMPANY

Reading, Massachusetts • Menlo Park, California • New York
Don Mills, Ontario • Wokingham, England • Amsterdam • Bonn
Sydney • Singapore • Tokyo • Madrid • San Juan • Milan • Paris

Library of Congress Cataloging-in-Publication Data
Date, C. J.
    Relational database writings, 1991–1994 / C. J. Date.
      p. cm.
    Includes bibliographical references and index.
    ISBN 0–201–82459–0
    1. Relational databases.
  QA76.9.D3D3726 1995
  005.75'6—dc20   94–34434
                                        CIP

Programs presented in this text are printed from
camera-ready material prepared by the author.

1 2 3 4 5 6 7 8 9 10-MA-99 98 97 96 95

I dedicate this book in sincerest respect
to the memory of the late, great Edward Abbey

About the Author

C. J. Date is an independent author, lecturer, and consultant, specializing in relational database systems. He was previously a database specialist at the IBM Santa Teresa Laboratory in San Jose, California, where he was involved in technical planning for the IBM relational products SQL/DS and DB2. He is best known for his books, in particular the *Relational Database Writings* series (of which the present book is the fourth) and *An Introduction to Database Systems,* currently in its sixth edition, which is the standard text in the field.

Preface

This book is the fourth in a series. Its predecessors were published by Addison-Wesley in 1986, 1990, and 1992, respectively. Like those earlier books, the present book consists of a collection of papers on the general topic of relational database technology—basically all those of my papers from the period 1991 to the present that seem to me to be worth preserving. The papers include four collaborative efforts, one with Hugh Darwen and three with David McGoveran.

The book is arranged into four principal parts, as follows:

    I.   Theory Is Practical!
    II. Relational Database Management
    III. The Problem of Missing Information
    IV. Relational *vs.* Nonrelational Systems

Each of these four parts has its own introduction, and I will leave further details of the papers to those introductions. There is also an afterword, containing the text of an interview I gave to *Data Base Newsletter* in 1994.

A brief note on the book's structure: As with the earlier books in this series, each of the chapters was originally intended to stand alone; thus, each typically contains sections, references, examples, etc., whose numbering is unique only within the chapter in question. To a very large degree, I have preserved the independence of individual chapters (editing out only the worst of the overlaps); thus, all references within a given chapter to (e.g.) Section 3 or Fig. 2 are to be taken as references to the indicated section or figure of the chapter in question.

Acknowledgments

Most of all, I would like to thank David McGoveran and Hugh Darwen for their major contributions to this book. I would also like to acknowledge the helpful comments received on earlier drafts of some of the chapters from various friends and colleagues: Nagraj Alur, Tanj Bennett, Charley Bontempo, Hugh Darwen, Mark Evans, Ron Fagin, Michael Jackson, John Kneiling, Adrian Larner, Albert Maier, Nelson Mattos, David McGoveran, Jim Panttaja, Mary Panttaja, Fabian Pascal, Arthur Ryman, Mike Sykes, Stephen Todd, Rick van der Lans, Anton Versteeg, Colin White, and Paul Winsberg. A special vote of thanks goes to David Stodder, Theresa Rigney, Roxane Fidler, and Andrea Pucky of *Database Programming & Design* magazine for their assistance and encouragement in connection with the papers in Part I, and to Ron Ross of *Data Base Newsletter* for allowing me to include his interview with me as the afterword. I would also like to thank my wife Lindy for her support throughout the production of this book and all its predecessors.

As for my editor, Elydia Davis, and the staff at Addison-Wesley, the best I can do is repeat what I said in the preface to earlier books in this series: Their assistance has been as friendly, obliging, and professional as it always is, and as I have come to expect. It is a pleasure to work with them.

Healdsburg, California   C. J. Date

Contents

PART I   THEORY IS PRACTICAL!

PART II   RELATIONAL DATABASE MANAGEMENT

PART III   THE PROBLEM OF MISSING INFORMATION

CHAPTER 9

Much Ado about Nothing   341

CHAPTER 10

A Note on the Logical Operators of SQL   363

PART IV   RELATIONAL *VS.* NONRELATIONAL SYSTEMS

CHAPTER 11
Essentiality   **379**

CHAPTER 12
An Inverted List System: DATACOM/DB   **387**

Publishing History

According to Date Installment Numbers 1–25
Originally published in *Database Programming & Design 5*, Numbers 9–12; *6*, Numbers 1–12; and *7*, Numbers 1–9 (September 1992 through September 1994).

An Overview of INGRES and QUEL
Originally published (in somewhat different form and with a slightly different title) in C. J. Date, *An Introduction to Database Systems: Volume I*, 5th edition, Addison-Wesley (1991).

The Primacy of Primary Keys: An Investigation
Originally published in *InfoDB 7*, No. 3 (Summer 1993).

A Normalization Problem
Originally published (in somewhat different form) in *The Relational Journal 4*, No. 2 (April/May 1992).

A New Database Design Principle
Originally published in *Database Programming & Design 7*, No. 7 (July 1994).

Updating Union, Intersection, and Difference Views
Originally published in *Database Programming & Design 7*, No. 6 (June 1994).

Updating Joins and Other Views
Originally published in *Database Programming & Design 7*, No. 8 (August 1994).

The Extended Relational Model RM/T
Originally published (in somewhat different form) in C. J. Date, *An Introduction to Database Systems: Volume I,* 5th edition, Addison-Wesley (1991).

The Third Manifesto
Previously unpublished.

Much Ado about Nothing
Originally published in *Database Programming & Design 6,* No. 10 (October 1993).

A Note on the Logical Operators of SQL
An earlier version of this paper was originally published (under the title "A Note on the Logical Operators of SQL: Part 1") in *The Relational Journal 5,* No. 1 (February/March 1993).

Essentiality
Originally published (in somewhat different form) in C. J. Date, *An Introduction to Database Systems: Volume I,* 5th edition, Addison-Wesley (1991).

An Inverted List System: DATACOM/DB
Originally published (in somewhat different form) in C. J. Date, *An Introduction to Database Systems: Volume I,* 5th edition, Addison-Wesley (1991).

A Hierarchic System: IMS
Originally published (in somewhat different form) in C. J. Date, *An Introduction to Database Systems: Volume I,* 5th edition, Addison-Wesley (1991).

A Network System: IDMS
Originally published (in somewhat different form) in C. J. Date, *An Introduction to Database Systems: Volume I,* 5th edition, Addison-Wesley (1991).

Frontend Subsystems
Originally published (in somewhat different form) in C. J. Date, *An Introduction to Database Systems: Volume I,* 5th edition, Addison-Wesley (1991).

Afterword: Marrying Objects and Relational
Originally published in two parts. Part I appeared in *Data Base Newsletter,* Vol. 22, No. 3 (May/June 1994), Part II in *Data Base Newsletter,* Vol. 22, No. 4 (July/August 1994).

PART **I**

THEORY IS PRACTICAL!

Introduction

Part I of this book contains the text—slightly revised here and there—of the first 25 installments of my regular column "According to Date," which has been appearing in the magazine *Database Programming & Design* every month since September 1992. (I may say that the title "According to Date" was not of my own choosing!) I have also included edited portions of the technical correspondence that occurred between readers and myself following some of those installments.

Basically, what I have been (and still am) trying to do in my *DBP&D* series is home in on a variety of theoretical aspects of relational technology, with the aim of explaining in lay terms just why those aspects are important and why they should be of interest to the database practitioner. Given that this was indeed the objective, the reader will appreciate the fact that the columns cover little in the way of really new ground compared with various previous publications of mine. Rather, the intent was to take issues that I had already considered more formally elsewhere and present them in a way that was deliberately less academic—more chatty, perhaps—than my usual style. In particular, I wanted the column to be a little easier to read than some of my other publications in this field, though whether I succeeded in that aim I must leave for the reader to judge.

I should add that I found the exercise of having to condense my thoughts on any particular subject into some 2,000 words or so a very valuable discipline, albeit one that was a little frustrating on occasion. For example, sometimes I could not develop themes as fully as I felt they really deserved (though when that happened, I usually cheated and divided the material up into a two- or three- part miniseries). And in a few places—I hope not too many—I might be accused of some slight oversimplification, again in the interests of space. But overall I think the discipline was good for me: It forced me to rein myself back, instead of indulging my usual tendency to try to spell out every last detail of every ramification of every topic. I hope the reader finds the resulting informal discussions useful and worthwhile.

Let me close this introduction by acknowledging the support I received with this series of columns from the editorial staff at *Database Programming & Design*—especially *DBP&D* Editor David Stodder, whose idea the column originally was, and my series editors Theresa Rigney, Roxane Fidler, and Andrea Pucky. I would also like to thank those readers who took the trouble to write in with comments and questions. A special word of thanks goes to Jim Panttaja, who read most of the installments in draft form and offered much helpful advice, some of which I followed and some of which I did not . . . Again, my thanks to all.

Theory Is Practical!

This is the first installment of what I hope will be a regular series in *Database Programming & Design*. I had better start by making it clear right at the outset that the series will probably be a trifle opinionated! I had been looking for some time for the right forum in which to air a variety of personal opinions, ideas, comments, suggestions, observations, etc., all on the general topic of databases, and so I was very pleased when David Stodder [*DBP&D* Editor] approached me at DB/Expo in San Francisco in March 1992 and offered me the opportunity to write this regular column.

Opinionated it may be, but I hope the series will also be *educational* . . . My primary objective, in the lectures I give and the classes I run, and in the books and papers I write, is always to *teach* (some might say preach). At the same time, I hope readers will also find the series entertaining, and of course useful, and on occasion challenging.

DATABASE THEORY

Enough of the preamble; let's get down to business. If there is a common theme that will run throughout this series, it is that **THEORY IS PRACTICAL**. I

Originally published in *Database Programming & Design 5*, No. 9 (September 1992). Reprinted by permission of Miller Freeman Inc.

choose this theme very deliberately, because so many people seem to believe the opposite, namely that, as Ted Codd puts it, "If something is theoretical, it cannot be practical." The truth is that theory—at least, the theory I'm talking about here, which is database theory, of course—is most definitely very practical indeed. Furthermore, much of it is not only practical, it is fundamental, straightforward, simple, useful, and it can be *fun* (as I hope to show over the next few months).

Of course, we really don't have to look any further than the relational model itself to find the most striking possible illustration of my thesis. Indeed, it really should not be necessary to have to defend the notion that theory is practical, in a context such as ours—namely, a *multibillion dollar industry* that is totally founded on one great theoretical idea. But I suppose the cynic's position would be "Yes, but what has theory done for me lately?" In other words, those of us who do think theory is important must be continually justifying ourselves to our critics. So in this first installment I would like to begin by mentioning one recent theoretical result that does indeed have obvious practical relevance.

A NEW NORMALIZATION THEOREM

"Everyone knows" that databases should ideally be designed such that all base tables are in the "ultimate"—i.e., fifth—normal form (5NF). The trouble is, few people have a good understanding of normal forms beyond third (3NF). And in between 3NF and 5NF lie all the complexities of *Boyce-Codd normal form* (BCNF), *multivalued dependence* (MVD), *fourth normal form* (4NF), *join dependence* (JD), and *fifth normal form* itself. These concepts are all so daunting, at least on the surface, that database texts and courses often don't even try to teach them but just stop at 3NF—and commercial database designs often stop there too, for much the same reason.

However, it turns out that in many cases it is possible to have our cake and eat it too—that is, it is possible to achieve 5NF without having to worry about those daunting concepts—thanks to a new theorem proved recently by Ron Fagin of IBM Research:

3NF and all keys simple implies 5NF

More precisely, if table T (a) is in 3NF and (b) is such that every key consists of exactly one column, then T is automatically in 5NF. (By "key" here, I mean what is more properly called a *candidate* key, i.e., a unique identifier. Every base table has at least one candidate key, of course, namely the primary key, but there might be others—called *alternate* keys—as well.)

Here, then, we have a very nice result that can easily be applied in practical design situations: All the designer has to do is aim for tables that satisfy requirements (a) and (b), and those tables will automatically be in 5NF. All of the "daunting concepts" referred to above can simply be ignored for such tables. Furthermore, that same nice result can also easily be incorporated into a mechanical database design tool—both as a criterion for checking the level of normalization of a given table and as a heuristic for preferring one design over another.

Of course, I don't mean to suggest that keys with more than one column are always avoidable, nor that they necessarily should be avoided, even if they can be. The complexities of BCNF, MVDs, etc., will always be relevant in some cases. What I am saying, however, is that here we have an accurate, simple characterization of a wide class of situations in which those complexities are *not* relevant, and hence situations in which the database designer's life is made a little easier.

3NF AND BCNF

While I'm on the subject of normalization, let me mention a nice definition of 3NF, due to Carlo Zaniolo, that some readers might not have seen before—a definition that has the virtue of being accurate, too, unlike some "definitions" I've seen recently. I assume the reader already understands the concept of functional dependence (FD), but let me review it briefly. We say that column C of table T is *functionally dependent* on some set of columns X of T (written $X \rightarrow C$) if and only if, whenever two rows of T have the same value for X, they also have the same value for C. For example, in the employees table

```
EMP { EMP#, SALARY, DEPT#, DEPTMGR }
```

we have the FD DEPT# $\rightarrow$ DEPTMGR, because any two employees that have the same department number must necessarily have the same department manager (assuming, of course, that every department has just one manager).

Also, we say that an FD is "trivial" if there is no way it can possibly not be true. An example is DEPT# $\rightarrow$ DEPT#; another is {EMP#,DEPT#} $\rightarrow$ DEPT#. In fact, an FD $X \rightarrow C$ is trivial if and only if the right-hand side C is contained within the left-hand side X. Of course, the term "contained" here includes the case where the container and the contained are one and the same; that is, the statement "X contains X" is true.

Here then is Zaniolo's definition:

■ Let T be a table, let X be any set of columns of T, and let C be any single column of T. Then T is in 3NF if and only if, for every FD $X \rightarrow C$ in T, at least one of the following is true:

1. X contains C (so the FD is trivial)

2. X contains a key of T

3. C is contained in a key of T

Incidentally, if we drop possibility number 3, the definition becomes a definition of *BCNF*. In other words, BCNF means that every nontrivial FD is "an arrow out of a key"; 3NF means that every nontrivial FD *either* is an arrow out of a key *or* has a target that is contained within a key. Note that BCNF implies 3NF; of course, this is well known, but the fact that a definition of BCNF can be obtained from a definition of 3NF by dropping one possibility makes it immediately and transparently obvious.

A MEDIAN PROBLEM

By now some readers might be thinking that this theory stuff is all much too eso- teric (if indeed they have even read this far and not given up in disgust). That's the trouble with theory, of course: In its attempt to be absolutely precise (which it naturally must be, to be worthy of the name), it has to adopt precise and formal definitions, and precise and formal notation, and the net effect is that it often looks very obscure and very complex. But frequently the ideas and insights underlying that precision and formalism are intuitively quite simple (as well as being very important and—I repeat—very practical). We will doubtless encounter more ex- amples of this phenomenon as this series progresses.

In an attempt to lighten the atmosphere a little, however, I will refrain from all further mention of theory (for now!) and close with a real SQL problem that you might like to try your hand at:

- Given table *T* with (numeric) column *C,* write a sequence of SQL statements to compute the median of the values in column *T.C. Note:* In general, the *median* can be found by sorting the values into sequence and then taking ei- ther the middle value or the arithmetic mean of the middle two values, de- pending on whether the number of values is odd or even. (With acknowledg- ments to Richard Hoffman of the IBM OS/2 Database Manager development team.)

I would like to include such "puzzle corner" problems as a regular feature of this column. I will give a solution to this particular problem in a future installment (Installment Number 6).

The Importance of Closure

Last month I said that my theme for this series was going to be "theory is practical." This month I want to examine another simple theoretical idea, namely **closure,** that has numerous far-reaching practical implications. Now, readers will certainly be familiar with the basic idea of closure, even if they don't know the term, because closure is a fundamental feature of ordinary arithmetic. We all know, for example, that if we add or multiply two numbers together, or subtract one number from another, we get another number. We say that numbers form a *closed system* under the operators +, −, ∗, etc., because if we take any two numbers and apply one of those operators to them, we get another number as the result. (Well, actually, there's one little exception, of course: The result of dividing a number by zero is *not* another number. I'll come back to this point later.)

One absolutely crucial consequence of the foregoing is as follows. Because the *output* from any arithmetic operation is the same kind of object as the *input,* we can use that *output* as *input* to another operation. In other words, we can write **nested arithmetic expressions**. Another way of saying the same thing is that, wherever we are allowed (in the context of an arithmetic expression) to write a number, we are also allowed to write another arithmetic expression in parentheses.

Originally published in *Database Programming & Design 5,* No. 10 (October 1992). Reprinted by permission of Miller Freeman Inc.

For example, in the expression "$a * b$," we can replace a or b by, say, "$(c + d)$"; and then we can replace c or d by another expression; and so on.

CLOSURE IN THE RELATIONAL MODEL

One of the most important facets of the relational model is, precisely, the fact that it is a closed system—because, of course, the result of performing any relational operation (join, project, union, etc.) is *another relation*. And the significance of this fact is precisely analogous to the significance of arithmetic closure as discussed above: We can write **nested relational expressions**. For instance, we can write an expression that is a projection of a restriction of a join, etc., etc. And this point in turn has all kinds of important consequences. In the rest of this installment, I want to explore a few of those consequences.

VIEW PROCESSING

A view definition is basically nothing more than a *named relational expression*. For example, the SQL view definition

```
CREATE VIEW CLERKS AS
        SELECT E#, D#, SALARY
        FROM    EMP
        WHERE   JOB = 'Clerk' ;
```

is just SQL-style syntax for a certain named relational expression (actually a projection of a restriction, with name CLERKS). When we write a query against this view—for example:

```
SELECT E#, SALARY
FROM    CLERKS
WHERE   D# = 'D2' ;
```

we are again just using SQL-style syntax for a certain relational expression *that refers to the view by name*. And what the system does in processing this query is *replace the view name by the expression that defines the view*—thus converting the query against the view to an equivalent query against the underlying base data instead. Note that it is the closure property that makes this replacement process legal (i.e., views work precisely because of closure). What we get, conceptually, is an expression that looks like this:

```
SELECT E#, SALARY
FROM    ( SELECT E#, D#, SALARY
          FROM    EMP
          WHERE   JOB = 'Clerk' )
WHERE   D# = 'D2' ;
```

And this can now be simplified to:

```
SELECT  E#, SALARY
FROM    EMP
WHERE   JOB = 'Clerk'
AND     D# = 'D2' ;
```

Of course, this example is very simple, and probably familiar in concept to most readers already. What is important to understand is that, from a theoretical standpoint, the process just described (replacing the reference to the view by the expression that defines the view) *always* works. In SQL, by contrast (at least, in SQL as implemented in many products today, and in the SQL standard), it does *not* always work. This is because SQL does *not* fully support the relational closure property—SQL expressions cannot be arbitrarily nested.*

Because of this failure on the part of SQL to adhere to the underlying theory, life gets more difficult for both users and implementers:

- **Implementers** either have to adopt a variety of *ad hoc* tricks, or else admit that certain queries don't work, or both. In DB2, for example, some queries are handled by what IBM calls "view merge" (this is the replacement technique described above); others are handled by "view materialization" (in which a copy of the view table is actually built and the query run against that copy); and others don't work at all.

- Furthermore, it is not at all easy to characterize precisely those queries that work in DB2 and those that do not—which makes the **user's** life much harder.

SAVING QUERY RESULTS

Another consequence of closure that we are all familiar with is *the ability to save query results*. Because the result of any query is always a table, we can save it *as* a table. (Have you ever stopped to think how awkward it would be if a query result was anything else?) *Snapshots* (unfortunately not supported in most of today's systems) are a useful generalization of this idea. Here is an example:

```
CREATE SNAPSHOT CLERKS AS
       SELECT E#, D#, SALARY
       FROM   EMP
       WHERE  JOB = 'Clerk'
       REFRESH EVERY DAY ;
```

Creating a snapshot is much like executing a query, except that the result of that query is saved in the database under the specified name (CLERKS in the example). The definition of the snapshot and the time of its creation are saved in the catalog. Periodically (EVERY DAY in the example) the snapshot is "re-

---

*These remarks were true of the version of the standard that was current at the time this installment was first written, namely SQL/89. The problem was fixed in the next version, SQL/92.

freshed"—i.e., its current value is discarded, the query is reexecuted, and the result of that reexecution becomes the new value. Thus, snapshot CLERKS represents the data as it was at most 24 hours ago.

Snapshots have many uses and advantages, but space does not permit me to go into details here. Let me just point out that snapshots are fundamentally what is needed for **decision support** systems.

DATA INDEPENDENCE

Here is another seemingly very simple point that has far-reaching implications. Because of closure, *there is no reason why a base table need be identical to a stored table*; it is sufficient that the base table be **derivable** from the stored tables by means of some relational expression. Thus, for example, we might store the join of two base tables (for performance reasons); ORACLE does this today. Or we might store a base table as two disjoint restrictions (again for performance reasons); DB2 does this today. And there is no reason in principle why the differences between stored and base tables should not be much greater than these two rather simple examples might suggest.

Unfortunately, however, most products today provide very little support for this idea; that is, most products today provide very much less **data independence** than relational technology is theoretically capable of. And this is precisely why we run into the notorious *denormalization* issue. Now, denormalization (for performance reasons) is certainly sometimes necessary, but *it should be done at the physical storage level, NOT at the logical (base table) level.* Because most systems today essentially equate stored and base tables, however, there tends to be much confusion over this simple point; furthermore, of course, denormalization usually has the side-effect of corrupting an otherwise clean logical design, with well-known undesirable consequences.

Note: One specific illustration of the idea that stored and base tables need not be the same is provided by **fragmentation,** a performance tactic much discussed in the context of distributed systems. The idea is to divide a given base table into distinct subtables (*fragments*) and then to store different fragments at different sites (e.g., to store rows for Dallas employees at the Dallas site and rows for Seattle employees at the Seattle site). The assumption is that most transactions will involve only local data, and hence that fragmentation will reduce the load on the communication network and improve overall performance.

CONCLUSION

There are numerous other aspects of closure (especially optimization) that I'd like to discuss, but I'm running out of space. I'm sure I'll be touching on some of those aspects in future installments. Let me conclude for now with three brief items:

1. I pointed out earlier that division by zero violates arithmetic closure—and we all know the problems that result from that violation (zero-divide exceptions, etc.). I'm pleased to be able to tell you that true relational systems do *not* suffer from any such nasty exceptions. *Note:* Installments Nos. 7 and 19 are relevant to this observation.

2. Whenever we add any new operators to a relational system, we *must* preserve the relational closure property! ORACLE's CONNECT BY extension to SQL is unfortunately an example of a violation of this requirement (it produces a result that is not a relation).

3. (This month's puzzle corner:) In ordinary arithmetic the number 0 has the property that $a + 0 = a$ for all numbers a. We say that 0 is the *identity* with respect to "+". Likewise, the number 1 is the identity with respect to "∗". What is the identity in the relational model with respect to join and Cartesian product?

TECHNICAL CORRESPONDENCE

I received a number of written comments on this installment when it was first published. First of all, Dr. Tom Johnston of Johnston Consulting, Atlanta, Georgia, took me to task on my statement that it was sufficient that base tables be derivable from stored tables by means of relational expressions. To quote his letter:

> "Relational operators transform relational objects into other relational objects. But [stored tables] are not relational objects and therefore are not subject to relational constraints. . . . The only constraint that *is* required [on the process of deriving base tables from stored tables] is that it be specifiable declaratively."

In other words, the process of deriving base tables from their stored counterparts is not limited to using relational operators only but can make use of any number of other transformations as well. I agree with this position, of course; what I was trying to do with my original statement was just to stress the point that there did not have to be a one-to-one correspondence between base and stored tables.

Second, another reader, Ms. Amy Siegel of Montclair, New Jersey, pointed out that I seemed to be contradicting myself: In an earlier book (*A Guide to DB2,* 4th edition, by C. J. Date and Colin J. White, Addison-Wesley, 1993, page 296) I had stated that a stored table *is* the physical representation of a base table. Now, I could wriggle out of this one by pretending that this latter statement refers to DB2 specifically (it is indeed true of DB2 specifically); however, I've made the same kind of statement in other, less specific contexts also, so that excuse really won't do. The fact is, this is an area (like so many others) in which my own understanding has grown over the years, and all I can do is admit my earlier error. As I wrote in this book's predecessor (*Relational Database Writings 1989–1991,* by C. J. Date and Hugh Darwen, Addison-Wesley, 1992, page 52):

". . . honesty compels me to confess that I might be partly responsible for [this] confusion: In several books . . . I have said that a base table physically exists, in the sense that there exist physically stored records . . . that directly represent that base table in storage. My apologies to any reader who may have been led astray by such remarks in the past. *Mea culpa.*"

Finally, Mr. Lawrence James of the EPA, Research Triangle Park, North Carolina, wrote to disagree with my claim that ORACLE's CONNECT BY violated relational closure. The following is an edited extract from his letter:

(Begin quote)

The result of an SQL statement using CONNECT BY is a table and can be used in another SQL statement. For example, I can create an SQL view:

```
CREATE VIEW JONES_EMP AS
       SELECT   E#, D#, SALARY
       FROM     EMP
       CONNECT BY PRIOR E# = MGR_E#
       START WITH E_NAME = 'Jones' ;
```

This view gives E#, D#, and SALARY for all employees that are subordinate to Jones, at any level. We can then write a query on this view:

```
SELECT E#, SALARY
FROM   JONES_EMP
WHERE  SALARY > 50000 ;
```

This will retrieve all employees under Jones with a salary greater than $50,000. The system processes this query—at least conceptually—by replacing the view name by the view definition and then simplifying the resulting statement to:

```
SELECT   E#, SALARY
FROM     EMP
WHERE    SALARY > 50000
CONNECT BY PRIOR E# = MGR_E#
START WITH E_NAME = 'Jones' ;
```

The CONNECT BY clause does have restrictions on its use with subqueries and joins, but it does generate a table as its result and thus satisfies the definition of closure.

(End quote)

I responded to this letter as follows:

I am grateful to Mr. James for having raised this issue. It's true, of course, that
CONNECT BY does produce a table as its result. The trouble is, however, that
table is *ordered* (furthermore, that ordering is usually "essential"; see Part IV of
this book, Chapter 11, for an explanation of this term). True relational tables, by
contrast, are not so ordered. Thus, the CONNECT BY result is not a true relational
table, and closure is violated.

By way of example, consider the bill-of-materials table shown in Fig. 1,
which is a relational representation of the tree shown in Fig. 2. The ORACLE
"part explosion" query

```
SELECT   LEVEL, MINORP#
FROM     BM
CONNECT BY MAJORP# = PRIOR MINORP#
START    WITH MAJORP# = 'P1' ;
```

will give a result that looks as shown in Fig. 3 (corresponding to a depth-first
traversal of the tree). And part of the meaning of this result is conveyed, not by
explicit data values, but rather by the *sequence* of rows in the table. Note in particular that the two rows of the form (2,P4) are *not* duplicates of one another, because
they have different meanings—one of them shows (by virtue of its position in row
sequence) that part P4 occurs at level 2 as an immediate component of part P2, the
other shows (again by virtue of its position in row sequence) that part P4 also
occurs at level 2 as an immediate component of part P3. Let me point out also that
the table has no primary key.

If this result table is now fed as input to another operation, then the information represented by the ordering of the rows will simply be lost. A trivial illustration is provided by the operation DISTINCT, which will actually eliminate one of
the two (2,P4) rows, thus quite definitely causing information to be lost. (It will
also destroy the relative sequence of the other rows, causing additional information to be lost as well.) So the relational closure property most certainly has been
violated in this example.

The difference between Mr. James's example and mine is that in his case the

BM	MAJORP#	MINORP#
	P1	P2
	P1	P3
	P2	P3
	P2	P4
	P3	P4

Fig. 1 The bill-of-materials table

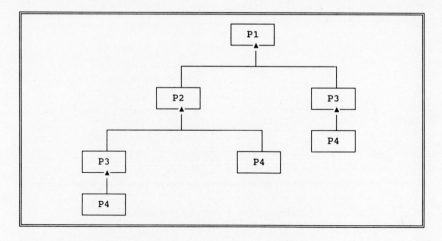

Fig. 2 Tree corresponding to Fig. 1 (with repeated nodes)

graph of the data—an organization chart—is a true hierarchy, in which each node has at most one parent. In my example, by contrast, there are nodes with more than one parent; for instance, as already mentioned, part P4 is an immediate component of part P2 and also an immediate component of part P3 (see Fig. 4). If the graph is a true hierarchy, the ordering in a CONNECT BY result *might* not matter (i.e., it might be "inessential")—whether it matters or not depends on the precise form of the query. (In fact it does matter in Mr. James's specific queries.) If on the other hand the graph is not a true hierarchy, then the ordering definitely will matter, and closure definitely will be violated.

LEVEL	MINORP#
1	P2
2	P3
3	P4
2	P4
1	P3
2	P4

Fig. 3 ORACLE "part explosion" result

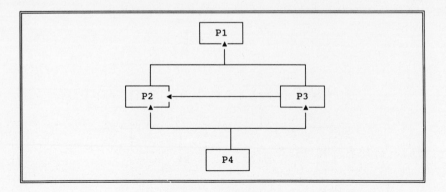

Fig. 4   "Tree" corresponding to Fig. 1 (without repeated nodes)

What's in a Name?

Last month I discussed the topic of *closure.* You will recall that closure in a relational context simply means that the result of every relational operation (join, project, union, etc.) is another relation. But what's a relation?

WHAT'S A RELATION?

Regrettably, the fact is not widely appreciated that every relation has *two parts,* which I will refer to as the *heading* and the *body*—where the heading is the column names and the body is the data. In Fig. 1, for example, the heading is the row { E#, SAL, D#, JOB } and the body is the five rows of data.

The body of a relation changes over time as a result of INSERT, UPDATE, and DELETE operations, but the heading does not change. (Well, it is true that some systems do allow you to change the heading by adding columns, dropping columns, and so on, but for present purposes such changes can be regarded as replacing the original relation by a new one with the same name. The point is not very relevant to the present discussion.)

If we are to take closure seriously, therefore, the result of every relational operation must have **a proper relational heading** (i.e., a proper set of proper

Originally published in *Database Programming & Design 5,* No. 11 (November 1992). Reprinted by permission of Miller Freeman Inc.

EMP	E#	SAL	D#	JOB
	E1	50K	D1	Clerk
	E2	45K	D1	Clerk
	E3	65K	D1	Guard
	E4	50K	D2	Guard
	E5	65K	D2	Clerk

Fig. 1 The EMP relation

column names). And why? *So that we can refer to those column names in subsequent operations*—e.g., in further relational operations nested deeper within the overall relational expression. For example, we could not even *write* an expression such as

```
rel-exp WHERE C = 3
```

if we did not know the names of the columns, such as C, of the result of evaluating *rel-exp*. In other words, we need a set of **column name inheritance rules** built into the system, such that if we know the column names of the input to any relational operation, we can predict the column names of the output from that operation.

Here is an example. Suppose we have two relations, the EMP relation from Fig. 1 and a DEPT relation with heading { D#, DNAME, BUDGET }. Then we can write an expression such as EMP JOIN DEPT; the result is the natural join of the two relations over department number (D#), with heading

```
{ E#, SAL, D#, JOB, DNAME, BUDGET }
```

In other words, the inheritance rule for JOIN is that the result has a heading consisting of the common column name(s) from the two operands (once, not twice), plus the other column names of the first operand, plus the other column names of the second operand.

The obvious question, of course, is: What if we want to do a join over columns with different names, or what if the operands have columns with the same name but those are not the columns we want to do the join over? To address such issues, we introduce a **column RENAME** operator. For example, suppose we want to do the same join as before, but the department number column in the DEPT relation is called DNO instead of D#. We can write:

```
EMP JOIN ( DEPT RENAME DNO AS D# )
```

Conceptually, the inner expression DEPT RENAME DNO AS D# returns a relation identical to DEPT, except that the DNO column is renamed D#; the JOIN operator then returns the desired overall result, as before.

What I'm proposing, therefore, is a revised version of the relational algebra in which:

- The column RENAME operator is supported
- Operations such as JOIN are done on the basis of matching column names
- All result relations have proper column names

This is not the place to go into details; a detailed discussion can be found in my book *An Introduction to Database Systems,* 6th edition, Addison-Wesley, 1995. Suffice it to say that such a version of the algebra would enable us to avoid all kinds of mistakes found in today's products, including anonymous columns, duplicate column names, ordinal position dependence, alphabetic ordering dependence, operand ordering dependence, and improper and/or unpredictable column names such as

```
EXPRESSION3
EMP.JOB
A.B.C. ... .Z.JOB
MAX.SAL
MAX(SAL)
+.A
+.A+
+.A+B
```

(etc., etc.). *Every* relation would have proper column names.

EXTEND AND SUMMARIZE

I have now laid the groundwork for introducing two very important operators, EXTEND and SUMMARIZE. Note first that the original relational algebra did not include any arithmetic or other scalar computation. Of course, real products do—I can certainly say "SELECT A+B . . ." in SQL, for example—but, strictly speaking, such capabilities are beyond the original scope of the relational algebra. Thus, we need to extend the algebra appropriately. The clean way of doing this is with the **EXTEND** operator:

```
EXTEND rel ADD scalar-exp AS col
```

For example:

```
EXTEND EMP ADD ( 0.2 * SAL ) AS INCR
```

This expression—note that it *is* an expression, not a "command" or statement—returns a relation that is identical to relation EMP except that it has an additional column called INCR, with value in any given row equal to 0.2 times the salary value in that same row. And since the result is (of course) another relation, with a proper relational heading, we can go on and apply other relational operators to it. For example, we can project it over the E# and INCR columns to produce a relation containing just employee numbers with their corresponding "increment" (INCR) values.

Note too that—because of closure—the *rel* operand of EXTEND can be *any relational expression,* in general. The same is not true of the SQL analog (which thus violates the closure property):

```
SELECT ... , 0.2 * SAL
FROM   EMP ;
```

For example, the *rel* operand in this SQL version cannot be the union of two relations.*

Note too that in the SQL version the result column corresponding to the expression 0.2 ∗ SAL has no name, at least in SQL/89 (another violation of closure). As a result, the SQL expression cannot be a subexpression nested within some larger expression, in general.

The EXTEND operator can be thought of as adding "row-wise" computation to the relational algebra. The **SUMMARIZE** operator adds "column-wise" computation:[†]

```
SUMMARIZE rel BY ( cols ) ADD aggregate-exp AS col
```

For example:

```
SUMMARIZE EMP BY ( D# ) ADD AVG ( SAL ) AS AVGSAL
```

This expression returns a relation with two columns, D# and AVGSAL, containing one row for each distinct value D# value in EMP; the AVGSAL value in any given row is the average salary for the indicated department. Here is the SQL analog:

```
SELECT D#, AVG ( SAL )
FROM   EMP
GROUP  BY D# ;
```

Note, however, that (at least in the SQL/89 standard) the "average salary" result column has no name (another closure violation). Note too that for SUMMARIZE the *rel* operand can be any relational expression, in general, whereas the same is not true for the SQL version (yet another closure violation). The consequences of

---

*The criticisms of SQL's support for EXTEND in this column were true of the version of SQL that was current at the time the column was first written, namely SQL/89; the problem was fixed in the next version, SQL/92. Analogous comments apply to the discussion of SUMMARIZE also.

[†]When this installment first appeared, it showed SUMMARIZE as having a GROUPBY clause instead of a BY clause.

these violations are analogous to those previously discussed under EXTEND; for example, it is not possible in SQL to apply a function such as AVG to a column of a union, and it is also not possible to nest an expression such as the one shown above as a subexpression within some larger expression, in general.

Incidentally, these failures (and others like them) on the part of SQL explain why certain queries against certain views don't work in some SQL systems. I touched on this point in last month's installment.

CONCLUSION

The foregoing discussions serve to illustrate another general point. I claimed in the first installment of this series that "theory is practical." I have to admit, however, that it does seem to be hard to convince people of the truth of this claim, perhaps because it tends to be quite difficult to point to some specific practical benefit that accrues from adhering to some specific theoretical prescription. On the other hand, it is, as we have seen, all too easy to show what goes wrong if that theoretical prescription is ignored! Indeed, as I've written elsewhere, relational systems are at their least attractive precisely at the points where they depart from the prescriptions of the underlying theory.

I will close as usual with a small puzzle. We are given the relation

```
EDT { E, D, T, ... }
    PRIMARY KEY { D, T }
```

where E is an event, D is a date, and T is a time. Note that the "same" E can appear any number of times in the relation. A given E is said to be a *winner* if no other E occurs on that D more times than the given E does. Use the operators discussed in this month's installment to produce the relation

```
RESULT { E, N }
      PRIMARY KEY { E }
```

containing one row for each winner E, such that for a given E, N is the number of days on which E was a winner. (For extra credit, you might like to try the same problem in SQL. Which is easier? Why?)

Why Three-Valued Logic Is a Mistake

"Everyone knows" that SQL's approach to the problem of missing information is based on **3-valued logic** (3VL). Many readers will also know that I am opposed to the 3VL approach. And out of all the many reasons for my opposition, the most important is *wrong answers*. It bothers me a great deal—and it should bother you too—that we are getting wrong answers out of our SQL systems. Furthermore, the problem is not fixable!—so long as we stay with 3VL, we will keep on getting wrong answers.

Before going any further, let me make it quite clear that my argument here is not so much with SQL *per se;* rather, it is with the underlying theory, namely 3VL, on which SQL is based. Does 3VL therefore constitute an exception to my oft-repeated claim that "theory is practical"?

Well, of course the theory in question has to be *GOOD* theory! "Good" in this context means that the theory must have a sensible *interpretation*; that is, there must exist some sensible and generally accepted correspondence between the specifics of the theory in question and phenomena in the real world. And it is my contention that 3VL does not possess any such interpretation.

Originally published under the title "Why Accept Wrong Answers?" in *Database Programming & Design 5,* No. 12 (December 1992). Reprinted by permission of Miller Freeman Inc.

BACKGROUND

I assume that readers are familiar with the following aspects of the 3VL approach:

- The use of special markers called **nulls** to represent the fact that some piece of information is missing for some reason

- The fact that if A is null or B is null or both, then a comparison such as $A \; \theta \; B$ (where θ is a comparison operator such as =, <, >, etc.) evaluates, not to *true* or *false,* but to *unknown* (this is why the logic is 3-valued—*unknown* is "the third truth-value")

- The behavior of the logical operators AND, OR, and NOT, as summarized in the following truth tables ($t = true, f = false, u = unknown$):

```
AND| t u f     OR | t u f     NOT|
---+------     ---+------     ---+---
 t | t u f      t | t t t      t | f
 u | u u f      u | t u u      u | u
 f | f f f      f | t u f      f | t
```

- The fact that when we apply a WHERE clause to some table, we get only those rows for which the conditional expression in that WHERE clause evaluates to *true,* not to *false* and not to *unknown*

WRONG ANSWERS OF THE FIRST KIND

"Wrong answer" queries come in many shapes and forms. One of the simplest and best known is illustrated by the following example:

```
SELECT E#
FROM    EMP
WHERE   JOB = 'Clerk'
OR NOT  JOB = 'Clerk' ;
```

The real world answer to this query is clearly "all employee numbers" (it is surely true of every employee that the job either is or is not "Clerk"). In 3VL, however, we will not get the employee number for any employee whose job is null. Thus, the answer that 3VL says is correct is not the answer that is correct in the real world.

Now, this example is so simple, and so familiar, that it is easy to overlook the seriousness of the error. A typical reaction on the part of 3VL proponents is "Well, of course, if you really wanted all of the employees, you should have added OR JOB IS NULL." I will return to this point in a moment. First, however, let us consider a slightly more complex example, based on the database of Fig. 1 (the "—" in that figure is meant to represent a null).

Consider the following expression, which I will refer to as *EXP1*:

DEPT	D#		EMP	E#	D#
	D2			E1	--

Fig. 1 The DEPT-EMP database

```
DEPT.D# = EMP.D#
AND EMP.D# = 'D1'
```

For the only two rows in the database, this expression evaluates to *unknown,* as the reader can easily verify. It follows that the SQL query

```
SELECT  E#
FROM    DEPT, EMP
WHERE   NOT ( DEPT.D# = EMP.D#
             AND EMP.D# = 'D1' ) ;
```

will not retrieve the employee number E1 (in fact, it will return an empty result). *But note carefully that since employee E1 does have some (unknown) department, the "—" does stand for some real value, say d.* Now, either *d* is D1 or it is not. If it is, then expression *EXP1* evaluates (for the given data) to *false,* because the term DEPT.D# = EMP.D# evaluates to *false.* Alternatively, if *d* is not D1, expression *EXP1* also evaluates (for the given data) to *false,* because the term EMP.D# = 'D1' evaluates to *false.* In other words, expression *EXP1* is always *false* in the real world, *regardless of what real value the "--" stands for.* Hence "NOT (*EXP1*)" is *true* in the real world, and the real world answer to the query is E1.

Once again, therefore, we see that the answer that 3VL says is correct is not the answer that is correct in the real world. In other words, 3VL does not behave in accordance with the way the real world behaves; that is, as I claimed earlier, it does not have a sensible *interpretation.*

WRONG ANSWERS OF THE SECOND KIND

Let me now return to the simple "Clerk" example. The general point illustrated by that example is that the truth-valued expression "*p* OR NOT *p,*" which is identically true in two-valued logic (2VL), is *not* identically true in 3VL. And, of course, there are numerous other examples of expressions that are identically true in 2VL but not in 3VL. Here are a few more:

- $x = x$
- $x > y$ AND $y > z$ implies $x > z$
- T JOIN $T = T$
- If T and U have the same heading, then T INTERSECT $U = T$ JOIN U

Now, when such a list is shown to the aforementioned 3VL proponents, the typical reaction is "So what? I'm never going to write a query that says WHERE $x = x$, or that joins a table to itself over all columns (etc., etc.). So who cares?" Needless to say, this is the *WRONG REACTION!* The point is, simple identities such as those just listed lie at the heart of the various **laws of transformation** that are used to convert queries into some more efficient form—laws, be it noted, that are used both by the *system* (when doing optimization) and by *users* (when figuring out the "best" way to state the query). And if the identities don't work, then the laws don't work. And if the laws don't work, then the transformations don't work. And if the transformations don't work, then accidents will happen.

What do I mean, "accidents"? I mean that now we have the potential for a *different kind* of wrong answer. The first kind, to repeat, arises because what 3VL thinks is correct is incorrect in real world terms. By contrast, the second kind arises because either the system or the user might be performing invalid transformations, with the result that the query the system is executing is not the query the user wanted.

Now, it is true that this second kind of wrong answer is (in principle) avoidable, but in practice it is *not* avoided. There are SQL products on the market today that perform invalid transformations. And even if there weren't, it is a virtual certainty that users would perform invalid transformations anyway.

The importance of all this cannot be overstressed. Once we know that *some* answers produced by the system might be wrong, *all bets are off*—ALL answers become suspect. And, to repeat, the problem is not fixable. So long as the system is using 3VL, "Type 1" wrong answers are guaranteed, and "Type 2" wrong answers are extremely likely as well.

WHAT IS THE SOLUTION?

The problem that nulls and 3VL are supposed to solve, namely the missing information problem, is certainly important, but I hope I have demonstrated that nulls and 3VL are not a satisfactory solution. So what do we do? The answer is that *we do what we do in the real world*—we use *default values*. For example, if we have a form to fill out, say a census form, and we are unable to answer some question on that form for some reason, we typically respond with a blank value —or a dash, or "N/A," or a question mark, etc. And each of these possible entries is, precisely, a special default value that is agreed by convention to bear a special interpretation. What we most certainly do not do is respond with a 3VL-style null. **There is no such thing as a "null" in the real world**.

The default values scheme means (among other things) that we stay firmly in two-valued logic, and the wrong answers caused by 3VL as discussed above cannot occur. Space precludes further explanation here; more details are given in the book *Relational Database Writings 1989–1991*, by C. J. Date and Hugh Darwen, Addison-Wesley, 1992.

I will return to the topic of nulls and 3VL next month—there is still a lot to be said. For now, however, let me leave you with this month's puzzle:

- Given the database of Fig. 1 (and assuming that EMP.D# is a foreign key matching DEPT.D#), show the 3VL and real-world answers to the following pseudoSQL query:

```
SELECT  E#
FROM    EMP
WHERE   MAYBE ( D# = 'D1' ) ;
```

(This is only "pseudoSQL" because it involves the logical operator MAYBE. MAYBE is defined to return *true* if its operand evaluates to *unknown, false* if its operand evaluates to *true* or *false*.)

TECHNICAL CORRESPONDENCE

When this installment first appeared, I received a letter from Leonard Gallagher, FIPS SQL Project Leader for the National Institute of Standards and Technology (NIST) in Gaithersburg, Maryland. Here are some edited extracts from that letter:

(Begin quote)

I strongly disagree with the conclusion that three-valued logic leads to "wrong answers" . . .

It is not practical to use default values for missing information in columns where every value of the data type already has a meaning, as is the case in many numeric columns . . .

An inexperienced SQL programmer may experience some confusion when first confronted with truth tables for three-valued logic. This confusion flows from the fact that NOT(*true*) is defined to be *false* instead of the **sometimes** more intuitively pleasing (*false* OR *unknown*), and that NOT(*unknown*) is defined to be *unknown* instead of the **sometimes** more intuitively pleasing (*true* OR *false*). Many of the confusing examples in the column derive from intentional obfuscation of these distinct alternatives for negation . . .

The second example examines a database in which an employee's department number is null. An unstated assumption is that the null really means the department number exists, but is missing because it is not known at the moment. This is an invalid assumption with the given schema and data. Instead, the null could mean that the value is missing because it really does not exist at all. For example, the president of a company often is not assigned to any department . . . Date's conclusion that the result is *false* is incorrect because it is based on an invalid existence assumption . . .

I close by noting that [the SQL/92 standard] provides an understandable and intuitively pleasing answer to the puzzle corner problem. The pseudoSQL query

```
SELECT  E#
FROM    EMP
WHERE   MAYBE ( D# = 'D1' ) ;
```

is easily [represented] in standard SQL by the query

```
SELECT  E#
FROM    EMP
WHERE   D# = 'D1' IS NOT FALSE ;
```

(End quote)

I responded to these comments as follows:

First, Leonard Gallagher "strongly disagrees" with my conclusion that three-valued logic (3VL) "leads to wrong answers." Well, naturally I "strongly disagree" with Gallagher! He makes a number of specific points that I wish to respond to in more detail, but the overriding and most serious criticism of his letter is that it fails to address *any* of the major objections to 3VL raised in my original column:

- The fact that 3VL does not have a sensible interpretation
- The fact that 3VL is virtually certain to lead to incorrect expression transformations on the part of either the system or the user (and probably both)
- The fact that 3VL and nulls are *not* what we use in the real world

Let me now turn to some points of detail.

1. Note first how much more complicated the question of data *interpretation* becomes in 3VL. (*Note:* The general question of data interpretation is discussed in more detail in Installment No. 7.) Consider, e.g., the relation EMP, with heading { E#, D# }. If we stay in 2VL (no nulls allowed), the interpretation of this relation is simply

"Employee E# works in department D#."

Or to spell it out more precisely:

"E# identifies an employee and D# identifies a department and employee E# works in department D#."

But if D# can be null, the interpretation becomes:

"E# identifies an employee and employee E# works in a department and *either* D# identifies that department *or* E#'s department number is unknown."*

And the more columns that can be null, the more complicated the interpreta-

---

*This interpretation assumes that the intended meaning of null is "value exists but is unknown"—see paragraph 7. In fact, since these remarks were first written, I have seriously come to doubt whether such an interpretation is even *well-formed*. See Chapter 20 of my book *An Introduction to Database Systems*, 6th edition, Addison-Wesley, 1995.

tion becomes, of course. *Exercise:* (a) State the interpretation for a relation EMP, with heading { E#, D#, JOB, SAL }, if any or all of D#, JOB, and SAL can be null; (b) state the interpretation for the projection of this latter EMP relation over D# and JOB. (I'm not at all sure how to answer part (b) of this exercise myself.)

Please note that the foregoing is *not* just an academic issue. The interpretation of a given relation is what the relation *means;* it is the *criterion for membership* in that relation. Users have to carry that meaning in their heads whenever they use the relation for any purpose whatsoever—in particular, when they insert new rows into the relation.

2. While I'm on the subject of projection, let me mention another well-known anomaly that arises over nulls. The question is whether or not two nulls are duplicates of one another. Advocates of 3VL approach this question as follows: For purposes of duplicate elimination (e.g., in PROJECT and UNION), they answer "yes"; for purposes of comparison (e.g., in RESTRICT and JOIN), they answer "no." How can this discrepancy be justified?

3. Gallagher points out that default values cannot be used for missing information in columns where every value of the data type already has a meaning. Of course this is correct. I omitted consideration of this case from my original column for space reasons; it is discussed further in my book *Relational Database Writings 1989–1991,* Addison-Wesley, 1992 (page 346). Here let me just say that it does not invalidate the overall idea of using default values.

4. I reject Gallagher's claim that default values are unpractical, since default values are precisely what we use all the time in the real world.

5. I **vigorously deny** the accusation that "many of the confusing examples in [my] column derive from intentional obfuscation . . ."! Gallagher does not seem to appreciate that his point about "distinct alternatives for negation" is *exactly* the point I'm trying to make when I say that 3VL does not have a sensible interpretation. The point is, the NOT of 3VL is *not* the "not" of ordinary English. The NOT of 3VL supports one of the "distinct alternatives for negation" and not the other.

   I further remark that in the paragraph where he makes this accusation, Gallagher makes use of the expressions "*false* OR *unknown*" and "*true* OR *false*" . . . I cannot resist pointing out that the OR in these expressions is not the OR of 3VL, it's the "or" of ordinary English. So there are "distinct alternatives" for conjunction, too.

6. Gallagher will doubtless now point out that the foregoing is precisely the reason why the constructs IS TRUE, IS NOT TRUE (etc.) were introduced in the SQL/92 standard, and of course he will be correct in so doing. But note that IS TRUE (etc.) are really additional truth-valued operators, just like NOT,

AND, and OR. So the 3VL user has to deal with six new operators, over and above the usual three operators of 2VL. Furthermore, those new operators suffer from several intuitively undesirable properties. For example, the expressions

```
NOT ( EMP.D# = 'D1' )
```

and

```
( EMP.D# = 'D1' ) IS NOT TRUE
```

are not interchangeable (because, if EMP.D# is null, the first evaluates to *unknown* and the second to *true*). In other words, "NOT TRUE" and "NOT (TRUE)" are different!

7. Gallagher is quite right in saying that (in my second example) I omitted to state the assumption that the null meant that the department number exists but is unknown. I apologize if this omission confused anybody. I feel the omission was justified, however, given the well-known fact that the behavior of nulls in SQL, and in 3VL generally, *has been defined all along* in accordance with this intended interpretation of "null."

8. Finally, I cannot resist pointing out that Gallagher himself has fallen into *EXACTLY* the kind of trap that I was warning about in my column!—his solution to the puzzle corner problem is incorrect ("IS NOT FALSE" in his solution should be replaced by "IS UNKNOWN"). It seems to me that there is probably a moral here.

Nothing in Excess

In my column last month I promised "more next time" on the subject of nulls and three-valued logic (3VL), and here it is. Now, although I think the whole 3VL approach is fundamentally misguided, it is of course necessary for present purposes to assume until further notice that we have agreed to abide by it. Furthermore, despite the fact that many of the points to be discussed are really just more nails in the 3VL coffin, they still need to be understood, if only because most of today's products do at least attempt to support 3VL. They can be regarded as areas to watch out for, or traps for the unwary.

unknown IS NOT THE SAME AS NULL

The first point to note is that *unknown* is not the same as null—i.e., the *unknown* truth value is not the same as "truth value unknown"! Suppose x is a logical variable, i.e., a variable of data type "truth value." (Of course, SQL doesn't support such a data type, but it should.) The possible values of x are, precisely, *true, false,* and *unknown*. If I say "x is *unknown*," I mean that the value of x is **known to be** *unknown*. If I say "x is null," I mean that the value of x is **not known**. So *unknown* and null are not the same thing.

To put it a different way: If x is *unknown*, then "$x = x$" yields *true;* if x is null, then "$x = x$" yields *unknown*.

Originally published in *Database Programming & Design 6*, No. 1 (January 1993). Reprinted by permission of Miller Freeman Inc.

Incidentally, SQL3 (the proposed follow-on to the SQL/92 standard) has fallen into this trap. It includes a truth value data type, called BOOLEAN; however, BOOLEAN comprises only two values, *true* and *false,* and the third truth value, *unknown,* is represented (quite incorrectly!) by null. To understand the seriousness of this flaw, the reader might care to meditate on the analogy of an "integer" data type that used null instead of zero to represent zero.

LOGICAL OPERATORS

Note: I am indebted to David McGoveran for drawing my attention to the ideas of this section.

In 2VL, there are exactly four possible monadic logical operators—one that maps both *true* and *false* into *true,* one that maps them both into *false,* one that maps *true* into *false* and vice versa (this is our old friend NOT, of course), and one that leaves them both unchanged. Likewise, there are exactly 16 possible dyadic logical operators, as indicated by the following table:

```
    |  t    f
----+-----------
 t  | t/f  t/f
 f  | t/f  t/f
```

Explanation: Replacing each of the four *t/f* specifications in the table by either *t* or *f* yields the definition of exactly one dyadic operator, because it defines the output for every possible combination of inputs. There are obviously 16 distinct ways of making the replacements.

What about 3VL? Well, there are 27 (= 3 ∗ 3 ∗ 3) possible monadic operators, because each of the three possible inputs *true, false,* and *unknown* can map to each of the three possible outputs *true, false,* and *unknown.* And there are *19,683* (= three to the ninth power) possible dyadic operators:

```
    |   t      u      f
----+---------------------
 t  | t/u/f  t/u/f  t/u/f
 u  | t/u/f  t/u/f  t/u/f
 f  | t/u/f  t/u/f  t/u/f
```

The general picture is summarized in the table below (using ∗∗ for exponentiation):

	monadic ops	dyadic ops
2VL	4	16
3VL	27	19,683
4VL	256	4,294,967,296
...	...	....
nVL	n ∗∗ n	n ∗∗ (n^2)

Now, in the case of 2VL, the four monadic operators and 16 dyadic operators can all be formulated in terms of suitable combinations of NOT and either AND or OR (this month's puzzle corner: prove this statement), so it isn't necessary to support all 20 operators explicitly. For 3VL, the following questions arise:

- What is a suitable set of *primitive* operators?
- What is a suitable set of *useful* operators?

There are also some obvious problems of proof, testing, debugging, usability, and so forth. *Note:* Regarding the distinction between "primitive" and "useful," observe that for 2VL either of the sets { NOT, AND } and { NOT, OR } is *primitive,* but the set { NOT, AND, OR } is more *useful.*

Perhaps this is the place to mention that in his "Relational Model, Version 2," Codd is requiring support not just for 3VL but also for *4*VL (in order to support an additional kind of null). Analogous (but considerably worse) difficulties clearly arise.

Incidentally, questions such as those above have never, so far as I know, been addressed by proponents of 3VL in the open database literature.*

SOME SQL ERRORS

I said last month that SQL was based on 3VL. While this statement is essentially true, it is important to realize that SQL doesn't get it quite right!—i.e., SQL manages to introduce certain additional flaws, over and above the flaws that are inherent in 3VL *per se.* Space does not permit detailed discussion here, but let me at least give a list of such flaws. *Note:* The following list is *not* exhaustive.

- The SQL EXISTS operator is not a faithful representation of the "existential quantifier" of 3VL, because it never returns *unknown.* What makes matters worse is that, in those situations where the correct 3VL answer is *unknown,* the SQL EXISTS operator returns *true* in some cases and *false* in others.
- SQL converts an empty set to null in the context of a scalar subquery comparison. Thus, if the EMP table *does* include employee E1 and does *not* include employee E7, we might incorrectly conclude from the following query that employees E1 and E7 have the same job:

```
SELECT  *
FROM    EMP
WHERE   JOB <> ( SELECT JOB
                 FROM    EMP
                 WHERE   E# = 'E7' ) ;
```

---

*See "A Note on the Logical Operators of SQL" (elsewhere in this volume) for further discussion.

- The result of applying any of the SQL aggregate functions (except COUNT) to an empty set is null (COUNT does correctly return zero; SUM should return zero also, MAX and MIN should return "minus infinity" and "plus infinity," respectively, and AVG should give "undefined"). *Note:* See Installment No. 8 for further discussion.

- The IS NULL operator is not powerful enough—its operand should be any scalar expression, not just a column name (an illustration of *closure* applied to scalar expressions, incidentally). *Note:* This problem is fixed in SQL/92.

- SQL definitely does not support all of the 19,710 possible logical operators of 3VL; in particular, it does not support MAYBE (see last month's installment). *Note:* MAYBE is supported in SQL/92, in the form of IS UNKNOWN.

The foregoing flaws in SQL have the potential of causing what we might call "wrong answers of the third kind" (see last month's installment for an explanation of the first two kinds).

unknown IS NOT A TRUTH VALUE (I)

It's time we dropped the pretense that we think 3VL is A Good Thing. The following riddle illustrates the point nicely: How many legs does a dog have, if we call a tail a leg? The answer, of course, is *four,* not five. Calling a tail a leg doesn't make it a leg.

So how many truth values are there? The answer, of course, is *two,* namely *true* and *false.* We might *SAY* that *unknown* is "a third truth value," but that doesn't make it one. After all, I might *say* that oggle-poggle is another integer, but that doesn't make it one; it has absolutely no effect on the set of all integers. Likewise, the set of all truth values just *IS* the set { *true, false* }, and there is nothing more to be said.

If we are given some proposition, say the proposition "Employee E1 works in department D1," then that proposition is either *true* or *false.* I might not know which it is, but it *is* one of the two (if it isn't, it isn't a proposition). Let's assume, in fact, that I don't know which it is. Then I certainly might say, informally, that the truth value of the proposition is unknown to me; but that "unknown" is a very different kind of object from the truth values *true* and *false* themselves. And pretending that it is the same kind of object—in other words, pretending that we have "three truth values"—is bound to lead to problems of interpretation (as of course it does).

An analogy might help. Suppose we have a box containing, let's say, 100 marbles. Now, I might not know how many marbles there are in the box, and I might therefore say that "the number of marbles is unknown" (or even "null"?); but that certainly doesn't mean that "unknown" is another integer, nor that 100 and "unknown" are the same thing. Does it?

unknown IS NOT A TRUTH VALUE (II)

A topic that we definitely need to discuss in this column sometime soon is *tables with no columns at all.** Yes, I'm serious! Without getting into a lot of detail, let me just make the following series of claims:

- Tables with no columns are important.
- A table with no columns can have either no rows at all or exactly one row. These are the only possibilities. If it has no rows at all, it is TABLE_DUM; if it has one row, it is TABLE_DEE (with acknowledgments to Hugh Darwen).
- TABLE_DUM corresponds to *false* and TABLE_DEE corresponds to *true*.

So what corresponds to *unknown?*

TECHNICAL CORRESPONDENCE

Among the letters I received when this installment was first published—several of which agreed with me that as a general principle nulls and 3VL were best avoided altogether—was one from Dr. Codd, who certainly did *not* agree with that position. His letter, and my response to it, grew into a somewhat lengthy debate that subsequently appeared as an article in its own right in a later issue of *Database Programming & Design* (see "Much Ado about Nothing," elsewhere in this volume).

Also, one reader, Joe Celko, wrote to offer some comments on multivalued logic in general. The following is a slightly edited version of his letter:

(Begin quote)

It is worth noting that multivalued logic is just as well defined as two-valued logic. The following scheme was proposed by Łukasiewicz in 1920. Any number of truth values can exist if we agree to represent them by numeric values in the range 0 (*absolutely false*) and 1 (*absolutely true*). We can then define generalized implication and negation operators, as follows:

```
p IMPLIES q  ≡  1 if p ≤ q
p IMPLIES q  ≡  1 - (p - q) if p > q
NOT p        ≡  1 - p
```

From these operators, we derive:

```
p OR q   ≡  (p IMPLIES q) IMPLIES q

p AND q  ≡  NOT (NOT p OR NOT q)

p IFF q  ≡  (p IMPLIES q) AND (q IMPLIES p)

MAYBE p  ≡  (NOT p) IMPLIES p
```

---

*See Installments Nos. 7 and 19.

Such systems have been shown to be consistent. And surprise! They look just like the SQL operators that Chris Date dislikes so much.

(End quote)

I responded to this letter as follows:

I thank Joe Celko for his comments. Let me make my position on this subject as clear as I possibly can. I don't "dislike" the three-valued logic (3VL) operators. I don't dispute the claim that 3VL (or *n*VL for arbitrary *n* greater than two) might be well-defined. I don't dispute the claim that such logics might be consistent. What I do dispute is the claim that such logics are useful for the purpose at hand— namely, dealing with missing information in databases. In Installment Number 4, I showed that answers that were correct according to 3VL were not necessarily correct in the real world. Hence, if we use a 3VL-based DBMS, we will sometimes get answers out of the system that are wrong. Further, there is no reliable way of knowing when the answers are wrong and when not. This state of affairs should be sufficient to persuade any reasonable person that 3VL is a disastrously bad approach to the problem we are trying to solve.

Also, I dispute some specific points of detail in Celko's letter.

1. First, the 3VL of SQL is not the 3VL of Łukasiewicz. Łukasiewicz's operators do not "look just like the SQL operators." In particular, if *p* is *unknown,* then Łukasiewicz defines "*p* IMPLIES *p*" to be *true,* whereas I think SQL would define it as "(NOT *p*) OR *p*," which is *unknown.* What is more, SQL's 3VL includes quantification.

2. Second, Celko's formula for MAYBE is wrong (if *p* is *true,* MAYBE *p* should be *false,* but Celko's formula gives *true*). In fact, I am extremely doubtful as to whether negation and (SQL-style) implication are sufficient to generate MAYBE (and a host of other 3VL operators).*

---

*As mentioned in an earlier footnote, I have discussed this question in more detail elsewhere—see "A Note on the Logical Operators of SQL," elsewhere in this volume.

Answers to Puzzle Corner Problems (Installment Numbers 1–5)

It's about time I gave some answers to the problems I've been including in the "puzzle corner" of previous installments in this series. My thanks and acknowledgments to those readers who wrote in with solutions of their own.

THE MEDIAN PROBLEM

Source: "Theory Is Practical!" (Installment Number 1).

Problem statement: Given table *T* with (numeric) column *C*, write a sequence of SQL statements to compute the median of the values in column *T.C. Note:* The median can be found by sorting the values into sequence and then taking either the middle value or the arithmetic mean of the middle two values, depending on whether the number of values is odd or even.

Solution:

Originally published under the title "Shedding Some Light" in *Database Programming & Design* 6, No. 2 (February 1993). Reprinted by permission of Miller Freeman Inc.

```
INSERT INTO T1 ( C )
       SELECT T.C FROM T
       UNION  ALL
       SELECT T.C FROM T ;

INSERT INTO T2 ( C )
       SELECT DISTINCT T1.C FROM T1
       WHERE  ( SELECT  COUNT (*)
                FROM    T )
          <= ( SELECT  COUNT (*)
                FROM    T1 X
                WHERE   X.C >= T1.C )
       AND    ( SELECT  COUNT (*)
                FROM    T )
          <= ( SELECT  COUNT (*)
                FROM    T1 X
                WHERE   X.C <= T1.C ) ;

INSERT INTO T3 ( M )
       SELECT AVG ( T2.C ) FROM T2 ;
```

Table *T3* (one column, one row) contains the desired result.

Explanation: First, we can avoid the slight awkwardness of not knowing whether column *T.C* contains an odd or even number of values by virtue of the following fact: The median of any given sequence of values, *S1* say, is the same as that of the "doubled up" sequence *S2* that is obtained from *S1* by replacing each value in *S1* by two copies of that value; however, sequence *S2* necessarily contains an even number of values. The purpose of the first INSERT above is to create a table *T1* that is a "doubled up" version of table *T*.

The second and third INSERTs make use of the following simple theorem, the proof of which is left as a subsidiary exercise for the reader.

Theorem: We are given the "doubled up" sequence

$$S = x[0] \leq x[1] \leq \ldots \leq x[2n-1]$$

such that $x[2i] = x[2i+1]$ for $i = 0, 1, \ldots, n-1$ (note that the median $M = (x[n-1] + x[n])/2$).

Let x be any value in S.

Let hx and lx be, respectively, the number of values in $S \geq x$ and the number of values in $S \leq x$.

Let y be any x such that $hx \geq n$ and $lx \geq n$ (note that this condition applies to $x[n-1]$ and $x[n]$ in particular, and does *not* apply to any x not equal to either $x[n-1]$ or $x[n]$).

Let $y[0] \leq y[1] \leq \ldots \leq y[2m-1]$ be all such y's. Note that every value in this sequence of y's will be equal to either $x[n-1]$ or $x[n]$—i.e., the sequence will contain at most two distinct values. Then the median M is the arithmetic mean of all distinct values in this sequence of y's. ∎

Comments:

1. Naturally I ignore the possibility that the given sequence (i.e., column *T.C*) might contain nulls.

2. For brevity I've omitted the necessary CREATE TABLEs for the intermediate and final result tables *T1, T2,* and *T3.*

3. I'm using the SQL/92 dialect of SQL, because SQL/89 simply throws too many irrelevant obstacles in the way of a straightforward solution. Specifically, I've assumed that it is acceptable (a) to use UNION in INSERT . . . SELECT and (b) to have subqueries on both sides of a scalar comparison operator in a WHERE clause. (As a matter of fact, SQL/92 would allow the entire solution to be collapsed into a single—albeit complex—SELECT statement, which among other things would obviate the need for the explicit tables *T1, T2,* and *T3.*)

4. The observant reader will note that I'm violating one of my own precepts in this solution, in that I'm explicitly allowing tables to include duplicate rows! I've argued on many occasions and in many places that duplicate rows should be avoided. But we were specifically asked for an *SQL* solution to the problem. Because the fundamental data object in SQL is not a set but a *bag,* SQL makes it hard to "do it clean" and comparatively easy to "do it dirty." The reader should not infer that we *must* use duplicate rows in order to deal with problems such as the one under discussion, nor that duplicate rows in general are a good thing.

   Note: In case the terminology is unfamiliar to the reader, I should explain that sets and bags are both unordered collections of elements; the difference is that sets never contain duplicates, whereas bags sometimes do.

5. What happens if table *T* is empty? What is the median of an empty sequence of values? The answer clearly is *undefined* (just as the average of an empty bag is undefined). The SQL solution above unfortunately gives null in this case, however.

Note added on republication: I should mention that—to my chagrin—the "solution" I originally gave for this problem in *Database Programming & Design* had not one but two bugs in it! First, I omitted the ALL from the UNION ALL in the first INSERT; second, I omitted the DISTINCT in the second INSERT (several readers spotted these errors). I can't help remarking on the fact that both of my errors had to do with duplicates—more support for my position that duplicates are *bad news.* See Installment Number 17 for further discussion.

THE IDENTITY PROBLEM

Source: "The Importance of Closure" (Installment Number 2).

Problem statement: In ordinary arithmetic the number 0 has the property that

$a + 0 = a$ for all numbers a. We say that 0 is the *identity* with respect to "+". Likewise, the number 1 is the identity with respect to "*". What is the identity in the relational model with respect to join and Cartesian product?

Solution: I will discuss this one in detail in my column next month.

THE WINNERS PROBLEM

Source: "What's in a Name?" (Installment Number 3).

Problem statement: We are given the relation

```
EDT { E, D, T, ... }
   PRIMARY KEY { D, T }
```

where E is an event, D is a date, and T is a time. Note that the "same" E can appear any number of times in the relation. A given E is said to be a *winner* if no other E occurs on that D more times than the given E does. Use relational algebra operators to produce the relation

```
RESULT { E, N }
      PRIMARY KEY { E }
```

containing one row for each winner E, such that for a given E, N is the number of days on which E was a winner.

Solution:

```
T1  :=  SUMMARIZE EDT BY ( E, D ) ADD COUNT AS CT ;
/* T1 {  E, D, CT } -- E occurs CT times on D                  */

T2  :=  SUMMARIZE T1 BY ( D ) ADD MAX ( CT ) AS CT ;
/* T2 { D, CT } -- CT is max no. of times any E occurs on D  */

T3  :=  T1 JOIN T2 ;
/* T3 { E, D, CT } -- E occurs CT times on D and no distinct */
/* E' occurs more than CT times on D                         */

T4  :=  SUMMARIZE T3 BY ( E ) ADD COUNT AS N ;
/* T4 { E, N } -- N is no. of days on which E is a winner   */
```

Table *T4* is the desired RESULT table.

Comments:

1. For simplicity I've broken the overall problem into a sequence of separate relational assignments. Note that if the system includes a delayed evaluation feature (as did, e.g., the PRTV prototype at the IBM Scientific Centre, Peterlee, England), then such a step-at-a-time approach need have no negative performance implications.

2. I haven't shown any declarations for the result tables *T1, T2, T3,* and *T4*. In

fact, a good implementation of the relational algebra would not *require* any such declarations!—a topic I might return to in a future installment.*

3. Here is an SQL analog of the foregoing solution (without annotation). I've collapsed the second and third steps from the relational algebra solution into a single INSERT statement in this SQL version.

```
INSERT  INTO T1 ( E, D, CT )
        SELECT E, D, COUNT (*)
        FROM   EDT
        GROUP  BY E, D ;

INSERT  INTO T3 ( E, D )
        SELECT E, D
        FROM   T1
        WHERE  CT =
               ( SELECT MAX ( CT )
                 FROM   T1 T2
                 WHERE  T1.D = T2.D ) ;

INSERT  INTO RESULT ( E, N )
        SELECT E, COUNT (*)
        FROM   T3
        GROUP  BY E ;
```

THE THREE-VALUED LOGIC PROBLEM

Source: "Why Three-Valued Logic Is a Mistake" (Installment Number 4).

Problem statement: Given the DEPT-EMP database shown in Fig. 1 (and assuming that EMP.D# is a foreign key matching DEPT.D#), show the three-valued logic (3VL) and real world answers to the following pseudoSQL query:

```
SELECT E#
FROM   EMP
WHERE  MAYBE ( D# = 'D1' ) ;
```

Note: The query is only "pseudoSQL" because it involves the logical operator MAYBE. MAYBE is defined to return *true* if its operand evaluates to *unknown,* *false* if its operand evaluates to *true* or *false*.

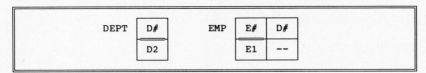

Fig. 1 The DEPT-EMP database

---

*Not in any of the installments included in the present book, however.

Solution: The 3VL answer is "E1" (employee E1's department number is null, shown as "--" in the figure). The real-world answer, by contrast, is no employee numbers at all; since EMP.D# is a foreign key, employee E1's department number cannot possibly be D1, because no such department exists. Hence the expression in the WHERE clause *must* evaluate to *false* in the real world. Once again we see that 3VL does not match reality!

OPERATORS OF TWO-VALUED LOGIC

Source: "Nothing in Excess" (Installment Number 5).

Problem statement: The four monadic and 16 dyadic operators of two-valued logic can all be formulated in terms of suitable combinations of NOT and either AND or OR. Prove this statement.

Solution: First, let *f(A)* be the monadic operator under consideration. The four possibilities are as follows:

```
f(A)    ≡    A
f(A)    ≡    NOT(A)
f(A)    ≡    A OR NOT(A)
f(A)    ≡    A AND NOT(A)
```

Now let *f(A,B)* be the dyadic operator under consideration. The 16 possibilities are as follows:

```
f(A,B)    ≡    A OR NOT(A) OR B OR NOT(B)
f(A,B)    ≡    A AND NOT(A) AND B AND NOT(B)
f(A,B)    ≡    A
f(A,B)    ≡    NOT(A)
f(A,B)    ≡    B
f(A,B)    ≡    NOT(B)
f(A,B)    ≡    A OR B
f(A,B)    ≡    A AND B
f(A,B)    ≡    A OR NOT(B)
f(A,B)    ≡    A AND NOT(B)
f(A,B)    ≡    NOT(A) OR B
f(A,B)    ≡    NOT(A) AND B
f(A,B)    ≡    NOT(A) OR NOT(B)
f(A,B)    ≡    NOT(A) AND NOT(B)
f(A,B)    ≡    (NOT(A) OR B) AND (NOT(B) OR A)
f(A,B)    ≡    (NOT(A) AND B) OR (NOT(B) AND A)
```

Incidentally, to see that we don't need both AND and OR, observe that, e.g.,

```
A OR B  ≡  NOT(NOT(A) AND NOT(B))
```

TECHNICAL CORRESPONDENCE

Several readers offered comments on or alternative solutions to the foregoing problems (in some cases both).

The Median Problem Revisited

The solution I gave for this problem above suffered from the drawback that it explicitly "took advantage" of the fact that SQL permits duplicate rows. The following solution, which is based on an idea described in a letter from Joe Celko, does not suffer from the same drawback.

```
SELECT AVG ( DISTINCT T.C ) AS M
FROM   T
WHERE  T.C IN
     ( SELECT MIN ( T.C )
       FROM   T
       WHERE  T.C IN
            ( SELECT TB.C
              FROM   T TA, T TB
              WHERE  TB.C <= TA.C
              GROUP  BY TB.C
              HAVING COUNT (*) <=
                   ( SELECT ( COUNT (*) / 2 ) + 0.5
                     FROM   T ) )
       UNION
       SELECT MAX ( T.C )
       FROM   T
       WHERE  T.C IN
     ( SELECT TB.C
       FROM   T TA, T TB
       WHERE  TB.C >= TA.C
       GROUP  BY TB.C
       HAVING COUNT (*) <=
            ( SELECT ( COUNT (*) / 2 ) + 0.5
              FROM   T ) ) ) ;
```

Explanation: Let $T*$ consist of the rows of table T ordered by ascending values of column *T.C,* and let the number of rows in $T*$ (or T) be n. Define LOW to be the first $n/2$ rows of $T*$ if n is even, or the first $(n+1)/2$ rows of $T*$ if n is odd; similarly, define HIGH to be the last $n/2$ rows of $T*$ if n is even, or the last $(n+1)/2$ rows of $T*$ if n is odd. Then the nested SELECT–FROM–WHERE beginning "SELECT MIN" returns the lowest value in HIGH, and the nested SELECT–FROM–WHERE beginning "SELECT MAX" returns the highest value in LOW. The median is the average (arithmetic mean) of these two values.

Note: Like the solution I gave originally, this solution is in fact not quite 100 percent correct. This is because, if table T is empty, the median should be *undefined,* but the SQL statement above incorrectly gives null.

Celko also points out in his letter that his approach can be adjusted to find arbitrary *quantiles.* For example, it could be used to divide the given sequence into four equal-sized subsequences, and thereby to find (e.g.) the *top quartile.* (In case you are not familiar with this concept, here is a rough definition: The top quartile of a sequence of values S is a value, v say, from S such that only 25 percent of the values in S are greater than or equal to v.)

The Winners Problem Revisited

The following single-statement SQL solution to the winners problem is due to Henry Pikner of the Federal Reserve Bank, New York:

```
SELECT  E, COUNT ( DISTINCT D )
FROM    EDT EDT1
WHERE   E IN
       ( SELECT E
         FROM    EDT EDT2
         WHERE   EDT2.D = EDT1.D
         GROUP   BY E
         HAVING COUNT (*) >=ALL ( SELECT  COUNT (*)
                                  FROM    EDT EDT3
                                  WHERE   EDT3.D = EDT1.D
                                  GROUP   BY E ) )
GROUP BY E ;
```

2VL Operators Revisited

Several correspondents, including once again Joe Celko, pointed out that in fact the operators of 2VL can all be formulated in terms of the *single* logical operator NOR, also known as the *Sheffer stroke* (usually written as a single vertical bar, "|"). Here is the truth table for this operator:

	t	f
t	f	f
f	f	t

As the truth table suggests, the operator is equivalent to "NOT . . . AND NOT . . . ." It can be thought of as "neither nor" ("neither the first operand nor the first operand is *true*"). Now we can define the familiar operators NOT, AND, and OR in terms of this operator:

```
NOT(A)   ≡  A|A
A AND B  ≡  (A|A) | (B|B)
A OR B   ≡  (A|B) | (A|B)
```

For example, let's take a look at the "*A* AND *B*" case:

A	B	A|A	B|B	(A|A) | (B|B)
t	t	f	f	t
t	f	f	t	f
f	t	t	f	f
f	f	t	t	f

This truth table shows that the expression (*A*|*A*)|(*B*|*B*) is equivalent to *A* AND *B*, because its final column is identical to the column in the truth table that defines AND:

A	B	A AND B
t	t	t
t	f	f
f	t	f
f	f	f

Since I've already shown how the operators of 2VL can all be formulated in terms of NOT, AND, and OR, the conclusion follows. *Subsidiary exercise for the reader:* NOR is thus a "generating" operator for the whole of 2VL. Can you find an operator that performs an analogous function for 3VL?

Tables with No Columns

I have some unfinished business to attend to. In my column a couple of months ago I mentioned the idea of *tables with no columns at all,* and I claimed among other things that such tables were not only possible but important. As you know, a "table" is really just a picture—an approximate picture, at that—of the mathematical construct called a *relation*. And, you see, a relation is defined to have a **set** of attributes (or columns, if you prefer) and a **set** of tuples (or rows, if you prefer).

As soon as we realize that sets are involved, we need to consider the possibility that the sets in question might be empty. In mathematics, empty sets are very definitely still sets, and theorems that hold true of sets in general are required to hold true (as far as possible) for empty sets in particular. As Hugh Darwen puts it: "When mathematicians discover rules that seem to hold true for any value of n, they detest it if $n = 0$ turns out to be an exception. So do computer programmers, for whom the undefined division-by-zero is a famous *bête noire,* and who don't like having to use a language that has forgotten to support, for instance, arrays with zero elements."

So a table should certainly be allowed to have an empty set of rows or an empty set of columns. The "empty set of rows" case is familiar, of course; it's just like a file with no records, and it's what we mean when we talk, perhaps a trifle

Originally published in *Database Programming & Design 6,* No. 3 (March 1993). Reprinted by permission of Miller Freeman Inc.

sloppily, about an "empty table." But the "empty set of columns" case is much less familiar.

TABLES AND PREDICATES

Before I can discuss this latter case any further, I need to digress for a moment to talk about *tables and predicates*. First, a **predicate** is just a *truth-valued function.* For example, the function "IN (*element, set*)," which returns *true* if the specified element is a member of the specified set and *false* otherwise, is a 2-place predicate (i.e., a truth-valued function with two parameters). Replacing the parameters by arguments—say the values "3" and "{ 9, 3, 4 }"—yields a *proposition,* i.e., an *instantiation* of the predicate, which might be *true* or *false,* in general (it's *true* in the example, of course). Likewise, the 2-place predicate > (*x,y*)—more conventionally written *x* > *y*—returns *true* if and only if the *x*-argument is greater than the *y*-argument.

Turning now to tables: The important point here is that **every table represents a certain predicate**. For instance, table EMP, with heading { E#, SAL, D# }, represents the 3-place predicate

   "Employee E# earns salary SAL and works in department D#."

Loosely speaking, this predicate is what the table *means.* Each row in the table—e.g., the row (E1,50K,D1)—represents a proposition (i.e., an instantiation of the predicate, with values replacing the parameters) that evaluates to *true.* In fact, a given combination of values (*e,s,d*) appears as a row in the table if the corresponding proposition is *true,* and does not appear in the table if the corresponding proposition is *false.* (In particular, if the table is empty, i.e., has no rows, then the meaning is that there does not exist a combination of values (*e,s,d*) such that the corresponding proposition is *true.*)

TABLES WITH NO COLUMNS

Let me now get to the main point of this discussion. Consider the table ES, with heading { E#, SAL }, that is derived from table EMP by "projecting away" column D#. The predicate for this table is

   *"**THERE EXISTS** a department D# **SUCH THAT** employee E# earns salary SAL and works in department D#."*

Thus, "projecting away" a given column is equivalent to introducing a "THERE EXISTS . . . SUCH THAT"—i.e., an *existential quantifier*—for that column into the predicate.

Now let's "project away" column E# from ES. We're left with a table S, say, with heading { SAL }, and with predicate

> *"THERE EXISTS a department D# SUCH THAT **THERE EXISTS** an employee E# **SUCH THAT** employee E# earns salary SAL and works in department D#."*

And now let's "project away" column SAL, to yield table Z, say. Table Z has *no columns at all*—its heading is the empty set, { }—and its predicate is

> *"THERE EXISTS a department D# SUCH THAT THERE EXISTS an employee E# SUCH THAT **THERE EXISTS** a salary SAL **SUCH THAT** employee E# earns salary SAL and works in department D#."*

This predicate is actually a proposition (or 0-place predicate)—it has no parameters and evaluates to *true* or *false*, unequivocally. To be specific, it evaluates to *true* if the original table EMP had any rows in it, and *false* if that table was empty.

TABLE_DUM AND TABLE_DEE

So . . . We have arrived at the notion that a table with no columns, like table Z above, is certainly acceptable from a logical standpoint. But is it *useful*? Well, of course, the answer is YES, but in order to show this I first have to consider the question of whether such a table can have any *rows*.

Note first that any such rows must be *0-tuples* (i.e., rows with no column values at all). You see, a tuple (or row) is a set too, a set of column values; and since the empty set is (as always) a perfectly respectable set, the notion of a 0-tuple is likewise perfectly respectable. Note further that there is really only one 0-tuple, because all 0-tuples are duplicates of one another! It follows that a table with no columns can have *AT MOST ONE ROW,* namely the 0-tuple. (Naturally we are interested here only in proper relational tables, which do not permit duplicate rows.)

Our table Z, therefore, can contain either one row or no rows at all; these are the only possibilities. It will contain one row if the original table EMP had any rows (and the existence of that one row means that the 0-place predicate corresponding to Z evaluates to *true*); it will contain no rows if table EMP contained no rows (and that lack of rows means that the 0-place predicate corresponding to Z evaluates to *false*). Note, incidentally, that this is all perfectly consistent with the rules for the projection operator—any projection of a table with no rows is a table with no rows, any projection of a table with one or more rows is a table with one or more rows, but with redundant duplicates eliminated.

So important are the only two possible 0-column tables that we have pet names for them: We call the one with no rows TABLE_DUM, and we call the other one TABLE_DEE (these names are due to Hugh Darwen). And, as we have seen, TABLE_DUM corresponds to *false,* or *no;* TABLE_DEE corresponds to *true,* or *yes.* This is why they're so important!—indeed, they are fundamental. One of the reasons that yes/no questions (e.g., "Does employee E1 work in department D1?") are hard to deal with in SQL is precisely because SQL does not support tables with no columns. *Note:* To remember which table is which, note that the "E"s of DEE correspond to the "E" of YES.

By the way, it is a little difficult to draw pictures of TABLE_DUM and TABLE_DEE! This is where the pictorial representation of a relation as a table breaks down slightly. Although (as we have seen) the concept of a relation with no attributes is utterly respectable, the concept of a table with no columns is somewhat counterintuitive, to say the least.

EFFECT ON RELATIONAL ALGEBRA

Have you ever wondered why the relational algebra operation *product* (more correctly, *Cartesian* product) is so called? One of the reasons is that it does behave in some respects like multiplication in ordinary arithmetic. And in ordinary arithmetic, the number 1 is the *identity* with respect to multiplication; i.e., it satisfies the property that $a * 1 = 1 * a = a$ for all numbers a. So what is the identity in the relational algebra with respect to Cartesian product?

The answer, as you will easily see, is TABLE_DEE, because T TIMES DEE = DEE TIMES $T = T$ for all tables T. The product T TIMES DEE, for example, has the same heading as T, and its body consists of all possible concatenations of a row of T with a row—actually the only row—of DEE. (As an aside, note that T TIMES DUM = DUM TIMES T = a table with the same heading as T but with no rows at all. Thus TABLE_DUM behaves a little bit like zero with respect to ordinary multiplication.)

TABLE_DEE is also the identity with respect to JOIN. And so I've now answered the puzzle corner problem from the second installment in this series ("The Importance of Closure"). For this month's puzzle corner, you are invited to consider the effects of DEE and DUM on the other relational algebra operations (restrict, project, union, intersection, difference, division, extend, summarize).

There is a great deal more to be said about TABLE_DUM and TABLE_DEE —in particular, I've only just begun to show how useful these tables can be in practice—but *(sigh)* once more I've run out of space . . .

Empty Bags and Identity Crises

Let B be a "bag" (*aka* a multiset—i.e., an unordered collection, possibly containing duplicates) of N numbers. We learned in Computer Programming 101 that the following code will compute the sum of those numbers:

```
SUM := 0 ;
for each X in B do
    SUM := SUM + X ;
```

Note the initialization step, which sets SUM to 0. In choosing this initial value, we are tacitly making use of the fact that 0 is the **identity** with respect to "+" (a concept I've mentioned in this series before). That is, 0 is the number that has the property that $X + 0 = 0 + X = X$ for all numbers X. Now, what happens if N is 0, i.e., the bag B is empty? The answer, of course, is that the final value of SUM is just its initial value, *viz.* 0. Thus we can say that *the sum of no numbers at all is 0* (the identity with respect to "+").

Exactly analogous reasoning shows that the *product* of no numbers at all is 1, the identity with respect to "*". And the *count* of no numbers at all is obviously 0. What about the *average?* Well, the average is the sum divided by the count, i.e., 0/0, which is *undefined*.

Originally published in *Database Programming & Design 6,* No. 4 (April 1993). Reprinted by permission of Miller Freeman Inc.

So now we have found some more SQL errors! In SQL, the COUNT of an empty bag is (correctly) defined to be 0; however, the SUM and AVG are both incorrectly defined to be null (SUM should give 0 and AVG should give an error). And if SQL supported a PRODUCT function, the PRODUCT of an empty bag would probably be defined to be null also (to judge by past mistakes), whereas it should in fact be 1.

MAXIMUM AND MINIMUM

Suppose we were asked to find, not the SUM, but the MAX of the numbers in *B*:

```
MAX := "minus infinity" ;
for each X in B do
    if X > MAX then MAX := X ;
```

"Minus infinity" here stands for the smallest possible value of *X* (i.e., the smallest value in the domain of *X*). It is not quite accurate to say that "minus infinity" is the identity with respect to ">", but it does play a somewhat analogous role, and it thus makes sense to define the MAX of no values at all to be "minus infinity." Similarly, "plus infinity" (the largest value in the applicable domain) plays an analogous role with respect to "<", and the MIN of no values at all is thus "plus infinity." SQL, by contrast, defines both the MAX and the MIN of an empty bag to be null.

LOGICAL OPERATORS

It is not just arithmetic operators such as "+" and "∗" that have identities. For example, the identity with respect to "‖" (string concatenation) is the empty string. And the identity with respect to the logical operator OR is *false;* that is, *p* OR *false* = *false* OR *p* = *p* for all truth-valued expressions *p*. For example, "*X* > *Y* OR *false*" means exactly the same as "*X* > *Y*": If *X is* greater than *Y,* then both expressions evaluate to *true,* otherwise they both evaluate to *false.*

It follows that the logical operator EXISTS applied to an empty bag yields *false* (and SQL does get this one right). The reason is that EXISTS is essentially just an iterated OR. To see this, consider what happens if *B* is empty in the following code, which is intended to test whether there exists a number in *B* that is greater than 3:

```
EXISTS := false ;
for each X in B do
    if X > 3 then EXISTS := true ;
```

Likewise, the identity with respect to AND is *true,* and this is why the logical operator FORALL (not supported by SQL, at least not directly) applied to an empty bag yields *true*—even when that result does not seem very intuitive! For example, "all giraffes living at the bottom of the sea are bright purple" is *true,* because the bag "all giraffes living at the bottom of the sea" is empty. Come to that, "all giraffes living at the bottom of the sea are bright orange" is *true* as well.*

A CONSEQUENCE OF THE SQL ERRORS

Let me go back to MAX and MIN for a moment. One consequence of SQL's incorrect treatment of those functions is that certain expression transformations that ought to be valid are in fact not valid in SQL. Here is an example, based on the well-known suppliers-and-parts database. The query is "Retrieve parts whose weight is greater than that of every Paris part."

First version (correct):

```
SELECT P.*
FROM   P
WHERE  P.WEIGHT >ALL
     ( SELECT P.WEIGHT
       FROM   P
       WHERE  P.CITY = 'Paris' ) ;
```

Transformed version:

```
SELECT P.*
FROM   P
WHERE  P.WEIGHT >
     ( SELECT MAX ( P.WEIGHT )
       FROM   P
       WHERE  P.CITY = 'Paris' ) ;
```

These two queries really ought to be equivalent; in the real world, if "$X >$ ALL(Y)" is *true,* then certainly "$X >$ MAX(Y)" is *true,* and vice versa. However, the transformation is not valid in SQL. Suppose the argument Y is in fact empty— i.e., there are no parts in Paris at all. In the first formulation, then, the subquery returns an empty bag; the expression in the WHERE clause of the outer SELECT thus evaluates to *true* for every part (the > ALL operator behaves like FORALL in this respect), and so every part is retrieved. In the second formulation, however, the subquery returns a null; the expression in the WHERE clause of the outer SELECT thus evaluates to *unknown* for every part, and so no parts are retrieved at all.

Note: In case the reader has forgotten, perhaps I should repeat the point from an earlier installment in this series that if transformations that ought to be valid are in fact not valid, then (as I put it previously) accidents will happen. Specifically, "wrong answers of the third kind" become a definite possibility, and even a likelihood. Refer to Installment Numbers 4 and 5 for further discussion.

---

*Perhaps a more convincing (or at least more familiar) illustration is provided by statements such as the following: "Dropping table T causes all rows of T to be automatically deleted." No one will object that this statement makes no sense if table T happens to be empty.

CARTESIAN PRODUCT

We saw last month that the identity in the relational algebra with respect to Cartesian product is TABLE_DEE, because *T* TIMES DEE = DEE TIMES *T* = *T* for all tables *T*. (Recall that TABLE_DEE is a table with no columns and one row, and its partner TABLE_DUM is a table with no columns and no rows.)

So the Cartesian product of no tables at all must be TABLE_DEE!

Now, SQL does provide functions such as SUM whose argument is a bag of *scalars*. Does it provide a Cartesian product "function" whose argument is a bag of *tables?* Yes, it does! For example, in the expression

```
SELECT ...
FROM    DEPT, EMP
WHERE   ... ;
```

the FROM clause is nothing more than SQL-style syntax for a Cartesian product "function" with argument a bag of two tables (DEPT and EMP).

It follows that, just as the argument bag of scalars in SUM is allowed to be empty, so the argument bag of tables in FROM should be allowed to be empty also. That is, we ought to be able to write a FROM clause that mentions *no tables at all*. And the result of executing such a FROM clause would be the identity with respect to Cartesian product, namely TABLE_DEE.

If this were possible, then we might write, e.g.,

```
SELECT CURRENT_TIME
FROM    ;
```

instead of the kind of silly thing we have to write today:

```
SELECT DISTINCT CURRENT_TIME
FROM    /* arbitrary table */ EMP ;
```

(And note moreover that table EMP must not be empty if this latter query is to work!) Furthermore, if we adopt the obvious convention that a FROM clause with no operands could be omitted entirely, our original query could be simplified to just

```
SELECT CURRENT_TIME ;
```

which is—at last—beginning to look fairly user-friendly. After all, why should we have to pretend that we are selecting from some table, when the item(s) being selected really don't come from any table at all?

Exercise: What would the following produce?

```
SELECT CURRENT_TIME
WHERE  1 = 0 ;
```

CONCLUSION

Not all dyadic operators have identities; for example, subtraction does not, because there is no number Z, say, such that $Z - X = X$ for all numbers X. (To be more precise, subtraction does not have a *left* identity. It does have a *right* identity, namely 0, because $Z - 0 = Z$ for all numbers Z.) Likewise, the logical "exclusive OR" operator does not have an identity either. However, I've tried to show that whenever we introduce a function whose argument is a bag (regardless of whether we use functional notation or some other syntactic style), we ought to consider what happens when that argument bag is empty. And when the function is essentially just shorthand for some iterated dyadic operator, as with SUM, EXISTS, Cartesian product, etc., then we should ensure that the empty argument case returns the appropriate identity, if there is one.

This month's puzzle corner: Give the correct "empty argument" treatment for each of the following functions. *Note:* In Cases 1–4 the argument is intended to be a bag of numbers; in Cases 5–6 it is a bag of tables all having the same (specified) heading.

1. Sum of the squares
2. Standard deviation
3. Median
4. Geometric mean
5. Union
6. Intersection

TECHNICAL CORRESPONDENCE

Quite a few readers were unhappy with my claim that the sum of an empty bag of numbers should be zero! For example, Chia-Pei Chang of Columbus RT Control Inc., Worthington, Ohio, wrote as follows (somewhat edited):

(Begin quote)

I find myself in serious disagreement . . . [Date's] reasoning appears to be flawed. [From the "Computer Programming 101" code for computing the sum of the numbers in a bag B] it is deduced that the sum of an empty bag is 0 . . . [but] the following code will also compute the sum over B:

```
COUNTER := 0 ;
for each X in B do
    begin ;
        if COUNTER = 0 then SUM := X ;
                       else SUM := SUM + X ;
        COUNTER := COUNTER + 1 ;
    end ;
```

[With this code] if *B* is empty, the sum remains undefined. Hence, it is dubious to say that "intuitive programming" should lead us to believe that the sum of an empty bag is 0 . . .

Of course, Date does not use [his Computer Programming 101 code] to prove his statement—it only provides a springboard [from] which one can delve into a more rigorous mathematical discussion. [His] claim that the sum of no numbers equals the additive identity is unfounded, however . . . Addition is a function—let's call it *f*—which takes two numbers and returns one number. The question to ask is "What is the return value of *f* when it is not called?" . . . The answer is *there is no return value*. It is similar to handing someone a blank sheet of paper and asking what number is written upon it. Seems like a very Zen question, doesn't it? However one chooses to think about the question, clearly the answer is **not** 0.

(End quote)

Well, of course, Chang is quite right to say that I was not using my code to *prove* that the sum of an empty bag should be zero—I was using it only to motivate the subsequent discussion. But I do feel bound to point out that my code abides by the principle—see Installment Number 7—that the zero case is treated just like any other (it is *not* treated as an exception), whereas Chang's code violates this principle. In any case, I feel free to *define* a SUM function that returns the sum of the numbers in *B* if *B* is nonempty and 0 otherwise. And it is my position that this function is more useful in practice than the SQL-style SUM that returns NULL if *B* is empty. Similarly for the other aggregate functions.

The problem with Chang's idea of having these functions returning nothing at all (and therefore raising an error) if the argument is empty is that then we can have a failure in the middle of a large complicated query or computation. Indeed, this fact was the original motivation for SQL returning null in such cases—i.e., *don't* fail in the middle, but let the computation continue. The trouble is, null is a disastrously bad thing to return in such a situation.

Another correspondent, Holo Devnani of Richmond Hill, Ontario, Canada, made a similar point to Chang's (with a similar piece of code). Devnani also objected to my defining the product of no numbers at all to be 1 (the identity with respect to "*"): "We know that product is repeated sum (e.g., $5 * 4 = 5 + 5 + 5 + 5$); so, if the sum is 0, how do we get the product to be 1? This implies that we can create something out of nothing. I believe this is against the known laws of physics."

To these criticisms I respond as follows: First (to repeat), I did not intend my "Computer Programming 101" code to be seen as a *proof* of the fact that (e.g.) the sum of an empty bag is zero; I simply meant it to serve as a strong motivating example for my *definition* of that fact. As for the question "If the sum is 0, how do we get the product to be 1?": A special case of the product of no numbers at all is provided by the expression n^0 (*n* to the power zero) for arbitrary *n*. And mathematics texts agree universally that this expression evaluates to 1. Another example is provided by the expression 0! (factorial 0), also universally taken to be 1.

The Power of the Keys

Readers will recall that *closure* in a relational context simply means that the result of every relational operation (join, project, union, etc.) is another relation. And in an earlier installment in this series ("What's in a Name?", Installment Number 3) I explained that relations have two parts, a heading and a body, and hence that the result of every relational operation must have a proper relational heading (i.e., a proper set of proper column names), as well as a proper relational body. Now I want to extend the idea of closure still further.

CANDIDATE KEYS

As well as a heading and a body, every relation has one or more *candidate keys*. A candidate key for a given relation R is basically just a unique identifier for R. More precisely, a subset, K say, of the columns of R is said to be a candidate key for R if and only if it satisfies the following two properties:

- *Uniqueness:*
  At any given time, no two rows of R have the same value for K.

Originally published in *Database Programming & Design 6*, No. 5 (May 1993). Reprinted by permission of Miller Freeman Inc.

■   *Irreducibility:*
No proper subset of *K* satisfies the uniqueness property.

Note that (as already stated) *every* relation does have at least one candidate key, because relations do not permit duplicate rows, and therefore the set of all columns, at least, does satisfy the uniqueness property. To see why we insist on the irreducibility property, consider relation EMP (see Fig. 1). In that relation, the combination { E#, SAL } is certainly "unique"—no two rows ever have the same value for { E#, SAL } at the same time—but it is not irreducible, because column E# is "unique," all by itself. If the system knew only that { E#, SAL } values were unique and did *not* know that E# values were unique, then it would enforce the wrong integrity constraint; for example, it would incorrectly permit the insertion of the row (E1,40K,D1,Clerk). Thus, the combination { E#, SAL } is "too big" to be a candidate key.

It is very important to understand that *all* relations, not just base relations, have candidate keys (hereinafter abbreviated to just *keys*). In the case of base relations specifically, it is normal to choose one key as the *primary* key (and any others are then said to be *alternate* keys), but this point is not very important for present purposes; so far as we are concerned here, all keys are equally significant.

KEY INHERITANCE

Now, if it is true that every relation has one or more keys, then a strong argument can be made that the system ought to know those keys (I will present such an argument in a moment). In the case of base relations, of course, the keys will be specified as part of the database definition. But what about other (i.e., derived) relations? For example, suppose we join the EMP relation of Fig. 1 to some other

EMP	E#	SAL	D#	JOB
	E1	50K	D1	Clerk
	E2	45K	D1	Clerk
	E3	65K	D1	Guard
	E4	50K	D2	Guard
	E5	65K	D2	Clerk

Fig. 1   The EMP relation

relation, say relation DEPT, with heading { D#, DNAME, BUDGET }. What keys exist in the result?

Clearly, what we need is a set of **key inheritance rules,** by which the system can deduce the keys for the result of an arbitrary relational operation. An example would be a rule that says that E# is a key for the result of the EMP-DEPT join referred to above. Given such a set of rules, the system would be able to deduce the keys for the result of *any relational expression.* And, indeed, such a set of rules can be and has been defined. This is not the place to go into details; the specifics can be found in Hugh Darwen's paper "The Role of Functional Dependencies in Query Decomposition" in our joint book *Relational Database Writings 1989– 1991,* Addison-Wesley, 1992.

PROBLEMS THAT COULD BE SOLVED

A system that implemented Darwen's rules would be in a position to solve a number of problems that exist in today's products, as I will now show. The problems in question are essentially all consequences of the fact that SQL today is driven by *syntax,* not *semantics* (keys, of course, being a "semantic" notion).

1. *The GROUP BY problem:* Consider the following query:

```
SELECT  DEPT.D#, BUDGET, AVG ( SAL )
FROM    DEPT, EMP
WHERE   DEPT.D# = EMP.D#
GROUP   BY DEPT.D# ;
```

This query is illegal in SQL, because column BUDGET is mentioned in the SELECT clause and not the GROUP BY clause. In other words, SQL does not understand that BUDGET is "single-valued per group"—i.e., that departments have only one budget. However, Darwen's rules show that D# is a key of the result relation, as well as of relation DEPT. If the system realized this fact, it could see that it is logically unnecessary to require BUDGET to be included in the GROUP BY clause as well as the SELECT clause.

Incidentally, it seems to me that this example provides a nice (albeit simple) vindication of my "theory is practical" claim. The **user** wants to write the query as shown, because it seems to make sense. The **theoretician** says yes, you can write it that way, it does make sense. It's the **pragmatist**—the *ad hoc,* no nonsense, don't-waste-my-time-with-theory person—who says no, you can't write it that way, it doesn't make sense! So here theory is definitely practical, and "pragma" is *un*practical. Analogous remarks apply to the other examples below.

2. *The DISTINCT problem:* Consider this query:

```
SELECT DISTINCT E#, D#, SAL
FROM    EMP ;
```

Note: The DISTINCT here, though logically unnecessary, is certainly not wrong. It might have been generated by some frontend—e.g., a natural language interpreter—"playing safe."

Some SQL implementations will perform badly on this query, because they will carry out an expensive and redundant sort to eliminate the (nonexistent) duplicate rows. Furthermore, if the expression is in fact a view definition, then SQL will say that the view in question is nonupdatable, because of the DISTINCT. However, it is obvious that E# is a key of the result (as well as a key of relation EMP). If the system realized this fact, it could see that the DISTINCT is effectively a no-op; no sort would be needed, and (in the view definition case) updates on the view could easily be supported.

3. *The expression transformation problem:* Here is a somewhat more complex example. Consider the following two expressions:

```
SELECT DEPT.D#, DEPT.BUDGET
FROM    DEPT, EMP
WHERE   DEPT.D# = EMP.D#
AND     EMP.E# = 'E1' ;

SELECT DEPT.D#, DEPT.BUDGET
FROM    DEPT
WHERE   DEPT.D# IN
    ( SELECT EMP.D#
      FROM    EMP
      WHERE   EMP.E# = 'E1') ;
```

These two expressions are semantically equivalent—both represent "department number and budget for the department employing employee E1"—but they are (obviously) syntactically different. Most SQL implementations will fail to recognize the semantic equivalence—and hence interchangeability—of the two expressions, and will accordingly perform differently on the two. Moreover, there is at least one system, namely DB2, in which a view defined using the first expression is considered to be updatable, whereas a view defined using the second is not. But Darwen's rules can be used to show that the two expressions are indeed semantically equivalent; again, therefore, a system understanding those rules will be able to behave "intelligently." (Space does not permit me to go into more details on this one, unfortunately.)

4. *The view updatability problem:* Consider the following view definition:

```
CREATE VIEW ESB AS
    SELECT E#, SAL, BUDGET
    FROM    EMP, DEPT
    WHERE   EMP.D# = DEPT.D# ;
```

Most SQL systems (and the SQL/92 standard) consider this view to be non-updatable. However, Darwen's rules tell us that E# is a key of the view (as well as of EMP), and hence that the view is at least updatable with respect to columns E# and SAL.*

FUNCTIONAL DEPENDENCIES

I have said that Darwen's rules allow the system to deduce keys for the result of any relational expression. While this statement is undeniably true, it would be very wrong of me to leave matters at that. What Darwen's rules actually do is allow the system to deduce the *functional dependencies* (FDs) that hold in the result of any relational expression. Here is a definition of functional dependency (repeated from the first installment in this series): Column C of relation R is *functionally dependent* on some set of columns X of R (written $X \to C$) if and only if, whenever two rows of R have the same value for X, they also have the same value for C. And, you see, when we say that keys are "unique," what we mean, precisely, is that if K is a key of relation R, then the FD $K \to C$ holds true for ALL columns C of R. Hence, if the system knows the FDs, it can deduce the keys! But knowing the FDs actually means *more* than just knowing the keys. This is another candidate topic for some future installment.

Note: Darwen's work on FD and key inheritance makes use of the following theorem. Let A, B, C, and D be subsets of the set of columns of relation R such that $A \to B$ and $C \to D$. Then (using "$\cup$" for union and "$-$" for set difference) $A \cup (C - B) \to B \cup D$. This month's puzzle (harder than usual!): Prove this theorem.

---

*See Chapters 5 and 6 in Part II of this book for an extended discussion of view updatability.

Expression Transformation (Part 1 of 2)

In several previous installments in this series I've mentioned the idea of transforming a given relational expression into another, logically equivalent expression. Such transformations constitute one of the two great ideas at the heart of relational optimization (the other, beyond the scope of the present discussion, being *database statistics*). In this installment and the next, I want to examine the question of expression transformation in some detail.

AN EXAMPLE

I will start with a simple example, in order to give some idea of the dramatic performance improvements that can be achieved by means of a suitable expression transformation. The example makes use of the well-known suppliers-and-parts database, which includes two relations, S (suppliers), with primary key { S# }, and SP (shipments), with primary key { S#, P# }. The query is:

```
( SP JOIN S ) WHERE P# = 'P2'
```

Originally published under the title "Inside Relational Optimizers" in *Database Programming & Design 6*, No. 6 (June 1993). Reprinted by permission of Miller Freeman Inc.

(loosely, "find supplier information for suppliers who supply part P2, together with the corresponding quantities"). Suppose the database contains 100 suppliers and 10,000 shipments, of which 50 are for part P2. If the system were simply to evaluate the expression by brute force, without any optimization at all, the sequence of events would be as follows:

1. *Join relations SP and S (over S#).* This step involves reading the 10,000 shipment rows; reading each of the 100 supplier rows 10,000 times (once for each of the 10,000 shipments); constructing an intermediate result consisting of 10,000 joined rows; and writing those 10,000 joined rows back out to the disk.

2. *Restrict the result of Step 1 to just the rows for part P2.* This step involves reading 10,000 rows but produces a relation consisting of only 50 rows, which I assume can be kept in main memory.

The following procedure is equivalent to the one just described, in the sense that it produces the same final result, but is obviously much more efficient:

1. *Restrict relation SP to just the rows for part P2.* This step involves reading 10,000 rows but produces a relation consisting of only 50 rows, which again I assume can be kept in main memory.

2. *Join the result of Step 1 to relation S (over S#).* This step involves the retrieval of the 100 supplier rows (once only, not once per P2 shipment, because all the P2 shipments are in memory). The result contains 50 rows (still in main memory).

The first of these two procedures involves a total of 1,030,000 row I/O's, whereas the second involves only 10,100. It is clear, therefore, that if we take "number of row I/O's" as our performance measure, then the second procedure is a little over 100 times better than the first. (In practice, of course, it is *page* I/O's that matter, not row I/O's, but we can ignore this refinement for present purposes.) It is also clear that we would like the implementation to use the second procedure rather than the first!

ANALYSIS

Just as the first procedure above is effectively a direct implementation of the original relational expression, so the second is effectively a direct implementation of the relational expression

```
( SP WHERE P# = 'P2' ) JOIN S
```

These two expressions are thus semantically equivalent, but as we have seen they have very different performance implications. Hence, if the system is presented with the first expression, we would like it to **transform** that expression into the second before evaluating it. And this is what expression transformation is all about. The relational algebra, being a high-level formalism, is subject to various formal **laws** of transformation. For example, there is a law that says that a join followed by a restriction can be transformed into a restriction followed by a join (I was using this law in the example). And a good relational optimizer will know these laws, and will apply them—because, of course, the performance of a query ideally should *not* depend on the specific syntax used to express that query in the first place.

So we see that expression transformation is capable of yielding dramatic performance improvements (a factor of over 100 to 1 in the case at hand). Thus, optimizability, in the sense of expression transformation, is actually a *strength* of relational systems: It is precisely the fact that relational queries are expressed at a high semantic level that makes them optimizable in the first place. (At the risk of beating a dead horse, let me point out how difficult—impossible?—it would be to optimize the query if it had been expressed in old-fashioned, prerelational, row-at-a-time procedural code.) On the other hand, of course, the example also shows that the optimization must be done!—for otherwise the system will probably display unacceptable performance. This is why I've stated elsewhere that optimization represents "both a challenge and an opportunity for relational systems."

Note, incidentally, that the transformations we are talking about can be applied without any regard for either actual data values or physical storage structures (indexes, etc.) in the database as stored. In other words, such transformations represent optimizations that are *virtually guaranteed to be good,* regardless of what the database physically looks like.

LAWS OF TRANSFORMATION

Space does not permit an exhaustive discussion of all of the possible laws of transformation here. I will therefore concentrate on a few important cases and key points. First, the law I used in the example was actually a specific case of a more general law, called the **distributive** law. We say that the monadic operator *f distributes* over the dyadic operator • if $f(A•B) = f(A) • f(B)$ for all A and B. In ordinary arithmetic, for example, SQRT (square root) distributes over multiplication, because

```
SQRT ( A * B )  =  SQRT ( A ) * SQRT ( B )
```

for all A and B. Therefore an arithmetic expression optimizer can always replace either of these expressions by the other when doing arithmetic expression transformation. (As a counterexample, SQRT does *not* distribute over addition, because the square root of $A + B$ is not equal to the sum of the square roots of A and B, in general.)

In relational algebra, the restriction operator distributes over union, intersection, and difference. It also distributes over join, provided the restriction condition consists, at its most complex, of the AND of two separate conditions, one for each of the two join operands. In the case of the original expression in the example, this requirement was indeed satisfied—in fact, the restriction condition was very simple and applied to just one of the operands—and so we could use the distributive law to replace the expression by a more efficient equivalent. The net effect was that we were able to "do the restriction early." Doing restrictions early is almost always a good idea, because it serves to reduce the number of rows to be scanned in the next operation in sequence, and probably reduces the number of rows in the output from that next operation too.

Here are a couple more specific cases of the distributive law, this time involving projection. First, the project operator distributes over union and intersection (but not difference!). Second, it also distributes over join, so long as all of the joining columns are included in the projection. These laws can be used to "do projections early," which again is usually a good idea, for reasons similar to those given above for restrictions.

Two more important general laws are the laws of **commutativity** and **associativity**. We say that the dyadic operator • is *commutative* if $A \bullet B = B \bullet A$ for all A and B. In ordinary arithmetic, for example, multiplication and addition are commutative, but division and subtraction are not. In relational algebra, union, intersection, and join are all commutative, but difference and division are not. So, for example, if a query involves a join of two relations A and B, the commutative law tells us that it doesn't matter which of A and B is taken as the "outer" relation and which the "inner." The system is therefore free to choose (say) the smaller relation as the "outer" one in computing the join.

Note: It is only fair to the reader to point out that join is, very regrettably, *not* commutative in SQL!—owing to the fact that SQL attaches significance to the left-to-right sequence of columns in a table (so that *A* JOIN *B* and *B* JOIN *A* differ in their result column sequences; recall that left-to-right column sequence is not part of the relational model). At best, this unfortunate fact makes life harder for both users and the system; at worst, it degrades performance.

Anyway, let's get back to our main discussion. We say that the dyadic operator • is *associative* if $A \bullet (B \bullet C) = (A \bullet B) \bullet C$ for all A, B, C. In arithmetic, multiplication and addition are associative, but division and subtraction are not. In relational algebra, union, intersection, and join are all associative, but difference and division are not. So, for example, if a query involves a join of three relations $A, B,$ and C, the associative and commutative laws together tell us that we can join the relations together in any order we like. The system is thus free to decide which of the various possible sequences is most efficient.

CONCLUDING REMARKS

In closing (for now), let me emphasize the fundamental importance of **closure** to everything we have been discussing. Closure means that we can write nested expressions, which means in turn that a single query can be represented by a single expression, not by a multistatement procedure; thus, the optimizer does not have to perform any flow analysis. Also, those nested expressions are recursively defined in terms of subexpressions, which permits the optimizer to adopt a variety of "divide and conquer" evaluation tactics. And, of course, the various general laws I've been discussing (distributivity, etc.) would not even begin to make sense if we did not have the closure property.

I will have more to say on this topic in my column next month. For now, let me leave you with this month's puzzle, namely as follows: Prove the following statements (making them more precise, where necessary).

- A sequence of restrictions against a given relation can be transformed into a single restriction.
- A sequence of projections against a given relation can be transformed into a single projection.
- A restriction of a projection can be transformed into a projection of a restriction.

One last question: The union operator is said to be **idempotent,** because *A* UNION *A* ≡ *A* for all *A*. As you might expect, idempotence can also be useful in expression transformation. Which other relational operators (if any) are idempotent?

Expression Transformation (Part 2 of 2)

Last month I discussed the basic idea of expression transformation, and explained the crucial relevance of that idea to relational optimization. In particular, I showed how the general laws of *distributivity, commutativity,* and *associativity* applied to relational operators such as projection and join. In this installment I want to explore several further aspects of this same general issue.

OTHER TYPES OF EXPRESSION

It is not just relational expressions that are subject to transformation laws. For instance, we already know from last month that certain transformations are valid for **arithmetic** expressions; e.g., the expression

    A * B + A * C

can be transformed into

    A * (B + C)

Originally published under the title "Relational Optimizers Part II" in *Database Programming & Design 6,* No. 7 (July 1993). Reprinted by permission of Miller Freeman Inc.

by virtue of the fact that "$*$" distributes over "$+$". A relational optimizer needs to know about such transformations because it will encounter arithmetic expressions in the context of the relational EXTEND operator (see "What's in a Name?", Installment Number 3).

Note, incidentally, that this example illustrates a slightly more general form of distributivity. Last month, I defined distributivity in terms of a *monadic* operator distributing over a *dyadic* operator; I said that the monadic operator f distributes over the dyadic operator $\bullet$ if $f(A \bullet B) = f(A) \bullet f(B)$ for all A and B. In the case at hand, however, "$*$" and "$+$" are both *dyadic* operators. In general, we say that the dyadic operator $*$ distributes over the dyadic operator $\bullet$ if $A * (B \bullet C) = (A * B) \bullet (A * C)$ for all A, B, C (in the example above, take $*$ as "$*$" and $\bullet$ as "$+$").

Let me turn now to **truth-valued** expressions. Suppose A and B are columns of two distinct relations. Then the truth-valued expression

```
A > B AND B > 3
```

(which might be part of a query) is clearly equivalent to—and can therefore be transformed into—the following:

```
A > B AND B > 3 AND A > 3
```

The equivalence is based on the fact that the comparison operator "$>$" is **transitive**. Note that this transformation is certainly worth making, because it enables the system to perform an additional restriction (using the condition "$A > 3$") before doing the greater-than join required by the condition "$A > B$". To repeat a point I made last month, doing restrictions early is generally a good idea; having the system *infer* additional "early" restrictions, as here, is also a good idea.

Note: The technique just discussed is implemented in IBM's DB2 product (among others), where it is referred to as "predicate transitive closure."

Here is another example: The truth-valued expression

```
A > B OR ( C = D AND E < F )
```

can be transformed into

```
( A > B OR C = D ) AND ( A > B OR E < F )
```

(this transformation makes use of the fact that OR distributes over AND). More generally, any truth-valued expression can be transformed into an equivalent expression in what is called **conjunctive normal form** (CNF). A CNF expression is an expression of the form

```
C1 AND C2 AND ... AND Cn
```

where each of *C1, C2, . . . , Cn* is, in turn, a truth-valued expression (called a *conjunct*) that involves no ANDs. The advantage of CNF is that a CNF expression is *true* only if every conjunct is *true;* equivalently, it is *false* if any conjunct is *false.*

Since AND is *commutative* (*A* AND *B* is the same as *B* AND *A*), the optimizer can evaluate the individual conjuncts in any order it likes; in particular, it can do them in order of increasing difficulty (easiest first). As soon as it finds one that is *false,* the whole process can stop.

Furthermore, in a parallel processing environment, it might even be possible to evaluate all of the conjuncts in parallel. Again, as soon as one yields *false,* the whole process can stop.

It follows from all of the above that the optimizer needs to know about properties such as distributivity that apply, not only to **relational** operators such as join, but also to **comparison** operators such as ">"; **logical** operators such as AND and OR; **arithmetic** operators such as "+"; and probably others as well.

SEMANTIC TRANSFORMATIONS

For my next example, I return to the suppliers-and-parts database (see last month's installment). Consider the following expression:

```
( SP JOIN S ) [ P# ]
```

("join relations SP and S over S# and project the result over P#"; the square brackets represent the projection operation). Now, the join here is a *foreign-to-primary-key join;* it matches a foreign key in relation SP with the primary key of relation S. It follows that every row of relation SP does join to some row in relation S; every row of relation SP therefore does contribute a P# value to the overall result. In other words, there is no need to do the join!—the expression can be simplified to just

```
SP [ P# ]
```

("project relation SP over P#").

And, of course, this transformation will give a wonderful improvement in performance (in general), because joins are not free (in general).

Note very carefully, however, that this transformation is valid *only* because of the semantics of the situation. In general, each of the operands in a join will include some rows that have no counterpart in the other operand, and hence do not contribute to the overall result. In general, therefore, transformations such as the one just illustrated are not valid. In the case at hand, however, every row of relation SP *must* have a counterpart in relation S, because of the integrity constraint (actually a referential constraint) that says that every shipment must have a supplier, and so the transformation is valid after all.

A transformation that is valid only because a certain integrity constraint is in force is called a **semantic** transformation (and the resulting optimization is called a semantic optimization). Now, it is important to understand that *any integrity constraint whatsoever* can be used in semantic optimization (i.e., the technique is not limited to just referential constraints). Suppose, for example, that the suppliers-and-parts database is subject to the constraint "All red parts must be stored in London," and consider the query:

Find suppliers who supply only red parts and are located in the same city as at least one of the parts they supply.

This is a fairly complex query! By virtue of the integrity constraint, however, we see that it can be transformed into the much simpler form:

Find London suppliers who supply only red parts.

We could easily be talking about several orders of magnitude improvement in performance here. (*Exercise for the reader:* Give formulations of these two queries in (a) the relational algebra, (b) SQL.)

So far as I know, few products if any do much in the way of semantic optimization at the time of writing. In fact, most don't even support the ability to *state* the integrity constraints, except for a few special cases (e.g., referential constraints). But they should! First of all, of course, we want the system to *enforce* those constraints, a topic I plan to return to sometime soon.* Second, we have seen how those constraints could be used to obtain *major* performance improvements— much greater improvements, very likely, than are obtained by any of today's more traditional optimization techniques.

OPTIMIZATION INHIBITORS

There is one last topic I want to mention before leaving the subject of expression transformation, and that is *optimization inhibitors*. The fact is, DBMS products today do include certain features that inhibit the optimizer's ability to do expression transformation. And users should at least be aware of those features, even though (in most cases) there's not much they can do about them! The features in question are:

1. Duplicate rows
2. Three-valued logic (3VL)
3. SQL's implementation of 3VL
4. Dynamically deferred constraints

Item #1 here is a big topic in its own right, one that I want to discuss in detail in a future installment;[†] here I will just say that duplicate rows should be avoided, for performance reasons if for no other. Items #2 and #3 I've discussed in previous installments (see Installment Numbers 4 and 5); in particular, I showed how they

---

*See Installment Numbers 14–16.
[†]Installment Number 17.

could lead to what I called *wrong answers of the second and third kind,* respectively, precisely because of their unfortunate impact on expression transformation. (I might also mention that I was tacitly ignoring 3VL in my discussion of truth-valued expressions above. The transformations I was talking about don't all work with 3VL.)

So that leaves just item #4, **dynamically deferred constraints**. As you might expect, this item is relevant to *semantic* optimization. When I was discussing semantic optimization, I was tacitly assuming that the integrity constraints in question were always enforced, and thus always satisfied by the database. Some systems, however, provide a means for the user to *disable* certain constraints at any time, and then later to (re)*enable* them, again at any time; IBM's SQL/DS is a case in point. And while the constraint is disabled, it's not being enforced (that's the whole idea, of course). But note the implication: When the constraint is not being enforced, there is no guarantee that it is satisfied by the database. And this state of affairs can occur at any time. And the optimizer does not know when it might occur. So the optimizer cannot use the constraint to do semantic transformations! (and we have just shot ourselves in the foot).

Note: The situation is not so bad if COMMIT forces all constraints back into the enabled mode (as it does in the SQL/92 standard), because the optimizer then does at least know that all constraints are satisfied at transaction boundaries. But if constraints can stay disabled across transaction boundaries, as they can in SQL/DS, then their usefulness for semantic optimization purposes is severely undermined.

I will close with this month's puzzle, which is (mostly) repeated from Installment Number 4 ("Why Three-Valued Logic Is a Mistake") and is intended to illustrate *wrong answers of the second kind.* The database is shown in Fig. 1 (the "—" represents a null); the two tables DEPT and EMP are meant to satisfy the obvious primary-to-foreign-key relationship.

Now consider the SQL query:

```
SELECT  E#
FROM    DEPT, EMP
WHERE   NOT ( DEPT.D# = EMP.D#
              AND EMP.D# = 'D1' ) ;
```

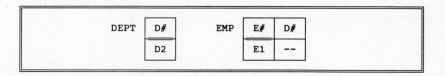

Fig. 1 The DEPT-EMP database

Show (a) the correct real-world answer to this query, (b) the answer delivered by the query as stated, and (c) the answer delivered if the optimizer applies "predicate transitive closure."

Answers to Puzzle Corner Problems (Installment Numbers 7–11)

My column this month is devoted once again to answering the various outstanding "puzzle corner" problems from previous installments. Thanks again to those readers who wrote in with their own solutions.

THE DEE AND DUM PROBLEM

Source: "Tables with No Columns" (Installment Number 7).

Problem statement: What are the effects of DEE and DUM on the relational algebra operations union, intersection, difference, restrict, project, division, extend, and summarize?

Solution: The following discussion is based on material from Hugh Darwen's chapter on DEE and DUM in our joint book *Relational Database Writings 1985–1989,* Addison-Wesley, 1990.

First, perhaps I should remind the reader that DEE and DUM are the only

Originally published under the title "Solving the Puzzles" in *Database Programming & Design 6,* No. 8 (August 1993). Reprinted by permission of Miller Freeman Inc.

possible instances of a relation with no columns. DEE has exactly one row (the 0-tuple) and DUM has no rows at all. Now, the only possible relations that are compatible with DEE and DUM for the purposes of union, intersection, and difference are DEE and DUM themselves. We have:

```
union  | DEE DUM      intersection | DEE DUM      difference | DEE DUM
-------+--------      -------------+--------      -----------+--------
  DEE  | DEE DEE              DEE  | DEE DUM             DEE | DUM DEE
  DUM  | DEE DUM              DUM  | DUM DUM             DUM | DUM DUM
```

In the case of difference, the first operand is shown at the left of the table and the second at the top (for the other operators, of course, the operands are interchangeable). Note how reminiscent these tables are of the truth tables for OR, AND, and AND NOT, respectively; of course, the resemblance is not a coincidence!

Turning now to restrict and project, we have:

- Any restriction of DEE yields DEE if the restriction condition is *true,* DUM if it is *false*.
- Any restriction of DUM yields DUM.
- Projection of any table over no columns yields DUM if the original table is empty, DEE otherwise. In particular, projection of DEE or DUM, necessarily over no columns at all, returns its input.

The following remarks on division assume a *generalized form* of the division operator (one that permits any table to be divided by any table)—another topic for future discussion!*

- Any table *T* divided by DEE yields *T*.
- Any table *T* divided by DUM yields an empty table with the same heading as *T*.
- DEE divided by any table *T* yields *T*.
- DUM divided by any table *T* yields an empty table with the same heading as *T*.
- Any nonempty table divided by itself yields DEE. An empty table divided by itself yields DUM.

Extend and summarize:

- Extending DEE or DUM to add a new column yields a relation of one column and the same number of rows as its input.

---

*See Installment Number 20.

■ Summarizing DEE or DUM (necessarily over no columns at all) yields a relation of one column and the same number of rows as its input.*

THE EMPTY ARGUMENT PROBLEM

Source: "Empty Bags and Identity Crises" (Installment Number 8).

Problem statement: Give the correct "empty argument" treatment for each of the following functions. *Note*: In Cases 1–4 the argument is intended to be a bag of numbers; in Cases 5–6 it is a bag of tables all having the same (specified) heading.

1. Sum of the squares
2. Standard deviation
3. Median
4. Geometric mean
5. Union
6. Intersection

Solution:

1. 0
2. Undefined
3. Undefined
4. 1
5. An empty table with the specified heading
6. A table with the specified heading and with body equal to the Cartesian product of all underlying domains

Regarding Case 3 (median), refer to the discussion of the median in my previous collection of answers (Installment Number 6).

Note: In the same installment (Number 8), I also asked what the following hypothetical SQL query would produce:

```
SELECT CURRENT_TIME
WHERE  1 = 0 ;
```

The answer, of course, is a table of one column and no rows. The query is equivalent to the relational algebra expression

---

*Regarding summarize, note that if (a) the operand is DUM rather than DEE, and (b) the aggregate expression involves AVG or any other operator that is undefined for an empty operand, the effect will be to raise an exception. See the section "Technical Correspondence" at the end of this installment.

```
EXTEND DUM ADD CURRENT_TIME AS X
```

except that the SQL version yields a column with no user-known name.

THE GENERAL UNIFICATION THEOREM

Source: "The Power of the Keys" (Installment Number 9).

Problem statement: Darwen's work on FD and key inheritance makes use of the following theorem. Let A, B, C, and D be subsets of the set of columns of relation R such that $A \rightarrow B$ and $C \rightarrow D$. Then (using "$\cup$" for union and "$-$" for set difference) $A \cup (C - B) \rightarrow B \cup D$. Prove this theorem.

Solution: The following discussion is excerpted from Hugh Darwen's chapter on the subject in our joint book *Relational Database Writings 1989–1991*, Addison-Wesley, 1992. Space does not permit much explanation; refer to that book for background and further details.

First we state, without proof, some simple theorems that we need to use in the proof (here "$\equiv$" means *if and only if* or *is equivalent to*, "$\Rightarrow$" means *if . . . then . . .* or *implies*).

- *Self-determination:* $A \rightarrow A$
- *Joint dependence:* $A \rightarrow B \;\&\; A \rightarrow C \equiv A \rightarrow B \cup C$
- *Transitivity:* $A \rightarrow B \;\&\; B \rightarrow C \Rightarrow A \rightarrow C$
- *Composition:* $A \rightarrow B \;\&\; C \rightarrow D \Rightarrow A \cup C \rightarrow B \cup D$

Proof:

1. $A \rightarrow B$	(given)
2. $C \rightarrow D$	(given)
3. $A \rightarrow B \cap C$	(by joint dependence and 1)
4. $C - B \rightarrow C - B$	(self-determination)
5. $A \cup (C - B) \rightarrow (B \cap C) \cup (C - B)$	(by composition, 3, 4)
6. $A \cup (C - B) \rightarrow C$	(simplifying 5)
7. $A \cup (C - B) \rightarrow D$	(by transitivity, 6, 2)
8. $A \cup (C - B) \rightarrow B \cup D$	(by composition, 1, 7)

This completes the proof. ∎

EXPRESSION TRANSFORMATION PROBLEMS

Source: "Expression Transformation" (Part 1, Installment Number 10; Part 2, Installment Number 11).

Problem statement: Prove the following statements (making them more precise, where necessary).

- A sequence of restrictions against a given relation can be transformed into a single restriction.
- A sequence of projections against a given relation can be transformed into a single projection.
- A restriction of a projection can be transformed into a projection of a restriction.

Solution: I will content myself with simply making the statements more precise (the proofs are very easy). First, if *C1* and *C2* are both restriction conditions for relation *R,* then the following two expressions are obviously equivalent:

```
( R WHERE C1 ) WHERE C2

R WHERE C1 AND C2
```

Second, if *L1* is a subset of the heading of relation *R* and *L2* is a subset of *L1,* then the following two expressions are obviously equivalent:

```
( R [ L1 ] ) [ L2 ]

R [ L2 ]
```

Both of the transformations just illustrated can be useful during view processing. Recall from "The Importance of Closure" (Installment Number 2) that the first step in processing a query against a view is to replace the view name by the expression that defines the view. Thus, if a view *V* is defined as (say) *R* WHERE *C1,* and the user issues a query of the form *V* WHERE *C2,* this first step will yield an expression of the form (*R* WHERE *C1*) WHERE *C2.* The optimizer can then go on to simplify this expression to the form *R* WHERE *C1* AND *C2.* And this simplification is certainly worthwhile, because it implies a single scan over the relation *R,* whereas the unsimplified form implies two separate scans.

Incidentally, this discussion also serves to illustrate another general point, namely that many of the laws of transformation used by the optimizer are useful, not so much in transforming the original query, but rather in transforming the output from a previous transformation. In other words, what the optimizer does is transform the original query, then transform the output from that transformation, then transform the output from *that* transformation, and so on, until it reaches a point where it judges—according to some builtin set of heuristics—that it has reached the "optimal" representation of the original query.

To complete the discussion of the original problem: If *L* and *C* are, respectively, a subset of the heading of relation *R* and a restriction condition for relation

R that involves only columns mentioned in *L,* then the following two expressions are obviously equivalent:

```
R [ L ] WHERE C

( R WHERE C ) [ L ]
```

Note that it is generally a good idea to do restrictions before projections, because the effect of the restriction will be to reduce the size of the input to the projection, and hence reduce the amount of data that needs to be sorted for duplicate elimination purposes.

In the same installment, I also asked which relational operators other than union were *idempotent.* (Union is said to be idempotent because A UNION $A \equiv A$ for all A.) It turns out that intersection and natural join are the only other idempotent operators (within the relational algebra as usually defined).

Note: I should mention in passing that, very regrettably, these operators are *not* idempotent in SQL!—owing to the unfortunate fact that SQL permits duplicate rows. Thus, e.g., if table A contains just two rows and those rows happen to be identical, then A UNION A contains just *one* row. By the way, SQL's UNION ALL doesn't help, either; A UNION ALL A contains *four* rows!

The final problem was as follows: We are given the database shown in Fig. 1 (the "—" represents a null); the two tables DEPT and EMP are meant to satisfy the obvious primary-to-foreign-key relationship. We are also given the SQL query:

```
SELECT E#
FROM    DEPT, EMP
WHERE   NOT ( DEPT.D# = EMP.D#
              AND EMP.D# = 'D1' ) ;
```

Show (a) the correct real-world answer to this query, (b) the answer delivered by the query as stated, and (c) the answer delivered if the optimizer applies "predicate transitive closure."

Solution: In English, the query means, loosely, "Find employee numbers for employees who are not in department D1." The point about the problem is that there is no way the null in the D# position in table EMP can possibly stand for D1, because department D1 does not exist. Thus, (a) the real-world answer to the

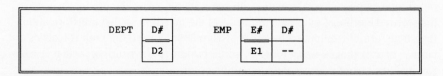

Fig. 1 The DEPT-EMP database

query is E1; (b) the answer delivered by the query as stated, however, is empty; (c) if predicate transitive closure is applied, the answer delivered is E1. (*Note:* Predicate transitive closure will extend the parenthesized conditional expression to include the term AND DEPT.D# = 'D1'.)

Note, however, that the fact that answers (a) and (c) are the same is a fluke! Predicate transitive closure *does not work*— i.e., the transformation is invalid, in general—under three-valued logic. At the risk of beginning to sound like a broken record, therefore, I will point out that once again we see that three-valued logic does not match reality.

TECHNICAL CORRESPONDENCE

I received a letter from David M. Fyffe of Microsoft Corp., Redmond, Washington, asking for further clarification of what should happen if an aggregate operator is applied to an empty bag and the result is *undefined*. Let's take a look at an example:

```
SUMMARIZE EMP BY ( D# )
          ADD AVG ( SAL )
          AS AVGSAL
```

If table EMP is empty (i.e., contains no rows), the average salary is undefined and the AVG invocation will raise an exception. However, a good language—following ALGOL 60—would include the following construct as a legal expression (and I would certainly want such a construct in *my* database language!):

```
IF exp1 THEN exp2 ELSE exp3
```

Here *exp1* is a conditional expression and *exp2* and *exp3* are type-compatible expressions. The overall expression evaluates to *exp2* if *exp1* is *true* and to *exp3* if *exp1* is *false*. (Incidentally, SQL/92 does provide something like this construct via its new CASE operator.)

Then—assuming that table EMP cannot be guaranteed to be nonempty—I would rewrite the SUMMARIZE example above as follows:

```
SUMMARIZE EMP BY ( D# )
ADD ( IF IS_EMPTY ( EMP ) THEN 0
ELSE AVG ( SAL ) )
AS AVGSAL
```

(assuming that 0 is the answer we want if the AVG argument turns out to be empty).

In the "Technical Correspondence" section of an earlier installment (Installment Number 8), I pointed out that one of the original motivations for SQL's defining the AVG (etc.) of an empty bag to be null—instead of raising an exception—was to avoid the possibility of a failure "in the middle of a large complicated query or computation." I submit that the mechanism sketched above provides a much superior approach to this same problem. It is superior because (a) it avoids the need for nulls and three-valued logic, (b) it does not usurp a decision that rightfully should be the user's, and (c) it provides the user with finer-grained control of exceptional situations.

How We Missed the Relational Boat

Between the idea
And the reality . . .
Falls the Shadow

—The Hollow Men (T. S. Eliot)

It is undeniably true that today's relational products—perhaps "relational" products, with relational in quotes, would be more apt—have failed in all too many ways to realize the full potential of relational technology. And the reason for this sorry state of affairs is, of course, that "relational products" today means, very specifically, **SQL** products. There is an enormous gulf between what the relational model prescribes or recommends and what the SQL language actually supports— and it is that gulf that is directly responsible for the aforementioned sorry situation.

Perhaps unsurprisingly, this issue is one that I feel very strongly about! The community sees SQL products and thinks they are relational. Hence, SQL flaws are seen as relational flaws, and legitimate criticisms of *products* are taken, quite erroneously, as criticisms of *the relational model* instead. I believe it is high time the community was made aware **IN NO UNCERTAIN TERMS** that SQL is very far from being truly relational. In this month's column, therefore, I would like to identify some of the many ways in which SQL departs from the prescriptions of the model—with the hope that the overall quality of debate in this area might thereby be raised somewhat.

Note added on republication: I wish I had made it clearer when this installment was first published that my criticisms were not aimed so much at the original

---

Originally published under the title "How SQL Missed the Boat" in *Database Programming & Design* 6, No. 9 (September 1993). Reprinted by permission of Miller Freeman Inc.

SQL language designers in IBM. Those people made a reasonably good job of what they were trying to do at the time, which was, primarily, to design *some* interface for a relational prototype (System R) that would serve to convince the world that relational database management was a viable technology—in particular, that a relational system could be built with acceptable performance. Rather, my criticisms are directed at the *process* by which a prototype language that is demonstrably flawed can be elevated lock, stock, and barrel (without any significant attempt to correct its obvious shortcomings) to commercial product and standard status.

PRELIMINARY REMARKS

As usual, there are several things I need to get out of the way before I can get on with my real message. Perhaps the most important from a practical perspective is the first one:

1. Even though SQL has so many problems, I am *NOT* saying you should not invest in an SQL DBMS! EVERYONE has to "get with" SQL—it's the only game in town. And indeed, SQL is unquestionably much better than what we had before (e.g., DL/I). What is so frustrating is that it could have been much better again—*at no extra cost* (in fact, I suspect it would have been cheaper to do it right).

2. It is possible to criticize SQL on numerous additional counts, over and above its shortcomings *vis-à-vis* the relational model; indeed, I've done so myself elsewhere (see references [5] and [6]). As I put it in reference [6]: "There are well-established principles for the design of languages, but there is little evidence that SQL was designed in accordance with any such principles" (slightly paraphrased). In other words, SQL is a fairly bad language *qua* language, quite apart from its relational shortcomings. Here, however, I want to examine it from a purely relational perspective.

3. E. F. Codd has also criticized SQL from a relational perspective. In his book [1], he identifies the following three "serious flaws" in SQL:

   - It permits duplicate rows.

   - Its attempt to use "IN subquery" as a way to avoid the need for certain constructs of the relational algebra and/or relational calculus was inadequately investigated at the time—and, of course, it subsequently failed. (An ironic failure, incidentally, since the "IN subquery" construct was the major justification for the existence of SQL in the first place.)

   - It does not support three-valued logic (3VL) adequately, and it does not support four-valued logic (4VL) at all.

I certainly agree with Codd on the first of these points. I also agree with him on the second, though this one is really more of a general language design criticism than it is a relational one (it is the direct cause of much of the very unfortunate and debilitating *redundancy* that permeates the SQL language [5,6]). Third, I also agree that SQL's support for 3VL is flawed; however, as I've explained in this series before, I think the whole idea of using multi-valued logic as a basis for dealing with missing information is misguided anyway, and hence Codd and I are somewhat at odds on this one. In any case, SQL suffers from many, many more relational flaws than just these three, as I will show.

4. I make little claim for originality in what follows; many other people have also discussed SQL's relational shortcomings, notably Hugh Darwen in references [2] and [3].

5. Please note that my criticisms are directed primarily at the **Full SQL/92** level of SQL. Current products, which support a much lower level of SQL than Full SQL/92, suffer from numerous other defects as well! And let no one think the criticisms are "purely academic," by the way. On the contrary, every one of them has very direct practical implications—not least in the huge amount of 3GL code that needs to be written (and maintained) in order to circumvent the problems.

6. Space does not permit detailed discussion of each and every criticism in the list. Rather, my aim is just to provide a kind of catalog of the issues, for purposes of subsqent reference. The reader will probably realize that it would be possible to write a whole book on this subject! Maybe I will, some day.

7. Finally, my basis for comparison purposes is the relational model as described in reference [4]. I will structure my discussion into *objects, operators,* and *integrity,* although the boundaries between these categories are not totally clearcut, as the reader will quickly see.

OBJECTS

Domains: Informally, we can divide domains into two kinds, system-defined and user-defined. System-defined domains are simply the builtin data types (INTEGER, FLOAT, etc.); user-defined domains are, precisely, user-defined data types, of potentially arbitrary complexity. Regarding system-defined domains, here I will only remark that SQL, incredible though it may seem, does not support the most fundamental data type of all!—namely, a Boolean or truth-valued data type. This is one reason why yes/no queries are so awkward in SQL; it is also the reason why there are no *true* and *false* literals, and why you cannot write "SELECT EXISTS(. . .)" to test for the existence of something.

As for user-defined domains, it is obvious that SQL does not allow users to define their own data types (in any significant sense of that term) *at all.* Specifically, therefore, SQL does not support:

- Strong typing, including in particular checking that the operands of a *comparison* are of the same type (as a consequence, SQL also does not have a proper notion of "union-compatibility")

- Subtypes and supertypes, with type inheritance

- User-defined operators or functions (for both system- and user-defined types)

- Conversions from one user-defined type to another

Note: SQL/92 did add support for a construct it calls a domain (it also added a CAST operator for converting a specified scalar value to a specified data type or specified domain). However, those SQL/92 "domains" would much better be referred to as just "shared column definitions," since that is effectively all they are. They are certainly not true user-defined data types, with all that that term implies.

Tables: SQL tables are not necessarily relations, because they do not necessarily prohibit duplicate rows (I've already promised to address this topic in more detail in a future installment,* so I will omit further discussion here). In addition:

- Candidate and primary key declarations (for *base* tables) are optional, not required.

- All SQL tables have a left-to-right column ordering.

- Although every column in every *named* table (i.e., base table or view) has a user-known name that is unique within the table in question, such is not always the case for *unnamed* tables (i.e., intermediate and final result tables).

- SQL tables must have at least one column—i.e., TABLE_DEE and TABLE_DUM are not supported (see "Tables with No Columns," Installment Number 7). As a consequence, SELECT-lists and FROM-lists must both be nonempty.

- Values in columns of tables cannot be tables in turn—i.e., tables cannot be nested; this is another topic we need to discuss in detail some time soon!†

- Although SQL does now support the definition of views of arbitrary complexity and queries of arbitrary complexity against such views—neither of which it did prior to SQL/92—it still does not support view updating as fully or systematically as it should.

---

*See Installment Number 17.

†Unfortunately not in any of the installments included in this volume. The interested reader is referred to Hugh Darwen's paper "Relation-Valued Attributes" in our joint book *Relational Database Writings 1989–1991,* Addison-Wesley, 1992.

- SQL does not support snapshots.

- SQL has no direct support for table assignment (i.e., the ability to assign a specified derived table to a specified named table).

- SQL has no direct support for table comparison (e.g., the ability to test two tables for equality).

OPERATORS

Closure: SQL does not adequately support the relational closure property with respect to either (a) column naming (see "What's in a Name?", Installment Number 3), or (b) key inheritance (see "The Power of the Keys," Installment Number 9). The consequences of these omissions are legion; some of them were spelled out in the earlier installments just mentioned.

Fundamental properties violated: Because SQL tables possess a left-to-right column ordering, the SQL NATURAL JOIN operation is not commutative—i.e., *A* NATURAL JOIN *B* is not the same as *B* NATURAL JOIN *A*. And because SQL tables permit duplicate rows, the SQL NATURAL JOIN, UNION, and INTERSECT operations are not idempotent—e.g., *A* UNION *A* is not the same as just *A*.

Missing operators: SQL's support for the column RENAME operator is inadequate (see "What's in a Name?", Installment Number 3), because its use is optional where it should be compulsory. SQL also does not support the generalized version of restriction (see reference [4]). It also does not directly support the universal quantifier FORALL, nor any form of DIVIDE operator. (Regarding this latter, however, it is only fair to point out that there is some debate as to what such direct support for DIVIDE should look like. This is another topic that I've already promised to address in a future installment.)* It also does not directly support any "single-row" INSERT, UPDATE, or DELETE operators (which are admittedly not primitive, but can be very useful in practice—again, see reference [4]). And finally, it does not support recursive queries (needed for bill of materials and similar applications).

Empty-table errors: SQL makes very heavy weather over empty tables (i.e., tables with no rows). For example, SELECT–FROM–HAVING on an empty table incorrectly yields one group instead of zero groups. The aggregate functions SUM, AVG, MAX, and MIN applied to an empty table all incorrectly yield null (see "Empty Bags and Identity Crises," Installment Number 8). And in the context of a

---

*See Installment Number 20.

scalar-to-subquery comparison, an empty table is incorrectly converted to a single-row, single-column table containing a null (see "Nothing in Excess," Installment Number 5).

Problems related to 3VL: I've already said that I don't think 3VL support is a good idea anyway. However, I do think that if it *is* supported, then it should be supported *right* (insofar as that may be possible). Here are some places where SQL's support is at best problematic:

- The SQL EXISTS operator is not a faithful representation of the existential quantifier of 3VL, because it never returns *unknown,* even when *unknown* is the logically correct result.

- The SQL UNIQUE operator (which is intended to test whether the rows of a specified SQL table are all distinct) also never returns *unknown,* even when *unknown* is the logically correct result.

- The NOT in IS NOT TRUE, IS NOT FALSE, and IS NOT UNKNOWN is not the NOT of 3VL, because (e.g.) "IS NOT TRUE" means "IS FALSE OR IS UNKNOWN," whereas "NOT TRUE" in 3VL means "FALSE."

- It is not known whether SQL's support is *complete,* in the sense that it supports all of the 19,710 possible logical operators of 3VL (see "Nothing in Excess," Installment Number 5). *Exercise for the reader:* Determine whether SQL's support is indeed complete or not.*

- I remark also in passing that the possibility that some component within a multicolumn key value (candidate or foreign) can be null while some other component is not leads to an inordinate amount of complexity in the rules governing the behavior of such keys.

Finally, SQL does not adequately support a user-defined default value mechanism that would allow users to avoid the snares and pitfalls of 3VL if they wanted to (see reference [7] for a discussion of what such adequate support might look like).

INTEGRITY

I plan to discuss the general question of integrity in a series of installments beginning next month. Here I will just summarize the major issues regarding SQL's support for integrity *vis-à-vis* the requirements of the relational model.

- SQL's support for domain constraints is unnecessarily and undesirably complex, and indeed confuses some very fundamental concepts that would be better kept separate.

---

*See "A Note on the Logical Operators of SQL" elsewhere in this volume.

- SQL does not support transition constraints.

- Its support for deferred constraints is at least partly procedural, not declarative.

- It does not provide any direct support for declaring (and hence exploiting) functional dependencies.

- It does not support empty keys (i.e., keys—candidate or primary or foreign— that involve no columns).

- It does not support integrity constraints of any kind against nonbase tables (e.g., declaration of candidate keys for a view).

FURTHER ISSUES

There is one more major item to add to the foregoing shameful litany—namely, SQL's **lack of orthogonality**. Now, this is a criticism of SQL/89 and today's products rather than a criticism of SQL/92 *per se,* but it is so important that I would be very remiss if I didn't at least mention it here. A full explanation of the significance of the term "orthogonality" is unfortunately beyond the scope of the present discussion; however, I must and will point out two immediate consequences of the lack of same in SQL/89.

1. Relational algebra expressions can be nested to arbitrary depth, but the corresponding SQL expressions cannot (see "The Importance of Closure," Installment Number 2, and "What's in a Name?", Installment Number 3).

2. SQL aggregate function references cannot be nested at all (e.g., there is no direct way to find the average of a collection of sums).

Both of these shortcomings have the consequence that some queries are impossible to express. What makes matters worse is that it's not even easy to say which ones are possible and which impossible, owing to the *ad hoc* and redundant nature of the language. Thus, it is often very difficult to figure out whether or not a given query can even be done in SQL!

Now, the improved orthogonality of SQL/92 goes part way to addressing the foregoing problems—i.e., the desired nesting effect can be achieved via certain circumlocutions—but those circumlocutions are often of such byzantine complexity that quite simple real-world queries can still be grotesquely difficult to express. See reference [8] for several illustrations.

Finally, there is another issue that needs to be raised but does not fit neatly into any of the three categories "objects," "operators," or "integrity" (rather, it spans all three), and that is the issue of *a clean logical/physical separation.* Now, the SQL/92 standard quite rightly limits itself to logical matters only. Real products, however, add all kinds of *ad hoc* "physical" features to their implementation of those logical matters in the interests of "completeness," "efficiency," "pragmatism," and so forth, with serious negative consequences. It goes without saying that such "physical" features would never be exposed to the user in a true relational system; the standard should have been expressly *pro*scriptive with respect to such matters, as well as being *pre*scriptive with respect to logical matters.

CONCLUDING REMARKS

I hope I've said enough to show (as I claimed at the outset) that SQL is very far from being truly relational. However, it is perhaps only fair to point out that the SQL/92 standard does not *claim* to be relational. Indeed, the term "relation" is never mentioned in the standard document at all! Of course, this fact does *NOT* constitute an acceptable excuse for the shortcomings identified above (and would not do so even if it were not the case that SQL originally *was* intended, quite definitely, to be relational).

I will close as always with a puzzle corner problem, due this month to my friend David McGoveran. We are given a set of tables T1, T2, . . . , TN. Each row in each table is either *valid* or *invalid* for some reason (i.e., either does or does not represent a true proposition about "the real world"). We are also given another table T0 with two columns, TABLE (value a table name) and VALIDITY (value an integer). The row (Ti,n) appears in T0 if and only if the statement "exactly n rows are valid in table Ti" is valid ($0 \leq n \leq$ the number of rows in Ti). All tables are initially empty. Can we or can we not insert the row (T0,0) into table T0?

A COMMENT ON REPUBLICATION

When I first published this installment, I fully expected to be inundated by letters from outraged defenders of the *status quo*. It seems to me an interesting comment on the situation that the number of such letters I received was exactly *zero*.

REFERENCES

1. E. F. Codd, *The Relational Model for Database Management Version 2* (Reading, Mass.: Addison-Wesley, 1990).

2. Hugh Darwen (writing as Andrew Warden), "Adventures in Relationland," in C. J. Date, *Relational Database Writings 1985–1989* (Reading, Mass.: Addison-Wesley, 1990).

3. Hugh Darwen, "The Askew Wall," in C. J. Date and Hugh Darwen, *Relational Database Writings 1989–1991* (Reading, Mass.: Addison-Wesley, 1992).

4. C. J. Date, "Notes Toward a Reconstituted Definition of the Relational Model Version 1 (RM/V1)," in C. J. Date and Hugh Darwen, *Relational Database Writings 1989–1991* (Reading, Mass.: Addison-Wesley, 1992).

5. C. J. Date, "What's Wrong with SQL?", in *Relational Database Writings 1985–1989* (Reading, Mass.: Addison-Wesley, 1990).

6. C. J. Date, "Some Principles of Good Language Design" and "A Critique of the SQL Database Language," both in *Relational Database: Selected Writings* (Reading, Mass.: Addison-Wesley, 1986).

7. C. J. Date, "The Default Values Approach to Missing Information," in C. J. Date and Hugh Darwen, *Relational Database Writings 1989–1991* (Reading, Mass.: Addison-Wesley, 1992).

8. David McGoveran, "The Database Connectivity Benchmark Specification" (Boulder Creek, Calif.: Alternative Technologies, 1993).

A Matter of Integrity (Part 1 of 3)

Everyone knows that data integrity is important. I have recently been surprised to discover, however, that what many people do *not* seem to know is that it is possible, and highly desirable, for integrity to be managed **declaratively** instead of procedurally. In Installment Number 11, I promised I would address the topic of integrity soon, and the time is clearly ripe.

Before I go any further, let me make it clear that I am concerned here with integrity constraints of *arbitrary complexity*—what some people call "business rules." I am *not* limiting myself to such matters as entity and referential integrity, which are merely special cases of the more general problem. For example, I would like to be able to declare an integrity constraint that says that no employee is allowed to earn more than his or her manager (see the section "Single *vs.* Multi-Row Rules" later). I definitely do not want to have to write procedural code to enforce this constraint.

Note: I have written on this subject before, notably in references [2] and [3]. Much of the material of this month's column (and that of the next two months—this is a big subject!) is based on material from those two sources.

Originally published under the title "A Matter of Integrity" in *Database Programming & Design 6*, No. 10 (October 1993). Reprinted by permission of Miller Freeman Inc.

DECLARATIVE *VS.* PROCEDURAL

If you go back to E. F. Codd's very first (1969) paper on relational theory [1], you will find a brief discussion of the idea of stating integrity constraints declaratively. And many, many subsequent books and papers, by Codd and many other people, have elaborated on this theme. Indeed, relational advocates have always taken it as an article of faith that declarative integrity support was a *sine qua non* for a good relational system.

(In fact, of course, the foregoing is just a special case of the more general relational position that declarative support, if feasible, is better than procedural support for *anything*. In a nutshell, declarative support means that the system does the work instead of the user. This is why we have declarative queries, declarative view definitions, declarative cursor definitions, and so on.)

Of course, most relational products have not provided much in the way of declarative integrity support. Some vendors, in fact, have quite specifically emphasized the opposite approach!—*viz.*, procedural support, using stored or triggered procedures (an issue I will return to in Part 3 of this discussion, the month after next). Perhaps this state of affairs accounts for the claims we sometimes hear to the effect that "integrity is not part of the relational model" or "the relational model has no semantics" (and many similar misconceptions). To protect the guilty I will not give any specific quotes and sources here, but I have, as I said earlier, been very surprised at the lack of understanding displayed by numerous writers in this area, even quite recently.

INTEGRITY RULES

Let's begin by looking at a simple example:

```
CREATE INTEGRITY RULE ER3
      FORALL EMP ( EMP.SAL > 0 )
      ON ATTEMPTED VIOLATION REJECT ;
```

This statement, which is expressed in a hypothetical language originally proposed in reference [3] (somewhat modified here), is basically nothing more than a longwinded way of saying that employee salaries must be positive. I have deliberately spelled it out in detail, however, in order to illustrate the point that in general integrity rules have (at least) *three components,* as follows:

1. A **name** (ER3—"employee rule 3"— in the example). The rule will be registered in the system catalog under this name. The name will also appear in any diagnostics produced by the system in response to an attempted violation of the constraint.

2. The **constraint** itself, specified by means of a truth-valued expression of, in

general, arbitrary complexity.* (Note that the constraint *per se* is actually just one component of the overall rule. Informally, however, the terms "integrity constraint" and "integrity rule" are often used as if they were synonymous.)

Note: In the example, the constraint says that *all* employees must have salary greater than zero (because of the *universal quantifier* FORALL EMP). Of course, it is sufficient in practice just to check the newly inserted or updated salary, not all salaries. But this can be regarded as an optimization!—conceptually, at least, it is nevertheless still necessary to talk about "all" salaries. It is, however, possible to define a syntactic simplification (the detailed rationale is beyond the scope of the present discussion) by which FORALL quantifiers can optionally be omitted, and I will adopt this simplification in most of the examples that follow.

3. A **violation response,** specified by the ON ATTEMPTED VIOLATION clause, telling the system what to do if the constraint evaluates to *false.* In the example, the violation response is simply to reject the offending INSERT or UPDATE (and to provide suitable diagnostic information, of course); such a response will surely be the one most commonly required in practice, so we might as well make it the default. But in general the response could be a procedure of arbitrary complexity.

SOME RELATED CONCEPTS

Now that I've introduced the basic idea, there are a few other matters to get out of the way before we can continue. The fact is, a very great deal of confusion surrounds this subject. First, integrity is sometimes confused with either **recovery** or **concurrency,** though it really should not be (most of today's products are quite strong on recovery and concurrency, but not on integrity). The differences among the three concepts can be summarized as follows:

- To say that the database is in a state of **integrity** means, precisely, that the database is *correct,* in the sense that it does not violate any known integrity constraint. In other words, we regard the database as correct if and only if it satisfies the logical AND of all known constraints. Clearly, however, a system that does not support much in the way of constraint declaration will have only a very weak sense of what it means for the database to be "correct."

- **Recovery** refers to the process of restoring the database to some previous "correct" state after some error (e.g., a hardware or software failure) has destroyed the current state, or at least rendered the current state suspect. But, of

---

*Actually the truth-valued expression is not quite "arbitrary" —it must be what is called a *closed WFF,* meaning that it cannot include any variables that are not at least implicitly quantified.

course, that restored state will only be "correct" in the system's own, probably rather weak, sense of that term as explained in the previous paragraph.

- **Concurrency** refers to the ability to have multiple transactions executing in parallel. Now, it is well known that concurrency, if not properly controlled, can lead to errors; that is, two concurrent transactions, each correct in itself, might interfere with one another in such a manner as to produce an overall result that is not correct. Systems that provide proper concurrency control, however, guarantee that such interference cannot occur. Note, however, that such systems typically do not concern themselves with the question as to whether individual transactions are correct in themselves; they merely guarantee that errors are not *introduced* by executing transactions in parallel.

Integrity is also sometimes confused with **security;** certainly the terms are frequently heard together in database contexts, though the concepts are actually quite distinct. Briefly, *security* refers to the protection of data against unauthorized disclosure, alteration, or destruction; *integrity,* to repeat, refers to the correctness of the data. In other words—to put it a little glibly—security means protecting the database against unauthorized users; integrity means protecting it against *authorized* users!

A CLASSIFICATION SCHEME

Now let's get back to our major theme. In reference [2] I proposed a systematic and comprehensive classification scheme for integrity rules. I would like to sketch the salient features of that scheme here, because I think it can help to clarify many of the issues in this general area.

> *Note added on republication: Since this series of three installments was first published, I have changed my mind (again!) on the specifics of the classification scheme. The papers on view updating and "a new database design principle" elsewhere in this volume give a brief overview of the revised scheme; it is also described in some detail in reference [4]. Some of the details of the discussion that follows are thus now a little out of date—but not dramatically so. I plan to revisit this whole area in a future installment in my* Database Programming & Design *series.*

First, we divide integrity rules into **domain** *vs.* **table** rules. The domain integrity rule for a given domain is, precisely, the definition of the set of values that go to make up that domain. It therefore constrains the values that can appear in any column defined on the domain in question. Of course, those columns can be subject to additional constraints as well, which are logically ANDed with the domain constraint (see the next section).

Note: To say that a domain integrity rule defines the set of values that make up the domain in question is to say, in effect, that the rule simply *enumerates* those values. Usability might dictate that, syntactically, the values be specified by, e.g., a range expression (*a* TO *b*) or a picture (999–99–9999), but such shorthands are, conceptually, nothing *but* shorthands for explicit enumeration.

Now let me turn to *table* rules. Table rules are conveniently divided into **single-** *vs.* **multi-row** rules. Furthermore, they can also be divided into **state** *vs.* **transition** rules, and into **immediate** *vs.* **deferred** rules. Let's examine each of these categories in turn.

SINGLE- *vs.* MULTI-ROW RULES

A **single-row** rule is a rule that applies to the values within each individual row of a given base table—i.e., a rule for which the constraint can be tested for a given row by examining just that row in isolation. In other words, the constraint—if we ignore the initial FORALL quantifier—is a *restriction condition*. Here is an example:

```
CREATE INTEGRITY RULE ER7
       IF EMP.JOB = 'Pgmr'
       THEN EMP.SAL < 50000 ;
```

("programmers must earn less than $50,000").

A very common special case of a single-row rule is what might be called a single-**scalar** rule—that is, a single-row rule in which the constraint applies to just one scalar value within each individual row. Integrity rule ER3 above ("salaries must be positive") is an example of such a rule. (*Note:* Syntactically, the constraint within a single-scalar rule will refer to just one column of the relevant base table, so such rules are sometimes called single-*column* rules.) In practice, single-row rules are very often single-scalar rules; perhaps for this reason, some products do support simple single-scalar rules (such as range checks or "nulls not allowed"), but do not support the more general single-row rules.

A **multi-row** rule is a rule that applies to the *combination* of any number of rows from any number of base tables (in other words, the constraint is a truth-valued expression of arbitrary complexity, instead of being limited to just a restriction condition). Here is an example ("no department with budget less than $1,000,000 can have an employee with salary greater than $100,000"):

```
CREATE INTEGRITY RULE DE20
       IF DEPT.BUDGET < 1000000
       AND DEPT.DEPT# = EMP.DEPT#
       THEN EMP.SAL ≤ 100000 ;
```

And here is another ("no employee is allowed to earn more than his or her manager"):

```
CREATE INTEGRITY RULE EE2
        IF EMP2.MGR_EMP# = EMP1.EMP#
        THEN EMP2.SAL ≤ EMP1.SAL ;
```

EMP1 and EMP2 here both represent rows of the employees table EMP.

STATE *vs.* TRANSITION RULES

All of the examples we have seen so far have been **state** rules—they have been concerned with correct *states* of the database. Sometimes, however, it is necessary to consider **transitions** from one state to another. For example:

```
CREATE INTEGRITY RULE E26
        IF EMP'.E# = EMP.E#
        THEN EMP'.SAL <= EMP.SAL ;
```

("employee salaries must never decrease"). *Explanation:* Here I am introducing the convention that a *primed* identifier such as EMP′ is understood to refer to the applicable table as it was *prior to the update under consideration.* Note that up to this point I have tacitly been assuming that all identifiers refer to the applicable table as it is *after* the applicable update. Thus the constraint in the example means:

> *If EMP′ and EMP are employee rows before and after the update, respectively, and if they have the same employee number (so they are in fact "the same" row), then the salary of EMP′ must be less than or equal to that of EMP.*

IMMEDIATE *vs.* DEFERRED RULES

Finally, all of the examples we have seen so far have also been **immediate** rules—that is, rules that are checked "immediately" whenever an update is performed that might violate them. Sometimes, however, it is necessary to **defer** the checking to some later time (typically commit time). For example:

```
CREATE INTEGRITY RULE DNE
        AT COMMIT
        EXISTS EMP ( EMP.DEPT# = DEPT.DEPT# )
        ON ATTEMPTED VIOLATION ROLLBACK ;
```

("every department must have at least one employee"). The checking here has to be deferred (this is the meaning of the specification AT COMMIT) to allow new departments to be created—because, of course, a new department will obviously violate the rule when it is first created, so such creation must be followed by an operation to assign at least one employee to the new department before the integrity check is done. Note that the violation response has been specified as

ROLLBACK; indeed, there's not much else that makes sense—we certainly cannot leave the database in an incorrect state. In fact, we might as well define the default violation response for a deferred rule to be ROLLBACK.

CONCLUDING REMARKS

I have now laid the groundwork for discussion of numerous further integrity-related matters. However, I have run out of space, so I will have to leave those topics to next month or the month after. So let me close with this month's puzzle corner problem, which in the interests of light relief has nothing to do with databases at all (instead, it's a simple—slightly infamous—geometry problem). You are given an isosceles triangle ABC, with angles A = 20°, B = C = 80°. Draw a line from B to meet AC at D (between A and C), such that angle CBD = 50°. Draw a line from C to meet AB at E (between A and B), such that angle BCE = 60°. Draw a line connecting D and E. Find angle DEC. *Note:* This problem requires only an elementary knowledge of high-school geometry, but you still might want to set yourself a time limit! Don't try it on your employer's time.

REFERENCES

1. E. F. Codd, "Derivability, Redundancy, and Consistency of Relations Stored in Large Data Banks." IBM Research Report RJ599 (August 19th, 1969).

2. C. J. Date, "A Contribution to the Study of Database Integrity," in *Relational Database Writings 1985–1989* (Reading, Mass.: Addison-Wesley, 1990).

3. C. J. Date, "Integrity," in *An Introduction to Database Systems: Volume II* (Reading, Mass.: Addison-Wesley, 1983).

4. C. J. Date, "Integrity," in *An Introduction to Database Systems,* 6th edition (Reading, Mass.: Addison-Wesley, 1995).

A Matter of Integrity (Part 2 of 3)

Last month I introduced a scheme for classifying integrity rules. Fig. 1 should be sufficient to jog your memory on the basics of that scheme. Just to review quickly, integrity rules are divided into *domain vs. table* rules, *state vs. transition* rules, and *immediate vs. deferred* rules. *Table* rules are further subdivided into *single- vs. multi-row* rules. Also, don't forget *single-scalar* (also known as *single-column*) rules, which are an important special case of single-row rules in general.*

Fig. 1 also spells out an aspect of the classification scheme that I did not discuss in detail last month—namely, which combinations of categories are valid? *Y* means the indicated combination is valid, *N* means it isn't. In particular, note from the figure that domain rules are always state rules, never transition rules, because a given scalar value that is submitted as a candidate for placement in a given column either *is* or is *not* a value from the relevant domain, and that's basically all that can be said about it. For exactly the same reason, domain rules are always immediate, never deferred. You should take a few moments to convince yourself that the other entries in the figure are all equally reasonable.

There are a couple of other preliminary remarks that I should have made last time but couldn't for space reasons, so let me make them here:

Originally published under the title "A Matter of Integrity, Part II" in *Database Programming & Design 6*, No. 11 (November 1993). Reprinted by permission of Miller Freeman Inc.

*Let me remind the reader that I have revised the specifics of the integrity classification somewhat since Installment Numbers 14–16 were first published. As a result, some of the details of the discussion that follows are a little out of date—but not dramatically so.

	immediate state	immediate transition	deferred state	deferred transition
domain	Y	N	N	N
single-row	Y	Y	N	N
multi-row	Y	Y	Y	Y

Fig. 1 The classification scheme summarized

1. It has been suggested that if the DBMS did in fact allow you to specify integrity rules declaratively, as I am proposing, then something like 90 percent of a typical database definition would consist of such rules! Which represents a huge amount of procedural code you wouldn't have to write any more (in effect, the system would write that code instead). Thus, declarative integrity support is a very important direction for DBMS product development.

2. Integrity is also an important consideration at database design time. That is, database design is not just a matter of getting the data structures right—integrity rules need to be specified too. Having a language in which to express such rules is thus very desirable!

SOME SYNTACTIC CONSIDERATIONS

Since the most general (multi-row) rules don't logically belong to any specific base table, symmetry suggests that they should be specified separately—i.e., by separate, standalone CREATE INTEGRITY RULE statements, as I was suggesting last month. And then, since at least some rules need to be specified in this standalone manner, parsimony suggests that *all* rules be specified in this same way—i.e., the language should not be cluttered up with multiple distinct ways of doing the same thing.

However, this approach, although conceptually clean, unfortunately makes certain simple cases—arguably the commonest ones in practice, too—unduly cumbersome. For example:

```
CREATE INTEGRITY RULE ECK1
      IF EMP2.EMP# = EMP1.EMP#
      THEN SAME ( EMP1, EMP2 ) ;
```

Translation: "If EMP1 and EMP2 have the same employee number, then EMP1 and EMP2 are in fact the same employee"; EMP1 and EMP2 here both represent rows of the employees table EMP, and I have had to invent a builtin function SAME that returns *true* if its two arguments denote the same row and *false* otherwise. All this means is that employee numbers are unique!—i.e., EMP# is a candidate key. A declaration of the form

```
ECK1 CANDIDATE KEY ( EMP# )
```

(part of the declaration of the EMP base table) would obviously be more user-friendly.

So we might well want to define a few syntactic shorthands. Candidates for such shorthands include the following.

- Any *single-scalar* rule could be specified as part of the relevant column declaration. Example:

```
SALARY DECIMAL (8,2) ...
       ER3 SALARY > 0
```

Compare the analogous example in last month's column, and note that the optional FORALL EMP specification and scoping parentheses can now be dropped, and so can the explicit EMP qualifier.

- Any *single-row* rule could be specified as part of the relevant base table declaration. Example:

```
CREATE TABLE EMP ...
       ER7 IF JOB = 'Pgmr'
           THEN SAL < 50000
```

Again the optional FORALL EMP specification, the scoping parentheses, and the explicit EMP qualifiers can all be dropped (once again, compare the analogous example in last month's column).

- Certain important special multi-row rules can also be abbreviated conveniently—namely, candidate key (including *primary* key) specifications, foreign key specifications, and functional dependency specifications. I'll examine these cases a little more carefully in the next section.

It is very important to understand, however, that each of the foregoing shorthands *is* only a shorthand. Conceptually, each of them is defined in terms of an expansion into a general integrity rule in the hypothetical language sketched in last month's column.

KEYS AND FUNCTIONAL DEPENDENCIES

It might surprise you to realize that a candidate key specification is indeed (as just indicated) a multi-row rule, since it must by definition involve just one table. But it is. Rule ECK1 in the previous section (first version) is sufficient to illustrate the point: The rule has to be expressed in terms of several (actually two) rows of the table in question. In other words, a candidate key rule says something like "if two rows have the same value for the candidate key, then those two rows are really the same row." As we have seen, such a rule can conveniently be abbreviated to a simple CANDIDATE KEY specification. And, in an exactly analogous manner, a primary key rule can conveniently be abbreviated to a simple PRIMARY KEY specification.

Similar remarks apply to functional dependencies (FDs). For example, in order to state that column B of table T is functionally dependent on some column A of T, in our general integrity language we would have to say something like:

```
CREATE INTEGRITY RULE TFD1
       IF   T1.A = T2.A ;
       THEN T1.B = T2.B ;
```

("whenever two rows of T have the same value for A, they also have the same value for B"). The obvious abbreviation is:

```
TFD1 A → B
```

(part of the declaration of table T).

As for foreign keys: Since two tables are involved—the referencing table and the target table—foreign key specifications are obviously multi-row (even if the two tables are in fact one and the same!). A general integrity language foreign key specification might thus look something like this:

```
CREATE INTEGRITY RULE EDFK
       FORALL EMP ( EXISTS DEPT
                  ( DEPT.DEPT# = EMP.DEPT# ) ) ;
```

Partly because of the asymmetry inherent in foreign key specifications, however, it is simple (and "natural"?) to abbreviate them—for example:

```
EDFK FOREIGN KEY ( DEPT# )
     REFERENCES DEPT
```

(part of the declaration of table EMP). Note, incidentally, that I am deliberately ignoring the "referential action" portion of a foreign key specification. Referential actions lead us into the realm of *triggered procedures* (or rather, declarative specification of such procedures), a topic that is beyond the scope of the present discussion.

ENTITY AND REFERENTIAL INTEGRITY

The relational model is usually described as including two general integrity rules, the entity integrity rule and the referential integrity rule (abbreviated below as EI and RI, respectively). Here are their definitions:

- *EI:* No component of the primary key of a base table is allowed to accept nulls.

  Note: You will often hear statements to the effect that the entity integrity rule says that every row of every base table must possess a unique primary key value. It does not. What it does say—to repeat—is that no such row can possess a primary key value that is wholly or partly null.

- *RI:* The database must not contain any unmatched foreign key values (where an "unmatched foreign key value" is a nonnull foreign key value for which there does not exist an equal value of the primary key in the relevant target table).

The point I would like to make here is that these "rules" are different in kind from all of the examples I have shown previously, both this month and last month. First, note that unlike all those other rules, these two are not specific to any particular database. In fact, they are really **metarules**—i.e., rules about rules; that is, they are rules that tell me that in any particular database I have to have certain rules that *are* specific to that database, in order to conform to the requirements of the relational model. In the departments-and-employees database, for example, I have to have a rule that says employee numbers in the EMP table cannot be null, in order to conform to the entity integrity (meta)rule. (This is a single-row, immediate, state rule, by the way.) Similarly, I have to have a multi-row rule that says that department numbers in the EMP table have to match department numbers in the DEPT table, in order to conform to the referential integrity metarule.

As a matter of fact, the relational model includes another metarule (not often articulated) that is actually more fundamental than the other two. This is the *column* integrity metarule, which states that every scalar value in every column must be a value from the relevant domain. Because of this metarule, I have to have a database-specific rule that says, for example, that every employee number in the EMP# column in the base table EMP comes from the domain also called EMP#.

THE CLASSIFICATION SCHEME REVISITED

Before going any further, I would like to take a slightly closer look at the integrity rule classification scheme, in order to address certain objections that might legitimately be raised concerning it. The fact is, it would be conceptually possible to simplify the scheme in certain respects, as I will now show. However, I will also argue against such simplifications on the grounds of pragmatism.

First of all, the split between single- and multi-row rules is indeed purely a pragmatic one. The fact is, single-row rules are syntactically easier to express, as we have seen, and they are likely to be easier and more efficient to enforce, than multi-row rules are (in general). For such reasons, it is convenient to think of them as a separate category. However, there is no *fundamental* distinction between single- and multi-row rules.

Second, given that **transactions** are defined as (among other things) units of integrity, there is an argument that says that all rules should be deferred, not immediate—i.e., all integrity checking should be done at commit time, because the database is only required to be "correct" *at transaction boundaries*. Again I would argue against this position on pragmatic (rather than logical) grounds. For example, it would be very annoying to have to wait until end-of-transaction to discover that the employee number you entered five minutes ago was invalid.

As a matter of fact, there is also a counterargument that says that all rules should be immediate, not deferred! This is because deferred rules can be simulated with immediate rules, while the converse is not true. For example, the rule that every department must have at least one employee (which I gave last month as an example of a deferred rule) could be expressed as follows:

```
CREATE INTEGRITY RULE DNE
       FORALL DEPT ( EXISTS EMP ( EMP.DEPT# = DEPT.DEPT# )
                     OR
                     EXISTS TEMP ( true ) )
       ON ATTEMPTED VIOLATION ROLLBACK ;
```

Here TEMP is a table that (at any given time) contains either one row or no rows. If it contains one row, then integrity rule DNE is satisfied. In order to trigger the "real" check (to make sure that every department really does have an employee), all we have to do is to delete the single row from TEMP.

Next, there is an argument that says that we do not need both state and transition rules, because any state rule can be regarded as a transition rule in which the previous value of the data in question is "don't care" (thanks to Geoff Martin of Monash University, Melbourne, Australia, for pointing this out to me). Once again, however, I would argue that the state *vs.* transition distinction is useful for pragmatic reasons.

And one final terminological point: Single- and multi-row rules are sometimes known as single- and multi-*variable* rules—where "variable" means a variable of what's called "the tuple relational calculus"; i.e., it's a variable that represents a row (tuple) of some table (relation). For example, the multi-row rule EDFK shown earlier:

```
CREATE INTEGRITY RULE EDFK
       FORALL EMP ( EXISTS DEPT
                  ( DEPT.DEPT# = EMP.DEPT# ) ) ;
```

is a multi-variable rule (in fact, there are exactly two variables here—EMP, which represents a row of the employees table, and DEPT, which represents a row of the departments table).

CONCLUDING REMARKS

This is a good place to break off our discussion for now; I will finish it next month. So once again I will close with a puzzle corner problem (nothing to do with integrity *per se,* though—unlike last month's puzzle—it does at least have something to do with databases!): Given table SP { S#, P# } showing which suppliers (S#) supply which parts (P#), give (a) an SQL solution, (b) a relational algebra solution, to the problem of finding all pairs of supplier numbers, S*x* and S*y* say, such that S*x* and S*y* supply exactly the same set of parts each (with acknowledgments to Fatma Mili of Oakland University, Rochester, Michigan). *Note:* You will probably find it much easier to produce the SQL solution than the relational algebra solution, owing to a very unfortunate omission from the original relational algebra. You might want to give some thought to the question of what that omission might be.

A Matter of Integrity (Part 3 of 3)

This month's column sees the conclusion of my three-part discussion of integrity support. There are three outstanding issues I want to address: integrity support in SQL, integrity support in object-oriented systems, and integrity support via stored procedures.

SQL/89 SUPPORT

SQL/89 added an optional *Integrity Enhancement Feature* (IEF) to the original standard SQL/86. IEF consists of three pieces:

1. User-defined default values
2. CHECK constraints
3. UNIQUE, PRIMARY KEY, and FOREIGN KEY specifications

Of these, only Nos. 2 and 3 are relevant to the present discussion. Here is an example of No. 2:

```
CREATE TABLE EMP ...
        CHECK ( JOB <> 'Pgmr' OR SAL < 50000 )
```

Originally published under the title "A Matter of Integrity, Part III" in *Database Programming & Design 6,* No. 12 (December 1993). Reprinted by permission of Miller Freeman Inc.

In terms of our integrity rule classification scheme, an IEF CHECK constraint represents an *immediate, state, single-row* rule. Note, moreover, that the rule is *unnamed* and has *no explicit violation response* (the implicit violation response is, of course, REJECT). As the example indicates, a CHECK constraint is specified as a clause within the relevant base table declaration; there is also a shorthand for single-*scalar* constraints, which can be specified as part of the relevant *column* declaration. *Note:* The specification NOT NULL (already supported in SQL/86) is defined to be shorthand for a specific simple single-scalar constraint.

Now let's turn to the major IEF component, namely UNIQUE, PRIMARY KEY, and FOREIGN KEY specifications. The following are all valid IEF declarations:

- `UNIQUE ( EMP# )`

- `PRIMARY KEY ( EMP# )`

- `FOREIGN KEY ( DEPT# ) REFERENCES DEPT`

Each of these specifications could appear as a clause within the declaration of base table EMP. (There are also some syntactic shorthands that can be used when the candidate key, primary key, or foreign key is single-column. I omit the details here.) Again, each example represents an unnamed, immediate, state rule, with no explicit violation response; however, the rules are now of course (special cases of) *multi-row* rules. Note, incidentally, that IEF's FOREIGN KEY specifications do not include any explicit referential action; implicitly, the only referential action supported is NO ACTION [*sic*]—details beyond the scope of the present discussion.

IEF's integrity support suffers from a number of detailed deficiencies, especially with respect to nulls, but overall it does represent a step in the right direction. The trouble is, the step is only a small one, and in any case it is optional: A vendor does not have to support IEF in order to be SQL/89-compliant. So let's move on to take a look at the integrity support provided in the newest version of SQL, namely SQL/92.

SQL/92 SUPPORT

In addition to the features already present in IEF, SQL/92 includes support for the following:

- Integrity rule names
- Domain rules
- General multi-row rules
- Deferred checking

There is still no support for transition rules or for explicit violation responses (except for certain referential actions, such as CASCADE; I omit these for space reasons). However, all integrity rules are at least now named (if the user does not supply an explicit name, the system will provide one anyway).

Turning to domain rules: Here I will just say that SQL/92's support —not just for domain integrity *per se* but for domains in general—is simultaneously too weak and too complex! This is not the place to go into too much detail; suffice it to say that (as I mentioned a couple of months ago) I think it would be much clearer not to use the term "domain" at all for the SQL construct, but rather to use some quite distinct term—perhaps just "shared column declaration," since that is effectively all it is. Regarding "domain" integrity support specifically, here are some of the problems:

- I explained in Part 1 of this three-part series that a domain integrity rule conceptually just enumerates the values in that domain. SQL/92, however, allows a "domain" integrity rule to involve a truth-valued expression *of arbitrary complexity*. This unwarranted permissiveness muddles and muddies some very fundamental concepts. For example, if domain D is defined to draw its values from column C of table T, then WHAT IS THE DOMAIN OF COLUMN $T.C$? I recommend strongly that users not "take advantage" of this very strange aspect of SQL/92.

     Note: If you really do want to say that a given "domain" draws its values from some column C of some table T—and hence constrain all columns defined on that domain accordingly—you can achieve the desired effect in a clean manner by suitable use of the conventional foreign key mechanism.

- Numerous complications arise if a domain integrity rule is dropped (via ALTER DOMAIN) or a domain is dropped altogether (via DROP DOMAIN). I omit the details here; the interested reader can find a complete explanation in *A Guide to the SQL Standard,* 3rd edition, by C. J. Date and Hugh Darwen, Addison-Wesley, 1993.

Moving on to general-purpose multi-row rules: It is of course a good thing that these are now supported. The trouble is, they are supported in two quite distinct ways!—and this fact leads to certain traps for the unwary. First, they can be expressed as standalone "assertions." For example:

```
CREATE ASSERTION DE20 CHECK
      ( NOT EXISTS
          ( SELECT *
            FROM   DEPT
            WHERE  DEPT.BUDGET < 1000000
            AND    EXISTS
                ( SELECT *
                  FROM   EMP
                  WHERE  EMP.DEPT# = DEPT.DEPT#
                  AND    EMP.SAL > 100000 ) )
```

("no department with budget less than \$1,000,000 can have an employee with salary greater than \$100,000").

Alternatively, we can state the same rule as part of the declaration of table EMP or table DEPT (or indeed *any* base table, come to that)—for example:

```
CREATE TABLE DEPT ...
      CONSTRAINT DE20 CHECK
   ( DEPT.BUDGET < 1000000 OR
     NOT EXISTS
        ( SELECT *
          FROM    EMP
          WHERE   EMP.DEPT# = DEPT.DEPT#
          AND     EMP.SAL > 100000 ) )
```

So the first problem is simply *redundancy:* There are many different ways of doing the same thing (usually not a good idea).

The second problem is as follows: If integrity rule *R* is specified as part of the declaration of base table *T,* then *R* is *always* satisfied when *T* is empty, no matter what form *R* takes—even if it takes the form "*T* must not be empty"! To be specific, if table *T* is empty, the following (standalone) "assertion" *will* be violated:

```
CREATE ASSERTION TNE CHECK
     ( EXISTS ( SELECT * FROM T ) )
```

whereas the following "base table constraint" will *not:*

```
CREATE TABLE T ... CONSTRAINT TNE CHECK
     ( EXISTS ( SELECT * FROM T ) )
```

The problem is, specifically, that SQL/92 allows "base table constraints" to be of arbitrary complexity, instead of limiting them to just those that make sense in such a context (essentially single-row rules, plus certain special-case multi-row rules such as PRIMARY KEY).

Now let me briefly describe SQL/92's support for deferred checking. Basically, any integrity rule can be declared to be DEFERRABLE or NOT DEFERRABLE; if it is DEFERRABLE, it can further be declared to be INITIALLY DEFERRED or INITIALLY IMMEDIATE, which defines its state at start-of-transaction. DEFERRABLE rules can be dynamically switched on and off by means of the statement

```
SET CONSTRAINTS constraints [ IMMEDIATE | DEFERRED ]
```

COMMIT forces all constraints into the IMMEDIATE state. And, of course, integrity rules are checked only when they are in the IMMEDIATE state.

As you can see, the foregoing support is at least partly procedural. My preference would be for fully declarative support, as indicated in the first installment of this three-part series.

One final remark regarding SQL/92: You will notice that there is no direct (i.e., shorthand) support for declaring functional dependencies (FDs). This could be unfortunate, since a knowledge of FDs on the part of the system is needed if the system is to be able to display certain "intelligent" forms of behavior. See "The Power of the Keys" (Installment Number 9).

OBJECT-ORIENTED SUPPORT

Consider once again the rule that says that no department with budget less than $1,000,000 can have an employee with salary greater than $100,000. In a relational system, this rule will be stated and enforced declaratively, as we have seen:

```
CREATE INTEGRITY RULE DE20
       IF DEPT.BUDGET < 1000000
       AND DEPT.DEPT# = EMP.DEPT#
       THEN EMP.SAL ≤ 100000 ;
```

In an object-oriented (OO) system, by contrast, code to enforce this rule must be included in the various *methods*—i.e., procedures—that are used to maintain the database. To be specific, appropriate code must be included in at least all of the following:

- Method for hiring an employee
- Method for updating an employee's salary
- Method for updating a department's budget
- Method for moving an employee to a new department

Points arising:

1. We have obviously lost the possibility of the system determining when to do the checking for itself.
2. How do we ensure that all necessary methods include all necessary enforcement code?
3. How do we ensure that all update access is via those methods (to avoid the possibility of bypassing the enforcement code)?
4. How do we ensure uniformity of error messages (a) across all methods involved in enforcing "the same" constraint; (b) across all constraints (e.g., all referential constraints) that bear a strong family resemblance?
5. If the constraint changes, how do we find all methods that need to be rewritten?
6. How do we ensure that the enforcement code is correct?
7. How do we do deferred (AT COMMIT) integrity checking?
8. How do we query the system to find all constraints that apply to a given object or combination of objects?

9. Will the constraints be enforced during load and other utility processing?

10. What about semantic optimization (i.e., using integrity constraints to simplify queries—see Installment Number 11)?

11. What about optimization and performance of the integrity checking code itself?

12. What about user productivity—during both application creation and application maintenance?

13. ISN'T THIS ALL A BIG STEP BACKWARD? (Yes, it is!)

Indeed, these are some of the reasons why I do not unreservedly embrace OO technology. I do think that OO technology includes some good ideas, and that relational systems need to be enhanced to incorporate those good ideas, but *not* at the expense of incorporating the bad ones as well—and procedural integrity support I do think is a very bad idea.

STORED PROCEDURE SUPPORT

In Part 1 of this three-part discussion, I mentioned the point that most relational products do not currently provide declarative integrity support (except for certain special cases, such as referential constraints), and moreover that some vendors quite specifically emphasize the opposite approach—namely, procedural support, using **stored** (or **triggered**) procedures. Now, I certainly agree that stored and triggered procedures are useful for a wide variety of purposes. However, I do *not* agree that they represent the preferred approach to the integrity problem. My reason for adopting this position is essentially that such procedures play much the same role in a relational system as methods do in an OO system!—and so all of my criticisms of OO systems above apply, *mutatis mutandis.*

CONCLUDING REMARKS

There is much, much more that could be said on the subject of data integrity, but I hope I have covered enough ground over the last three months to give you an idea of the importance, scope, and potential of good declarative integrity support. I will wind up (as always) with a puzzle, taken this time from the book *A Guide to the SQL Standard* mentioned earlier. It has to do with the effect of nulls on integrity constraints in SQL/92. Let *CK* be some candidate key, possibly involving multiple columns, for some base table *T,* and let *ck2* be a new value for *CK* that some user is attempting to introduce into table *T.* That attempt will fail if *ck2* is the same as some value for *CK, ck1* say, that already exists within table *T.* What then does it mean for the two values *ck1* and *ck2* to be "the same"? More specifically, you are asked to give precise interpretations for each of the following three statements:

1. *ck1* and *ck2* are "the same" for the purposes of a comparison condition (e.g., in a WHERE clause)
2. *ck1* and *ck2* are "the same" for the purposes of candidate key uniqueness
3. *ck1* and *ck2* are "the same" for the purposes of duplicate elimination (e.g., in UNION)

Toil and Trouble

I've indicated several times in this series that duplicate rows (hereinafter usually abbreviated to just *duplicates*) are, and always were, a mistake in SQL. In fact, it is my position that (a) duplicate rows should never have been permitted in the first place, but (b) given that they *were* permitted, they ought to be avoided in practice. It is time I gave some solid reasons for this position.

THE CAT FOOD EXAMPLE

The following extract from an article by David Beech [1] is typical of the arguments that are advanced by duplicate-row advocates.

> *For example, the row "cat food 0.39" could appear three times [on a supermarket checkout receipt] with a significance that would not escape many shoppers . . . At the level of abstraction at which it is useful to record the information, there are no value components that distinguish the objects. What the relational model does is force people to lower the level of abstraction, often inventing meaningless values to be inserted in an extra column whose*

Originally published in *Database Programming & Design* 7, No. 1 (January 1994). Reprinted by permission of Miller Freeman Inc.

purpose is to show what we knew already, that the cans of cat food are distinct.

Apart from the remark regarding "lowering the level of abstraction," which is just arm-waving, this seems to me to be exactly the straw-man argument I gave in reference [3], under the heading "Why Duplicates Are Good (?)"—to wit:

1. Duplicates occur naturally in practice.
2. Given that this is so, it is a burden to have to invent some artificial identifier in order to distinguish between them.

In a subsequent section of reference [3] entitled "Why Duplicates Are Bad: The Fundamental Issue," I went on to refute this argument as follows:

1. Individual objects *must* be identifiable (i.e., distinguishable from all other objects)—for if an object is not identifiable, then it is impossible even to talk about it, let alone perform any kind of operation upon it or use it for any sensible purpose. In other words, objects must have **identity**.

2. In a collection of objects in which there are no duplicates (i.e., a mathematical set), objects obviously do have identity, because they are in fact **self-identifying**. For example, in the set of integers {3,6,8,11}, there is no ambiguity as to which element of the set is "6" and which is "8" (etc.). However, in the collection (3,6,6,8,8,8,11), which is certainly not a mathematical set (it is a *multiset* or *bag* instead), we cannot make an analogous statement; both "6" and "8" are now ambiguous.

3. So what *is* the identification mechanism in a collection that permits duplicates (i.e., a bag)? For example, in the bag just shown, how can we distinguish the two "6"s from one another? Note that there must still *be* an identification mechanism; if we cannot distinguish the two "6"s from one another somehow, **we cannot even tell that there are two of them.** In other words, we would not even know that there *were* any duplicates in the first place!

Now, a common reaction to this argument is "But I really *don't* need to distinguish among the duplicates—all I want to do is to be able to count them." The point I'm trying to make is that you do need to distinguish them, even just to count them. This point is crucial, of course, and I really don't know how to make it any more strongly than I already have.

How then do we distinguish duplicates such as the two "6"s in the bag shown above? The answer, of course, is that we do so *by their relative position;* we say something like "this 6 is **here** and that 6 is over **there**," or "this is the **first** 6 and that one is the **second**."

And so we have now introduced a totally new concept, one that is quite deliberately omitted from the relational model: *positional addressing.* Which means that we are now quite beyond the pale!—i.e., we have moved quite outside the cozy framework of relational theory. Which means that there is *no guarantee whatsoever* that any results that hold within that framework still apply. For example, does JOIN still work? (As a matter of fact, it doesn't.) What about UNION? PROJECT? SUMMARIZE? Are the theorems of normalization still valid? What about the quantifiers EXISTS and FORALL? What about the rules for functional dependency inheritance? What about expression transformation and optimization? Etc., etc., etc.

Furthermore, we now definitely need certain additional operators, such as "retrieve the *n*th row" or "insert this new row *here*" or "move this row from *here* to *there*." In my opinion, these operators constitute a much greater burden for the user than does the occasional need to invent an artificial identifier.

The relational model, by contrast, adopts the position that, since objects do have to be identifiable *somehow,* then we might as well represent their identity in exactly the same way as everything else—namely, by values in columns. (Especially as there will often be a "natural" identifier that is such a column value anyway, which means that the problem of having to invent an artificial value might not arise very often in practice.) In this way we can stay securely within the context of relational theory, and all of the desirable properties of that theory will thus be directly applicable.

To return for a moment to the argument of reference [1], Beech continues:

> *We are not being less than respectable mathematically if we consider collections containing duplicates, because mathematicians deal with such collections, called* multisets *or . . .* bags.

The point here seems to be that the usual advantage claimed for the relational model, to the effect that the model is at least mathematically respectable, can be claimed by the duplicate-row advocates for their "model" too. But all of the mathematical "bag theory" treatments I've seen start off by assuming that there is a way to count duplicates! And that assumption, I contend, effectively means that *bags* are defined in terms of *sets*—each bag element really has a hidden identifying tag that distinguishes it somehow, and the bag is really a *set* of tag/element pairs. I see no advantage, and definite disadvantages, in introducing this extra level of complexity.

EXPRESSION TRANSFORMATION

The foregoing argument should be sufficient (I hope) to show why I think it was a mistake—for both theoretical *and practical* reasons—to include duplicate support in SQL in the first place. Now I would like to go on to argue that, even though duplicates *are* supported, you should take care to avoid them in practice. (The

P	P#	PNAME	SP	S#	P#
	P1	Screw		S1	P1
	P1	Screw		S1	P1
	P1	Screw		S1	P2
	P2	Screw			

Fig. 1 A database with duplicates

following argument is also paraphrased from reference [3], and is based on an example originally due to Nat Goodman.)

The fundamental point is that—as I've hinted above, and as I've also pointed out in a couple of earlier installments in this series—expression transformations that are valid in a relational context are *not* necessarily valid in the presence of duplicates. Here is an example. Consider the database shown in Fig. 1.

Perhaps I should begin by asking the question: What does it *mean* to have three "(P1,Screw)" rows in table P and not two or four or seventeen? It must mean *something,* for if it means nothing, then why are the duplicates there in the first place? To paraphrase a point first nicely made by Codd (in a live presentation): If something is true, saying it twice doesn't make it any *more* true.

So let's assume that there is indeed some meaning attached to the existence of duplicates, even though that meaning (whatever it is) is hardly very explicit. (I note in passing, therefore, that duplicates contravene another of the objectives of the relational model, namely the objective of *explicitness*—the meaning of the data should be made as explicit as possible. The presence of duplicates implies that part of the meaning is hidden.) In other words, given that duplicates do have some meaning, there are presumably going to be business decisions made on the basis of the fact that (e.g.) there are three "(P1,Screw)" rows in table P, and not two or four.

Now consider the following query: "List part numbers for parts that either are screws or are supplied by supplier S1, or both." Here are some candidate SQL formulations for this query, together with the output produced in each case.*

```
1. SELECT  P#
   FROM    P
   WHERE   PNAME = 'Screw'
   OR      P# IN
         ( SELECT  P#
           FROM    SP
           WHERE   S# = 'S1') ;
```

---

*Thanks to Jim Panttaja of Panttaja Consulting Group Inc., Healdsburg, California, for checking these results for me, using Microsoft SQL Server Release 4.2a running on OS/2.

Result: P1 * 3, P2 * 1.

```
2. SELECT  P#
   FROM    SP
   WHERE   S# = 'S1'
   OR      P# IN
         ( SELECT  P#
           FROM    P
           WHERE   PNAME = 'Screw');
```

Result: P1 * 2, P2 * 1.

```
3. SELECT  P.P#
   FROM    P, SP
   WHERE   ( S# = 'S1' AND
             P.P#  =  SP.P# )
   OR      PNAME = 'Screw' ;
```

Result: P1 * 9, P2 * 3.

```
4. SELECT  SP.P#
   FROM    P, SP
   WHERE   ( S# = 'S1' AND
             P.P#  =  SP.P# )
   OR      PNAME = 'Screw' ;
```

Result: P1 * 8, P2 * 4.

```
5. SELECT  P#
   FROM    P
   WHERE   PNAME = 'Screw'
   UNION   ALL
   SELECT  P#
   FROM    SP
   WHERE   S# = 'S1' ;
```

Result: P1 * 5, P2 * 2.

```
6. SELECT  DISTINCT P#
   FROM    P
   WHERE   PNAME = 'Screw'
   UNION   ALL
   SELECT  P#
   FROM    SP
   WHERE   S# = 'S1' ;
```

Result: P1 * 3, P2 * 2.

```
7. SELECT  P#
   FROM    P
   WHERE   PNAME = 'Screw'
   UNION   ALL
   SELECT  DISTINCT P#
   FROM    SP
   WHERE   S# = 'S1' ;
```

Result: P1 * 4, P2 * 2.

8.
```
SELECT DISTINCT P#
FROM    P
WHERE   PNAME = 'Screw'
OR      P# IN
        ( SELECT P#
          FROM    SP
          WHERE   S# = 'S1') ;
```

Result: P1 * 1, P2 * 1.

9.
```
SELECT DISTINCT P#
FROM    SP
WHERE   S# = 'S1'
OR      P# IN
        ( SELECT P#
          FROM    P
          WHERE   PNAME = 'Screw');
```

Result: P1 * 1, P2 * 1.

10.
```
SELECT P#
FROM    P
GROUP   BY P#, PNAME
HAVING  PNAME = 'Screw'
OR      P# IN
        ( SELECT P#
          FROM    SP
          WHERE   S# = 'S1') ;
```

Result: P1 * 1, P2 * 1.

11.
```
SELECT P.P#
FROM    P, SP
GROUP   BY P.P#,PNAME,S#,SP.P#
HAVING  ( S# = 'S1' AND
          P.P#  =  SP.P# )
OR      PNAME = 'Screw' ;
```

Result: P1 * 2, P2 * 2.

12.
```
SELECT P#
FROM    P
WHERE   PNAME = 'Screw'
UNION
SELECT P#
FROM    SP
WHERE   S# = 'S1' ;
```

Result: P1 * 1, P2 * 1.

The obvious first point to make is that the twelve different formulations produce nine different results!—different, that is, with respect to their *degree of duplication*. (I make no claim, incidentally, that either the twelve different formulations or the nine different results are the only ones possible—indeed, they are not, in general.) Thus, if the user really cares about duplicates, then he or she needs to be *extremely* careful in formulating the query appropriately.

Furthermore, of course, analogous remarks apply to the system itself: Because different formulations can produce different results, the system optimizer too has to be *extremely* careful in its task of expression transformation (i.e., transforming one formulation into another). In other words, duplicate rows act as a significant *optimization inhibitor* (see Installment Number 11). Here are some implications of this point:

- First, the optimizer code itself is harder to write, harder to maintain, and probably more buggy—all of which conspires to make the product simultaneously more expensive and less reliable.
- Second, system performance is likely to be worse than it might otherwise be.
- Third, the user is going to have to get involved in performance issues; e.g., the user might have to spend time and effort on figuring out the best way to state a given query.

(The obvious puzzle corner problem for this month is to try out the twelve formulations, and any others you can think of, on your own DBMS. You might discover some interesting things about your optimizer! Incidentally, I should mention here that I have certainly encountered products that do not handle the degree of duplication correctly in all cases—presumably because they are making some expression transformations that are technically incorrect.)

The foregoing state of affairs is particularly frustrating in view of the fact that (in most cases) the user probably does *not* really care how many duplicates appear in the result. In other words, (a) different formulations produce different results, as demonstrated above; however, (b) the differences are probably irrelevant from the user's point of view; *BUT* (c) the optimizer is not aware of this latter fact and is therefore prevented—unnecessarily—from performing the transformations it would like to perform.

On the basis of examples like the foregoing, I would conclude (among other things) that users should *always* ensure that query results contain no duplicates—e.g., by specifying DISTINCT at appropriate points in the query—and thus simply forget about the whole problem. (And if this advice is followed, of course, then there can be no good reason for having duplicates in the database in the first place.)

Note: The alternative in SQL to SELECT DISTINCT is SELECT ALL (and SELECT ALL is unfortunately the default). The discussion of the foregoing sections suggests that a more apt alternative might have been SELECT *in*DISTINCT . . . On a more serious note: The trouble is, of course, that SELECT DISTINCT takes longer to execute than SELECT ALL, in general, even if the DISTINCT is effectively a "no-op." But this problem arises because SQL systems are typically unable to optimize properly over duplicate elimination, owing to their lack of knowledge of key inheritance (see "The Power of the Keys", Installment Number 9).

CONCLUSION

Duplicate row support should be dropped. A strategy for doing so gracefully was outlined by Codd in his book [2]:

1. Implement an installation-time switch in the DBMS so that the DBA can specify whether duplicates are to be eliminated (a) in all cases—i.e., automatically—or (b) only on user request;

2. Announce that support for case (b) will be dropped in (say) two or three years' time;

3. Drop that support at the appropriate time, simultaneously upgrading the optimizer to take advantage of the now guaranteed lack of duplicates.

TECHNICAL CORRESPONDENCE

After this installment first appeared, I received a long letter from Robert A. Alps of Evanston, Illinois. Mr. Alps made so many points in his letter that I decided to devote a complete installment to replying to him (that installment is due to appear after this book is published). However, I would like to deal with one of his comments here. In the body of the present installment, I claimed that mathematical "bag theory" treatments usually start by assuming that there is a way to count duplicates, and I further claimed that that assumption effectively means that *bags* are defined in terms of *sets*. Alps countered by claiming that, on the contrary, it should indeed be possible to construct a theory of bags that does not require that initial assumption.

I now feel that the question of whether that initial assumption is necessary is a red herring (and it was probably wrong of me to raise it in the first place). The point rather is that—regardless of whether or not that initial assumption is necessary—bag theory:

- Must be more complex than set theory;
- Includes set theory as a proper subset;*
- Is reducible to set theory.

Occam's Razor would thus clearly suggest that we stay with sets and not get into the unnecessary complexities of bags.

I also received a letter from Chuck Reinke of Concord, California, who felt that I had not responded satisfactorily to the cat food example. He suggested the following:

---

*Perhaps I should say a proper *subbag*.

Let's consider rats *and* ratlets. *Whenever there's a new litter, I want to create an entry for each new ratlet. When just born they are indistinguishable . . . Yet, as they grow, I can distinguish certain ones by color or behavior— it's time to assign them a unique key.*

As Date would have it, prior to this stage ratlets should be banned from relational representation. Assigning each ratlet an arbitrary unique key implies nonexistent information, that the ratlets are distinguishable . . . The inadequacy of SQL is a poor argument for prohibiting duplicates in relational design. I want to keep track of practical real-world information, not create mathematical abstractions of Aristotelian purity.

Space constraints required me to keep my response short, so I refrained from pointing out that (a) the arguments against duplicates had nothing to do with the inadequacies of SQL *per se,* and (b) "keeping track of practical real-world information" in a database *necessarily* involves creating some kind of "mathematical abstraction." Instead, I simply replied as follows.

(Begin quote)

The obvious design for the ratlets problem is:

```
LITTERS ( LITTER_ID, #_OF_RATLETS )
        PRIMARY KEY ( LITTER_ID )

RATLETS ( RATLET_ID, LITTER_ID )
        PRIMARY KEY ( RATLET_ID )
        FOREIGN KEY ( LITTER_ID ) REFERENCES LITTERS
```

When there's a new litter, we make the obvious entry in LITTERS. When an individual ratlet becomes "interesting" (unlike Mr. Reinke, I do not say "distinguishable," because distinguishability presupposes identity), we make the obvious entry in RATLETS.

Anyone who still believes in duplicates should be asked to write out one googol times, "There's no such thing as a duplicate."

(End quote)

REFERENCES

1. David Beech, "New Life for SQL," *Datamation* (February 1st, 1989).

2. E. F. Codd, *The Relational Model for Database Management Version 2* (Reading, Mass.: Addison-Wesley, 1990).

3. C. J. Date, "Why Duplicate Rows Are Prohibited," in *Relational Database Writings 1985–1989* (Reading, Mass.: Addison-Wesley, 1990).

Answers to Puzzle Corner Problems (Installment Numbers 13–17)

My column this month is devoted once again to answering the various outstanding "puzzle corner" problems from previous installments. Thanks again to those readers who wrote in with their own solutions.

THE PARADOX OF EPIMENIDES

Source: "How We Missed the Relational Boat" (Installment Number 13).

Problem statement: We are given a set of tables T1, T2, . . . , TN. Each row in each table is either *valid* or *invalid* for some reason (i.e., does or does not represent a true proposition about "the real world"). We are also given another table T0 with two columns, TABLE (value a table name) and VALIDITY (value an integer). The row (Ti,n) appears in T0 if and only if the statement "exactly n rows are valid in table Ti" is valid ($0 \leq n \leq$ the number of rows in Ti). All tables are initially empty. Can we or can we not insert the row (T0,0) into table T0?

Solution: You will probably have realized that this is the well-known Paradox of

Originally published under the title "Putting the Pieces Together" in *Database Programming & Design* 7, No. 2 (February 1994). Reprinted by permission of Miller Freeman Inc.

Epimenides ("this statement is false") in relational form. If we do insert the row (T0,0), then by definition it must be the case that there are no valid rows in table T0, in which case the row (T0,0) is not valid, and so it should not have been inserted. If we cannot insert the row, then there are no valid rows in table T0, and so it should be possible to say as much by inserting the row after all.

Incidentally, a problem of this same general nature manifests itself in connection with optimization. The optimizer typically has a set of tables available to it in the catalog containing various pieces of information that are useful for optimization purposes (e.g., "column *T.B* is functionally dependent on column *T.A*"). Can the optimizer use the information in those tables to optimize access to those tables themselves? (With acknowledgments to David McGoveran, who first drew my attention to this problem.)

THE TRIANGLE PROBLEM

Source: "A Matter of Integrity" (Part 1, Installment Number 14).

Problem statement: We are given an isosceles triangle ABC, with angles A = 20°, B = C = 80°. Draw a line from B to meet AC at D (between A and C), such that angle CBD = 50°. Draw a line from C to meet AB at E (between A and B), such that angle BCE = 60°. Draw a line connecting D and E. Find angle DEC.

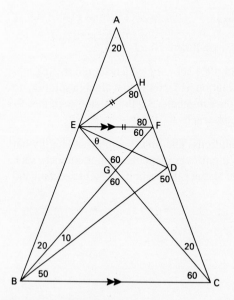

Fig. 1 Isosceles triangle ABC

Solution: Let the angle to be found—i.e., DEC—be θ (see Fig. 1). Draw EF parallel to BC to meet AC at F. Draw BF and let BF and CE meet at G. Draw EH to meet AF at H (between A and F), such that EH = EF. Then it is easy to see that:

```
EHF = EFH = 80°;
BDC = 50°;
EFG = FGE = GEF = BGC = CBG = 60°;
FED = 60° - θ;
FDE = θ + 20°.
```

Then:

```
CDB = CBD (= 50°), so CD = CB;
CBG = CGB (= 60°), so CB = CG;
hence CD = CG = x, say.

EAC = ECA (= 20°), so EA = EC = y, say;
hence GE = CE - CG = y - x.

EFG = EGF (= 60°), so EF = EG = y - x;
EH = EF, so EH = y - x.

CEH = CEF + FEH
    = 60° + 20° = 80°
    = CHE, so CH = CE = y;
hence DH = CH - CD = y - x = EH;
hence HED = HDE;
i.e., 80° - θ = θ + 20°;
so θ = 30°.  ■
```

THE SUPPLIER-PAIRS PROBLEM

Source: "A Matter of Integrity" (Part 2, Installment Number 15).

Problem statement: Given table SP { S#, P# } showing which suppliers (S#) supply which parts (P#), give (a) an SQL solution, (b) a relational algebra solution, to the problem of finding all pairs of supplier numbers, Sx and Sy say, such that Sx and Sy supply exactly the same set of parts each.

Solution (SQL): I will give two SQL solutions. The first is somewhat lengthy but essentially straightforward—basically, it retrieves pairs of supplier numbers such that there is no part supplied by the first and not the second, or by the second and not the first:

```
SELECT SA.S# AS SX, SB.S# AS SY
FROM   S SA, S SB
WHERE  SA.S# < SB.S#
AND    NOT EXISTS
       ( SELECT *
         FROM   P PC
         WHERE  EXISTS
                ( SELECT *
                  FROM   SP SPA
                  WHERE  SPA.S# = SA.S#
```

```
         AND      SPA.P# = PC.P#
         AND      NOT EXISTS
                ( SELECT *
                  FROM    SP SPB
                  WHERE   SPB.S# = SB.S#
                  AND     SPB.P# = PC.P# ) )
    OR   EXISTS
       ( SELECT *
         FROM    SP SPA
         WHERE   SPA.S# = SB.S#
         AND     SPA.P# = PC.P# )
         AND     NOT EXISTS
                ( SELECT *
                  FROM    SP SPB
                  WHERE   SPB.S# = SA.S#
                  AND     SPB.P# = PC.P# ) ) ) ;
```

The second SQL solution, which is due to Henry Pikner of the Federal Reserve Bank in New York, is more succinct, but relies on a somewhat different perception of the logic of solving the problem. The intuitive interpretation of this one is left as a subsidiary exercise for the reader.

```
SELECT SA.S# AS SX, SB.S# AS SY
FROM   SP SA, SP SB
WHERE  SA.S# < SB.S#
AND    SA.P# = SB.P#
GROUP  BY SA.S#, SB.S#
HAVING COUNT (*) =
     ( SELECT COUNT(*)
       FROM    SP
       WHERE   SP.S# = SA.S# )
AND    COUNT (*) =
     ( SELECT COUNT(*)
       FROM    SP
       WHERE   SP.S# = SB.S# ) ;
```

Solution (relational algebra): The following solution is due to Hugh Darwen.

```
T1   :=   ( SP RENAME S# AS SX ) [ SX, P# ] ;
T2   :=   ( SP RENAME S# AS SY ) [ SY, P# ] ;
T3   :=   T1 [ SX ] ;
T4   :=   T2 [ SY ] ;
T5   :=   T1 TIMES T4 ;
T6   :=   T2 TIMES T3 ;
T7   :=   T1 JOIN T2 ;
T8   :=   T3 TIMES T4 ;
T9   :=   SP [ P# ] ;
T10  :=   T8 TIMES T9 ;
T11  :=   T10 MINUS T7 ;
T12  :=   T6 INTERSECT T11 ;
T13  :=   T5 INTERSECT T11 ;
T14  :=   T12 [ SX, SY ] ;
T15  :=   T13 [ SX, SY ] ;
T16  :=   T14 UNION T15 ;
T17  :=   T7 [ SX, SY ] ;
T18  :=   T17 MINUS T16 ;
ANS  :=   T18 WHERE SX > SY ;
```

This is very complicated! And the principal reason for the complexity is that the original relational algebra did not provide any direct support for *relational comparisons* (e.g., the ability to test two relations for equality). However, this omission can and should be remedied. I will have more to say on this matter in a future installment.*

THE COMPARISON PROBLEM

Source: "A Matter of Integrity" (Part 3, Installment Number 16).

Problem statement: What does it mean in SQL/92 for two values *ck1* and *ck2* (possibly composite) to be "the same"? More specifically, you are asked to give precise interpretations for each of the following three statements:

1. *ck1* and *ck2* are "the same" for the purposes of a comparison condition (e.g., in a WHERE clause)
2. *ck1* and *ck2* are "the same" for the purposes of candidate key uniqueness
3. *ck1* and *ck2* are "the same" for the purposes of duplicate elimination (e.g., in UNION)

Solution: It turns out that no two of these statements are equivalent! No. 1 is defined in accordance with the rules of three-valued logic; No. 2 is defined in accordance with the rules for the UNIQUE condition; and No. 3 is defined in accordance with SQL's definition of duplicates. Suppose, for example, that the values *ck1* and *ck2* are simple (i.e., noncomposite) and are in fact both null. Then No. 1 gives *unknown,* No. 2 gives *false,* and No. 3 gives *true.* However, it is at least true that if No. 1 gives *true,* No. 2 must necessarily give *true,* and if No. 2 gives *true,* then No. 3 must necessarily give *true.*

It is probably worth pointing out explicitly that the three statements are all equivalent in the absence of nulls—yet another reason why nulls should be avoided, in my opinion. For further discussion and information, see the book *A Guide to the SQL Standard,* 3rd edition, by C. J. Date and Hugh Darwen, Addison-Wesley, 1993.

THE DUPLICATES PROBLEM

Source: "Toil and Trouble" (Installment Number 17).

Problem statement: You were asked to try out as many different formulations as you could think of for a specific query against a specific database containing du-

---

*See Installment Number 21.

plicates (the database itself, the query, and twelve candidate formulations being given).

Solution: It is obviously impossible to give a "solution" to this problem here. However, I would like to ask a subsidiary (or follow-up) question: Did you notice any differences in response time for different formulations? Probably the database was too small for any such differences to be immediately obvious, but if your system provides a simple way of measuring response times accurately, you might want to carry out some additional experiments . . .

TECHNICAL CORRESPONDENCE

An attendee at one of my seminars, Steve Hnizdur of Reliance Mutual, Tunbridge Wells, England, wrote to draw my attention to the surprising fact (surprising to me, at any rate) that there was a generalized version of the triangle problem, as follows.

Problem statement: We are given a triangle ABC—*not* necessarily isosceles, please note—with angles $A = \alpha$ ($\alpha < 60$), $B = \alpha + 60°$, and therefore $C = 120° - 2\alpha$. Draw a line from B to meet AC at D (between A and C), such that angle ABD $= 30°$. Draw a line from C to meet AB at E (between A and B), such that angle ACE $= 30° - (\alpha/2)$. Draw a line connecting D and E. Find angle DEC.

Solution: Let the angle to be found—i.e., DEC—be θ (see Fig. 2). Draw CF (equal in length to CB) to meet AB at F; F might or might not be between A and B, depending on the value of α. Draw a line connecting F and D. Then it is easy to see that:

```
BCF = 180° - 2(α + 60°) = 60° - 2α;
FCA = 120° - 2α - (60° - 2α) = 60°;
BDC = 180° - (30° + α) - (120° - 2α) = 30° + α
    = DBC;
so CD = BC;
so CD = CF;
so triangle CFD is equilateral.
```

Also:

```
FCE = 60° - (30° - (α/2)) = 30° + (α/2);
FEC = 180° - (90° - (3α/2)) - (60° + α) = 30° + (α/2)
    = FCE;
so FE = FC;
so FE = FD.

EFD = 180° - DFE - CFB
    = 180° - 60° - (60° + α) = 60° - α;
hence FED = (180° - EFD)/2 = 60° + (α/2);
hence θ = FED - FEC
        = 60° + (α/2) - 30° - (α/2)
        = 30°. ■
```

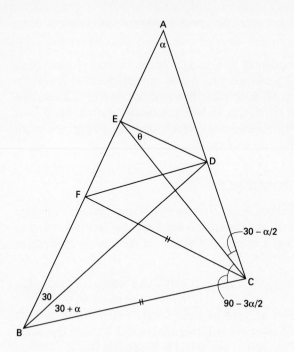

Fig. 2   Generalized triangle ABC

How interesting that the value of θ does not depend on the value of α! To get back to the original special case problem, we take α to be 20°, and then angles B and C are both 80°, and the triangle is therefore isosceles. Note, however, that it is not the fact that the triangle is isosceles *per se* that is important in that special case, but simply the fact that angles A and B have certain specific values (and therefore angle C does too). To repeat, it's only because the values of angles B and C happen to be equal that the triangle happens to be isosceles. However, the fact that the triangle *is* isosceles does allow us to adopt another approach to the problem in that special case (as we saw in my original solution).

More on DEE and DUM

I first discussed TABLE_DEE and TABLE_DUM, those two very special tables that have no columns at all, in this series a year ago ("Tables with No Columns," Installment Number 7). Let me quickly remind you of some of DEE and DUM's salient features:

1. DEE is the one that contains just one row (the 0-tuple); DUM contains no rows at all.

2. DEE corresponds to *true,* or *yes,* and DUM corresponds to *false,* or *no.*

3. DEE is the identity with respect to TIMES and JOIN; that is, DEE TIMES T = T TIMES DEE = T for all tables T (and similarly for JOIN).

A couple of corollaries arise immediately:

- Regarding Point 2 above, I mentioned in Installment Number 7 that one of the reasons that yes/no queries are hard to deal with in SQL is precisely because SQL does not support tables with no columns. For example, the following SQL expression—*IF* it were legal—would represent the yes/no query "Does employee E1 work in department D1?":

```
SELECT /* no columns at all */
FROM    DEPT NATURAL JOIN EMP
WHERE   D# = 'D1'
AND     E# = 'E1' ;
```

Originally published in *Database Programming & Design 7,* No. 3 (March 1994). Reprinted by permission of Miller Freeman Inc.

The answer is *yes* if the "SELECT *no columns* . . ." yields DEE and *no* if it yields DUM. Unfortunately, however, empty SELECT-lists are illegal in SQL.

■   Regarding Point 3, I showed in "Empty Bags and Identity Crises" (Installment Number 8) that it follows from this point that we ought to be able to write a FROM clause that mentions no tables at all, and the result of executing such a FROM clause would be, precisely, TABLE_DEE. If this were possible, then we might write, e.g.,

```
SELECT CURRENT_TIME
FROM    /* no tables at all */ ;
```

Unfortunately, however, empty FROM-lists, like empty SELECT-lists, are illegal in SQL.

I closed Installment Number 7 by saying that there was much more to be said about DEE and DUM. Hence this month's column.

A MATTER OF INTERPRETATION

Some readers have complained that the concept of a table with no columns is rather confusing! Such readers should try asking themselves the following question: What would ordinary arithmetic be like without the concept of zero? You see, tables with no columns play a role in the relational algebra that is very much analogous to the role that zero plays in ordinary arithmetic. In both cases, in fact, the concept is *crucial*.

Another point I've found to cause some confusion is the following. DEE and DUM are, of course, the only possible values that can be assumed by a zero-column table, and we sometimes express this fact by saying (rather sloppily) that they are "the only possible zero-column tables." But many distinct zero-column tables can have DEE or DUM as their *value*—implying that DEE and DUM can have many distinct **interpretations** or **meanings**.

An analogy might help. In the familiar suppliers-and-parts database, the two tables SC (projection of suppliers over supplier cities) and PC (projection of parts over part cities) might conceivably look as shown in Fig. 1. These two tables obviously have the same value, but their meaning is quite different. For example, the fact that London appears in table SC means "There exists at least one London *supplier,*" while the fact that London appears in table PC means "There exists at least one London *part.*"

In exactly the same way, two tables might both have DEE (say) as their value, but the meaning would be quite different in the two cases. In other words, the

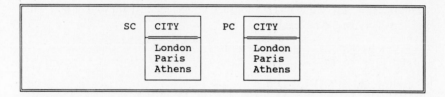

Fig. 1 Tables SC and PC

meaning of DEE and DUM *depends on context*—just as the meaning of *yes* and *no* depends on context, come to that.

SOME MORE SQL ERRORS

I've already pointed out that SQL does not allow either the SELECT-list or the FROM-list to be empty. What makes these omissions slightly surprising is that SQL does (tacitly) allow one of its other clauses to have an empty operand list! The clause in question is GROUP BY. For example, the SQL query

```
SELECT  AVG ( SALARY ) AS ASAL
FROM    EMP ;
```

is—at least conceptually—shorthand for the following:

```
SELECT  AVG ( SALARY ) AS ASAL
FROM    EMP
GROUP   BY /* no columns at all */ ;
```

Explanation: Assume for the moment that table EMP does include at least one row. Then every one of those EMP rows has the same value for the (empty) set of grouping columns—namely, the 0-tuple. There is thus exactly one group in the "grouped table" that is the intermediate result, and so there is exactly one row in the final result. If on the other hand table EMP is empty, then there are no rows to be grouped, and hence no groups, and hence no rows in the final result.

Note: Actually, SQL (at least the SQL standard) falls into another trap in this area. If the SELECT statement includes a HAVING clause but no GROUP BY clause, the original table is treated as a grouped table that contains exactly one group. But—as the foregoing discussion shows—if the original table is empty, it should be treated as a grouped table that contains no groups at all, not "exactly one" group.

Let me revert to the question of empty SELECT-lists and empty FROM-lists for a moment. If SQL did in fact permit such things, then—believe it or not!—the following query would be legal:

```
SELECT /* no columns at all */
FROM   /* no tables at all  */ ;
```

The result would be TABLE_DEE.

Now, we have just seen that SQL—very reasonably—allows a GROUP BY clause in which the "GROUP-BY-list" is empty to be totally omitted. If we applied the same convention to the FROM clause and the SELECT clause, the earlier example of an empty FROM-list would reduce to:

```
SELECT CURRENT_TIME ;
```

The example of an empty SELECT-list would reduce to:

```
FROM   DEPT NATURAL JOIN EMP
WHERE  D# = 'D1'
AND    E# = 'E1' ;
```

And the "believe it or not!" example would become slightly more unbelievable still:

```
;
```

On a more serious note, let me point out a couple more SQL problems arising from its lack of support for DEE and DUM. First, it is not possible to create a base table with no columns (i.e., it is not possible for CREATE TABLE to include no column definitions). Such a facility might be exactly what you would like at database design time, when you might want to specify a new entity type without having to be bothered (yet) with any properties that entity type might possess.

Second, it is not possible (e.g.) to ALTER TABLE T DROP COLUMN C . . . if C happens to be the only column of T. (Perhaps this is not a burning issue, but it's at least worth mentioning in passing as another minor anomaly.)

EMPTY KEYS

What is the primary key for DEE and DUM?

Perhaps I should let you meditate on this question for a while before I go on to discuss it in detail. In fact, I don't want to discuss it in detail right away; rather, I want to take a detour into *functional dependencies* (FDs) and come back to the original question in a few moments.

Let me remind you of the definition of functional dependency. We say that column C of table T is *functionally dependent* on some set of columns X of T (written $X \rightarrow C$) if and only if, whenever two rows of T have the same value for X, they also have the same value for C.

Notice in this definition that X is a *set* of columns. As soon as we realize this fact, we should immediately ask: What happens if that set is empty?—i.e., if X is the empty set (usually written "ϕ")? Well, if the FD $\phi \to C$ holds in T, it must be true that every row of T has the same value for C—because every row certainly has the same value for ϕ, namely the 0-tuple.

Now suppose that the FD $\phi \to C$ holds for *all* columns C of T. Then ϕ must be a candidate key for T!—because (as I explained in "The Power of the Keys," Installment Number 9) if K is a set of columns of T such that (a) $K \to C$ holds true for all columns C of T, and (b) no subset of K possesses the same property, then K is a candidate key for T. And if ϕ is a candidate key, it must be the *only* candidate key (and hence the primary key)—because any other set of columns of T would necessarily include ϕ as a proper subset, and would therefore violate the *irreducibility* requirement for candidate keys.

So we have arrived at the idea that a table T can quite legitimately have ϕ as its primary key. (Note that I'm still talking about tables in general here, not necessarily just the special tables DEE and DUM.) Observe, however, that any such table is constrained to contain *at most one row*. This is because, if it contained more than one row, each of those rows would contain the same value (the 0-tuple) for the empty set of columns, and we would have a primary key uniqueness violation on our hands!

The notion that a primary key can be empty (i.e., contain no columns) turns out to be crucially important in Darwen's work on functional dependency and candidate key inheritance (see "The Power of the Keys," Installment Number 9, for further discussion). Furthermore, empty keys can also be useful in database design. It is often the case that the entity type at the top of some hierarchy of entity types is constrained to have just one instance; for example, in the COMPANY–DIVISION–DEPARTMENT–EMPLOYEE hierarchy, there should be just one row in the COMPANY table. Specifying ϕ as the primary key for the COMPANY table can be used to achieve the desired effect. (Note that, e.g., COMPANY_NAME is *not* the true primary key—though most people would probably say it was—because it does not satisfy the irreducibility requirement for candidate keys. What is more—precisely because it doesn't satisfy that irreducibility requirement—pretending that COMPANY_NAME is the primary key also doesn't capture the constraint that the table can contain at most one row.)

Now, we already know that TABLE_DEE and TABLE_DUM are constrained to contain at most one row (in fact, of course, DEE contains exactly one row and DUM contains no rows at all). Indeed—as I'm sure you've realized by now—the empty set ϕ is the primary key for both DEE and DUM. So (thank goodness!) DEE and DUM, like all other relational tables, most certainly do possess at least one candidate key each (in fact they possess *exactly* one candidate key each). To repeat a point, however, do not fall into the trap of thinking that DEE and DUM are the only tables that can have an empty key.

CONCLUDING REMARKS

The discussions of the previous section point to yet another SQL error, or at least an omission—namely, the fact that SQL does not support empty keys. Now, one thing I didn't mention explicitly in those discussions was the following: Since (as we have seen) a primary key can be empty, a foreign key can therefore be empty as well! That is, a table *T2* might include a foreign key *FK* that references a table *T1* via *T1*'s primary key *PK,* where *PK* is in fact empty. For this month's puzzle corner, you are invited to think about the consequences of this idea, and in particular to try to answer the question: Could empty foreign keys be useful in practice?

I would like to close by acknowledging my heavy debt in this area to Hugh Darwen. Much of this month's column is based on his chapter "The Nullologist in Relationland" in our joint book *Relational Database Writings 1989–1991,* Addison-Wesley, 1992. For further reading on this topic, I recommend that chapter wholeheartedly.

Divide—and Conquer?

Of all the operators in the relational algebra, the divide operator has the reputation—perhaps justified—of being the hardest to understand. What is more, it also suffers from certain shortcomings that conspire to make it a trifle unsatisfactory in certain ways; in fact, it doesn't even quite do the job it was originally designed to do. This month, I want to try and demystify this rather annoying operator, and consider what might be done to overcome its various drawbacks. *Note:* Much of the following material is based on an earlier joint paper (reference [2]) by myself and Hugh Darwen.

AN INFORMAL EXAMPLE

According to Codd [1], the divide operator was explicitly introduced into the relational algebra as a counterpart to the universal quantifier FORALL in the relational calculus. Thus, it was specifically intended as a basis for dealing with "FORALL-type" queries. Consider, for example, the usual suppliers-and-parts database, in which tables { S#, . . . }, P { P#, . . . }, and SP { S#, P#, . . . } represent suppliers, parts, and shipments of parts by suppliers, respectively. Consider also

Originally published in *Database Programming & Design 7*, No. 4 (April 1994). Reprinted by permission of Miller Freeman Inc.

the query "Find supplier numbers for suppliers who supply all parts." Here is a straightforward formulation of this query in the relational calculus:

```
S.S# WHERE FORALL P EXISTS SP
            ( SP.S# = S.S# AND SP.P# = P.P# )
```

("supplier numbers where, for all parts, there exists a shipment saying that the supplier supplies the part").

Here, by contrast, is the relational algebra expression that would most commonly be given as a representation of this query (in fact, this very example is often used as an introduction to the use of the divide operator—indeed, I've used it this way myself many times):

```
SP [ S#, P# ] DIVIDEBY P [ P# ]
```

Explanation: The expression SP[S#,P#] represents the projection of the shipments table SP over columns S# and P#, and thus yields the set of all supplier-number/ part-number pairs such that the indicated supplier supplies the indicated part. The expression P[P#] represents the projection of the parts table P over column P#, and thus yields the set of all part numbers. By dividing the latter into the former, we obtain the set of all supplier numbers that are paired in table SP with *every* part number from table P—in other words, we get supplier numbers for suppliers who supply all parts, as required. Or do we? I'll come back to this question later.

CODD'S DIVIDE

Here then is a definition of Codd's original divide operator:

■ Let tables *A* and *B* have headings {*X,Y*} and {*Y*}, respectively. (*X* and *Y* here represent *sets* of columns; *Y* is all the columns of *B,* and *X* is all the columns of *A* not included in *B*. Note that the heading of *B* must be a subset of the heading of *A*.)

■ Then the division of *A* by *B, A* DIVIDEBY *B,* is a table with heading {*X*} and with body consisting of all rows {*X:x*} such that a row {*X:x,Y:y*} appears in *A* for all rows {*Y:y*} appearing in *B*.

Note to the reader: It would probably be a good idea to check the explanation given earlier for the relational algebra solution to the "suppliers who supply all parts" problem to ensure that that explanation does indeed conform to this definition.

Now, divide as just defined is not a primitive operator. To be specific, the expression *A* DIVIDEBY *B* is semantically equivalent to the following more complex expression:

```
A [ X ] MINUS ( ( A [ X ] TIMES B ) MINUS A ) [ X ]
```

Or to spell it out one step at a time:

```
T1    :=   A [ X ] ;
T2    :=   T1 TIMES B ;
T3    :=   T2 MINUS A ;
T4    :=   T3 [ X ] ;
ANS   :=   T1 MINUS T4 ;
```

TODD'S DIVIDE

As we have seen, Codd's divide required the heading of the divisor to be a subset of the heading of the dividend. Stephen Todd of the IBM UK Scientific Centre in Peterlee, England, subsequently defined a more general form of divide that allowed any table to be divided by any table, regardless of whether the divisor's heading was a subset of the dividend's or not. Suppose we extend the suppliers-and-parts database to include a table PJ showing which parts (P#) are used in which projects (J#). Then the expression

```
SP [ S#, P# ] DIVIDEBY PJ [ P#, J# ]
```

gives S#-J# pairs such that supplier S# supplies all parts used in project J#; by contrast, the expression

```
PJ [ J#, P# ] DIVIDEBY SP [ P#, S# ]
```

gives J#-S# pairs such that project J# uses all parts supplied by supplier S#. (Or do they? Again, I'll come back to this question later.)

Here is the definition of Todd's divide:

- Let tables *A* and *B* have headings {*X,Y*} and {*Y,Z*}, respectively.

- Then the division of *A* by *B*, *A* DIVIDEBY *B*, is a table with heading {*X,Z*} and with body consisting of all rows {*X:x,Z:z*} such that a row {*X:x,Y:y*} appears in *A* for all rows {*Y:y,Z:z*} appearing in *B*.

(As before, it is probably worth checking the examples given above against this definition.)

Like Codd's divide, Todd's divide can be defined in terms of other operations, as follows:

```
( A [ X ] TIMES B [ Z ] ) MINUS
( ( A [ X ] TIMES B ) MINUS ( A JOIN B ) ) [ X, Z ]
```

Step-at-a-time version:

```
T1    :=   A [ X ] ;
T2    :=   B [ Z ] ;
T3    :=   T1 TIMES T2 ;
T4    :=   T1 TIMES B ;
T5    :=   A  JOIN  B ;
T6    :=   T4 MINUS T5 ;
T7    :=   T6 [ X, Z ] ;
ANS   :=   T3 MINUS T7 ;
```

PROBLEMS WITH THE FOREGOING

I've already indicated that divide suffers from certain problems. To be specific:

1. Codd's divide and Todd's divide both have difficulties over empty sets and related matters—which is why I hinted that the informal characterizations of the various examples given earlier were all slightly inaccurate.

2. Furthermore, the corrected versions of those examples are not of the form *A* DIVIDEBY *B* for any *A* and *B* whatsoever. That is, they are not divides!— which is why I stated earlier that divide does not quite do the job it was meant to. This criticism applies to both Codd's and Todd's version.

3. Todd's divide is not quite a generalized version of Codd's—which implies, quite apart from anything else, that we should definitely not use the same syntax *A* DIVIDEBY *B* for both.

Now let's examine each of these problems in turn.

THE FIRST PROBLEM

To illustrate the first problem, I will go back to Codd's divide, but consider a slightly more complex example: "Find supplier numbers for suppliers who supply all *purple* parts." The following expression, a little surprisingly, does NOT give the right answer:

```
SP [ S#, P# ] DIVIDEBY ( P WHERE COLOR = 'Purple' ) [ P# ]
```

Why doesn't this work? Well, let's assume that in fact no purple parts exist at all. Then *every supplier supplies all of them!* This is because (as I explained in "Empty Bags and Identity Crises," Installment Number 8) the universal quantifier FORALL applied to an empty set always yields *true*—even when that *true* result does not seem very intuitive. As I put it in that earlier installment: The statement "all giraffes living at the bottom of the sea are bright purple" is *true,* because the set "all giraffes living at the bottom of the sea" is empty. Thus, "all purple parts are supplied by supplier S*x*" is *true* if the set of all purple parts is empty—and it is *true* no matter who supplier S*x* happens to be (i.e., it is true for *every* supplier).

To repeat, therefore: If there are in fact no purple parts, then *all* suppliers supply all of them—**even suppliers who supply no parts at all**. And if there are any suppliers who supply no parts at all, those suppliers will be represented in the suppliers table S but *not* in the shipments table SP. There is thus no way the expression shown above can produce such a supplier, because it extracts supplier numbers from table SP, *not* from table S.

As for Todd's divide, space does not permit me to go into details here; suffice it to say that it suffers from precisely analogous problems. What this all means is that neither Codd's divide nor Todd's divide is exactly the counterpart to the universal quantifier that it was originally intended to be.

Now, at this point you might well be thinking that this is all a very tiny problem indeed, one that is scarcely worth bothering about in practice. But let me remind you that we are talking here about the relational model, the **principal virtue** of which is supposed to be that it is soundly based on what is known formally as *first-order logic*. Indeed, the relational calculus consists of an applied form of that logic, and the relational algebra in turn is intended to be precisely equivalent to the relational calculus—equivalent, that is, in the sense that every expression of the algebra has a precise equivalent in the calculus and vice versa.

As the foregoing discussion shows, however, this equivalence between the algebra and the calculus is not as straightforward a matter as we would like it to be. To revert to our original query ("suppliers who supply all parts"), the calculus and algebraic formulations given were *not* equivalent. In fact, the algebraic formulation does not truly correspond to the informal characterization "suppliers who supply all parts"—instead, it corresponds to the characterization "suppliers who *supply at least one part* and in fact supply all parts." Perhaps more significantly, the expression

```
SP [ S#, P# ] DIVIDEBY ( P WHERE COLOR = 'Purple' ) [ P# ]
```

does not correspond to the characterization "suppliers who supply all purple parts"—instead, it corresponds to the characterization "suppliers who *supply at least one part* and in fact supply all purple parts."

Thus we can see that there are—at the very least—certain traps for the unwary in the use of the divide operator. More specifically, the most obviously intuitive formulation of a given FORALL-type query, using divide, is very often *not* the formulation that is logically correct. This is a serious pyschological issue, if not a logical one.

THE SECOND PROBLEM

It is not difficult to find a correct formulation of these FORALL-type queries. To see that this is so, consider first the step-at-a-time expansion of the previous (incorrect) formulation of the the query "Find supplier numbers for suppliers who supply all purple parts." For simplicity, let's assume that we have already constructed a table PP that contains just the part numbers of purple parts—i.e., PP is table P restricted to purple parts and then projected over P#.

```
T1  :=  SP [ S# ] ;
T2  :=  T1 TIMES PP ;
T3  :=  T2 MINUS SP ;
T4  :=  T3 [ S# ] ;
ANS :=  T1 MINUS T4 ;
```

All we have to do to convert this to a correct solution is to replace "SP[S#]" in the first step by "S[S#]" instead, so that supplier numbers are extracted from the set of *all* supplier numbers (in table S) instead of just from the set of supplier numbers for suppliers who supply at least one part (in table SP). This corrected solution will produce the right answer even if there are no purple parts—i.e., even if table PP is empty (you should take a moment to convince yourself that this is so).

The trouble is, the revised (correct) sequence is no longer of the form *A* DIVIDEBY *B* for any *A* and *B* at all—i.e., it does not match the definition template for divide. In other words, it isn't a divide.

Now, it would be possible to define a new relational algebra operator whose definition template does match the corrected sequence; indeed, I suggested exactly such an operator in reference [2]. However, it would certainly not be appropriate to call that new operator "divide"! Codd did not choose the name "divide" arbitrarily—he chose it because of the following nice property:

```
( A TIMES B ) DIVIDEBY B  ≡  A
```

(i.e., if we form the product of tables *A* and *B* and then divide the result by table *B,* we get back to table *A* again; DIVIDEBY is a kind of inverse of TIMES). With the hypothetical new operator, by contrast, there would be three operands (S, SP, and PP in the example), and no analogous property would or could possibly hold. The name "divide" would thus no longer be very apt.

Remarks analogous to the above apply to Todd's divide also. I omit the details for space reasons.

THE THIRD PROBLEM

The third problem is that Codd's divide is *not* a special case of Todd's divide in the (presumably unusual) situation in which the divisor is empty. In fact, it is easy to see from the step-at-a-time definitions that if *B* is empty, then Codd's divide gives the projection of *A* over *X,* while Todd's divide gives an empty result. (The same is true for the revised operations suggested in reference [2].) As stated earlier, therefore, the two operators *cannot* logically be given the same name.

CONCLUDING REMARKS

Given all of the foregoing difficulties, the idea of avoiding divide altogether begins to look distinctly attractive! In next month's installment, I will discuss *relational comparison operators,* which (among other things) can be used for exactly this purpose. Until then, let me leave you with this month's puzzle corner problem, which is simply to give SQL equivalents for each of the divide examples we have been discussing. This exercise might give you increased respect for the divide operator!—despite the various shortcomings of that operator that we have been examining above.

REFERENCES

1. E. F. Codd, "Relational Completeness of Data Base Sublanguages," in R. Rustin (ed.), *Data Base Systems,* Courant Computer Science Symposia Series 6 (Englewood Cliffs, N.J.: Prentice-Hall, 1972).

2. C. J. Date and Hugh Darwen, "Into the Great Divide," in *Relational Database Writings 1989–1991* (Reading, Mass.: Addison-Wesley, 1992).

Relational Comparisons

In Installment Number 15, I asked the following as a puzzle corner problem:

■   Given relation SP { S#, P# } showing which suppliers (S#) supply which parts (P#), give (a) an SQL solution, (b) a relational algebra solution, to the problem of finding all pairs of supplier numbers, Sx and Sy say, such that Sx and Sy supply exactly the same set of parts each.

I remarked also that it would probably be easier to find the SQL solution than the relational algebra solution, owing to a very unfortunate omission from the original relational algebra. And in Installment Number 18, I explained that the omission in question was *relational comparison operators*. In this installment, I want to examine this issue in some detail.

THE BASIC IDEA

When designing a programming language, it is a good principle, as soon as you introduce a new type of object (for example, strings, reals, tuples, arrays, sets, etc.), immediately to ask yourself two questions:

Originally published under the title "Relations Beyond Compare" in *Database Programming & Design* 7, No. 5 (May 1994). Reprinted by permission of Miller Freeman Inc.

1. What does it mean to **assign** one object of this type to another?
2. What does it mean to **compare** two objects of this type?

Now, when Codd was designing the original relational model—and the relational model is, after all, effectively nothing more than a rather abstract programming language—the major object type he introduced was, of course, the relation. And he remembered the first of these two questions, and did include a relational assignment operator in the model; but he very unfortunately forgot the second, with the result that there was no direct way (in the model as originally defined) of comparing two relations—for instance, testing them for equality, or testing to see whether one was a subset of the other. And as we know, one consequence of this omission was that certain queries were extremely awkward to express.

However, the omission is easily repaired. In a nutshell, all we need to do is:

1. Decide what kind of relational comparisons we would like to be able to perform—that is, what new comparison operators we need;
2. Define a new kind of *conditional* or *truth-valued* expression that incorporates those comparison operators;
3. (Orthogonality!) Permit those conditional expressions to be used wherever conditional expressions are currently permitted—which means, primarily, in *restrict* operations. *Note:* Technically speaking, a restrict operation that includes such a conditional expression is no longer a genuine restrict operation!—but we can defer discussion of this nicety to a future installment.*

Regarding the first step, it is fairly obvious that the operators we need are things like "equals," "subset of," "proper subset of," "superset of," "proper superset of," and so on. Regarding the other two steps, read on!

NEW CONDITIONAL EXPRESSIONS

Specific syntax is not important, of course, but we need some specific syntax in order to discuss examples. So let me define a new kind of conditional expression, a *relational comparison,* with syntax as follows:

```
rel-exp-1   rel-θ   rel-exp-2
```

Here *rel-exp-1* and *rel-exp-2* are arbitrary relational algebra expressions, and *rel-θ* is any of the following comparison operators:

$=$ (equals)
$\neq$ (not equals)

---

*Unfortunately not one of those included in this volume. The interested reader is referred to Chapter 6 of my book *An Introduction to Database Systems,* 6th edition, Addison-Wesley, 1995.

≤   (subset of)
<   (proper subset of)
≥   (superset of)
>   (proper superset of)

Note: The two comparands (that is, the results of evaluating *rel-exp-1* and *rel-exp-2*) must be "union-compatible"—another topic I plan to discuss in detail in this series sometime soon.* For present purposes, all this means is that they must have *identical headings;* that is, they must have the same column names, and corresponding columns must be defined on the same domain.

I should point out too that the choice of operator symbols is perhaps a little unwise, since, e.g., the negation of "*A* is a proper subset of *B*" is certainly not "*A* is a superset of *B*" (i.e., "<" and "≥" are not inverses of each other). However, I'll stay with these symbols for the purposes of the present discussion.

Here then are a couple of examples, based on the familiar suppliers-and-parts database, with relations S { S#, . . . , CITY } (suppliers), SP { S#, P#, . . . } (shipments), and P { P#, . . . , CITY } (parts).

1. `S [ CITY ] = P [ CITY ]`

   Meaning: Is the projection of suppliers (S) over CITY the same as the projection of parts (P) over CITY?

2. `S [ S# ] > SP [ S# ]`

   Meaning (considerably paraphrased): Are there any suppliers who don't supply any parts?

SOME RESTRICTION EXAMPLES

First let me remind you of the general form of the restrict operation, which is as follows:

   `( rel-exp ) WHERE cond-exp`

Here *rel-exp* is an arbitrary relational algebra expression and *cond-exp* is a conditional expression. (If *rel-exp* is just a relation name, the enclosing parentheses can be omitted.) If *R* is the result of evaluating *rel-exp,* then the overall result of the restriction is, of course, those rows of *R* for which *cond-exp* evaluates to *true.*

Now let's take a look at some restriction examples in which *cond-exp* is, specifically, a relational comparison.

Example 1: Find suppliers who supply all parts.

---

*See Installment Numbers 22 and 23.

The usual expression given for this query involves the relational divide operator:

```
( SP [ S#, P# ] DIVIDEBY P [ P# ] ) JOIN S
```

However, this is not a totally accurate representation of the query, for reasons explained in my column last month. The following, by contrast, is not only arguably easier to understand, it is also correct!

```
T   := SP RENAME S# AS X ;
ANS := S WHERE ( T WHERE X = S# ) [ P# ] = P [ P# ] ;
```

Explanation:

1. The first step results in a relation T that is identical to relation SP except that attribute S# has been renamed as X. The purpose of this step is simply to avoid a naming clash that would otherwise arise in the second step.

2. For a given supplier S*n,* say, in relation S, the expression

```
( T WHERE X = S# ) [ P# ]
```

   evaluates to a relation with one column (P#), giving part numbers for all parts supplied by supplier S*n*. Note in particular that if supplier S*n* supplies no parts at all, then this single-column relation will contain zero rows.

3. This single-column relation is then tested for equality with the relation (also having the single column P#) giving part numbers for all the parts that exist, represented by the expression P[P#]. And this test will yield *true* if and only if the set of part numbers for parts supplied by S*n* is equal to the set of part numbers for all parts that exist.

4. The overall result is thus, precisely, those rows of relation S representing suppliers who supply all parts.

Of course, we can write the entire query as a single expression if we like:

```
S WHERE ( ( SP RENAME S# AS X ) WHERE X = S# ) [ P# ] = P [ P# ]
```

Subexpressions such as the one illustrated in the example—

```
( ( SP RENAME S# AS X ) WHERE X = S# ) [ P# ]
```

(that is, expressions involving a column renaming, followed by an equality comparison that compares that renamed column with a column of the "outer" relation that has the same name as the renamed column before the renaming, followed by a projection)—are needed sufficiently often in practice that it seems worthwhile to introduce an appropriate shorthand. Let us therefore agree to define

```
( MATCHING rel-exp ) [ cols ]
```

(where *rel-exp* is an arbitrary relational expression and *cols* is a list of columns of the result of evaluating that expression) to be an expression that is permitted as a comparand within a restriction, with interpretation as follows: First, let the restriction be

```
R1 WHERE C1
```

and let *C1* be a relational comparison in which one comparand is

```
( MATCHING R2 ) [ cols ]
```

Let the set of columns common to *R1* and *R2* be *Y*. Then the appearance of the subexpression "(MATCHING *R2*[*cols*])" within *C1* is defined to be shorthand for the expression

```
( ( R2 RENAME Y AS X ) WHERE X = Y ) [ cols ]
```

for some arbitrary name *X*. With this simplification, the overall expression for "suppliers who supply all parts" becomes just

```
S WHERE ( MATCHING SP ) [ P# ] = P [ P# ]
```

Example 2: Suppose the suppliers-and-parts database is extended to include the relations J { J#, . . . } (projects) and PJ { P#, J#, . . . } (which shows which parts are used in which projects). Then the expressions

```
( ( S TIMES J ) WHERE ( MATCHING SP ) [ P# ] ≥
                       ( MATCHING PJ ) [ P# ] ) [ S#, J# ]
```

and

```
( ( S TIMES J ) WHERE ( MATCHING SP ) [ P# ] ≤
                       ( MATCHING PJ ) [ P# ] ) [ S#, J# ]
```

yield (a) a relation with heading { S#, J# } such that supplier S# supplies all parts used in project J#, and (b) a relation with heading { J#, S# } such that project J# uses all parts supplied by supplier S#, respectively. Compare the (incorrect!) formulations of these queries using Todd's divide operator (see last month's column).

Example 3 (the pairs-of-suppliers problem from the introduction): We have seen that this query is quite difficult to express in the "classical" relational algebra. However, the ability to do relational comparisons makes it very straightforward. Let RX denote relation S with column S# renamed as SX, projected over that renamed column, and let RY be defined analogously. Then the required result is given by

```
( RX TIMES RY ) WHERE ( SP WHERE S# = SX ) [ P# ] =
                      ( SP WHERE S# = SY ) [ P# ]
```

Appending an additional condition—"AND SX < SY"—would produce a slightly tidier result; specifically, it would (a) eliminate pairs of the form (Sx,Sx), and (b) ensure that the pairs (Sx,Sy) and (Sy,Sx) do not both appear.

SOME MORE SHORTHANDS

One particular comparison that is needed very often in practice is a comparison between a given relation and an empty relation—i.e., a test to see whether the given relation contains zero rows. Once again, therefore, it seems worthwhile to introduce a shorthand. So let me define a truth-valued function

```
IS_EMPTY ( rel-exp )
```

which returns *true* if the result of evaluating *rel-exp* is empty, and *false* otherwise.

Another common requirement is to be able to test whether a given row *r* appears within a given relation *R*. Assuming that we can construct a relation containing a specified row by enclosing the specified row in set brackets { }, the following relational comparison will do the trick:

```
{r} ≤ R
```

However, the following shorthand—which will be very familiar to you if you know SQL, of course—is a little more user-friendly:

```
r IN R
```

Note that IN here is really the *set membership* operator, usually written ∈.

ADDITIONAL BENEFITS

I've shown that the availability of relational comparisons greatly simplifies the formulation of certain queries. In fact, I will go further: If we had relational comparisons, we wouldn't need the quantifiers! This is because

```
EXISTS x ( p )  ≡  NOT ( IS_EMPTY ( x WHERE p ) )
```

and

```
FORALL x ( p )  ≡  IS_EMPTY ( x WHERE NOT ( p ) )
```

In other words, any query that can be expressed using quantifiers can alternatively be expressed using relational comparisons instead. This is a nice bonus, since many people find the quantifiers a little intimidating.

For essentially the same reason, if we had relational comparisons, we wouldn't need the divide operator either (I mentioned this point last month).

Note: In fact, we don't absolutely *need* the quantifiers anyway, thanks to the availability of the aggregate function COUNT. This is because

```
EXISTS x ( p )  ≡  COUNT ( x WHERE p ) > 0
```

and

```
FORALL x ( p )  ≡  COUNT ( x WHERE p ) = COUNT ( x )
```

I'm not a fan of the idea of replacing quantified expressions by COUNT-style expressions, but it would be wrong of me not to mention the possibility.

Another application of relational comparisons is the following. I've argued in this series before that relational systems really ought to support a Boolean or truth-valued data type. If such a data type *were* supported, then any assignment-type operation in which the target is of type Boolean (and note that read and write are both "assignment-type operations"!) could make use of a relational comparison expression to specify the source (right-hand side) of that assignment.

CONCLUDING REMARKS

The idea of relational comparisons is not new. They were included, a trifle tentatively, in the original specification of SQL [1], though they never made it through to the commercial or standard versions of the language. They were also included in a set of database extensions to PL/I proposed by a colleague, Paul Hopewell, and myself in 1970 [2]. However, I'm not aware of any implementation of the relational algebra *per se* that includes support for such comparisons. I've tried to show that such an implementation might be a nice thing to have.

Here to close is this month's puzzle corner problem. Assume that we have a version of the relational algebra that does include relational comparisons. Give algebraic expressions for the following queries:

1. Find suppliers who supply at least all parts supplied by supplier S2.
2. Find supplier numbers for suppliers who supply at least all parts supplied by at least one supplier who supplies at least one London part.

You might like to try giving SQL solutions as well.

REFERENCES

1. Donald D. Chamberlin and Raymond F. Boyce, "SEQUEL: A Structured English Query Language," in *Proc. ACM SIGMOD Workshop on Data Description, Access and Control,* Ann Arbor, Mich. (1974).

2. C. J. Date and P. Hopewell, "Functional Specifications for PL/I Data Base Support" (IBM internal report, October 1970).

Domains, Relations, and Data Types (Part 1 of 2)

Last month, when I was discussing relational comparisons, I said that the two comparands had to be **union-compatible**. I went on to say that what this meant was that the comparands had to have the same column names, and corresponding columns had to be defined on the same domain. This month, I want to examine this idea more closely—but I want to approach it in a slightly roundabout manner. I'll start by elaborating on the relational *domain* concept.

DOMAINS

"Everyone knows" that a domain is a conceptual pool of values from which various columns in various tables draw their actual values. Here, for example, is part of the definition of the suppliers-and-parts database (I follow the recommended discipline of giving each column the same name as its underlying domain wherever possible):

Originally published under the title "Domains, Relations, and Data Types" in *Database Programming & Design 7*, No. 6 (June 1994). Reprinted by permission of Miller Freeman Inc.

```
CREATE DOMAIN S#   CHAR(5) ;
CREATE DOMAIN CITY CHAR(15) ;
CREATE DOMAIN P#   CHAR(6) ;

CREATE TABLE S
  ( S#    S#   NOT NULL,
    ..... ,
    CITY CITY NOT NULL,
  PRIMARY KEY ( S# ) ) ;

CREATE TABLE P
  ( P#    P#   NOT NULL,
    ..... ,
    CITY CITY NOT NULL,
  PRIMARY KEY ( P# ) ) ;

CREATE TABLE SP
   ( S#    S#   NOT NULL,
     P#    P#   NOT NULL,
     ..... ,
   PRIMARY KEY ( S#, P# ), ... ) ;
```

Actually, I would prefer not to use SQL for my examples, because (as I explained in Installment Number 13) SQL "domains" are very far from being true relational domains—they're really little more than shared column definitions. True relational domains, by contrast, are really *data types*—possibly builtin or system-defined, more generally **user-defined**. Many programming languages support the concept of user-defined data types. In Pascal, for example, I can say

```
type Day = ( Sun, Mon, Tue, Wed, Thu, Fri, Sat ) ;
```

And then I can say, for example,

```
var Today : Day ;
```

Here *Day* is very much like a relational domain, and *Today* is very much like a column defined on that domain (it is certainly the case that the "column" *Today* is restricted to values from the "domain" *Day*).

The fact that a domain is really a data type means that there is a great deal more to the concept than is generally realized. However, I'll have to defer discussion of the full implications of this fact until next month. For now, the important point is the following:

If I write a comparison such as A > B *(where* A *and* B *are scalar values), then—because of the fundamental semantics of the data type notion— EITHER (a)* A *and* B *must be of the same type (that is, come from the same domain), OR (b) there must be some conversion function known to the system such that* A *and* B *can at least be converted to the same type.*

In PL/I, for example, the comparison *A > B* is legal if and only if either (a) *A* and *B* are of the same type (say both FIXED DECIMAL) or (b) if one is convertible to the type of the other (say *A* is FIXED DECIMAL and *B* is FLOAT). *Note:*

Please do **NOT** infer from this example that domains are limited to simple things like FIXED DECIMAL or FLOAT; they're not. I'll discuss this point in detail next month.

I'll also come back to the question of conversion between types (or domains) next month; for now, to keep things simple, let's just assume that in a comparison such as $A > B$, the comparands A and B must be of *exactly* the same type. For a relational DBMS, the implication is that the system should reject any relational request that calls for a comparison—either explicit, as in restrict, or implicit, as in divide—between values from different domains. For example:

```
SELECT  S.*
FROM    S
WHERE   NOT EXISTS
      ( SELECT *
        FROM    SP
        WHERE   SP.P# = S.S# ) ;
```

The user here is presumably trying to find suppliers who supply no parts; by mistake, however—probably just a slip of the fingers—he or she has typed "SP.P#" instead of "SP.S#" in the inner WHERE clause. The effect is to request an invalid (cross-domain) comparison, and it would be a friendly act on the part of the DBMS *not* just to execute the query, but instead to point out to the user that the query does not seem to make sense.

Note: In his book [1], Codd calls for "domain check override" (DCO) versions of the relational operators, which allow comparisons to be performed even when the comparands are from different domains. In the foregoing example, for instance, attaching a clause such as "IGNORE DOMAIN CHECKS" to the SQL request would cause the query to be executed despite the user's typing error. But I do not subscribe to the DCO idea, for reasons I'll discuss in detail next month.

Recognizing that a domain is really a data type allows us to recognize also that it is not just comparison operations to which the concept is relevant (despite the emphasis on such operations in most of the database literature). For example, it is certainly relevant to **assignment** (which—as I pointed out last month—includes all read and write operations); that is, the source and target in an assignment must be of the same type (same domain). Which raises the question: What is the type (domain) of the result of an arbitrary expression?—since, of course, the source for an assignment is, in general, an expression of arbitrary complexity. For example, consider the following SQL UPDATE operation, which involves the assignment of the value of a rather complicated scalar expression to column position T.C within the row(s) to be updated:

```
UPDATE T
   SET C = ( X + Y - Z ) * W + 3 ... ;
```

This is yet another question I'm going to have to defer (I'm building up rather a large backlog here, but never mind). But let me just point out that this example also indicates that the whole business of domains or data types is relevant to *all* operations—not just to comparisons and assignments, but also to computational operations such as +, −, ∗, ‖, and so on.

RELATIONS

I've said that domains are really data types. It would be more accurate to say they are **scalar** data types (*aka* atomic, or basic, or primitive, data types). Now, programming languages additionally recognize certain **composite** data types (*aka* nonatomic, or aggregate, or structured, data types), which are built up out of other data types (which can be scalar or composite in turn) by means of certain **type constructors**. For example, arrays and lists are type constructors; thus, we can construct a composite data type that is an array of integers, or a list of arrays of integers, or an array of lists of arrays of character strings, etc., etc.

By the same token, relations constitute a type constructor in the relational model. If I create a new relation (perhaps via CREATE TABLE in SQL), I am— among other things—creating a new composite data type "set of rows," where the rows in turn are all of a certain composite type, namely the type specified by the heading of the new relation (see the next section below).

It follows that, just as (a) when I compare two scalars, those two scalars must be of the same scalar type, so (b) when I compare two relations (see last month's installment), those two relations must be of the same *composite* type (or be such that one can be converted to the type of the other—but we agreed to ignore the possibility of conversions until further notice). This fact is the origin of the notion of **union-compatibility**. (*Note:* "Union-compatibility" is the usual term; as you can see, however, it is really nothing more than a special case of the well-understood programming language notion of *type* compatibility.) In the dialect of the relational algebra we have been using in this series (see "What's in a Name?", Installment Number 3), we say that two relations *A* and *B* are "union-compatible" if and only if they have exactly the same *heading*—that is, they have the same column names, and corresponding columns are defined on the same domain (as explained in the opening to this month's column).

Furthermore, it should be clear that with relations, just as with scalars, the notion of type (or "union") compatibility applies to much more than just comparison operations. To be specific:

- It applies to relational *assignments*. In other words, if I assign relation *B* to relation *A*, then *A* and *B* must be union- compatible—which again raises questions about the type of the result of an arbitrary expression, since (of course) *B* can be a relational expression of arbitrary complexity, in general.

- It applies to certain operations of the relational algebra—specifically union, intersection, and difference operations. In other words, if I form the union or intersection or difference of two relations *A* and *B*, then *A* and *B* must be union-compatible. And (again) what is the type of the result?

Note: "Union-compatibility" is really *not* a very good term. For one thing, the concept does not apply only to union, as we have just seen. For another, different DBMSs, different languages, and different writers all have different definitions of the concept; the definition of reference [1], for example, is much more *ad hoc* than the one given above. It really would be better to stay with the more conventional programming language term **type-compatible** instead.

ROWS

So far, we have discussed *domains* (or scalar types), also *relations* (which are not themselves types but are certainly *of* some [composite] type), but we have skipped over *rows,* which likewise are of some [composite] type (**row** is another type constructor). Basically, a row is a set of ordered pairs

```
{ < C1:v1 >, ..., < Cn:vn > }
```

in which each Ci is a column name and each vi is a scalar from the unique domain Di corresponding to column Ci. Each row thus has a type, namely the Cartesian product of the domains Di (speaking a little loosely). So the notions of type and type compatibility apply to rows also. Without going into details, I will just remark that these notions apply in the following contexts among others:

- When doing row comparisons (for example, testing two rows for equality);
- When testing a row for membership in a relation (via IN or ϵ);
- When checking a referential constraint—which involves comparing two *sub-rows,* in general (i.e., values of a given foreign key and the corresponding primary key)—but a "subrow" can of course be regarded as a row in its own right.

CONCLUDING REMARKS

Well, I've left myself a lot of clearing up to do next month! I will close for now with this month's puzzle corner problem, which (by way of light relief) has nothing to do with databases at all. Here it is. A ladder of length 35 feet leans up against a vertical wall. A cubical box, 12 feet on a side, fits exactly under the ladder (that is, with one edge of the box tucked tightly into the right angle between the wall and the floor, the diagonally opposite edge just touches the ladder). How far is the base of the ladder from the wall?

REFERENCE

1. E. F. Codd, *The Relational Model for Database Management Version 2* (Reading, Mass.: Addison-Wesley, 1990).

Domains, Relations, and Data Types (Part 2 of 2)

I will begin this month by examining **domains** specifically. To date, domains have typically neither been properly implemented, nor properly understood (these two facts are not unrelated, of course). As explained last month, however, a domain is fundamentally just a scalar data type, possibly system-defined (like FIXED DECIMAL or FLOAT), more generally user-defined (like S# or P# in the suppliers-and-parts database).

DEFINING A DOMAIN

So what kind of domain support do we really need? First of all, of course, we need the ability to define a new domain (CREATE DOMAIN in SQL). At a minimum, such a definition must allow the user to specify:

- The **name** of the new domain
- The **representation** of the new domain in terms of previously known domains (as a trivial example, supplier numbers might be represented as charac-

---

Originally published under the title "Domains, Relations, and Data Types, Part II" in *Database Programming & Design 7*, No. 7 (July 1994). Reprinted by permission of Miller Freeman Inc.

ter strings—but note that the representation might be in terms of previously known *user-defined* domains, not just system-defined domains)

■ Any relevant domain-level **integrity rules** (see "A Matter of Integrity," Installment Numbers 14–16)

We also need the ability to specify the legal **operators** that apply to the new domain. However, I don't think such specifications are properly part of the domain definition *per se,* for reasons to be discussed later. Before I can get to that question, however, I need to say something about this business of "domain check override."

"DOMAIN CHECK OVERRIDE"

As I explained last month, domains constrain comparisons. For instance, the comparison SP.S# = S.S# is clearly valid (the comparands are both from the same domain), while the comparison SP.P# = S.S# is *not* valid, because the comparands are from different domains. I also mentioned, however, that Codd has proposed "domain check override" (DCO) versions of the relational operators, which would allow comparisons to be performed even when the comparands are from different domains; a DCO version of join, for example, would cause the join to be done even if the joining columns are not from the same domain (see reference [1]).

The justification for DCO operations is that there will be occasions when the user knows more than the system does. In dealing with the query "Are any of our suppliers also customers of ours?" (for example), it might well be necessary to compare a supplier number and a customer number, and it might equally well be the case that supplier numbers and customer numbers are two different domains. And if this is indeed a reasonable query, then the system must certainly not prevent the user from asking it! So we do need a way of overriding domain checks on occasion. As I stated last month, however, I don't think that "DCO operations" are the appropriate way of dealing with this requirement, for the following reasons.

Consider first the comparison

```
P.WEIGHT > SP.QTY
```

(part weight *vs.* shipment quantity). Assuming that weights and quantities are different domains, we can surely agree that this comparison is invalid. But suppose we write it slightly differently:

```
P.WEIGHT - SP.QTY > 0
```

According to reference [1], this revised comparison is valid!—the system now does *not* perform the necessary domain checking, but merely confirms that all values concerned are "of the same basic data type" (in the example, they are all numbers). In other words, the two comparisons, which are clearly identical from a logical point of view, have—according to reference [1]—different semantics! Now, this *cannot* be correct, or acceptable. So we see first that there is something suspect in reference [1]'s notion of domain checking, which implies *a fortiori* that there is something fishy in the DCO idea too.

Next, consider the comparisons

1. S.S# = 'X3'
2. P.P# = 'X3'
3. S.S# = P.P#

Of these three:

1. The first is valid, and might even evaluate to *true;*
2. The second is valid, and might even evaluate to *true;*
3. The third is not valid.

In other words, we can apparently have three values *x, y,* and *z,* say, such that *x = z* is *true* and *y = z* is *true* and yet *x = y* is not *true*—in fact, we can't even legitimately *write x = y!* So what is going on?

What is going on, of course, is **implicit data type conversion**. In the first comparison, the character string literal value "X3" is implicitly converted to type S#, and the comparison is between two supplier numbers—which is clearly valid. In the second comparison, the "X3" is implicitly converted to type P#, and the comparison is between two part numbers, which again is clearly valid. But in the third case, *there is no conversion known to the system* that can convert a supplier number to a part number or *vice versa,* and so the comparison fails on a type error.

(Let me note in passing that some people would argue strongly that conversions should always be explicit, never implicit. As a matter of fact, I have considerable sympathy for this position. For present purposes, however, I will continue to assume that conversions can indeed be implicit.)

So . . . S# and P# are really user-defined data types (as I keep saying), each defined on the underlying system-defined data type "character string." Part of the process of defining S# and P# is to define **conversion functions** for converting a character string to a supplier number or part number, as applicable; these functions are used implicitly by the system in dealing with expressions such as the two valid comparisons discussed above. In addition, the user might also provide a function—let's call it CHAR—for "going the other way" (that is, for converting a supplier number or part number to a character string). Then, if we really did want to test a supplier number and a part number for (say) equality, presumably what we really want to know is whether *their character string representations* are the same:

```
CHAR ( S.S# ) = CHAR ( P.P# )
```

This kind of mechanism—using either implicit or explicit conversion functions—provides the "domain check override" capability, but does so in a manner that is systematic (not *ad hoc*) and fully orthogonal.

Note: This whole area is one of several where the database community would have done well to have paid more attention to the programming languages community. The fact is, the entire business of data types (including type compatibility and conversions) has been very well understood in the languages world for something like 30 years. And we in the database world could have benefited from that experience, instead of trying to reinvent the wheel (and getting it wrong into the bargain). In fact, if the early database researchers, designers, and developers had paid more attention to programming language ideas, we might not have had some of the database problems we do have today.

OTHER OPERATORS

We can now see that the usual statement to the effect that "the domains must be the same" for a comparison is a very crude approximation to what is really needed. First of all, the rule should be, rather, that if the domains are *not* the same, then there must at least exist a conversion function (known to the system) for converting one to the other. Second, such rules don't apply just to comparison operators! For example, consider the following expressions:

1. `P.WEIGHT + SP.QTY`
2. `P.WEIGHT * SP.QTY`

The first of these (I presume) makes little sense, and it would be nice if the DBMS would reject it. The second, on the other hand, does make sense: It represents the computation of the total weight for all parts involved in the shipment. (The result, therefore, might very well be considered as also belonging to the domain of weights—that is, being of type WEIGHT.)

Complete support for the domain notion would thus include at least all of the following:

1. The ability to specify, for each domain, the valid monadic operators that apply to values from that domain. This will tell the system (among other things) that a character string can be converted to a supplier number.

2. The ability to specify, for each pair of domains, the valid dyadic operators that apply to pairs of values, one from each of those two domains. This will tell the system, for example, that the expressions SP.S# = S.S# and P.WEIGHT $*$ SP.QTY are valid, and (by exclusion) that the expressions SP.P# = S.S# and P.WEIGHT + SP.QTY are invalid.

   Note: Now I can explain why I don't think the operator specifications should be included as part of the domain definition *per se*. The point is, of course, that operators in general apply to *combinations* of domains, not just to a single domain. For instance, should the definition of "∗" (multiplication) be included in the definition of the WEIGHT domain or the QTY domain? The best answer is surely "neither of the above."

3. More generally, the ability to specify, for each combination of *n* domains, the valid *n*-adic operators that apply to collections of *n* values, one from each of those *n* domains.

4. The ability to specify, for each valid operator, the domain of the result of that operator. This will tell the system, for example, that multiplying P.WEIGHT by SP.QTY will produce another weight.

The foregoing implies that the system will know exactly which scalar expressions are legal and which not. It will also know (for those that are legal) the domain of the result. (I mentioned last month that the system needed to know the type of the result of an arbitrary expression; now we see how this can be done.)

Observe that the foregoing also implies that the set of domains (for a given database or other operational unit of "data in the aggregate") must be a *closed set*. That is, the domain of the result of every legal scalar expression must be one of the domains that is known to the system.

Note: In particular, that closed set of domains *must* include the domain of truth values! It is almost incredible that SQL actually allows you to write certain expressions—namely, conditional expressions—that evaluate to a data type that is not one of those known to SQL. See "How We Missed the Relational Boat" (Installment Number 13).

What all the foregoing amounts to is what the programming languages people call **strong typing**. Strong typing implies, among other things, that (a) everything *has* a type, and (b) whenever we write an expression OF ANY KIND, the system checks that *either* the operands of each operator are of the right type for that operator *or* there exist appropriate conversion functions for converting them to the right type. And—at the risk of pointing out the obvious—strong typing is a good idea, because it allows errors to be caught at compile time instead of at run time (or perhaps never!).

Finally, of course, everything I've been discussing extends in an obvious way from scalars to *rows* and *relations* (in particular, to the notion of "union-compatibility"). I omit the details here for space reasons.

WHAT IS A SCALAR?

I don't know whether you've noticed, but so far I've said nothing at all about the nature of the values that can appear inside a domain, except to refer to them as "scalars." Actually those values can be **anything at all!** We tend to think of them as being very simple (numbers, strings, etc.), but there is nothing in the relational model that requires them to be limited to such simple forms. Thus, we can have domains of engineering drawings, domains of legal documents, domains of geometric objects, etc., etc. The only requirement is that any internal structure those values might possess must be *invisible to the DBMS*—that is, the values are indeed scalar (or "atomic") so far as the DBMS is concerned.

And here we are beginning to get into another large topic. What I'm saying here is that, in the relational database world, a domain is (in general) a user-defined data type *of arbitrary complexity*. Now, if we look at the object-oriented (OO) world, we find that one of the fundamental OO concepts, the *object class,* is (in general) a user-defined data type of arbitrary complexity! In other words, domains and object classes are essentially the same thing. And so we have here the key to marrying the two technologies (relational and OO) together. This is very obviously another topic that I need to discuss in detail some other time.*

PUZZLE CORNER

As usual, I'll close with a puzzle corner problem. Unlike last month, the problem this month is at least a database problem, though it does not have much to do with the topic of this month's column as such. Let R be a relation of degree n (that is, a relation with n columns). Then:

1. How many different projections of R are there?
2. What is the maximum number of functional dependencies that can possibly hold in R?
3. What is the maximum number of candidate keys that R can possibly have?

REFERENCE

1. E. F. Codd, *The Relational Model for Database Management Version 2* (Reading, Mass.: Addison-Wesley, 1990).

---

*That installment is not included in this volume, unfortunately. However, the topic is discussed in "The Third Manifesto" (see Part II of this book, Chapter 8).

Answers to Puzzle Corner Problems (Installment Numbers 19–23)

My column this month is devoted once again to answering the various outstanding "puzzle corner" problems from previous installments. Thanks as usual to those readers who wrote in with their own solutions.

EMPTY FOREIGN KEYS

Source: "More on DEE and DUM" (Installment Number 19).

Problem statement: Since a primary key can be empty, a foreign key can obviously be empty as well; that is, a table *T2* might include a foreign key *FK* that references a table *T1* via *T1*'s primary key *PK,* where *PK* is in fact empty. You are invited to think about the consequences of this idea, and in particular to try to answer the question: Could empty foreign keys be useful in practice?

Solution: The following discussion is paraphrased from Hugh Darwen's chapter "The Nullologist in Relationland" in our joint book *Relational Database Writings 1989–1991,* Addison-Wesley, 1992.

Originally published under the title "A Solution for Every Problem" in *Database Programming & Design* 7, No. 8 (August 1994). Reprinted by permission of Miller Freeman Inc.

Note first that *T2* can be *any table whatsoever,* since the empty set of columns is a subset of the heading of every table. In other words, any table whatsoever can reference table *T1*. The referential constraint will be satisfied whenever *T1* is nonempty—that is, contains a single row (it can't have more than one row, by definition!), and will be violated whenever *T1* is empty but *T2* is nonempty.

In particular, any table whatsover can reference TABLE_DEE or TABLE_DUM. Referencing TABLE_DEE achieves nothing—the constraint could be violated only if TABLE_DEE were empty, which by definition it is not. On the other hand, a table that references TABLE_DUM is, perhaps usefully, constrained to be empty. For a specific suggestion of a situation —a little too complex to discuss here—where such a constraint might be useful, see the chapter by Hugh Darwen already mentioned.

DIVIDE IN SQL

Source: "Divide—and Conquer?" (Installment Number 20).

Problem statement: You are asked to give SQL equivalents of the following relational algebra expressions. Note that—as explained in Installment Number 20— the informal characterizations given with these expressions are *not* 100 percent accurate.

1. `SP [ S#, P# ] DIVIDEBY P [ P# ]`

   ("supplier numbers for suppliers who supply all parts")

2. `SP [ S#, P# ] DIVIDEBY PJ [ P#, J# ]`

   ("S#-J# pairs such that supplier S# supplies all the parts used in project J#")

3. `PJ [ J#, P# ] DIVIDEBY SP [ P#, S# ]`

   ("J#-S# pairs such that project J# uses all parts supplied by supplier S#")

4. `SP [ S#, P# ] DIVIDEBY ( P WHERE COLOR = 'Purple' ) [ P# ]`

   ("supplier numbers for suppliers who supply all purple parts")

Solutions:

1. An exact SQL analog is:

```
SELECT  DISTINCT SPX.S#
FROM    SP SPX
WHERE   NOT EXISTS
        ( SELECT *
          FROM    P
          WHERE   NOT EXISTS
                  ( SELECT *
                    FROM    SP SPY
                    WHERE   SPY.S# = SPX.S#
                    AND     SPY.P# = P.P# ) ;
```

An *accurate* characterization of this formulation is "Find supplier numbers for suppliers who supply *at least one part and in fact supply* all parts"). To obtain what is presumably the result actually desired, it would be sufficient to replace the line "FROM SP SPX" by the line "FROM S SPX". The resulting formulation could and probably should then be cosmetically improved to yield:

```
SELECT  S.S#
FROM    S
WHERE   NOT EXISTS
      ( SELECT *
        FROM    SP
        WHERE   NOT EXISTS
              ( SELECT *
                FROM    P
                WHERE   SP.S# = S.S#
                AND     SP.P# = P.P# ) ;
```

(in other words, the supplier numbers should be extracted from table S instead of table SP). For the remaining cases, I will give SQL solutions to the query actually intended rather than precise analogs of the relational algebra expressions.

2. S#-J# pairs such that supplier S# supplies all the parts used in project J#:

```
SELECT  S.S#, J.J#
FROM    S, J
WHERE   NOT EXISTS
      ( SELECT *
        FROM    P
        WHERE   NOT
              ( NOT EXISTS
                  ( SELECT *
                    FROM    PJ
                    WHERE   PJ.J# = J.J#
                    AND     PJ.P# = P.P# )
              OR  EXISTS
                  ( SELECT *
                    FROM    SP
                    WHERE   SP.S# = S.S#
                    AND     SP.P# = P.P# ) ) ) ;
```

3. J#-S# pairs such that project J# uses all parts supplied by supplier S#:

```
SELECT  J.J#, S.S#
FROM    J, S
WHERE   NOT EXISTS
      ( SELECT *
        FROM    P
        WHERE   NOT
              ( NOT EXISTS
                  ( SELECT *
                    FROM    SP
                    WHERE   SP.S# = S.S#
                    AND     SP.P# = P.P# )
              OR  EXISTS
                  ( SELECT *
                    FROM    PJ
                    WHERE   PJ.J# = J.J#
                    AND     PJ.P# = P.P# ) ) ) ;
```

4. Supplier numbers for suppliers who supply all purple parts (this is just a slight variation on the first example):

```
SELECT  S.S#
FROM    S
WHERE   NOT EXISTS
      ( SELECT *
        FROM    SP
        WHERE   NOT EXISTS
              ( SELECT *
                FROM    P
                WHERE   SP.S# = S.S#
                AND     SP.P# = P.P#
                AND     P.COLOR = 'Purple' ) ) ;
```

RELATIONAL COMPARISONS

Source: "Relational Comparisons" (Installment Number 20).

Problem statement: Assume that we have a version of the relational algebra that does include relational comparisons. Give algebraic expressions for the following queries:

1. Find suppliers who supply at least all parts supplied by supplier S2.
2. Find supplier numbers for suppliers who supply at least all parts supplied by at least one supplier who supplies at least one London part.

You might like to try giving SQL solutions as well.

Solutions:

```
1. S WHERE ( MATCHING SP ) [ P# ] ≥
            ( SP WHERE S# = 'S2' ) [ P# ]
2.  T1   :=  ( S RENAME S# AS SX ) [ SX ] ;
    T2   :=  ( SP JOIN P ) WHERE CITY = 'London';
    T3   :=  ( T2 RENAME S# AS SY ) [ SY ] ;
    T4   :=  T1 TIMES T3 ;
    T5   :=  T4 WHERE ( SP WHERE S# = SX ) [ P# ] ≥
                      ( SP WHERE S# = SY ) [ P# ] ;
    ANS  :=  T5 [ SX ];
```

Or as a single nested expression:

```
( ( ( ( S RENAME S# AS SX ) [ SX ]
      TIMES
      ( ( SP JOIN P ) WHERE CITY = 'London' )
          RENAME S# AS SY ) [ SY ] )
    WHERE ( SP WHERE S# = SX ) [ P# ] ≥
          ( SP WHERE S# = SY ) [ P# ] ) [ SX ]
```

Alternative solution, based on a somewhat different perception of the query (and making use of the "IN" shorthand):

```
( SP WHERE P# IN
  ( SP WHERE S# IN
    ( SP WHERE P# IN
      ( P WHERE CITY = 'London')
          [ P# ] ) [ S# ] ) [ P# ] ) [ S# ]
```

SQL versions:

1.
```
SELECT  S.*
FROM    S
WHERE   NOT EXISTS
        ( SELECT SPY.*
          FROM    SP SPY
          WHERE   SPY.S# = 'S2'
          AND     NOT EXISTS
                  ( SELECT SPZ.*
                    FROM    SP SPZ
                    WHERE   SPZ.S# = S.S#
                    AND     SPZ.P# = SPY.P# ) ) ;
```

2.
```
SELECT  DISTINCT SP.S#
FROM    SP
WHERE   SP.P# IN
        ( SELECT SP.P#
          FROM    SP
          WHERE   SP.S# IN
                  ( SELECT SP.S#
                    FROM    SP
                    WHERE   SP.P# IN
                            ( SELECT P.P#
                              FROM    P
                              WHERE   P.CITY = 'London' ) ) ) ;
```

This is (not surprisingly) very similar to the second algebraic solution.

THE LADDER PROBLEM

Source: "Domains, Relations, and Data Types" (Part 1, Installment Number 22).

Problem statement: A ladder of length 35 feet leans up against a vertical wall. A cubical box, 12 feet on a side, fits exactly under the ladder (that is, with one edge tucked tightly into the right angle between the wall and the floor, the diagonally opposite edge just touches the ladder). How far is the base of the ladder from the wall?

Solution: This is a surprisingly difficult problem! The obvious approach is to say something like: Let the distance from the base of the ladder to the wall be x and the distance from the base of the wall to the top of the ladder be y (see Fig. 1). Then we clearly have

$$x^2 + y^2 = 35^2 = 1225$$

by Pythagoras's theorem. Also, by similar triangles, we obviously have

$$(x - 12)/12 = 12/(y - 12)$$

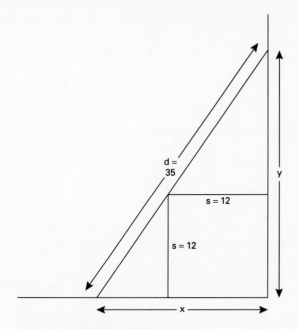

Fig. 1 The ladder and the box

From this latter equation, we obtain $y = 12x(x - 12)$; substituting for y in the first equation and rearranging, we get

$$x^4 - 24x^3 - 937x^2 + 29400x = 176400$$

which doesn't exactly look encouraging! (Do you know the general solution for a quartic equation?) Clearly, this approach doesn't work very well.

So let's try again. One good idea is to work entirely in symbols until the last moment; this technique allows us more easily to spot symmetries or other properties that might be helpful. So let's use d for the length of the ladder and s for the side of the box. The two initial equations then become

1. $x^2 + y^2 = d^2$
2. $(x - s)/s = s/(y - s)$

Second, since (as we have seen) rewriting Equation 2 in terms of expressions in Equation 1 didn't seem very fruitful, let's try the opposite tack: rewriting Equation 1 in terms of expressions in Equation 2. Since $x = (x - s) + s$ and $y = (y - s) + s$, we can rewrite Equation 1 as

$$((x - s) + s)^2 + ((y - s) + s)^2 = d^2$$

Dividing both sides by s^2 and simplifying, we get

$$((x - s)/s)^2 + 2(x - s)/s + 1 +$$
$$((y - s)/s)^2 + 2(y - s)/s + 1 = (d/s)^2$$

Now let $(x - s)/s = z$. Then $(y - s)/s = 1/z$; substituting and simplifying, we get

$$(z + 1/z)^2 + 2(z + 1/z) = (d/s)^2$$

This is a quadratic in $z + 1/z$, which we can solve to obtain

$$z + 1/z = \sqrt{((d/s)^2 + 1)} - 1$$
$$= \sqrt{((35/12)^2 + 1)} - 1)$$
$$= 37/12 - 1$$
$$= 25/12$$

whence we have $z =$ either 4/3 or 3/4. It follows that $x =$ either 21 feet or 28 feet. (There are two solutions because the original problem is obviously symmetric in x and y. When $x = 21$, $y = 28$, and *vice versa*.)

PROPERTIES OF RELATIONS

Source: "Domains, Relations, and Data Types" (Part 2, Installment Number 23).

Problem statement: Let R be a relation of degree n (that is, a relation with n columns). Then:

1. How many different projections of R are there?
2. What is the maximum number of functional dependencies that can possibly hold in R?
3. What is the maximum number of candidate keys that R can possibly have?

Solution:

1. Every projection of R is taken over some subset of the set of columns of R. Since a set of cardinality n has 2^n possible subsets, there are 2^n different projections of the given relation. Note that this count includes the *identity* projection (the projection on all n columns, which yields a result that is identical to R) and the *nullary* projection (the projection on no columns at all, which yields TABLE_DUM if R is empty and TABLE_DEE otherwise).

2. A functional dependency (FD) is basically a statement of the form $A \rightarrow B$, where A and B are each subsets of the set of columns of R. Since (again) a set of cardinality n has 2^n possible subsets, each of A and B has 2^n possible values, and hence an upper limit on the number of possible FDs is 2^{2n}. Note, however, that this count includes many *trivial* FDs (FDs where the right-hand side B is a subset of the left-hand side A).

3. Let m be the largest integer $\geq n/2$. Relation R will have the maximum possible number of candidate keys if either (a) every distinct set of m columns is a candidate key or (b) n is odd and every distinct set of $m-1$ columns is a candidate key. Either way, it follows that the maximum number of candidate keys in R is $n! / (m! * (n-m)!)$.

Here are examples to illustrate the two cases:

```
ELEMENTS ( NAME ... , SYMBOL ... , ATOMIC# ... )
CANDIDATE KEY ( NAME )
CANDIDATE KEY ( SYMBOL )
CANDIDATE KEY ( ATOMIC# )

MARRIAGES ( WIFE ... , HUSBAND ... , WEDDING_DATE ... )
CANDIDATE KEY ( WIFE, HUSBAND )
CANDIDATE KEY ( HUSBAND, WEDDING_DATE )
CANDIDATE KEY ( WEDDING_DATE, WIFE )
```

I'm assuming in this second example that no two distinct marriages involve the same husband and wife.

Many Happy Returns!

This month marks the second anniversary of this column. It also, near enough, marks the **25th** anniversary of the relational model!—Codd's very first paper on relational matters, an IBM Research Report, was dated August 19th, 1969 [6]. So this month, instead of taking my usual approach of homing in on some specific aspect of the relational model and examining it in detail, it seemed appropriate to step back a little and take stock, and in particular to pay tribute to Codd's tremendous achievement in getting the whole world to "go relational." In what follows, therefore, I would like to offer a personal perspective on what seem to me to be some of the major events in relational history.

CODD'S ORIGINAL CONTRIBUTION

Throughout the 1970s, Codd published an extraordinary series of original papers [7–11] that elaborated and built on the ideas first articulated in reference [6]. Those papers provided the foundation for just about everything we think of as relational today. **The importance of that work cannot be overestimated**. Today's multibillion dollar relational database industry owes its existence—

Originally published in *Database Programming & Design 7*, No. 9 (September 1994). Reprinted by permission of Miller Freeman Inc.

indeed, many of us (myself not least) owe our livelihoods and our very careers—to the contributions that Codd made in those original papers.

Of course, I don't mean to suggest that nobody else contributed to relational development during the 1970s. Nor do I mean to suggest that Codd's papers got every last detail exactly right, or that Codd himself foresaw every last implication of his ideas. But such a state of affairs is normal and natural when such a major invention first sees the light of day (think of the telephone, or the automobile, or television—or computers themselves, come to that).

Before I go any further, therefore, let me briefly mention a few important contributions made by other early workers in the field:

- The work of Hall, Todd, and others at the IBM Scientific Centre in the UK on the IS/1 and PRTV prototypes [16,22]

- The work of Chamberlin, Traiger, and others at IBM Research in San Jose, California, on the System R prototype [3,5]

- The work of Zloof at IBM Research in Yorkstown Heights, New York, on the Query-By-Example prototype [23]

- The work of Stonebraker, Wong, and others at UC Berkeley on the INGRES prototype [19,20]

- The work of Armstrong, Fagin, and others on dependency theory [1,14]

Some people might be a little surprised at the inclusion of IS/1 and PRTV in this list. Certainly those prototypes are not as well known as the other contributions mentioned. This situation is undeserved, however, and also somewhat unfortunate, given that IS/1 and PRTV got so many things right that later prototypes—and products—subsequently got wrong.

Anyway, the various prototype activities mentioned above led to significant developments in such areas as data independence, query compilation, optimization, security, integrity, view support, user interface design, and many others—and, of course, they paved the way for all of the numerous products we see in the marketplace today.

THE HISTORICAL CONTEXT

We are so used to relational technology these days, and think of it as being so "obvious" and "natural," that I suspect that many current database practitioners don't even know what the database scene was like when Codd published his first papers. ("Those who don't know history are doomed to repeat it"? Certainly there are signs that some of the early, prerelational mistakes are being made all over again in a new context . . . But that's far too big a topic to pursue here.)

By way of illustrating what the prerelational scene was in fact like, here is a quote from the documentation for a certain well-known prerelational system (no prizes):

> *Logically deleting a logical child prevents further access to the logical child using its logical parent. Unidirectional logical child segments are assumed to be logically deleted. A logical parent is considered logically deleted when all its logical children are physically deleted. For physically paired logical relationships, the physical child paired to the logical child must also be physically deleted before the logical parent is considered logically deleted.*

You see?

Another striking example appears in reference [12], where a simple application—a machine shop scheduling application—is coded in both CODASYL and a relational language. For full details of the example, the reader is referred to the original paper [12]; here just let me make the following observations.

- The CODASYL solution involved over 60 statements, including 15 GO TOs, 12 IFs, and well over 20 distinct database statements (FINDs, GETs, STOREs, etc.). The relational solution, by contrast, involved just *three* statements—one SELECT, one (COBOL) MOVE, and one INSERT, in SQL terms. (And in fact the relational solution could have been reduced to a single INSERT ... SELECT statement, if desired.)

- The CODASYL "solution"—which was not created by the authors of reference [12] but was taken from a document that was intended as a CODASYL *tutorial*—included at least two bugs!

The example (along with many, many others like it) thus clearly showed that relational systems can tremendously simplify problems of database access.

There's another point I'd like to make here, too. The relational model is not just "a better CODASYL." In a way, the early relational advocates (and I certainly include myself in this camp) did themselves a major disservice in the early days. You see, we had to try and convince the world at large that relations were a viable technology, one that really could solve the same kinds of problems that hierarchies and networks could solve; and so we necessarily got into the business of *comparing* relational technology and those old, prerelational technologies. In so doing, however, we unwittingly reinforced the idea that relations and hierarchies and networks were all the same kind of thing ... with the further implication that if relations did replace hierarchies and networks, something else could come along and replace relations in turn.

I now believe strongly that such a perception is WRONG. **Relational really is different**. "Relational *vs.* nonrelational" is an apples-and-oranges comparison; it is not like comparing, say, PL/I and COBOL, or Smalltalk and C++, or even COBOL and C++. The relational model consists of a *set of abstract principles* upon which *any* modern DBMS—regardless of whether it "looks relational on the outside"—really ought to be based. Debates on the relative merits of relational and nonrelational technology usually miss this fundamental point.

Anyway, you can see that the historical context was a mess . . . and you would think that anyone with a good and reasonable proposal for getting us out of that mess would be welcomed with open arms. Well, you'd be wrong.

THE BATTLES FOR ACCEPTANCE

Codd spent a significant portion of his time in the 1970s and early 1980s fighting for his ideas, both in the community at large and—perhaps more significant at the time—inside IBM in particular. And the struggles were very much uphill. Here, for example, is (the gist of) a response Codd received from an IBM manager to whom he had written suggesting that relational database should be seriously considered as part of IBM's longterm database strategy:

> *My staff and I have found your comments interesting. In order to provide a more thorough and in-depth analysis on their applicability as a requirement for future database systems, we respectfully request that you provide the following:*
>
> 1. *A clear definition of relational databases: their structure, access technique, programming methods, compatibility, and comparison with our current database standard DL/I*
>
> 2. *Economic justification of a business case*
>
> 3. *Account scenarios and experience of users in today's environment, with names, descriptions, performance, and function provided*
>
> 4. *Account of application descriptions of users in the future, by industry and application type, if possible*
>
> 5. *Description of compatibility with CODASYL*

This, in 1975 . . . !

Turning to battles outside of IBM: The most visible example was *The Great Debate,* which was the outcome of a challenge issued by Ted Codd (with my support) to Charles Bachman, the best-known proponent of the CODASYL network approach. The debate was held at the ACM SIGMOD meeting in Ann Arbor, Michigan, May 1974. Here is a quote from a review of the event published in *Communications of the ACM* in June that year: *". . . the whole session must certainly be put down as a milestone event of the kind too seldom witnessed in [the computing] field"* [2].

Well, these examples—despite the fact that they represent just the tip of a very large iceberg—should be sufficient to give some idea of the kind of battles that Codd got himself involved in. Thank goodness, he won. And so did we all.

SOME MAJOR MILESTONES

It's very hard to say which historical events are major and which not. IBM's announcement of DB2, for example, was obviously "major" in some respects, but perhaps not so major as the internal IBM meeting at which the decision was made to devote resources to the project that led to that announcement. Thus, some "major" events were not very visible at the time, or were not very obviously "major" at the time they occurred. But I don't think anybody would quarrel with the following perhaps rather conservative list:

■   Publication of Codd's paper in *Communications of the ACM* (1970)

In my opinion, the publication of this paper [7] was *the* most significant event in the whole history of database technology. It was this paper that put database research on a solid scientific footing.

One particular consequence of the publication of reference [7] was that numerous prototype implementations got under way. Among these I should mention:

■   MacAIMS (1970–71)

I include MacAIMS mainly as a matter of historical interest. Certainly it would be wrong to imply that the MacAIMS effort was a consequence of the publication of reference [7]. In fact, the MacAIMS system was built at MIT more or less at the same time as, and in parallel with, (and at least partly independently of) Codd's original work [15,21]. It's an interesting example of that phenomenon where ideas seem to float around the stratosphere and get picked up by several people independently at pretty much the same time—as with, for example, the almost simultaneous development of the differential calculus by Leibniz and Newton, or the almost simultaneous discovery of Neptune by Leverrier and Adams. However, the MacAIMS people didn't seem to recognize the full importance of what they had, and they never really followed through. Nevertheless, it would be wrong to ignore their pioneering efforts here.

■   IS/1 and PRTV (1971–75)

I mentioned this work previously.

■   The Great Debate (1974)

I've already discussed this one too.

■   System R (early-mid 1970s)

The System R prototype was built in IBM Research, San Jose. It was extremely successful in showing that a relational system could be built with reasonable performance. It pioneered the compilation approach adopted by many products today, also certain aspects of optimization (particularly the use of database statistics in access path selection). The success of System R was probably the principal reason IBM management signed on to the idea of building a relational product . . . and the rest is history, as they say.

■ INGRES (early-mid 1970s)

INGRES was the other "big" 1970s prototype. It was very influential in the academic world, and of course it too—like System R—led directly to a commercial product. Like System R, it was a pioneer in a number of fields, not least the field of optimization. In particular, its query language QUEL was in my opinion (and in that of many other people) far superior to IBM's query language SQL. Unlike System R, however, INGRES had the misfortune of not being built in IBM; if it had been, we might now have had a much better relational standard than we do.

■ Early product announcements (1979–83)

These marked the first signs of maturity in the field, when research started to become engineering.

■ Tandem NonStop SQL (1987)

Early relational systems, while certainly providing great improvements over prerelational systems in such areas as usability, flexibility, data independence, productivity, ease of prototyping, and so forth, did not provide the kind of performance needed for high-volume production applications. And some people claimed they never would. The following (contemporary, genuine) quote is quite typical:

Why Large On-Line Relational Systems Don't (and May Not Ever) Yield Good Performance (title of a paper by William Inmon [17])

Tandem's NonStop SQL was the first product to expose this performance myth for what it was—a myth. As I wrote at the time [13]: *"A genuine relational DBMS has finally demonstrated transaction rates equal to or better than the rates of the fastest nonrelational DBMSs—rates in the hundreds or even thousands of transactions per second."* (Subsequently, of course, several other vendors also demonstrated such transaction rates, and we began to get into the *benchmark wars*—but that's another story.)

■ SQL/86, SQL/89, SQL/92, . . .

I suppose these also have to be regarded as major milestones (some might say millstones). I make no further comment here.

THE FUTURE

What of the future? Well, despite the phenomenal success of relational technology in the marketplace, we are—predictably enough—seeing something of a "relational backlash" right now. To quote reference [4]:

> *It is hard for relational advocates, having been on the leading edge for 10 to 12 years, to wake up and find that fashion has moved on to something else. The temptation is to tell the upstarts they don't know what they're talking about.*

The author is referring, of course, to the widespread current brouhaha regarding object-oriented (OO) systems. But he unwittingly puts his finger on the nub of the problem when he refers to "fashion." An acquaintance of mine from the UK, Adrian Larner, sums the matter up very nicely [18]:

> *I am, I regret to say, resigned to the transient triumph of OO: Fashion is more powerful than reason, for reason is not the property of any vested interest. We should count ourselves lucky that for some while now, fashion and reason have coincided in relational. But—once again—we have failed to learn from our successes.*

However, I am *not* so resigned! What we need to do is to take the *good* ideas of OO (but not the bad ones, of which there are more than a few) and incorporate them into relational systems. In my opinion, there are exactly two such "good ideas":

- User-defined data types
- Inheritance

Detailed discussion of how to incorporate these ideas into relational systems would be out of place here; suffice it to say that (as I indicated in my column last month) *domains are the key*. I've already promised to discuss this issue in more depth in a future installment. Here I content myself with the following remarks:

- A relational system that implemented domains properly would be able to do all the things that OO advocates claim their systems can do and relational systems cannot.
- The whole reason we are hearing so much about OO systems is precisely because the relational vendors have failed to step up to the challenge of implementing the relational model properly.
- And that failure in turn stems from a failure to understand what the relational model is really all about.

So I expect (or at least hope) that the future will see "proper" relational systems, with "proper" domain support, that are capable of doing the good things that OO promises. Certainly it would be a tremendous shame to walk away from 25 years of relational research and development.

REFERENCES

1. W. W. Armstrong, "Dependency Structures of Data Base Relationships," Proc. IFIP Congress, Stockholm, Sweden (August 1974).

2. Robert Ashenhurst, "A Great Debate," *CACM 17,* No. 6 (June 1974).

3. M. M. Astrahan *et al.,* "System R: Relational Approach to Database Management," *ACM TODS 1,* No. 2 (June 1976)

4. Charles Babcock, "Relational Backlash," *Computerworld* (June 28th, 1993).

5. M. W. Blasgen *et al.,* "System R: An Architectural Overview," *IBM Sys. J. 20,* No. 1 (February 1981).

6. E. F. Codd, "Derivability, Redundancy, and Consistency of Relations Stored in Large Data Banks," IBM Research Report RJ599 (August 19th, 1969).

7. E. F. Codd, "A Relational Model of Data for Large Shared Data Banks," *CACM 13,* No. 6 (June 1970); republished in *CACM 26,* No. 1 (January 1982).

8. E. F. Codd, "A Data Base Sublanguage Founded on the Relational Calculus," Proc. 1971 ACM SIGFIDET Workshop on Data Description, Access, and Control (November 1971).

9. E. F. Codd, "Further Normalization of the Data Base Relational Model," in *Data Base Systems,* Courant Computer Science Symposia Series 6 (Englewood Cliffs, N.J.: Prentice-Hall, 1972).

10. E. F. Codd, "Relational Completeness of Data Base Sublanguages," in *Data Base Systems,* Courant Computer Science Symposia Series 6 (Englewood Cliffs, N.J.: Prentice-Hall, 1972).

11. E. F. Codd, "Extending the Database Relational Model to Capture More Meaning," *ACM TODS 4,* No. 4 (December 1979).

12. E. F. Codd and C. J. Date, "Interactive Support for Nonprogrammers: The Relational and Network Approaches," Proc. 1974 ACM SIGMOD Workshop on Data Description, Access, and Control, Vol. II, Ann Arbor, Michigan (May 1974). Republished in C. J. Date, *Relational Database: Selected Writings* (Addison-Wesley, 1986).

13. C. J. Date, "R.I.P. The Relational Performance Myth," *Computerworld* (March 30th, 1987).

14. R. Fagin, "Normal Forms and Relational Database Operators," Proc. 1979 ACM SIGMOD International Conference on Management of Data, Boston, Mass. (May/June 1979).

15. R. C. Goldstein and A. J. Strnad, "The MacAIMS Data Management System," Proc. 1970 ACM SICFIDET Workshop on Data Description and Access (November 1970).

16. P. A. V. Hall, P. Hitchcock, and S. J. P. Todd, "An Algebra of Relations for Ma-

chine Computation," Conference Record of the 2nd ACM Symposium on Principles of Programming Languages, Palo Alto, Calif. (January 1975).

17. William Inmon, "Why Large On-Line Relational Systems Don't (And May Not Ever) Yield Good Performance," *System Development* (April 1986).

18. Adrian Larner, private communication (1993).

19. M. R. Stonebraker, E. Wong, P. Kreps, and G. D. Held, "The Design and Implementation of INGRES," *ACM TODS 1,* No. 3 (September 1976).

20. Michael Stonebraker (ed.), *The INGRES Papers: The Anatomy of a Relational Database Management System* (Reading, Mass.: Addison-Wesley, 1986).

21. A. J. Strnad, "The Relational Approach to the Management of Data Bases." Proc. IFIP Congress, Ljubljana, Yugoslavia (August 1971).

22. S. J. P. Todd, "The Peterlee Relational Test Vehicle—A System Overview," *IBM Sys. J. 15,* No. 4 (1976).

23. M. M. Zloof, "Query By Example," Proc. National Computer Conference (May 1975).

RELATIONAL DATABASE MANAGEMENT

Introduction

Part II contains some of the most original material in the book. Specifically, it includes the first papers to describe:

- The systematic and completely general new approach to view updating developed by David McGoveran and myself in 1993;

- A new "scientific" database design principle, also developed by David McGoveran and myself in 1993.

These papers also contain the first discussion of a new classification scheme for integrity constraints, a scheme that seems to me more satisfactory (because again more systematic) than others I have seen in the literature—including earlier schemes of my own.

This part of the book also includes the paper I wrote on the primacy (?) of primary keys, in which I first challenged—a trifle hesitantly—one of the principal orthodoxies of the relational approach.

Another original paper in this part of the book is "The Third Manifesto," an attempt by Hugh Darwen and myself to lay the foundation for a true rapprochement between object-oriented and relational database technology—a topic that seems even more timely now than it was when we first wrote the paper.

The remaining papers describe the INGRES prototype and the relational language QUEL, discuss some issues arising in connection with the use of functional dependencies (FDs) for database design, and present a tutorial introduction to the extended form of the relational model known as RM/T.

CHAPTER **1**

An Overview of INGRES and QUEL

ABSTRACT

This paper provides an introduction to the principal features of the relational language QUEL, which was the primary interface to both the original ("University") INGRES prototype and the first few releases of the Commercial INGRES product.

COMMENTS ON REPUBLICATION

Of the numerous relational database languages developed during the 1970s, there were two that were clearly paramount, namely SQL from IBM Research and QUEL from the University of California at Berkeley. Each was the primary interface to a major relational prototype—System R in the case of SQL, and INGRES in the case of QUEL. (As the reader will be aware, both of these prototypes later led to commercial products.) And because of the importance of these two prototypes, earlier editions of my book *An Introduction to Database Systems* included material on both of them, and hence on both SQL and QUEL.

Originally published (in somewhat different form) in my book *An Introduction to Database Systems: Volume I,* 5th edition, pages 221–243 (Addison-Wesley, 1991). Reprinted by permission.

For reasons that need not concern us here, QUEL was subsequently eclipsed in the mainstream database world by SQL, and today no commercial product (so far as I know) continues to support QUEL as its sole or primary interface. However, QUEL does still form the basis of a certain amount of database research, and examples expressed in QUEL do still appear in the research literature from time to time. Moreover, many people, myself included, regard QUEL as technically superior to SQL in certain respects. I therefore feel that database professionals ought to have at least a basic familiarity with the major features of QUEL. Since space did not permit the retention of the INGRES/QUEL material in the most recent edition (the sixth) of *An Introduction to Database Systems* (Addison-Wesley, 1995), I decided to revise it appropriately for inclusion in the present book.

1. BACKGROUND

The relational language QUEL ("Query Language") was the primary interface to both the original INGRES prototype [5,9] and the first few releases of the Commercial INGRES product [2]. The INGRES prototype was developed in the mid to late 1970s at the University of California at Berkeley. (The name INGRES, pronounced *ingress,* originally stood for "Interactive Graphics and Retrieval System".) The INGRES prototype—now usually called *University INGRES* to distinguish it from the Commercial INGRES product—became widely available in university environments in the late 1970s and early 1980s, both in the United States and elsewhere. In addition, of course, an active program of research and development continues at Berkeley to this day, and much of that activity is a direct or indirect outgrowth of the original INGRES research.

In the early 1980s, a company called Relational Technology Inc. (later renamed Ingres Corporation and acquired by The ASK Group Inc.) was formed to develop and market a commercial version of INGRES. University INGRES ran on DEC PDP machines under the UNIX operating system; Commercial INGRES runs on a variety of different machines under a variety of different operating systems, including (e.g.) DEC VAX machines under either UNIX or VMS, IBM System/370 machines and similar under VM, IBM Personal Computers and similar under PC/DOS, and numerous other machines under UNIX. In this paper I will generally not bother to distinguish between the University and Commercial versions, except where the distinctions are important; the generic name INGRES should thus be taken to refer to both, barring explicit statements to the contrary.

Note: As already indicated, INGRES originally supported QUEL, not SQL. Like just about every other product on the market, INGRES does now support SQL, but that support was added later. The present paper concentrates on QUEL specifically, of course, but it does assume that the reader has some prior knowledge of SQL. Comparisons between QUEL and SQL will be drawn from time to time. Also, the reader might find it instructive to try giving SQL analogs of some of the QUEL examples.

Like SQL, QUEL can be used both as an interactive query language (via the INGRES **Terminal Monitor**) and also as a database programming language embedded within a variety of host languages (via **Embedded QUEL** or EQUEL). And here we run into a point of difference between the University and Commercial versions of the system. University INGRES was an *interpretive* system; in other words, the two operations of

1. Producing an optimized *query plan* for a given QUEL request, and
2. Executing that plan,

were not as sharply separated as they would be in a compiling system. Now, interpretation does have its advantages, the following among them:

- The elaborate compilation/recompilation mechanism of a compiling system like IBM's DB2 is not needed.
- The optimizer always produces code that is in accordance with the current state of the database.
- Operations such as dropping an index or other object do not require any additional system activity to track utilization of the dropped object.
- Furthermore, the optimizer might in fact produce better code, precisely because it operates in terms of more current information.

The disadvantage, of course, is that repetitively executed programs must be optimized every time they are run. The Commercial version therefore provides two features to address this problem:

1. First, if a given database request is to be executed several times during a single program run, that request can optionally be optimized just once (on its first execution within that program run) instead of every time it is executed. See the discussion of the **REPEAT option** in Section 6.
2. Second, the **stored procedure** facility provides a way for an application program to invoke a procedure (i.e., subroutine) that in fact has been compiled ahead of time, rather as in a conventional compiling system like DB2. Again, see Section 6 for further discussion.

The Suppliers-and-Parts Database

The running example throughout this paper, and indeed throughout most of this book, is the well-known suppliers-and-parts database. Fig. 1 shows a set of sample values for this database; subsequent examples will actually assume these specific

S	S#	SNAME	STATUS	CITY
	S1	Smith	20	London
	S2	Jones	10	Paris
	S3	Blake	30	Paris
	S4	Clark	20	London
	S5	Adams	30	Athens

P	P#	PNAME	COLOR	WEIGHT	CITY
	P1	Nut	Red	12	London
	P2	Bolt	Green	17	Paris
	P3	Screw	Blue	17	Rome
	P4	Screw	Red	14	London
	P5	Cam	Blue	12	Paris
	P6	Cog	Red	19	London

SP	S#	P#	QTY
	S1	P1	300
	S1	P2	200
	S1	P3	400
	S1	P4	200
	S1	P5	100
	S1	P6	100
	S2	P1	300
	S2	P2	400
	S3	P2	200
	S4	P2	200
	S4	P4	300
	S4	P5	400

Fig. 1 The suppliers-and-parts database (sample values)

values, where it makes any difference. For further explanation (if needed), see, e.g., reference [3].

2. DATA DEFINITION

The QUEL data definition statements are as follows:

```
CREATE      —   creates a base table
INDEX       —   creates an index
DEFINE VIEW —   creates a view
DESTROY     —   destroys a base table, index, or view
MODIFY      —   changes the storage structure of a base table or index
```

There is no QUEL analog of the SQL "ALTER TABLE" function. Views are discussed in Section 5; the other features are the subject of the present section.

CREATE

The general syntax for CREATE is as follows:

```
CREATE base-table ( column-definition-commalist )
```

where a *column-definition* in turn takes the form:

```
column  =  data-type [ NOT NULL ]
```

(Note that QUEL does not support primary or foreign keys at the time of writing, so there are no primary or foreign key definition clauses.) Here is an example:

```
CREATE S ( S#      = CHAR(5)   NOT NULL,
           SNAME   = CHAR(20)  NOT NULL,
           STATUS  = I2        NOT NULL,
           CITY    = CHAR(15)  NOT NULL )
```

The following are the principal scalar data types supported by QUEL:

I1, I2, I4	binary integers of 1, 2, 4 bytes respectively
F4, F8	floating point numbers of 4, 8 bytes respectively
MONEY	dollars and cents, 16 digits, with assumed decimal point two digits from the right
CHAR(*n*)	fixed length character string of *n* characters
VARCHAR(*n*)	varying length character string of maximum length *n* characters
DATE	date and time, representing either an absolute value such as "14-Mar-91 10:30 am" or an interval such as "2 months 14 days 10 hours 30 minutes"

Note that different INGRES base tables can have significantly different storage representations. They are automatically created as "heaps" (that is, new rows are stored wherever there happens to be room); however, the storage structure for any given base table can be changed to some other form, say to an indexed (BTREE) structure, at any time after that base table is created. Furthermore, the storage structure can subsequently be changed as often as desired. See the discussion of MODIFY below.

INDEX

The INDEX statement is used to create additional indexes on the stored form of a given base table, over and above the index (if any) that already exists as part of that base table's principal storage structure. The syntax is:

```
INDEX ON base-table IS index ( column-commalist )
```

For example:

```
INDEX ON S IS XSC ( CITY )
```

An index created via an INDEX operation is initially stored as an ISAM structure (again, see the discussion of MODIFY below), but can later be modified to some other structure just as a base table can. In fact, an index created via INDEX is generally regarded as just a special kind of stored table in INGRES.

DESTROY

Syntax:

```
DESTROY table-commalist
```

where each *table* is the name of a base table or index (or view). Examples:

```
DESTROY S, P, SP
DESTROY XSC
```

(We are assuming in the second example that XSC is an index name.) If a base table or view is destroyed, all views and indexes on that base table or view are automatically destroyed also.

MODIFY

The MODIFY operation is used to change the storage structure for a given base table or index (in other words, to reorganize that base table or index in storage). The syntax is:

```
MODIFY table TO structure [ UNIQUE ] [ ON column-commalist ]
```

where *table* identifies a base table or an index, and *structure* is one of the following:

```
BTREE       CBTREE
HASH        CHASH
ISAM        CISAM
HEAP        CHEAP
HEAPSORT    CHEAPSORT
```

Explanation: The optional "C" prefix—as in, e.g., CBTREE—specifies that the data is to be compressed on the disk. BTREE, HASH, and HEAP are self-explanatory. (*Note:* HASH uses a standard INGRES-supplied division/remainder algorithm.) ISAM ("indexed sequential access method") is somewhat similar to BTREE, but is a less dynamic structure (in practice BTREE is usually—but not invariably—preferable to ISAM). Finally, HEAPSORT causes the rows to be sorted into a specified order at the time of the MODIFY; however, the sort order is not maintained in the face of subsequent updates (e.g., new rows are still added wherever there happens to be room, as in HEAP).

Examples:

1. MODIFY P TO CHEAP

2. MODIFY SP TO HEAPSORT ON S#:A, P#:D

   The rows of the stored form of base table SP are physically sorted into descending P# order within ascending S# order. If neither ":A" nor ":D" is specified, ":A" is assumed by default; these specifications can be used only with HEAPSORT (and CHEAPSORT). UNIQUE cannot be specified for HEAPSORT (or CHEAPSORT), nor for HEAP (or CHEAP).

3. MODIFY S TO BTREE UNIQUE ON S#

   The stored form of base table S is sorted into S# order and a B-tree is built on that column. No two rows of S are allowed to have the same S# value (the MODIFY will fail—i.e., the storage structure will remain unchanged—if that constraint is already violated by existing rows).

4. MODIFY SP TO CHASH UNIQUE ON S#, P#

The stored form of base table SP is reorganized into a hash-addressed structure, compressed, with hash access via values of the column combination (S#,P#). No two rows of SP are allowed to have the same value for that combination (the MODIFY will fail if that constraint is already violated by existing rows).

Note: The MODIFY operation removes duplicate rows from the table *in all cases* (i.e., regardless of whether UNIQUE is specified), except for HEAP and CHEAP. Furthermore, duplicate rows can be introduced only into tables stored as HEAP or HEAPSORT (or CHEAP or CHEAPSORT). INGRES tables thus always satisfy a "no duplicates" constraint, except for the various heap structures (which are best regarded as anomalous anyway, since most tables will usually have one of the other structures in practice). The optional UNIQUE specification represents a *stronger* constraint; in effect, it says that rows are to be unique, not just on the combination of all of their columns, but rather on the combination of some specified subset of their columns.

Two further points:

1. MODIFY also includes certain additional parameters, not discussed here, that have to do with such things as the amount of free space to be left in each page on the disk. Of course, INGRES automatically applies appropriate default values if such parameters are left unspecified.

2. MODIFY automatically destroys any indexes on the table being modified. Thus it might be necessary to follow the MODIFY by an appropriate set of INDEX operations.

3. DATA MANIPULATION: RETRIEVAL OPERATIONS

The QUEL data manipulation statements are as follows:

```
RETRIEVE
APPEND
REPLACE
DELETE
```

This section discusses retrieval operations, the next discusses update operations. In both cases, the examples focus on those aspects of QUEL that are significantly different from their SQL counterpart (or that do not have such a counterpart).

First of all, then, RETRIEVE. The general syntax is:

```
RETRIEVE [ UNIQUE ] ( target-commalist )
[ WHERE    condition ]
[ SORT BY  column-commalist ]
```

where each *target* is basically an *assignment* of the form

```
[ unqualified-name = ] scalar-expression
```

The optional *"unqualified-name ="* portion of such an assignment can be omitted only if the result of evaluating the scalar expression has an obvious inherited name. UNIQUE is the QUEL analog of DISTINCT in SQL; likewise, SORT BY is the QUEL analog of ORDER BY in SQL, except that SORT BY implies UNIQUE. *Note:* A target commalist of the form *T.*ALL is also permitted as a shorthand for the commalist *T.C1, T.C2, . . . , T.Cn,* where *C1, C2, . . . , Cn* are all the columns of table *T* (analogous to "SELECT *" in SQL).

Simple Retrievals and Joins

3.1 Qualified Retrieval. Get supplier number and status for suppliers in Paris with status > 20.

```
RETRIEVE ( S.S#, S.STATUS )
WHERE     S.CITY = "Paris"
AND       S.STATUS > 20
```

Notice that all references to columns in the database (in the target commalist and in the WHERE clause) *must* be appropriately qualified; in contrast to SQL, there is no FROM clause from which to derive any implicit qualification. The condition in the WHERE clause can include the comparison operators =, <>, >, >=, <, and <=; the Boolean operators AND, OR, and NOT; and parentheses to indicate a desired order of evaluation.

3.2 Saving the Result of a Query. Get supplier number and status for suppliers in Paris with status > 20 (as in Example 3.1), and save the result in base table TEMP.

```
RETRIEVE INTO TEMP ( S.S#, S.STATUS )
WHERE     S.CITY = "Paris"
AND       S.STATUS > 20
```

INGRES automatically creates a new base table called TEMP, with columns S# and STATUS, and saves the result of the query in that table. Table TEMP must not exist prior to execution of the RETRIEVE.

3.3 Retrieval of Computed Values. For all parts, get the part number and the weight of that part in grams (part weights are given in table P in pounds).

```
RETRIEVE ( P.P#, EXPLANATION = "Weight in grams =",
                 GMWT = P.WEIGHT * 454 )
SORT BY GMWT, P#:D
```

Result:

P#	EXPLANATION	GMWT
P5	Weight in grams =	5448
P1	Weight in grams =	5448
P4	Weight in grams =	6356
P3	Weight in grams =	7718
P2	Weight in grams =	7718
P6	Weight in grams =	8626

It is necessary to introduce names for the second and third columns of the result here, because there are no obvious names they can inherit. Such introduced names can then be referenced in the SORT BY clause (but not in the WHERE clause, unfortunately). Note, incidentally, that—as the phrase "second and third columns of the result" suggests—we are relying on the fact that columns of tables have a left-to-right ordering in QUEL; the literal strings in the EXPLANATION column would not make much sense if they did not appear at the appropriate point in the row.

In general, expressions in the target commalist (and in the WHERE clause) can involve, not only column names and literals and the usual operators (+, −, ∗, /, parentheses), but also exponentiation, string concatenation, and a wide array of scalar builtin functions—e.g., SIN, COS, SQRT, INTERVAL (for date arithmetic), and so on.

3.4 Partial-Match Retrieval. Get all parts whose names begin with the letter C.

```
RETRIEVE ( P.ALL )
WHERE     P.PNAME = "C*"
```

The following special characters can be used to specify partial match retrieval in a string comparison:

- The character "?" matches any single character.
- The character "∗" matches any sequence of zero or more characters.
- The string "[*xyz*]" (where *xyz* is any set of characters) matches any character in *xyz*.

Note: A special character can be made to behave like an ordinary character—i.e., the special interpretation can be disabled—by preceding it by a backslash character.

3.5 Simple Equijoin. Get all combinations of supplier and part information such that the supplier and part in question are located in the same city.

```
RETRIEVE ( S.ALL, P.ALL )
WHERE     S.CITY = P.CITY
```

3.6 Join of Three Tables. Get all pairs of city names such that a supplier located in the first city supplies a part stored in the second city.

```
RETRIEVE UNIQUE ( S.CITY, P.CITY )
WHERE     S.S# = SP.S#
AND       SP.P# = P.P#
```

Notice that this query references a table (SP) in the WHERE clause that is not mentioned in the target commalist.

3.7 Joining a Table with Itself. Get all pairs of supplier numbers such that the two suppliers concerned are colocated.

```
RANGE OF FIRST IS S
RANGE OF SECOND IS S

RETRIEVE ( FIRST.S#, SECOND.S# )
WHERE     FIRST.CITY = SECOND.CITY
AND       FIRST.S#   < SECOND.S#
```

The two RANGE statements define FIRST and SECOND as explicit **range variables,** each ranging over table S. By contrast, all range variables in previous examples have been implicit.

Aggregates and Aggregate Functions

Like SQL, QUEL provides a set of aggregate operators to operate on the collection of values in some column of some table. The available operators are COUNT, SUM, AVG, MAX, and MIN (more or less as in SQL); COUNTU, SUMU, and AVGU, where the "U" stands for "unique" (e.g., QUEL "SUMU" is analogous to SQL "SUM (DISTINCT . . .)"); and ANY (analogous to SQL "EXISTS"—see the subsection "Quantification" below). The general syntax for an aggregate operator reference is as follows:

```
aggregate ( scalar-expression [ WHERE condition ] )
```

Since an aggregate operator returns a scalar value, it can appear in the target commalist or in the WHERE clause wherever a scalar literal is allowed.

3.8 Aggregate in the Target List. Get the total number of suppliers.

```
RETRIEVE ( X = COUNT ( S.S# ) )
```

Note that a name (here X) must be supplied for the result.

3.9 Aggregate in the Target List. Get the total number of suppliers currently supplying parts.

```
RETRIEVE ( Y = COUNTU ( SP.S# ) )
```

3.10 Aggregate in the Target List. Get the total quantity of part P2 supplied.

```
RETRIEVE ( Z = SUM ( SP.QTY WHERE SP.P# = "P2" ) )
```

3.11 Aggregate in the WHERE Clause. Get supplier numbers for suppliers with status value less than the current maximum status value in the S table.

```
RETRIEVE ( S.S# )
WHERE     S.STATUS < MAX ( S.STATUS )
```

Note that there are two different "S"s here (as there would also be in the analogous SQL formulation). The following version makes the point explicit:

```
RANGE OF SX IS S, SY IS S

RETRIEVE ( SX.S# )
WHERE     SX.STATUS < MAX ( SY.STATUS )
```

In general, any range variables (implicit or explicit) appearing inside the argument to an aggregate are *purely local to that aggregate;* they are distinct from any range variable that might happen to have the same name but appears outside the aggregate—*unless* they are mentioned in a BY clause within the aggregate argument (see the next example).

3.12 Use of the BY Clause. For each part supplied, get the part number and the total shipment quantity for that part.

```
RETRIEVE ( SP.P#, X = SUM ( SP.QTY BY SP.P# ) )
```

The action of the BY clause is somewhat analogous to that of the GROUP BY clause in SQL—but only somewhat. First of all, note that an aggregate operator whose argument includes a BY clause is referred to in QUEL (rather confusingly!) as an aggregate **function**. The value of such a function is not just a single scalar value, but rather an entire collection of such values, one for each distinct value of the column identified in the BY clause. (Assume for simplicity that the BY clause does in fact identify just a single column; the generalization to more than one column is tedious but straightforward.) Thus, a query involving an aggregate function is conceptually evaluated in two stages, as follows.

1. First, the aggregate function itself is evaluated, to yield an intermediate result table (AF, say). In the example, table AF looks like this:

AF	BY	AGG
	P1	600
	P2	1000
	P3	400
	P4	500
	P5	500
	P6	100

   Table AF contains two columns, one ("AGG") giving the aggregated values (the sums, in the case at hand) and the other ("BY") giving the corresponding values of the BY column.

2. Now the original query is altered (again conceptually) to read as follows:

```
RETRIEVE UNIQUE ( SP.P#, X = AF.AGG )
WHERE      SP.P# = AF.BY
```

   That is, (a) a UNIQUE specification is inserted, unless one is already present; (b) the aggregate function in the target commalist is replaced by a reference to the "aggregate values" column in table AF; and (c) a WHERE clause is appended to the query, specifying an equality join condition between the BY column specified in the original query and the "by-values" column in table AF. The altered query is then evaluated to yield the desired overall result.

Note that the effect of appending the join condition to the query is to make the range variables that were mentioned in the BY clause known outside the aggregate function. In other words, such variables are *not* purely local to the aggregate function. Any other range variables referenced inside the aggregate function are, however, still purely local.

3.13 Aggregate Function in the WHERE Clause. Get part numbers for all parts supplied by more than one supplier.

```
RETRIEVE ( SP.P# )
WHERE    COUNT ( SP.S# BY SP.P# ) > 1
```

Note that this query would typically require a HAVING clause in SQL. In QUEL, by contrast, all "HAVING-type" conditions are expressed by means of a conventional WHERE clause that includes an aggregate function (as in the example).

3.14 Nested Aggregate Functions. Get the average of the total quantities in which each part is supplied.

```
RETRIEVE ( X = AVG ( SUM ( SP.QTY BY SP.P# ) ) )
```

This query has no direct analog in SQL, because SQL aggregate functions cannot be nested. (*Exercise:* Why not?)

3.15 Aggregate Functions in an Arithmetic Expression. For each supplier, get the supplier number and a count of the parts not supplied by that supplier.

```
RETRIEVE ( S.S#, X = COUNT ( P.P# ) -
                     COUNT ( SP.P# BY S.S#
                             WHERE SP.S# = S.S# ) )
```

The first COUNT returns the total number of parts, the second returns the number supplied by this supplier.

Note, incidentally, that the column we choose to do the counting on in a COUNT reference is arbitrary; any column of the relevant table would suffice. For some reason QUEL does not permit a COUNT reference of the form "COUNT (*T*.ALL . . .)."

Quantification

3.16 Query Involving Existential Quantification. Get supplier names for suppliers who supply part P2.

```
RETRIEVE ( S.SNAME )
WHERE    S.S# = SP.S#
AND      SP.P# = "P2"
```

Any range variable mentioned in the WHERE clause and not in the target commalist is considered to be *implicitly* quantified by the existential quantifier (EXISTS in SQL). Thus the foregoing query can be paraphrased:

"Get supplier names such that there exists a shipment with the same supplier number and with part number P2."

The aggregate function ANY can be used if desired to make the quantification more explicit:

```
RETRIEVE ( S.SNAME )
WHERE    ANY ( SP.S# BY S.S#
                  WHERE S.S# = SP.S#
                  AND   SP.P# = "P2" ) = 1
```

ANY returns the value 0 if its argument set is empty, the value 1 otherwise. In practice there is little point in using the "ANY (. . .) = 1" form, since such a query can always be expressed more simply without using ANY at all, as the example above illustrates. However, the "ANY (. . .) = 0" form *is* sometimes necessary, since it is QUEL's analog of the *negated* form NOT EXISTS in SQL. See Examples 3.17 and 3.18 below.

Note: ANY resembles COUNT in that the column over which we choose to compute the function—column SP.S#, in the example—is arbitrary; any column of the relevant table would suffice. Note too that the conditions ANY(. . .) = 0 and COUNT(. . .) = 0 are functionally identical. However, the ANY form is preferable, in that it is a more "natural" formulation (it is closer to the natural language expression "there does not exist any"). It also has the potential for more efficient evaluation.

3.17 Query Using ANY (. . .) = 0. Get supplier names for suppliers who do not supply part P2.

```
RETRIEVE ( S.SNAME )
WHERE    ANY ( SP.S# BY S.S#
                  WHERE S.S# = SP.S#
                  AND   SP.P# = "P2" ) = 0
```

Note that the following formulation does *not* produce the desired result. (Why not? What *does* it produce?)

```
RETRIEVE ( S.SNAME )
WHERE    S.S# = SP.S#
AND      SP.P# <> "P2"
```

3.18 Query Using ANY (. . .) = 0. Get supplier names for suppliers who supply all parts.

```
RETRIEVE ( S.SNAME )
WHERE  ANY ( P.P# BY S.S#
                WHERE ANY ( SP.P# BY S.S#, P.P#
                               WHERE S.S# = SP.S#
                               AND   SP.P# = P.P# ) = 0 ) = 0
```

Querying the Catalog

Like all relational systems, INGRES has a system catalog that contains information concerning tables, columns, indexes, etc., and users can query that catalog using the retrieval operator of their regular query language, in this case the RETRIEVE statement of QUEL. However, QUEL also provides a special HELP statement, which can be regarded as a convenient shorthand for certain predefined catalog RETRIEVE operations (except that HELP also displays its output in a more readable format than the conventional RETRIEVE operation does). For example, the operation

```
HELP SP
```

displays information regarding table SP (its columns and their data types, its storage structure, etc.). Likewise, the operation

```
HELP
```

(with no operand) displays a list of all user tables (as opposed to system tables) in the database.

4. DATA MANIPULATION: UPDATE OPERATIONS

QUEL includes three update operations—APPEND, REPLACE, and DELETE—with syntax as follows:

```
APPEND TO table ( target-commalist ) [ WHERE condition ]

REPLACE range-variable ( target-commalist ) [ WHERE condition ]

DELETE range-variable [ WHERE condition ]
```

The *range-variable* in REPLACE and DELETE can be either an explicit range variable (introduced via an explicit RANGE statement) or a table name, which acts as an implicit range variable.

4.1 Single-Row APPEND. Add part P7 (city Athens, weight 24, name and color at present unknown) to base table P.

```
APPEND TO P ( P# = "P7", CITY = "Athens", WEIGHT = 24 )
```

The name and color in the new row will be set to null, since no other value has been explicitly specified (assuming for the sake of the example that NOT NULL does not apply to these columns). Note that column names on the left of the equals signs in an APPEND target commalist must *not* be explicitly qualified. They can be regarded as being implicitly qualified by the table name that appears following the keyword APPEND.

4.2 Multi-Row APPEND. Suppose base table NEWSP has the same columns (S#,

P#, and QTY) as base table SP. Copy all rows of NEWSP for which the quantity is greater than 1000 into SP.

```
APPEND TO SP ( S#  = NEWSP.S#,
               P#  = NEWSP.P#,
               QTY = NEWSP.QTY )
WHERE  NEWSP.QTY > 1000
```

4.3 Single-Row REPLACE. Change the color of part P2 to yellow and increase its weight by 5.

```
REPLACE P ( COLOR = "Yellow", WEIGHT = P.WEIGHT + 5 )
WHERE    P.P# = "P2"
```

As with APPEND, column names on the left of the equals signs in the target commalist must not be explicitly qualified. They can be regarded as being implicitly qualified by the range variable name that appears following the keyword REPLACE.

4.4 Multi-Row REPLACE. Double the status of all suppliers in London.

```
REPLACE S ( STATUS = 2 * S.STATUS )
WHERE    S.CITY = "London"
```

4.5 REPLACE Referring to Another Table. Set the shipment quantity to zero for all suppliers in London.

```
REPLACE SP ( QTY = 0 )
WHERE    SP.S# = S.S#
AND      S.CITY = "London"
```

4.6 Updating One Table from Another. Suppose base table SP has an additional column, TOTWT, representing total shipment weight. Compute the values for this column by multiplying the quantity for each shipment by the corresponding part weight.

```
REPLACE SP ( TOTWT = SP.QTY * P.WEIGHT )
WHERE    SP.P# = P.P#
```

4.7 Single-Row DELETE. Delete supplier S5.

```
DELETE S WHERE S.S# = "S5"
```

4.8 Multi-Row DELETE. Delete all shipments with quantity greater than 300.

```
DELETE SP WHERE SP.QTY > 300
```

5. VIEWS

Views in QUEL are fairly similar to views in SQL. Here is an example of a QUEL view definition:

```
DEFINE VIEW LONSUPPS
     ( S#      = S.S#,
       SNAME   = S.SNAME,
       STATUS  = S.STATUS
       CITY    = S.CITY )
       WHERE   S.CITY = "London"
```

The general syntax is:

```
DEFINE VIEW view ( target-commalist ) [ WHERE condition ]
```

One difference from SQL (at least as SQL was originally defined) is that new names need be specified explicitly for the columns of the view only in the cases where there is no "obvious" name that could be inherited (or where there would otherwise be ambiguity). Here is a modified version of the example above that illustrates the point:

```
DEFINE VIEW LONSUPPS
     ( S#, SNAME, STATUS, LONDON = S.CITY )
       WHERE S.CITY = "London"
```

Here is an example of a RETRIEVE operation against (the first version of) LONSUPPS:

```
RANGE OF LS IS LONSUPPS

RETRIEVE ( LS.ALL )
WHERE     LS.STATUS < 25
```

The process of converting such a retrieval into an equivalent retrieval on the underlying base table(s) is known in INGRES as **query modification** [8]. The converted form looks like this:

```
RANGE OF LS IS S

RETRIEVE ( S# = LS.S#, SNAME = LS.SNAME,
           STATUS = LS.STATUS, CITY = LS.CITY )
WHERE     LS.STATUS < 25
AND       LS.CITY = "London"
```

The converted form is then executed in the usual way, of course. In a similar manner, the update operation

```
RANGE OF LS IS LONSUPPS

REPLACE LS ( STATUS = LS.STATUS + 10 )
WHERE     LS.STATUS < 15
```

is converted by the query modification process into

```
RANGE OF LS IS S

REPLACE LS ( STATUS = LS.STATUS + 10 )
WHERE     LS.STATUS < 15
AND       LS.CITY = "London"
```

Similarly for APPEND and DELETE operations.

Views are dropped by the same DESTROY operation that is used to drop base tables and indexes. For example:

```
DESTROY LONSUPPS
```

QUEL's behavior with respect to data manipulation operations on views is similar but not identical to that of SQL. As far as retrieval operations are concerned, QUEL is definitely superior, because the syntax of QUEL is more systematic than that of SQL; thus, for example, many view retrievals that would fail in SQL (at least as originally defined) work perfectly well in QUEL. However, when it comes to update operations, QUEL is just as *ad hoc*—though in different ways—as SQL is.

6. EMBEDDED QUEL

An *embedded QUEL* (EQUEL) preprocessor is available for the languages Ada, C, COBOL, FORTRAN, BASIC, Pascal, and PL/I. Here is an example of an EQUEL statement:

```
##    REPLACE S ( STATUS = X )
##    WHERE   S.S# = Y
```

The initial ## characters are required for all source lines that are to be processed by the EQUEL preprocessor, including declarations of host language variables (such as X and Y in the example). For instance, if the REPLACE above were part of a FORTRAN program, then the corresponding declarative statements might look as follows:

```
##    DECLARE

##    INTEGER * 2       X
##    CHARACTER * 5     Y
```

The DECLARE statement is needed to warn the preprocessor that a block of declarations is to follow.

Host language variables can be used in EQUEL statements for any or all of the following:

- Target variables for RETRIEVE
- Range variable names
- Table and column names
- Column values and literals within expressions and conditions
- Complete expressions and conditions

For the first category, of course, host variables *must* be used, and they can be of any appropriate data type. For the remaining categories, the host variables must be of type character string.

Note that the foregoing list of possibilities is considerably more extensive than the corresponding list for embedded SQL. Observe in particular that host language variables can be used to supply entire expressions and conditions. For example:

```
##   CHARACTER * 25    CONDITN

     CONDITN = ' S.CITY = "London" '

##   REPLACE S ( STATUS = 2 * S.STATUS )
##   WHERE   CONDITN
```

Feedback information after execution of any EQUEL statement can be obtained via the special operation INQUIRE_INGRES. For example:

```
##   INQUIRE_INGRES ( Z = ERRORNO )
```

The *error number* for the most recently executed EQUEL statement is returned in host variable Z. An error number of zero indicates successful execution.

Here is another example:

```
##   INQUIRE_INGRES ( N = ROWCOUNT )
```

The number of rows retrieved (or replaced or . . .) in the most recently executed EQUEL statement is returned in host variable N.

The dialect of EQUEL supported in Commercial INGRES includes a set of cursor facilities that are similar but not identical to those of embedded SQL. University INGRES, by contrast, had no notion of cursors. Instead, the problem of multi-row retrieval was handled by means of a construct called a **RETRIEVE loop**. For example (FORTRAN again):

```
##   DECLARE

##   CHARACTER * 5    X
##   INTEGER * 4      Y
##   CHARACTER * 6    Z

     Z = 'P5'

##   RETRIEVE ( X = SP.S#, Y = SP.QTY )
##   WHERE    SP.P# = Z
##   {
         process X and Y
##   }
```

University INGRES assumed that all RETRIEVE operations were potentially multi-row; there was thus no analog of the embedded SQL "singleton SELECT" (though there is in Commercial INGRES). In the example, the RETRIEVE is executed using the current value of the host variable Z (P5, in the example). The code between the braces ("process X and Y") is then executed once for each row in the retrieved set. That code must not include any other database operations.

When all rows have been processed, control goes to the statement following the closing brace. The statement

```
##     ENDRETRIEVE
```

can be used to exit from the RETRIEVE loop "early," i.e., to force control to go the statement following the closing brace before all retrieved rows have been processed.

It might be helpful to compare the foregoing ideas with the SQL cursor mechanism. The EQUEL RETRIEVE acts like a combination of the SQL cursor declaration and OPEN; exit from the loop (either explicitly, via ENDRETRIEVE, or implicitly, after all rows have been processed) is analogous to CLOSE. FETCH is completely implicit; the target variables are specified in the "OPEN" (i.e., RETRIEVE), not in a separate FETCH statement. There is no analog of the SQL UPDATE/DELETE CURRENT operations; nor can any other database operation be executed from within the RETRIEVE loop. Note too that EQUEL imposes some *syntactic* constraints on the structure of the program. Specifically, the loop source code *must* immediately follow the RETRIEVE statement, and the statement to be executed first on exit from the loop *must* be the one immediately following the loop source code.

To conclude this brief look at EQUEL, we remind the reader of the two features of Commercial INGRES—mentioned in Section 1—that overcome to some extent the performance disadvantage of interpretation, namely (a) the REPEAT option and (b) stored procedures.

1. First, the REPEAT option. Normally, each EQUEL statement is processed by the INGRES optimizer at the time it is encountered during flow of control through the executing program. Thus, if the same statement is executed repeatedly (e.g., if it is inside a program loop), it will be optimized repeatedly also—clearly an undesirable state of affairs. The REPEAT option is intended to alleviate this problem. Consider the following example:

```
##     REPEAT REPLACE S ( STATUS = @X )
##            WHERE   S.S# = @Y
```

The first time this statement is executed, it is optimized in the usual way. In addition, the REPEAT option causes the optimizer to *save the resulting query plan*. If the statement is subsequently encountered again, INGRES will then reuse the saved plan instead of generating a new one. In the example, host variables X and Y are considered to be **parameters** (indicated by the prefix "@" symbols); each time the statement is encountered, it will be executed using the current values of those variables. Parameters are allowed wherever literals are allowed.

The foregoing scheme can be characterized, loosely, as "compile on first use." The optimization is still being done at run time, not prior to run time as in a full compiling system, but it is done only once per program execution instead of once per *statement* execution.

2. Second, stored procedures.* A stored procedure is a collection of statements—database operations, plus declarations of local variables, flow of control statements such as IF and WHILE, and so forth—that is compiled ahead of time and stored in the database. Such procedures can be invoked from an application program as subroutines. Note that stored procedures not only provide the benefits of compilation, they also to serve to reduce the amount of communication between the application and the DBMS (i.e., between the client and the server).

Finally, a few miscellaneous points:

■ An EQUEL program can process only one INGRES database at a time.† The EQUEL statement

```
##    INGRES database
```

must be executed to "open" the required database before it can be used. Likewise, the EQUEL statement

```
##    EXIT
```

must be used to "close" the database after it is finished with. (The program can then go on to open another database, if it chooses.)

■ Analogs of the SQL COMMIT and ROLLBACK operations are provided. The details are beyond the scope of this discussion.

■ Embedded SQL includes a special set of facilities ("dynamic SQL") to assist in the writing of online applications. EQUEL has comparatively little need of such facilities, since EQUEL is *always* "dynamic" (in the sense that the various components of an EQUEL statement can all be represented by host variables whose values can change with time). The only difficulty occurs with target commalists. For example, given only the facilities sketched in this section so far, there is no way to construct a RETRIEVE statement for which the number of values retrieved per row is not known until run time. EQUEL therefore provides a special function, the PARAM function, for dealing with exactly this problem (i.e., PARAM supports the dynamic construction of target commalists).

■ Last, EQUEL also provides an extensive set of facilities known as

---

*Stored procedures are available as part of INGRES's SQL support, not its QUEL support.

†Under INGRES/STAR, however (the distributed database version of the Commercial INGRES product), that "one database" can be a virtual object that spans any number of real databases.

EQUEL/FORMS to assist in the construction of the screen and dialog management portions of an online application. For details the reader is referred to the INGRES documentation.

EXERCISES

1. Fig. 2 shows some sample values for an extended form of the suppliers-and-parts database called the *suppliers-parts-projects* database. Write an appropriate set of QUEL definitional statements for this database.

The remaining exercises are all based on the suppliers-parts-projects database. In each case you are asked to write a QUEL statement for the indicated operation.

2. Get full details of all projects.

3. Get full details of all projects in London.

4. Get supplier numbers for suppliers who supply project J1.

5. Get all shipments where the quantity is in the range 300 to 750 inclusive.

S

S#	SNAME	STATUS	CITY
S1	Smith	20	London
S2	Jones	10	Paris
S3	Blake	30	Paris
S4	Clark	20	London
S5	Adams	30	Athens

P

P#	PNAME	COLOR	WEIGHT	CITY
P1	Nut	Red	12	London
P2	Bolt	Green	17	Paris
P3	Screw	Blue	17	Rome
P4	Screw	Red	14	London
P5	Cam	Blue	12	Paris
P6	Cog	Red	19	London

J

J#	JNAME	CITY
J1	Sorter	Paris
J2	Display	Rome
J3	OCR	Athens
J4	Console	Athens
J5	RAID	London
J6	EDS	Oslo
J7	Tape	London

SPJ

S#	P#	J#	QTY
S1	P1	J1	200
S1	P1	J4	700
S2	P3	J1	400
S2	P3	J2	200
S2	P3	J3	200
S2	P3	J4	500
S2	P3	J5	600
S2	P3	J6	400
S2	P3	J7	800
S2	P5	J2	100
S3	P3	J1	200
S3	P4	J2	500
S4	P6	J3	300
S4	P6	J7	300
S5	P2	J2	200
S5	P2	J4	100
S5	P5	J5	500
S5	P5	J7	100
S5	P6	J2	200
S5	P1	J4	100
S5	P3	J4	200
S5	P4	J4	800
S5	P5	J4	400
S5	P6	J4	500

Fig. 2 The suppliers-parts-projects database (sample values)

6. Get all part-color/part-city combinations.

7. Get all supplier-number/part-number/project-number triples such that the indicated supplier, part, and project are all colocated.

8. Get all supplier-number/part-number/project-number triples such that the indicated supplier, part, and project are not all colocated.

9. Get all supplier-number/part-number/project-number triples such that no two of the indicated supplier, part, and project are colocated.

10. Get part numbers for parts supplied by a supplier in London.

11. Get part numbers for parts supplied by a supplier in London to a project in London.

12. Get all pairs of city names such that a supplier in the first city supplies a project in the second city.

13. Get part numbers for parts supplied to any project by a supplier in the same city as that project.

14. Get project numbers for projects supplied by at least one supplier not in the same city.

15. Get all pairs of part numbers such that some supplier supplies both the indicated parts.

16. Get the total number of projects supplied by supplier S1.

17. Get the total quantity of part P1 supplied by supplier S1.

18. For each part being supplied to a project, get the part number, the project number, and the corresponding total quantity.

19. Get part numbers of parts supplied to some project in an average quantity of more than 320.

20. Get project names for projects supplied by supplier S1.

21. Get colors of parts supplied by supplier S1.

22. Get part numbers for parts supplied to any project in London.

23. Get project numbers for projects using at least one part available from supplier S1.

24. Get supplier numbers for suppliers supplying at least one part supplied by at least one supplier who supplies at least one red part.

25. Get supplier numbers for suppliers with a status lower than that of supplier S1.

26. Get project numbers for projects whose city is first in the alphabetic list of such cities.

27. Get project numbers for projects supplied with part P1 in an average quantity greater than the greatest quantity in which any part is supplied to project J1.

28. Get supplier numbers for suppliers supplying some project with part P1 in a quantity greater than the average shipment quantity of part P1 for that project.

29. Get project numbers for projects not supplied with any red part by any London supplier.

30. Get project numbers for projects supplied entirely by supplier S1.

31. Get part numbers for parts supplied to all projects in London.

32. Get supplier numbers for suppliers who supply the same part to all projects.

33. Get project numbers for projects supplied with at least all parts available from supplier S1.

34. Get all cities in which at least one supplier, part, or project is located.

35. Get part numbers for parts that are supplied either by a London supplier or to a London project.

36. Get supplier-number/part-number pairs such that the indicated supplier does not supply the indicated part.

37. Get all pairs of supplier numbers, Sx and Sy say, such that Sx and Sy supply exactly the same set of parts each. (Thanks to a correspondent, Fatma Mili of Oakland University, Rochester, Michigan, for this problem.)

REFERENCES AND BIBLIOGRAPHY

1. Eric Allman, Michael Stonebraker, and Gerald Held,"Embedding a Relational Data Sublanguage in a General Purpose Programming Language," Proc. ACM SIGPLAN/ SIGMOD Conference on Data: Abstraction, Definition, and Structure, Salt Lake City, Ut. (March 1976). Joint Issue: *ACM SIGPLAN Notices 11,* Special Issue / *ACM SIGMOD Bulletin FDT 8,* No. 2 (1976). Republished in reference [7].

2. C. J. Date, *A Guide to INGRES* (Reading, Mass.: Addison-Wesley, 1987).

A comprehensive description and analysis of the Commercial INGRES product as of 1987.

3. C. J. Date, "An Introduction to Relational Databases," in *An Introduction to Database Systems,* 6th edition (Reading, Mass.: Addison-Wesley, 1995).

4. P. Hawthorn and M. R. Stonebraker, "Performance Analysis of a Relational Data Base Management System," Proc. 1979 ACM SIGMOD International Conference on Management of Data, Boston, Mass. (May/June 1979). Republished in reference [7].

This paper reports on the conclusions drawn from running a set of benchmark queries against University INGRES. Queries are divided into two categories, "data-intensive" and "overhead-intensive." The benchmarks show that the two categories have such widely differing characteristics that it might be difficult to build a single system that can handle both well. However, the paper also shows that significant performance improvements are achievable in both cases by means of "some combination of" extended memory, read-ahead techniques (sometimes called *sequential prefetch*), and parallel processing.

5. G. D. Held, M. R. Stonebraker, and E. Wong, "INGRES—A Relational Data Base System," Proc. NCC 44, Anaheim, Calif. (Montvale, N.J.: AFIPS Press, May 1975).

The first paper to describe University INGRES. Includes a preliminary definition of QUEL.

6. G. D. Held and M. R. Stonebraker, "Storage Structures and Access Methods in the Relational Data Base Management System INGRES," Proc. ACM Pacific, San Francisco, Calif. (April 1975).

7. Michael Stonebraker (ed.), *The INGRES Papers: The Anatomy of a Relational Database Management System* (Reading, Mass.: Addison-Wesley, 1986).

A collection of some of the major papers from the University INGRES project, edited and annotated by one of the original INGRES designers. (References [1], [4], and [9–

11] are included in this book.) To the present writer's knowledge, this is the only book available that describes the design and implementation of a full-scale relational DBMS in detail. Essential reading for the serious student.

8. M. R. Stonebraker, "Implementation of Integrity Constraints and Views by Query Modification," Proc. ACM SIGMOD International Conference on Management of Data, San Jose, Calif. (May 1975).

9. M. R. Stonebraker, E. Wong, P. Kreps, and G. D. Held, "The Design and Implementation of INGRES," *ACM TODS 1,* No. 3 (September 1976). Republished in reference [7].

A detailed description of University INGRES.

10. Michael Stonebraker *et al.*, "Performance Enhancements to a Relational Database System," *ACM TODS 8,* No. 2 (June 1983). Republished in reference [7].

Analyzes the effects of four possible performance-motivated changes to University INGRES (or to its environment): dynamically compiling QUEL requests, implementing frequently executed INGRES routines in microcode, replacing the UNIX file system by a specially tailored (INGRES-specific) system, and replacing UNIX entirely by a special-purpose operating system. (The term "dynamic compilation" means compilation at run time. The idea is that, even though optimization is still done at run time instead of at some prior time, the optimizer should nevertheless produce compiled code instead of acting as a pure interpreter.) Benchmark experiments indicate that dynamic compilation and using a specially tailored file system would both be very beneficial, but that the other two changes would be of only limited usefulness. Note that Commercial INGRES does in fact use a form of dynamic compilation.

11. M. R. Stonebraker, "Retrospection on a Data Base System," *ACM TODS 5,* No. 2 (June 1980). Republished in reference [7].

An account of the history of the University INGRES project (to January 1979). The emphasis is on mistakes and lessons learned, rather than on successes.

ANSWERS TO SELECTED EXERCISES

```
1. CREATE S ( S#     = CHAR(5)   NOT NULL,
              SNAME  = CHAR(20)  NOT NULL,
              STATUS = I2        NOT NULL,
              CITY   = CHAR(15)  NOT NULL )

   CREATE P ( P#     = CHAR(6)   NOT NULL,
              PNAME  = CHAR(20)  NOT NULL,
              COLOR  = CHAR(6)   NOT NULL,
              WEIGHT = I2        NOT NULL,
              CITY   = CHAR(15)  NOT NULL )

   CREATE J ( J#     = CHAR(4)   NOT NULL,
              JNAME  = CHAR(10)  NOT NULL,
              CITY   = CHAR(15)  NOT NULL )
   CREATE SPJ ( S#   = CHAR(5)   NOT NULL,
                P#   = CHAR(6)   NOT NULL,
                J#   = CHAR(4)   NOT NULL,
                QTY  = I4 )

   MODIFY S TO BTREE UNIQUE ON S#
```

```
    MODIFY P TO BTREE UNIQUE ON P#

    MODIFY J TO BTREE UNIQUE ON J#

    MODIFY SPJ TO BTREE UNIQUE ON S#, P#, J#
```

2. `RETRIEVE ( J.ALL )`

3. `RETRIEVE ( J.ALL ) WHERE J.CITY = "London"`

4. ```
   RETRIEVE ( SPJ.S# )
   WHERE     SPJ.J# = "J1"
   ```

5. ```
   RETRIEVE ( SPJ.ALL )
   WHERE     SPJ.QTY >= 300
   AND       SPJ.QTY <= 750
   ```

6. `RETRIEVE UNIQUE ( P.COLOR, P.CITY )`

7. ```
   RETRIEVE ( S.S#, P.P#, J.J# )
   WHERE     S.CITY = P.CITY
   AND       P.CITY = J.CITY
   AND       J.CITY = S.CITY
   ```

8. ```
   RETRIEVE ( S.S#, P.P#, J.J# )
   WHERE     S.CITY <> P.CITY
   OR        P.CITY <> J.CITY
   OR        J.CITY <> S.CITY
   ```

9. ```
   RETRIEVE ( S.S#, P.P#, J.J# )
   WHERE     S.CITY <> P.CITY
   AND       P.CITY <> J.CITY
   AND       J.CITY <> S.CITY
   ```

10. ```
    RETRIEVE ( SPJ.P# )
    WHERE     SPJ.S# = S.S#
    AND       S.CITY = "London"
    ```

11. ```
    RETRIEVE ( SPJ.P# )
    WHERE     SPJ.S# = S.S# AND S.CITY = "London"
    AND       SPJ.J# = J.J# AND J.CITY = "London"
    ```

12. ```
    RETRIEVE ( S.CITY, J.CITY )
    WHERE     S.S# = SPJ.S# AND SPJ.J# = J.J#
    ```

13. ```
    RETRIEVE ( SPJ.P# )
    WHERE     SPJ.S# = S.S#
    AND       SPJ.J# = J.J#
    AND       S.CITY = J.CITY
    ```

14. ```
    RETRIEVE ( SPJ.J# )
    WHERE     SPJ.S# = S.S#
    AND       SPJ.J# = J.J#
    AND       S.CITY <> J.CITY
    ```

15. ```
    RANGE OF SPJX IS SPJ
    RETRIEVE ( SPJ.P#, SPJX.P# )
    WHERE     SPJ.S# = SPJX.S#
    AND       SPJ.P# < SPJX.P#
    ```

16. `RETRIEVE ( X = COUNTU ( SPJ.J# WHERE SPJ.S# = "S1" ) )`

17. ```
    RETRIEVE ( Y = SUM ( SPJ.QTY WHERE SPJ.S# = "S1"
                            AND    SPJ.P# = "P1" ) )
    ```

18. ```
    RETRIEVE ( SPJ.P#, SPJ.J#, Z = SUM ( SPJ.QTY
                            BY SPJ.P#, SPJ.J# ) )
    ```
    ```

```
19. RETRIEVE ( SPJ.P# )
    WHERE     AVG ( SPJ.QTY BY SPJ.P#, SPJ.J# ) > 320

20. RETRIEVE ( J.JNAME )
    WHERE     J.J# = SPJ.J#
    AND       SPJ.S# = "S1"

21. RETRIEVE ( P.COLOR )
    WHERE     P.P# = SPJ.P#
    AND       SPJ.S# = "S1"

22. RETRIEVE ( SPJ.P# )
    WHERE     SPJ.J# = J.J#
    AND       J.CITY = "London"

23. RANGE OF SPJX IS SPJ

    RETRIEVE ( SPJ.J# )
    WHERE     SPJ.P# = SPJX.P#
    AND       SPJX.S# = "S1"

24. RANGE OF SPJX IS SPJ, SPJY IS SPJ

    RETRIEVE ( SPJ.S# )
    WHERE     SPJ.P# = SPJX.P#
    AND       SPJX.S# = SPJY.S#
    AND       SPJY.P# = P.P#
    AND       P.COLOR = "Red"

25. RANGE OF SX IS S

    RETRIEVE ( S.S# )
    WHERE     S.STATUS < SX.STATUS
    AND       SX.S# = "S1"

26. RETRIEVE ( J.J# )
    WHERE     J.CITY = MIN ( J.CITY )

27. RETRIEVE ( SPJ.J# )
    WHERE     SPJ.P# = "P1"
    AND       AVG ( SPJ.QTY BY SPJ.P#, SPJ.J# ) >
              MAX ( SPJ.QTY WHERE SPJ.J# = "J1" )

28. RETRIEVE ( SPJ.S# )
    WHERE     SPJ.P# = "P1"
    AND       SPJ.QTY > AVG ( SPJ.QTY BY SPJ.P#, SPJ.J# )

29. RETRIEVE ( J.J# )
    WHERE     ANY ( SPJ.S# BY J.J#
                    WHERE SPJ.S# = S.S# AND S.CITY = "London"
                    AND   SPJ.P# = P.P# AND P.COLOR = "Red"
                    AND   SPJ.J# = J.J# ) = 0
```

30.–33. Left as exercises for the reader.

```
34. RETRIEVE INTO TEMP ( S.CITY )
    APPEND   TO   TEMP ( P.CITY )
    APPEND   TO   TEMP ( J.CITY )
    RETRIEVE UNIQUE ( TEMP.CITY )
```

QUEL does not directly support the UNION operator.

35.–37. Left as exercises for the reader.

The Primacy of Primary Keys: An Investigation

ABSTRACT

This paper examines two distinct but interrelated issues:

1. First, among the set of candidate keys that a given relation might possess, the relational model ascribes a primal role to an arbitrarily chosen member of that set called the **primary** key.

2. Second, relational database design methodologies (though not the relational model *per se*) tend to suggest, again a trifle arbitrarily, that a given real-world entity type should be represented inside the database by "the same" primary key wherever it appears.

As indicated, these two recommendations—some might call them **rules**—both involve a certain degree of arbitrariness. That being so, can those recommen-

Originally published in *InfoDB 7,* No. 3 (Summer 1993). Reprinted by permission of Database Associates International.

dations or rules be fully justified in practice? This paper considers this question in depth.

COMMENTS ON REPUBLICATION

As the Abstract indicates, the purpose of this paper is to examine certain aspects of relational technology that (as the body of the paper puts it) have always been the source of some slight embarrassment to relational advocates. The aspects in question are as follows:

1. The rule that says every (base) relation must have, very specifically, a primary key, instead of just having one or more *candidate* keys;

2. The rule that says that every entity should be represented by "the same" primary key value throughout the database.

The reason for the embarrassment is that these rules tend to smack more of dogma than logic, as we shall see. Indeed, the original paper grew out of my own increasing dissatisfaction with the seeming lack of solid justification for the orthodox relational position on these matters; as a friend of mine put it, these are the areas where in live presentations "you talk quickly and hope no one will notice." For my part, I wanted to try to clarify in my own mind exactly what the issues were, and getting those issues down in writing was (as always) a great help in the clarification process. This paper, with its somewhat heretical conclusion, was the result.

Note: Perhaps I should explain immediately that the "heretical conclusion" is that, while the rules in question can be seen as good guidelines that should certainly be followed in the majority of practical situations, they are indeed only guidelines, and sometimes there are good reasons for violating them. As far as my own examples elsewhere in this book are concerned, I have usually, but *not* invariably, abided by those guidelines.

1. INTRODUCTION

As explained in the Abstract, this paper is concerned with two distinct issues. The first is as follows: Among the set of candidate keys that a given relation might possess, the relational model ascribes a primal role to a particular member of that set, which it calls the **primary** key. And, if the set of candidate keys actually does include more than one member, then the choice of which is to be primary is essentially arbitrary. As Codd puts it in reference [3]: *"The normal basis [for making the choice] is simplicity, but this aspect is outside the scope of the relational model."* But why should it be necessary to make such a choice in the first place?— i.e., why, in those cases where a genuine choice does exist, is it necessary, or desirable, to introduce such an element of arbitrariness?

Furthermore, the relational model goes on to insist that all references (via foreign keys) to a given relation must always be to that relation's primary key specifically, never to an alternate key.* Thus we see that a decision that is essentially arbitrary in the first place—namely, the choice of primary key—might lead to arbitrary restrictions on subsequent decisions as well; that is, it might constrain the set of decisions as to what can and cannot be a legal foreign key, in ways that might not have been foreseen when that first decision (the primary key decision) was made.

The second issue is as follows: Relational database design methodologies (though not the relational model *per se*) usually require a given real-world entity type to be represented by "the same" primary key wherever it appears in the database. But, again, this requirement does seem on the face of it to involve a certain degree of arbitrariness. Again, the question has to be: Why is the rule necessary?—or, rather, *is* the rule in fact necessary?

These two issues are indeed (as stated in the Abstract) "distinct but interrelated." Until further notice, however, I will concentrate on the first one only.

2. KEYS IN THE RELATIONAL MODEL

Let me begin by taking a closer look at the relevant concepts of the relational model. First, here is a definition of **candidate** key:[†]

- **Definition:** A candidate key for a given relation R is a subset of the attributes of R, say K, such that at any given time:

  1. *Uniqueness property:*
     No two distinct tuples of R have the same value for K.

  2. *Irreducibility property:*
     No proper subset of K has the uniqueness property.

Perhaps I should elaborate on the second of these two requirements briefly. Basically, the point is that if we were to declare a "candidate key" that was not irreducible in this sense, the system would not be aware of the true state of affairs, and thus would not be able to enforce the (very important) associated integrity constraint. For example, suppose employee numbers are globally unique, but we declare the combination {EMP#,DEPT#}—instead of EMP# alone—as a candidate key for the EMPLOYEE relation. Then the system will not enforce the con-

---

*An **alternate** key is a candidate key that is not the primary key.

[†]Please note that the logical notion of a candidate key should not be confused with the physical notion of a "unique index," even though the latter is very often used to implement the former. A candidate key is a unique identifier, and furthermore is required to be unique "for all time"; it is not just a matter of what unique indexes happen to exist at some particular moment.

straint that employee numbers are globally unique; instead, it will enforce only the weaker constraint that employee numbers are unique *within department.*

Note: Irreducibility is referred to as **minimality** in most of the relational literature (including previous writings of my own). However, "minimality" is not really the *mot juste,* because to say that candidate key *K1* is "minimal" does not mean that another candidate key *K2* cannot be found that has fewer components; it is entirely possible that (e.g.) *K1* has four components and *K2* only two.

Turning now to primary keys: Primary keys are so called precisely because they are supposed to *be* primary. That is, a given relation might have any number of candidate keys—at least one, of course—but (in the case of a base relation, at any rate) we are supposed to choose exactly one of those candidates and make it the primary key. And primary keys are then defined to be the tuple-level **addressing mechanism** within the relational model. As I put it in reference [5]:

> *"The only system-guaranteed way of pinpointing some specific tuple [within some specific base relation] is by its primary key value."*

In that same reference [5] I also stated:

> *". . . in practice, it is the primary key that is the really significant one; candidate [keys] and alternate keys are merely concepts that necessarily arise during the process of defining the more important concept* **primary key.***"*

The fact is, however, that the idea of singling out one particular candidate key for special treatment along the lines just indicated has always been the source of some slight embarrassment to relational advocates (myself included). One of the strongest arguments in favor of the relational model has always been its claim to a solid theoretical foundation. And, whereas this claim is quite clearly justified in most respects, the primary *vs.* alternate key distinction—i.e., the idea of having to choose one member from a set of equals to be somehow "more equal than the others"—has always seemed to rest on grounds that do not enjoy the same degree of theoretical respectability. Certainly there does not seem to be any *formal* justification for the distinction, nor any formal way of making the choice. To repeat the quote from reference [3]: *"The normal basis [for making the choice] is simplicity,* **but this aspect is outside the scope of the relational model"** (emphasis added).

Thus we see that the distinction between primary and alternate keys (hereinafter referred to as *the PK:AK distinction*) introduces an unpleasant note of arbitrariness, artificiality, and asymmetry into what is otherwise a formally defined system. As I will show later, it can also serve to introduce an unpleasant degree of arbitrariness, artificiality, and asymmetry into the database itself. What is more, it can also lead to an undesirable and unnecessary distinction between base and derived relations, as we will see.

3. ARGUMENTS IN DEFENSE OF THE PK:AK DISTINCTION

Before we go on to consider some of these unfortunate consequences of the PK:AK distinction in detail, we should first examine the arguments in its defense. Since I am on record as a defender of that distinction myself [6,7], perhaps I should begin by summarizing my own arguments! The following points 1–5 are taken from a paper I wrote in 1984 entitled "Why Every Relation Should Have Exactly One Primary Key" [6]. *Note:* In the interests of accuracy I should explain that reference [6] actually offered six arguments, not five, but the extra one was merely a matter of terminology and is irrelevant for present purposes.

1. Dropping the PK:AK distinction would imply (among other things) that the entity integrity rule [2] would have to be extended to apply to all candidate keys (all candidate keys in base relations, at any rate), thereby further complicating the relational model. However, I have argued elsewhere [11] that the entity integrity rule should be dropped anyway, so in my opinion this point becomes at best moot.

2. "The discipline of using the same symbol to identify a given entity everywhere it is referenced . . . allows the system to recognize the fact that those references do all refer to the same thing." This statement is clearly true, but I now feel that the discipline in question should be treated as a **design guideline** rather than a hard and fast requirement. See the various examples later in this paper (in particular, the applicants-and-employees example) for some illustrations of situations in which it might be desirable not to follow such a guideline in practice.

   Anyway, this argument is not an argument to support the position of the paper's title (i.e., that every relation should have "exactly one" primary key); rather, it is an argument to support the position that every relation that has anything to do with the given entity type should have, or should reference, "the same" primary key. In other words, it is addressing the second of the two issues under discussion in the present paper, not the first! I must have been a little confused in 1984.

3. The next point was that "metaqueries"—i.e., queries against the catalog—can be more difficult to formulate if entities are identified in different ways in different places. For example, consider what is involved in formulating the metaquery "Which relations refer to employees?" if employees are sometimes referred to by employee serial number and sometimes by social security number.

   The idea here is basically that the discipline referred to under point 2 above can be beneficial for the user as well as the system. Again, however, it seems to me that we are really talking about guidelines, not absolute requirements—and in any case the argument is again addressing the second, not the first, of the issues of concern to the present paper.

4. The next point was not exactly an argument *for* the PK:AK distinction, but rather a criticism of an argument *against* it. That latter argument went as follows: Suppose some user is prevented, for security reasons, from seeing some primary key; then that user needs access to the data by some alternate key instead; so why make the PK:AK distinction in the first place?

   I still don't find this latter argument very convincing, but of course criticizing an argument *against* some position doesn't prove that the contrary position is correct!

5. The final point was an appeal to Occam's Razor ("no unnecessary concepts"). In effect, I was arguing that to treat all candidate keys as equals was to complicate the addressing scheme unnecessarily. But it might well be argued that Occam's Razor applies the other way around, and that it is the concepts of primary key and alternate key that are unnecessary!—i.e., all we really need is **candidate** keys.

In a nutshell, the arguments of reference [6] no longer seem to me very compelling; the only one that still appears to have any validity is the one summarized under points 2 and 3 above, which (as I have already stated) is not really an argument for the PK:AK distinction anyway. Moreover, I now feel that the position supported by that particular argument should be seen more as a matter of discipline than as an inviolable rule (again, see later for examples to justify this position).

I remark in passing, incidentally, that I did hedge my bets somewhat in 1984! Here is another quote [6]:

> *"Note that if we can agree on [retaining the PK:AK distinction] for now, there is always the possibility of eliminating that distinction (if desirable) at some future time. And note moreover that this argument does not apply in the opposite direction: Once we are committed to [treating all candidate keys equally], a system that requires a distinguished primary key will forever be [nonstandard]."*

Although I did not express it in such terms at the time, this quote is effectively an appeal to the **Principle of Cautious Design** [10], a principle that I do still strongly believe in. Indeed, it seems to me that the very fact that I am able to shift my position on the PK:AK distinction now—which is indeed what I am doing —can be regarded as a vindication of that principle.

Before closing this section, I remark that Codd also is on record as a defender of the PK:AK distinction (not surprisingly, since he originated it): *"Severe problems would arise . . . if any relation whatsoever were permitted to have more than one primary key* [sic] *. . . The consequences of permitting more than one primary key . . . for a single base relation [would be] disastrous"* [3]. He gives an example involving employees with "several distinct responsibilities"—project management, department management, inventory management, etc.—and goes on to say that *"comparing for equality of identifiers from distinct columns is intended to establish that one and the same employee is involved . . . This objective is dealt a severe blow if the types of identifiers used for employees can be different depending on which pair of employee-identifying columns is selected for the comparison."* It can be seen that this argument is essentially the same as that given under points 2 and 3 above, which (a) as I have already indicated, is slightly confused, and (b) as we will see later, does not fully stand up under close scrutiny anyway.

4. RELATIONS WITH MULTIPLE CANDIDATE KEYS

Now let us consider some reasonably realistic examples of relations having more than one candidate key. The first is taken from reference [5]; it concerns a relation EXAM with attributes STUDENT, SUBJECT, and POSITION. The meaning of an EXAM tuple {STUDENT:s,SUBJECT:j,POSITION:p} is that student s was examined in subject j and achieved position p in the class list. For the sake of the example, let us assume that there are no ties (that is, no two students obtained the same position in the same subject). Then, clearly, if we know the student and the subject, there is exactly one corresponding position; equally, if we know the subject and the position, there is exactly one corresponding student. Hence {STUDENT,SUBJECT} and {SUBJECT,POSITION} are both candidate keys:

```
EXAM ( STUDENT, SUBJECT, POSITION )
    CANDIDATE KEY ( STUDENT, SUBJECT )
    CANDIDATE KEY ( SUBJECT, POSITION )
```

Here is another example, essentially isomorphic to the previous one but with perhaps a more familiar interpretation:

```
MARRIAGE ( HUSBAND, WIFE, DATE_OF_MARRIAGE )
        CANDIDATE KEY ( HUSBAND, DATE_OF_MARRIAGE )
        CANDIDATE KEY ( WIFE, DATE_OF_MARRIAGE )
```

And here is another (again essentially similar), based on the simple airline application of reference [12]:

```
ROSTER ( DAY, HOUR, GATE, PILOT )
      CANDIDATE KEY ( DAY, HOUR, GATE )
      CANDIDATE KEY ( DAY, HOUR, PILOT )
```

How do we choose the primary key in cases such as these? What grounds are there for choosing one candidate key over the other? (*Note:* I can say *the* other because each example involves exactly two candidate keys, but in general, of course, this need not be the case.) Reference [3]'s criterion of "simplicity" does not seem to be of any assistance here. Note too that whichever we choose, we wind up with an unpleasant and unnatural asymmetry; e.g., in the second example, why should husbands and wives be treated differently? Why should we be forced to introduce such asymmetry? Asymmetry is usually not a good idea. *"Try to treat symmetrically what is symmetrical, and do not destroy wantonly any natural symmetry"* [17].

Now, in all of the foregoing examples the candidate keys were composite (i.e., involved more than one attribute) and overlapped (i.e., had at least one attribute in common). Lest it be thought that it is only when candidate keys overlap that there might be difficulty in choosing the primary key, let me give a counter-example (taken from reference [5]). Suppose we have a relation ELEMENTS representing the table of chemical elements. Then every element has a unique *name,* a unique *symbol* (e.g., the symbol for lead is "Pb"), and a unique *atomic number.* The relation thus clearly has three distinct candidate keys, all of which are "simple" (in the sense that each involves just a single attribute), and hence, obviously, none of them overlaps either of the others. On what grounds do we choose one of these three candidate keys as the primary key? It seems to me that a good case could be made for any one of them, depending on circumstances.

To pursue this example a moment longer: Whichever candidate key we do choose as the primary key, we might then be faced with the need to have a foreign key in some other relation that references an alternate key in the ELEMENTS relation. I will return to the question of foreign keys referencing alternate keys later.

Here is another familiar (perhaps all too familiar) example of a relation with several candidate keys, all of which are simple:

```
TAX_BRACKETS ( LOW, HIGH, PERCENTAGE )
             CANDIDATE KEY ( LOW )
             CANDIDATE KEY ( HIGH )
             CANDIDATE KEY ( PERCENTAGE )
```

Numerous further examples could be given (several can be found in reference [5]), but by now the point is presumably clear: Not only are there no formal criteria for choosing one candidate key over another (in those cases where there is a choice), but sometimes there do not appear to be any informal criteria either. Thus, it really does not seem appropriate to insist that such a choice must *always* be made, even if it is appropriate in many cases (even most cases).

There is another (important) point that needs to be mentioned, a more formal point than most of the ones discussed so far: Over the past 20 years, a great deal of research has been carried out on such matters as **dependency theory and further normalization, view updatability, optimization** (including in particular **semantic** optimization), and **usability** (see, e.g., references [1,4,13,14,15]). And in all of this research it is **candidate** keys, not primary keys, that play the crucial role. (Indeed, this must be the case, precisely because the research in question is formal.) Given that this is so, it really does not seem appropriate to insist *formally* on the primacy of primary keys—though, to repeat, it might be appropriate to recommend it *in*formally.

Yet another point I would like to make is that the PK:AK distinction leads to an undesirable and unnecessary differentiation between base relations and other relations. This is because, according to Codd [3], the relational model *requires* distinguished primary keys for base relations, *permits* (but does not require) them for views and snapshots, and considers it *"completely unnecessary* for primary keys to be declared or deduced" for other relations (italics as in the original). In fact, reference [3] goes so far as to suggest that relations other than base relations might not even *possess* a primary key, which surely raises serious questions about the concept in the first place. My position on these matters is rather different:

- First, I am adamant that **every** relation, base or derived, does have at least one **candidate** key (because, of course, no relation ever permits duplicate tuples).

- Second, I would insist that every **base** relation have at least one candidate key that is explicitly declared (preferably, of course, all such candidate keys should be explicitly declared).

- Usually, a given base relation will have, very specifically, an explicitly declared **primary** key, but I would not insist on this as a hard requirement.

- In contrast to Codd's stated position, I agree strongly with Darwen [4] that the system definitely *should* be able to deduce candidate keys for derived relations.

- The previous point notwithstanding, I also believe that it should be possible to declare candidate keys—not just primary keys—for derived relations (in particular for views and snapshots), for reasons I have previously given in references [11] and [12].

5. THE INVOICES-AND-SHIPMENTS EXAMPLE

I now turn my attention to a more elaborate example, taken from reference [9]. The application concerns invoices and shipments, and there is a one-to-one relationship between these two entity types—each shipment has exactly one invoice and each invoice has exactly one shipment. Here then is the "obvious" database design:

```
INVOICE   ( INV#, SHIP#, INV_DETAILS )
          PRIMARY KEY ( INV# )
          ALTERNATE KEY ( SHIP# )
          FOREIGN KEY ( SHIP# ) REFERENCES SHIPMENT

SHIPMENT ( SHIP#, INV#, SHIP_DETAILS )
          PRIMARY KEY ( SHIP# )
          ALTERNATE KEY ( INV# )
          FOREIGN KEY ( INV# ) REFERENCES INVOICE
```

So the database structure is as shown in Fig. 1.

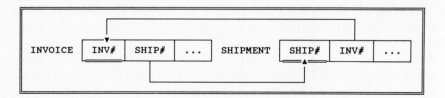

Fig. 1   The invoices-and-shipments database

Observe that each of the two relations has two candidate keys, INV# and SHIP#. However, I assume we can agree that the "natural" primary key for INVOICE is INV# and the "natural" primary key for SHIPMENT is SHIP#. Attributes INVOICE.SHIP# and SHIPMENT.INV# are then alternate keys. Furthermore, of course, each of those alternate keys is also a foreign key, referring to the primary key of the other relation.

One problem with the foregoing design is as follows. Clearly, the database is required to satisfy the constraint—let me call it *C*—that if the INVOICE relation shows invoice *i* as corresponding to shipment *s,* then the SHIPMENT relation must show shipment *s* as corresponding to invoice *i* (and vice versa); in other words, the pair {INV#:*i*,SHIP#:*s*} must appear in INVOICE if and only if the pair {SHIP#:*s*,INV#:*i*} appears in SHIPMENT. But the design above does not capture or enforce this constraint. For example, the configuration of values in Fig. 2 is permitted by that design and yet violates the constraint. The constraint therefore needs to be separately stated and separately enforced.

> *Aside:* It might be thought that if we pretended that the primary key for both relations was the *combination* {INV#,SHIP#}, and if we further defined each of those fake "primary keys" to be a foreign key referencing the other, then this constraint would be taken care of automatically. As we have seen, however, the relational model requires primary keys—or, more generally, candidate keys—to be irreducible, in the sense that they do not include any attributes that are irrelevant for unique identification purposes. We have also seen

INVOICE	INV#	SHIP#	...	SHIPMENT	SHIP#	INV#	...
	i1	s1	...		s1	i2	...
	i2	s2	...		s2	i1	...

Fig. 2   "Legal" values that violate constraint *C*

that there are good reasons for this requirement. In other words, the combination {INV#,SHIP#} simply *is not* a candidate key, let alone the primary key, for either of the two relations, and we would be lying if we told the system otherwise. Indeed, if the combination {INV#,SHIP#} were truly a candidate key, then the relationship between invoices and shipments would be many-to-many, which it isn't. *End of aside.*

Note too that, as the foregoing discussion of constraints indicates, this design involves some **redundancy:** Every pair of {INV#,SHIP#} values appearing in either one of the two relations also necessarily appears in the other. Now, we could avoid this redundancy by combining the two relations into one:

```
INV_SHIP ( INV#, SHIP#, INV_DETAILS, SHIP_DETAILS )
         PRIMARY KEY ( INV# )
         ALTERNATE KEY ( SHIP# )
```

By eliminating the redundancy, moreover, we have also eliminated the need to state and enforce the additional integrity constraint *C* mentioned above. Furthermore, we could if we like define the original INVOICE and SHIPMENT relations as views—specifically, projection views—of the base relation INV_SHIP, thus allowing the user still to regard invoices and shipments as distinct entities. This revised design thus does enjoy certain advantages over the "obvious" version. (Note, however, that there might be some difficulty over updating those projection views. Detailed discussion of this point is beyond the scope of this paper.)

On the other hand, there are some disadvantages too. Observe first that we have had to make an asymmetric decision once again, choosing INV# over SHIP#—arbitrarily—as the primary key for INV_SHIP. Second, suppose further that shipments have certain subsidiary information that invoices do not; e.g., suppose that shipments are containerized, each shipment involving several containers. Then a new CONTAINER relation is needed:

```
CONTAINER ( CONT#, SHIP#, ... )
          PRIMARY KEY ( CONT# )
          FOREIGN KEY ( SHIP# ) REFERENCES INV_SHIP ( SHIP# )
```

And so we have a foreign key referencing an alternate key!—which is prohibited by the relational model, as we know.

Now, can we avoid this violation of the prescriptions of the relational model? Well, of course, the answer is clearly *yes*. There are various ways in which this might be done:

1. We could go back to the two-relation design (thereby reintroducing the data redundancy and the need for the additional constraint, however).

2. We could replace SHIP# by INV# in the CONTAINER relation. However, this approach seems very artificial (containers have nothing to do with invoices *per se*), and moreover introduces an unpleasant level of indirection

into the design (the shipment for a given container would be accessible only via the corresponding invoice).

3. We could leave the CONTAINER relation as it is, but replace the foreign key specification by an explicit statement of the constraint that every SHIP# value in CONTAINER must also appear in INV_SHIP (using a suitable general purpose integrity language, such as that described in reference [8]). But it does seem a pity to have to deal with a constraint that is so similar to a "true" foreign key constraint in such a roundabout manner; indeed, it could be argued that the effect is again to introduce an undesirable asymmetry (foreign keys that reference primary keys being treated in one manner and "foreign keys" that reference alternate keys being treated in quite another).

4. We could introduce an artificial primary key (IS#, say) for INV_SHIP, and use that as the foreign key in the CONTAINER table—which would still involve a level of indirection, as in paragraph 2 above, but would at least reintroduce the symmetry that was lost when we arbitrarily chose INV# as the primary key for INV_SHIP.

To summarize: None of these four "workaround" approaches seems totally satisfactory. The example thus appears to show that—if we wish to avoid redundancy and arbitrariness and artificiality and asymmetry and indirectness—then we need to be able to treat primary and alternate keys as equals, and we need to be able to have foreign keys that reference alternate keys. In other words, we need to ignore the differences between primary and alternate keys, and simply consider them all as candidate keys. Please note carefully, however, that I am NOT saying that the apparent need in this example to violate certain relational precepts cannot be avoided; what I am saying is that I don't see a good way to avoid it, nor a good reason for adopting a bad way. I would therefore like to suggest that the precepts in question should be treated as strong guidelines but *not* as inviolable rules.

6. ONE PRIMARY KEY PER ENTITY TYPE?

I turn now to the second of the two issues mentioned in the Abstract, viz: Entities of a given type are usually required "to be identified in precisely the same way across the entire database" [3]. What this means, loosely speaking, is that there will typically be:

■ A single "anchor" relation for the given entity type, having some particular primary key;

together with

■ Zero or more subsidiary relations giving further information about entities of that type, each having a foreign key that refers back to the primary key of the anchor relation.

I will refer to this requirement as the "one primary key for one entity type" requirement. Several obvious questions arise:

- Might there not be a good reason to have more than one anchor relation for a given entity type—perhaps corresponding to different **roles** for that entity type?

- If there are several such anchor relations, might there not be a good reason to have different primary keys in different anchor relations—thus implying that the same entity might be identified in different ways in different contexts?

- Hence, might there not be a good reason to have different **foreign** keys in different relations that, again, identify the same entity in different ways in different contexts?

- Finally, might there not even be a good reason to have several distinct identifiers, all of equal weight, for the same entity in the *same* relation?

We have already seen many examples in this paper in which the answer to the last of these questions is *yes*. In order to examine the other questions, let us consider another example.

7. THE APPLICANTS-AND-EMPLOYEES EXAMPLE

This example—which is based on a real-world situation, incidentally—concerns applicants for jobs in a certain enterprise. Relation APPLICANTS is used to keep a list of such applicants:

```
APPLICANTS ( APP#, NAME, ADDR, ... )
           PRIMARY KEY ( APP# )
```

The *applicant number* (APP#), which is unique to the applicant, is assigned at the time the applicant applies for the job, and constitutes the obvious primary key for the relation (in fact, of course, it is the only candidate key).

Next, several further relations are used to keep subsidiary applicant information (previous jobs held, list of references, list of dependants, etc.). I consider just one of these here, the "previous jobs held" relation (APPLICANT_JOBS):

```
APPLICANT_JOBS ( APP#, EMPLOYER, JOB, START_DATE, END_DATE, ... )
               PRIMARY KEY ( APP#, START_DATE )
               ALTERNATE KEY ( APP#, END_DATE )
               FOREIGN KEY ( APP# ) REFERENCES APPLICANTS
```

Notice, incidentally, that once again we are faced with an arbitrary choice of primary key, but this is not the point I want to examine here.

Now, when a job applicant is successful, he or she is assigned an *employee number* (EMP#), unique to the employee, and information regarding the new employee (job title, department number, phone number, etc.) is recorded in an EMPLOYEES relation:

```
EMPLOYEES ( EMP#, JOB, DEPT#, PHONE#, ... )
          PRIMARY KEY ( EMP# )
```

Now we have two distinct anchor relations, APPLICANTS and EMPLOYEES, such that **the very same entity** (i.e., a given person) is identified by an APP# value in one of the two and by an EMP# value in the other. Of course, it is true that the two relations represent different person **roles:** A given tuple in the APPLICANTS relation represents a given person in an applicant role and the corresponding tuple in the EMPLOYEES relation represents the same person in an employee role—but the fact remains that there is just a single entity involved.

But this is not the end of the story. Clearly, the EMPLOYEES relation needs to refer back to the APPLICANTS relation somehow. Thus, we need to introduce an APP# foreign key into the EMPLOYEES relation:

```
EMPLOYEES ( EMP#, JOB, DEPT#, PHONE#, APP#, ... )
          PRIMARY KEY ( EMP# )
          ALTERNATE KEY ( APP# )
          FOREIGN KEY ( APP# ) REFERENCES APPLICANTS
```

Note that we have two candidate keys once again!—namely, EMP# and APP#. This point will be relevant in a few moments; for now, however, let me just ignore it.

Next, of course, we will need additional relations to carry subsidiary information for employees (salary history, benefit details, etc.). Here is the salary history relation:

```
SAL_HIST ( EMP#, SALARY_DATE, SALARY, ... )
         PRIMARY KEY ( EMP#, SALARY_DATE )
         FOREIGN KEY ( EMP# ) REFERENCES EMPLOYEES
```

Now we have the very same entity being not only *identified,* but also *referenced,* by an EMP# value in one relation (SAL_HIST) and by an APP# value in others (APPLICANT_JOBS, EMPLOYEES). In other words, the database structure is as shown in Fig. 3.

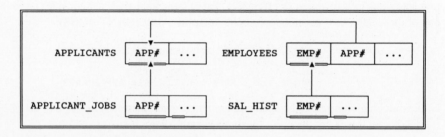

Fig. 3 The applicants-and-employees database

Now, we could avoid the apparent need for two different identifiers (APP# and EMP#) for the same entity type by regarding EMPLOYEES as a subtype of APPLICANTS; after all, every employee is an applicant, while the converse is not true. In this way we could use APP# as the primary key for the EMPLOYEES relation, treating EMP# as an alternate key (or even dropping it altogether), and replace EMP# by APP# in the SAL_HIST relation (see Fig. 4).

But why should the enterprise change its way of doing business, just because of a piece of relational dogma ("one primary key for one entity type")? To be specific, why should it not be allowed to identify applicants by applicant number and employees by employee number—even though applicants and employees are all persons, and indeed every employee is also an applicant?

Aside: Another possibility would be to introduce a PERSONS relation and then regard both APPLICANTS and EMPLOYEES as subtypes of PERSONS. I leave the details as an exercise for the reader; I simply remark that this approach basically doesn't solve anything, even if we invent a PERSON# as the primary key of PERSONS. On the other hand, I *would* definitely recommend the supertype/subtype approach when "the same" primary key is involved everywhere (e.g., if we were dealing with EMPLOYEES and PROGRAMMERS and SYSTEM_PROGRAMMERS and APPLICATION_ PROGRAMMERS, etc., etc., all identified by EMP#). *End of aside.*

To summarize: The foregoing example seems to show that there might be occasions on which it is indeed desirable (a) to have several anchor relations for "the same" entity type, and (b) to have a different primary key in each of those anchor relations, and (c) to have different foreign keys matching those different primary keys in different subsidiary relations. Again, please note that I am NOT saying that the apparent need here to violate the rule "one primary key for one entity type" cannot be avoided. What I am saying is that I don't see a good way to avoid it, nor do I see a good reason for adopting a bad way. Again, therefore, I

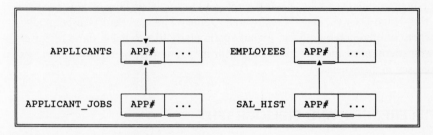

Fig. 4 Using APP# as the primary key for EMPLOYEES

would like to suggest that the "one primary key for one entity type" precept should be treated as a very strong guideline, but *not* as an inviolable rule.

8. CONCLUSION

In this paper I have presented a number of pragmatic arguments for:

- Relaxing the *formal* requirement that every base relation have a distinguished candidate key called the primary key
- Relaxing the *formal* requirement that every foreign key refer specifically to a primary key instead of to an alternate key
- Relaxing the *informal* requirement that there be exactly one anchor relation for each entity type

Of course, I am well aware that if (e.g.) we open up the relational model to drop the requirement that some candidate key be distinguished as the primary key—and accordingly allow a foreign key to reference any candidate key—then we simultaneously open the door to the possibility of bad database designs. That is why I recommend retaining precepts such as "entities of a given type should be identified in the same way across the entire database" as **rules of thumb,** or guidelines for good database design. In other words, such precepts should be violated only if there is some really good reason for doing so. But I do accept that sometimes such good reasons will exist.

There is one final piece of unfinished business I have to attend to. In a previous paper [7] I criticized the SQL standard [16] for permitting foreign keys to reference alternate keys as well as primary keys. As this paper shows, I no longer feel that such criticism is valid, and I hereby withdraw it, with apologies.

ACKNOWLEDGMENTS

I would like to thank an attendee at one of my seminars, Suzan Saginian, for supplying me with the applicants-and-employees example, and my reviewers Nagraj Alur, Hugh Darwen, David McGoveran, Colin White, and Paul Winsberg, all of whom offered helpful advice. I would particularly like to thank those reviewers who encouraged me to "go public" with the somewhat heretical opinions expressed in this paper.

REFERENCES AND BIBLIOGRAPHY

1. A. V. Aho, Y. Sagiv, and J. D. Ullman, "Efficient Optimization of a Class of Relational Expressions," *ACM TODS 4,* No. 4 (December 1979).

2. E. F. Codd, "Extending the Database Relational Model to Capture More Meaning," *ACM TODS 4,* No. 4 (December 1979).

3. E. F. Codd, "Domains, Keys, and Referential Integrity in Relational Databases," *InfoDB 3,* No. 1 (Spring 1988).

4. Hugh Darwen, "The Role of Functional Dependence in Query Decomposition," in C. J. Date and Hugh Darwen, *Relational Database Writings 1989–1991* (Reading, Mass.: Addison-Wesley, 1992).

5. C. J. Date, *An Introduction to Database Systems: Volume I* (5th edition) (Reading, Mass.: Addison-Wesley, 1990).

6. C. J. Date, "Why Every Relation Should Have Exactly One Primary Key," in *Relational Database: Selected Writings* (Reading, Mass.: Addison-Wesley, 1986).

7. C. J. Date, "Referential Integrity and Foreign Keys," in *Relational Database Writings 1985–1989* (Reading, Mass.: Addison-Wesley, 1990).

8. C. J. Date, "A Contribution to the Study of Database Integrity," in *Relational Database Writings 1985–1989* (Reading, Mass.: Addison-Wesley, 1990).

9. C. J. Date, "A Note on One-to-One Relationships," in *Relational Database Writings 1985–1989* (Reading, Mass.: Addison-Wesley, 1990).

10. C. J. Date, "The Principle of Cautious Design," in C. J. Date and Hugh Darwen, *Relational Database Writings 1989–1991* (Reading, Mass.: Addison-Wesley, 1992).

11. C. J. Date, "Notes Toward a Reconstituted Definition of the Relational Model Version 1 (RM/V1)," in C. J. Date and Hugh Darwen, *Relational Database Writings 1989–1991* (Reading, Mass.: Addison-Wesley, 1992).

12. C. J. Date, "A Normalization Problem" (in this volume).

13. C. J. Date and Ronald Fagin, "Simple Conditions for Guaranteeing Higher Normal Forms in Relational Databases," in C. J. Date and Hugh Darwen, *Relational Database Writings 1989–1991* (Reading, Mass.: Addison-Wesley, 1992). Also published in *ACM TODS 17,* No. 3 (September 1992).

14. Umeshwar Dayal and Philip A. Bernstein, "On the Correct Translation of Update Operations on Relational Views," *ACM TODS 7,* No. 3 (September 1982).

15. Ronald Fagin, "Normal Forms and Relational Database Operators," Proc. ACM SIGMOD International Conference on Management of Data, Boston, Mass. (May/June 1979).

16. International Organization for Standardization (ISO), *Database Language SQL,* Document ISO/IEC 9075:1989. Also published as American National Standards Institute (ANSI) Document ANSI X3.135-1989.

17. G. Polya, *How to Solve It* (2nd edition) (Princeton, N.J.: Princeton University Press, 1971).

A Normalization Problem

ABSTRACT

We examine a simple problem of normalization and use it to make some observations on the subject of database design and explicit integrity constraint declaration.

COMMENTS ON REPUBLICATION

The normalization problem referred to in this chapter's title was originally posed by Joe Celko in reference [1]. I originally wrote the short paper that follows as a response to that problem, and more specifically as an attempt to clarify in my own mind exactly what was wrong with the five solutions provided along with the problem in the original reference [1].

The original problem statement concluded with the words "This problem will give you respect for a database normalizer tool you probably never had" (I assume the phrase "you probably never had" is to be understood as qualifying "respect," not "a database normalizer tool.") On the contrary!—if I am to take it that the five solutions provided in reference [1] are what some database normalizer tool would

Originally published (in somewhat different form) in *The Relational Journal 4*, No. 2 (April/May 1992). Reprinted with permission.

actually give me, then the problem serves rather to increase my suspicion of such tools. So I agree there is a valuable lesson to be learned here, but I'm not sure it's the lesson the author of reference [1] had in mind.

1. PROBLEM STATEMENT

The problem to be discussed is taken from a recent article in *Database Programming & Design* [1]. We are given a self-explanatory set of functional dependencies (FDs) for a simple airline application, as follows:*

```
 1. { FLIGHT } → DESTINATION
 2. { FLIGHT } → HOUR
 3. { DAY, FLIGHT } → GATE
 4. { DAY, FLIGHT } → PILOT
 5. { DAY, HOUR, GATE } → DESTINATION
 6. { DAY, HOUR, GATE } → FLIGHT
 7. { DAY, HOUR, GATE } → PILOT
 8. { DAY, HOUR, PILOT } → DESTINATION
 9. { DAY, HOUR, PILOT } → FLIGHT
10. { DAY, HOUR, PILOT } → GATE
```

Reference [1] states the requirement as follows: "Try to find all five 3NF database schemas in these relationships." Two points arise immediately.

1. First, I feel compelled to criticize the sloppiness with which the requirement is expressed (especially since—as I have previously remarked on more than one occasion—one of the objectives of the relational model was precisely to inject some precision and clarity into the database field). To be specific:

   · The problem as stated tends to suggest that there are *exactly* five solutions (or "3NF schemas"), which is manifestly not the case.

   · The requirement should preferably be stated in terms of BCNF (if not 5NF), rather than 3NF. (In practice, of course, people frequently say "3NF" when what they really mean is BCNF. See the next section for formal definitions of these terms.)

   · It's not the "schema" (as that term is used in reference [1]) that is 3NF, but rather the relations that are defined within that schema.

   · The schemas are not "in" the "relationships"; rather, they *represent* them.

   · The use of the term "relationships" to refer to FDs, though unusual, is not

---

*Throughout this paper I adopt the familiar convention by which the braces enclosing the single member of a singleton set can optionally be omitted, thus writing, e.g., A for {A}.

exactly incorrect, but there is an obvious possibility of confusion with "relations," and it would have been better to use another term (perhaps "FDs").

2. Second, the form in which the problem is stated is typical of such problems in general—that is, the reader is presented with a set of FDs as *input* and is asked to come up with an appropriate relational design as *output*. However:

- I have argued elsewhere [4] that FDs have no meaning outside the context of some containing relation, and hence that it would be more correct, or more accurate, to regard the input as a "universal relation" [8] that *satisfies* the given set of FDs, and the output as a certain *nonloss decomposition* of that universal relation.

- Starting with a set of FDs—one in which the FDs are not all independent of one another, at that—is generally *not* a good way to do database design! Some top-down methodology, such as that described in reference [2], is to be preferred in practice.

2. DEFINITIONS OF 3NF AND BCNF

I assume that the objectives and advantages of third normal form (3NF), and more particularly Boyce-Codd normal form (BCNF), are too well known to need rehearsing here (as indicated above, I am assuming that it is BCNF, not just 3NF, that we are really being asked to aim for). Tutorial presentations on such matters can be found in many places (see, e.g., reference [4]). To avoid any confusion that might otherwise arise over terms, however, I will at least give precise definitions here of the 3NF and BCNF concepts. *Note:* Several equivalent definitions of these terms can be given, but the following are the most satisfactory for our purposes.

Let R be a relation (more accurately, relation *schema*), let X be any subset of the set of attributes of R, and let A be any single attribute of R. Then:

1. R is in *3NF* if and only if, for every FD $X \rightarrow A$ satisfied by R, at least one of the following is true:
   a. X includes A (so the FD is trivial)
   b. X includes a candidate key of R
   c. A is included in some candidate key of R
2. R is in *BCNF* if and only if, for every FD $X \rightarrow A$ satisfied by R, at least one of the following is true:
   a. X includes A (so the FD is trivial)
   b. X includes a candidate key of R

To put matters more intuitively (albeit less precisely): BCNF means that every nontrivial FD is "an FD out of a candidate key" [4]; 3NF means that every nontrivial FD is *either* an FD out of a candidate key *or* an FD in which the dependent attribute is a component of some candidate key. Note that BCNF implies 3NF.

3. PROBLEM SOLUTION

The first thing to do is to rewrite the given set of FDs in an obvious way, combining Nos. 1 and 2, Nos. 3 and 4, Nos. 5–7, and Nos. 8–10, to yield the following revised set (note the renumbering):

1. { FLIGHT } → { DESTINATION, HOUR }
2. { DAY, FLIGHT } → { GATE, PILOT }
3. { DAY, HOUR, GATE } → { DESTINATION, FLIGHT, PILOT }
4. { DAY, HOUR, PILOT } → { DESTINATION, FLIGHT, GATE }

Because of FD No. 1, we can drop the dependent attribute DESTINATION from the right-hand side in each of Nos. 3 and 4, yielding as our final simplified set of FDs the following:

1. { FLIGHT } → { DESTINATION, HOUR }
2. { DAY, FLIGHT } → { GATE, PILOT }
3. { DAY, HOUR, GATE } → { FLIGHT, PILOT }
4. { DAY, HOUR, PILOT } → { FLIGHT, GATE }

The most immediately obvious attempt at a design would thus involve four relations, one for each of the four FDs, with the primary key of each relation comprising the set of attributes on the left-hand side of the corresponding FD. Of these four relations, however, the ones corresponding to FDs Nos. 3 and 4 are clearly not BCNF, because they both satisfy the additional FD FLIGHT → HOUR—see the definition of BCNF, earlier—and hence both involve some data redundancy. The "obvious" design thus involves just two relations, corresponding to FDs Nos. 1 and 2:

```
FDH ( FLIGHT, DESTINATION, HOUR )
    PRIMARY KEY ( FLIGHT )

DFGP ( DAY, FLIGHT, GATE, PILOT )
    PRIMARY KEY ( DAY, FLIGHT )
```

These two relations are both BCNF, as the reader can easily confirm.

In addition, we need two explicitly declared integrity constraints, corresponding to FDs Nos. 3 and 4. We might express these constraints as follows:

```
IF ( f1,t1,h ), ( f2,t2,h ) ∈ FDH AND
   ( d,f1,g,p1 ), ( d,f2,g,p2 ) ∈ DFGP
THEN f1 = f2 AND p1 = p2

IF ( f1,t1,h ), ( f2,t2,h ) ∈ FDH AND
   ( d,f1,g1,p ), ( d,f2,g2,p ) ∈ DFGP
THEN f1 = f2 AND g1 = g2
```

I am assuming here that the DBMS supports some kind of calculus-based language for declaring integrity constraints (as described in, e.g., reference [3]). *Explanation:* The first of these two declarations says, in English, that if (a) two rows of FDH have the same HOUR *h,* and (b) two rows of DFGP, one each for the two FLIGHTs *f1* and *f2* in the two FDH rows, have the same DAY *d* and GATE *g,* then (c) the two FDH rows must be the same and (d) the two DFGP rows must be the same—in other words, if we know the HOUR, DAY, and GATE, then the FLIGHT and PILOT are determined. The second declaration is analogous. (I will have more to say on the question of integrity constraints—specifically, on how to declare them—toward the end of this paper.)

Note: Of course, attribute FLIGHT of relation DFGP is a foreign key, referencing the primary key FLIGHT of relation FDH. Reference [1] does not mention foreign keys at all, and so I will ignore them too (mostly); I remark, however, that the process of identifying foreign keys is a very important part of database design in practice (i.e., database design is not just a matter of getting the relations right —*integrity constraints* are a crucial aspect too). I remark further that if reference [1] had in fact taken foreign keys into account, some of the problems with its proposed solutions (see the next section below) would have become obvious very quickly.

4. THE FIVE PROPOSED SOLUTIONS

I now turn to the five "solutions" proposed in reference [1] ("solutions" in quotes, because it will turn out that none of them is in fact acceptable as a good database design). *Note:* The reader will soon see that the discussions that follow are somewhat repetitious. This is because the section as a whole is not meant to be read exhaustively—rather, it is intended to serve as a source for future reference. The reader might prefer to go directly to the end of the section, where the flaws in the five solutions are summarized in tabular form.

1. The first solution of reference [1] looks like this:

```
DEPARTURES ( FLIGHT, DESTINATION, HOUR )
    PRIMARY KEY ( FLIGHT )

WEEKLY_ROSTER ( DAY, HOUR, GATE, FLIGHT, PILOT )
    PRIMARY KEY ( DAY, HOUR, GATE )
```

DEPARTURES here is the same as our FDH; WEEKLY_ROSTER corresponds to FD No. 3, and as I have already explained is not BCNF. But that is not the only problem with this design. To spell out the problems in detail:

■ WEEKLY_ROSTER has an additional (but undeclared) candidate key, *viz.* {DAY,HOUR,PILOT}. Because it is not declared, the candidate key constraint cannot be maintained by the DBMS.

- WEEKLY_ROSTER has another undeclared candidate key, *viz.* {DAY,FLIGHT}. Because it is not declared, the candidate key constraint cannot be maintained by the DBMS.

- WEEKLY_ROSTER has an additional (but undeclared) FD, *viz.* FLIGHT → HOUR. Because it is not declared, it cannot be maintained by the DBMS.

- Because of the FD FLIGHT → HOUR, WEEKLY_ROSTER is not BCNF. As a result, WEEKLY_ROSTER includes some internal redundancy (the fact that a given FLIGHT operates at a given HOUR appears seven times in the relation, in general—once for each possible value of DAY).

- Because of the FD FLIGHT → HOUR again, the design involves some redundancy across the two relations. Specifically, the fact that a given FLIGHT operates at a given HOUR appears not only seven times in the WEEKLY_ROSTER relation but once in the DEPARTURES relation as well.

2. Here is the second solution from reference [1]:

```
DEPARTURES ( FLIGHT, DESTINATION, HOUR )
   PRIMARY KEY ( FLIGHT )

WEEKLY_ROSTER ( DAY, HOUR, PILOT, FLIGHT, GATE )
   PRIMARY KEY ( DAY, HOUR, PILOT )
```

This solution is very similar to the first; the difference is that WEEKLY_ROSTER now corresponds to FD No. 4 instead of No. 3. The problems with this design are essentially identical to those discussed under the first solution above, *mutatis mutandis.*

3. Here is the third solution from reference [1]:

```
DEPARTURES ( FLIGHT, DESTINATION, HOUR )
   PRIMARY KEY ( FLIGHT )

GATE_PILOT_SCHEDULE ( DAY, FLIGHT, GATE, PILOT )
   PRIMARY KEY ( DAY, FLIGHT )

GATE_FLIGHT_SCHEDULE ( DAY, HOUR, GATE, FLIGHT )
   PRIMARY KEY ( DAY, HOUR, GATE )

PILOT_FLIGHT_SCHEDULE ( DAY, HOUR, PILOT, FLIGHT )
   PRIMARY KEY ( DAY, HOUR, PILOT )
```

DEPARTURES here is the same as our FDH and GATE_PILOT_SCHEDULE is the same as our DFGP. The other two relations correspond to FDs Nos. 6 and 9, respectively, in the *original* (unsimplified) set of FDs. The problems with this design are as follows:

- GATE_FLIGHT_SCHEDULE has an additional (undeclared) candidate key, *viz.* {DAY,FLIGHT}. Because it is not declared, the candidate key constraint cannot be maintained by the DBMS.

- GATE_FLIGHT_SCHEDULE has an additional (undeclared) FD, *viz*. FLIGHT → HOUR. Because it is not declared, it cannot be maintained by the DBMS.

- Because of the FD FLIGHT → HOUR, GATE_FLIGHT_SCHEDULE is not BCNF.

- PILOT_FLIGHT_SCHEDULE has an additional (undeclared) candidate key, *viz*. {DAY,FLIGHT}. Because it is not declared, the candidate key constraint cannot be maintained by the DBMS.

- PILOT_FLIGHT_SCHEDULE has an additional (undeclared) FD, *viz*. FLIGHT → HOUR. Because it is not declared, it cannot be maintained by the DBMS.

- Because of the FD FLIGHT → HOUR, PILOT_FLIGHT_SCHEDULE is not BCNF.

- The design involves a grossly excessive amount of cross-relation redundancy. The details are left as an exercise for the reader.

4. Here is the fourth solution from reference [1]:

```
DEPARTURES ( DESTINATION, HOUR )
   PRIMARY KEY ( FLIGHT )

GATE_FLIGHT_SCHEDULE ( DAY, FLIGHT, GATE )
   PRIMARY KEY ( DAY, FLIGHT )

GATE_PILOT_SCHEDULE ( DAY, HOUR, GATE, PILOT )
   PRIMARY KEY ( DAY, HOUR, GATE )

PILOT_FLIGHT_SCHEDULE ( DAY, HOUR, PILOT, FLIGHT )
   PRIMARY KEY ( DAY, HOUR, PILOT )
```

DEPARTURES here is the same as our FDH, except that attribute FLIGHT is missing (this is presumably just a typo, since FLIGHT is given as the primary key). GATE_FLIGHT_SCHEDULE is the same as our DFGP, except that attribute PILOT is missing (this is probably *not* just a typo). The other two relations correspond to FDs Nos. 7 and 9, respectively, in the original unsimplified set. Problems:

- GATE_PILOT_SCHEDULE has an additional (undeclared) candidate key, *viz*. {DAY,HOUR,PILOT}. Because it is not declared, the candidate key constraint cannot be maintained by the DBMS.

- PILOT_FLIGHT_SCHEDULE has an additional (undeclared) candidate key, *viz*. {DAY,FLIGHT}. Because it is not declared, the candidate key constraint cannot be maintained by the DBMS.

- PILOT_FLIGHT_SCHEDULE has an additional (undeclared) FD, *viz*. FLIGHT → HOUR. Because it is not declared, it cannot be maintained by the DBMS.

- Because of the FD FLIGHT → HOUR, PILOT_FLIGHT_SCHEDULE is not BCNF.

- The symmetry between GATEs and PILOTs has been destroyed.

- Again the design involves a great deal of cross-relation redundancy. Again the details are left as an exercise for the reader.

  5. Here is the fifth solution from reference [1]:

```
DEPARTURES ( DESTINATION, HOUR )
    PRIMARY KEY ( FLIGHT )

DUTY_ROSTER ( DAY, FLIGHT, PILOT )
    PRIMARY KEY ( DAY, FLIGHT )

GATE_FLIGHT_SCHEDULE ( DAY, HOUR, GATE, FLIGHT )
    PRIMARY KEY ( DAY, HOUR, GATE )

GATE_PILOT_SCHEDULE ( DAY, HOUR, PILOT, GATE )
    PRIMARY KEY ( DAY, HOUR, PILOT )
```

DEPARTURES here is the same as our FDH, except that attribute FLIGHT is missing (again, this is presumably just a typo, since FLIGHT is given as the primary key). DUTY_ROSTER is the same as our DFGP, except that attribute GATE is missing (this is probably *not* just a typo). The other two relations correspond to FDs Nos. 6 and 10 in the original (unsimplified) set. Problems:

- GATE_FLIGHT_SCHEDULE has an additional (undeclared) candidate key, *viz.* {DAY,FLIGHT}. Because it is not declared, the candidate key constraint cannot be maintained by the DBMS.

- GATE_FLIGHT_SCHEDULE has an additional (undeclared) FD, *viz.* FLIGHT → HOUR. Because it is not declared, it cannot be maintained by the DBMS.

- Because of the FD FLIGHT → HOUR, GATE_FLIGHT_SCHEDULE is not BCNF.

- GATE_PILOT_SCHEDULE has an additional (undeclared) candidate key, *viz.* {DAY,HOUR,GATE}. Because it is not declared, the candidate key constraint cannot be maintained by the DBMS.

- The symmetry between GATEs and PILOTs has been destroyed.

- Once again the design involves much cross-relation redundancy. Once again the details are left as an exercise for the reader.

In short: None of the foregoing five designs is the "obvious" one; none of them is complete (each omits two candidate key declarations and at least one additional integrity constraint); none of them is fully BCNF (each includes at least one nonBCNF relation); and each of them involves some cross-relation redundancy, as well as the intra-relation redundancy that results from having relations that are not BCNF.

These criticisms are summarized in the table in Fig. 1 (where for reasons of space DAY, FLIGHT, GATE, HOUR, and PILOT are abbreviated to D, F, G, H, and P, respectively). It might help to point out that the relation names are "solution-local"; e.g., relation GATE_PILOT_SCHEDULE in solution No. 4 is not quite the same as relation GATE_PILOT_SCHEDULE in solution No. 5 (they have different primary keys).

Solution No.	Undeclared CKs	Undeclared FDs	Not BCNF
1	{D,H,P} & {D,F} in WEEKLY_ ROSTER	F → H in WEEKLY_ ROSTER	WEEKLY_ ROSTER
2	{D,H,G} & {D,F} in WEEKLY_ ROSTER	F → H in WEEKLY_ ROSTER	WEEKLY_ ROSTER
3	{D,F} in GATE_ FLIGHT_ SCHEDULE	F → H in GATE_ FLIGHT_ SCHEDULE	GATE_ FLIGHT_ SCHEDULE
	{D,F} in PILOT_ FLIGHT_ SCHEDULE	F → H in PILOT_ FLIGHT_ SCHEDULE	PILOT_ FLIGHT_ SCHEDULE
4	{D,F} in PILOT_ FLIGHT_ SCHEDULE	F → H in PILOT_ FLIGHT_ SCHEDULE	PILOT_ FLIGHT_ SCHEDULE
	{D,H,P} in GATE_ PILOT_ SCHEDULE		
5	{D,F} in GATE_ FLIGHT_ SCHEDULE	F → H in GATE_ FLIGHT_ SCHEDULE	GATE_ FLIGHT_ SCHEDULE
	{D,H,G} in GATE_ PILOT_ SCHEDULE		

Fig. 1 The "solutions" of reference [1] summarized

5. DECLARING INTEGRITY CONSTRAINTS

Despite my criticisms of its proposed solutions, reference [1] does serve one useful purpose, as follows: It shows very clearly why, although the discipline of normalization is helpful, in that it enables us (among other things) to represent certain integrity constraints—specifically, certain FDs—very simply, it does not in general enable us to represent *all* constraints (not even all FDs) in that simple manner. Thus, there will be times when explicit declaration of additional constraints is necessary. In the case at hand, we had to give explicit declarations for two such additional constraints, *viz.* (to repeat):

```
IF ( f1,t1,h ), ( f2,t2,h ) ∈ FDH AND
   ( d,f1,g,p1 ), ( d,f2,g,p2 ) ∈ DFGP
THEN f1 = f2 AND p1 = p2

IF ( f1,t1,h ), ( f2,t2,h ) ∈ FDH AND
   ( d,f1,g1,p ), ( d,f2,g2,p ) ∈ DFGP
THEN f1 = f2 AND g1 = g2
```

These two constraints correspond to FDs Nos. 3 and 4 in the simplified set (despite the fact that they don't look very much like FDs; I will return to this point in a moment). As mentioned earlier in this paper, the constraints are expressed in relational calculus. But of course most DBMSs today do not support relational calculus, they support SQL; and, unfortunately, SQL systems provide *no way at all* of expressing explicit constraints such as those I have been discussing, other than in procedural code, if the level of SQL supported is no greater than that of the current standard [9]. They can, however, be expressed in "SQL/92" [10], the likely follow-on to that current standard.* This is what the two constraints above might look like in SQL/92:

```
CREATE ASSERTION DHGFP
CHECK ( NOT ( EXISTS ( SELECT * FROM FDH FDH1 WHERE
              EXISTS ( SELECT * FROM FDH FDH2 WHERE
              EXISTS ( SELECT * FROM DFGP DFGP1 WHERE
              EXISTS ( SELECT * FROM DFGP DFGP2 WHERE
                       FDH2.HOUR = FDH1.HOUR AND
                       DFGP1.FLIGHT = FDH1.FLIGHT AND
                       DFGP2.FLIGHT = FDH2.FLIGHT AND
                       DFGP2.DAY = DFGP1.DAY AND
                       DFGP2.GATE = DFGP1.GATE AND
                     ( FDH1.FLIGHT <> FDH2.FLIGHT OR
                       DFGP1.PILOT <> DFGP2.PILOT ) ) ) ) ) ) )

CREATE ASSERTION DHPFG
CHECK ( NOT ( EXISTS ( SELECT * FROM FDH FDH1 WHERE
              EXISTS ( SELECT * FROM FDH FDH2 WHERE
              EXISTS ( SELECT * FROM DFGP DFGP1 WHERE
              EXISTS ( SELECT * FROM DFGP DFGP2 WHERE
```

---

*"Likely follow-on" was correct when this paper was first written. SQL/92 is now (1994) the current standard.

```
          FDH2.HOUR = FDH1.HOUR AND
          DFGP1.FLIGHT = FDH1.FLIGHT AND
          DFGP2.FLIGHT = FDH2.FLIGHT AND
          DFGP2.DAY = DFGP1.DAY AND
          DFGP2.PILOT = DFGP1.PILOT AND
        ( FDH1.FLIGHT <> FDH2.FLIGHT AND
          DFGP1.GATE <> DFGP2.GATE ) ) ) ) ) ) )
```

The relational calculus formulations seem preferable! (Actually, this part of SQL/92 is patterned fairly closely on the relational calculus. The trouble is, however, that certain useful features of the calculus are missing, including in particular the universal quantifier FORALL and the logical implication operator IF . . . THEN . . . It is these omissions that make the SQL/92 declarations so verbose—not to mention hard to understand.)

Now, I have already mentioned the fact that the calculus versions of the constraints do not look much like functional dependencies, even though they do in fact correspond to FDs Nos. 3 and 4 in the simplified set. But what if we had the ability to declare candidate keys (primary keys and alternate keys) for *views,* or, more generally, for relational *expressions* of any kind? Consider the following example. First let me repeat the database design:

```
FDH ( FLIGHT, DESTINATION, HOUR )
    PRIMARY KEY ( FLIGHT )

DFGP ( DAY, FLIGHT, GATE, PILOT )
    PRIMARY KEY ( DAY, FLIGHT )
```

Now let V be a view, defined as the foreign-to-primary-key natural join of these two relations (i.e., the join over FLIGHT):

```
CREATE VIEW V AS ( FDH JOIN DFGP )
```

(using a hybrid of SQL and the syntax of reference [5]). If we could additionally declare candidate keys for this view, thus—

```
CREATE VIEW V AS ( FDH JOIN DFGP )
       CANDIDATE KEY ( DAY, HOUR, GATE )
       CANDIDATE KEY ( DAY, HOUR, PILOT )
```

—then these two declarations would serve very nicely to define integrity constraints (FDs) Nos. 3 and 4 in the simplified set! Thus, the discussions of this paper provide another argument in support of a position I have previously argued in reference [6], to the effect that it should be possible to declare candidate keys for views as well as for base relations. Note that the candidate keys in question—i.e., in the example under discussion—certainly cannot be inferred from the FDs that hold only within (not across) the underlying base relations.

Note: One reviewer (Hugh Darwen) pointed out that SQL/92 almost does provide the ability to declare candidate keys for arbitrary relational expressions, thanks to its new UNIQUE condition. Loosely speaking, the conditional expression UNIQUE(*T*), where *T* is an arbitrary SQL/92 table expression, returns *true* if and only if *T* evaluates to a genuine relation (i.e., the result of evaluating *T* does not contain any duplicate rows). Hence:

```
CREATE ASSERTION DHGFP
CHECK ( UNIQUE ( SELECT DAY, HOUR, GATE
                 FROM   FDH NATURAL JOIN DFGP ) )

CREATE ASSERTION DHPFG
CHECK ( UNIQUE ( SELECT DAY, HOUR, PILOT
                 FROM   FDH NATURAL JOIN DFGP ) )
```

There is one final issue I would like to raise regarding constraint declarations (more specifically, *candidate key* declarations, which are of course an important special case of constraint declarations in general). As we saw, every one of the solutions of reference [1] involved some undeclared candidate keys; in the first solution, for example, relation WEEKLY_ROSTER had an explicitly declared primary key {DAY,HOUR,GATE} and two undeclared alternate keys {DAY,HOUR,PILOT} and {DAY,FLIGHT}. Now, it *might* be argued that {DAY,FLIGHT} is the "natural" choice for the primary key here—despite the fact that it was not so chosen by reference [1]—because it involves the fewest attributes. But there seems to be no good reason for choosing either of the other two over its rival, and indeed any such choice introduces an unpleasant degree of arbitrariness and asymmetry into the situation. I intend to examine this issue in more detail in a future paper [7]; here I would just like to say that I no longer feel as confident as I once did regarding the primacy of primary keys.

ACKNOWLEDGMENTS

I would like to thank Joe Celko for posing the original problem, and my reviewers Hugh Darwen, David McGoveran, and (especially) Paul Winsberg for their helpful comments on an earlier draft.

REFERENCES AND BIBLIOGRAPHY

1. Joe Celko, "Back to the Future," *Database Programming & Design 4,* No. 12 (December 1991).

2. C. J. Date, "A Practical Approach to Database Design," in *Relational Database: Selected Writings* (Reading, Mass.: Addison-Wesley, 1986).

3. C. J. Date, "Integrity," in *An Introduction to Database Systems,* 6th edition (Reading, Mass.: Addison-Wesley, 1995).

4. C. J. Date, "Further Normalization I: 1NF, 2NF, 3NF, BCNF," in *An Introduction to Database Systems,* 6th edition (Reading, Mass.: Addison-Wesley, 1995).

5. C. J. Date, "Relational Algebra," in *An Introduction to Database Systems,* 6th edition (Reading, Mass.: Addison-Wesley, 1995).

6. C. J. Date, "Notes Toward a Reconstituted Definition of the Relational Model Version 1 (RM/V1)," in C. J. Date and Hugh Darwen, *Relational Database Writings 1989–1991* (Reading, Mass.: Addison-Wesley, 1992).

7. C. J. Date, "The Primacy of Primary Keys: An Investigation" (in this volume).

8. Ronald Fagin, Alberto O. Mendelzon, and Jeffrey D. Ullman, "A Simplified Universal Relation Assumption and Its Properties," *ACM TODS 7,* No. 3 (September 1982).

9. International Organization for Standardization (ISO), *Database Language SQL,* Document ISO/IEC 9075:1989. Also published as American National Standards Institute (ANSI) Document ANSI X3.135-1989.

10. International Organization for Standardization (ISO), *Database Language SQL,* Document ISO/IEC 9075:1992. Also published as American National Standards Institute (ANSI) Document ANSI X3.135-1992.

A New Database Design Principle

ABSTRACT

A new database design principle is proposed, having to do with **isomorphic tables**—that is, tables that "are the same shape," meaning (loosely) that they are defined on the same domains.

COMMENTS ON REPUBLICATION

The work described in this chapter and the next two was done jointly by David McGoveran and myself during 1993. David was the primary author on the present chapter and I was the primary author on the other two (and I am grateful to David for agreeing to let me republish all three in the present volume).

It was the view update question discussed in Chapters 5 and 6 that was the overall spur to our work. I had been developing the outlines of a new approach to view updating, one that enjoyed several nice properties and overall looked quite

Originally published in *Database Programming & Design 7,* No. 7 (July 1994). Reprinted by permission of David McGoveran, Alternative Technologies, Boulder Creek, California, and Miller Freeman Inc.

promising, but I kept running into the problem that the approach I was proposing could occasionally lead to strange results. Then David pointed out that those strange results occurred only if the database design was "strange" too in a certain sense, and proposed a new design principle that said, in effect "Don't design databases in this strange way." And that observation led directly to the production of the original versions of these three chapters.

Note: Despite the foregoing, I must make it clear that avoiding view update anomalies is far from being the sole benefit that accrues from the new design principle. Indeed, I would claim that, like the principles of further normalization, the new principle injects a little rigor into a field (database design) that—as I have written elsewhere—is still very much of an art, not a science [2].

1. INTRODUCTION

The purpose of this paper is to present and describe a new—and, we believe, very fundamental—database design principle. Like the well-known principles of normalization, our principle can be seen in part as a systematic means of avoiding redundancy, and thereby avoiding certain update anomalies that might otherwise occur. Although the principle is very simple, we have not previously seen it articulated in published form; in fact, the experience of one of us (McGoveran) suggests that the principle is quite often violated in practice. We briefly explore some of the consequences of such violations.

2. THE LOVES-HATES EXAMPLE

We begin with a simple example. Consider the following database:

```
CREATE DOMAIN PERSONS ... ;

CREATE BASE TABLE LOVES
     ( X DOMAIN ( PERSONS ),
       Y DOMAIN ( PERSONS ) ... ) ;

CREATE BASE TABLE HATES
     ( X DOMAIN ( PERSONS ),
       Y DOMAIN ( PERSONS ) ... ) ;
```

The intended semantics are, of course, that the row $<x,y>$ appears in LOVES only if "x loves y" is true, and the row $<x,y>$ appears in HATES only if "x hates y" is true. *Note:* Throughout this paper we use a modified form of conventional SQL syntax, for reasons of simplicity and explicitness.

Now suppose the row <Romeo,Juliet> is to be inserted into this database. The user responsible for the INSERT will presumably insert the row into base table LOVES. **Note carefully, however, that he or she could just as easily have inserted the row into base table HATES instead**. It is only because the user had some additional information—namely, the knowledge that "Romeo loves Juliet" is true—that he or she decided to insert the row into LOVES and not into HATES. Since that additional information is not known to the DBMS, the "decision procedure" for deciding whether a given row should be inserted into LOVES or HATES is likewise not known to the DBMS. In other words, part of the meaning of the database is **concealed from the system**.

Note, moreover, that it is not just the DBMS that is affected by this concealment. **Exactly the same information is being concealed from other users as well**. That is, given the same row <Romeo,Juliet>, another user will be just as unable to decide which of LOVES and HATES the row is to go into if he or she does not have the necessary extra information (*viz.*, that "Romeo loves Juliet" is true). To put the point another way: Suppose we are told that for a certain pair of persons x and y either "x loves y" is true or "x hates y" is true, but we are not told which. In general, then, we will only be able to tell which of the two possibilities is in fact the case by looking to see which of the two base tables the row <x,y> appears in.

Note further that even when we have found which table the row <x,y> appears in, we still don't really know which of the two possibilities is the case—we know only that the row appears in LOVES or HATES, as the case may be. And lest the reader object that we surely *do* now know which possibility is the case, since the necessary information is represented by the **names** of the two base tables involved (LOVES and HATES), let us now rename those tables ABC and XYZ, respectively. Now can you tell which of "x loves y" and "x hates y" is true? The answer, of course, is that you can tell only if you know that ABC "means" *loves* and XYZ "means" *hates*. In fact, of course, there is nothing to stop us renaming LOVES as HATES and HATES as LOVES . . . *Now* can you tell?

Before attempting to draw any conclusions from the foregoing, let us move on to examine another example.

3. THE EMPLOYEES EXAMPLE

Suppose we have a database concerning employees, in which every employee has a (unique) employee number EMP#, a name ENAME, a department number DEPT#, and a salary SAL. Further, suppose that we decide (for some reason—the precise reason is not important for the moment) to represent employees by *two* base tables, EMPA and EMPB, where:

- EMPA contains rows for employees in department D1;

- EMPB contains rows for employees who are either not in department D1 or have a salary in excess of 33K.

See Fig. 1 for some sample values.

EMPA				EMPB			
EMP#	ENAME	DEPT#	SAL	EMP#	ENAME	DEPT#	SAL
E1	Lopez	D1	25K	E2	Cheng	D1	42K
E2	Cheng	D1	42K	E3	Finzi	D2	30K
				E4	Saito	D2	45K

Fig. 1 Base tables EMPA and EMPB (first version): sample values

The reader will surely agree that this is a bad design. But why exactly is it bad? Some insight into this question can be gained by considering the following scenario. Suppose first of all that we start off with an empty database (i.e., base tables EMPA and EMPB both contain no rows at all). Suppose next that we are asked to insert information regarding employee E2 (name Cheng, department D1, salary 42K) into this database. We construct the row

```
< E2, Cheng, D1, 42K >
```

But which base table do we put it in? The answer, obviously, has to be **both** (as suggested by Fig. 1). It has to be both, because the new row satisfies both (a) the criterion for membership in EMPA (the department number is D1), and (b) the criterion for membership in EMPB (the salary is greater than 33K). After all, if the row were to be inserted into just one of the two base tables, the question is which one? There are no grounds, except arbitrary ones, for choosing either table over the other.

(In fact, if we put the row into just one of the tables—say EMPA and not EMPB—we could be accused of a **contradiction**. For the appearance of the row in EMPA would mean that Cheng works in department D1 and earns 42K, while the simultaneous nonappearance of the row in EMPB would mean that Cheng either does not work in department D1 or does not earn more than 33K.)

Thus we see that one reason the design is bad is that it leads to **redundancy:** The very same information is represented twice, in two distinct base tables.

Of course, it is fairly easy to see what causes the redundancy in this particular example. To be specific, there is a certain **lack of independence** between the two base tables EMPA and EMPB, inasmuch as "their meanings overlap" (it is possible for the same row to satisfy the membership criterion for both). Lack of independence between objects is generally to be avoided if possible, because it implies that changes to one will require changes to the other as well. For instance, a DELETE on one table might require a DELETE on another (as is indeed the case in our EMPA-EMPB example, if we wish to delete the information for employee E2).

Thus it looks as if a good design principle might be "Don't have tables whose meanings overlap"—and indeed, so it is. Before we can make this principle more precise, however, we need to examine the question of the meaning of a table in greater depth. Note in particular that the principle as just—very loosely!—articulated is not sufficient in itself to explain what is wrong with the LOVES-HATES example discussed earlier.

4. INTEGRITY CONSTRAINTS

In order to discuss what tables mean, we must first digress for a few moments to consider the general issue of **integrity constraints**. We classify such constraints into four kinds, namely domain constraints, column constraints, table constraints, and database constraints,* as follows:

- A **domain** constraint is just the definition of the set of values that go to make up the domain in question; in other words, it effectively just enumerates the values in the domain. *Note:* We mention domain constraints merely for completeness—they play no part in the database design principle that is the primary focus of this paper.

- A **column** constraint states that the values appearing in a specific column must be drawn from some specific domain. For example, consider base table EMPB from the previous section. The columns of that table are subject to the following column constraints:

```
e.EMP#   IN EMP#_DOM
e.ENAME  IN NAME_DOM
e.DEPT#  IN DEPT#_DOM
e.SAL    IN US_CURRENCY_DOM
```

  Here *e* represents an arbitrary row of the table and EMP#_DOM, NAME_ DOM, etc., are the names of the relevant domains.

- A **table** constraint states that a specific table must satisfy some specific condition, where the condition in question refers **solely** to the table under consideration—i.e., it does not refer to any other table, nor to any domain. For example, here are two table constraints for the base table EMPB:

```
1. e.DEPT# ≠ 'D1' OR e.SAL > 33K
2. IF e.EMP# = f.EMP# THEN e.ENAME = f.ENAME
                      AND   e.DEPT# = f.DEPT#
                      AND   e.SAL   = f.SAL
```

The first of these is self-explanatory. The second says that if two rows *e* and *f* have the same EMP# value, then they also have the same ENAME value, the

---

*This classification is slightly different (but not dramatically so) from that previously given by one of the present authors (Date) in references [3] and [4].

same DEPT# value, and the same SAL value—in other words, they are the same row. (Of course, this is just a longwinded way of saying that EMP# is a candidate key. Naturally we assume that all tables do have at least one candidate key!— i.e., duplicate rows are not permitted.)

Note: Observe that we talk of table constraints in general, not just base table constraints. The point is, **all** tables, base or otherwise, are subject to table constraints, as the authors have discussed in detail elsewhere [5]. For present purposes, however, it is indeed base table constraints in particular that are of primary interest; for the remainder of this paper, therefore, we will take the unqualified term "table constraint" to mean a base table constraint specifically, barring explicit statements to the contrary.

■ A **database** constraint states that the overall database must satisfy some specific condition, where the condition in question can refer to as many tables as desired. For example, suppose the database of Fig. 1 were extended to include a departments table DEPT. Then the referential constraints from EMPA and EMPB to that table DEPT would both be database constraints (they would both in fact refer to exactly two tables).

5. THE QUESTION OF MEANING

Now we can get back to our discussion of what tables (and indeed databases) **mean**. The first point is that every table—be it a base table, a view, a query result, or whatever—certainly does have an associated meaning. And, of course, users must be aware of those meanings if they are to use the database correctly and effectively. For example, the meaning of base table EMPB is something like the following:

> *"The employee with the specified employee number (EMP#) has the specified name (ENAME), works in the specified department (DEPT#), and earns the specified salary (SAL). Furthermore, either the department number is not D1 or the salary is greater than 33K (or both). Also, no two employees have the same employee number."*

Formally, the foregoing "meaning" is an example of what is called a **predicate**, or truth-valued function—a function of four arguments, in this particular case. Substituting values for the arguments is equivalent to **invoking** the function (or "instantiating" the predicate), thereby yielding an expression that evaluates to either *true* or *false*. For example, the substitution

```
EMP# = 'E3'   ENAME = 'Finzi'   DEPT# = 'D2'   SAL = 30K
```

yields the value *true*. By contrast, the substitution

```
EMP# = 'E3'   ENAME = 'Clark'   DEPT# = 'D2'   SAL = 25K
```

yields the value *false*. And at any given time, of course, the table contains exactly those rows that make the predicate evaluate to *true* at that time.

It follows from the foregoing that if (for example) a row is presented as a candidate for insertion into some table, the DBMS should accept that row only if it does not cause the corresponding predicate to be violated. More generally, the predicate for a given table represents the **criterion for update acceptability** for that table—that is, it constitutes the criterion for deciding whether or not some proposed update is in fact valid (or at least plausible) for the given table. In other words, such a predicate corresponds to what we earlier referred to as the *membership criterion* for the table in question.

In order for it to be able to decide whether or not a proposed update is acceptable for a given table, therefore, the DBMS needs to be aware of the predicate for that table. Now, it is of course not possible for the DBMS to know **exactly** what the predicate is for a given table. In the case of base table EMPB, for example, the DBMS has no way of knowing *a priori* that the predicate is such that the row <E3,Finzi,D2,30K> makes it *true* and the row <E3,Clark,D2,25K> does not; it also has no way of knowing exactly what certain terms appearing in that predicate (such as "works in" or "earns") mean. However, the DBMS certainly **does** know a reasonably close approximation to that predicate. To be specific, it knows that, if a given row is to be deemed acceptable, all of the following must be true:

- The EMP# value must be a value from the domain of employee numbers
- The ENAME value must be a value from the domain of names
- The DEPT# value must be a value from the domain of department numbers
- The SAL value must be a value from the domain of US currency
- Either the DEPT# value is not D1 or the SAL value is greater than 33K (or both)
- The EMP# value is unique with respect to all such values in the table

In other words, for a base table such as EMPB, the DBMS does at least know all the integrity constraints (column constraints and table constraints) that have been declared for that base table. Formally, therefore, we can **define** the (DBMS-understood) "meaning" of a given base table to be the logical AND of all column constraints and table constraints that apply to that base table (and it is this meaning that the DBMS will check whenever an update is attempted on the base table in question). For example, the formal meaning of base table EMPB is:

```
        e.EMP#  IN EMP#_DOM AND
        e.ENAME IN NAME_DOM AND
        e.DEPT# IN DEPT#_DOM AND
        e.SAL   IN US_CURRENCY_DOM AND
( e.DEPT# ≠ 'D1' OR e.SAL > 33K ) AND
( IF e.EMP# = f.EMP# THEN e.ENAME = f.ENAME AND
                          e.DEPT# = f.DEPT# AND
                          e.SAL   = f.SAL )
```

We will refer to this expression—let us call it PE—as **the table predicate** for base table EMPB.

Incidentally, note how the foregoing remarks serve to point up once again the fundamental importance of the relational **domain** concept. Relational vendors should be doing all within their power to incorporate proper domain support into their DBMS products. It is perhaps worth pointing out too that "proper domain support" here does **not** mean support for the very strange construct called "domains" in the SQL/92 standard.

To return to the main thread of our discussion: As indicated above, in order for the DBMS to be able to decide whether or not a given update is acceptable on a given table, the DBMS needs to be aware of the table predicate that applies to the table in question. Now, the DBMS certainly is aware of the relevant predicate in the case of a base table, as we have just seen. But what about **derived** tables—e.g., what about views? What is the table predicate for a derived table? Clearly, what we need is a set of rules such that if the DBMS knows the table predicate(s) for the input(s) to any relational operation, it can deduce the table predicate for the output from that operation. Given such a set of rules, the DBMS will then know the table predicate for all possible tables.

It is in fact very easy to state such a set of rules—they follow immediately from the definitions of the relational operators. For example, if A and B are any two type-compatible tables* and their respective table predicates are PA and PB, then the table predicate PC for table C, where C is defined as A INTERSECT B, is obviously (PA) AND (PB); that is, a row r will appear in C if and only if it appears in both A and B—i.e., if and only if $PA(r)$ and $PB(r)$ are both true. So if, for example, we define C as a view and try to insert r into that view, r must satisfy both the table predicate for A and the table predicate for B, or the INSERT will fail (see reference [5]).

Here is another example: The table predicate for the table that results from the **restriction** operation

```
T WHERE condition
```

is (PT) AND *(condition)*, where PT is the table predicate for T. For example, the table predicate for EMPB WHERE SAL < 40K is

```
( PE ) AND ( SAL < 40K )
```

where PE is the table predicate for EMPB as defined earlier.

Stating the table predicates corresponding to the other relational operators is left as an exercise for the reader.

---

*Type-compatibility is usually referred to as **union**-compatibility in the literature. We prefer our term for reasons that are beyond the scope of the present discussion.

We conclude this section by remarking that—although it is somewhat irrelevant to the main theme of this paper—the overall database has a formal meaning too, just as the individual base tables do. The meaning of the database—the **database predicate** for that database—is essentially the logical AND of all individual table predicates for the (named) tables in that database, together with all database constraints that apply to that database.

6. TABLES WITH OVERLAPPING MEANINGS

Now we can pin down what we mean when we say that the meanings of two tables overlap. Let *A* and *B* be any two tables, with associated table predicates *PA* and *PB*, respectively. Then the meanings of *A* and *B* are said to **overlap** if and only if some row *r* can be constructed such that *PA(r)* and *PB(r)* are both true.

Given this definition, our new design principle—

```
Within a given database, no two distinct base tables should
have overlapping meanings.
```

—is now precise.

However, two very important corollaries of the principle are perhaps not immediately obvious, and are in any case worth stating explicitly. The first has to do with **isomorphic tables**. For the purposes of this paper, we define two tables

```
A { A1, ..., An }
B { B1, ..., Bn }
```

to be **isomorphic** if and only if there exists a one-to-one correspondence between the columns of *A* and the columns of *B*, say *A1:B1, . . . , An:Bn*, such that in each pair of columns *Ai:Bi* ($i = 1, . . . , n$) the two columns are defined on the same domain. *Note:* Two tables that are type-compatible are certainly isomorphic, but tables can be isomorphic without necessarily being type-compatible. This is because type-compatibility as we define it requires the two tables to have identical column names [2].

Here then is the first corollary:

- *Two tables cannot possibly have overlapping meanings if they are not isomorphic.*

It follows that—as stated in the Abstract—our design principle applies specifically to isomorphic tables. However, we caution the reader that the tables in question are not necessarily base tables! Refer to the section "An Important Clarification" later in this paper.

The second corollary is as follows:

■   *When a given row* r *is presented for insertion into the database, the DBMS should be able to decide for itself which table (if any) that row* r *belongs to.*

In other words, the process of inserting a row can be regarded as a process of inserting that row **into the database** (rather than into some specific table), provided the design principle is adhered to.

   Note: On being informed of this point, the reader might very well respond "So what?"—relational languages always require the user to specify the target table on an INSERT, so what is the advantage of having the system be able to figure out for itself what the target table is? One answer to this question is that the specified target table might be a **view**. Consider an INSERT into a view *V* defined as the union of two tables *A* and *B*. As the present authors have discussed in detail elsewhere [5], it is very desirable that the system be able to decide for itself which of *A* and *B* the new row belongs to.

7. THE EXAMPLES REVISITED

Now let us revisit the examples discussed earlier in the paper. First of all, the EMPA-EMPB design is clearly bad, since the meanings of the two tables clearly overlap. But suppose we were to redefine those tables as follows:

■   EMPA contains rows for employees in department D1;

■   EMPB contains rows for employees not in department D1.

See Fig. 2 for some sample values.

   The meanings of the tables now do not overlap. However, **the design is still bad if the DBMS is not aware of that fact**. That is, if the table predicates for the two tables **as stated to the DBMS** do not include the terms

```
... AND e.DEPT# = 'D1' ...    /* for EMPA */
... AND e.DEPT# ≠ 'D1' ...    /* for EMPB */
```

then the meanings still do overlap so far as the DBMS is concerned. In other words, the word "meaning" in our design principle refers specifically to the

EMPA				EMPB			
EMP#	ENAME	DEPT#	SAL	EMP#	ENAME	DEPT#	SAL
E1	Lopez	D1	25K	E3	Finzi	D2	30K
E2	Cheng	D1	42K	E4	Saito	D2	45K

Fig. 2   Base tables EMPA and EMPB (second version): sample values

"meaning" as understood by the DBMS (of course), **not** necessarily to the meaning as understood by the user.

What about the LOVES-HATES example? Well, here are the table predicates for the design as originally given:

```
r.X IN PERSONS AND r.Y IN PERSONS    /* for LOVES */
r.X IN PERSONS AND r.Y IN PERSONS    /* for HATES */
```

(where r is an $<x,y>$ row). These two predicates are identical, of course, and therefore most certainly do overlap!* In fact, the example is not really different in kind from the EMPA-EMPB example (second version) just discussed.

Here by contrast is a revised design that does not violate our design principle:

```
CREATE DOMAIN PERSONS ... ;
CREATE DOMAIN L_OR_H VALUES { 'loves', 'hates' } ;

CREATE BASE TABLE LOVES
    ( X DOMAIN ( PERSONS ),
      R DOMAIN ( L_OR_H ),
      Y DOMAIN ( PERSONS ) ... ) ;

CREATE BASE TABLE HATES
    ( X DOMAIN ( PERSONS ),
      R DOMAIN ( L_OR_H ),
      Y DOMAIN ( PERSONS ) ... ) ;
```

The table predicates are now as follows (and should be so defined to the DBMS):

```
r.X IN PERSONS AND r.Y IN PERSONS
            AND r.R = 'loves'    /* for LOVES */

r.X IN PERSONS AND r.Y IN PERSONS
            AND r.R = 'hates'    /* for HATES */
```

To insert the information that Romeo loves Juliet, it is now necessary to insert the row <Romeo,loves,Juliet>. Note, incidentally, that there is nothing to stop us inserting the row <Romeo,hates,Juliet> as well! In fact, the two three-column base tables LOVES and HATES might as well now be replaced by a single base table that is the union of the two. (*Exercise for the reader:* What would the corresponding table predicate be?) An analogous remark applies to the EMPA-EMPB example (second version) above.

8. AN IMPORTANT CLARIFICATION

The message of this paper thus far might be summed up as follows: Whenever your database design includes two distinct base tables that are isomorphic, be sure that the DBMS-understood meanings of those two tables do not overlap. This rule

---

*The same would still be true if we renamed the X and Y columns (say) L1 and L2 in LOVES and H1 and H2 in HATES (the tables would still be isomorphic). Consider, for example, what would happen on an attempt to insert a row into the union of the two tables.

(or discipline) is easy to state and easy to apply, and it would be nice if matters stopped right there. Unfortunately, however, there is one important ramification that we have so far overlooked. Consider the tables EMPX and EMPY shown in Fig. 3.

EMPX	EMP#	ENAME	DEPT#		EMPY	EMP#	ENAME	SALARY
	E1	Lopez	D1			E1	Lopez	25K
	E2	Cheng	D1			E2	Cheng	42K
	E3	Finzi	D2			E3	Finzi	30K
	E4	Saito	D2			E4	Saito	45K

Fig. 3   Base tables EMPX and EMPY: sample values

It should be clear that the design of that figure is once again a bad one, because of the redundancy it implies. Here, however, the overlap in meaning occurs, not between the two tables EMPX and EMPY, but rather between the two **projections** of those tables over EMP# and ENAME. Clearly, therefore, we need to extend our design principle to deal with such a situation, as follows:

> Let A and B be any two base tables in the database. Then there must not exist nonloss decompositions of A and B into A1, A2, ..., Am and B1, B2, ..., Bn *(respectively)* such that two distinct projections in the set A1, A2, ..., Am, B1, B2, ..., Bn *have overlapping meanings.*

By the term "nonloss decomposition" (of some given table), we mean, of course, a decomposition of that table—according to the well-known principles of normalization—into a set of projections such that (a) the given table can be reconstructed by joining those projections back together again, and (b) none of those projections is redundant in that reconstruction process.

Note: This refined version of our design principle in fact subsumes the original version, because one "nonloss decomposition" of any given table *T* is the set of projections consisting of just the "identity projection" *T* itself. In other words, if we agree to refer to tables that have projections whose meanings overlap as having meanings that *partially* overlap, then *total* overlap is just a special case (i.e., two tables that have totally overlapping meanings certainly have partially overlapping meanings, *a fortiori*).

9. CONCLUDING REMARKS

There are several remarks to be made by way of conclusion.

- First, readers might be tempted to think that our new design principle is very obvious and really just common sense. And in a way they would be right. But the principles of normalization (third normal form, etc.) are likewise "obvious and just common sense." The point is, however, that the principles of normalization take those common sense ideas and **provide a precise, accurate characterization of those intuitive concepts**. In a similar manner, our new design principle provides a precise, accurate characterization of certain additional intuitive concepts.

- At least one of the present authors (McGoveran) has not only encountered genuine database designs in which the principle has been flouted (despite the fact that it is "really just common sense"), he has also encountered database practitioners and database "experts" who have expressly recommended flouting that principle. Indeed, we have probably all seen designs such as the following—

```
ACTIVITIES_88 { ENTRY#, DESCRIPTION, AMOUNT, NEW_BALANCE }
ACTIVITIES_89 { ENTRY#, DESCRIPTION, AMOUNT, NEW_BALANCE }
ACTIVITIES_90 { ENTRY#, DESCRIPTION, AMOUNT, NEW_BALANCE }
ACTIVITIES_91 { ENTRY#, DESCRIPTION, AMOUNT, NEW_BALANCE }
ACTIVITIES_92 { ENTRY#, DESCRIPTION, AMOUNT, NEW_BALANCE }
ACTIVITIES_93 { ENTRY#, DESCRIPTION, AMOUNT, NEW_BALANCE }
```

  (etc., etc.)—in which activities for different years are kept in different tables.

- In a design such as the one just illustrated, part of the (informal, user-understood-but-not-DBMS-understood) meaning of the database is **encoded in the table names**. Such a design can thus be seen as violating Codd's "Information Principle" [1], which can be stated as follows:

  All information in the database must be cast explicitly in terms of values in tables and in no other way.

  Our design principle—at least, that part of it that recommends against the use of names to carry meaning—can thus be seen as a corollary (though not a very obvious one) of Codd's Information Principle.*

- Note that adherence to our design principle has the consequence that if A and B are any two type-compatible base tables, then it will be true for all time that:

```
A UNION B      is a disjoint union
A INTERSECT B  is empty
A MINUS B      is equal to A
```

- Adherence to our principle also has the very desirable consequence that the

---

*Some readers might be aware of the fact that in his further discussion of the Information Principle, Codd goes on to point out that names too are "cast in terms of values": "Even . . . names are represented as character strings in [certain tables that] are normally part of the builtin database catalog" (reference [1], page 31). This fact is something of a red herring, however; in no way does it invalidate our new design principle.

rules given in reference [5] for updating union, intersection, and difference views work very well and never produce what we referred to in that paper as "surprising results."

■   One final **and very important** remark: The new design principle is equally applicable to the design of what might be called "individual user databases"—that is, an individual user's perception (as defined by views and/or base tables) of some underlying shared database. In other words, such an "individual user database" ought not to include any views and/or base tables whose meanings overlap (even partially), for essentially all of the same reasons that the shared database ought not to include any base tables whose meanings overlap (even partially).

ACKNOWLEDGMENTS

The authors would like to thank Hugh Darwen, Fabian Pascal, and Paul Winsberg for their helpful comments on earlier drafts of this paper.

REFERENCES AND BIBLIOGRAPHY

1. E. F. Codd, *The Relational Model for Database Management Version 2* (Reading, Mass.: Addison-Wesley, 1990).

2. C. J. Date, *An Introduction to Database Systems* (6th edition) (Reading, Mass.: Addison-Wesley, 1995).

3. C. J. Date, "A Matter of Integrity" (in three parts) (in this volume).

4. C. J. Date, "A Contribution to the Study of Database Integrity," in *Relational Database Writings 1985–1989* (Reading, Mass.: Addison-Wesley, 1990).

5. C. J. Date and David McGoveran, "Updating Union, Intersection, and Difference Views" (in this volume).

APPENDIX A:
A REMARK ON DEFAULTS

Section 8 of this paper discussed "an important clarification" to the first version of our design principle, having to do with *projections* of the given base tables. Unfortunately, another important clarification is also required, having to do with **column defaults.** This second clarification was included in the original draft of the paper but was omitted from the version published in *Database Programming & Design.* We therefore discuss it in this appendix.

First of all, relational systems typically permit the user to insert partial rows into the database; if the user does not provide a value for some particular column, then the system completes the row by placing a default value* in that column position. For example, suppose we are given a variation on the usual suppliers-and-parts database, in which base tables S (suppliers) and P (parts) look like this:

```
S  { ID#, STATUS, CITY }
P  { ID#, COLOR, WEIGHT, CITY }
```

Then the INSERT operation—

```
INSERT ( ID# = 'S6', CITY = 'Tucson' )
INTO   S ;
```

—might cause the system to complete the row by placing the value 0 in the STATUS position (if 0 is defined as the default for column S.STATUS) before inserting the new row into the suppliers table S.

Now consider the partial row <X5,Tucson>, where "X5" is an ID number and "Tucson" is a CITY value. Unless we have appropriate additional information, we cannot immediately tell whether this is a partial suppliers (S) row or a partial parts (P) row. It follows that if, e.g., we define a view as follows—

```
CREATE VIEW V AS ( SELECT ID#, CITY FROM S )
                  UNION
                  ( SELECT ID#, CITY FROM P ) ;
```

—and we try to insert the row <X5,Tucson> into this view, then all the system can do is attempt to insert an appropriately completed row into both table S and table P. And if columns S.STATUS, P.COLOR, and P.WEIGHT all do possess a corre-

---

*Possibly NULL in SQL. We do not wish to get sidetracked into a discussion of the problems of nulls here; for present purposes, it is irrelevant whether the default is null or something else.

sponding default value (i.e., none of them has "defaults not allowed"), the effect will indeed be to insert "an appropriately completed row" into both tables [5].

It follows from the foregoing that our design principle requires some slight refinement, as follows:

> Let A' and B' be any two base tables in the database, and let A and B be the projections of A and B (respectively) over all columns that do not have a default value (i.e., all columns that have "defaults not allowed"). Then there must not exist nonloss decompositions of A and B into A1, A2, ..., Am and B1, B2, ..., Bn (respectively) such that two distinct projections in the set A1, A2, ..., Am, B1, B2, ..., Bn have overlapping meanings.

This refined version of the design principle subsumes both previous versions.

Updating Union, Intersection, and Difference Views

ABSTRACT

A new and systematic approach to the problem of updating relational views is described. The approach is then applied to views whose definition involves union, intersection, and difference operators.

COMMENTS ON REPUBLICATION

I am not alone in thinking that the treatment of view updating within the overall theory of relational databases has always been rather unsatisfactory for one reason or another. As Nat Goodman puts it in reference [14]: ". . . there is no theory behind any of this. Each [rule] seems intuitively correct, but there is no overall framework. It would be better to have a general rule that states what a correct view

Originally published in *Database Programming & Design 7*, No. 6 (June 1994). Reprinted by permission of David McGoveran, Alternative Technologies, Boulder Creek, California, and Miller Freeman Inc.

update algorithm has to do, and then derive the special rules for each case from that general rule. Without this, the [rules] feel like a crazy patchwork of exceptions and special notes. In some cases, two or more [rules] are equally sensible . . ." (and so on).

In the paper that follows, we (i.e., David McGoveran and myself) present such a general rule. We then derive the special rules for unions, intersections, and differences from that general rule. (We derive the special rules for the other relational operators in the next chapter.)

It is perhaps of interest to say that these proposals grew out of my attempts to come up with a view updating scheme that would treat the semantically equivalent views *V1* = *A* INTERSECT *B* and *V2* = *A* MINUS (*A* MINUS *B*) equivalently—in particular, taking into account the fact that the definition of *V1* is symmetric in *A* and *B* while the definition of *V2* is not. The key observation (obvious, after the fact!) turned out to be that **at all times, every table *T* must satisfy the table predicate that applies to *T***. It follows (to spell it out in detail) that when an update is performed on any table *T:*

- *Before* the update, table *T* cannot include any row(s) that cause the table predicate for *T* to be violated.

- *After* the update, table *T* cannot include any row(s) that cause the table predicate for *T* to be violated.

Thus, for example, if a row *r* is presented for insertion into *V* = *A* MINUS *B,* then row *r:*

- Must satisfy the predicate for *A* (for otherwise it cannot appear in *A* and hence cannot appear in *A* MINUS *B a fortiori*);

- Must not satisfy the predicate for *B* (for otherwise it might already appear in *B,* in which case inserting it into *A* will cause it *not* to appear in *A* MINUS *B*);

- Must not already appear in *A* (for otherwise we will be attempting to insert a duplicate row);

- *Cannot* already appear in *B* (because it does not satisfy the predicate for *B*).

Note: The foregoing statements are slightly simplified; as the body of the paper explains, it's not really *rows* that have to satisfy predicates, it's *tables.* Also, regarding the second of the bullet items above, the alert reader might suggest that if *r* does already appear in *B,* the desired effect (of inserting *r* into *A* MINUS *B*) might be achieved by *deleting* it from *B* before (if necessary) inserting it into *A.* We reject this possibility for reasons explained in the body of the paper (see in the section "Further Principles," especially Principle No. 7).

Portions of this material previously appeared in somewhat different form in reference [5]. Also—to repeat from the "Comments on Republication" in

Chapter 4—I am grateful to David McGoveran for allowing me to republish the material in the present book.

1. INTRODUCTION

Historically, the question of view updatability has typically been treated in a fairly *ad hoc* manner. Certainly this is the case:

- In the SQL standard (see references [1], [9], and especially [4]), and
- In today's commercial SQL products (see, e.g., references [11] and [16]), and
- Even—to some extent—in the more research-oriented technical literature (see, e.g., references [2–3], [14], and [18]).

It is not at all unusual, for example, to find that a given DBMS will

- Prohibit updates on a view that is logically updatable, or
- Permit updates on a view that is logically not updatable, or
- Implement view updates in a logically incorrect way,

or—most likely in practice!—do all of the above, depending on circumstances.

The lack of a systematic approach to the problem is further underscored by the undue emphasis that has historically been laid on restriction, projection, and join views (see, e.g., references [8], [12–13], and [15]). Union, intersection, and difference views, which are—or should be—at least as important in practice, have received comparatively little attention.

The authors of this paper have recently developed a systematic and formal approach to the view updating problem. In this paper, we present an informal introduction (emphasis on "informal"!) to that formal approach. We also illustrate the approach as it applies to union, intersection, and difference views specifically. A forthcoming paper [10] will deal with joins and other kinds of views.

2. INTEGRITY CONSTRAINTS

Note: The material of this section and the next is mostly repeated from reference [17]. We retain the two sections in this republished version, however, in order to keep the chapter reasonably self-contained.

Before we can get into the specifics of our approach, we need to lay some groundwork. The first point—and this one is ABSOLUTELY CRUCIAL—is that **every table has an INTERPRETATION or MEANING**. In order to explain this point, we must first digress for a moment to consider the general issue of **integrity constraints**. For the purposes of this discussion, it is convenient to classify such constraints into four kinds, namely domain constraints, column constraints, table constraints, and database constraints,* as follows:

- A **domain** constraint is just the definition of the set of values that go to make up the domain in question; in other words, it effectively just enumerates the values in the domain. *Note:* We mention domain constraints merely for completeness—they play no part in the view updating scheme that is the primary focus of this paper.

- A **column** constraint states that the values appearing in a specific column must be drawn from some specific domain. For example, consider the employees base table

```
EMP { EMP#, ENAME, DEPT#, SAL }
```

(see Fig. 1 for a sample tabulation). The columns of that table are subject to the following column constraints:

```
e.EMP#  IN EMP#_DOM
e.ENAME IN NAME_DOM
e.DEPT# IN DEPT#_DOM
e.SAL   IN US_CURRENCY_DOM
```

Here *e* represents an arbitrary row of the table and EMP#_DOM, NAME_DOM, etc., are the names of the relevant domains. *Note:* Throughout this paper we use a modified form of conventional SQL syntax, for reasons of simplicity and explicitness.

- A **table** constraint states that a specific table must satisfy some specific condition, where the condition in question refers **solely** to the table under consideration—i.e., it does not refer to any other table, nor to any domain. For example, here are two table constraints for the base table EMP:

EMP	EMP#	ENAME	DEPT#	SAL
	E1	Lopez	D1	25K
	E2	Cheng	D1	42K
	E3	Finzi	D2	30K
	E4	Saito	D2	45K

Fig. 1 Base table EMP (sample values)

---

*This classification is slightly different (but not dramatically so) from that previously given by one of the present authors (Date) in references [6] and [7].

```
1. IF e.DEPT# = 'D1' THEN e.SAL < 44K
2. IF e.EMP# = f.EMP# THEN e.ENAME = f.ENAME
                      AND   e.DEPT# = f.DEPT#
                      AND   e.SAL   = f.SAL
```

The first of these says that employees in department D1 must have a salary less than 44K. The second says that if two rows e and f have the same EMP# value, then they must also have the same ENAME value, the same DEPT# value, and the same SAL value—in other words, they must be the same row (this is just a longwinded way of saying that EMP# is a candidate key).

Note: Observe that we talk of table constraints in general, not just base table constraints. The point is, **all** tables, base or otherwise, are subject to table constraints, as we will see later.

■ For the purposes of this paper we define a database to be some user-defined— or DBA-defined—collection of named tables (base tables and/or views). A **database** constraint, then, states that the database in question must satisfy some specific condition, where the condition in question can refer to as many named tables as desired. For example, suppose the database containing base table EMP were extended to include a departments base table DEPT. Then the referential constraint from EMP to DEPT would be a database constraint (referring, as it happens, to exactly two base tables).

Here is another example of a database constraint (also referring to the same two base tables):

```
d.BUDGET > 2 * SUM ( e WHERE e.DEPT# = d.DEPT#, SAL )
```

Here d and e represent an arbitrary DEPT row and an arbitrary EMP row, respectively. The constraint says that every department has a budget that is at least twice the sum of all salaries for employees in that department.

Note: Unlike column constraints and base table constraints, which can always be checked **immediately** (i.e., after each individual update operation), database constraints must—at least conceptually—be **deferred** (i.e., checked at end-of-transaction). In practice there will be many cases where database constraints too can be checked immediately, but such "early" checking should be regarded as nothing more than an optimization.

3. TABLE PREDICATES

Now we can get back to our discussion of what tables **mean**. As we stated previously, every table—be it a base table, a view, a query result, or whatever—certainly does have an associated meaning. And, of course, users must be aware of those meanings if they are to use the database effectively (and correctly). For example, the meaning of table EMP is something like the following:

"The employee with the specified employee number (EMP#) has the specified name (ENAME), works in the specified department (DEPT#), and earns the specified salary (SAL). Furthermore, if the department number is D1, then the salary is less than 44K. Also, no two employees have the same employee number."

(This statement is not very precise, but it will serve for the moment.)

Formally, this statement is an example of what is called a **predicate,** or truth-valued function—a function of four arguments, in this particular case. Substituting values for the arguments is equivalent to **invoking** the function (or "instantiating" the predicate), thereby yielding an expression that evaluates to either *true* or *false.* For example, the substitution

```
EMP# = 'E1'   ENAME = 'Lopez'   DEPT# = 'D1'   SAL = 25K
```

yields the value *true.* By contrast, the substitution

```
EMP# = 'E1'   ENAME = 'Abbey'   DEPT# = 'D3'   SAL = 45K
```

yields the value *false.* And at any given time, of course, the table contains exactly those rows that make the predicate evaluate to *true* at that time.

It follows from the foregoing that if (for example) a row is presented as a candidate for insertion into some table, the DBMS should accept that row only if it does not cause the corresponding predicate to be violated. More generally, the predicate for a given table represents the **criterion for update acceptability** for that table—that is, it constitutes the criterion for deciding whether or not some proposed update is in fact valid (or at least plausible) for the given table.

In order for it to be able to decide whether or not a proposed update is acceptable for a given table, therefore, the DBMS needs to be aware of the predicate for that table. Now, it is of course not possible for the DBMS to know **exactly** what the predicate is for a given table. In the case of table EMP, for example, the DBMS has no way of knowing *a priori* that the predicate is such that the row <E1,Lopez,D1,25K> makes it *true* and the row <E1,Abbey,D3,45K> does not; it also has no way of knowing exactly what certain terms appearing in that predicate (such as "works in" or "earns") really mean. However, the DBMS certainly **does** know a reasonably close approximation to that predicate. To be specific, it knows that, if a given row is to be deemed acceptable, all of the following must be true:

- The EMP# value must be a value from the domain of employee numbers
- The ENAME value must be a value from the domain of names
- The DEPT# value must be a value from the domain of department numbers
- The SAL value must be a value from the domain of US currency
- If the DEPT# value is D1 then the SAL value must be less than 44K
- The EMP# value is unique with respect to all such values in the table

In other words, for a base table such as EMP, the DBMS does at least know all the integrity constraints (column constraints and table constraints) that have been declared for that base table. Formally, therefore, we can **define** the (DBMS-understood) "meaning" of a given base table to be the logical AND of all column constraints and table constraints that apply to that base table (and it is this meaning that the DBMS will check whenever an update is attempted on the base table in question). For example, the formal meaning of base table EMP is the following:

```
        e.EMP#   IN EMP#_DOM AND
        e.ENAME  IN NAME_DOM AND
        e.DEPT#  IN DEPT#_DOM AND
        e.SAL    IN US_CURRENCY_DOM AND
( IF e.DEPT# = 'D1' THEN e.SAL < 44K ) AND
( IF e.EMP# = f.EMP# THEN e.ENAME = f.ENAME AND
                         e.DEPT# = f.DEPT# AND
                         e.SAL   = f.SAL )
```

We will refer to this expression—let us call it PE—as **the table predicate** for base table EMP.

So much for base tables. But what about **derived** tables—in particular, what about views? What is the table predicate for a derived table? Clearly, what we need is a set of rules such that if the DBMS knows the table predicate(s) for the input(s) to any relational operation, it can deduce the table predicate for the output from that operation. Given such a set of rules, the DBMS will then know the table predicate for all possible tables, and will thus be able to decide the acceptability or otherwise of an arbitrary update on an arbitrary table (derived or base).

It is in fact very easy to state such a set of rules—they follow immediately from the definitions of the relational operators. For example, if A and B are any two type-compatible tables* and their respective table predicates are PA and PB, then the table predicate PC for table C, where C is defined as A INTERSECT B, is obviously (PA) AND (PB); that is, a row r will appear in C if and only if it appears in both A and B—i.e., if and only if $PA(r)$ and $PB(r)$ are both *true*. So if, for example, we define C as a view and try to insert r into that view, r must satisfy both the table predicate for A and the table predicate for B, or the INSERT will fail (see the section "Updating Intersections and Differences" later for further discussion).

Here is another example: The table predicate for the table that results from the **restriction** operation

```
T WHERE condition
```

is (PT) AND (*condition*), where PT is the table predicate for T. For example, the table predicate for EMP WHERE DEPT# = 'D1' is

```
( PE ) AND ( DEPT# = 'D1' )
```

---

*Type-compatibility is usually referred to as **union**-compatibility in the literature. We prefer our term for reasons that are beyond the scope of the present discussion.

where PE is the table predicate for EMP as defined earlier.

Stating the table predicates corresponding to the other relational operators is left as an exercise for the reader.

4. FURTHER PRINCIPLES

There are several further principles that must be satisfied by any systematic view updating mechanism. Space does not permit much elaboration on these principles here, but most of them are readily understandable on intuitive grounds anyway.

1. All tables must be genuine relations—i.e., duplicate rows are not permitted.

2. The updatability or otherwise of a given view is a semantic issue, not a syntactic one—i.e., it must not depend on the particular form in which the view definition happens to be stated. For example, the following two view definitions are semantically identical:

```
CREATE VIEW V AS
EMP WHERE DEPT# = 'D1' OR SAL > 33K ;

CREATE VIEW V AS
( EMP WHERE DEPT# = 'D1' ) UNION ( EMP WHERE SAL > 33K ) ;
```

Obviously, both of these views should be updatable. The SQL standard, however, and most of today's SQL products, adopt the *ad hoc* position that the first is updatable and the second is not.

3. It follows from the previous point that the view updatability rules must work correctly in the special case when the "view" is in fact a base table. This is because any base table *B* is semantically indistinguishable from a view *V* that is defined as *B* UNION *B*, or *B* INTERSECT *B*, or *B* MINUS *C* (if *C* is another base table that has no rows in common with *B*), or *B* WHERE *true*, or any of several other expressions that are identically equivalent to just *B*. Thus, for example, the rules for updating a union view, when applied to the view *V* = *B* UNION *B*, must yield exactly the same result as if the updates had been applied directly to the base table *B*.

4. The rules must preserve symmetry where applicable. For example, the delete rule for an intersection view *V* = *A* INTERSECT *B* must not arbitrarily cause a row to be deleted from *A* and not from *B*, even though such a one-sided delete would certainly have the effect of deleting the row from the view. Instead, the row must be deleted from both *A* and *B*.

5. The rules must take into account any applicable triggered actions, such as cascade DELETE. *Note:* For numerous well-documented reasons we would prefer such triggered actions to be specified *declaratively*, not procedurally. However, the view updating rules *per se* do not impose any such requirement.

6. For reasons of simplicity among others, it is desirable to regard UPDATE as shorthand for a DELETE-then-INSERT sequence (i.e., just as syntactic sugar), and we will so regard it later in this paper. This shorthand is acceptable **provided** it is understood that:

   - No checking of table predicates is done "in the middle of" any given update; that is, the expansion of UPDATE is DELETE-INSERT-check, not DELETE-check-INSERT-check. The reason is, of course, that the DELETE portion might temporarily violate the table predicate while the UPDATE overall does not. For instance, suppose table T contains exactly 10 rows, and consider the effect of "UPDATE row r" on T if T's table predicate says that T must contain at least 10 rows.

   - Triggered actions are likewise never performed "in the middle of" any given update (in fact they are done at the end, immediately prior to the table predicate checking).

   - The shorthand requires some slight refinement (beyond the scope of the present paper) in the case of projection views. See reference [10].

   We remark that treating UPDATEs as DELETEs-then-INSERTs implies that we regard UPDATEs as replacing entire rows, not as replacing individual values within such a row.

7. All update operations on views are implemented by the same kind of update operations on the underlying tables. That is, INSERTs map to INSERTs and DELETEs to DELETEs (we can ignore UPDATEs, thanks to the previous point). For suppose, contrariwise, that there is some kind of view—say a union view—for which (say) INSERTs map to DELETEs. Then it must follow that INSERTs **on a base table** must also sometimes map to DELETEs! This is because (as already observed under No. 3 above) the base table B is semantically identical to the union view $V = B$ UNION B. An analogous argument applies to every other kind of view also (restriction, projection, intersection, etc.). The idea that an INSERT on a base table might really be a DELETE we take to be self-evidently absurd; hence our position that (to repeat) INSERTs map to INSERTs and DELETEs to DELETEs.

8. In general, the rules when applied to a given view V will specify the operations to be applied to the table(s) on which V is defined. And those rules must work correctly even when those underlying tables are themselves derived tables in turn. In other words, the rules must be capable of **recursive application**.

9. The rules cannot assume that the database is well designed (e.g., fully normalized). However, they might on occasion produce a slightly surprising result if the database is **not** well designed—a fact that can be seen in itself as an additional argument in support of good design. We will give some examples of such "slightly surprising results" later in this paper.

5. UPDATING UNIONS

The general principles articulated in the previous section apply to all kinds of updates on all kinds of tables. In particular, they apply to updates on joins, restrictions, projections, etc. For the remainder of this paper, however, we concentrate on the question of updates on unions, intersections, and differences specifically (unions in this section, intersections and differences in the next). We begin with a few preliminary remarks.

1. We assume we are updating a table defined by means of an expression of the form *A* UNION *B* or *A* INTERSECT *B* or *A* MINUS *B* (as appropriate), where *A* and *B* are arbitrary relational expressions (i.e., they are not necessarily base tables). *A* and *B* must be type-compatible.

2. The table predicates corresponding to *A* and *B* are *PA* and *PB*, respectively.

3. Several of the view update rules refer to the possibility of **side-effects**. Now, it is well known that side-effects are usually undesirable; the point is, however, that side-effects might be unavoidable if *A* and *B* happen to be overlapping subsets of the same underlying table, as will frequently be the case with union, intersection, and difference views.

4. We limit our attention to single-row updates only, for simplicity.

Important caveat: The reader must understand that considering single-row updates only is in fact an **over**simplification, and indeed a distortion of the truth. Relational operations are always set-at-a-time; a set containing a single row is merely a special case. What is more, a multi-row update is sometimes **required** (i.e., some updates cannot be simulated by a series of single-row operations). And this remark is true of both base tables and views, in general. For example, suppose table EMP includes two additional employees, E8 and E9, and is subject to the constraint that E8 and E9 must have the same salary. Then a single-row UPDATE that changes the salary of just one of the two will necessarily fail.

Since our objective in this paper is merely to present an **informal** introduction to our ideas, we will (as stated) describe the update rules in terms of single-row operations. But the reader should not lose sight of the foregoing important caveat.

Here then is the INSERT rule for *A* UNION *B:*

■   The new row must satisfy *PA* or *PB* or both. If it satisfies *PA*, it is inserted into *A* (note that this INSERT might have the side-effect of inserting the row into *B* also). If it satisfies *PB*, it is inserted into *B*, unless it was inserted into *B* already as a side-effect of inserting it into *A*.

Note: The specific procedural manner in which the foregoing rule is stated ("insert into *A*, then insert into *B*") should be understood purely as a pedagogic device; it should not be taken to mean that the DBMS will execute exactly that procedure in practice. Indeed, the principle of symmetry—No. 4

from the "Further Principles" section—implies as much, because neither *A* nor *B* has precedence over the other. Analogous remarks apply to all of the rules discussed in this paper.

Explanation:

- The new row must satisfy at least one of *PA* and *PB* because otherwise it does not qualify for inclusion in *A* UNION *B*—i.e., it does not satisfy the table predicate, *viz.* (*PA*) OR (*PB*), for *A* UNION *B*. (As an aside, we note also that the new row must not already appear in either *A* or *B,* because otherwise we would be trying to insert a row that already exists.)
- If the requirements of the previous paragraph are satisfied, the new row is inserted into whichever of *A* or *B* it logically belongs to (possibly both).

Examples:

Let view UV be defined as

```
( EMP WHERE DEPT# = 'D1' ) UNION ( EMP WHERE SAL > 33K )
```

Fig. 2 shows a sample tabulation of this view, corresponding to the sample tabulation of EMP shown in Fig. 1.

UV	EMP#	ENAME	DEPT#	SAL
	E1	Lopez	D1	25K
	E2	Cheng	D1	42K
	E4	Saito	D2	45K

Fig. 2 View UV (sample values)

- Let the row to be inserted be <E5,Smith,D1,30K>. This row satisfies the table predicate for EMP WHERE DEPT# = 'D1' (though not the table predicate for EMP WHERE SAL > 33K). It is therefore inserted into EMP WHERE DEPT# = 'D1'. Because of the rules regarding INSERT on a restriction (which are fairly obvious and are not spelled out in detail here), the effect is to insert the new row into the EMP base table.
- Now let the row to be inserted be <E6,Jones,D1,40K>. This row satisfies the table predicate for EMP WHERE DEPT# = 'D1' **and** the table predicate for

EMP WHERE SAL > 33K. It is therefore logically inserted into both. However, inserting it into either of the two restrictions has the side-effect of inserting it into the other anyway, so there is no need to perform the second INSERT explicitly.

Now suppose EMPA and EMPB are two distinct **base** tables, EMPA representing employees in department D1 and EMPB representing employees with salary > 33K (see Fig. 3); suppose view UV is defined as EMPA UNION EMPB, and consider again the two sample INSERTs previously discussed. Inserting the row <E5,Smith,D1,30K> into view UV will cause that row to be inserted into base table EMPA, presumably as required. However, inserting the row <E6,Jones,D1,40K> into view UV will cause that row to be inserted into **both** base tables! This result is logically correct, although arguably counterintuitive (it is an example of what we called a "slightly surprising result" earlier). **It is the authors' position that such surprises can occur only if the database is badly designed**. In particular, it is our position that a design that permits the very same row to appear in—i.e., to satisfy the table predicate for—two distinct base tables is by definition a bad design. This (perhaps controversial!) position is elaborated elsewhere [17].

EMPA				EMPB			
EMP#	ENAME	DEPT#	SAL	EMP#	ENAME	DEPT#	SAL
E1	Lopez	D1	25K	E2	Cheng	D1	42K
E2	Cheng	D1	42K	E4	Saito	D2	45K

Fig. 3 Base tables EMPA and EMPB (sample values)

Note: To pave the way for an understanding of reference [17], the reader might care to meditate on the fact that the two base tables EMPA and EMPB already both contain the row <E2,Cheng,D1,42K>. How did this state of affairs arise?

We turn now to the DELETE rule for *A* UNION *B:*

■   If the row to be deleted appears in *A,* it is deleted from *A* (note that this DELETE might have the side-effect of deleting the row from *B* also). If it (still) appears in *B,* it is deleted from *B*.

Examples to illustrate this rule are left as an exercise for the reader. Note that (in general) deleting a row from *A* or *B* might cause a cascade DELETE or some other triggered action to be performed.

Finally, the UPDATE rule:

■ The row to be updated must be such that the updated version satisfies *PA* or *PB* or both. If the row to be updated appears in *A*, it is deleted from *A* **without** performing any triggered actions (cascade DELETE, etc.) that such a DELETE would normally cause, and likewise **without** checking the table predicate for *A*. Note that this DELETE might have the side-effect of deleting the row from *B* also. If the row (still) appears in *B*, it is deleted from *B* (again without any triggered actions or table predicate checks). Next, if the updated version of the row satisfies *PA*, it is inserted into *A* (note that this INSERT might have the side-effect of inserting the updated version into *B* also). Finally, if the updated version satisfies *PB*, it is inserted into *B*, unless it was inserted into *B* already as a side-effect of inserting it into *A*.

This UPDATE rule essentially consists of the DELETE rule followed by the INSERT rule, except that (as indicated) no triggered actions or table predicate checks are performed after the DELETE (any triggered actions associated with the UPDATE are conceptually performed after all deletions and insertions have been done, just prior to the table predicate checks).

It is worth pointing out that one important consequence of treating UPDATEs in this fashion is that a given UPDATE can effectively cause a row to move from one table to another. Given the database of Fig. 3, for example, updating the row <E1,Lopez,D1,25K> within view UV to <E1,Lopez,D2,40K> will delete the existing row for Lopez from EMPA and insert the updated row for Lopez into EMPB.

6. UPDATING INTERSECTIONS AND DIFFERENCES

Here now are the rules for updating *A* INTERSECT *B*. This time we simply state the rules without further discussion (they follow the same general pattern as the union rules). Again, examples to illustrate the various cases are left as an exercise for the reader.

■ **INSERT:** The new row must satisfy both *PA* and *PB*. If it does not currently appear in *A*, it is inserted into *A* (note that this INSERT might have the side-effect of inserting the row into *B* also). If it (still) does not appear in *B*, it is inserted into *B*.

■ **DELETE:** The row to be deleted is deleted from *A* (note that this DELETE might have the side-effect of deleting the row from *B* also). If it (still) appears in *B*, it is deleted from *B*.

■ **UPDATE:** The row to be updated must be such that the updated version satisfies both *PA* and *PB.* The row is deleted from *A* without performing any triggered actions or table predicate checks (note that this DELETE might have the side-effect of deleting it from *B* also); if it (still) appears in *B,* it is deleted from *B,* again without any triggered actions or table predicate checks. Next, if the updated version of the row does not currently appear in *A,* it is inserted into *A* (note that this INSERT might have the side-effect of inserting the row into *B* also). If it (still) does not appear in *B,* it is inserted into *B.*

And here are the rules for updating *A* MINUS *B:*

- **INSERT:** The new row must satisfy *PA* and not *PB.* It is inserted into *A.*
- **DELETE:** The row to be deleted is deleted from *A.*
- **UPDATE:** The row to be updated must be such that the updated version satisfies *PA* and not *PB.* The row is deleted from *A* without performing any triggered actions or table predicate checks; the updated version of the row is then inserted into *A.*

7. CONCLUDING REMARKS

We have described a systematic approach to the view updating problem in general, and have applied that approach to the question of updating union, intersection, and difference views in particular. A critical aspect of our approach is that a given row can appear in a given table only if that row does not cause the table predicate for that table to be violated, and this observation is just as true for a view as it is for a base table. In other words, the table predicate for a given table constitutes the **criterion for update acceptability** for that table.

Regarding the rules for union, intersection, and difference views specifically, the following desirable properties of our approach are worth calling out explicitly:

1. Each kind of view supports all three update operations (INSERT, UPDATE, DELETE). By contrast, other proposals (see, for example, the proposals of references [3] and [14]) allow, e.g., DELETE but not INSERT on a union view, implying that the user might be able to delete a row from a given view and then not be able to insert that very same row back into that very same view.

2. Certain important equivalences are preserved. For example, the expressions *A* INTERSECT *B* and *A* MINUS (*A* MINUS *B*) are semantically identical and should thus display identical update behavior if treated as view definitions, and so they do (exercise for the reader!).

3. For union and difference, INSERT and DELETE are always inverses of each other; however, for intersection they might not be (quite). For instance, if *A* and *B* are distinct base tables, inserting row *r* into *V* = *A* INTERSECT *B* might

cause *r* to be inserted into *A* only (because it is already present in *B*); subsequently deleting *r* from *V* will now cause *r* to be deleted from both *A* and *B*. (On the other hand, deleting *r* and then reinserting it will always preserve the *status quo*.) However, it is once again the authors' position that such an asymmetry can arise only if the database is badly designed (in particular, if the design permits the very same row to satisfy the table predicate for two distinct base tables). See reference [17].

Of the foregoing, we remark that Nos. 1 (support for all three update operations) and 3 (INSERT and DELETE inverses of each other) might be regarded as two more principles that a systematic view updating mechanism really ought to satisfy if possible. No. 2 (certain equivalences preserved) is in fact a special case of the second of the principles already stated in the section "Further Principles" earlier.

Finally, we note that (of course) few DBMS products today support any kind of updates at all on union, intersection, and difference views. It is our hope that this paper can serve as a guideline to be followed (a) by vendors in adding the necessary support to their products; (b) by the SQL standards committees in their efforts to develop the next iteration of the SQL standard known informally as "SQL3." In the meantime, DBAs and application programmers who have to develop workaround solutions (using, perhaps, stored or triggered procedures) to the problems caused by the current lack of support would be well advised to adhere to the principles described in the foregoing sections.

ACKNOWLEDGMENTS

The authors would like to thank Nagraj Alur, Hugh Darwen, Fabian Pascal, and Paul Winsberg for their helpful comments on earlier drafts of this paper.

REFERENCES AND BIBLIOGRAPHY

1. International Organization for Standardization (ISO), *Database Language SQL,* Document ISO/IEC 9075:1992. Also available as American National Standards Institute (ANSI) Document ANSI X3.135-1992.

2. D. D. Chamberlin, J. N. Gray, and I. L. Traiger, "Views, Authorization, and Locking in a Relational Data Base System," Proc. NCC *44,* Anaheim, Calif. (Montvale, N.J.: AFIPS Press, 1975).

3. E. F. Codd, *The Relational Model for Database Management Version 2* (Reading, Mass.: Addison-Wesley, 1990).

4. Hugh Darwen, "Without Check Option," in C. J. Date and Hugh Darwen, *Relational Database Writings 1989–1991* (Reading, Mass.: Addison-Wesley, 1992).

5. C. J. Date, *An Introduction to Database Systems* (6th edition) (Reading, Mass.: Addison-Wesley, 1995).

6. C. J. Date, "A Matter of Integrity" (in three parts) (in this volume).

7. C. J. Date, "A Contribution to the Study of Database Integrity," in *Relational Database Writings 1985–1989* (Reading, Mass.: Addison-Wesley, 1990).

8. C. J. Date, "Updating Views," in *Relational Database: Selected Writings* (Reading, Mass.: Addison-Wesley, 1986).

9. C. J. Date and Hugh Darwen, *A Guide to the SQL Standard* (3rd edition) (Reading, Mass.: Addison-Wesley, 1993).

10. C. J. Date and David McGoveran, "Updating Joins and Other Views" (in this volume).

11. C. J. Date and Colin J. White, *A Guide to DB2* (4th edition) (Reading, Mass.: Addison-Wesley, 1992).

12. Umeshwar Dayal and Philip A. Bernstein, "On the Correct Translation of Update Operations on Relational Views," *ACM TODS 7,* No. 3 (September 1982).

13. A. L. Furtado and M. A. Casanova, "Updating Relational Views," in W. Kim, D. Reiner, and D. Batory (eds.), *Query Processing in Database Systems* (New York, N.Y.: Springer Verlag, 1985).

14. Nathan Goodman, "View Update Is Practical," *InfoDB 5,* No. 2 (Summer 1990).

15. Arthur M. Keller, "Algorithms for Translating View Updates to Database Updates for Views Involving Selections, Projections, and Joins," Proc. 4th ACM SIGACT-SIGMOD Symposium on Principles of Database Systems, Portland, Ore. (March 1985).

16. David McGoveran and C. J. Date, *A Guide to SYBASE and SQL Server* (Reading, Mass.: Addison-Wesley, 1992).

17. David McGoveran and C. J. Date, "A New Database Design Principle" (in this volume).

18. M. R. Stonebraker, "Implementation of Views and Integrity Constraints by Query Modification," Proc. ACM SIGMOD International Conference on Management of Data, San Jose, Calif. (May 1975).

Updating Joins and Other Views

ABSTRACT

A recent paper by the present authors [5] described a new and systematic approach to the problem of updating relational views, and discussed the application of that approach to views based on the operators union, intersection, and difference. The present paper completes the discussion by considering views based on other operators, such as join.

COMMENTS ON REPUBLICATION

See the "Comments on Republication" in the previous chapter. *Note:* Portions of this material previously appeared in somewhat different form in reference [3]. Also, I am (again) grateful to David McGoveran for allowing me to republish the material in the present book.

Originally published in *Database Programming & Design 7,* No. 8 (August 1994). Reprinted by permission of David McGoveran, Alternative Technologies, Boulder Creek, California, and Miller Freeman Inc.

1. INTRODUCTION

The problem of view updating has been the subject of considerable study for many years. In reference [5], the present authors described an approach to the problem that seems more satisfactory (i.e., more systematic and more robust) than previous proposals, and applied that approach to the particular case of union, intersection, and difference views. The emphasis in that paper on those operators was deliberate—it was our feeling that union, intersection, and difference, though important, had been largely neglected in most previous work; moreover, we also felt that a strong feature of our scheme was precisely the fact that it treated those operators correctly. However, we clearly need to show how our approach applies to joins and other operators as well. Hence the present paper.

Note: The discussions of this paper, like those of reference [5], are quite informal. It is our intention to produce a formal description of our scheme as soon as time permits.

2. PRELIMINARIES

We assume the reader has already seen this paper's predecessor [5]. Here we just summarize the major points from that paper, for ease of subsequent reference. Refer to the previous paper for further explanation.

The major contribution of the earlier paper was the identification of a series of principles that must be satisfied by any systematic view updating mechanism. Of those principles, the first and overriding one is as follows:

1. *A given row can appear in a given table only if that row does not cause the table predicate for that table to be violated—and this observation is just as true for a view as it is for a base table.*

The **table predicate** for a given table is, loosely speaking, "what the table means"; it is the **criterion for update acceptability** for that table. In other words, the table predicate for a given table constitutes the criterion for deciding whether or not some proposed update is in fact valid, or at least plausible, for that table. In the case of a base table, the table predicate is the logical AND of all column constraints and table constraints that apply to the base table in question. In the case of a derived table, the table predicate is derived in a straightforward way from the table predicate(s) for the table(s) from which the table in question is derived; for example, the table predicate PC for $C = A$ INTERSECT B is (PA) AND (PB), where PA and PB are the table predicates for A and B, respectively.

The remaining principles are as follows.

2. All tables must be genuine relations (i.e., duplicate rows are not allowed).

3. The updatability or otherwise of a given view is a semantic issue, not a syn-

tactic one (i.e., it must not depend on the particular form in which the view definition happens to be stated).

4. The view updatability rules must work correctly in the special case when the "view" is in fact a base table.

5. The rules must preserve symmetry where applicable.

6. The rules must take into account any applicable triggered actions, such as cascade DELETE.

7. For most purposes, UPDATE can be regarded as shorthand for a DELETE-then-INSERT sequence. Note, however, that it must be understood that no checking of table predicates is done "in the middle of " any given update; that is, the expansion of UPDATE is DELETE-INSERT-check, not DELETE-check-INSERT-check. It must also be understood that triggered actions are likewise never performed "in the middle of" any given update. Finally, it must also be understood that some slight refinement is required to the foregoing shorthand in the case of projection views (see the section "Updating Projections" later for further discussion).

8. All update operations on views are implemented by the same kind of update operations on the underlying tables. That is, INSERTs map to INSERTs and DELETEs to DELETEs (we can ignore UPDATEs, thanks to the previous point).

9. The rules must be capable of recursive application.

10. The rules cannot assume that the database is well designed (though they might on occasion produce a slightly surprising result if the database is *not* well designed—a fact that can be seen in itself as an additional argument in support of good design).

11. If a view is updatable, there should be no *prima facie* reason for permitting some updates but not others (e.g., DELETEs but not INSERTs).

12. INSERT and DELETE should be inverses of each other, where possible.

We now discuss the application of the foregoing principles to the updating of views whose definition involves relational operations other than union, intersection, and difference. The major operators we consider are restriction, projection, extension, and join. As in reference [5], we limit our attention to single-row updates only, for simplicity; however, we must first repeat the following remarks from that paper.

> *"Important caveat: The reader must understand that considering single-row updates only is in fact an oversimplification, and indeed a distortion of the truth. Relational operations are always set-at-a-time; a set containing a single row is merely a special case. What is more, a multi-row update is some-*

*times **required** (i.e., some updates cannot be simulated by a series of single-row operations). And this remark is true of both base tables and views, in general. For example, suppose [the employees table EMP is subject to the constraint that employees] E8 and E9 must have the same salary. Then a single-row UPDATE that changes the salary of just one of the two will necessarily fail.*

"Since our objective in this paper is merely to present an informal introduction to our ideas, we will (as stated) describe the update rules in terms of single-row operations. But the reader should not lose sight of the foregoing important caveat."

One final preliminary remark: We should make it clear at the outset that for the operators under consideration here, our rules (or some of them, at any rate) will probably not look all that different from those found in other proposals—at least at first glance. Nevertheless, we claim that our rules are still more systematic than (for example) those of the SQL standard, and in any case part of the point is that our rules must be seen as a package; i.e., the rules for join (etc.) discussed in this paper cannot be separated from the rules discussed in reference [5] for union (etc.).

3. THE SUPPLIERS-AND-PARTS DATABASE

All examples in this paper are based on the familiar suppliers-and-parts database [3]. See Fig. 1 for a simplified database definition and Fig. 2 for a set of sample data values.

Notation: Throughout this paper we use italic upper-case letters *A, B, ...* from near the beginning of the alphabet to refer generically to tables, and italic upper-case letters *X, Y, ...* from near the end of the alphabet to refer generically to columns of such tables. The table predicates for *A, B, ...* are *PA, PB, ...*, respectively. We use italic lower-case letters *a, b, ...* to refer generically to rows of tables *A, B, ...*, respectively.

4. UPDATING RESTRICTIONS

First of all, note that the table predicate for the table that results from the restriction operation (also known as a selection operation)

```
A WHERE condition
```

```
CREATE DOMAIN S#      ... ;
CREATE DOMAIN NAME    ... ;
CREATE DOMAIN STATUS  ... ;
CREATE DOMAIN CITY    ... ;
CREATE DOMAIN P#      ... ;
CREATE DOMAIN COLOR   ... ;
CREATE DOMAIN WEIGHT  ... ;
CREATE DOMAIN QTY     ... ;

CREATE BASE TABLE S
    ( S#       DOMAIN ( S# ),
      SNAME    DOMAIN ( NAME ),
      STATUS   DOMAIN ( STATUS ),
      CITY     DOMAIN ( CITY ) )
    PRIMARY KEY ( S# ) ;

CREATE BASE TABLE P
    ( P#       DOMAIN ( P# ),
      PNAME    DOMAIN ( NAME ),
      COLOR    DOMAIN ( COLOR ),
      WEIGHT   DOMAIN ( WEIGHT ),
      CITY     DOMAIN ( CITY ) )
    PRIMARY KEY ( P# ) ;

CREATE BASE TABLE SP
    ( S#       DOMAIN ( S# ),
      P#       DOMAIN ( P# ),
      QTY      DOMAIN ( QTY ) )
    PRIMARY KEY ( S#, P# )
    FOREIGN KEY ( S# ) REFERENCES S
    FOREIGN KEY ( P# ) REFERENCES P ;
```

Fig. 1 The suppliers-and-parts database (data definition)

S

S#	SNAME	STATUS	CITY
S1	Smith	20	London
S2	Jones	10	Paris
S3	Blake	30	Paris
S4	Clark	20	London
S5	Adams	30	Athens

SP

S#	P#	QTY
S1	P1	300
S1	P2	200
S1	P3	400
S1	P4	200
S1	P5	100
S1	P6	100
S2	P1	300
S2	P2	400
S3	P2	200
S4	P2	200
S4	P4	300
S4	P5	400

P

P#	PNAME	COLOR	WEIGHT	CITY
P1	Nut	Red	12	London
P2	Bolt	Green	17	Paris
P3	Screw	Blue	17	Rome
P4	Screw	Red	14	London
P5	Cam	Blue	12	Paris
P6	Cog	Red	19	London

Fig. 2 The suppliers-and-parts database (sample values)

(where *condition* is, specifically, a restriction condition [3]) is

```
( PA ) AND ( condition )
```

For example, the table predicate for the restriction S WHERE CITY = 'London' is

```
( PS ) AND ( CITY = 'London' )
```

where PS is the table predicate for the suppliers table S. It follows that (for example) any row *r* presented for insertion into a view defined by means of this restriction must be such that the conditions PS(*r*) and *r*.CITY = 'London' both evaluate to *true,* or the INSERT will fail.*

Here then are the update rules for *A* WHERE *condition:*

- **INSERT:** The new row must satisfy both *PA* and *condition.* It is inserted into *A.*

- **DELETE:** The row to be deleted is deleted from *A.*

- **UPDATE:** The row to be updated must be such that the updated version satisfies both *PA* and *condition.* The row is deleted from *A* without performing any triggered actions or table predicate checks. The updated version of the row is then inserted into *A.*

Examples:

Let view LS be defined as

```
S WHERE CITY = 'London'
```

Fig. 3 shows a sample tabulation of this view, corresponding to the sample tabulation of S shown in Fig. 2.

- An attempt to insert the row <S6,Green,20,London> into LS will succeed. The new row will be inserted into table S, and will therefore be effectively inserted into the view as well.

- An attempt to insert the row <S1,Green,20,London> into LS will fail, because it violates the table predicate for table S—specifically, it violates the uniqueness constraint on the primary key S.S# for table S.

- An attempt to insert the row <S6,Green,20,Athens> into LS will fail, because it violates the restriction condition CITY = 'London'.

- An attempt to delete the LS row <S1,Smith,20,London> will succeed. The row will be deleted from table S, and will therefore be effectively deleted from the view as well.

---

*In SQL, however, such an attempt will fail only if the CREATE VIEW statement explicitly includes the specification WITH CHECK OPTION—i.e., by default, it will **not** fail. See reference [2] for some criticisms of this state of affairs.

LS	S#	SNAME	STATUS	CITY
	S1	Smith	20	London
	S4	Clark	20	London

Fig. 3   View LS (sample values)

- An attempt to update the LS row <S1,Smith,20,London> to <S6,Green, 20,London> will succeed. An attempt to update that same row <S1,Smith, 20,London> to either <S2,Smith,20,London> or <S1,Smith,20,Athens> will fail—in the first case because it violates the primary key uniqueness constraint on table S, in the second case because it violates the restriction condition CITY = 'London'.

5. UPDATING PROJECTIONS

Again we start by considering the relevant table predicate. Let the columns of table *A* be partitioned into two disjoint groups, *X* and *Y* say. Regard each of *X* and *Y* as a single **composite** column. It is clear, then, that a given row <*x*> will appear in the projection *A*[*X*] if and only if there exists some value *y* from the domain of *Y*-values such that the row <*x,y*> appears in *A*. For example, consider the projection of table S over S#, SNAME, and CITY. Every row <*s#,sname,city*> appearing in that projection is such that there exists a status value *status* such that the row <*s#,sname,status,city*> appears in table S.

Here then are the update rules for *A*[*X*]:

- **INSERT:** Let the row to be inserted be <*x*>. Let the default value of *Y* be *y** (it is an error if no such default value exists, i.e., if *Y* has "defaults not allowed"). The row <*x,y*> (which must satisfy *PA*) is inserted into *A*.

  Note: Since candidate keys will usually (but not invariably—see reference [4]) have "defaults not allowed," a projection that does not include all candidate keys of the underlying table will usually not permit INSERTs.

- **DELETE:** All rows of *A* with the same *X*-value as the row to be deleted from *A*[*X*] are deleted from *A*.

  Note: In practice, it will usually be desirable that *X* include at least one candidate key of *A*, so that the row to be deleted from *A*[*X*] is derived from

---

*A default value might be NULL in SQL. We do not wish to get sidetracked into a discussion of the problems of nulls here; for present purposes, it is irrelevant whether the default is null or something else. See reference [6] for further discussion.

exactly one row *a* of *A*. However, there is no logical reason to make this a hard requirement. (Analogous remarks apply in the case of UPDATE also— see below.)

- **UPDATE:** Let the row to be updated be <*x*> and let the updated version be <*x'*>. Let *a* be a row of *A* with the same *X*-value *x*, and let the value of *Y* in row *a* be *y*. All such rows *a* are deleted from *A* without performing any triggered actions or table predicate checks. Then, for each such value *y*, row <*x',y*> (which must satisfy *PA*) is inserted into *A*.

   Note: It is here that the "slight refinement" mentioned in Principle No. 7 in the "Preliminaries" section shows itself. Specifically, observe that the final "INSERT" step in the UPDATE rule reinstates the previous *Y*-value in each inserted row—it does **not** replace it by the applicable default value, as a standalone INSERT would.

Examples:

Let view SC be defined as

```
SC [ S#, CITY ]
```

Fig. 4 shows a sample tabulation of this view, corresponding to the sample tabulation of S shown in Fig. 2.

- An attempt to insert the row <S6,London> into SC will succeed, and will have the effect of inserting the row <S6,*n*,*t*,London> into table S, where *n* and *t* are the default values for columns S.SNAME and S.STATUS, respectively.

- An attempt to insert the row <S1,London> into SC will fail, because it violates the table predicate for table S—specifically, it violates the uniqueness constraint on the primary key S.S# for table S.

- An attempt to delete the row <S1,London> from SC will succeed. The row for S1 will be deleted from table S.

- An attempt to update the SC row <S1,London> to <S1,Athens> will succeed;

SC	S#	CITY
	S1	London
	S2	Paris
	S3	Paris
	S4	London
	S5	Athens

Fig. 4   View SC (sample values)

the effect will be to replace the row <S1,Smith,20,London> in table S by the row <S1,Smith,20,Athens>—**not** by the row <S1,*n,t*,Athens>, please observe.

■ An attempt to update that same SC row <S1,London> to <S2,London> will fail (why, exactly?).

Consideration of the case in which the projection does not include a candidate key of the underlying table—for example, the projection of table S over STATUS and CITY—is left as an exercise for the reader.

6. UPDATING EXTENSIONS

The reader might perhaps be unfamiliar with the relational EXTEND operator. Here is a brief explanation, taken from reference [3]. Basically, EXTEND takes a specified table and—conceptually, at least—returns a new (derived) table that is similar to the original table but includes an additional column, values of which are obtained by evaluating some specified computational expression. For example, we might write:

```
EXTEND P ADD ( WEIGHT * 454 ) AS GMWT
```

Assuming sample values for table P as given in Fig. 2, the result of this expression is as shown in Fig. 5. (The assumption is that WEIGHT values are given in pounds; the expression WEIGHT * 454 will convert those weights to grams.) Note that there is an exact one-to-one correspondence between rows of the extension and rows of the underlying table.

In general, the table predicate *PE* for the table *E* that results from the extension operation

```
EXTEND A ADD exp AS X
```

P#	PNAME	COLOR	WEIGHT	CITY	GMWT
P1	Nut	Red	12	London	5448
P2	Bolt	Green	17	Paris	7718
P3	Screw	Blue	17	Rome	7718
P4	Screw	Red	14	London	6356
P5	Cam	Blue	12	Paris	5448
P6	Cog	Red	19	London	8626

Fig. 5 An example of EXTEND

is as follows:

```
PA ( a ) AND e.X = exp ( a )
```

Here *e* is a row of table *E* and *a* is the projection of that row *e* over all columns of *A*. In stilted English:

> "Every row *e* in the extension is such that (a) the row *a* that is derived from *e* by projecting away the value *e.X* satisfies *PA,* and (b) that value *e.X* is equal to the result of applying the expression *exp* to that row *a.*"

For example, the table predicate for the extension of table P shown in Fig. 5 is as follows:

> "Every row *<p#,pname,color,weight,city,gmwt>* in the extension is such that (a) the row *<p#,pname,color,weight,city>* satisfies the table predicate for P, and (b) the value *gmwt* is equal to the value 454 ∗ *weight.*"

Here then are the update rules for *E* = EXTEND *A* ADD *exp* AS *X:*

- **INSERT:** Let the row to be inserted be *e; e* must satisfy *PE*. The row *a* that is derived from *e* by projecting away the value *e.X* is inserted into *A*.
- **DELETE:** Let the row to be deleted be *e*. The row *a* that is derived from *e* by projecting away the value *e.X* is deleted from *A*.
- **UPDATE:** Let the row to be updated be *e* and let the updated version be *e'; e'* must satisfy *PE*. The row *a* that is derived from *e* by projecting away the value *e.X* is deleted from *A* without performing any triggered actions or table predicate checks. The row *a'* that is derived from *e'* by projecting away the value *e'.X* is inserted into *A*.

Examples (refer to Fig. 5):

- An attempt to insert the row <P7,Cog,Red,12,Paris,5448> will succeed, and will have the effect of inserting the row <P7,Cog,Red,12,Paris> into table P.
- An attempt to insert the row <P7,Cog,Red,12,Paris,5449> will fail (why?).
- An attempt to insert the row <P1,Cog,Red,12,Paris,5448> will fail (why?).
- An attempt to delete the row for P1 will succeed, and will have the effect of deleting the row for P1 from table P.
- An attempt to update the row for P1 to <P1,Nut,Red,10,Paris,4540> will succeed; the effect will be to replace the row <P1,Nut,Red,12,London> in table P by the row <P1,Nut,Red,10,Paris>.
- An attempt to update that same row to a row for P2 (with all other values unchanged) or a row in which the GMWT value is not equal to 454 times the WEIGHT value will fail (in each case, why?).

7. UPDATING JOINS

Most previous treatments of the view update problem—including those by one of the present authors (Date)—have argued that the updatability or otherwise of a given join depends, at least in part, on whether the join is one-to-one, one-to-many, or many-to-many. By contrast, it is the contention of the present paper that joins are **always** updatable. Moreover, the update rules are identical in all three cases, and are essentially quite straightforward.

What makes this claim plausible—startling though it might seem at first sight—is the new perspective on the problem that is afforded by adoption of the fundamental principle stated at the beginning of the "Preliminaries" section. Broadly speaking, the overall objective of support for the view mechanism has always been to make views look as much like base tables as possible, and this objective is indeed a laudable one. With regard to view update specifically, however:

- It is usually assumed (implicitly) that it is always possible to update an individual row of a base table independently of all the other rows in that base table.

- By contrast, it is manifestly **not** always possible to update an individual row of a view independently of all the other rows in that view. For example, Codd shows in reference [1] that it is not possible to delete just one row from a certain join, because the effect would be to leave a table that "is not the join of any two tables whatsoever" (which means that the result could not possibly satisfy the table predicate for the view). And the approach to such view updates historically has always been to reject them altogether, on the grounds that it is impossible to make them look completely like base table updates.

Our approach is rather different. We recognize the fact that even with a base table, it is not always possible to update individual rows independently of all the rest. (Consider what would happen, for example, if the suppliers base table were subject to the constraint that either suppliers S1 and S4 both appear or neither of them does.) Typically, therefore, we accept those view updates that have historically been rejected, interpreting them in an obvious and logically correct way to apply to the underlying table(s); we accept them, moreover, in full recognition of the fact that updating those underlying tables might well have side-effects on the view—**side-effects that are, however, required in order to avoid the possibility that the view might violate its own table predicate**.

With that preamble out of the way, let us now get down to detail. In what follows, we first define our terms. Then we present the update rules for joins. Then we consider the implications of those rules for each of the three cases (one-to-one, one-to-many, many-to-many) in turn.

First of all, then—following reference [3]—we take the term "join" to mean

natural join specifically. Let the columns of table A be partitioned into two disjoint groups, X and Y say. Likewise, let the columns of table B be partitioned into two disjoint groups, Y and Z say. Now suppose that the columns of Y (only) are common to the two tables, so that the columns of X are "the other columns" of A and the columns of Z are "the other columns" of B. Suppose also that corresponding columns of Y (i.e., columns with the same name) are defined on the same domain. Finally, regard each of X, Y, and Z as a single **composite** column. Then the expression

    A JOIN B

yields a table with columns $\{X,Y,Z\}$ consisting of all rows $<x,y,z>$ such that the row $<x,y>$ appears in A and the row $<y,z>$ appears in B. The table predicate PJ for $J = A$ JOIN B is thus

    PA (a) AND PB (b)

where for a given row j of the join, a is the "A-portion" of j (i.e., the row that is derived from j by projecting away the value $j.Z$) and b is the "B-portion" of j (i.e., the row that is derived from j by projecting away the value $j.X$). In other words:

> "Every row in the join is such that the A-portion satisfies PA and the B-portion satisfies PB."

For example, the table predicate for the join of tables S and SP over S# is as follows:

> "Every row $<s\#,sname,status,city,p\#,qty>$ in the join is such that the row $<s\#,sname,status,city>$ satisfies the table predicate for S and the row $<s\#,p\#,qty>$ satisfies the table predicate for SP."

Here then are the update rules for $J = A$ JOIN B:

- **INSERT:** The new row j must satisfy PJ. If the A-portion of j does not appear in A, it is inserted into A.* If the B-portion of j does not appear in B, it is inserted into B.

  Note: As in reference [5], the specific procedural manner in which the foregoing rule is stated ("insert into A, then insert into B") should be understood purely as a pedagogical device; it should not be taken to mean that the DBMS will execute exactly that procedure in practice. Indeed, the principle of symmetry—No. 5 from the "Preliminaries" section—implies as much, because neither A nor B has precedence over the other. Analogous remarks apply to all of the other rules below.

---

*Note that this INSERT might have the side-effect of inserting the B-portion into B also, as with INSERTs on, e.g., unions or intersections (see reference [5]). Analogous remarks apply to the DELETE and UPDATE rules also; for brevity, we do not bother to spell out all such possibilities here.

- **DELETE:** The *A*-portion of the row to be deleted is deleted from *A* and the *B*-portion is deleted from *B*.

- **UPDATE:** The row to be updated must be such that the updated version satisfies *PJ*. The *A*-portion is deleted from *A*, without performing any triggered actions or table predicate checks, and the *B*-portion is deleted from *B*, again without performing any triggered actions or table predicate checks. Then, if the *A*-portion of the updated version of the row does not appear in *A*, it is inserted into *A*; if the *B*-portion does not appear in *B*, it is inserted into *B*.

Let us now examine the implications of these rules for the three different cases.

Case 1 (one-to-one):

The term "one-to-one" here would more accurately be "(one-or-zero)-to-(one-or-zero)." In other words, there is a DBMS-known integrity constraint in effect that guarantees that for each row of *A* there is at most one matching row in *B* and *vice versa*. More precisely, the set of columns *Y* over which the join is performed must include a subset (not necessarily a proper subset) *K*, say, such that *K* is a candidate key for *A* and a candidate key for *B*.

Examples:

- For a first example, the reader is invited to consider the effect of the foregoing rules on the join of the suppliers table S to itself over supplier numbers (only).

- By way of a second example, suppose the suppliers-and-parts database includes another base table, SR { S#, REST }, where S# identifies a supplier and REST identifies that supplier's favorite restaurant. Assume that not all suppliers in table S are represented in table SR. The reader is invited to consider the effect of the foregoing rules on the join of tables S and SR (over S#). What difference would it make if a given supplier could be represented in table SR and not in table S?

Case 2 (one-to-many):

The term "one-to-many" here would more accurately be "(zero-or-one)-to-(zero-or-more)." In other words, there is a DBMS-known integrity constraint in effect that guarantees that for each row of *B* there is at most one matching row in *A*. Typically, what this means is that the set of "common columns" *Y* over which the join is performed must include a subset (not necessarily a proper subset) *K*, say, such that *K* is a candidate key for *A* and a matching foreign key for *B*.*

---

*If this is in fact the case, and if (as we would strongly recommend [6]) that foreign key has "nulls not allowed," we can replace the phrase "zero or one" by "exactly one."

Examples:

Let view SSP be defined as

```
S JOIN SP
```

(this is a foreign-key-to-matching-candidate-key join, of course). Sample values are shown in Fig. 6.

■ An attempt to insert the row <S4,Clark,20,London,P6,100> into SSP will succeed, and will have the effect of inserting the row <S4,P6,100> into table SP (thereby adding a row to the view).

■ An attempt to insert the row <S5,Adams,30,Athens,P6,100> into SSP will succeed, and will have the effect of inserting the row <S5,P6,100> into table SP (thereby adding a row to the view).

■ An attempt to insert the row <S6,Green,20,London,P6,100> into SSP will succeed, and will have the effect of inserting the row <S6,Green,20,London> into table S and the row <S6,P6,100> into table SP (thereby adding a row to the view).

Note: Suppose for the moment that it is possible for SP rows to exist without a corresponding S row. Suppose moreover that table SP already includes some rows with supplier number S6 (but not one with supplier number S6 and part number P1). Then the INSERT in the example just discussed will have the effect of inserting some additional rows into the view—namely, the join of the row <S6,Green,20,London> and those previously existing SP rows for supplier S6.

SSP	S#	SNAME	STATUS	CITY	P#	QTY
	S1	Smith	20	London	P1	300
	S1	Smith	20	London	P2	200
	S1	Smith	20	London	P3	400
	S1	Smith	20	London	P4	200
	S1	Smith	20	London	P5	100
	S1	Smith	20	London	P6	100
	S2	Jones	10	Paris	P1	300
	S2	Jones	10	Paris	P2	400
	S3	Blake	30	Paris	P2	200
	S4	Clark	20	London	P2	200
	S4	Clark	20	London	P4	300
	S4	Clark	20	London	P5	400

Fig. 6 View SSP (sample values)

- An attempt to insert the row <S4,Clark,20,Athens,P6,100> into SSP will fail (why?).

- An attempt to insert the row <S5,Adams,30,London,P6,100> into SSP will fail (why?).

- An attempt to insert the row <S1,Smith,20,London,P1,400> into SSP will fail (why?).

- An attempt to delete the row <S3,Blake,30,Paris,P2,200> from SSP will succeed, and will have the effect of deleting the row <S3,Blake,30,Paris> from table S and the row <S3,P2,200> from table SP.

- An attempt to delete the row <S1,Smith,20,London,P1,300> from SSP will "succeed" (see the note below) and will have the effect of deleting the row <S1,Smith,20,London> from table S and the row <S1,P1,300> from table SP.

    Note: Actually the overall effect of this attempted DELETE will depend on the foreign key delete rule from SP.S# to S.S#. If the rule is RESTRICT the overall operation will fail. If it is CASCADE it will have the side-effect of deleting all other SP rows for supplier S1 as well. Other possibilities are left as an exercise for the reader.

- An attempt to update the SSP row <S1,Smith,20,London,P1,300> to <S1,Smith,20,London,P1,400> will succeed, and will have the effect of updating the SP row <S1,P1,300> to <S1,P1,400>.

- An attempt to update the SSP row <S1,Smith,20,London,P1,300> to <S1,Smith,20,Athens,P1,400> will succeed, and will have the effect of updating the S row <S1,Smith,20,London> to <S1,Smith,20,Athens> and the SP row <S1,P1,300> to <S1,P1,400>.

- An attempt to update the SSP row <S1,Smith,20,London,P1,300> to <S6,Smith,20,London,P1,300> will "succeed" (see the note below) and will have the effect of updating the S row <S1,Smith,20,London> to <S6,Smith, 20,London> and the SP row <S1,P1,300> to <S6,P1,300>.

    Note: Actually, the overall effect of this attempted update will depend on the foreign key update rule from SP.S# to S.S#. The details are left as another exercise for the reader.

Case 3 (many-to-many):

The term "many-to-many" here would more accurately be "(zero-or-more)-to-(zero-or-more)." In other words, there is no DBMS-known integrity constraint in effect that guarantees that we are really dealing with a Case 1 or Case 2 situation.

Examples:

Let view SCP be defined as

S JOIN P

(join of S and P over CITY—a many-to-many join). Sample values are shown in Fig. 7.

■ Inserting the row <S7,Brown,15,Oslo,P8,Wheel,White,25> will succeed, and will have the effect of inserting the row <S7,Brown,15,Oslo> into table S and the row <P8,Wheel,White,25,Oslo> into table P (thereby adding the specified row to the view).

■ Inserting the row <S1,Smith,20,London,P7,Washer,Red,5> will succeed, and will have the effect of inserting the row <P7,Washer,Red,5,London> into table P (thereby adding **two** rows to the view—the row <S1,Smith,20, London,P7,Washer,Red,5> (as specified) and the row <S4,Clark,20,London, P7,Washer,Red,5>).

■ Inserting the row <S6,Green,20,London,P7,Washer,Red,5> will succeed, and will have the effect of inserting the row <S6,Green,20,London> into table S and the row <P7,Washer,Red,5,London> into table P (thereby adding **six** rows to the view).

■ Deleting the row <S1,Smith,20,London,P1,Nut,Red,12> will succeed, and will have the effect of deleting the row <S1,Smith,20,London> from table S and the row <P1,Nut,Red,12,London> from table P (thereby deleting **four** rows from the view).

Further examples are left as an exercise for the reader.

SC

S#	SNAME	STATUS	CITY	P#	PNAME	COLOR	WEIGHT
S1	Smith	20	London	P1	Nut	Red	12
S1	Smith	20	London	P4	Screw	Red	14
S1	Smith	20	London	P6	Cog	Red	19
S2	Jones	10	Paris	P2	Bolt	Green	17
S2	Jones	10	Paris	P5	Cam	Blue	12
S3	Blake	30	Paris	P2	Bolt	Green	17
S3	Blake	30	Paris	P5	Cam	Blue	12
S4	Clark	20	London	P1	Nut	Red	12
S4	Clark	20	London	P4	Screw	Red	14
S4	Clark	20	London	P6	Cog	Red	19

Fig. 7   The join of S and P over CITY

8. CONCLUDING REMARKS

We have applied the systematic view updating scheme first described in reference [5] to the question of updating restriction, projection, extension, and join views. Regarding join views in particular, we offer the following additional comments:

- It is well known that intersection is a special case of natural join. To be specific, if tables A and B are type-compatible,* the expressions A INTERSECT B and A JOIN B are semantically identical; they should thus display identical update behavior if treated as view definitions, and so they do (exercise for the reader!).

- It is well known also that Cartesian product is a special case of natural join. To be specific, if tables A and B have no common columns at all, the expressions A TIMES B and A JOIN B are semantically identical; they should thus display identical update behavior if treated as view definitions, and so they do (another exercise for the reader).

- The reader will observe that we have said nothing regarding θ-**joins**. The reason is, of course, that θ-join is not a primitive operation; in fact, it is defined as a restriction of a Cartesian product. The update rules for θ-join can therefore be derived from the rules for restriction and Cartesian product.

We have now discussed all of the operators that are usually regarded as part of the relational algebra except for RENAME, SUMMARIZE, and DIVIDE [3]. **RENAME** is trivial. Regarding **SUMMARIZE,** we remark that (in general) the SUMMARIZE operation is not information-preserving—that is, there is no unambiguous reverse mapping from the result of a SUMMARIZE back to the original table. As a consequence, views whose definition involves SUMMARIZE are (in general) not updatable. Finally, **DIVIDE** (like θ-join) is not primitive, and hence the relevant update rules can be derived from those already given (specifically those for difference, projection, and Cartesian product); the details are left as yet another exercise for the reader, but we observe that in practice it seems likely that most division views will not be updatable at all (why, exactly?).

One final observation: Throughout this paper and its predecessor [5], we have implied, but never quite stated explicitly, that the target of a given update operation need not be a named table (i.e., a base table or a view), but can instead be **any arbitrary relational expression**. By way of illustration, suppose we have a view LSSP defined as

```
( S WHERE CITY = 'London' ) JOIN SP
```

With our usual sample values, an attempt to insert the row <S6,Green,20,

---

*Type-compatibility is usually referred to as **union**-compatibility in the literature. We prefer our term for reasons that are beyond the scope of the present discussion.

London,P6,100> into this view will succeed (it will have the effect of inserting the row <S6,Green,20,London> into table S and the row <S6,P6,100> into table SP). More precisely, the first of these two rows—<S6,Green,20,London>—will be inserted, not directly into base table S, but rather into the restriction S WHERE CITY = 'London'; the rule for inserting a row into a restriction will then come into play, with the desired final effect. The point is, however, that the target of the intermediate INSERT is represented by a restriction expression, not by a named relation.

It follows that there is no reason why the syntax of the usual INSERT, DELETE, and UPDATE operations need be limited (as it is in SQL today, for example) to designating the relevant target table by means of a table name. Rather, it should be extended to permit that target to be designated by means of an arbitrary relational expression.

ACKNOWLEDGMENTS

The authors would like to thank Hugh Darwen, Fabian Pascal, and Paul Winsberg for their helpful comments on earlier drafts of this paper.

REFERENCES AND BIBLIOGRAPHY

1. E. F. Codd, "Recent Investigations in Relational Data Base Systems," Proc. IFIP Congress, Stockholm, Sweden (August 1974).

2. Hugh Darwen, "Without Check Option," in C. J. Date and Hugh Darwen, *Relational Database Writings 1989–1991* (Reading, Mass.: Addison-Wesley, 1992).

3. C. J. Date, *An Introduction to Database Systems* (6th edition) (Reading, Mass.: Addison-Wesley, 1995).

4. C. J. Date, "Notes Toward a Reconstituted Definition of the Relational Model Version 1 (RM/V1)," in C. J. Date and Hugh Darwen, *Relational Database Writings 1989–1991* (Reading, Mass.: Addison-Wesley, 1992).

5. C. J. Date and David McGoveran, "Updating Union, Intersection, and Difference Views" (in this volume).

6. David McGoveran, "Nothing from Nothing" (in four parts), *Database Programming & Design 6,* No. 12 and *7,* Nos. 1–3 (December 1993–March 1994).

The Extended Relational Model RM/T

ABSTRACT

This paper provides a tutorial introduction to the major features of RM/T [3]. RM/T is an extended form of the original relational model that is specifically intended to address the issue of *semantic modeling*. The paper also describes the application of certain RM/T ideas to the problem of database design.

COMMENTS ON REPUBLICATION

Most present-day database design methodologies make use of some kind of *entity/relationship model* (E/R model). Most such methodologies also make use of *entity/relationship diagrams* (E/R diagrams). The E/R model and E/R diagrams were originally introduced by Chen in reference [2]; since the publication of that

Originally published (in considerably different form) in my book *An Introduction to Database Systems: Volume I,* 5th edition, pages 593–613 (Addison-Wesley, 1991). Reprinted by permission.

paper, however, literally dozens of other writers have proposed refined, revised, and otherwise revamped versions of the E/R model.

In reference [3], Codd proposed an extended version of the relational model, called RM/T, that was specifically intended to be a more formal, more precise attack on the same problem that the various versions of the E/R model were addressing. And several database professionals (this writer included) find RM/T to be superior to the E/R model in certain respects. By the time RM/T arrived on the scene, however, the E/R model was already firmly established, at least in the commercial world; probably for that reason, RM/T has so far had comparatively little influence on database technology in general or database design methodologies in particular.

Despite the foregoing state of affairs, I do feel that database professionals ought to have at least a basic familiarity with the major features of RM/T. Since space did not permit the retention of the RM/T material in the most recent edition (the sixth) of my book *An Introduction to Database Systems* (Addison-Wesley, 1995), I decided to revise it appropriately for inclusion in the present book.

1. INTRODUCTION

Readers are assumed to be familiar with the basic idea of semantic modeling and its application to database design. In particular, they are assumed to have some knowledge of *the entity/relationship model* (E/R model), which forms the basis of most approaches to database design in widespread use today. They are also assumed to have some familiarity with *entity/relationship diagrams* (E/R diagrams). Tutorial discussions of all of these topics can be found in reference [6].

In this paper, by contrast, we describe another important attack on the semantic modeling problem, *viz.* the **extended relational model** known as **RM/T** (T for Tasmania, where the ideas were first publicly presented). Section 2 presents an overview of the principal concepts of RM/T, and Section 3 then shows how RM/T can be used to do database design. Section 4 offers a brief analysis and comparison of the E/R and RM/T approaches. Finally, Section 5 presents a brief summary.

2. AN OVERVIEW OF RM/T

The extended relational model RM/T was introduced by Codd in reference [3]. It can be regarded as a competitor to the entity/relationship model, inasmuch as (a) like the E/R model, it represents an attack on the semantic modeling problem, and (b) again like the E/R model, it can be used as the basis for a systematic database design methodology. An extended tutorial description of RM/T (or at least certain aspects thereof), incorporating a number of refinements and improvements developed by Codd and the present author since the original publication of reference [3], can be found in reference [12]. This section forms a brief introduction to some of the material discussed in more detail in reference [12]. The reader is warned that the treatment below is necessarily an overview only; for more information, see either of the references already mentioned [3,12].

Now, we will be discussing some of the differences between RM/T and the E/R model in detail later, in Section 4. However, one immediate difference is that RM/T makes no unnecessary distinctions between entities and relationships; a relationship is regarded merely as a special kind of entity. A second difference is that the structural and integrity aspects of RM/T are more extensive, and are defined more precisely, than those of the E/R model. A third difference is that RM/T includes its own special operators, over and above the operators of the basic relational model (which are the only operators defined for the E/R model, so far as this writer is aware). *Note:* Much additional work remains to be done in this last area, however, as we shall see.

In outline, then, RM/T works as follows:

- First, entities (including "relationships") are represented by *E-relations* and *P-relations,* both of which are special forms of the general *n*-ary relation. E-relations are used to record the fact that certain **entities** exist, and P-relations are used to record certain **properties** of those entities.

- Second, a variety of relationships can exist among entities—for example, entity types *A* and *B* might be linked together in an **association** (i.e., a many-to-many relationship), or entity type *Y* might be a **subtype** of entity type *X* (i.e., every instance of *Y* might necessarily also be an instance of *X*). RM/T includes a formal **catalog** structure (details beyond the scope of this paper) by which such relationships can be made known to the system; the system is thus able to enforce the various **integrity constraints** that are implied by the existence of such relationships.

- Third, a number of high-level **operators** are provided to facilitate the manipulation of the various RM/T objects (E-relations, P-relations, catalog relations, etc.).

An Example

Fig. 1 is an E/R diagram for a simple manufacturing company (it is based on a figure from reference [2] and is intended to be more or less self-explanatory). The reader might find it helpful to study that figure in conjunction with the discussions in the remainder of this section. We will also use that same figure as a basis for the database design discussions in Section 3.

The Entity Classification Scheme

RM/T provides an **entity classification scheme,** which in many respects constitutes the most significant aspect—or, at least, the most immediately visible aspect—of the entire model. Entities are divided into three categories, namely *kernels, characteristics,* and *associations:*

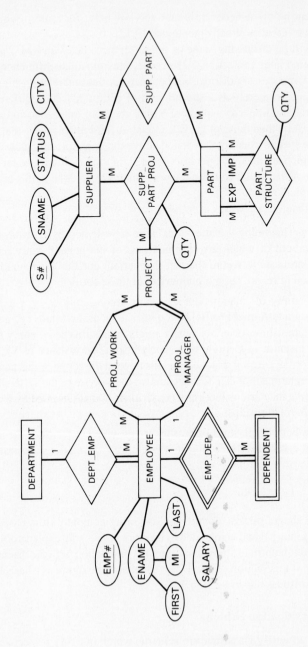

Fig. 1 Entity/relationship diagram (example)

- **Kernel entities:** Kernel entities are entities that have *independent existence;* they are "what the database is really all about." In other words, kernels are entities that are neither characteristic nor associative (see below). In terms of the example of Fig. 1, suppliers, parts, projects, employees, and departments would typically all be kernel entities.

- **Characteristic entities:** A characteristic entity is an entity whose primary purpose is to describe or "characterize" some other entity. For example, an employee dependent (meaning a child or other family member) might be a characteristic of an employee. Characteristics are *existence-dependent* on the entity they describe. The entity described can be kernel, characteristic, or associative.

- **Associative entities:** An associative entity is an entity whose function is to represent a *many-to-many* (or many-to-many-to-many, etc.) *relationship* among two or more other entities. For example, a shipment is an association between a supplier and a part. The entities associated can each be kernel, characteristic, or associative.

The primary purpose of the entity classification scheme is to impose some structure on the real world, which might otherwise appear to be just an amorphous jumble of facts. A secondary purpose is to introduce some discipline into the integrity enforcement scheme (see later). Both of these aspects are of major significance in database design, of course.

In addition to the foregoing:

- Entities (regardless of their classification) can also have **properties;** for example, parts have weights, departments have budgets, shipments have quantities.

- In particular, any entity (again, regardless of its classification) can have a property whose function is to identify or **designate** some other related entity; for example, each employee will typically designate some corresponding department entity. Entities such as employees in this example are said to be *designative.* A designation thus represents a many-to-one relationship between two entities.

  Note: It follows from the foregoing that a characteristic entity is in fact a special case of a designative entity; it is really nothing more than a designating entity that happens to be existence-dependent on the entity it designates. Thus, employee dependents are characteristics of employees—they designate employees and are existence-dependent on them. Employees, by contrast, are *not* characteristics of departments—although they designate departments, they are not existence-dependent on them.

  We conclude this subsection by relating the foregoing concepts to their E/R analogs. Loosely speaking, a kernel corresponds to an E/R "regular entity," a characteristic to an E/R "weak entity," and an association to an E/R "relationship" (many-to-many variety only). However, these correspondences are only approximate. For example, it is far from clear whether the E/R model permits a participant in a relationship to be a relationship in turn. (And if it does, incidentally, it is also far from clear how to draw the corresponding E/R diagram. Presumably there will be two diamonds connected by a straight line—but which of them represents the participant?) It is also not clear whether an E/R relationship can have subtypes (see later), whereas an RM/T association certainly can.

Surrogates

By definition, any database contains representatives of certain real-world entities (e.g., suppliers, parts, and shipments, in the case of the suppliers-and-parts database). Since entities are distinguishable in the real world, their representatives in the database must also be distinguishable. In the basic relational model, this identification function is performed by user-defined, user-controlled primary keys*—"user keys" for short. In RM/T, by contrast, it is performed by *system-*controlled primary keys, or **surrogates**.

The advantages of surrogates are discussed at length in reference [14] (where the concept was introduced) and references [3] and [12]; for present purposes, it is sufficient to understand that, in RM/T, *all primary keys and all foreign keys are surrogates*. The basic idea is as follows. When the user creates a new entity representative in the database—e.g., when the user executes the INSERT statement

```
INSERT { { < S#     : 'S1'      >,
            < SNAME  : 'Smith'   >,
            < STATUS :  20       >,
            < CITY   : 'London' > } }
  INTO   S ;
```

—the system generates a new surrogate value (*alpha,* say) for the new entity (supplier S1, in the example). The value *alpha* is unique with respect to all surrogate values that exist or ever have existed in the database; furthermore, it is guaranteed never to change and never to be reassigned. All references inside the system to supplier S1 will be via the value *alpha.* (References outside the system, by contrast, will probably continue to be via the value S1.)

Two immediate consequences of the RM/T surrogate idea are worth calling out explicitly. First, note that primary and foreign keys in RM/T are always non-composite (such keys therefore never overlap). Second, note that foreign keys in RM/T always reference, not just some base relation, but very specifically an E-relation (see the next subsection for an explanation of E-relations).

---

*We are assuming here that (in those cases where there is a choice) we are following the discipline of selecting one candidate key as the primary key (see reference [5]). In fact the point is irrelevant anyway in the present context, as will quickly become clear.

E-Relations

The database contains one **E-relation** for each entity type. The E-relation for a given entity type is a unary (single-attribute) relation that lists the surrogates for all entities of that type currently existing in the database. The primary purpose of an E-relation is thus to record the existence of the entities in question, and hence to serve as a central reference point for all other entries in the database that concern those entities in any way.

By way of example, let us consider an RM/T version of suppliers-and-parts. The database will include three E-relations, which might look as shown in Fig. 2 (where we assume that we currently have two suppliers, three parts, and five shipments). Each E-relation is given the same name as the corresponding entity type; the single attribute in each case has a name that is obtained by appending a trailing "¢" to the relation name. (In fact, all attributes whose values are surrogates—which is to say, precisely, all primary keys and all foreign keys—are given names that include a trailing "¢", partly for ease of recognition and partly for other reasons that are beyond the scope of this discussion.)

We will continue this example in the next subsection below.

P-Relations

The property types for a given entity type are represented by a set of **P-relations**. In the case of suppliers, for example, we might have the three P-relations:

```
SKN  ( S¢, S#, SNAME )
     PRIMARY KEY ( S¢ )
     FOREIGN KEY ( S¢ ) REFERENCES S

ST   ( S¢, STATUS )
     PRIMARY KEY ( S¢ )
     FOREIGN KEY ( S¢ ) REFERENCES S

SC   ( S¢, CITY )
     PRIMARY KEY ( S¢ )
     FOREIGN KEY ( S¢ ) REFERENCES S
```

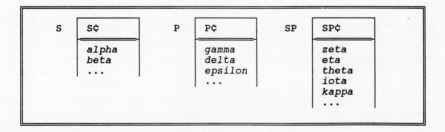

Fig. 2 E-relations for suppliers-and-parts (RM/T version)

The precise manner in which properties are grouped into P-relations is left to the discretion of the database designer: At one extreme all properties might be bundled together into a single (*n*-ary) P-relation, at the other extreme each property might have a (binary) P-relation of its own. Purely for the sake of the example— not for any really good reason—we have arranged the properties for suppliers into the three P-relations SKN, ST, and SC as indicated above. Thus, for the two suppliers *alpha* and *beta* (who we assume are actually suppliers S1 and S2), the P-relations might look as shown in Fig. 3.

Similarly for parts (details left as an exercise for the reader). What about shipments? Shipments are of course an associative entity type; for a given shipment, the properties to be represented in the database are as follows:

■ the surrogate for the relevant supplier (S)

■ the surrogate for the relevant part (P)

■ the relevant quantity (QTY)

Note that there is no longer any need for shipments to have a supplier number or part number property—the supplier and part for a given shipment are identified by surrogates, not by user keys.* One advantage of this scheme, incidentally, is that there is now never any need to cascade a change in a supplier number or part number value down to the shipments for that supplier or part (in fact, foreign key update rules now become totally irrelevant and need not be specified).

SKN	S¢	S#	SNAME	ST	S¢	STATUS
	alpha	S1	Smith		alpha	20
	beta	S2	Jones		beta	10
	...	..	.....		...	..

SC	S¢	CITY
	alpha	London
	beta	Paris
	...	...

Fig. 3 P-relations for suppliers (RM/T version)

---

*An analogous remark applies to designations (not illustrated by the suppliers-and-parts example). For example, employees would typically have a DEPT¢ property, not a DEPT# property. Likewise for characteristics; as pointed out earlier, a characteristic entity is really just a designating entity that happens to be existence-dependent on the entity it designates.

For simplicity, let us assume that all three shipment properties are represented in a single P-relation:

```
SPSPQ   ( SP¢, S¢, P¢, QTY )
        PRIMARY KEY ( SP¢ )
        FOREIGN KEY ( S¢ ) REFERENCES S
        FOREIGN KEY ( P¢ ) REFERENCES P
```

Some possible values are shown in Fig. 4.

SPSPQ	SP¢	S¢	P¢	QTY
	zeta	alpha	gamma	300
	eta	alpha	delta	200
	theta	alpha	epsilon	400
	iota	beta	gamma	300
	kappa	beta	delta	400
	...	...	...	...

Fig. 4 P-relation for shipments (RM/T version)

Subtypes and Supertypes

A given entity can be of several types simultaneously. For example, a given employee entity might simultaneously be an instance of the EMPLOYEE entity type, an instance of the PROGRAMMER entity type, an instance of the APPLICATION_ PROGRAMMER entity type, and so on. We say that PROGRAMMER is a **subtype** of the EMPLOYEE **supertype**, APPLICATION_PROGRAMMER is a **subtype** of the PROGRAMMER **supertype,** and so on (see Fig. 5).

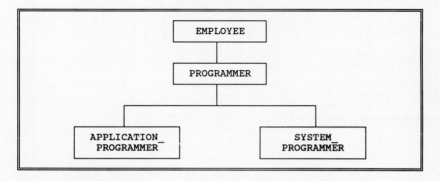

Fig. 5 Subtypes and supertypes (example)

All *properties* of a given supertype apply automatically to all of that supertype's subtypes, but the converse is not true. For example, all properties of employees apply automatically to programmers (but the converse is not true). In particular, all *designations* that apply to employees apply automatically to programmers, but the converse is not true; programmers might have designations of their own that do not apply to employees in general. Likewise, (a) all *characteristics* of employees are automatically characteristics of programmers, but the converse is not true; (b) all *associations* in which employees participate are automatically associations in which programmers participate, but the converse is not true.

Fig. 6 shows some possible E- and P-relations for the EMPLOYEE and PROGRAMMER entity types (only). Note in this example that Jacob (surrogate *omicron*) is a programmer who has presumably not yet been trained in any programming language.

One last remark concerning supertypes and subtypes: A subtype of a *kernel* entity type is still a kernel entity type. Likewise, a subtype of an *association* is still an association, and a subtype of a *characteristic* is still a characteristic.

Integrity Rules

RM/T includes six new integrity rules. They are numbered 3–8, since Rules 1 and 2 (the entity and referential integrity rules) of the basic relational model still apply. We remark however that Rules 4–8 can all be seen as special cases of the existing Rule 2. We remark also that the rules might be better regarded as "metarules" (see reference [6]).

EMPLOYEE

EMPLOYEE¢
lambda
mu
nu
xi
omicron

EMPLOYEE_PROPS

EMPLOYEE¢	E#	ENAME
lambda	E1	Lopez
mu	E2	Cheng
nu	E3	Finzi
xi	E4	Saito
omicron	E5	Jacob

PROGRAMMER

PROGRAMMER¢
lambda
xi
omicron

PROGRAMMER_PROPS

PROGRAMMER¢	LANG
lambda	COBOL
xi	C

Fig. 6 E- and P-relations for EMPLOYEE and PROGRAMMER

3. **Entity integrity in RM/T:** E-relations accept insertions and deletions but not updates (because surrogates never change).

4. **Property integrity:** A property cannot exist in the database unless the entity it describes is also in the database.

5. **Characteristic integrity:** A characteristic entity cannot exist in the database unless the entity it describes is also in the database.

6. **Association integrity:** An associative entity cannot exist in the database unless each entity participating in the association is also in the database.*

7. **Designation integrity:** A designative entity cannot exist in the database unless the entity it designates is also in the database.[†]

8. **Subtype integrity:** A subtype entity cannot exist in the database unless it also exists in the database as the corresponding supertype entity.

Refer to Codd's paper [3] or reference [12] for further discussion.

Operators

One thing that sets RM/T apart from most other proposals in the semantic modeling area is that it includes, not only a set of objects and rules as described above, but also a corresponding set of **operators**. Those operators permit (among other things) the definition of widely varying user views over a common underlying database; moreover, they allow those definitions to be comparatively independent of the precise structure of that database.

For example, suppose the suppliers-and-parts database is represented by E- and P-relations as sketched in the foregoing subsections. Now, it would be possible, using only the operators of the *basic* relational model, to provide user views of suppliers, parts, and shipments as the familiar three *n*-ary relations S (degree 4), P (degree 5), and SP (degree 3), in which all surrogates are concealed and only user keys show through. (Note, incidentally, that such a capability implies a requirement to be able to update certain join views.) However:

- Each of those three view definitions would have to be thought out and formulated independently.

- Each would involve several distinct relational algebra operations.

- Moreover, each would be highly sensitive to changes in the RM/T-level definition of the database. For example, consider the effect of breaking the suppliers P-relation SKN into two P-relations, one each for S# and SNAME.

---

*Except—according to reference [12]—where it is explicitly stated that such a participant can legally be specified as "unknown." We now feel this possibility requires more study.

[†]Except—according to reference [12]—where it is explicitly stated that the designated entity can legally be specified as "unknown." We now feel this possibility requires more study.

RM/T, by contrast, provides a single operator, the *PROPERTY* operator, whose effect is to gather together *all* the immediate properties for a specified entity type into a single *n*-ary relation, regardless of how many properties there are, regardless of how those properties are grouped into P-relations, and regardless of the naming structure of those P-relations. Thus the three view definitions could each involve just that one operator, and the problems outlined above would not arise.

Having said that, we should now stress the point (already mentioned in the introduction to this section) that the operators of RM/T as currently defined must be regarded as *preliminary only;* a considerable amount of additional definitional work is needed before they can be regarded as being in any final kind of form. For that reason we do not discuss them any further here. The interested reader is referred to references [3] and [12] for more information.

3. DATABASE DESIGN WITH RM/T

We now present an introduction to a database design methodology that was developed by the present author using the ideas—at least, the structural and integrity ideas—of RM/T as a foundation. The methodology is described in more detail in reference [10]. Also, reference [8] discusses an extension to the methodology to deal with one specific problem, namely the problem of one-to-one relationships, and references [9] and [11] provide an extensive set of discussions and recommendations regarding the use of foreign keys (foreign keys play a critical role in the methodology, as will be seen).

The methodology does depart slightly from the prescriptions of RM/T in two respects:

1. It permits the use of surrogate keys but does not insist on them. In other words, user-defined, user-controlled primary keys (possibly even composite keys) are allowed, at the discretion of the database designer. The pros and cons of surrogates are discussed in some detail in reference [14].

2. It does not insist on one E-relation plus zero or more separate P-relation(s) for each entity type, but rather allows all of those relations to be collapsed into a single relation.

In outline, the methodology involves the following steps:

- Deciding the kernels
- Deciding the associations
- Deciding the designations
- Deciding the characteristics
- Deciding the properties
- Deciding the supertypes and subtypes

Of course, the steps can be performed in any sequence, and in practice a certain amount of repetition will be necessary (database design is always an iterative process). However, we will follow the sequence as shown above in order to impose some structure on the discussion. We will use the example of Fig. 1 in the previous section to illustrate the ideas. (Note, incidentally, that it is perfectly acceptable to use E/R diagrams to represent a database design, even if we choose not to use the ideas of the E/R model *per se* in the design process. This point is elaborated in Section 4.)

Kernels

The kernel entities are the *independent* entities; as Section 2 put it, they are "what the database is really all about." The kernels in the example of Fig. 1 are as follows:

```
DEPARTMENT
EMPLOYEE
SUPPLIER
PART
PROJECT
```

Each kernel entity type maps into a base relation. The database will thus contain five base relations, say DEPT, EMP, S, P, and J, corresponding to these five kernels. Furthermore, of course, each of those base relations will have a primary key—DEPT#, EMP#, S#, P#, and J#, say—corresponding to the kernel identifiers in the real world. We will document these facts by writing an appropriate set of data definition statements, or at least the beginnings of such a set of statements.* Here, for example, is the statement for the DEPT relation (in outline):

```
CREATE BASE RELATION DEPT
     ( DEPT# DOMAIN ( DEPT# ) ... )
       PRIMARY KEY ( DEPT# ) ;
```

The others are left as an exercise for the reader to complete. *Note:* The domains need to be documented too. We omit detailed discussion of this aspect here.

Associations

Associations are many-to-many (or many-to-many-to-many, etc.) relationships among other entities. Those other entities, in turn, can be kernels, or characteristics, or associations, or any combination. In the example, the associations are as follows:

---

*In other words, we are suggesting the use of DDL statements as a means for recording design decisions. DDL statements are not the only way of performing this function, of course, but whatever formalism is used must be functionally equivalent to such statements. Our use of DDL statements in the present section should be interpreted in this light.

```
PROJ_WORK (associates employees and projects)
SUPP_PART (associates suppliers and parts)
SUPP_PART_PROJ (associates suppliers, parts, and projects)
PART_STRUCTURE (associates parts and parts)
```

Each associative entity type also maps into a base relation. We therefore introduce four more base relations corresponding to these four associations. Let the relation for the SUPP_PART association be SP (the usual suppliers-and-parts relation). We defer for a moment the question of the primary key for this relation, and concentrate instead on the matter of the *foreign* keys that are necessary in order to identify the participants in the association:

```
CREATE BASE RELATION SP
    ( S# ... , P# ... , ... )
    .....
        FOREIGN KEY ( S# ) REFERENCES S
        FOREIGN KEY ( P# ) REFERENCES P ;
```

Clearly, the relation must include two foreign keys (S# and P#) corresponding to the two participants (suppliers and parts), and those foreign keys must reference the corresponding participant relations S and P. Furthermore, an appropriate set of foreign key rules—a nulls rule, a delete rule, and an update rule—must be specified for each of those foreign keys (see reference [6] for a tutorial explanation of such rules). In the case of relation SP, we might specify the following foreign key rules (the specific rules shown are only by way of illustration, of course):

```
CREATE BASE RELATION SP
    ( S# ... , P# ... , ... )
    .....
        FOREIGN KEY ( S# ) REFERENCES S
                    NULLS NOT ALLOWED
                    DELETE RESTRICTED
                    UPDATE CASCADES
        FOREIGN KEY ( P# ) REFERENCES P
                    NULLS NOT ALLOWED
                    DELETE RESTRICTED
                    UPDATE CASCADES ;
```

Turning now to the question of the primary key: An association *is* an entity; it can have characteristics, and/or participate in other associations; it might therefore need to be referenced from other places in the database; it therefore needs a primary key. So what is the primary key for an association?

- One possibility would be to take the combination of the participant-identifying foreign keys (S# and P#, in the case of SP)—*if* that combination has a unique value for each instance of the relationship (which might or might not be the case, but usually is), and *if* it has "nulls not allowed" (which also might or might not be the case, but usually is),* and *if* the database designer has no objection to composite primary keys (which might or might not be the case).

---

*We assume here that we wish to enforce the entity integrity rule for relation SP. See reference [6].

■   Alternatively, a new noncomposite attribute, or surrogate—"shipment number" say—might be introduced to serve as the primary key.

For the sake of the example, we will go with the first of these two possibilities, and so add the clause

```
PRIMARY KEY ( S#, P# )
```

to the CREATE BASE RELATION statement for relation SP.

Consideration of the PROJ_WORK, PART_STRUCTURE, and SUPP_ PART_PROJ associations is left as an exercise for the reader.

Designations

A designation is a many-to-one relationship between two other entities. Those other entities, in turn, can be kernels, or characteristics, or associations, or any combination. In the example, there are three designations:

```
PROJ_MANAGER (projects designate managers)
DEPT_EMP (employees designate departments)
EMP_DEP (dependents designate employees)
```

Of these three, however, the last really represents a *characteristic* relationship, because employee dependents are existence-dependent on employees (remember from Section 2 that a characteristic entity is a special case of a designating entity in which the designating entity is existence-dependent on the designated entity). By contrast, there is no such existence dependence in the case of PROJ_ MANAGER or DEPT_EMP. We will discuss characteristics in a moment; for now, let us concentrate on the DEPT_EMP relationship.

Designations do *not* cause the introduction of new relations. Rather, a designation is represented simply by a foreign key in the relation for the designating entity, referencing the designat*ed* entity. In the case of DEPT_EMP, for example:

```
CREATE BASE RELATION EMP
    ( EMP#  ... , DEPT# ... , ... )
      PRIMARY KEY ( EMP# )
      FOREIGN KEY ( DEPT# ) REFERENCES DEPT
                  NULLS  ...
                  DELETE ...
                  UPDATE ... ;
```

The foreign key rule possibilities for a foreign key that represents a designation are the same as those for a foreign key that represents a participant in an association (in general).

Note: For the sake of the present exposition, we will assume that one-to-one relationships (which in any case are not all that common in practice) are treated in exactly the same way as many-to-one relationships. Reference [8] contains an extended discussion of the special problems of the one-to-one case.

Characteristics

A characteristic is an entity that "characterizes" (or describes)—and is existence-dependent on—some other entity. The entity characterized can be a kernel, or an association, or another characteristic. As already explained, the relationship from the characteristic to the entity characterized is really a designation; however, the foreign key rules for that designation *must* be as follows:

```
NULLS NOT ALLOWED
DELETE CASCADES
UPDATE CASCADES
```

These three rules together capture and reflect the necessary existence dependence. Here is an example:

```
CREATE BASE RELATION DEPENDENT
    ( EMP# ... )
      .....
        FOREIGN KEY ( EMP# ) REFERENCES EMP
                    NULLS NOT ALLOWED
                    DELETE CASCADES
                    UPDATE CASCADES ;
```

What about the primary key? Like an association, a characteristic *is* an entity; it can participate in associations, and/or have other characteristics; it might therefore need to be referenced from other places in the database; it therefore needs a primary key. Once again, it turns out we have a choice:

- One possibility is to take the combination of the foreign key that identifies the entity being characterized (the "target entity"), together with the attribute that distinguishes different characteristics within that target entity—*if* (once again) the database designer has no objection to composite primary keys.

- Alternatively, we might introduce a new, noncomposite attribute (a surrogate).

For the sake of the example again, we will go with the first of the two possibilities, and so add the clause

```
PRIMARY KEY ( EMP#, DEP_NAME )
```

(where DEP_NAME is the name of the employee's dependent) to the CREATE BASE RELATION statement for relation DEPENDENT.

Properties

A property is just a piece of information that describes an entity in some way—for example, the budget for a department, or the salary for an employee, or the birthday of a dependent, or the quantity of a shipment. A domain is identified for each property, and attributes representing those properties are assigned to the relations for the entities they most immediately describe, in accordance with the well-known principles of further normalization. Data definitions are written for all such domains and attributes. We omit the details here; see reference [10] for further discussion.

Supertypes and Subtypes

Since Fig. 1 does not involve any supertypes and subtypes, we now switch to the example of Fig. 5. Each entity type in that figure will map into a base relation of its own; each such relation will contain attributes corresponding to the properties that apply at the relevant position within the type hierarchy (and hence to all subordinate positions, by inheritance, but not to any superior positions). Let us concentrate on the relations, EMP and PGMR say, corresponding to the entity types EMPLOYEE and PROGRAMMER:

```
CREATE BASE RELATION EMP
     ( EMP#    ... , DEPT# ... , SALARY ... , ... )
       PRIMARY KEY ( EMP# ) ;

CREATE BASE RELATION PGMR
     ( EMP#    ... , LANG   ... , ... )
       PRIMARY KEY ( EMP# )
       FOREIGN KEY ( EMP# ) REFERENCES EMP ... ;
```

Here the attribute LANG represents the property "primary programming language," which applies only to those employees that happen to be programmers. Observe that relations EMP and PGMR both have the same primary key (EMP#), and furthermore that the primary key for the subtype (PGMR) also serves as foreign key, referring back to the primary key of the supertype (EMP). Deciding an appropriate set of foreign key rules for that foreign key is left as an exercise for the reader. Consideration of the other entity types in Fig. 5 (APPLICATION_PROGRAMMER and SYSTEM_PROGRAMMER) is left as an exercise also.

4. COMPARISON WITH THE E/R MODEL

The E/R and RM/T models represent competing approaches to the problem of semantic modeling in general and the problem of database design in particular. Now, the reader will probably have realized that we prefer the RM/T approach, and might be wondering why—especially since (a) the E/R approach is far more widely used in practice, and in any case (b) the two approaches might not seem all that different, at least to the extent that we have described them. But in fact there are some significant differences, as we now explain. *Note:* The following discussion is elaborated in reference [7].

The E/R Model as a Foundation for the Relational Model?

We begin by considering the E/R approach from a slightly different perspective. It is probably obvious to the reader that the ideas of the E/R approach, or something very close to those ideas, must have been the informal underpinnings in Codd's mind when he originally developed the formal relational model. As explained in reference [6], the overall approach to semantic modeling involves four broad steps, which we can summarize as follows:

1. Identify useful semantic concepts
2. Devise formal objects
3. Devise formal integrity rules
4. Devise formal operators

Observe that these four steps are also applicable to the design of the *basic* relational model (and indeed to any formal data model), not just to extended models such as RM/T. In other words, in order for Codd to have constructed the (formal) basic relational model in the first place, he must have had some (informal) "useful semantic concepts" in his mind, and those concepts must basically have been those of the E/R model, or something very like them. Indeed, Codd's own writings support this contention. In his very first paper on the relational model [4], we find the following:

> *"The set of entities of a given entity type can be viewed as a relation, and we shall call such a relation an* entity type relation . . . *The remaining relations . . . are between entity types and are . . . called* inter-entity relations . . . *An essential property of every inter-entity relation is that [it includes at least two foreign keys that] either refer to distinct entity types or refer to a common entity type serving distinct roles."*

Here Codd is clearly proposing that relations be used to model both "entities" and "relationships." But—and it is a very big but—the point is that *relations are formal objects, and the relational model is a formal system.* The essence of Codd's contribution was that he found a good *formal* model of certain aspects of the real world.

In contrast to the foregoing, the entity/relationship model is *not* (or, at least, not primarily) a formal model. Instead, it consists primarily of a set of *in*formal concepts, corresponding to Step 1 (only) of the four steps mentioned above. (Furthermore, what formal aspects it does possess do not seem to be significantly different from the corresponding aspects of the basic relational model—see the further discussion of this point in the next subsection below.) And while it is unquestionably useful to have an armory of "Step 1" concepts at one's disposal for database design (and other) purposes, the fact remains that database designs cannot be completed without the formal objects and rules of Steps 2 and 3, and numerous other tasks cannot be performed at all without the formal operators of Step 4.

Please note that the foregoing remarks are not intended to suggest that the E/R model is not useful. It is. But it is not the whole story. Moreover, it is a little strange to realize that the first published description of the *in*formal E/R model appeared several years after the first published description of the *formal* relational model, given that (as we have seen) the latter was originally founded on some rather E/R-like ideas.

Is the E/R Model a Data Model?

In the light of the discussions above, it is not even clear that the E/R "model" is truly a data model at all, at least in the sense in which the relational model is a data model (i.e., a formal system involving structural, integrity, and manipulative aspects). Certainly the term "E/R modeling" is usually taken to mean, primarily, the process of deciding the *structure* of the database (although it does include consideration of certain integrity aspects also). However, a charitable reading of Chen's original paper would suggest that the E/R model *is* a data model, but one that is essentially just *a thin layer on top of the basic relational model* (it is certainly not a candidate for replacing the relational model, as some people seem to think). We justify this claim as follows.

- First, the fundamental E/R data object—that is, the fundamental *formal* object, as opposed to the informal objects "entity," "relationship," etc.—is the *n*-ary relation.

- The E/R operators are basically the operators of the relational algebra. (Actually, reference [2] is not very clear on this point, but it seems to propose a set of operators that are strictly less powerful than those of the relational algebra; for example, there is apparently no union and no explicit join.)

- It is in the area of integrity that the two approaches differ from each other somewhat: The E/R model includes a set of *builtin* integrity rules, corresponding to some—but not all—of the foreign key rules discussed in reference [6]. Thus, where a "pure" relational system would require the user to formulate certain foreign key rules explicitly, an E/R system would require only that the user state that a given relation represents a certain kind of relationship, and certain foreign key rules would then be implicitly understood.

Entities *vs.* Relationships

We have suggested several times already that "relationships" are best regarded merely as a special kind of entity. In contrast, it is a *sine qua non* of the E/R approach that the two concepts be distinguished somehow. In this writer's opinion, any approach that insists on making such a distinction is seriously flawed, because *the very same object* can quite legitimately be regarded as an entity by some users and a relationship by others. Consider the case of a marriage, for example:

- From one perspective, a marriage is clearly a relationship between two people (sample query: "Who was Elizabeth Taylor married to in 1975?");

- From another perspective, a marriage is equally clearly an entity in its own right (sample query: "How many marriages have been performed in this church since April?").

If the design methodology insists on the "entity *vs.* relationship" distinction, then (at best) the two interpretations will be treated asymmetrically (i.e., "entity" queries and "relationship" queries will take quite different forms); at worst, one interpretation will not be supported at all (i.e., one class of query will be impossible to formulate).

As a further illustration of the point, consider the following statement from a tutorial on the E/R approach in reference [13]:

> *"It is common* initially *to represent some relationships as attributes [meaning, specifically, foreign keys] during conceptual schema design and then to convert these attributes into relationships as the design progresses and is better understood."*

But what happens if an attribute *becomes* a foreign key at some later time?—i.e., if the database evolves after it has already been in existence for some period of time? If we take this argument to its logical conclusion, database designs should involve only relationships, no attributes at all!

RM/T Is a Formal Model

In sharp contrast to all of the above, RM/T *is* a formal model. It is true that it has an informal set of underpinnings—the entity and property notions, the classification of entities into kernels and characteristics and associations, the type hierarchy concept, and so forth. However, it is also true that it has a formal set of objects (E- and P-relations, plus others not discussed in this paper), a formal set of integrity rules (see Section 2), and a formal set of operators (not discussed in any detail in this chapter). In other words, like the basic relational model (of which it is an extension), it addresses Steps 2–4 of the "overall approach to semantic modeling," not just Step 1. In particular, the fact that it provides a formal set of objects and integrity rules means that the RM/T-based design methodology sketched in Section 3, which is based on those formal concepts, is more precise, more systematic, and less arbitrary than the E/R methodology described earlier in this paper. This in a nutshell is our reason for preferring it.

In connection with the foregoing, the point is worth repeating that Chen's original paper [2] actually contained two distinct, and more or less independent, proposals: It proposed the E/R model *per se,* and it also proposed **the E/R diagramming technique**. The popularity of the E/R model can probably be attributed more to the existence of that diagramming technique than to any other cause. But the point is, it is not necessary to adopt all of the ideas of the *model* in order to use the *diagrams;* it is quite possible to use the diagrams as a basis for *any* design methodology—an RM/T-based methodology, for example, as we saw in Section 3. Arguments regarding the relative suitability of the E/R and other models as a basis for database design often seem to miss this point.

5. SUMMARY

In this paper we have examined the extended version of the relational model known as **RM/T**. Like the original model, RM/T includes **objects, integrity rules,** and **operators** (though it is only fair to point out that the operators portion requires more work and is best regarded as preliminary at this time). As an informal basis for its formal constructs, RM/T makes use of an **entity classification scheme,** which divides entities into **kernels, characteristics,** and **associations:**

- *Kernel* entities are "what the database is really all about"; they have independent existence.

- *Characteristic* entities "characterize" or describe other entities (and are existence-dependent on those other entities). Those other entities can be kernel or associative or characteristic in turn.

- *Associative* entities are many-to-many (or many-to-many-to-many, etc.) relationships among other entities. Those other entities can be kernels or characteristics or associations or any combination.

Further, any entity can have **properties,** and any entity can **designate** another entity (and that other entity can be kernel or characteristic or associative).

We illustrated all of the foregoing ideas by showing what the suppliers-and-parts database might look like in RM/T. We also briefly described RM/T's approach to **subtypes** and **supertypes**.

Next, we showed how the ideas of RM/T could serve as the basis for a database design methodology, and we offered some comparisons between RM/T and the entity/relationship model.

There is one final point that is worth calling out explicitly. Despite the unfortunate fact that the whole field of semantic modeling is still somewhat subjective, there is one specific area in which ideas from that field can be very relevant and useful today—namely, the *data dictionary* area. The data dictionary can be regarded in some respects as "the database designer's database"; it is after all a database in which the database designer records his or her design decisions [1]. The study of semantic modeling can thus be extremely useful in the design of the dictionary system, because it identifies the kinds of object the dictionary itself needs to support and "understand"—for example, entity classes (such as RM/T's kernels, characteristics, and associations), integrity rules (such as the rules of RM/T), entity supertypes and subtypes, and so forth.

EXERCISES

1. Define the following RM/T terms:

kernel
characteristic
association
designation
surrogate
E-relation
P-relation

2. Give examples of:

   a. an association in which one of the participants is a characteristic;
   b. an association in which one of the participants is another association;
   c. an association that designates another entity;
   d. an association that has a subtype;
   e. a subtype that has a characteristic that does not apply to the supertype.

3. Sketch an RM/T version of any database with which you might be familiar.

4. Use the concepts and constructs of RM/T to design a dictionary structure for any DBMS with which you might be familiar. If possible, perform this exercise first for a relational DBMS, and then for a nonrelational one. To what extent can your two solutions be integrated?—in other words, is it possible to define a "generic" dictionary structure that can handle both DBMSs?

REFERENCES AND BIBLIOGRAPHY

1. Frank W. Allen, Mary E. S. Loomis, and Michael V. Mannino, "The Integrated Dictionary-Directory System," *ACM Comp. Surv. 14,* No. 2 (June 1982).

A tutorial on the data dictionary, with a brief survey of available products as of 1982.

2. Peter Pin-Shan Chen, "The Entity-Relationship Model—Toward a Unified View of Data," *ACM TODS 1,* No. 1 (March 1976). Republished in M. Stonebraker (ed.), *Readings in Database Systems* (San Mateo, Calif.: Morgan Kaufmann, 1988).

3. E. F. Codd, "Extending the Database Relational Model to Capture More Meaning," *ACM TODS 4,* No. 4 (December 1979).

In addition to the aspects of RM/T discussed briefly in the body of this chapter, this paper includes proposals for including time considerations and various kinds of data aggregation (see references [15–16]) in the overall activity of semantic modeling.

4. E. F. Codd, "Derivability, Redundancy, and Consistency of Relations Stored in Large Data Banks," IBM Research Report RJ599 (August 19th, 1969).

5. C. J. Date, "The Primacy of Primary Keys: An Investigation" (in this volume).

6. C. J. Date, *An Introduction to Database Systems* (6th edition) (Reading, Mass.: Addison-Wesley, 1995).

7. C. J. Date, "Entity/Relationship Modeling and the Relational Model," in C. J. Date and Hugh Darwen, *Relational Database Writings 1989–1991* (Reading, Mass.: Addison-Wesley, 1992).

Elaborates on the discussions of Section 4.

8. C. J. Date, "A Note on One-to-One Relationships," in *Relational Database Writings 1985–1989* (Reading, Mass.: Addison-Wesley, 1990).

An extensive discussion of the problem of one-to-one relationships, which turn out to be rather more complicated than they might appear at first sight.

9. C. J. Date, "Referential Integrity and Foreign Keys. Part I: Basic Concepts; Part II: Further Considerations," in *Relational Database Writings 1985–1989* (Reading, Mass: Addison-Wesley, 1990).

10. C. J. Date, "A Practical Approach to Database Design," in *Relational Database: Selected Writings* (Reading, Mass.: Addison-Wesley, 1986).

In addition to explaining the design methodology sketched in Section 3 of this chapter in a little more depth, this paper also offers a brief discussion of a set of miscellaneous design issues: vectors, codes and flags, field overloading, etc.

11. C. J. Date, "Referential Integrity," Proc. 7th International Conference on Very Large Data Bases, Cannes, France (September 1981). Republished in revised form in *Relational Database: Selected Writings* (Reading, Mass: Addison-Wesley, 1986).

12. C. J. Date, "The Extended Relational Model RM/T," Chapter 6 of *An Introduction to Database Systems: Volume II* (Reading, Mass.: Addison-Wesley, 1983).

13. Ramez Elmasri and Shamkant B. Navathe, *Fundamentals of Database Systems* (Redwood City, Calif.: Benjamin/Cummings, 1989).

14. P. Hall, J. Owlett, and S. J. P. Todd, "Relations and Entities," in J. W. Klimbie and K. L. Koffeman (eds.), *Data Base Management* (New York, N.Y.: North-Holland, 1974).

The paper that first introduced the idea of surrogates (incorporated later into RM/T).

It is perhaps worth emphasizing the point that surrogates are *not* (as some writers seem to think) "tuple IDs." For one thing—to state the obvious—tuple IDs identify tuples and surrogates identify entities, and there is certainly nothing like a one-to-one correspondence between the two. In fact, there is a one-to-one correspondence between entities and tuples *only* in the case of E-relations (in RM/T terms). It follows that tuples in base relations other than E-relations, and tuples in derived relations, have *no* obvious correspondence to surrogates at all.

Furthermore, tuple IDs have performance connotations, while surrogates do not; access to a tuple via its tuple ID is assumed to be fast (we are assuming here that [base relation] tuples map fairly directly to physical storage, as is in fact the case in most of today's relational products). Also, tuple IDs are usually concealed from the user, while surrogates are usually not; in other words, it is not possible to store a tuple ID as an attribute value, while it certainly is possible to store a surrogate as an attribute value.

In a nutshell: Surrogates are a logical concept; tuple IDs are a physical concept.

15. J. M. Smith and D. C. P. Smith, "Database Abstractions: Aggregation," *CACM 20,* No. 6 (June 1977).

16. J. M. Smith and D. C. P. Smith, "Database Abstractions: Aggregation and Generalization," *ACM TODS 2,* No. 2 (June 1977).

The proposals of these two papers [15] and [16] had a significant influence on RM/T, especially in the area of subtypes and supertypes.

The Third Manifesto

All logical differences are big differences

—Wittgenstein (attrib.)

ABSTRACT

We present a manifesto for the future direction of data and database management systems. The manifesto consists of a series of prescriptions, proscriptions, and "very strong suggestions."

COMMENTS ON REPUBLICATION

The paper that follows was written jointly by Hugh Darwen and myself in 1994. However, we had been discussing the subject matter for several years before we got around to setting our ideas down on paper. And our motive for writing those ideas down is, I think, pretty much self-explanatory: Both of us were (and are) very much concerned over the direction in which the field of database manage-

The version of the paper published here is a late draft (the original is dated September 9th, 1994). Reprinted by permission of Hugh Darwen. *Author's addresses:* Hugh Darwen, darwen@vnet.ibm.com (e-mail), Warwick Software Development Laboratory, IBM United Kingdom Ltd., PO Box 31, Warwick CV34 5JL, England, phone (44) 926-464398 (voice), (44) 926-410764 (fax); C. J. Date, PO Box 1000, Healdsburg, CA 95448, USA, phone (1) 707/433-6523 (voice), (1) 707/433-7322 (fax). Readers are invited to write indicating briefly whether they support or oppose the ideas expressed herein.

ment seems to be headed, and both of us felt that something had to be done to try and stem the tide of irrationality that seems to be rising on all sides. Database management is, after all, a field that does enjoy a solid and respectable scientific foundation; it would be a great pity—and a great mistake—to abandon that foundation now in the pursuit of false idols.

One small point of an editorial nature: As the reader will quickly discover, the paper consists in large part of a series of prescriptions and proscriptions. In some cases, whether a particular point is treated as a prescription or a proscription is a trifle arbitrary. For example, the proscription that there be no tuple-at-a-time operations could equally well have been stated as a prescription that all operations be set-at-a-time. I hope this slight degree of arbitrariness will not detract from the paper's overall message and comprehensibility.

Finally, it goes without saying that I am grateful to Hugh Darwen for agreeing to let me republish the paper in this book.

1. INTRODUCTION

This is a manifesto regarding the future of data and database management systems. It is intended to follow and, we hope, supersede two previous manifestos [1,34]—hence our choice of title. Reference [1], in spurning the Relational Model of Data, ignores its importance and significance and also, we think, fails to give firm direction. Reference [34], while correctly espousing the Relational Model, fails to mention and emphasize the hopelessness of continuing to follow a commonly accepted perversion of that model, namely SQL, in fond pursuit of the Relational Model's ideals. By contrast, we feel strongly that any attempt to move forward, if it is to stand the test of time, must *reject SQL unequivocally*. However, we do pay some attention to the question of what to do about today's SQL legacy.

2. BACK TO THE FUTURE

We seek a firm foundation for the future of data. We do not believe that the database language SQL is capable of providing such a foundation. Instead, we believe that any such foundation must be firmly rooted in the **Relational Model of Data,** first presented to the world in 1969 by E. F. Codd in reference [6].

We fully acknowledge the desirability of supporting certain features that have been much discussed in more recent times, including some that are commonly regarded as aspects of **Object Orientation**. We believe that these features are orthogonal to the Relational Model, and therefore that the Relational Model needs no extension, no correction, no subsumption, and, above all, no perversion, in order for them to be accommodated in some database language that could represent the foundation we seek.

Let there be such a language, and let its name be **D.***

D shall be subject to certain prescriptions and certain proscriptions. Some prescriptions arise from the Relational Model of Data, and we shall call these **Relational Model Prescriptions,** abbreviated to **RM Prescriptions.** Prescriptions that do not arise from the Relational Model we shall call **Other Orthogonal Prescriptions,** abbreviated to **OO Prescriptions.** We similarly categorize D's proscriptions.

We now proceed to itemize D's prescriptions and proscriptions. The RM Prescriptions and Proscriptions are not negotiable.[†] Unfortunately, the same cannot quite be said of the OO Prescriptions and Proscriptions, as there is not, at the time of writing, a clear and commonly agreed model for them to be based on. We do believe that OO has significant contributions to make in the areas of **user-defined data types** and **inheritance,** but there is still no consensus on an abstract model, even with respect to these important topics; thus, we have been forced to provide our own definitions in these areas. And it is only fair to warn the reader that inheritance, at least, raises a number of questions that still do not seem to have been satisfactorily answered in the open literature. As a result, our proposals in this area must necessarily be somewhat tentative at this time (see OO Prescriptions 2 and 3 and Appendix A).

As well as prescriptions and proscriptions, this manifesto includes some **Very Strong Suggestions,** also subdivided into RM and OO categories.

Two final preliminary remarks:

1. The version of the Relational Model that we espouse is, very specifically, that version first described in reference [21] and further refined (slightly) in reference [18]. Note, however, that the definitions given herein for *tuple* and *relation* represent a small improvement over the definitions given in those earlier publications.

2. In what follows, we deliberately do not go into a lot of detail on the various prescriptions, proscriptions, and suggestions. (We do sometimes offer a few explanatory comments on certain points, but all such commentary could be deleted without affecting the technical substance of our proposal.) It is our intention to follow this manifesto with a series of more specific papers describing various aspects of our proposal in more depth.

---

*No special significance attaches to this choice of name; we use it merely to refer generically to any language that conforms to the principles laid down in subsequent sections.

[†]Some might feel this statement to be excessively dogmatic. What we mean is that prescriptions and proscriptions that arise from the Relational Model are only as negotiable as the features of the Relational Model themselves are.

3. RM PRESCRIPTIONS

1. A **domain** is a named set of values. Such values, which shall be of arbitrary complexity, shall be manipulable *solely* by means of the operators defined for the domain(s) in question (see RM Prescription 3 and OO Proscription 3)— i.e., domain values shall be **encapsulated**. For each domain, a notation shall be available for the explicit specification (or "construction") of an arbitrary value from that domain.

    Comments:

    -   We treat the terms *domain* and *data type* (*type* for short) as synonymous and interchangeable. The term *object class* is also sometimes used with the same meaning, but we do not use this latter term.

    -   We refer to domain values generically as *scalar values* (*scalars* for short). Note, therefore, that we explicitly permit "scalar" values to be arbitrarily complex; thus, e.g., an array of stacks of lists of . . . (etc.) might be regarded as a scalar value in suitable circumstances.

2. Scalar values shall always appear (at least conceptually) with some accompanying identification of the domain to which the value in question belongs. In other words, scalar values shall be **typed**.

3. For each ordered list of n domains, not necessarily distinct ($n \geq 0$), D shall support the definition of the valid n-adic **operators** that apply to corresponding ordered lists of n values, one from each of those n domains. Every such operator definition shall include a specification of the domain of the **result** of that operator. Such operator definitions shall be logically distinct from the definitions of the domains to which they refer (instead of being "bundled in" with those definitions).

    Comments:

    -   We treat the terms *operator* and *function* as synonymous and interchangeable. The term *method* is also sometimes used with the same meaning, but we do not use this latter term.

    -   A function that directly or indirectly assigns to one of its arguments is known as a **mutator,** or simply as a function with side-effects. Such functions are generally deprecated, but they cannot be prohibited and they may be needed in connection with inheritance (see Appendix A). It is our intention that a warning be issued if the argument thus assigned to is in fact a system-created dummy.

4. Let V be a domain. The operators defined for V must necessarily include operators that expose the **actual representation** of values from V. Nothing in the syntax of such operators (other than their name) shall distinguish them from other operators that apply to values from V.

Comments:

- It is our intention (a) that operators that expose the actual representation be used only in the implementation of other operators, and (b) that this effect be achieved by means of the system's authorization mechanism. In other words, the actual representation of domain values should be hidden from most users.

- Let *V* be a domain. We remark that it will often be desirable to define a set of operators whose effect is to expose *one possible representation* (not necessarily the actual representation) for values from *V;* given such operators, the user will effectively be able to operate on values from *V* just as if the actual representation were exposed.

- Although the actual representation of domain values is not relevant to the specifications of this manifesto, it might be helpful to point out that if *v1* and *v2* are distinct values from domain *V,* nothing in the D language requires the actual representations of *v1* and *v2* to be the same.

5. D shall come equipped with certain builtin domains, including in particular the domain of **truth values** (*true* and *false*). The usual operators (NOT, AND, OR, IF . . . THEN . . . , IFF, etc.) shall be supported for this domain.

6. Let *H* be some tuple heading (see RM Prescription 9). Then it shall be possible to define a domain whose values are tuples with heading *H*—in other words, **TUPLE** shall be a valid type constructor. The operators defined for such a domain shall be, precisely, the set of tuple operators supported by D. Those operators shall include one for constructing a tuple from specified scalars and another for extracting specified scalars from a tuple. They shall also include tuple "nest" and "unnest" capabilities analogous to those described for relations in reference [10].

7. Let *H* be some relation heading (see RM Prescription 10). Then it shall be possible to define a domain whose values are relations with heading *H*—in other words, **RELATION** shall be a valid type constructor. The operators defined for such a domain shall be, precisely, the set of relational operators supported by D. Those operators shall include one for constructing a relation from specified tuples and another for extracting specified tuples from a relation. They shall also include relational "nest" and "unnest" capabilities along the lines described in reference [10].

Comment: Note that from the perspective of any relation that includes an attribute defined on such a domain, the "scalar" values in that domain are still (like all domain values) encapsulated. We explicitly do not espouse NF^2 ("NF squared") relations as described in, e.g., reference [33], which involve major extensions to the classical Relational Algebra.

8. The **equals** comparison operator ("=") shall be defined for every domain. Let

v1 and *v2* each denote some value from some domain, *V*. Then *v1* = *v2* is *true* if and only if *v1* and *v2* are the same member of *V*.

9. A **tuple,** *t*, is a set of ordered triples of the form *<A,V,v>*, where:

   - *A* is the name of an **attribute** of *t*. No two distinct triples in *t* shall have the same attribute name.
   - *V* is the name of the (unique) **domain** corresponding to attribute *A*.
   - *v* is a value from domain *V*, called the **attribute value** for attribute *A* within tuple *t*.

   The set of ordered pairs *<A,V>* that is obtained by eliminating the *v* (value) component from each triple in *t* is the **heading** of *t*. Given a tuple heading, a notation shall be available for the explicit specification (or "construction") of an arbitrary tuple with that heading.

10. A **relation,** *R*, consists of a *heading* and a *body*. The **heading** of *R* is a tuple heading *H* as defined in RM Prescription 9. The **body** of *R* is a set *B* of tuples, all having that same heading *H*. The attributes and corresponding domains identified in *H* are the **attributes** and corresponding **domains** of *R*. Given a relation heading, a notation shall be available for the explicit specification (or "construction") of an arbitrary relation with that heading.

    Comments:

    - Note that each tuple in *R* contains exactly one value *v* for each attribute *A* in *H;* in other words, *R* is in *First Normal Form,* 1NF.
    - We draw a sharp distinction between relations *per se* and relation *variables* (see RM Prescription 13). An analogous distinction applies to databases also (see RM Prescription 15). We recognize that these terminological distinctions will, regrettably, be unfamiliar to most readers; we adopt them nevertheless, in the interests of precision.

11. A **scalar variable of type *V*** is a variable whose permitted values are scalars from a specified domain *V*, the **declared domain** for that scalar variable. Creating a scalar variable *S* shall have the effect of initializing *S* to some scalar value—either a value specified explicitly as part of the operation that creates *S*, or some implementation-dependent value if no such explicit value is specified.

12. A **tuple variable of type *H*** is a variable whose permitted values are tuples with a specified tuple heading *H*, the **declared heading** for that tuple variable. Creating a tuple variable *T* shall have the effect of initializing *T* to some tuple value—either a value specified explicitly as part of the operation that creates *T*, or some implementation-dependent value if no such explicit value is specified.

13. A **relation variable**—**relvar** for short—**of type *H*** is a variable whose permitted values are relations with a specified relation heading *H*, the **declared heading** for that relvar.

14. Relvars are either *base* or *derived*. A **derived relvar** is a relvar whose value at any given time is a relation that is defined by means of a specified relational expression (see RM Prescriptions 18–20); the relational expression in question shall be such that the derived relvar is updatable according to the rules and principles described in references [16] and [27–28]. A **base relvar** is a relvar that is not derived. Creating a base relvar shall have the effect of initializing that base relvar to an empty relation.

    Comment: Base and derived relvars correspond to what are known in common parlance as "base relations" and "updatable views," respectively. Note, however, that we consider many more views to be updatable than have traditionally been so considered [27–28].

15. A **database variable—dbvar** for short—is a defined set of relvars. Every dbvar is subject to a set of **integrity constraints** (see RM Prescriptions 23 and 24). The value of a given dbvar at any given time is a set of ordered pairs $<R,r>$ (where R is a relvar name and r is the current value of that relvar), such that (a) there is one such ordered pair for each relvar in the dbvar, and (b) together, those relvar values satisfy the applicable constraints. Such a dbvar value is called a **database** (sometimes a *database state,* but we do not use this latter term).

16. Each **transaction** interacts with exactly one dbvar. However, distinct transactions can interact with distinct dbvars, and distinct dbvars are not necessarily disjoint. Also, a transaction can dynamically change its associated dbvar by adding and/or removing relvars (see RM Prescription 17).

    Comments:

    - One purpose of the dbvar concept is to define a scope for relational operations. That is, all relvars mentioned in any given relational expression (see RM Prescriptions 18–20) shall be contained within the same dbvar.
    - The set of all base relvars might be regarded as the "base" dbvar. Individual transactions, however, interact with a "derived" or "user" dbvar that consists (in general) of a mixture of base and derived relvars.
    - The mechanism for making and breaking the connection between a transaction and its unique corresponding dbvar is not specified in this manifesto.

17. D shall provide operators to **create** and **destroy** domains, variables (including in particular relvars), and integrity constraints. Every explicitly created domain, variable, or integrity constraint shall be named. Every base relvar shall have at least one **candidate key,** specified explicitly as part of the operation that creates that base relvar.

    Comment: The creation and destruction of dbvars (which we assume to be "persistent") is performed outside the D environment.

18. The **Relational Algebra** as defined in reference [18] shall be expressible without excessive circumlocution.

Comment: "Without excessive circumlocution" implies among other things that:

- Universal and existential quantification shall be equally easy to express. For example, if D includes a specific operator for relational **projection,** then it should also include a specific operator for the general form of relational **division** described (as DIVIDEBY PER) in reference [9].

- Projection over specified attributes and projection over all but specified attributes shall be equally easy to express.

19. Relvar names and explicit ("constructed") relation values shall both be legal relational expressions.

20. D shall provide operators to create and destroy named **functions** whose value at any given time is a relation that is defined by means of a specified relational expression. Invocations of such functions shall be permitted within relational expressions wherever explicit relation values are permitted.

    Comment: Such functions correspond to what are known in common parlance as "read-only views," except that we permit the relational expressions defining such "views" to be parameterized. Such parameters represent scalar values and are permitted within the defining relational expression wherever explicit scalar values are permitted. (It might be possible to support tuple and relation parameters also. See RM Very Strong Suggestion 7.)

21. D shall permit:

    a. (the value of) a tuple expression to be **assigned** to a tuple variable, and

    b. (the value of) a relational expression to be **assigned** to a relvar,

    provided in both cases that the requirements of *type compatibility* as described in reference [15] are satisfied.

    Comment: Of course, this prescription does not prohibit the additional provision of convenient shorthands such as INSERT, UPDATE, and DELETE as described in reference [18].

22. D shall support certain **comparison operators.** The operators defined for comparing tuples shall be "=" and "≠" (only); the operators defined for comparing relations shall include "=", "≠", "is a subset of" (etc.); the operator "∈" for testing membership of a tuple in a relation shall be supported. In all cases, the requirements of *type compatibility* as described in reference [15] shall be satisfied.

23. Any expression that evaluates to a truth value is called a **conditional expression**. Any conditional expression that is (or is logically equivalent to) a closed WFF of the Relational Calculus [18] shall be permitted as the specification of an **integrity constraint**. Integrity constraints shall be classified according to the scheme described in references [17] and [27–28] into **domain, attribute, relation,** and **database** constraints, and D shall support constraint inheritance as required by that scheme.

24. Every relvar has a corresponding **relation predicate** and every dbvar has a corresponding **database predicate,** as explained in references [17] and [27–28]. Relation predicates shall be satisfied at statement boundaries. Database predicates shall be satisfied at transaction boundaries.

    Comments:

    - These concepts, which we believe to be both crucial and fundamental, have unfortunately been very much overlooked in the past, and we therefore amplify them slightly here. Basically, a relation predicate is the logical AND of all integrity constraints that apply to the relvar in question, and a database predicate is the logical AND of all integrity constraints that apply to the dbvar in question. The point cannot be emphasized too strongly that it is *predicates,* not *names,* that represent data semantics.

    - To say that relation predicates shall be satisfied at statement boundaries is to say, precisely, that no relational assignment shall leave any relvar in a state in which its relation predicate is violated. To say that database predicates shall be satisfied at transaction boundaries is to say, precisely, that no transaction shall leave the corresponding dbvar in a state in which its database predicate is violated.

    - This prescription further implies that it shall not be possible to update an "updatable view" (i.e., derived relvar) in such a way as to violate the definition of that view. In other words, "updatable views" shall always be subject to what SQL calls CASCADED CHECK OPTION [26].

25. Every dbvar shall include a set of relvars that constitute the **catalog** for that dbvar. It shall be possible to assign to relvars in the catalog.

    Comment: This prescription implies that the catalog must be what is commonly known as "self-describing."

26. D shall be constructed according to well-established principles of good language design as documented in, e.g., reference [3].

    Comment: Arbitrary restrictions such as those documented in references [23–24] and [26], and all other *ad hoc* concepts and constructs, shall thus be absolutely prohibited.

4. RM PROSCRIPTIONS

The observant reader will note that many of the proscriptions in this section are logical consequences of the RM Prescriptions. In view of the unfortunate mistakes that have been made in SQL, however, we feel it is necessary to write down some of these consequences by way of clarification.

1. D shall include no construct that depends on the definition of some ordering

for the attributes of a relation. Instead, for every relation *R* expressible in D, the attributes of *R* shall be distinguishable by *name*.

Comment: This proscription implies no more anonymous columns, as in SQL's SELECT X + Y FROM T, and no more duplicate column names, as in SQL's SELECT X, X FROM T and SELECT T1.X, T2.X FROM T1, T2.

2. D shall include no construct that depends on the definition of some ordering for the tuples of a relation.

Comment: This proscription does not imply that such an ordering cannot be imposed for, e.g., presentation purposes; rather, it implies that the effect of imposing such ordering is to convert the relation into something that is not a relation (perhaps a sequence or ordered list).

3. For every relation *R,* if *t1* and *t2* are distinct tuples in *R,* then there must exist an attribute *A* of *R* such that the attribute value for *A* in *t1* is not equal to the attribute value for *A* in *t2.*

Comment: In other words, "duplicate rows" are absolutely, categorically, and unequivocally outlawed. What we tell you three times is true.

4. Every attribute of every tuple of every relation shall have a value that is from the applicable domain.

Comment: In other words—no more "nulls," and no more many-valued logic!

5. D shall not forget that relations with zero attributes are respectable and interesting, nor that candidate keys with zero components are likewise respectable and interesting.

6. D shall include no constructs that relate to, or are logically affected by, the "physical" or "storage" or "internal" levels of the system (other than the functions that expose the actual representation of domain values—see RM Prescription 4). If an implementer wants or needs to introduce any kind of "storage structure definition language," the statements of that language, and the mappings of dbvars to physical storage, shall be cleanly separable from everything expressed in D.

7. There shall be no tuple-at-a-time operations on relations.

Comments:

- INSERT, UPDATE, and DELETE statements, if provided, insert or update or delete (as applicable) a *set* of tuples, always; a set containing a single tuple is just a special case (though it might prove convenient to offer a syntactic shorthand for that case).

- Tuple-at-a-time retrieval (analogous to SQL's FETCH via a cursor)—though prohibited, and generally deprecated to boot—can effectively be performed, if desired, by converting the relation to an ordered list of tuples and iterating over that list.

- Tuple-at-a-time update (analogous to SQL's UPDATE and DELETE via a cursor) is categorically prohibited.

8. D shall not include any specific support for "composite domains" or "composite columns" (as proposed in, e.g., reference [4]), since such functionality can be achieved if desired through the domain support already prescribed. See reference [11].

9. "Domain check override" operators as documented in reference [4] are *ad hoc* and unnecessary and shall not be supported.

10. D shall not be called SQL.

5. OO PRESCRIPTIONS

1. D shall permit **compile-time type checking**.

   Comment: By this prescription, we mean that—insofar as feasible—it shall be possible to check at compilation time that no type error can occur at run time. This requirement does not preclude the possibility of "compile and go" or interpretive implementations.

2. **(Single inheritance)** If D permits some domain *V'* to be defined as a **subdomain** of some **superdomain** *V*, then such a capability shall be in accordance with some clearly defined and generally agreed model.

   Comments:

   - It is our hope that such a "clearly defined and generally agreed" inheritance model will someday be found. The term "generally agreed" is intended to imply that the authors of this manifesto, among others, shall be in support of the model in question. Such support shall not be unreasonably withheld.

   - We note that support for inheritance implies certain extensions to the definitions of *scalar variable, tuple variable, relation,* and *relvar.* It also seems to imply that OO Prescription 1 might need to be relaxed slightly. See Appendix A, which gives an outline of a possible model for inheritance that incorporates these points.

3. **(Multiple inheritance)** If D permits some domain *V'* to be defined as a subdomain of some superdomain *V*, then *V'* shall not be prevented from additionally being defined as a subdomain of some other domain *W* that is neither *V* nor any superdomain of *V* (unless the requirements of OO Prescription 2 preclude such a possibility).

4. D shall be **computationally complete**. That is, D may support, but shall not require, invocation from so-called "host programs" written in languages other than D. Similarly, D may support, but shall not require, the use of other programming languages for implementation of (user-defined) operators.

   Comment: We do not intend this prescription to undermine such matters as

D's optimizability unduly. Nor do we intend it to be a recipe for the use of procedural constructs such as loops to perform database queries or integrity checks. Rather, the point is that computational completeness will be needed (in general) for the implementation of user-defined functions. To be able to implement such functions in D itself might well be more convenient than having to make excursions into some other language—excursions that in any case are likely to cause severe problems for optimizers. Of course, we agree that it might prove desirable to prohibit the use of certain D features outside the code that implements such functions; on the other hand, such a prohibition might too severely restrict what can be done by a "free-standing" application program (i.e., one that does not require invocation from some program written in some other language). More study is needed.

5. Transaction initiation shall be performed only by means of an explicit **"start transaction"** operator. Transaction termination shall be performed only by means of a **"commit"** or **"rollback"** operator; "commit" must be explicit, but "rollback" can be implicit (if the transaction fails through no fault of its own).

    Comment: If transaction *T* terminates via commit ("normal termination"), changes made by *T* to the applicable dbvar are committed. If transaction *T* terminates via rollback ("abnormal termination"), changes made by *T* to the applicable dbvar are rolled back.

6. D shall support **nested transactions**—i.e., it shall permit a transaction *T1* to start another transaction *T2* before *T1* itself has finished execution, in which case:

    a. *T2* and *T1* shall interact with the same dbvar (as is in fact required by RM Prescription 16).

    b. D shall not preclude the possibility that *T1* and *T2* be able to execute asynchronously. However, *T1* shall not be able to complete before *T2* completes (in other words, *T2* shall be wholly contained within *T1*).

    c. Rollback of *T1* shall include the undoing of *T2* even if *T2* was committed.

7. Let *A* be an **aggregate** operator (such as SUM) that is essentially just shorthand for some iterated dyadic operator θ (the dyadic operator is "+" in the case of SUM). If the argument to *A* happens to be empty, then:

    a. if an identity value exists for θ (the identity value is 0 in the case of "+"), then the result of that invocation of *A* shall be that identity value;

    b. otherwise, the result of that invocation of *A* shall be undefined.

6. OO PROSCRIPTIONS

1. Relvars are not domains.

    Comment: In other words, we categorically reject the equation "relation =

object class" (more accurately, the equation "relvar = object class") espoused in, e.g., reference [32].

2. If attribute *A* of relation *R* is defined on domain *V,* then attribute *A* of relation *R* shall contain values of domain *V* and not pointers to such values.

   Comments:

   - In other words, we reject the idea that relations might contain *"object IDs"* instead of values. More generally, in fact, we reject the idea that scalar variables of any kind might contain "object IDs" instead of values, and hence the idea that "objects" might make use of pointers in order to share "subobjects."

   - In fact, we reject the idea that "objects" as seen by the user might have any kind of ID that is somehow distinct from the "object" value. We remark in passing that we also reject the idea that *tuples* as seen by the user might have "tuple IDs" that are somehow distinct from the tuple value (some writers seem to equate tuple IDs and object IDs).

3. Any *"public instance variable"* notation provided for operating on values in domains shall be mere syntactic shorthand for certain special function invocations (and perhaps "pseudovariable references," if such instance variables can appear on the left-hand side of assignment operations). There shall not necessarily be any direct correlation between such instance variables and the actual representation of the domain values in question.

4. D shall not include either the concept of *"protected"* (as opposed to private) instance variables or the concept of *"friends"* (see reference [29] for an explanation of these concepts).

   Comment: We believe the problem that such concepts are intended to address is better solved by means of the system's authorization mechanism.

7. RM VERY STRONG SUGGESTIONS

1. It should be possible to specify one or more **candidate keys** for each derived relvar. For each relvar (base or derived) for which candidate keys have been specified, it should be possible to nominate exactly one of those candidate keys as the **primary** key.

   Comment: Every relvar does have one or more candidate keys (of which at least one must be so designated by the user in the case of base relvars, as required by RM Prescription 17). Designation of one particular candidate key as primary is optional, however, for reasons explained in reference [20].

2. D should include support for **system-generated** keys along the lines described in references [7–8].

3. D should include some convenient declarative shorthand for expressing (a) **referential constraints** and (b) **referential actions** such as "cascade delete."

4. It is desirable, but thought not to be completely feasible, for the system to be able to compute the **candidate keys** of every relation R expressible in D, such that:

   a. candidate keys of R are inherited by R' when R is assigned to R', and

   b. candidate keys of R may be included in the information about R that is available to a user of D.

   D should provide such functionality, but without any guarantee that computed keys are not proper supersets of actual keys, or even that some superset (proper or otherwise) is discovered for every actual key. Implementations of D can thus compete with each other in their degree of success at discovering candidate keys.

   Comment: The recommendation that candidate keys should (as far as possible) be deduced for derived relations is partly but not wholly subsumed by RM Prescription 23, which requires a certain level of support for general constraint inheritance.

5. D should provide some convenient (nonprocedural) means of expressing **quota queries** (e.g., "find the three shortest employees"). Such a capability should not be bundled with the mechanism that converts a relation into an ordered list (see RM Proscription 2).

6. D should provide some convenient (nonprocedural) means of expressing the **generalized transitive closure** of a graph relation, including the ability to perform generalized *concatenate* and *aggregate* operations as described in reference [30].

7. D should permit the parameters to relation-valued functions to represent tuples and relations as well as scalars.

   Comment: We make this a suggestion merely, rather than a prescription, because we believe it requires further study at this time.

8. D should provide a mechanism for dealing with "missing information" along the lines of the default value scheme described in reference [22] (but based on domains rather than attributes).

   Comment: The term "default values" is perhaps misleading, inasmuch as it suggests an interpretation that was not intended—namely, that the value in question occurs so frequently that it might as well be the default. Rather, the intent is to use an appropriate "default" value, distinct from all possible genuine values, when no genuine value can be used. For example, if the genuine values of the attribute HOURS_WORKED are positive integers, the default value "?" might be used to mean that (for some reason) no genuine value is known. Note, therefore, that the domain for HOURS_WORKED is *not* the domain of positive integers.

9. **SQL** should be implementable in D—not because this is desirable *per se,* but so that a painless migration route might be available for current SQL users. To this same end, existing SQL databases should be convertible to a form that D programs can operate on without error.

Comment: The foregoing does not imply that D must be a superset of SQL, but rather that it should be possible to write a frontend layer of D code on top of D's true relational functionality that:

a. will accept SQL operations against converted SQL data; and

b. will give the results that SQL would have given if those SQL operations had been executed against the original unconverted SQL data.

We should stress that we believe it possible to construct such an SQL frontend without contravening any of the prescriptions and proscriptions laid down in this manifesto.

8. OO VERY STRONG SUGGESTIONS

1. Some form of **type inheritance** should be supported (in which case, see OO Prescriptions 2 and 3). In keeping with this suggestion, D should not include the concept of *implicit type conversion.*

   Comment: Implicit type conversion would undermine the objective of substitutability (see Appendix A).

2. "Collection" type constructors, such as **LIST, ARRAY,** and **SET,** as commonly found in languages supporting rich type systems, should be supported. (See also RM Prescription 7.)

3. If a collection type constructor, C, other than RELATION, is supported, then a conversion function, say C2R, should be provided for converting values of type C to relations, and an inverse function, say R2C, should also be provided, such that:

   a. $C2R(R2C(r)) = r$ for every relation r expressible in D;

   b. $R2C(C2R(c)) = c$ for every expressible value c of type C.

4. D should be based on the "single-level storage" model as described in, e.g., reference [25]. In other words, it should make no logical difference whether a given piece of data resides in main memory, secondary storage, tertiary storage, etc.

9. CONCLUDING REMARKS

We have presented a manifesto for the future direction of data and database management systems. Now perhaps is the time to confess that we do feel a little uncomfortable with the idea of calling what is, after all, primarily a technical document a "manifesto." According to *Chambers Twentieth Century Dictionary,* a manifesto is a "written declaration of the intentions, opinions, or motives" of some person or group (e.g., a political party). This particular written declaration, by contrast, is—we hope—a matter of science and logic, not mere "intentions, opinions, or motives." Given the historical precedents that led us to write this document, however, our title was effectively chosen for us.

By way of summary, we present an abbreviated mnemonic list of all of the prescriptions, proscriptions, and very strong suggestions discussed in the foregoing sections.

RM Prescriptions

1. Domains
2. Typed scalars
3. Scalar operators
4. Actual representation
5. Truth values
6. Type constructor TUPLE
7. Type constructor RELATION
8. Equality operator
9. Tuples
10. Relations
11. Scalar variables
12. Tuple variables
13. Relation variables (relvars)
14. Base *vs.* derived relvars
15. Database variables (dbvars)
16. Transactions and dbvars
17. Create/destroy operations
18. Relational algebra
19. Relvar names and explicit relation values
20. Relational functions
21. Relation and tuple assignment
22. Comparisons
23. Integrity constraints
24. Relation and database predicates
25. Catalog
26. Language design

RM Proscriptions

1. No attribute ordering
2. No tuple ordering
3. No duplicate tuples

4. No nulls
5. No nullological mistakes
6. No internal-level constructs
7. No tuple-level operations
8. No composite columns
9. No domain check override
10. Not SQL

OO Prescriptions

1. Compile-time type checking
2. Single inheritance (conditional)
3. Multiple inheritance (conditional)
4. Computational completeness
5. Explicit transaction boundaries
6. Nested transactions
7. Aggregates and empty sets

OO Proscriptions

1. Relvars are not domains
2. No object IDs
3. No "public instance variables"
4. No "protected instance variables" or "friends"

RM Very Strong Suggestions

1. Candidate keys for derived relvars
2. System-generated keys
3. Referential integrity
4. Candidate key inheritance
5. Quota queries
6. Transitive closure
7. Tuple and relation parameters
8. Default values
9. SQL migration

OO Very Strong Suggestions

1. Type inheritance
2. Collection type constructors
3. Conversion to/from relations
4. Single-level store

ACKNOWLEDGMENTS

We are grateful to the following friends and colleagues for numerous technical discussions and helpful comments on earlier drafts of this manifesto: Tanj Bennett, Charley Bontempo, Mark Evans, Ron Fagin, Michael Jackson, John Kneiling, Adrian Larner, Albert Maier, Nelson Mattos, David McGoveran, Jim Panttaja, Mary Panttaja, Fabian Pascal, Arthur Ryman, Mike Sykes, Stephen Todd, Rick van der Lans, and Anton Versteeg.

REFERENCES AND BIBLIOGRAPHY

1. Malcolm Atkinson *et al.*, "The Object-Oriented Database System Manifesto," Proc. First International Conference on Deductive and Object-Oriented Databases, Kyoto, Japan, 1989 (New York, N.Y.: Elsevier Science, 1990).

2. David Beech, "Collections of Objects in SQL3," Proc. 19th International Conference on Very Large Data Bases, Dublin, Ireland (August 1993).

See the annotation to reference [14].

3. Jon Bentley, "Little Languages," *CACM 29,* 8 (August 1986).

Illustrates and discusses the following "yardsticks of language design":

orthogonality
generality
parsimony
completeness
similarity
extensibility
openness

4. E. F. Codd, *The Relational Model for Database Management Version 2* (Reading, Mass.: Addison-Wesley, 1990).

Codd spent much of the late 1980s revising and extending his original model (which he now refers to as "the Relational Model Version 1" or RM/V1), and this book is the result. It describes "the Relational Model Version 2" (RM/V2). *Note:* We include this reference primarily so that we can make it clear that the version of the Relational Model espoused in the present manifesto is *not* "RM/V2," nor indeed "RM/V1" as Codd currently defines it. Rather, it is the version described in references [18] and [21].

5. E. F. Codd, "A Relational Model of Data for Large Shared Data Banks," *CACM 13,* 6 (June 1970). Republished in *Milestones of Research—Selected Papers 1958–1982* (CACM 25th Anniversary Issue), *CACM 26,* 1 (January 1983).

The first widely available description of the original Relational Model, by its inventor.

6. E. F. Codd, "Derivability, Redundancy, and Consistency of Relations Stored in Large Data Banks," IBM Research Report RJ599 (August 19th, 1969).

A preliminary version of reference [5].

7. Hugh Darwen, "The Duplicity of Duplicate Rows," in C. J. Date and Hugh Darwen, *Relational Database Writings 1989–1991* (Reading, Mass.: Addison-Wesley, 1992).

8. Hugh Darwen (writing as Andrew Warden), "The Keys of the Kingdom," in C. J. Date, *Relational Database Writings 1985–1989* (Reading, Mass.: Addison-Wesley, 1990).

9. Hugh Darwen and C. J. Date, "Into the Great Divide," in C. J. Date and Hugh Darwen, *Relational Database Writings 1989–1991* (Reading, Mass.: Addison-Wesley, 1992).

10. Hugh Darwen and C. J. Date, "Relation-Valued Attributes; *or,* Will the Real First Normal Form Please Stand Up?", in C. J. Date and Hugh Darwen, *Relational Database Writings 1989–1991* (Reading, Mass.: Addison-Wesley, 1992).

11. C. J. Date, "We Don't Need Composite Columns," *Database Programming & Design 8,* 5 (May 1995, to appear).

12. C. J. Date, "Oh Oh Relational . . . ," *Database Programming & Design 7,* 10 (October 1994).

A less formal presentation—really just a summary and sequence of position statements—of some of the material from reference [14].

13. C. J. Date, *An Introduction to Database Systems* (6th edition) (Reading, Mass.: Addison-Wesley, 1995).

14. C. J. Date, "Toward an OO/Relational Rapprochement," Chapter 25 of reference [13].

Explains in detail why the equation "domain = object class" is right and the equation "relvar = object class" is wrong, and describes the benefits that would accrue from a true rapprochement between relational and OO principles as advocated in the present manifesto. *Note:* References [3] and [32] are examples of papers that advocate the "relvar = object class" equation.

15. C. J. Date, "Domains, Relations, and Data Types," Chapter 19 of reference [13].

Lays the groundwork for understanding why the equation "domain = object class" is right (see reference [14]).

16. C. J. Date, "Views," Chapter 17 of reference [13].

17. C. J. Date, "Integrity," Chapter 16 of reference [13].

18. C. J. Date, "The Relational Model," Part II of reference [13].

19. C. J. Date, "How We Missed the Relational Boat," in this volume.

20. C. J. Date, "The Primacy of Primary Keys: An Investigation," in this volume.

21. C. J. Date, "Notes Toward a Reconstituted Definition of the Relational Model Version 1 (RM/V1)," in C. J. Date and Hugh Darwen, *Relational Database Writings 1989–1991* (Reading, Mass.: Addison-Wesley, 1992).

There are a few discrepancies (mostly minor) between the version of the Relational Model described in this paper and the version described in reference [13]. Where such discrepancies occur, reference [13] should be regarded as superseding.

22. C. J. Date, "The Default Values Approach to Missing Information," in C. J. Date

and Hugh Darwen, *Relational Database Writings 1989–1991* (Reading, Mass.: Addison-Wesley, 1992).

23. C. J. Date, "What's Wrong with SQL?", in C. J. Date, *Relational Database Writings 1985–1989* (Reading, Mass.: Addison-Wesley, 1990).

24. C. J. Date, "A Critique of the SQL Database Language," *ACM SIGMOD Record 14,* 3 (November 1984). Republished in C. J. Date, *Relational Database: Selected Writings* (Reading, Mass.: Addison-Wesley, 1986).

25. C. J. Date, "An Architecture for High-Level Language Database Extensions," Proc. ACM SIGMOD International Conference on Management of Data, Washington, D.C. (June 1976).

26. C. J. Date and Hugh Darwen, *A Guide to the SQL Standard* (3rd edition) (Reading, Mass.: Addison-Wesley, 1993).

This book is a tutorial reference to the current SQL standard ("SQL/92"). It contains numerous examples of violations of good language design principles. In particular, it includes an appendix (Appendix D) that documents "many aspects of the standard that appear to be inadequately defined, or even incorrectly defined, at this time."

27. C. J. Date and David McGoveran, "Updating Joins and Other Views," in this volume.

28. C. J. Date and David McGoveran, "Updating Union, Intersection, and Difference Views," in this volume.

29. Margaret A. Ellis and Bjarne Stroustrup, *The Annotated C++ Reference Manual* (Reading, Mass.: Addison-Wesley, 1990).

30. Nathan Goodman, "Bill of Materials in Relational Database," *InfoDB 5,* 1 (Spring/Summer 1990).

31. P. A. V. Hall, P. Hitchcock, and S. J. P. Todd, "An Algebra of Relations for Machine Computation," Conference Record of the 2nd ACM Symposium on Principles of Programming Languages, Palo Alto, Calif. (January 1975).

32. William Kelley and Won Kim, "Observations on the Current SQL3 Object Model Proposal (and Invitation for Scholarly Opinions)," available from UniSQL, Inc., 9390 Research Blvd., Austin, Texas 78759 (1994).

See the annotation to reference [14].

33. Mark A. Roth, Henry F. Korth, and Abraham Silberschatz: "Extended Algebra and Calculus for Nested Relational Databases," *ACM TODS 13,* 4 (December 1988).

34. Michael Stonebraker *et al.*, "Third Generation Database System Manifesto," *ACM SIGMOD Record 19,* 3 (September 1990).

APPENDIX A:
NOTES ON INHERITANCE

In this appendix we present some notes toward a possible model for the concepts of subdomain, superdomain, and type inheritance. Note carefully that we are concerned here with inheritance as it applies to *domains,* not relvars, and hence with inheritance as it applies to *operators,* not attributes* (and certainly not representations). Please note too that we restrict our attention to *single inheritance* only at this time; the concept of *multiple* inheritance leads to far too many questions that—as yet—do not seem to have any satisfactory answers. We do suspect that support for multiple inheritance will ultimately prove desirable, but at the time of writing we believe it would be premature to attempt to incorporate any such functionality into a robust formal model such as the one we are seeking.

We assume throughout what follows that domain V' has been defined to be a **subdomain** of some **superdomain** V. Then:

1. V and V' are not necessarily distinct; that is, every domain is both a subdomain and a superdomain of itself.

   Comment: Although the "actual" (internal) representation of domain values is not relevant to the model *per se,* it might be helpful to point out that if domains V and V' are in fact distinct, then the actual representation of values from V' does not have to be the same as that of values from V. For example, let V be ELLIPSE and V' be CIRCLE. Then ellipses might be represented by their two semiaxis lengths a and b, whereas circles might be represented by their radius r. (We assume for simplicity that all ellipses—and hence *a fortiori* all circles—are centered on the origin, and that their major and minor axes lie along the X- and Y-axis, respectively.)

2. Every subdomain of domain V' is also regarded as a subdomain of domain V. Every superdomain of domain V is also regarded as a superdomain of domain V'.

3. If V and V' are distinct, V' is said to be a **proper** subdomain of V, and V is said to be a **proper** superdomain of V'.

4. There must exist at least one **root** domain, i.e., a domain that has no proper superdomain. We do not assume that there exists exactly one root domain.

---

*The possibility of some kind of "relvar inheritance" support is not precluded, but is not discussed further in this manifesto.

5. If V' is a proper subdomain of V and there is no distinct domain V'' that is both a proper superdomain of V' and a proper subdomain of V, then V' is said to be an **immediate** subdomain of V, and V is said to be an **immediate** superdomain of V'.

6. Every operator defined for V shall also be defined for V'—the principle of (operator) **inheritance**. More precisely, let θ be an operator, and let $V1$, $V2, \ldots, Vn$ be the domains of the operands of that operator. Let Vi be any one of $V1, V2, \ldots, Vn$, and let Vi' be a proper subdomain of Vi. Then an operator with the same name θ shall also be defined—at least implicitly—such that:

   a. the domains of the operands of that operator are the same as the domains of the operands of the original operator, except for the replacement of Vi by Vi';

   b. the domain of the result of that operator is the same as that of the result of the original operator or some proper subdomain thereof.

From the user's point of view, the "same" operator θ will thus support several different combinations of domains for its operands—the principle of (operator) **polymorphism**.

Comments:

- The new operator will have to be explicitly defined—i.e., new implementation code will have to be written—only if *either* (a) the code needs direct access to the actual representation of values from domain Vi' and that representation is different from that of values from domain Vi, *or* (b) the domain of the result is a proper subdomain of that of the result of the original operator.

- The combination of (a) the operator name θ, (b) the names of some valid combination of operand domains $V1, V2, \ldots, Vn$ (in order), and (c) the name of the domain of the result, is sometimes referred to as a **signature**. Different signatures involving the same operator name thus correspond conceptually to different versions of the operator in question.

7. It follows from the principle of operator inheritance that within any expression, wherever a value of domain V is permitted, a value of any subdoma in V' of V shall also be permitted—the principle of **substitutability**.

Comment: Let S' and S be variables of types V' and V, respectively, and let θ be a polymorphic operator whose ith operand is of type (domain) V. Further, let the comparison

```
S  =  TREAT S' AS V
```

yield *true* (in other words, S and S' "have the same value"—see point 13 below). Then we assume that the expressions

```
θ ( ..., S', ... )
```

and

```
θ ( ..., TREAT S' AS V, ... )
```

yield "the same" result (except that the domain of the first result might be a proper subdomain of that of the second). In other words, if θ has to be reimplemented for V', we assume that such reimplementation does not change the semantics of θ. We note that this would-be requirement is not enforceable; we note also, however, that if it is violated, then substitutability makes no sense.

8. Let θ be a polymorphic operator, and let x be some expression that makes use of θ. Which specific implementation of θ to invoke in connection with evaluation of x will be determined (in general) on the basis of consideration of the domains of θ's operands. It shall be possible (in general) for every operand to participate in this process.

   Comment: In other words, D shall not require that such a determination be made on the basis of a single "distinguished" or "receiver" parameter.

9. The definition of **scalar variable** needs some extension if type inheritance is supported. Let scalar variable S be declared to be of type V (i.e., V is the declared domain for S—see RM Prescription 11). Because of substitutability, the value currently assigned to S at any given time can be a value from any subdomain V' of domain V; that current value is simultaneously regarded as being of type V' and of type V'' for all superdomains V'' (including domain V) of domain V'. V' is said to be the **current domain** (sometimes the **most specific** current domain) for S.

   Changing our notation slightly, we can thus model a scalar variable as a named ordered triple of the form $<DV,CV,v>$, where:

   - The **name** of the triple is the name of the variable (S in the example).
   - DV is the name of the **declared domain** for S.
   - CV (which changes with time) is the name of the **current domain** for S.
   - v (which changes with time) is a value from domain CV, called the **current value** for S.

   We will use the notation $DV(S)$, $CV(S)$, $v(S)$ to refer to the current values of the DV, CV, v components (respectively) of scalar variable S. Note that it must always be the case that $CV(S)$ is some subdomain (not necessarily a proper subdomain) of $DV(S)$. Note too that $v(S)$ is always a value from every proper superdomain of $CV(S)$ as well as being a value from $CV(S)$ *per se*.

10. The definition of **tuple variable** needs some extension if type inheritance is supported. Let T be a tuple variable with declared heading

```
{ <A1,DV1>, <A2,DV2>, ..., <An,DVn> }
```

(see RM Prescription 12). Then the permitted values of *T* are tuples of the form

```
{ <A1,CV1,v1>, <A2,CV2,v2>, ..., <An,CVn,vn> }
```

where:

- for all i $(1, 2, \ldots, n)$, CVi is a subdomain of DVi;
- for all i $(1, 2, \ldots, n)$, vi is a value from domain CVi.

The notation $DV(S)$, $CV(S)$, $v(S)$ introduced under point 9 above can be extended in an obvious way to refer to the (declared) heading domain DVi, the current domain CVi, and the current value vi, respectively, of attribute Ai of tuple variable *T* ("attribute $T.Ai$").

Comments:

- The definition of **relation** needs extending analogously. Let relation *R* have heading *H*. Let *T* be a tuple variable with that same heading *H*. Then the body *B* of *R* consists of a set of tuples with heading *H* (as before—see RM Prescription 10—but the term "tuples with heading *H*" now has an extended interpretation).

- The definition of **relvar** needs extending analogously. Let relvar *R* have heading *H*. Then the permitted values of *R* are relations with heading *H* (as before—see RM Prescription 13—but the term "relations with heading *H*" now has an extended interpretation).

11. **(Scalar assignment with inheritance)** Let *X* be some scalar variable and let *Y* denote the value of some scalar expression. Note that *Y* can be regarded as another scalar variable, either a user-declared variable (if the original scalar expression consists of a simple variable reference) or a system-declared variable (otherwise). In both cases $DV(Y)$ can be determined at compilation time (in accordance with RM Prescriptions 3 and 11); $CV(Y)$ and $v(Y)$, by contrast, cannot be determined until run time, in general. Now consider the assignment

```
X := Y
```

$DV(Y)$ must be a subdomain of $DV(X)$, otherwise the assignment is illegal (this is a compile-time check). If the assignment is legal, its effect is to set $CV(X)$ equal to $CV(Y)$ and $v(X)$ equal to $v(Y)$.

Comments:

- A function that directly or indirectly assigns to a variable (or part thereof) of domain *V* is sometimes known as a **mutator** for *V* (see RM Prescription 3).

- The rules for tuple and relation assignment can be derived in an obvious way from the rules just presented for scalar assignment. We omit the details here.

12. **(Scalar comparison with inheritance)** Let X and Y each be the value of some scalar expression. Note that each of X and Y can be regarded as denoting a simple scalar variable, as in point 11 above; hence $DV(X)$ and $DV(Y)$ can be determined at compilation time, while $CV(X)$, $v(X)$, $CV(Y)$, and $v(Y)$, by contrast, cannot (in general). Now consider the comparison

```
X = Y
```

$DV(X)$ must be a superdomain (not necessarily a proper superdomain) of $DV(Y)$ or *vice versa,* otherwise the comparison is illegal (this is a compile-time check). If the comparison is legal, its effect is to return *true* if $CV(X) = CV(Y)$ and $v(X) = v(Y)$, *false* otherwise.

Comments:

- The rules for other comparison operators ($<$, $\leq$, etc.) can be derived in an obvious way from the rules just presented for equality (always assuming that the semantics of these operators are not to be defined in some counter-intuitive fashion, as is—perhaps unfortunately—not impossible). We omit the details here.

- The rules for tuple and relation comparisons can be derived in an obvious way from the rules just presented for scalar comparisons. We omit the details here.

13. (With acknowledgments to Nelson Mattos:) A scalar expression of the form

```
TREAT scalar AS V
```

(or logical equivalent thereof) shall be supported. Here *scalar* is an arbitrary scalar expression and V is the name of a declared domain. Let X denote the value of the scalar expression. V must be either a subdomain or superdomain of $DV(X)$ (note that $DV(X)$ is known at compilation time, so this is a compile-time check). If the TREAT expression is legal *and* $CV(X)$ is a subdomain of V (this is a run-time check), then its value is a scalar, Y say, with $DV(Y) = CV(Y) = V$ and $v(Y) = v(X)$.

Comment: The intent of this prescription is to ensure that run-time type errors can occur only in the context of an invocation of the TREAT function. For example, let domain CIRCLE be defined as a subdomain of domain ELLIPSE, and let C and E be scalar variables with declared domains CIRCLE and ELLIPSE, respectively. Then the assignment

```
C := E
```

is illegal (because $DV(E)$ is not a subdomain of $DV(C)$). By contrast, the assignment

```
C  :=  TREAT E AS CIRCLE
```

(an example of **"treating down"**) is legal, and, if the current value of E is in fact of type CIRCLE, will have the effect of assigning that value to C. (More precisely, the expression TREAT E AS CIRCLE will yield a result, E' say, with $DV(E') = CV(E') = $ CIRCLE and $v(E') = v(E)$, and E' will then be assigned to C.) On the other hand, if the current value of E is only of type ELLIPSE, not CIRCLE, the TREAT function will raise a run-time type error.

Here is another example. As before, let domain CIRCLE be defined as a subdomain of domain ELLIPSE, and let C and E be variables with declared domains CIRCLE and ELLIPSE, respectively. Then the comparison

```
E  =  C
```

is legal but cannot possibly return *true* if the current value of E is only of type ELLIPSE, not CIRCLE. By contrast, the comparison

```
E  =  TREAT C AS ELLIPSE
```

(an example of **"treating up"**) will return *true* even if the current value of E is only of type ELLIPSE, not CIRCLE, provided that $v(E) = v(C)$. (More precisely, the expression TREAT C AS ELLIPSE will yield a result, C' say, with $DV(C') = CV(C') = $ ELLIPSE and $v(C') = v(C)$, and C' will then be compared with E.) Note that "treating up" cannot possibly raise a run-time type error.

Incidentally, note the implication that a value that is "only" of type ELLIPSE might in fact correspond to a circle "in the real world." In other words, to declare CIRCLE to be a subdomain of ELLIPSE is to partition the set of ellipses into those that the system knows are circles *vs.* those that it does not—*not* into those that are circles *vs.* those that are not.

Note further that we explicitly reject the concept sometimes called **specialization by constraint,** according to which a change in a variable's value might cause an "automatic" change in that variable's type. In the case of ellipses and circles, for example, the system might know that every circle has equal semiaxes, but it will *not* know that every ellipse with equal semiaxes should really be a circle; thus, updating ("mutating") a variable of type ELLIPSE such that its semiaxes are now equal does *not* automatically make that variable of type CIRCLE. One reason for rejecting such a possibility is as follows:

- Suppose the user defines *V1* and *V2* to be (the sole) immediate subdomains of domain *V*.

- Suppose further that the user states that a value from domain *V* is "really" a value from domain *V1* if it satisfies constraint *C1*, and a value from domain *V2* if it satisfies constraint *C2*.

- What happens if a given value from domain *V* satisfies both constraint *C1* and constraint *C2?*

14. A relational expression of the form

```
rel : IS_V ( attr )
```

(or logical equivalent thereof) shall be supported. Here *rel* is an arbitrary relational expression, *attr* is the name of an attribute of the result of that expression, and *V* is the name of a domain. The declared domain of *attr* must be a superdomain of *V* (this is a compile-time check). The value of the expression is defined to be a relation with (a) a heading the same as that of *rel*, except that the declared domain corresponding to attribute *attr* in that heading is *V*, and (b) a body consisting of those tuples of *rel* in which *attr* contains a value from *V*, except that the declared domain corresponding to attribute *attr* in each of those tuples is *V*.

Comment: The intent of this prescription is illustrated by the following example. Suppose relvar R includes an attribute X defined on domain VEHICLE, and suppose TRUCK is a proper subdomain of VEHICLE. Suppose further that PAYLOAD is an operator that applies to trucks but not to nontrucks. Then the expression

```
R:IS_TRUCK(X) WHERE PAYLOAD(X) > TONS(5)
```

will return those tuples of (the current value of) R that correspond to trucks with payload greater than 5 tons (say). By contrast, the expression

```
R WHERE PAYLOAD(X) > TONS(5)
```

is illegal (this is a compile-time check), since PAYLOAD is not defined for domain VEHICLE (and hence not for values of X that do not correspond to trucks).

We conclude this appendix with an abbreviated mnemonic list of the various points discussed above.

1. "Subdomain of" is reflexive
2. "Subdomain of" is transitive
3. Proper subdomains
4. Root domains
5. Immediate subdomains
6. Operator inheritance (polymorphism)

7. Substitutability
8. No "receiver parameters"
9. Scalar variables (extended definition)
10. Tuple variables (extended definition)
11. Scalar assignment with inheritance
12. Scalar comparison with inheritance
13. TREAT
14. Relational expression *rel*:IS_V(*attr*)

THE PROBLEM OF MISSING INFORMATION

PART 11

THE PROBLEM OF
MISSING INFORMATION

Introduction

Part IV of this book's predecessor, *Relational Database Writings 1989–1991*, was also entitled "The Problem of Missing Information," and I think I had better repeat what I said there:

> *[This part of the book] addresses, once again, the subject of missing information. This topic has already been discussed in two papers in the first book in this series and three in the second; indeed, in that second book I wrote that I was "a little embarrassed to be dredging up [this] hackneyed topic . . . yet again"—but here we go once more, with* five *papers this time. The topic is endless, it seems.*

Well, at least it's only two papers this time . . .

Actually, I would like to call the reader's attention to the recent series of papers by David McGoveran (with the generic title "Nothing from Nothing") on this same general topic:

- "What's Logic Got to Do with It?", *Database Programming & Design 6*, No. 12 (December 1993)

- "Classical Logic: Nothing Compares 2 U," *Database Programming & Design 7*, No. 1 (January 1994)

- "Can't Lose What You Never Had," *Database Programming & Design 7*, No. 2 (February 1994)

- "It's in the Way That You Use It," *Database Programming & Design 7*, No. 3 (March 1994)

To quote from David's overall introduction to these four papers: "[This] series addresses a crisis (and a *scandal*) of the relational model: the use of many-valued logic as a mechanism for handling missing information." The papers stress the use of careful database design to avoid the apparent need for "nulls" and three-valued logic.

Much Ado about Nothing

ABSTRACT

"A point/counterpoint on the tough issue of missing values, by Dr. E. F. Codd and C. J. Date" (*Database Programming & Design's* own description of this debate when it was first published).

COMMENTS ON REPUBLICATION

I mentioned in the "Technical Correspondence" section in Installment Number 5 of my *Database Programming & Design* series ("Nothing in Excess") that among the letters I received when that installment was first published was one from Dr. Codd, who certainly did not agree with my criticisms of nulls and three-valued logic. His letter, and my response to it, grew into a somewhat lengthy debate that subsequently appeared as an article in its own right in a later issue of *Database Programming & Design*. This is that article.

    Note: All footnotes in this chapter have been added in this republished version—they were not included in the artcle as originally published.

Originally published in *Database Programming & Design 6,* No. 10 (October 1993). Reprinted by permission of Miller Freeman Inc.

1. INTRODUCTION

(The introduction that follows is a slightly edited version of Database Programming & Design's *own introduction to the original debate.)*

Dr. E. F. Codd and C. J. Date are two of the best-known figures in the history, development, and exposition of what was a breakthrough concept in database technology: the relational model. Ever since the model was first defined by Codd in 1970, in his famous paper "A Relational Model of Data for Large Shared Data Banks," we have been reading, listening to, and interpreting their commentaries on it. While Codd and Date have agreed upon much during the course of the relational model's evolution and implementation, on some issues they definitely do not agree. One important disagreement—and the topic of this special article—centers on the issue of nulls and missing values, and the underlying theoretical problems of three- and four-valued logic.

Both have written extensively on these topics, as is noted in the "References and Bibliography" section at the end. The comments presented here were sparked by Date's columns in our magazine beginning last December, when he discussed the three-valued logic approach to missing information. Codd then sent us his criticisms of Date's writings; his commentary is presented here. Date then provided a rebuttal to specific points of Codd's, which follows Codd's remarks. Finally, we give Codd a chance to rebut Date's rebuttal.

For the reader's convenience, we kept Codd's commentary together, so it may be read as a whole. We noted throughout, however, where Date's specific rebuttals apply, and should be read. This way, the reader may follow Codd's comments all the way through, and then return to his essay, reading Date's rebuttals as appropriate.

At first, the issues may seem arcane and theoretical, but most developers and DBAs know they clearly are not, and merit serious debate. Missing values remain one of the toughest—and potentially, most dangerous—problems in database technology.

We begin with Dr. Codd's commentary.

2. CODD'S COMMENTARY

Although C. J. Date has been a strong supporter of the relational approach to database management for over 20 years, from time to time I have found that his criticisms of the relational model have been incorrect. I *do* agree with many of his criticisms of SQL: However, he often fails to make a clear distinction between SQL and the relational model. SQL came after the relational model was described; it was invented by a small IBM group in the Yorktown Heights [N.Y.] Research Laboratory. In my book, *The Relational Model for Database Management: Version 2* [1], I make it clear what semantic properties a relational language should have if it is to conform to the model, and label such a language *RL*. I also describe three major shortcomings of SQL (there are, of course, numerous others [2]):

- As a user option, SQL permits rows to occur within a single relation that are complete duplicates of each other. I call this a *tabular error* because it is based on two misconceptions:

  1. That relations and tables are in one-to-one correspondence, and
  2. That duplicate rows are essential to some applications.

- Full support of first-order predicate logic is sacrificed in the name of user friendliness. I call this a *pyschological mixup:* A logically sound language is absolutely necessary as a foundation. Any useful "user-friendly features" should be grafted as a layer on top, along with rigorously defined translation between layers.

- The treatment of missing information is wrong for two reasons:

  1. Support in the language for multivalued logic is grossly inadequate, and
  2. A user is permitted to designate a value that is acceptable to a column specifically to indicate the fact that some value is missing from that column. I call this latter error one of *missing-value misrepresentation.*

Date has criticized the multi-valued logic approach to missing values in the relational model, claiming it can lead to catastrophic errors. He has advocated the missing-value misrepresentation approach, which he calls the *default value* approach. In 1986, when Date had his original paper reprinted in the U.S., I prepared a technical response [3].

The ideas behind Date's default value approach came completely from pre-relational products that used single-record-at-a-time processing. The default-value approach appealed to RDBMS vendors because it placed all of the responsibility for the representation and handling of missing values in a relational database completely on the users. However, I think it is best described as a nonsolution to the problem, and a complete evasion of the issue. The approach contains no clear description of how missing values in a column are to be treated. That means that the treatment will often be invented by application programmers and buried in their programs. It also means that there are likely to be many different treatments buried in numerous programs.

Now that we are dealing with RDBMSs that employ multiple-record-at-a-time processing, this default-value approach is unacceptable for the following reasons:

1. The *meaning* of the fact that a value is missing from some part or column of a relational database is quite different from the meaning of a value that is legitimate within that part or column;

2. A single relational request can touch many different columns in a relational database, and therefore it is intolerable that in conceiving such a request the user should have to understand and cope with as many different representations and treatments of missing values as the columns that are touched. In a relational database, both the representation and treatment of missing values *must* be uniform across the entire database.

See Date's Rebuttal I

Date and other critics of multivalued logic claim that serious errors are inevitable if a multivalued logic is made available to users. However, such critics have failed to provide a single example of a *severely wrong* answer being delivered as a result of a multivalued logic. A result is severely incorrect if the logical expression is evaluated by the DBMS to be

- *True* when it is actually *false* or *unknown;* or
- *False* when it is actually *true* or *unknown.*

A result is *mildly incorrect* if the DBMS evaluates an expression as *unknown* when it is actually either *true* or *false.* In the paper in which I introduced three-valued logic (3VL) [4], I cited an example of a request *mildly mishandled* by 3VL: For some requests the condition would be evaluated as *unknown* when the correct answer was *true* or *false,* if the DBMS were unable to recognize tautologies. This example shows that simple 3VL should be augmented by some inferential capability. An example would be the following: Suppose that the birth year is recorded for most employees, but it is missing from the database for a few. Now, consider the request: Retrieve the serial numbers and names of employees for each of whom

1. The birth year is 1960, or
2. The birth year is earlier than 1960, or
3. The birth year is later than 1960.

Suppose the DBMS does NOT have the capability of recognizing that the whole condition must be *true* for every employee, whether the birth year happens to be missing or not. That is, it is unable to detect tautologies or contradictions. Then for those employees whose birth year is unknown, the DBMS comes up with *unknown* for each of the three subconditions. And, using the rule that for truth values

unknown OR *unknown* is *unknown,*

it evaluates the whole condition to be *unknown.* This is an example of a mild error.

This kind of error is just as likely to occur (and other kinds much more likely) if the responsibility for handling missing information is placed totally on the users.

See Date's Rebuttal II

Now, an obvious cure for this is to equip the DBMS not only with 3VL, but also with the capability of recognizing for any whole condition whether it is a tautology. This would be easy if only propositional logic were being supported. However, the relational model requires the more powerful predicate logic to be supported in specifying the condition part of a request. It is well known that it is a logically undecidable problem to determine whether an arbitrary formula in predicate logic is a tautology or a contradiction.

Therefore, it is pointless to search for an allegedly universal algorithm for detecting all possible tautologies and all possible contradictions. A reasonably good algorithm can be developed that will take care of at least all of the simple cases that will be encountered in commercial activities, and this algorithm should be incorporated into every RDBMS product. The RDBMS will then make mild errors only when a most unusual request is made. An RDBMS must admit its inability to deduce a sound response to a user request whenever this is impossible because of missing values. Also, present treatment by SQL of missing values is, in my opinion, totally unsatisfactory. For a more complete treatment of missing values and a refutation of Date's criticisms, refer to my book [5].

See Date's Rebuttal III

Date's argument that *true* and *false* are the only truth values, and that, therefore, *unknown* cannot be treated as a logical value makes no sense to me. After all, it is very common in mathematics to label unknown values by letters such as m, n, x, y, z. The fact that the letters m, n do not "look like" any of the integers does not prevent them from actually having integer values in an expression such as $m + n$, $m - n$, or an assertion that $m * m = m$. In any event, when dealing with missing values, an RDBMS must be able to determine whether NOT A, A OR B, and A AND B is *true, false,* or *unknown* when A, or B, or both are *unknown*.

Date's argument that the number of distinct functions from truth values to truth values is very large, and that fact makes 3VL and four-valued logic (4VL) unusable is ridiculous. After all, the number of distinct functions from integers to integers is infinite, because the number of distinct integers is infinite. However, no one in his right mind would use that as an argument that integers are unusable.

Taking the whole of Date's article into consideration, I completely reject Date's claims:

- To have inserted "more nails into the 3VL coffin";
- That it is time to drop the pretense that 3VL is a good thing.

> ### See Date's Rebuttal IV

3. DATE'S REBUTTAL I

Before I begin, let me make one thing crystal clear: My quarrel is not with the relational model. On the contrary, I felt at the time when it was first introduced (and I still feel) that the original model was a work of genius. All of us owe Dr. Codd a huge debt of gratitude for his major contribution. And, as the originator and "elder statesman" of relational theory, Codd always deserves the courtesy of very close attention to his remarks on relational matters.

So my quarrel is not with the relational model, but rather with *nulls* and *three-valued logic (3VL),* which—in a database context—were first discussed by Codd in 1979. It is true that Codd now regards 3VL as an integral part of the relational model, but I do not (and I am not alone in taking this position). Indeed, the whole question of how to handle missing information is largely independent of whether the underlying model is relational or something else. Thus, I would like to distinguish very carefully between what we might call "RM" (the original model, with two-valued logic) and "RM+3VL" (Codd's version, with three-valued logic). My quarrel, to repeat, is with the "3VL" portion of "RM+3VL."

Now, regarding Codd's first point (that default values misrepresent the fact that information is missing): I do not dispute this! However, I would make two points:

1. It is default values, not nulls, that we use in the real world, as I pointed out in my December 1992 column in *Database Programming & Design* [6].

2. Nulls misrepresent the semantics too (see below). In other words, I don't think we yet know how *not* to misrepresent the semantics; and given that this is so, I take the position that we should not undermine the solid foundation of the relational model with something as suspect as 3VL, when it demonstrably doesn't solve the problem anyway.*

Note: When I talk about "undermining the foundations of the relational model," what I mean is that a "relation" that includes nulls, whatever else it might be, is *not a relation!*—at least, not in the formal sense of that term. As a conse-

---

*In other words, I invoke the *Principle of Cautious Design*—see the article of that name in this book's predecessor, *Relational Database Writings 1989–1991,* by C. J. Date and Hugh Darwen (Addison-Wesley, 1992).

quence, the entire foundation crumbles; we can no longer be sure of *any* aspect of the underlying theory, and *all bets are off.* I cannot believe that Codd really wants to destroy the entire edifice that he has so painstakingly constructed over the years.

As for nulls also misrepresenting the semantics, consider the following two points:

■ A (Codd-style) 3VL system supports just one type of null, "value unknown." There is thus a strong likelihood that users will use that null for purposes for which it is not appropriate. For example, suppose employee Joe is not a sales-person and so does not qualify for a commission. Then Joe's commission is quite likely to be misrepresented as "value unknown" (it should of course be "value does not apply"). One simple consequence of this misrepresentation error is that Joe's total compensation (salary plus commission) will incor-rectly evaluate to "unknown" instead of to just the salary value.

What's more, an analogous argument will continue to apply so long as the system supports fewer types of null than are logically necessary. In other words, simply adding support for a "value does not apply" null might solve the specific problem mentioned in the previous paragraph, but it will not solve the general problem. Thus, a system that supports fewer types of null than are logically necessary is just as open to misuse—perhaps even more so—than a system that does not support nulls at all.

■ Now suppose the system supports two kinds of null, "value unknown" and "value does not apply" and *four*-valued logic (4VL), and suppose employee Joe's job is unknown. What do we do about Joe's commission? It surely must be null—the information is surely missing—but we don't know whether that null should be "value unknown" or "value does not apply." Perhaps we need another kind of null, and *five*-valued logic . . . This argument clearly goes on for ever, leading to an apparent requirement for *an infinite number of kinds of null.* What do we conclude from this state of affairs?

Next, regarding Codd's allegation that the default-value approach lacks a "clear description of how [default] values are to be treated": I have published sev-eral such descriptions over the past few years, the first in 1982, the most recent in 1992 [7].

Of course, Codd is quite right to warn of the dangers of *undisciplined* use of default values. That's why I have consistently advocated a *disciplined* approach. By the way, a system that supports nulls can still be used in an undisciplined way, as I have already shown. In fact, an argument can be made that such a system is *more* susceptible to lack of discipline, partly (a) because of the false sense of se-curity provided by the fact that nulls are supported ("Missing information? Don't worry about it, the system can handle it"), and partly (b) because

1. The system designers assume that users are going to use nulls, and therefore

2. They typically don't provide explicit system support for defaults, and therefore

3. Users who have made the (in my opinion, very sensible) decision to avoid nulls are on their own—the system doesn't help (in fact, it positively hinders).

Finally, I completely reject Codd's suggestion that the default values idea comes from prerelational systems—on the contrary, it comes from the real world, as I have already said. I also reject the suggestion that it has anything to do with "record-at-a-time" thinking—how to deal with missing information has nothing to do with whether the operators are record-at-a-time or set-at-a-time.

On behalf of the vendors, I also reject the suggestion that default values appealed to them "because it placed all of the responsibility on the users." Might it not have been that the vendors had their own misgivings concerning 3VL? In any case, I know of no vendor that actually supported a proper default values scheme before supporting 3VL. Moreover, a proper default values scheme does *not* "place all of the responsibility on the users." To contend otherwise is to misrepresent the semantics of the default values scheme.

4. DATE'S REBUTTAL II

First, a small point regarding Codd's claim that the *mild* error he notes "is just as likely to occur (and other kinds much more likely)" in a default values scheme. It seems to me that there is all the difference in the world between:

- Building a system—i.e., one based on 3VL—in which we *know* errors will occur, because the system has logical flaws in it, and

- Building a system that is at least logically correct but is open to misuse. *Any* system is open to misuse. That's why we have to have discipline.

Next, and more important: Contrary to Codd's claim that "[I] have failed to provide a single example of a severely wrong answer," I gave the following example in 1989 [8], and repeated it in my December 1992 column in *Database Programming & Design*. The database (DB1) is shown in Fig. 1 (the "-- represents "value unknown"). The query is:

```
SELECT  E#
FROM    DEPT, EMP
WHERE   NOT ( DEPT.D# = EMP.D# AND EMP.D# = 'D1' ) ;
```

It's not worth going through the example again in detail here. The basic point is that the expression in the WHERE clause is "actually *unknown*" (Codd's phrase-

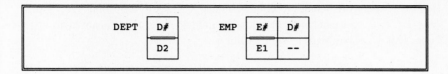

Fig. 1 Example database DB1

ology) but is treated as *false,* with the result that employee number E1 is not retrieved but in fact should be (the real-world answer to the query is E1). This is a
severe error by Codd's definition.

Please note too that the foregoing is a 3VL error, not just an SQL error. Paraphrasing slightly from Codd's book [9], he states: "Executing a query delivers
only those cases in which the condition part evaluates to *true*." This is tantamount
to treating *unknown* as *false.*

In case the reader is not convinced, let me give another example. The
database (DB2) is given in Fig. 2. The query is "Does anyone in department D1
earn a salary of 100K?" This query will involve a test to see whether the literal row
"<D1,100K>" appears in the projection of EMP over D# and SAL. In forming that
projection, however, the row "<D1,--->" will be eliminated [10]. Result: The 3VL
answer to the query is *false;* the real-world answer, by contrast, is *unknown.* This
is surely also a severe error by Codd's definition.

Finally, and much more important still: The whole business of "severe" *vs.*
"mild" errors is in any case surely nonsense. It seems to me that it is nothing more
than a rearguard attempt to shore up an already suspect position. After all, if we
were talking about integers instead of truth values, what would we think of a system that occasionally produced the answer 2 when the correct answer was 1 or 3?
And in what sense could this be any more acceptable than one that occasionally
produced 1 or 3 when the correct answer was 2?

Suppose the DBMS says that it *doesn't know* whether Country X is developing a nuclear weapon, whereas in fact Country X is *not* doing so; and suppose

EMP	E#	D#	SAL
	E1	D1	50K
	E2	D1	---

Fig. 2 Example database DB2

Country Y therefore decides to bomb Country X "back to the Stone Age," just in case. The error here can hardly be said to be mild. (This example is not to my taste; I choose it deliberately for its shock value.)

5. DATE'S REBUTTAL III

Here I would just like to raise a few questions.

1. What evidence is there that "a reasonably good algorithm can be developed"?

2. Is there a precise definition of the "simple cases" that such an algorithm will handle?

3. Is that definition intuitively understandable? In other words, will the user be able to predict with any confidence whether or not the DBMS is going to give the right answer to a given query?

4. If the answer to the previous question is no, then why would any user ever use the system for any purpose at all?

5. In fact, Codd is requiring the DBMS itself to "admit its inability to deduce a sound response to a user request" whenever applicable. In other words, he is asking for a decision procedure regarding the decidability of formulas in three-valued logic. What evidence is there that such a procedure exists?

6. What percentage of real-world queries that are "encountered in commercial activities" are "simple" in the foregoing sense?

7. What evidence exists to support the answer to the previous question?

8. If we are limited to using "simple" queries only, exactly what incremental value is the "RM+3VL" system providing over a prerelational, record-at-a-time system?

9. What does "commercial activities" include? Does it include financial applications? Manufacturing applications? Hardware and software design applications? Geographic and mapping applications? Document-handling applications? Medical applications? Chemical applications?

I think it is time to quote Wittgenstein again: *All logical differences are big differences.* (To my regret, I do not know the source of this quote. I would be grateful to any reader who could help.)

Now, turning to Codd's discussion of missing values in his book, and refutation of my views therein: Codd claims that his book "refutes my criticisms in detail." I don't think it does. The two major criticisms dealt with in his book are (1) "the alleged counterintuitive nature [of nulls and 3VL]" and (2) "the alleged breakdown of normalization."

■   Regarding (1), Codd does not address the counterintuitive nature of 3VL *per se,* but instead claims that default values are counterintuitive too. In doing so, incidentally, he confuses the semantics of the two very different expressions "not known" and "known not"—a trap that is all too easy to fall into, of course (indeed, this confusion is precisely one of the reasons why I claim that 3VL is counterintuitive). In an earlier paper [11], I gave an example of a (very simple!) query involving 3VL that Codd and I *both* seriously misinterpreted when we first discussed it (it was a somewhat lengthy discussion too, I might add). The misinterpretation rested once again on the distinction between "not known" and "known not." I stand by my contention that 3VL is difficult to deal with on an intuitive level.

- Regarding (2), I originally claimed that "the fundamental theorem of normalization" breaks down in the presence of nulls [12], and so it does. Codd's counterargument is unconvincing.

In any case, I have several other serious criticisms of 3VL that Codd's chapter does not address at all. They include (and this is not an exhaustive list):

- The fact that we apparently need an infinite number of types of null

- The semantic overloading or "misrepresentation" that will occur if not all types of null are supported (bound to be the case, given the previous point)

- The lack of a convincing justification for the different treatment of equality of nulls in comparisons *vs.* equality of nulls in duplicate elimination

- The fact that the (admittedly informal) argument in support of the entity integrity rule ("primary keys in base relations do not permit nulls") quite obviously extends to *every column in the database*—implying that nulls should be inadmissible *everywhere*

- If TABLE_DUM corresponds to *false* and TABLE_DEE corresponds to *true,* what corresponds to *unknown*? (see my March 1993 column in *Database Programming & Design* [13])

6. DATE'S REBUTTAL IV

Regarding my argument that there are only two truth values: Codd's counterargument here makes no sense to me. Is he suggesting that *unknown* is not a truth value after all, but just a variable whose actual value at any given time is either *true* or *false?* So we aren't really dealing with 3VL after all?

The only way I might make sense of Codd's position here is to interpret his remarks as actually *agreeing* with what I said in my January 1993 column (which I'm sure was not what he intended). Here's what I said in that column [14]:

(Begin quote)

How many truth values are there? The answer, of course, is *two,* namely *true* and *false*. We might *SAY* that *unknown* is a third truth value, but that doesn't make it one. After all, I might *say* that oggle-poggle is another integer, but that doesn't make it one; it has absolutely no effect on the set of all integers. Likewise, the set of all truth values just *IS* the set {*true*, *false*}, and there is nothing more to be said.

If we are given some proposition, say the proposition "Employee E1 works in department D1," then that proposition is either *true* or *false*. I might not know which it is, but it *is* one of the two (if it isn't, it isn't a proposition). Let's assume, in fact, that I don't know which it is. Then I certainly might say, informally, that the truth value of the proposition is unknown to me; but that "unknown" is a very different kind of object from the truth values *true* and *false* themselves. And pretending that it is the same kind of object—in other words, pretending that we have three truth values—is bound to lead to problems of interpretation (as of course it does).

(End quote)

Note: Of course, I understand the point that we are free to define a purely *formal* system in which there are as many "truth values" as we like. This does not alter the fact that, in the real world, the values *true* and *false* (on the one hand) and the value *unknown* (on the other) are totally different kinds of things.

Finally, regarding my argument concerning truth-valued functions: Here Codd both misrepresents my position and misses the point. My argument was not that because there were so many functions, we should not support 3VL; rather, it was that if we want to support 3VL, we should be sure that we support all possible 3VL functions. Now, in the case of integers, it is true that the total number of functions is infinite—*BUT* we know that any computable function is expressible in terms of a small number of primitive operators, so all we have to do is support those primitives properly. Likewise, in 2VL we know that all 2VL functions can be expressed in terms of a small (very small!) number of primitive operators, and so again all we have to do is support those primitives properly.

For 3VL, therefore, I was asking, first, for a suitable set of primitive operators that would guarantee that all 19,710 logical functions were supported (indeed, if any of those functions are *not* supported, then it cannot be claimed that the system we are dealing with is 3VL). I was also asking for a suitable set of *useful* operators (not necessarily the same thing as primitive operators). I was also asking for a proof of completeness. I was also raising questions of testing, debugging, and usability. And then I was asking the analogous questions all over again for 4VL, where there are over *four billion* possible functions. I believe these are serious questions that advocates of 3VL and 4VL are morally obliged to address.*

---

*In connection with this particular issue, see the paper "A Note on the Logical Operators of SQL" elsewhere in this volume.

Taking the whole of Codd's comments into consideration, I stand more firmly than ever by my original position.

7. REBUTTING THE REBUTTALS

(To close out this discussion, Dr. Codd offers some comments on Date's rebuttals.)

Just about every database contains missing values scattered over numerous parts of the database. For example, an employee's birthdate might have to be marked "missing but applicable," because it is at present unknown. Or, the employee's year-to-date commission may have to be marked as missing and inapplicable because he or she is not a salesperson.

Database management would be simpler if missing values didn't exist.* Unfortunately, for a variety of reasons, they do occur and need to be managed. C. J. Date's assertion that a relation containing missing values is not a relation is unacceptable. While relations that contain missing values are not normally encountered in mathematics, the same operators in the relational model continue to be applicable. Requests expressed in a relational language must be able to cope with missing values, without resorting to guessing.

With Date's default value approach, both the representation and treatment of missing values can be peculiar to the columns in which missing values are permitted. This might be acceptable in a single-record-at-a-time DBMS; it's clearly *not* in a multiple-record-at-a-time DBMS. The principal reason for adopting an approach that is *uniform across the entire database* is that a single relational request may involve data from numerous distinct columns of the database, and many of these columns are likely to be permitted to have missing values. Imagine a request that deals with 12 or more such columns: A significant part of formulating this request would involve detailed knowledge of the 12 or more representations and treatments of missing values, if the default value scheme were adopted.

For uniformity, one might look to support in hardware. Today's memory technology, however, can't distinguish between values to be taken seriously and those that are not—such as those left in some condition by some previous activity. Once a disk is formatted, the computer regards every bit as part of the value of something. In my relational model version 2 (RM/V2), any column in which missing values are permitted is assigned one extra byte to indicate, for each row, whether the associated value is:

1. To be treated seriously, or
2. Missing and applicable, or
3. Missing and inapplicable.

---

*I like this sentence!

IBM's DB2 partially supports this representation.

A basic ground rule in the relational model is that *the DBMS must NOT provide a definite response to a query when it is not certain about the response because values are missing.* I remember well when I first arrived in New York City to reside in the U.S. It was the fall of 1948 and I was looking vigorously for a job. Often I would have to ask people on the street how to get to specific parts of the city. I received detailed directions, but almost invariably these directions were wrong. I stopped asking and used street maps instead. Similarly, people who use a DBMS that *guesses* the answer to a query but delivers it as if it were not guessing are likely to abandon its use.*

Re: Date's Rebuttal I

In Date's Rebuttal I, he decries the inadequacies of three-valued logic (3VL), which I first discussed in 1979. In 1986, I proposed a significant improvement [3], which distinguished between two categories of missing database values:

1. Temporarily unknown

2. Inapplicable, and hence unknowable.

Semantics make this distinction necessary. I also proposed four-valued logic (4VL) and *additional general-purpose functions* to permit adequate handling of missing information. Date, in many of his examples, ignores both. This double oversight makes his examples merely cases of the incorrect use of the missing value machinery in RM/V2 [1].

In his Rebuttal I, Date asserts: "It is default values, not nulls, that we use in the real world." Arguments of this type can, and have, been used [*sic*] to delay every technical or scientific step forward. It could have been used to argue against the introduction of computers: "It is mental arithmetic that we use in the real world, not machines." The phrase "real world" is a serious trap, because what is real is continually changing.

Let's take one of Date's examples: A user enters data with an element missing, and he or she does not know whether the element is applicable or inapplicable. Date would claim that, as a consequence, we need a third kind of missing value. In his rebuttal, he goes on to say that we need more and more distinct types of missing values.

---

*I remark that "guessing the answer and delivering it as if it were not guessing" is exactly what SQL does when it applies an aggregate function such as AVG to a collection of values that happens to include some nulls. Suppose the user asks for the average salary of employees, and at least one employee is shown in the database as having a null salary. Then SQL simply ignores such employees and returns the average salary of the rest!—instead of responding "I don't know," which would be more honest. (It does admittedly return a warning code also, but there is no way to force the user to check for that code.)

I reject this sequence of arguments. In RM/V2, I discontinued using "null" because the term has been so often misinterpreted. As I pointed out earlier, missing values are either *A-marked* (applicable, presently unknown) or *I-marked* (inapplicable, hence unknowable). Let's assume we have an RDBMS that is faithful to RM/V2. As background, remember that:

- For each column other than a primary key column, the DBA may declare that A-marks be permitted or prohibited.

- For each column other than a primary or foreign key column, the DBA may declare that I-marks be permitted or prohibited.

- A-marks are weaker and more flexible than I-marks [1].

- A-marks likely occur more often than I-marks in a relational database that is in conceptual normal form *(p)* because *p* is the maximum percentage of I-marked values in any column, and *p* is normally set by the DBA to be considerably less than 1.

- Whenever a tuple is entered with a missing value, this value is A-marked in the database, unless an integrity constraint exists that clearly indicates an I-mark must be recorded.

In this example, we must assume that both types of marking are permitted in the pertinent column, and that no declared integrity constraint resolves the issue of whether an A-mark or I-mark should be used. Then RM/V2 marks the missing value as applicable. Later, if it is discovered that the value should have been I-marked, not A-marked, then the DBA or someone with suitable authorization changes the marking on this missing value. Thus, I fail to see the need for more than two kinds of markings.

Date also asserts that multivalued logic destroys the foundation upon which the Relational Model is built. I do not agree. There is no theoretical impairment and no loss of usability, whereas both scope and usability are lost if the default value scheme advocated by Date is adopted.

Date also asserts that normalization becomes invalid when multivalued logic is introduced. This is false, providing that this logic is introduced correctly (few RDBMSs do this today) and care is taken with its use. For example, if the RDBMS supported DBA-defined requests (few do), the DBA could define integrity constraints that will be stored in the catalog to enable the RDBMS to enforce the functional, multivalued, and inclusion dependencies discovered at database design time. However, the RDBMS must withhold the enforcement of these constraints from the *missing* tuple components until they are replaced by actual values. This enforcement should occur at the time of attempted replacement.

Finally, I oppose the use of default values only if it's done to represent that a value is missing. Default values may be useful in other contexts. For example, a bank teller shouldn't be required to re-enter his or her terminal identifier every time he or she enters a customer transaction. The terminal should handle this itself.

(Database Programming & Design gave me the opportunity to reply to Codd's additional comments, but it seemed to me that no further reply was warranted.)

TECHNICAL CORRESPONDENCE

The foregoing debate, perhaps not surprisingly, led to a number of letters from readers. In fact, more than one reader wrote in with attempts to salvage the idea that "automatic" null support be provided *without* having to stray beyond the boundaries of conventional two-valued logic (2VL). I regret that I did not find these attempts very convincing, and choose not to discuss them here.

Ceuan Clement-Davies from Frankfurt, West Germany, offered the following comment, which I cannot do better than quote *verbatim:*

"One thing struck me forcibly . . . [Codd's] remarks on tautologies seemed a significant admission. Since the example he gives [regarding birth years] isn't a tautology in Łukasiewicz's system (and any system of three-valued logic in which this was made to be a tautology would show unfortunate effects elsewhere), it isn't at all clear to me whether Codd is suggesting that a RDBMS should use *two-valued* logic to detect tautologies, and *three-valued* logic for everything else. This would be a curious mixture."

Stephen Ferg of the U.S. Department of Labor (Bureau of Labor Statistics) wrote claiming that:

1. The concept of null is deeply embedded in the relational model, and probably cannot be removed from it.

2. Nulls often, and in some cases must, have no semantic content whatever: They simply mean that there is no value in a given column of a given row.

He then went on to say (this is an edited extract from his letter):

(Begin quote)

Consider an EMP table with columns E#, ETYPE, and TOTSALES. ETYPE indicates whether the employee in question is a member of the sales staff . . . TOTSALES indicates the total number of sales the employee has made since the beginning of the year . . . For an employee not on the sales staff, TOTSALES will be null. For a sales employee, TOTSALES may be null until the employee files his or her first sales report (until then, the number is applicable, but unknown).

It is this kind of example that both Codd and Date seemed to have in mind during their debate. But there is another use for null that is far more important. Suppose we have two entities, EMP and DEPT, and a relationship, ASSIGNED,

EMP		ASSIGNED			DEPT
E#		E#	D#		D#
E1		E1	D1		D1
E2					D2

Fig. 3 The departments and employees database (first version)

with the constraint that (at any given time) each employee is assigned to at most one department. There are two employees (E1, E2) and two departments (D1, D2). E1 is assigned to D1, but E2 is not currently assigned to any department (E2 is on leave of absence and will be assigned to a department when [he or she] returns from that leave). A logically ideal implementation of this situation is shown in Fig. 3.

Because ASSIGNED is a many-to-one relationship, however, the ASSIGNED table and the EMP table have the same primary key. This permits the schema to be "optimized" by merging the two tables, so that ASSIGNED.D# becomes a foreign key in the EMP table, producing the structure shown in Fig. 4.

There are three things worth noting about Fig. 4.

1. First, such an optimized design is extremely common—so common that many database designers think of it as the ideal relational implementation of such a situation, rather than as an optimized implementation one step removed from the ideal implementation.

2. Second, such a design requires the use of nulls in foreign keys . . .

3. Third, in such a design a null has no semantic content whatever: It exists only because of optimization and implementation considerations . . . It is not the case that E2 cannot be assigned to a department, and it is not true that E2's department number is "missing" or "unknown" (as if such a number really

EMP		DEPT
E#	D#	D#
E1	D1	D1
E2	--	D2

Fig. 4 The departments and employees database (second version)

existed but we just don't know what it is). So . . . we have a third kind of null: It doesn't mean "inapplicable" and it doesn't mean "unknown"—it simply means that the column has no value.

Note that the design of Fig. 3 also does not avoid the need for a "simply no value" null: If we do a left outer join of the EMP and ASSIGNED tables in that figure, we will produce a result table that is exactly the same as the EMP table in Fig. 4. An outer join produces nulls because we ask the DBMS to show us data from one table even when no matching data can be found in another table. Such nulls have no meaning, no semantic content . . .

My conclusions:

1. Despite the difficulties with null that Date points out, we cannot have a relational model that is altogether free of null, so we had better learn to live with it.

2. Despite Codd's impulse to distinguish different kinds of null on semantic grounds, it is probably better just to let null mean "no value here" . . . [in order to avoid] the unmanageable complexities of 3-valued, 4-valued, . . . , *n*-valued logic.

(End quote)

My reactions to Ferg's letter are as follows.

First of all, I agree with Ferg that the design of Fig. 3 is preferable to that of Fig. 4. However, Ferg claims that nulls are "deeply embedded in the relational model and probably cannot be removed from it." But he provides no proof of this claim, and I could not possibly disagree with it more. (After all, the model survived very well without nulls for about ten years!) In fact, I challenge him to produce an example of a problem that appears to need nulls for its solution that cannot also be solved without them.

Ferg goes on to claim that nulls "often . . . have no semantic content whatever," but subsequently contradicts himself on this very point. In the example he uses to support his claim, the null department number in the EMP row <E2,—> certainly does have "semantic content"—it means, loosely, that the employee will be assigned to a department when [he or she] returns from leave of absence (Ferg's own words).

Later Ferg says that the nulls that appear in the result of an outer join also "have no meaning, no semantic content." Again I disagree. The point is not that the nulls have no meaning, but rather that (in such a result) different nulls have different meanings, as I have illustrated elsewhere (see "Watch Out for Outer Join," in C. J. Date and Hugh Darwen, *Relational Database Writings 1989–1991*, Addison-Wesley, 1992, pp. 328–330).

In any case, the question "Do nulls have semantic content?" is the wrong question to ask. The point is, operators (logical, computational, relational, or whatever) must be defined to deal with nulls *somehow*. And the behavior of those operators effectively DEFINES the semantics of nulls. In other words, nulls must always—necessarily—have *some* "semantic content." Ferg's suggestion that we should just let nulls mean "no value here" thus really makes no sense.

To pursue the previous point a moment longer: A large part of my objection to nulls is based on the fact that the particular "semantic content" defined by the operators of three-valued logic is of no practical value for the purpose at hand, because that "semantic content" does not mimic the way the real world works. As I put it in my original December 1992 column [6], answers that 3VL says are correct are often not the answers that are correct in the real world.

One further point: Ferg also gives an example in which the TOTSALES figure for a sales employee who has not yet filed a sales report is shown as null. It should of course be zero! This is another illustration of the kinds of mistakes that people are likely to make in a system that supports nulls. Indeed, SQL itself makes the same mistake when it defines the sum of an empty set to be null. See my April 1993 column "Empty Bags and Identity Crises" [15].

Another correspondent, Martin H. Rusoff of Banc One Financial Card Services in Columbus, Ohio, wrote as follows (again this is an edited extract):

(Begin quote)

It seems to me that the entire discussion is slightly off target . . . There are usually several alternatives to handling [missing information]. These can range from ignoring it up to taking exceptional measures to discover the missing data. Any of these could be automated, but it requires knowledge of what the data *means* and possibly *why it is missing* to decide the correct response. While this might be decided in the data model, more often it depends on the use to which the data will be put—i.e., on the *application*.

Example: Suppose we are given table EMP with a row as shown in Fig. 5, and we need to calculate the total amount needed to meet payroll. Then there are a number of possible responses:

EMP	E#	ENAME	GRADE	SALARY	COMMISSION
	E1	Smith	T4	--	--

Fig. 5 Example EMP row

- I don't know.

- Use the top and bottom figures for the salary for grade T4 to compute maximum and minimum amounts (a similar technique could be used to determine the commission, based on whether grade T4 is eligible for commission or not, and then looking at the maximum and minimum values in the database).

- Use a default of some kind, possibly calculated based on the maximums and minimums computed above.

- Ignore this employee.

- Use statistical data stored elsewhere to come up with probable amounts and then calculate a confidence [rating] for the entire result.

- Initiate exception processing to determine the answer, possibly then continuing to calculate the result ignoring the missing values.

Depending on the situation, any of these might be acceptable. However, an accountant would probably calculate the maximums after determining if a commission might apply and attach a note saying that the data was missing for certain listed individuals. I do not see how a database engine could decide this. *End of example*.

I fully agree that the current treatment is error prone . . . [However,] I am not sure that legislating 3VL, fuzzy logic (with ranges or probabilities), or using defaults is the right answer . . . In the end, it might be appropriate to always generate an error whenever a null is located and permit an application to rerun the query using additional qualifiers telling the database engine how to process the nulls.

Instead of debates of this kind, I would like to see an explanation of how the existing facilities can be used correctly to handle missing data.

(End quote)

I responded to these comments as follows:

I completely agree with Martin Rusoff that it will usually be the case that only the application can decide what to do when nulls are encountered. His example makes the point admirably. But I do not agree with him that "the entire discussion is slightly off target." To be candid, I will admit to a sneaking sympathy with this position—I know the debate must have seemed somewhat academic and not too relevant to the rough-and-tumble of day-to-day operations—but the fact is that such a perception is sadly mistaken.

First of all (as I have observed many times, in the pages of *Database Programming & Design* and elsewhere), **theory is practical!** That is, the theory on which a given DBMS is based necessarily has very practical consequences for the user of that DBMS. And if that theory is bad, the consequences will be bad too.

To see that this is so, it is sufficient to realize that it will often be the DBMS, not the application, that has to "decide what to do when nulls are encountered." I have argued this point before for the particular case of the optimizer component of the DBMS (see reference [6]). Note, moreover, that not all nulls "preexist" in base tables—some are generated dynamically (i.e., in the middle of executing a query). As a result, it is a virtual certainty that it will be the DBMS, not the application, that will have to decide how to deal with them. And the DBMS will typically not have the application-specific knowledge to enable it to make the correct application-specific decisions. Consequence: Wrong answers!

Also, of course, there is the point—admittedly only a psychological point, not a logical one, but a point that is very much a practical consideration—that users will be lulled into a false sense of security by the fact that the system can "handle" missing information. That is, applications often do *not* include the necessary logic to deal with nulls, even when they should, because the user is under the misapprehension that the system has taken that burden off the user's shoulders.

Finally, James R. Alexander of the Goochland-Powhatan Community Services Board, Goochland, Virginia, wrote as follows:

(Begin quote)

If I do not know the gender of Person A and I am asked "Is Person A female?", I respond "I don't know." However, if I am asked "Do you know if Person A is female?", I respond "No." The first question concerns Person A's gender, the second question concerns my knowledge of Person A's gender. A query of a database is certainly a question of the second type . . .

I have developed and been using for over three years a data collection engine which is the front-end for a database . . . This engine understands that every attribute has, in addition to its explicit domain, an implicit domain . . . composed of unknown, not applicable, and not represented (i.e., other), which are consistently represented by ?, !, and #, respectively. The human services organization I work for uses this data collection engine to maintain data for many typical business applications . . . We use various off-the-shelf reporting [programs], which employ two-valued logic, and we get correct results.

(End quote)

I could not agree more with Mr. Alexander. I said much the same thing in reference [11] (page 234): ". . . we obviously cannot ask the system questions about the real world *per se,* only about its knowledge of the real world as represented by values in the database." The critical point, as Mr. Alexander observes, is to stay within two-valued logic. I am glad to hear he has been using his technique successfully for several years.

REFERENCES AND BIBLIOGRAPHY

Note: The style used for references in this chapter differs from that in the rest of the book. It is, however, the style that was used when this article was first published.

1. E. F. Codd, *The Relational Model for Database Management Version 2* (Reading, Mass.: Addison-Wesley, 1990). RM/V2 treatment of missing values may be found in Chapters 8 and 9. For a discussion of the two types of missing values, see p. 191.

2. *Ibid.,* Chapter 23. *Author's note:* "This chapter describes adverse consequences of these errors, suggests corrective steps that DBMS vendors should apply, and precautionary steps users should take in the meantime."

3. E. F. Codd, "Missing Information (Applicable and Inapplicable) in Relational Databases," *ACM SIGMOD Record 15,* No. 4 (1986). See also E. F. Codd, "More Commentary on Missing Information," *ACM SIGMOD Record 15,* No. 5 (1986).

4. E. F. Codd, "Extending the Database Relational Model to Capture More Meaning," *ACM TODS 4,* No. 4 (September 1979).

5. E. F. Codd, Chapter 23 of *The Relational Model for Database Management Version 2* (Reading, Mass.: Addison-Wesley, 1990). *Author's note:* "Date's criticisms are refuted in detail in Chapter 9. (Unfortunately, in the first printing, two errors appeared in the truth table for logical OR on pages 182 and 236. These have been corrected.)"

6. C. J. Date, "Why Three-Valued Logic Is a Mistake" (in this volume).

7. C. J. Date, Section 5.5 ("Null Values") of *An Introduction to Database Management: Volume II* (Reading, Mass.: Addison-Wesley, 1982). A more recent treatment of this topic may be found in C. J. Date, "The Default Values Approach to Missing Information," in C. J. Date and Hugh Darwen, *Relational Database Writings 1989–1991* (Reading, Mass.: Addison-Wesley, 1992).

8. C. J. Date, "Three-Valued Logic and the Real World," *InfoDB 4,* No. 4 (Winter 1989). This article was republished in C. J. Date and Hugh Darwen, *Relational Database Writings 1989–1991* (Reading, Mass.: Addison-Wesley, 1990).

9. E. F. Codd, *The Relational Model for Database Management Version 2,* page 183 (Reading, Mass.: Addison-Wesley, 1990). (The quotation is a paraphrasing.)

10. *Ibid.,* page 189.

11. C. J. Date, "NOT Is Not "Not"! (Notes on Three-Valued Logic and Related Matters," in *Relational Database Writings 1985–1989* (Reading, Mass.: Addison-Wesley, 1990).

12. C. J. Date, Section 5.5 ("Null Values") of *An Introduction to Database Management: Volume II* (Reading, Mass.: Addison-Wesley, 1982).

13. C. J. Date, "Tables with No Columns" (in this volume).

14. C. J. Date, "Nothing in Excess" (in this volume).

15. C. J. Date, "Empty Bags and Identity Crises" (in this volume).

CHAPTER **10**

A Note on the Logical Operators of SQL

ABSTRACT

In reference [1] I raised the question of whether SQL supported, either directly or indirectly, all of the 19,710 possible logical operators of three-valued logic. For SQL as currently defined, the answer to this question is almost certainly *no*. However, this paper shows how SQL could be extended in such a way that—under a certain set of charitable assumptions—that answer could be changed to *yes*.

COMMENTS ON REPUBLICATION

I started my investigation into the question of whether SQL supported all of the logical operators of three-valued logic in 1992. After what seemed at the time to be a considerable amount of work, I convinced myself that in a certain sense SQL might be said to support all 27 *monadic* operators, at least; I therefore wrote up and published that result in a paper entitled "A Note on the Logical Operators of

Portions of this paper were originally published (in considerably different form) under the title "A Note on the Logical Operators of SQL (Part 1)" in *The Relational Journal 5*, No. 1 (February/March 1993). Reprinted with permission.

SQL (Part I)." It was my intention to produce "Part II" if and when I concluded my investigation into the 19,683 *dyadic* operators.

I spent a lot of time on this latter investigation off and on over the next several months, discussing the issue with numerous friends and colleagues, and even writing a program to resolve the issue by enumerating exactly those dyadic operators that SQL did support, before discovering that (again in a certain sense) the problem had in fact previously been solved. As a consequence, "Part II"— which I had anticipated being much longer than Part I—turned out to be very short, and hardly worth publishing as a standalone paper. The paper republished here, therefore, is effectively a combination of the original Part I and the previously unpublished Part II.

I should clarify what I mean by the term *support* in phrases such as "support all possible logical operators." The problem I was addressing, very specifically, was as follows:

- SQL does of course permit the use of *logical expressions* (also known as *conditional* or *truth-valued* expressions) in WHERE clauses and similar contexts, as is well known.

- Such logical expressions are constructed from certain primitive truth-valued expressions (e.g., simple comparisons such as $a = b$) and certain *logical operators* (also known as *connectives*) such as AND, OR, and NOT.

- SQL's logic is, very specifically, three-valued. So the question arises: Are there any logical expressions of that three-valued logic (3VL for short) that ought to be permissible within WHERE clauses and the like, but in fact are not permitted in WHERE clauses in SQL? In other words, are there any 3VL operators that are not directly included in SQL, and moreover cannot be simulated either?

If the answer to this question is *yes,* it would mean that SQL's 3VL support was (at best) incomplete; in fact, it could be argued that SQL thus did not really support 3VL at all.

1. INTRODUCTION

A *logical operator* (also known as a Boolean operator) is an operator whose operands and result are all truth-valued. Familiar examples include the operators AND, OR, and NOT.

Now, in two-valued logic (2VL), there are exactly two truth values, *true* and *false* (abbreviated *t* and *f*). As a consequence, there are exactly four possible *monadic* (single-operand) logical operators—one that maps both *true* and *false* into *true*, one that maps them both into *false*, one that maps *true* into *false* and vice versa (this is NOT, of course), and one that leaves them both unchanged. And there are exactly 16 possible dyadic (two-operand) operators, as indicated by the following table:

	t	f
t	t/f	t/f
f	t/f	t/f

Explanation: Replacing each of the four *t/f* specifications in the table by either *t* or *f* yields the definition of exactly one dyadic operator, because it defines the output for every possible combination of inputs. There are clearly 16 distinct ways of making the replacements, and hence 16 operators. The following table makes the same point in a different way:

A	B																
t	t	t	t	t	t	t	t	t	t	f	f	f	f	f	f	f	f
t	f	t	t	t	t	f	f	f	f	t	t	t	t	f	f	f	f
f	t	t	t	f	f	t	t	f	f	t	t	f	f	t	t	f	f
f	f	t	f	t	f	t	f	t	f	t	f	t	f	t	f	t	f

What about three-valued logic (3VL)? Well, here there are three truth values *true, false,* and *unknown* (abbreviated *t, f,* and *u,* respectively); hence there are $3 * 3 * 3 = 27$ possible monadic operators, because each of the three possible inputs *t, f,* and *u* can map to each of the three possible outputs *t, f,* and *u*. And there are three to the ninth power = 19,683 possible dyadic operators:

	t	u	f
t	t/u/f	t/u/f	t/u/f
u	t/u/f	t/u/f	t/u/f
f	t/u/f	t/u/f	t/u/f

More generally, in fact, *n*-valued logic involves *n to the power n* monadic operators and *n to the power* n^2 dyadic operators.

Now, in the case of 2VL, the four monadic operators and 16 dyadic operators can all be formulated in terms of suitable combinations of NOT and either AND or OR, so it is not necessary to support all 20 operators explicitly (see reference [2] for a proof of this statement). For 3VL—or indeed *n*VL for any *n* > 2—the following questions arise:

- What is a suitable set of *primitive* operators?
- What is a suitable set of *useful* operators?

(Regarding the distinction between "primitive" and "useful," observe that for 2VL either of the sets {NOT, AND} and {NOT, OR} is *primitive*, but the set {NOT, AND, OR} is more *useful*.)

In the case of SQL specifically (which does include some support for 3VL), the question becomes:

■   Do the logical operators that SQL directly supports constitute a *sufficient* set, in the sense that every possible 3VL operator can be obtained by means of some suitable combination of operators from that directly supported set?

This paper investigates this question. For reasons of simplicity, I will concentrate until further notice on the *monadic* 3VL operators specifically. The question of support for dyadic operators is discussed later.

2. SOME FURTHER PRELIMINARIES

There are a few more preliminary matters I need to get out of the way before I can proceed with the substance of the discussion.

1. Although SQL certainly does support several logical operators, the operands for those operators are not simple truth values but, rather, more general expressions that *evaluate* to a truth value. Thus, for example, in SQL I can write

    ```
    ( a = b ) IS UNKNOWN
    ```

    but I cannot write, e.g.,

    ```
    x IS UNKNOWN
    ```

    where x is a literal or simple variable. The reason is, of course, that SQL does not support a truth-valued data type. But it should! In what follows, therefore, I will adopt the convenient fiction that the operands to the logical operators can indeed be (truth-valued) literals or simple (truth-valued) variables. Note that the literal t (or *true*) can be simulated by a logical expression of the form "0 = 0" (say); likewise, the literal u (or *unknown*) can be simulated by a logical expression of the form "NULL = NULL", and the literal f (or *false*) can be simulated by a logical expression of the form "0 = 1".

    Note: I choose to ignore the fact that "NULL = NULL" is not a legal SQL expression (it is easy to construct a workaround).

2. It is convenient, and customary, to adopt a functional notation instead of genuine SQL syntax, and thus to write, e.g., IS UNKNOWN (x) instead of x IS UNKNOWN. I will follow this convention in this paper.

    Note: The "IS UNKNOWN" operator of SQL is in fact the MAYBE operator of reference [3].

3. Please note that the SQL operators IS NULL and IS NOT NULL are *not* logical operators. It is true that they return truth values, but their operands are not truth values. Note too that NULL is not the same as the u or *unknown* truth value (see reference [3] for further discussion of this point).

3. MONADIC OPERATORS SUPPORTED "DIRECTLY"

As indicated previously, I am limiting my attention (until further notice) to the monadic operators only. SQL provides direct support for seven of these, as follows:

SQL expression	abbreviation
NOT x	N(x)
x IS TRUE	IT(x)
x IS UNKNOWN	IU(x)
x IS FALSE	IF(x)
x IS NOT TRUE	INT(x)
x IS NOT UNKNOWN	INU(x)
x IS NOT FALSE	INF(x)

It is convenient to abbreviate the names of these operators as indicated. Here are the truth tables that define them:

N	
t	f
u	u
f	t

IT			IU			IF	
t	t		t	f		t	f
u	f		u	t		u	f
f	f		f	f		f	t

INT			INU			INF	
t	f		t	t		t	t
u	t		u	f		u	t
f	t		f	t		f	f

Note that IS NOT TRUE is the same as NOT(IS TRUE), and similarly for IS NOT UNKNOWN and IS NOT FALSE—indeed, this is how the "IS NOT" operators are defined. It follows that the operators supported by SQL, whatever else they might be, certainly do not constitute a *primitive* or minimal set.

Note: Just as IS UNKNOWN is equivalent to the MAYBE operator of reference [3], so IS NOT FALSE is equivalent to the TRUE_OR_MAYBE operator of that same reference.

The following logical operators are also supported in a manner that is indirect, but only slightly so:

operator	abbreviation
IDENTITY	I
TRUE	T
UNKNOWN	U
FALSE	F

IDENTITY returns its input; TRUE always returns *true;* UNKNOWN always returns *unknown;* and FALSE always returns *false.* In other words, the truth tables look like this:

```
I  |          T  |          U  |          F  |
t  | t        t  | t        t  | u        t  | f
u  | u        u  | t        u  | u        u  | f
f  | f        f  | t        f  | u        f  | f
```

These operators can be simulated in SQL by means of expressions of the form indicated below:

```
required        equivalent expression
--------        ---------------------
I(x)            x
T(x)            0 = 0
U(x)            x = y  (see below)
F(x)            0 = 1
```

In the case of U(x), I am assuming that (a) x is an arbitrary logical expression and (b) y is an arbitrary variable of type truth value whose value happens to be null.

The following table summarizes the situation so far; specifically, it indicates (by their abbreviated names) the eleven monadic operators that are supported "directly" in SQL.

```
        T   I     I I   I             U             I   I N     I     F
            N         N U               N   U         F
            F         U                 T

    t | t t t t  t t t t t  u u u u  u u u u u  f f f f  f f f f f
    u | t t t u  u u f f f  t t t u  u u f f f  t t t u  u u f f f
    f | t u f t  u f t u f  t u f t  u f t u f  t u f t  u f t u f
```

The sixteen operators that are *not* supported directly can conveniently be labeled by the initial letters of the truth values to which they map *true, unknown,* and *false* (in that order):

```
TTU     UTT     UUF     FTU
TUT     UTU     UFT     FUU
TUU     UTF     UFU     FUF
TFU     UUT     UFF     FFU
```

4. MONADIC OPERATORS SUPPORTED INDIRECTLY

I will now show that the sixteen "missing" monadic operators can all be simulated in SQL by means of suitable conjunctions (ANDs) or disjunctions (ORs) of supported operators. For completeness, here are the 3VL truth tables for AND and OR:

```
AND | t u f         OR | t u f
----+------        ----+------
 t  | t u f          t | t t t
 u  | u u f          u | t u u
 f  | f f f          f | t u f
```

First let me give an example. Suppose we wish to examine the conjunction of

INT and INU. The following truth table shows that that conjunction is equivalent to IF, because its final column is identical to the column in the truth table that defines IF; i.e., INT AND INU ≡ IF.

x	INT(x)	INU(x)	INT(x) AND INU(x)
t	f	t	f
u	t	f	f
f	t	t	t

Using this technique, it is easy to verify the following identities (among many others):

1. TTU ≡ U OR INF
2. TUT ≡ I OR N
3. TUU ≡ I OR U
4. TFU ≡ INU AND TTU
5. UTT ≡ U OR INT
6. UTU ≡ U OR IU
7. UTF ≡ UTT AND INF
8. UUT ≡ U OR N
9. UUF ≡ I AND U
10. UFT ≡ UUT AND INU
11. UFU ≡ U AND INU
12. UFF ≡ U AND IT
13. FTU ≡ INT AND TTU
14. FUU ≡ U AND N
15. FUF ≡ I AND N
16. FFU ≡ U AND IF

Since (a) this list includes a definition of every one of the sixteen "missing" operators, and (b) every one of those definitions is in terms of operators that have previously been defined, it follows that all 27 monadic operators are indeed expressible in SQL. ∎

5. DYADIC OPERATORS

Let me now turn to the dyadic operators—of which (as mentioned earlier) there are 19,683. Does SQL support all of these too?

Well, in a certain trivial (and **very** charitable) sense the answer to this question is *yes* also. This is because SQL (i.e., the current SQL standard known informally as SQL/92 [4]) does provide a CASE operator, one form of which is as follows:

```
CASE when-clause-list END
```

A "when clause" in turn takes the form:

```
WHEN logical-expression THEN scalar-expression
```

Let *x* and *y* be arbitrary logical expressions. Then the expression

```
CASE
    WHEN x IS TRUE    AND y IS TRUE    THEN truth-value-1
    WHEN x IS TRUE    AND y IS UNKNOWN THEN truth-value-2
    WHEN x IS TRUE    AND y IS FALSE   THEN truth-value-3
    WHEN x IS UNKNOWN AND y IS TRUE    THEN truth-value-4
    WHEN x IS UNKNOWN AND y IS UNKNOWN THEN truth-value-5
    WHEN x IS UNKNOWN AND y IS FALSE   THEN truth-value-6
    WHEN x IS FALSE   AND y IS TRUE    THEN truth-value-7
    WHEN x IS FALSE   AND y IS UNKNOWN THEN truth-value-8
    WHEN x IS FALSE   AND y IS FALSE   THEN truth-value-9
END
```

(where each of *truth-value-1, -2, . . . , -9* stands for one of the truth value literals *true, unknown,* and *false*) clearly represents an application of that particular dyadic operator whose definition is given by the truth table shown below to the two logical expressions *x* and *y*. (The *t/u/f* column at the left corresponds to *x,* the *t/u/f* row at the top corresponds to *y.*)

	t	u	f
t	truth-value-1	truth-value-2	truth-value-3
u	truth-value-4	truth-value-5	truth-value-6
f	truth-value-7	truth-value-8	truth-value-9

Note, however, that here we are definitely assuming that SQL does support a proper truth-valued data type and proper truth value literals.

However, we would obviously prefer not to have to write out the full definition of each dyadic operator every time we use it; what we want is to be able to define such an operator once only and thereafter simply appeal to that definition.

Part I of this paper as originally published stopped at this point with the words: "For this reason, I regard the issue of whether SQL supports the dyadic operators properly as still an open question." The next section discusses this "open question" further.

6. DYADIC OPERATORS REVISITED

First of all let me say that this section will be quite short, since it turns out that the problem it addresses has effectively already been solved! In our discussions prior to this point, we have seen that SQL can be said to support all 27 monadic 3VL operators, *provided* we make the charitable assumption that SQL supports a truth-valued data type (and does so, moreover, in a fully orthogonal manner). I will refer to this assumption as "Assumption *TV.*"

Now, it is necessary to make Assumption *TV* in order to permit the use of comparisons such as $x = y$ (where x and y are arbitrary logical expressions). Note in particular that if the value of y happens to be null, the expression $x = y$ can be used as an SQL representation of the monadic operator $U(x)$, with truth table as follows:

```
U
─────────
t │ u
u │ u
f │ u
```

This operator is known formally as *the Slupecki T-function* [5]. As can be seen, it returns the *unknown* truth-value u no matter what the truth value of its input. Now, according to reference [5], page 64, a 3VL system that supports all three of the following—

- the familiar NOT operator
- the Slupecki T-function
- the Łukasiewicz implication operator (see below)

—is *truth-functionally complete* (i.e., does indeed support all possible 3VL operators). Now, SQL obviously supports the NOT operator directly, and we have shown that it can be (charitably) regarded as supporting the Slupecki T-function also. As for Łukasiewicz implication, here first is the truth table for that operator:*

```
    │ t u f
────────────
t   │ t u f
u   │ t t u
f   │ t t t
```

Thus, the expression $LI(p,q)$, where LI is the Łukasiewicz implication operator, can be represented by the SQL expression

```
NOT ( p ) OR ( q ) OR ( p IS UNKNOWN AND q IS UNKNOWN )
```

It follows that—**under assumption *TV*—**SQL is truth-functionally complete. ∎

7. CONCLUDING REMARKS

Full, orthogonal support for a truth-valued data type needs to be incorporated into SQL with all due speed.

─────────────

*Łukasiewicz implication is different from the more familiar *material* implication, in which p IMPLIES q is identical to NOT(p) OR (q).

ACKNOWLEDGMENTS

I would like to thank David McGoveran for drawing my attention to the "3VL operators" problem in the first place and for discussing it with me at some length, and Hugh Darwen for challenging me to investigate the problem in detail. I would also like to thank David and Hugh for their comments on earlier drafts of this note, and David for numerous stimulating discussions on the subject of logic in general and 3VL in particular.

REFERENCES AND BIBLIOGRAPHY

1. C. J. Date, "Nothing in Excess" (in this volume).

2. C. J. Date, "Answers to Puzzle Corner Problems (Installment Numbers 1–5)" (in this volume).

3. C. J. Date, "NOT Is Not "Not"! (Notes On Three-Valued Logic and Related Matters)," in *Relational Database Writings 1985–1989* (Reading, Mass.: Addison-Wesley, 1990).

4. C. J. Date and Hugh Darwen, *A Guide to the SQL Standard* (3rd edition) (Reading, Mass.: Addison-Wesley, 1993).

5. Nicholas Rescher, *Many-Valued Logic* (New York, N.Y.: McGraw-Hill, 1969).

RELATIONAL VS. NONRELATIONAL SYSTEMS

Introduction

This part of the book consists almost exclusively of material that had to be dropped for space reasons from the most recent edition (the sixth) of my book *An Introduction to Database Systems* (Addison-Wesley, 1995). Most of that material deals with various precursors to the relational approach to database management—the inverted list approach, the hierarchic approach, and the network (CODASYL) approach. From the standpoint of theory, of course, those approaches are primarily of historical interest; from a practical standpoint, by contrast, they are still of considerable importance in the commercial world. Thus, practitioners certainly need to know something about them. And I would argue that theoreticians too need to have some knowledge of past developments; to repeat from an earlier chapter in this book, those who do not know history are doomed to repeat it. I therefore decided to revise the material appropriately for inclusion in the present book.

The bulk of this part of the book thus consists of three fairly lengthy chapters, as follows:

- Chapter 12 describes the inverted list approach and the inverted list system DATACOM/DB;
- Chapter 13 describes the hierarchic approach and the hierarchic system IMS;
- Chapter 14 describes the network approach and the network (CODASYL) system IDMS.

The chapters are written on the assumption that the reader does have some prior knowledge of relational systems—each includes a certain amount of analysis and assessment from a relational point of view and draws some comparisons with the corresponding aspects of relational technology. Despite this builtin bias, however, I am hopeful that the chapters can serve as useful standalone tutorials on the three major prerelational approaches (indeed, they have been used for exactly this purpose in their previous incarnations).

Of course, inverted lists, hierarchies, and networks (and the corresponding products) obviously differ from one another considerably at the detail level. Nevertheless, they do also share a number of common characteristics, among them the following.

1. First, of course, the various products have all been in existence longer—in some cases much longer—than the current round of relational products.

2. Second, those prerelational products were not developed on the basis of a

predefined abstract data model (the previous point notwithstanding). Instead, any such models were defined *after the event* by a process of abstraction or induction from existing implementations.* The relational model was the first example of a data model that was defined prior to any implementation— indeed, it was the first example of a data model, period. Relational systems were the first systems to be constructed in accordance with the prescriptions of a predefined abstract model.

3. Prerelational systems are at a lower level of abstraction than relational systems. In particular, they are all basically record-at-a-time systems (except as indicated in point 6 below). Of course, this state of affairs is a direct consequence of the fact that the systems were originally designed some considerable time ago. Comparing a relational system and a nonrelational system is in some ways analogous to comparing a more recent programming language such as Ada or APL to an older one such as COBOL; as time goes by, the level of abstraction tends to increase in database systems just as it does in programming languages (and for very similar reasons).

4. To pursue the point of the previous paragraph a little further: The "data models" for the various prerelational systems can be regarded as abstractions of certain familiar *storage* structures (with their associated operators). Loosely speaking, the inverted list model is an abstraction of the indexed file organization, and the hierarchic and network models are both abstractions of the pointer chain or parent/child file organization (with certain elements of hashing and indexing thrown in). If a relational system is to a prerelational system as Ada or APL is to COBOL, then a prerelational system is to a file management system as COBOL is to Assembler Language.

5. As a result of their record-at-a-time orientation, nonrelational systems are all fundamentally *programming* systems; the primary user in every case is an application programmer, typically using COBOL, who has to navigate manually through the database. Any "optimization" is generally performed by that application programmer, not by the system.

6. *End* users are supported by means of online application programs, either vendor-supplied (i.e., builtin) or installation-written (or possibly supplied by a third-party software vendor).

   Note: In connection with the foregoing, it is significant that just about every nonrelational system known to this writer—with the noteworthy exception of IMS—has been extended to include some kind of "relational" frontend (i.e., an additional software layer to support "relational" access, possibly by

---

*At the time of writing, the hierarchic approach is still the only one of the three ever to have been subjected to any *formal* analysis, so far as I am aware. See reference [3] in Chapter 13.

an end user, to a nonrelational database). "Relational" is in quotes here because it is certainly not the case that those frontends all provide the kind of function that can and should be expected of a true relational system. Furthermore, I should also mention that there are some very severe technical problems involved in trying to provide such a frontend (see reference [5] in Chapter 13).

7. Even if a nonrelational system can be extended to include a relational frontend as suggested above, there will still be a significant difference between such a system and a "pure" relational system, namely as follows: *In a nonrelational system, users can always access the database through the low-level, nonrelational (record-at-a-time) interface.* (Such access is not possible in a pure relational system, of course.) As a result, it might be possible to **subvert the system**—e.g., by bypassing certain relational security or integrity controls, or by creating or updating a database in such a way as to make it impossible to provide a pure relational view of that database.

A few words regarding the structure of these three chapters:

- In each case the chapter starts with a little background information on the approach (inverted list, hierarchic, or network) to be discussed.

- That background information is then followed by an attempt to define the underlying data model for that approach, before getting into details of the example system *per se*. (The reason I say "attempt" here is explained in point 2 above.)

- Next, the chapter gives an overview of the system and describes its basic data definition and data manipulation operators. It also briefly touches on the applicable storage structure in each case.

- At this point the descriptions diverge to discuss features that are specific to the particular system under consideration. In the case of IMS, for example, the chapter discusses *logical databases* and *secondary data structures.* The DATACOM/DB and IDMS chapters include a brief description of the product extensions that move those systems in the direction of relational support.

It goes without saying that a lot of detail is omitted in all three cases. The system descriptions are also considerably simplified in many places (in particular by not using genuine syntax, for the most part).

Finally, some words regarding the other two chapters in this part of the book:

- Chapter 11 discusses the concept of *essentiality,* which is helpful in understanding one very important aspect of the difference between relational and nonrelational systems in general. The reader will find it helpful to bear this concept in mind throughout the discussions of the inverted list, hierarchic, and network approaches that follow in the next three chapters.

■ Chapter 15 presents a tutorial overview of frontend subsystems. This is a topic that is somewhat independent of the question of whether the underlying system is relational or otherwise—though I would argue that it is at least easier to build a well-integrated, coherent set of such frontend subsystems if the foundation is indeed relational and not something else.

CHAPTER **11**

Essentiality

ABSTRACT

We discuss the notion of **essentiality,** which is crucial to understanding one of the key differences between relational and nonrelational databases.

COMMENTS ON REPUBLICATION

See the introduction to this part of the book.

1. INTRODUCTION

The concept of essentiality was introduced by Codd in reference [1] in order to help pin down a fundamental distinction between relational and nonrelational databases. Although the relational *vs.* nonrelational debates *per se* are by now mainly a matter of historical interest, the essentiality notion is still a great aid to clear thinking in certain contexts. The purpose of this short note is to describe and explain that notion.

Originally published (in considerably different form) in my book *An Introduction to Database Systems: Volume I,* 5th edition, pages 371–376 (Addison-Wesley, 1991). Reprinted by permission.

2. A HIERARCHIC DATABASE

The only data structure provided in the relational model is the relation itself. In order to appreciate the significance of this fact, it is necessary to have at least a superficial understanding of one or more other data structures that are not relational. We therefore present a very brief tutorial here on the **hierarchic** data structure* (since that structure is probably the next easiest to understand).

Consider the simple departments-and-employees database shown in relational form in Fig. 1. This database contains three department rows and five employee rows: Department D1 has two employees (E1 and E2), department D3 has three employees (E3, E4, and E5), and department D2 currently has no employees at all.

A hierarchic version of the same data is shown in Fig. 2 (column headings omitted to avoid unnecessary clutter). The hierarchic structure consists of three **trees** or **hierarchies,** one for each of the three departments. Each tree consists of:

- One department (DEPT) row,[†] plus

- One employee (EMP) row for each employee in that department, plus

- **Links** connecting those rows together appropriately (shown as vertical lines in Fig. 2).

The links can be thought of as *chains of pointers*—a pointer from each DEPT row to the first EMP row for that DEPT, a pointer from that EMP row to the next for the same DEPT, and so on, and finally a pointer from the last EMP row for a

DEPT			EMP			
DEPT#	DNAME	BUDGET	EMP#	ENAME	DEPT#	SALARY
D1	Sales	20M	E1	Lopez	D1	40K
D2	Dvpmt	9M	E2	Cheng	D1	42K
D3	Admin	18M	E3	Finzi	D3	30K
			E4	Saito	D3	35K
			E5	Jacob	D3	40K

Fig. 1 The departments-and-employees database (relational)

---

*This material is treated in more detail in reference [2]. It might be helpful to point out that the hierarchic data structure is really nothing more than a slight abstraction of the familiar parent/child *storage* structure (see, e.g., reference [4], Appendix A).

[†]We use the term "row" because it is familiar from relational systems. It is not the term normally used in hierarchic systems.

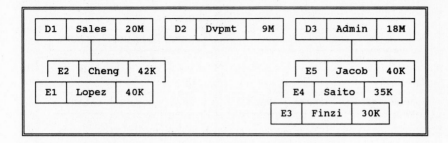

Fig. 2 The departments-and-employees database (hierarchic)

given DEPT back to the original DEPT row. *Note:* These pointers might be physically represented in storage by actual pointers or by some functionally equivalent method; however, the user can always *think* of the pointers as physically existing, regardless of the actual implementation.

In this hierarchic structure, DEPTs are said to be the **parent** rows and EMPs the **child** rows. In general, each parent row has zero or more corresponding child rows, and each child row has exactly one corresponding parent row. A child cannot exist in a hierarchy without its parent. Thus, if the user issues a request to delete a parent, then the DBMS must either automatically delete the children (if any) of that parent too, or it must reject the request if any such children exist. (In other words, hierarchies can in principle support either a CASCADES or a RESTRICTED delete rule, but not a NULLIFIES rule, in relational terms.)

Note carefully that the EMP rows of Fig. 2 do not include a DEPT# component. To find out what department a given employee is in, it is necessary to traverse the link from the applicable EMP row to the corresponding DEPT (parent) row. Likewise, to find all employees in a given department, it is necessary to traverse the link from the applicable DEPT row to the corresponding EMP (child) rows. In other words, the information that was represented by *foreign keys* in the relational version is represented by *links* in the hierarchic version; links are the hierarchic analog of foreign keys, speaking *very* loosely.

Now, the two diagrams above (Figs. 1 and 2) are of course *instance* diagrams—they show actual data values. By contrast, the (time-independent) *structure* of the two versions of the database is shown by the two structure diagrams in Fig. 3. In the hierarchic structure diagram (right half of the figure), we have labeled the department-employee link explicitly as DEPTEMP, for purposes of subsequent reference. That link (shown as a single line in Fig. 3) must be understood to represent multiple chains of multiple pointers each, just as the boxes in the same figure must be understood to represent multiple rows. *Note*: The meaning of the remark "DEPTEMP essential" in the figure will be explained in Section 4.

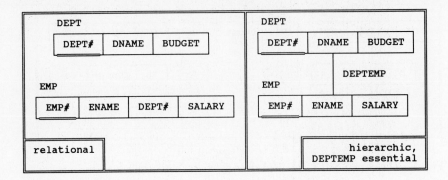

Fig. 3 Structure diagrams for departments-and-employees

3. QUERYING THE HIERARCHIC DATABASE

We now consider two sample queries against the departments-and-employees database. For each query we show a relational formulation (using SQL) and a hierarchic formulation (using a hypothetically extended version of SQL to cater for hierarchic structures).

Q1: Get employee numbers and employee names for employees with salary greater than 20K.

Relational:

```
SELECT  EMP#, ENAME
FROM    EMP
WHERE   SALARY > 20K ;
```

Hierarchic:

```
SELECT  EMP#, ENAME
FROM    EMP
WHERE   SALARY > 20K ;
```

Q2: Get employee numbers and employee names for employees with salary greater than 20K in department D3.

Relational:

```
SELECT  EMP#, ENAME
FROM    EMP
WHERE   SALARY > 20K
AND     DEPT# = 'D3' ;
```

Hierarchic:

```
SELECT  EMP#, ENAME
FROM    EMP
WHERE   SALARY > 20K
AND   ( SELECT DEPT#
        FROM   DEPT
        OVER   EMP ) = 'D3' ;
```

For query Q1 the two formulations are obviously identical. For query Q2, however, they are not. The relational formulation for Q2 still has the same basic form as for Q1 (SELECT–FROM–WHERE, with a simple restriction condition in the WHERE clause); the hierarchic formulation, by contrast, has to make use of a new language construct, namely the "OVER" clause (which is our hypothetical SQL representation of a link-traversing operation). The WHERE condition in that formulation is certainly not a simple restriction condition.

The examples thus illustrate the important point that the hierarchic data structure *fundamentally requires* certain additional data access operators. Note carefully too that those operators *are* additional; the operators needed for the relational structure are still needed as well, as query Q1 demonstrates. Note moreover that this point applies not only to all the other data manipulation operators (INSERT, DELETE, etc.) as well, but also to the definitional operators, the security operators, the integrity operators, etc., etc. The links of the hierarchic data structure thus serve only to add *complexity;* they certainly do not add any *power*—there is nothing that can be represented by a hierarchy (i.e., by rows and links) that cannot be represented by relations (i.e., by rows) alone.

Now, it is sometimes suggested that the complexity problems of the hierarchic structure can be reduced, if not eliminated, by reinstating the DEPT# component (i.e., the foreign key) in the EMP row as shown in Fig. 4. Given the revised hierarchy of that figure, query Q2 (hierarchic version) can now be formulated without using the OVER construct at all; in fact, the formulation becomes identical to the relational version. The reason is, of course, that the rows (both DEPT and EMP) in that revised hierarchy are identical to their relational counterparts; the database is now the same as the relational version, except for the presence of the DEPTEMP link. However, that link is now entirely redundant; there is no information represented by link DEPTEMP that is not also represented by the foreign key EMP.DEPT#, and the user can therefore ignore the link without any loss of function.

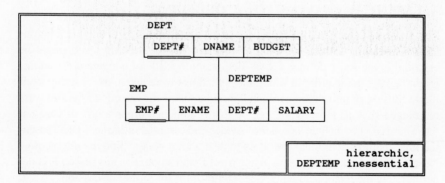

Fig. 4   Structure diagram for the departments-and-employees hierarchy (EMP.DEPT# reinstated)

4. RELATIONAL *vs.* NONRELATIONAL DATABASES

We can now explain the notion of **essentiality**. A data object is **essential** if its loss would cause a loss of information—by which we mean, very precisely, that *some relation would no longer be derivable*. For example, in the relational version of departments-and-employees, all data objects (the two rows and their seven components) are essential in this sense. Likewise, in the original hierarchic version (Fig. 3), all data objects (the two rows, their six components, and the link) are again essential. But in the revised hierarchy of Fig. 4, the rows and their components are essential *but the link is inessential*. There is no information that can be derived from that revised hierarchy that cannot be derived from the rows and their components alone. There is no logical need to use the link at all.

Note: It is sometimes argued that the opposite is the case—the DEPTEMP link is essential and the foreign key EMP.DEPT# is inessential. But that argument misses the point, which is that, since some row components *must* be essential, and nothing else need be (since everything *can* be represented by values in rows), then why involve anything else?

It is now possible to pin down an absolutely crucial difference between a relational database and any other kind of database, say a hierarchic database. In a relational database, the *only* essential data object is the relation itself (loosely speaking, the database is just rows and their components). In other kinds of database, **there must be at least one additional essential data object** (such as an essential link). For if there is not, then the database is really a relational database that happens to have certain access paths exposed (and there is no requirement that the user use those access paths, and the question arises as to why they are exposed anyway when others are not). And it is those additional essential data objects that lead to much (not all) of the complexity of nonrelational databases.*

5. ESSENTIAL *vs.* INESSENTIAL ORDERING

The concept of essentiality allows us to explain why it is significant that relations have no ordering to their rows. In an ordered file, the ordering itself might be essential in the sense defined above. For example, a file of temperature readings might be kept in the order in which those readings were taken; the ordering itself might thus carry information, which would be lost if the records of the file were rearranged (just as information can be lost if someone drops a box of cards, if those cards do not include a sequence field). And essential ordering, like an essential link, requires additional operators to deal with it—e.g., "find the nth record," "insert a record between records n and $n + 1$," and so on. For this reason it is not permitted in the relational model. See reference [5] for further discussion.

---

*A striking example in support of this claim appears in Chapter 14 (Example 5.8).

Note: It is sometimes suggested that *in*essential ordering might be acceptable, however. A file is said to be inessentially ordered if it is ordered on the basis of the value(s) of some field(s)—for example, the employee file might be ordered by employee number, but no information would be lost if the records were shuffled around. Some relational systems do in fact support ordering in this sense. Note, however, that relations *per se* are unordered by definition; it would be better to regard an "ordered relation" as a totally distinct kind of object—perhaps in fact as, precisely, a sequential file. In this regard, the SQL ORDER BY operation might best be thought of as converting a relation into such a file, rather than "ordering a relation."

In any case, even inessential data constructs can cause problems, because they do still carry information, even though they are inessential; for example, they might represent a security exposure. See reference [6] for further discussion of this point.

6. CONCLUDING REMARKS

Relational languages such as SQL always include four basic data manipulation operations (SELECT, INSERT, UPDATE, and DELETE in the case of SQL). And the fact that there *are* only four such operations is a consequence of the simplicity of the relational data structure. All data in a relational database is represented in exactly the same way, namely as values in column positions within rows of tables. Since there is only one way to represent anything, we need only one operator for each of the four basic manipulative functions (retrieve, insert, change, delete). By contrast, systems based on a more complex data structure fundamentally require $4n$ such operations, where n is the number of ways that data can be represented in that system. In CODASYL systems, for example [3], where data can be represented either as rows or as links between rows, we typically find a STORE operation to create a row and a CONNECT operation to create a link; a MODIFY operation to change a row and a RECONNECT operation to change a link;* an ERASE operation to destroy a row and a DISCONNECT operation to destroy a link; and so on.

REFERENCES AND BIBLIOGRAPHY

1. E. F. Codd and C. J. Date, "Interactive Support for Nonprogrammers: The Relational and Network Approaches," in C. J. Date, *Relational Database: Selected Writings* (Reading, Mass.: Addison-Wesley, 1986).

---

*In the interests of accuracy, we should mention that the specific CODASYL implementation described in reference [3] does not in fact support the RECONNECT operation.

2. C. J. Date, "A Hierarchic System: IMS" (in this volume).

3. C. J. Date, "A Network System: IDMS" (in this volume).

4. C. J. Date, *An Introduction to Database Systems* (6th edition) (Reading, Mass.: Addison-Wesley, 1995).

5. C. J. Date, "Why Duplicate Rows Are Prohibited," in *Relational Database Writings 1985–1989* (Reading, Mass.: Addison-Wesley, 1990).

6. C. J. Date, "Some Relational Myths Exploded," in *Relational Database: Selected Writings* (Reading, Mass.: Addison-Wesley, 1986).

CHAPTER **12**

An Inverted List System: DATACOM/DB

ABSTRACT

We present a tutorial overview of "the inverted list model" and a leading example thereof, DATACOM/DB from Computer Associates.

COMMENTS ON REPUBLICATION

See the introduction to this part of the book.

1. BACKGROUND

DATACOM/DB—or CA-DATACOM/DB, to give it its full name—is a product of Computer Associates (previously Applied Data Research) for IBM mainframes running MVS, VM, or VSE. It can be regarded as a typical example of an inverted

Originally published (in somewhat different form) in my book *An Introduction to Database Systems: Volume I,* 5th edition, pages 737–751 (Addison-Wesley, 1991). Reprinted by permission.

list DBMS. In this chapter we present a reasonably detailed overview of DATACOM/DB, in order to give some idea of what it is that constitutes a typical inverted list system. *Note:* As indicated in the introduction to this part of the book, no one has ever defined an abstract "inverted list data model," so far as this writer is aware. However, Section 2 below describes in an informal manner what such an abstract model might look like. The rest of the chapter then goes on to describe DATACOM/DB specifically.

The reader might find the following helpful as a guide to understanding systems like DATACOM/DB. Many relational systems—though not all—can be thought of as inverted list systems at the internal level. For example, IBM's DB2 can be thought of in such a way; that is, the *Stored Data Manager* component of DB2 provides what is essentially an "inverted list" set of functions—with the important difference that those functions are not exposed to the human user, but are instead used by other, higher-level DB2 components whose purpose in turn is to provide the true user interface (namely SQL) to the end user or application programmer. Thus an inverted list DBMS might loosely be regarded as a system comparable to the low-level component of a relational DBMS such as DB2, in which users operate directly at the record-at-a-time level instead of at the relational (set-at-a-time) level.

Note: Since the above was first written, DATACOM/DB has been extended to provide an SQL interface on top of the original inverted list interface. For obvious reasons, however, we restrict our attention in the present chapter to the inverted list interface specifically.

2. THE INVERTED LIST MODEL

Data Structure

An inverted list database is similar to a relational database—but a relational database at a low level of abstraction, a level at which the stored tables themselves **and also certain access paths to those stored tables** (in particular, certain indexes) are directly visible to the user. (Remember from the introduction to this part of the book that "user" here means an application programmer specifically.) Like a relational database, an inverted list database contains a collection of "tables" or files, and those "tables" or files are divided into rows (records) and columns (fields) as in the relational case. However, there are some significant differences too, of course:

1. First, the rows of an inverted list table, unlike the rows of a relational table, are considered to be **ordered** in some physical sequence. Note that this physical sequence is independent of any additional orderings that might be imposed on the table by means of indexes (see paragraph 3 below).

The fields within the rows or records are likewise considered to be ordered, left to right.

2. Next, an ordering might also be defined for the *total database,* in which (for example) all the rows of table *A* are considered to precede all the rows of table *B,* or the rows of tables *A* and *B* are considered to be interleaved in some specific way. We refer to this ordering as the **database sequence**. The physical sequence for a given table will be some subsequence of the overall database sequence.

3. For a given table, any number of **search keys** can be defined. A search key is an arbitrary field or field combination over which an index is to be built. Such indexes permit both direct and sequential access on the basis of search key values; in particular, of course, they support sequential access via an ordering that is different from the underlying physical sequence.

   Note that access via a search key and access via a nonindexed field are *different operations* (indeed, access via a nonindexed field might not even be possible, depending on the system). In other words, indexes are not "transparent to the user" in an inverted list system. However, the user is not responsible for *maintaining* those indexes—on the contrary, index maintenance is handled by the DBMS, just as it is in a relational system.

Data Manipulation

The data manipulation operators in any record-level system (inverted list or otherwise) are crucially dependent on the notion of **record addressing**. In general, the operators in such a system will fall into two broad classes:

1. Operators that establish addressability to some record in the database;
2. Operators that operate on the record at some previously established address.

We refer to operators in the first of these two categories variously as **search, locate,** or **find** operators. Such operators in turn fall into two subsidiary classes:

a. Operators that locate a record "out of the blue"— i.e., **direct** search operators.

b. Operators that locate a record in terms of its position relative to some previously established address—i.e., **relative** search operators.

Examples of all three cases follow.

■ An example of Case 1a—direct search operators—is "Locate the first record in physical sequence in table *T*." The system finds the requested record and returns its address in some designated program variable *P*.

■ An example of Case 1b—relative search operators—is "Locate the first record in physical sequence in table *T* following the record whose address is given by variable *P*." The system finds the requested record and returns its address in that same variable *P*.

- An example of Case 2—operators that operate on the record at some previously established address—is "Delete the record whose address is given by variable *P*."

We refer to variables such as *P* in these examples as "*database address* (or *pointer*) variables." They perform a function that is somewhat analogous to that of cursors in embedded SQL. A program can maintain addressability to any number of records at the same time by supplying enough database address variables.

Note carefully that, in the case of the search operators, the system needs to know the **access path** by which it is to locate the desired record, so that it can understand what is meant by terms such as "first" and "next." The access path in the examples above was physical sequence for table *T*. The other available access paths in an inverted list database are provided by (a) the total database sequence and (b) the defined indexes (i.e., the search keys). The access path for a given search operation is specified as follows:

- In the·case of a direct search operator (e.g., "locate first"), it is specified as one of the operands to the operation.
- In the case of a relative search operator (e.g., "locate next"), it is *not* specified as an operand. Instead, what happens is the following. When any search operator (direct or relative) is executed, the system returns, not only the address of the record found, but also certain control information to identify the access path that was used to locate that record. (Both the address and the control information are returned in the same database address variable *P*.) Thus, when a relative search operator specifies a particular variable *P* to identify the start point for the search, it is also implicitly specifying the access path along which that search is to be performed. The access path information in *P* must not be changed by the user.

It is normally not possible to go part way down one access path and then veer off on another.

Here then are some examples of typical inverted list operations (*T* is a table in the database, *K* is a search key for *T*, and *P* is a database address variable):

- LOCATE FIRST: Find the first record of *T* in physical sequence, and return its address (plus access path ID) in *P*.
- LOCATE FIRST WITH SEARCH KEY EQUAL: Find the first record of *T* in *K* sequence having a specified value for *K*, and return its address (plus access path ID) in *P*.

- LOCATE NEXT: Find the first record of T following the record identified by P (using the access path identified by P), and return its address in P.

- LOCATE NEXT WITH SEARCH KEY EQUAL: Find the first record of T following the record identified by P having the same value for K as that record (using the access path identified by P, which must be "K sequence"), and return its address in P.

- LOCATE FIRST WITH SEARCH KEY GREATER: Find the first record of T following the record identified by P and having a higher value for K than that record (using the access path identified by P, which must be "K sequence"), and return its address in P.

- RETRIEVE: Retrieve the record identified by P.

- UPDATE: Update the record identified by P.

- DELETE: Delete the record identified by P.

- STORE: Store a new record and return its address in P.

Data Integrity

Support for general integrity rules of arbitrary complexity is not included in the inverted list model. Some systems do provide some limited special-case support, allowing certain constraints—e.g., field uniqueness constraints—to be specified declaratively and enforced automatically, but most constraints will normally have to be enforced by the user (i.e., by installation-written procedural code). In particular, referential integrity is typically the user's responsibility.

3. AN OVERVIEW OF DATACOM/DB

We now proceed with our detailed examination of DATACOM/DB specifically. As mentioned in Section 1, DATACOM/DB runs on IBM mainframes under VSE, VM, and MVS. It provides a CALL-level interface for application programs written in any of the following languages: COBOL, PL/I, FORTRAN, RPG II, and System/370 Assembler Language. In the case of COBOL (only), it also provides an interface called DATACOM/DL—also known as COBOL/DL—which consists essentially of a set of extensions to COBOL that are expanded via a preprocessor into conventional CALLs.

A DATACOM/DB system can support up to 999 databases. Each database is defined by adding an appropriate set of descriptors to the DATACOM/DB dictionary (DATADICTIONARY). The definition process is performed interactively through a forms-based interface.* The descriptors for a given database specify (in effect) the DATACOM/DB versions of all three levels of the so-called

---

*See Chapter 15.

"ANSI/SPARC architecture"—internal, conceptual, and external—though the three are not always clearly distinguished. In particular, of course, the descriptors specify the tables, fields, and search keys involved in the database. *Note:* The DATACOM/DB term for search key is simply *key*. We will stay with the term "search key," however, in order to avoid confusion with the common relational use of the unqualified term "key" to mean the *primary* key specifically. DATACOM/DB does not have a notion of primary key *per se*.

The unit of access to a DATACOM/DB database is called an **element**. An element can be thought of as a "subrecord"; it consists of an arbitrary collection of contiguous fields from the record in question. Note the contiguity requirement; for example, given our usual supplier record with fields (in left-to-right order, remember!) S#, SNAME, STATUS, and CITY,* there are ten possible elements that can be defined—one covering the entire record, two involving three fields each, three involving two fields each, and four involving a single field each. Each element can be individually protected against unauthorized access. Retrieval operations can access any subset of the elements of the record, subject of course to the authorization controls just mentioned.

The remainder of this chapter has the following structure. Following this brief overview section, Section 4 explains the DATACOM/DB data definition process in a little more detail. At the same time, it also necessarily introduces certain aspects of the DATACOM/DB storage structure (since the user's view of the database is definitely affected by that structure, as we will see). Section 5 then discusses some of the most important DATACOM/DB data manipulation operations. Last, Section 6 describes the *Compound Boolean Selection* feature (CBS), an extension to the original DATACOM/DB base product that adds the beginnings of some relational functionality to that product.[†]

We do not have room in this chapter for a detailed discussion of such aspects of DATACOM/DB as recovery, concurrency, etc. We content ourselves instead with the following brief comments. First, the system does provide a set of recovery and concurrency controls, more or less conventional in nature. It also provides a set of security controls, both at the element level (as already mentioned) and also at the table and database levels. As for integrity, DATACOM/DB requires most integrity controls to be provided by user-written code; however, it is possible to specify for any given table that a certain search key, the "master key," must have DUPLICATES NOT ALLOWED (see Section 4).

---

*See Section 1 of Chapter 1 ("An Overview of INGRES and QUEL") if you need to refresh your memory regarding the suppliers-and-parts database.

[†]Following the acquisition of ADR in 1988 by Computer Associates, announcements were made to the effect that DATACOM/DB would be integrated with CA's own CA-UNIVERSE product (which was originally a QUEL-based relational DBMS) to produce a true SQL-based relational product. Details of that integration are beyond the scope of this chapter, but it should be noted that CA does now advertise DATACOM/DB as an SQL product.

We conclude this section with a brief survey of some of the frontend subsystems and other auxiliary products that run with DATACOM/DB:

- DATADICTIONARY (already mentioned)
- DATACOM/DL (already mentioned)
- DATACOM/DC (a DC manager)
- DATAQUERY (a relational query/update frontend, for both interactive and batch use)
- DATAREPORTER (a batch report writer)
- DATAENTRY (a generalized interactive data entry application)
- DATADESIGNER (a logical database design aid)
- IDEAL (an application development system, with relational operators for database access)

In addition, a distributed version of the product called CA:DB-STAR has also been released.

4. DATA DEFINITION

As explained in Section 2, indexing in an inverted list system such as DATACOM/DB is typically visible to the user. Any discussion of the DATACOM/DB logical data structure must therefore necessarily include some description of the corresponding physical storage structure also. Briefly, a DATACOM/DB database can be thought of as a collection of stored records, each stored record belonging to exactly one table, together with **a single** (B-tree) **index over all of the records in the database**. That single index actually supports *all* of the search keys in *all* of the tables in the database. By way of illustration, we give a DATACOM/DB version of the suppliers-and-parts database (with numerous details omitted, of course).

Note: For simplicity, we do not show genuine DATACOM/DB syntax. In fact, as mentioned in Section 3, data definition in DATACOM/DB is actually done interactively, via a forms-based interface to the ADR dictionary (DATADICTIONARY). For present purposes, however, it is obviously more convenient to show the definitions in a conventional linear manner.

First the suppliers table:

```
ADD TABLE S      TABLEID =  1
     FIELDS      S#      =  CL5
                 SNAME   =  CL20
                 STATUS  =  H
                 CITY    =  CL15
     ELEMENTS    S       =  ( S#,SNAME,STATUS,CITY )
                 S#      =  ( S# )
                 SNAME   =  ( SNAME )
```

```
                    STATUS  =  ( STATUS )
                    CITY    =  ( CITY )
       SEARCH KEYS  S#      =  ( S# )      KEYID = 1
                    CITY    =  ( CITY )    KEYID = 5
       MASTER KEY   S#      DUPLICATES NOT ALLOWED
                            UPDATES         ALLOWED
       NATIVE KEY   S#
```

Explanation:

- The TABLEID clause gives a unique internal identifier to the table (1, in the example).

- The FIELDS portion of the definition specifies the four fields of the table and their data types (DATACOM/DB supports the standard IBM System/370 data types: CL5 is a character string of length 5, H is halfword binary, etc.).

- The ELEMENTS portion defines five elements—one for each field in isolation and one for the combination of all four fields. For simplicity we have given each element the same name as the object from which it is derived.

- The SEARCH KEYS portion defines two search keys, S# (based on the S# field) and CITY (based on the CITY field); for simplicity, again, we have given each search key the same name as the field from which it is derived. The significance of the KEYID specifications will be explained in a moment.

- Finally, the MASTER KEY and NATIVE KEY clauses specify that the search key S# is both the **master key** and the **native key** for the suppliers table. Every table is required to have exactly one master key and exactly one native key (they do not have to be identical, though they are in our example). The significance of these two keys is as follows:

  a. The master key can optionally be specified "unique" (DUPLICATES NOT ALLOWED) and nonupdatable (UPDATES NOT ALLOWED). *Note:* In our example, we are ignoring the unfortunate DATACOM/DB restriction that if updates are allowed then duplicates must be allowed also (!).

  b. The native key controls the physical clustering of records of the table in storage (see later).

Now the parts table:

```
ADD TABLE P    TABLEID =  2
     FIELDS    P#      =  CL6
               PNAME   =  CL20
               COLOR   =  CL6
               WEIGHT  =  H
               CITY    =  CL15
     ELEMENTS  P       =  ( P#,PNAME,COLOR,WEIGHT,CITY )
               P#      =  ( P# )
               PNAME   =  ( PNAME )
               COLOR   =  ( COLOR )
               WEIGHT  =  ( WEIGHT )
```

```
                        CITY     =   ( CITY )
            SEARCH KEYS P#       =   ( P# )     KEYID = 2
                        COLOR    =   ( COLOR )  KEYID = 4
                        CITY     =   ( CITY )   KEYID = 5
            MASTER KEY  P#       DUPLICATES NOT ALLOWED
                                 UPDATES        ALLOWED
            NATIVE KEY  P#
```

Now we can explain the KEYID specification. Observe that the CITY search keys for the two tables S and P have been given the same search key ID, namely 5. **As far as DATACOM/DB is concerned, they are therefore the same search key**. The CITY index entries for suppliers in a particular city, say London, will be physically adjacent to the CITY index entries for parts in that same city (see the explanation of index structure below). As a result, queries of the form "Find suppliers and parts that are colocated" (which will have to make use of the index) will be reasonably efficient.

Finally the shipments table:

```
ADD TABLE SP        TABLEID =   3
    FIELDS          S#       =   CL5
                    P#       =   CL6
                    QTY      =   F
    ELEMENTS        SP       =   ( S#,P#,QTY )
                    S#       =   ( S# )
                    P#       =   ( P# )
                    QTY      =   ( QTY )
    SEARCH KEYS     S#       =   ( S# )     KEYID = 1
                    P#       =   ( P# )     KEYID = 2
                    SHIP#    =   ( S#,P# )  KEYID = 3
    MASTER KEY      SHIP#    DUPLICATES NOT ALLOWED
                             UPDATES        ALLOWED
    NATIVE KEY      S#
```

Note the SEARCH KEYS, MASTER KEY, and NATIVE KEY specifications here —in particular, note the search key IDs, and note the fact that S# is specified as the native key. Since S# is also the native key for table S, supplier and shipment records will be physically clustered together on the basis of matching supplier numbers. For example, shipment records for supplier S1 will be stored physically close to the supplier record for supplier S1. Furthermore, the supplier and shipment records for supplier S1 will precede and be close to those for supplier S2, those for S2 will precede and be close to those for supplier S3, and so on.

We are now in a position to explain the structure of the (single) DATACOM/DB index. Conceptually, that index is built on a single hypothetical composite field, made up as follows:

```
search key ID + search key value + table ID
```

Each index entry contains a value for this hypothetical field, together with a pointer to a corresponding record in the database. In our example, the search key IDs and table IDs are as follows:

```
search key IDs :    S#      1
                    P#      2
                    SHIP#   3
                    COLOR   4
                    CITY    5

table IDs       :   S       1
                    P       2
                    SP      3
```

The overall sequence of index entries is thus as indicated below (assuming the usual set of sample data values):

search key	value	table	pointer
S#	S1	S	pointer to S record for S1
S#	S1	SP	pointer to 1st SP record for S1
S#	S1	SP	pointer to 2nd SP record for S1
..	..	..	. . . . .
S#	S1	SP	pointer to last SP record for S1
S#	S2	S	pointer to S record for S2
S#	S2	SP	pointer to 1st SP record for S2
..	..	..	. . . . .
S#	S5	..	pointer to S record for S5
P#	P1	P	pointer to P record for P1
P#	P1	SP	pointer to 1st SP record for P1
..	..	..	. . . . .
..	..	..	. . . . .
P#	P6	SP	pointer to last SP record for P6
SHIP#	S1/P1	SP	pointer to SP record for S1/P1
..	..	..	. . . . .
SHIP#	S4/P5	SP	pointer to SP record for S4/P5
COLOR	Blue	P	pointer to 1st P record for Blue
..	..	..	. . . . .
COLOR	Red	P	pointer to last P record for Red
CITY	Athens	S	pointer to 1st S record for Athens
..	..	..	. . . . .
CITY	Rome	P	pointer to last P record for Rome

Points arising:

1. This single index does indeed provide the functionality of separate indexes on S.S#, SP.S#, SP.(S#,P#), etc.

2. Note that the index includes many entries per record, in general.

3. As already explained, the index entries for (e.g.) S.S# and SP.S# are interleaved in such a way as to provide a form of inter-file clustering (in the index entries themselves, that is, not in the data). Access via the index to a given S record and its corresponding SP records will thus be reasonably fast, because the relevant index entries, at least, will be physically close together. Analogous remarks apply to the index entries for P.P# and SP.P# and to the index entries for S.CITY and P.CITY.

4. Furthermore (again as already explained), a given S record and its corresponding SP records will also be stored physically close together, because S# has been defined as the native key for both tables. Analogous remarks do *not* apply to P records and their corresponding SP records, nor to S and P records for the same city (data can be physically clustered in one and only one way, of course).

5. Since every table must have at least one search key (because every table must have both a master key and a native key, not necessarily distinct), every record in the database is represented at least once in the index. Thus the index provides a total ordering over all records in the database, and programs can exploit that ordering in a variety of ways. Note, however, that (as already pointed out), a given record might appear several times in that total ordering.

5. DATA MANIPULATION

As explained in Section 2, the manipulative operators in an inverted list system such as DATACOM/DB fall into two broad classes, those that establish addressability ("search operators") and those that operate on the record at a previously established address. In addition, the search operators can be further subdivided into direct search operators and relative search operators. The following list is a brief summary of the principal DATACOM/DB operators, grouped in accordance with the foregoing classification. The list is not intended to be exhaustive; in particular, it does not include the operators of the Compound Boolean Selection feature, which will be discussed in Section 6.

Direct search operators:

```
GSETP  --  locate (and read) first record in physical sequence
LOCKX  --  locate first record with specified search key equal
           to specified value
LOCKY  --  locate first record with specified search key equal
           to or greater than specified value
REDKY  --  same as LOCKX + REDLE
RDUKY  --  same as LOCKX + RDULE
```

Relative search operators:

```
GETPS  --  locate (and read) next record in physical sequence
LOCNX  --  locate next record
LOCBR  --  locate previous record (backward search)
LOCNE  --  locate next record with same search key value
LOCNK  --  locate first record with greater search key value
LOCKL  --  locate first record with same or lower search key
           value (backward search)
REDNX  --  same as LOCNX + REDLE
RDUNX  --  same as LOCNX + RDULE
REDNE  --  same as LOCNE + REDLE
RDUNE  --  same as LOCNE + RDULE
```

Operators that operate on a previously located record:

```
REDLE  --  read located record
RDULE  --  read located record for update (set exclusive lock)
DELET  --  delete located record
UPDAT  --  update located record
RELES  --  release exclusive lock
```

And one more important operator:

```
ADDIT  --  store new record; does not establish addressability
```

Each of these operators takes three operands (among others that we choose to ignore): a *request area,* an *I/O area,* and an *element list* (in general—but not all operands are needed for all operations). The request area corresponds to what we called the database address variable in Section 2; it is used to hold position and access path information, and also a return code from the most recent operation that used this request area (blank means the operation was successful). The I/O area and element list are required for retrieval (GSETP, GETPS, RED*xx*, RDU*xx*), UPDAT, and ADDIT operations; the I/O area serves the obvious purpose, and the element list indicates the elements of the record that are to be retrieved, updated, or stored.

We now present a small set of manipulative examples (ignoring many details, however, and making use of a very much simplified syntax).

5.1 Direct Retrieval. Get the supplier record for supplier S4.

```
LOCKX  using request-area-1
       ( table = S,
         search-key = S#,
         value = 'S4' ) ;
REDLE  using request-area-1
       ( element-list = S ) ;
```

Or simply:

```
REDKY  using request-area-1
       ( table = S,
         search-key = S#,
         value = 'S4',
         element-list = S ) ;
```

5.2 Sequential Retrieval. Get part numbers for parts supplied by supplier S4.

```
LOCKY  using request-area-1
       ( table = SP,
         search-key = S#,
         value = 'S4' ) ;
while "record found" on request-area-1
do ;
   REDLE  using request-area-1
          ( element-list = P# ) ;
   LOCNE  using request-area-1 ;
end ;
```

5.3 Sequential Retrieval. Get part numbers for parts supplied by suppliers in London.

```
LOCKY   using request-area-1
        ( table = S,
          search-key = CITY,
          value = 'London' ) ;
while "record found" on request-area-1
do ;
   REDLE   using request-area-1
           ( element-list = S# ) ;
   LOCKY   using request-area-2
           ( table = SP,
             search-key = S#,
             value = S# value read in preceding REDLE ) ;
   while "record found" on request-area-2
   do ;
      REDLE   using request-area-2
              ( element-list = P# ) ;
      LOCNE   using request-area-2 ;
   end ;
   LOCNE   using request-area-1 ;
end ;
```

5.4 Sequential Retrieval. Get part numbers for parts supplied by suppliers with status 20 (compare example 5.3).

```
GSETP   using request-area-1
        ( table = S,
          element-list = S#, STATUS ) ;
while "record found" on request-area-1
do ;
   if STATUS = 20 then
   do ;
      LOCKY   using request-area-2
              ( table = SP,
                search-key = S#,
                value = S# value read in preceding REDLE ) ;
      while "record found" on request-area-2
      do ;
         REDLE   using request-area-2
                 ( element-list = P# ) ;
         LOCNE   using request-area-2 ;
      end ;
   end ;
   GETPS   using request-area-1
           ( element-list = S#, STATUS ) ;
end ;
```

Since STATUS has not been defined as a search key, searching for suppliers with status 20 has to be done by an exhaustive scan. We choose to perform that scan in physical sequence, for reasons of performance.

5.5 Update. Add 10 to the status for supplier S4.

```
LOCKX   using request-area-1
        ( table = S,
          search-key = S#,
          value = 'S4' ) ;
```

```
RDULE  using request-area-1
         ( element-list = STATUS ) ;
set STATUS = STATUS + 10 in I/O area ;
UPDAT  using request-area-1
         ( element-list = STATUS ) ;
```

Before a record can be updated (or deleted), it must first be retrieved with one of the RDU*xx* operations ("read for update").

5.6 Storing a New Record. Store a new supplier record (supplier number S6, name Robinson, status 35, city unknown).

```
move 'S6', 'Robinson', 35 to I/O area for request-area-1 ;
ADDIT  using request-area-1
         ( element-list = S#, SNAME, STATUS ) ;
```

The CITY field will be set to blanks in the new record.

6. THE COMPOUND BOOLEAN SELECTION FEATURE

The Compound Boolean Selection feature (CBS) was added to the original DATACOM/DB product in 1985 or thereabouts. The general objective of CBS is to provide increased flexibility and increased data independence at the application programming interface; as explained in Section 3, it can be regarded as a step toward converting DATACOM/DB into a true relational DBMS. A good way of explaining CBS (at perhaps rather a superficial level) is to compare it with embedded SQL. The major CBS operations, and their embedded SQL equivalents, are as follows:

- SELFR — "select first"

  SELFR is analogous to a combination of the embedded SQL operations DECLARE CURSOR, OPEN, and FETCH. Thus, one of the operands of SELFR is a *query* (not a CBS term), defining a set of records; that set is opened or "activated" (also not a CBS term), and the first record of that active set is retrieved. The defining query consists of a table name, a restriction condition, and an optional ordering specification.

- SELNR — "select next"

  SELNR is analogous to FETCH in embedded SQL, though it does also provide certain additional functions (to be discussed).

- SELSM — "select same"

  SELSM retrieves the current record (again). Embedded SQL has no equivalent of this function.*

---

*No longer true; SQL (i.e., SQL/92) now includes a statement of the form FETCH RELATIVE *n*, in which the value *n* = 0 is legal and has the effect of re-retrieving the current row.

- UPDAT/DELET — "update"/"delete"

  UPDAT and DELET are analogous in the CBS context to the embedded SQL operations UPDATE CURRENT and DELETE CURRENT, respectively.

- SELPR — "release set"

  SELPR is analogous to CLOSE in embedded SQL.

The foregoing operations clearly provide more function than the basic data manipulation facilities described in Section 5:

1. First, access paths—that is, *logical* access paths—do not have to be predefined but can be specified dynamically via the SELFR operation.

2. Second, those logical access paths can be defined in terms of arbitrary restriction conditions, involving any fields—they are not limited to simple conditions of the form "search key equal (or greater than or equal) to value." In fact, there is no reliance on predefined search keys at all.

3. Third, the ordering of those logical access paths can also be specified dynamically.

On the other hand, the fact that the condition in a path definition must be a simple restriction—in particular, the fact that it cannot involve a join—means that CBS alone still does not qualify DATACOM/DB as a true relational system.

The CBS feature provides a number of further facilities in addition to those sketched above:

1. First, the SELFR operation can optionally include the following specifications (not genuine CBS syntax):

   · UNIQUE (specifiable only if ordering is specified)

   Records with the same value for the ordering field(s) as the record most recently retrieved will be skipped over during subsequent retrieval requests.

   · COUNT

   The cardinality of the active set is returned.

   · n (quota)

   Subsequent retrieval requests will return "not found" after the first n records of the active set have been retrieved. This facility can be used—in conjunction with the dynamic ordering facility—to implement such retrievals as "Get the three heaviest parts" (for example).

   · FOR UPDATE

   An exclusive lock will be applied to each record as it is retrieved. FOR UPDATE is required if the retrieved record is subsequently to be updated or deleted. The lock will be released automatically on the next retrieval if the record has not in fact been updated or deleted. *Note:* FOR UPDATE can be specified on SELNR and SELSM as well as on SELFR.

2. Second, SELNR ("select next") can specify a "skip count." A skip count of +*n* causes SELNR to retrieve the record *n* positions after the current record in the active set. Similarly, a skip count of -*n* causes it to retrieve the record *n* positions before the current record. Skip counts of 0 and -32768 cause SELNR to retrieve the first record and the last record, respectively. SELFR initializes the skip count to +1.

3. Third, it is also possible to establish certain "interrupt limits" in SELFR. An example of an interrupt limit is "number of I/O's." If that number is exceeded during SELFR execution, control is returned to the application program with an appropriate return code in the request area. At that point the program can issue any one of the following operations:

   - SELPR, which cancels the SELFR entirely (no active set is established)
   - SELST, which stops execution of the SELFR but accepts the partially built active set as a basis for subsequent processing (SELNR, etc.)
   - SELCN, which continues building the active set (the interrupt counters are all reset, and might subsequently cause another interrupt during further execution of the same SELFR)

We conclude this section, and this chapter, by observing that the availability of the CBS feature clearly implies the existence of a query optimization component within the DATACOM/DB system. Detailed characteristics of that optimizer are unknown at the time of writing.

EXERCISES

1. Define a DATACOM/DB version of the suppliers-parts-projects database (see Exercise 1 in Chapter 1, "An Overview of INGRES and QUEL").

The remaining exercises are all based on the suppliers-parts-projects database. In each case you are asked to write a series of DATACOM/DB statements for the indicated operation. Use operators of the Compound Boolean Selection feature where appropriate.

2. Get S# values for suppliers who supply project J1.

3. Get S# values for suppliers who supply project J1 with a red part.

4. Get P# values for parts supplied to all projects in London.

5. Get J# values for projects not supplied with any red part by any London supplier.

6. Get P# values for parts supplied by at least one supplier who supplies at least one part supplied by supplier S1.

7. Get all pairs of CITY values such that a supplier in the first city supplies a project in the second city.

8. Change the color of all red parts to orange.

9. The quantity of P1 supplied to J1 by S1 is now to be supplied by S2 instead (in addition to any quantity of P1 that S2 already supplies to J1). Make all the necessary changes.

CHAPTER **13**

A Hierarchic System: IMS

ABSTRACT

We present a tutorial overview of "the hierarchic model" and the leading example
thereof, IBM's IMS.

COMMENTS ON REPUBLICATION

See the introduction to this part of the book.

1. BACKGROUND

IMS is an IBM program product for the MVS environment. It was one of the
earliest database systems to become commercially available—the first version of
the system ("IMS/360 Version 1") was released in 1968—and at the time of writing it is still one of the top two or three products, if not *the* top product, in the
mainframe marketplace, both in terms of number of systems installed and also in

Originally published (in somewhat different form) in my book *An Introduction to Database Systems:
Volume I,* 5th edition, pages 753–789 (Addison-Wesley, 1991). Reprinted by permission.

terms of user commitment.* We therefore use it as our example of the hierarchic approach.

Note: The full name of the current version of IMS is "Information Management System/Enterprise Systems Architecture (IMS/ESA) Database Manager," and IBM manuals invariably refer to it by this full name. However, we will continue to use the abbreviated form "IMS" in this chapter.

Hierarchic systems, like inverted list systems, were not originally constructed on the basis of a predefined abstract data model; rather, such a model was defined after the event by a process of abstraction from implemented systems (principally from IMS, in fact—see reference [3]). As with our discussion of inverted list systems in Chapter 12, however, it is convenient to discuss the abstract model first— even if such a discussion must necessarily be somewhat hypothetical—before embarking on a description of the details of IMS *per se*. Section 2 is therefore devoted to a discussion (fairly informal) of such a hypothetical model.

2. THE HIERARCHIC MODEL

Hierarchic Data Structure

A hierarchic database consists of an ordered collection of **trees**—more precisely, an ordered collection consisting of many **occurrences** of a single **type** of tree. We discuss types first, then go on to discuss occurrences later.

A *tree type* consists of a single **root** record type, together with an ordered collection of zero or more dependent (lower-level) subtree types. A subtree type in turn also consists of a single record type—the root of the subtree type—together with an ordered collection of zero or more lower-level dependent subtree types, and so on. The entire tree type thus consists of a hierarchic arrangement of record types. In addition, of course, record types are made up of field types in the usual way.

As an example, consider the education database[†] of Fig. 1, which contains information about the internal education system of a large industrial company. The company in question maintains an education department whose function is to run a number of training courses for the employees of the company; each course is offered at a number of different locations within the organization, and the database contains details both of offerings already given and of offerings scheduled to be given in the future. The database contains the following information:

- For each course: course number, course title, details of all immediate prerequisite courses, and details of all offerings

---

*Though DB2 is certainly running it close.

[†]We deliberately depart for a while from our usual suppliers-and-parts example.

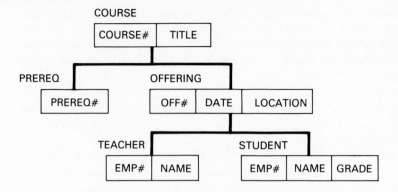

Fig. 1 Structure of the education database

- For each prerequisite course for a given course: course number for that prerequisite course
- For each offering of a given course: offering number, date, location, details of all teachers, and details of all students
- For each teacher of a given offering: employee number and name
- For each student of a given offering: employee number, name, and grade

The tree type for the education database has COURSE as its root record type and has two subtree types, rooted in the PREREQ and OFFERING record types, respectively (and note that this collection of subtree types is ordered—that is, the PREREQ subtree type definitely precedes the OFFERING subtree type, as the figure suggests). The subtree type rooted in PREREQ is "root only"; by contrast, the subtree type rooted in OFFERING in turn has two lower-level subtree types, both root only, rooted in the TEACHER and STUDENT record types, respectively. Again the subtree types are ordered.

The database thus contains five record types: COURSE, PREREQ, OFFERING, TEACHER, and STUDENT. COURSE (as already stated) is the root record type, the others are **dependent** record types. Furthermore, COURSE is said to be the **parent** record type for record types PREREQ and OFFERING, and PREREQ and OFFERING are said to be **child** record types for record type COURSE. Likewise, OFFERING is the parent record type for TEACHER and STUDENT, and TEACHER and STUDENT are child record types for OFFERING. The connection between a given child (type) and its corresponding parent (type) is called a **link** (type). *Note:* It is normal to drop the qualifiers "type" and "occurrence" whenever it is possible to do so without risk of ambiguity, though for the purposes of the present section we will continue to be specific (usually).

At this point it might be helpful to point out the principal—indeed, crucial— difference between a hierarchic structure such as that of Fig. 1 and the equivalent relational structure. That difference is as follows: **In a hierarchic database, certain information that would be represented in a relational database by foreign keys is represented instead by parent-child links**. In the education database, for example, the connection between OFFERINGs and COURSEs is represented, not by a COURSE# field in the OFFERING record, but rather by the COURSE-OFFERING link.* This difference in structure naturally leads to a difference in the operators also, as we will see.

So much for types; now we turn our attention to *occurrences*. The root/ parent/child (etc.) terminology just introduced for types carries over into occurrences too. Thus, each tree occurrence consists of a single root record occurrence, together with an ordered collection of zero or more occurrences of each of the subtree types immediately dependent on the root record type. Each of those subtree occurrences in turn also consists of a single record occurrence—the root of the subtree occurrence—together with an ordered collection of zero or more occurrences of each of the subtree types immediately dependent on that root record type, and so on. In other words, for any given occurrence of any given parent record type, there are n occurrences of each of its child record types (n greater than or equal to zero). For an illustration, see Fig. 2, which shows a single tree from the education database of Fig. 1—more accurately, of course, a single tree *occurrence*.

We explain the tree of Fig. 2 as follows. By definition, that tree contains a single COURSE occurrence (the root of the tree). That COURSE has two subordinate PREREQs and three subordinate OFFERINGs (more accurately, that COURSE *occurrence* has an *ordered collection* of two subordinate PREREQ *occurrences* and an *ordered collection* of three subordinate OFFERING *occurrences*). We say that the COURSE is a parent (occurrence), with two PREREQ children and three OFFERING children (i.e., child occurrences). Likewise, the first OFFERING is also a parent, with one TEACHER child and several STUDENT children (only three shown). The other two OFFERINGs have no TEACHER or STUDENT children at present. Furthermore, each parent (occurrence) is considered to be the parent in as many links (i.e., link occurrences) as that parent has children; the COURSE record in Fig. 2, for example, is the parent in two occurrences of the COURSE-PREREQ link and the parent in three occurrences of the COURSE-OFFERING link. Conversely, each child (occurrence) is the child in exactly one link (occurrence).

---

*Note, however, that in general not all such connections will be represented by links; on the contrary, some will still be represented by fields, as in a relational database. For example, field PREREQ.PREREQ# in Fig. 1 is a foreign key in the conventional relational sense.

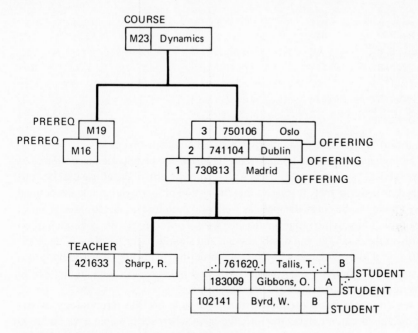

Fig. 2 Sample tree for the education database

In addition to the foregoing, there is one term that applies to occurrences and not to types—the term "twin." All occurrences of a given child type that share a common parent occurrence are said to be **twins**. Thus, for example, the three OFFERINGs in Fig. 2 are twins (even though there are three of them!). Note by contrast that the PREREQs in that figure are not twins of those OFFERINGs, because, although they have the same parent as those OFFERINGs, they are of a different type.

The reader will have observed the frequency with which the concept of ordering was mentioned during the foregoing explanations. In fact, the notion of ordering is critical to the hierarchic data structure. Consider some (sub)tree type T, with root record type R and subtree types $S1, S2, \ldots, Sn$ (in that order). Let t be an occurrence of T, with root r (an occurrence of R) and subtrees $s1, s2, \ldots, sn$ (occurrences of $S1, S2, \ldots, Sn$, respectively). Then we define the *hierarchic sequence* for t—recursively—to be that sequence obtained by taking record r first, followed by all of the records of $s1$ in hierarchic sequence, followed by all of the records of $s2$ in hierarchic sequence, ..., followed by all of the records of sn in hierarchic sequence. For example, the hierarchic sequence for the tree of Fig. 2 is as follows:

```
COURSE        M23
PREREQ        M16
PREREQ        M19
OFFERING        1
TEACHER    421633
STUDENT    102141
STUDENT    183009
    ..........
STUDENT    761620
OFFERING        2
OFFERING        3
```

(i.e., top-to-bottom, left-to-right order, also called depth-first order).

Note that each individual tree in the database can be regarded as a subtree of a hypothetical "system" root record. As a result, **the entire database can be considered as a single tree**. It follows that the notion of hierarchic sequence defined above applies to the entire database as well as to each individual (sub)tree. That is, the notion of hierarchic sequence defines a *total ordering* for the collection of all records in the database, and databases can and should be regarded as being (logically) stored in accordance with that total ordering. (This idea is particularly important in IMS, because many of the IMS manipulative operators are defined in terms of that total ordering. See Section 5.)

We conclude this subsection with a brief note on IMS terminology. In explaining the hierarchic data structure, we have wherever possible used common and fairly standard terms, such as "tree," "record," and so on. However, IMS uses *segment* in place of the more familiar "record," and refers to an entire tree of segments—somewhat confusingly—as a *database record*. The terms "tree," "subtree," and "link" are not used in IMS at all; however, they are convenient, and we will continue to use them in this chapter.

Hierarchic Data Manipulation

A hierarchic data manipulation language consists of a set of operators for operating on data represented in the form of trees. Examples of such operators include the following:

- An operator to locate a specific tree in the database—for example, an operator to locate the tree for course M23 (see Fig. 2);

- An operator to move from one such tree to the next—for example, an operator to step from the tree for course M23 to the tree that follows it in the hierarchic sequence of the database;

- Operators to move from record to record within such a tree by moving up and down the various hierarchic paths—for example, an operator to step from the COURSE record for course M23 to the first OFFERING record for that course;

- Operators to move from record to record in accordance with the hierarchic sequence of the database—for example, an operator to step from a TEACHER record for a particular OFFERING to a STUDENT record for that OFFERING or for some subsequent OFFERING;

■ An operator to insert a new record at a specified position within such a tree— for example, an operator to insert a new OFFERING into the tree for course M23;

■ An operator to delete a specified record—for example, an operator to delete a particular OFFERING from the tree for course M23;

and so on. Note that (as the examples suggest) such operators are typically all *record-level*. It is true that certain hierarchic systems do support certain set-level operators also, but such operators are outside the scope of "the hierarchic model," as that term is usually understood.

Hierarchic Data Integrity

The hierarchic model includes "automatic" support for certain forms of referential integrity, by virtue of the following rule: *No child is allowed to exist without its parent.* (The rule refers to occurrences, of course, not types.) For example, if a given parent is deleted, the system will automatically delete the entire (sub)tree that is rooted at that parent. Likewise, a child cannot be inserted unless its parent already exists. In relational terminology, therefore, we can say—a little loosely— that the hierarchic data structure automatically enforces the following "foreign key rules":

```
NULLS NOT ALLOWED
DELETE ... CASCADES
UPDATE ... CASCADES
```

IMS in particular supports certain additional rules by means of its logical database and secondary indexing facilities. See Sections 7 and 8.

3. AN OVERVIEW OF IMS

We turn now to IMS specifically. First, the definitional aspects. There are two principal definitional constructs in IMS, the **database description** (DBD) and the **program communication block** (PCB). We explain these two constructs in out- line as follows.

1. An IMS database is of course a hierarchic database,* in the sense of Section 2; it consists of a hierarchic arrangement of **segments** (i.e., records), and each

---

*At least from the user's point of view. Under some circumstances, however, the physical (stored) structure is more network-like (see Section 7).

segment in turn consists of an ordered collection of **fields**. Each such database is defined by means of a DBD, which specifies (among other things) the hierarchic structure of that database.

2. However, users deal, not with databases directly, but with *views* of those databases ("view" is not an IMS term). A given user's view of a given database consists basically of a "subhierarchy," derived from the underlying hierarchy by omitting certain segments and/or certain fields. Such a view is defined by means of a PCB, which specifies (among other things) the hierarchic structure of that view.

We can thus see that, *very* approximately, a DBD is the IMS equivalent of SQL's "CREATE TABLE" and a PCB is the IMS equivalent of SQL's "CREATE VIEW"—with the significant difference that CREATE TABLE and CREATE VIEW are dynamic operations and can be performed at any time, whereas DBD and PCB definition are static operations and require the execution of an IMS utility. Furthermore, the simple explanation above ignores two very important points:

- First, a given IMS database can be either **physical** or **logical**. A physical database has a DBD that directly describes the representation of that database in physical storage. A logical database, by contrast, has a DBD that describes the representation of that database in terms of one or more other (physical) databases; i.e., a "logical" DBD is defined in terms of one or more underlying "physical" DBDs. The referential integrity rules for a logical database are significantly more complex than those for a physical database. (The simple rule given in Section 2, to the effect that no record— i.e., segment—can exist without its parent, tacitly assumed that the database in question was physical, in IMS terms.)

- Second, if the DBD corresponding to a given PCB defines a database having one or more **secondary indexes,** then it is possible for that PCB to specify, not just a subhierarchy of the underlying hierarchy, but a **secondary data structure**. A secondary data structure is still a hierarchy, but a hierarchy in which the participant segments have been rearranged, possibly drastically. (A secondary index in IMS is a significantly more complex object than secondary indexes as usually understood, as we will see.)

As a result of these two considerations, the true IMS picture is considerably more complicated than our initial brief explanation might have suggested. For further details, see Sections 7 and 8.

We turn now to data manipulation. IMS is invoked via a CALL interface called DL/I (Data Language/I) from application programs written in PL/I, COBOL, or System/370 Assembler Language. Note, therefore, that (as usual in nonrelational systems) the user in IMS is definitely an *application programmer*; in this chapter, therefore, we restrict our use of the term "user" accordingly.

Note: The full IMS system includes, not only the DBMS component that is the principal topic of this chapter, but also a transaction manager and data communications (DC) component called the IMS/ESA Transaction Manager. In other words, IMS is a full "DB/DC system." The DC component provides facilities (a) to permit the user to define the mappings between byte string messages and the physical layout of those messages on the terminal ("Message Formatting Services"), and (b) to allow programs to send and receive such messages ("DL/I DC calls," so called to distinguish them from DL/I database or DB calls). However, details of such facilities are beyond the scope of this chapter.

The remainder of the chapter has the following structure. After this preliminary overview section, Section 4 explains IMS data definition (i.e., the DBD and PCB constructs); note, however, that the more complex aspects—logical databases and secondary indexing—are not discussed at all until Sections 7 and 8. Section 5 describes IMS data manipulation (i.e., the DL/I database calls). Section 6 then presents a necessarily brief introduction to IMS storage structures. Next, as already indicated, Sections 7 and 8 describe the logical database and secondary index features omitted from Section 3. Finally, Section 9 presents a few concluding remarks.

There is no room in this chapter for a detailed discussion of such topics as recovery, concurrency, etc. We content ourselves with the following brief remarks:

- *Recovery:* The recovery features of IMS are both extensive and sophisticated, and include all of the features (transaction, system, and media recovery) expected of a full-function database system.

- *Concurrency:* IMS concurrency control is based on record (segment) locking, though certain additional controls are also provided. However, IMS does not automatically support full two-phase locking but rather a protocol that more nearly resembles the "cursor stability" (CS) protocol of DB2. In terms of the SQL standard (i.e., SQL/92), this means—*very* roughly speaking!—that IMS supports the isolation level READ COMMITTED, not SERIALIZABLE.

- *Security:* Just as views can be used to hide information in a relational system, so PCBs can be used (though not so flexibly) to hide information in IMS. PCBs are also used to specify the DL/I operations (get, insert, etc.) the user is allowed to execute on the "view." In addition, IMS provides a range of facilities (password checking, etc.) to ensure that specific transactions can be invoked only by specific end users and/or from specific terminals.

- *Integrity:* IMS will optionally enforce certain field uniqueness constraints (see Section 4). In addition (as already indicated), certain referential integrity constraints are supported directly by the hierarchic data structure itself (together with certain explicit insert/update/delete rules, in the case of logical databases; see Section 7).

IMS also possesses a fairly extensive family of related products, as is only to be expected for a system that has been available for as long as IMS has. Such products include a data dictionary, query interfaces (both interactive and batch), an application generator, design aids, testing and debugging aids, measurement and tuning tools, and many other facilities. Such products are available from several other vendors in addition to IBM.

To conclude this section, we stress the point that our treatment of IMS in this chapter is necessarily very superficial. Many details are simply ignored. As a result, our explanations might make the system appear unrealistically straightforward! The fact is, IMS is a very complex system—complex, that is, not only internally, but externally too; the user interface to IMS is *extremely* complicated. And needless to say it is precisely the details— the numerous special cases, exceptions, interdependencies, etc., that the user has to learn and deal with—that give rise to all the complexity. Indeed, one of Codd's motivations for developing the relational model in the first place was precisely to escape from the complexities of systems such as IMS [4].

4. DATA DEFINITION

As explained in the previous section, there are two major definitional constructs in IMS, the database description (DBD) and the program communication block (PCB). We discuss the DBD first. Fig. 3 shows a possible DBD for the education database. (We remind the reader that we are ignoring numerous details in this chapter; in particular, Fig. 3 does not show details of how the database is mapped to physical storage. However, some of those details will be discussed briefly in Section 6.)

```
 1     DBD       NAME=EDUCPDBD
 2     SEGM      NAME=COURSE,BYTES=36
 3     FIELD     NAME=(COURSE#,SEQ),BYTES=3,START=1
 4     FIELD     NAME=TITLE,BYTES=33,START=4
 5     SEGM      NAME=PREREQ,PARENT=COURSE,BYTES=3
 6     FIELD     NAME=(PREREQ#,SEQ),BYTES=3,START=1
 7     SEGM      NAME=OFFERING,PARENT=COURSE,BYTES=21
 8     FIELD     NAME=(OFF#,SEQ),BYTES=3,START=1
 9     FIELD     NAME=DATE,BYTES=6,START=4
10     FIELD     NAME=LOCATION,BYTES=12,START=10
11     SEGM      NAME=TEACHER,PARENT=OFFERING,BYTES=24
12     FIELD     NAME=(EMP#,SEQ),BYTES=6,START=1
13     FIELD     NAME=NAME,BYTES=18,START=7
14     SEGM      NAME=STUDENT,PARENT=OFFERING,BYTES=24
15     FIELD     NAME=(EMP#,SEQ),BYTES=6,START=1
16     FIELD     NAME=NAME,BYTES=18,START=7
17     FIELD     NAME=GRADE,BYTES=1,START=25
```

Fig. 3 DBD (many details omitted) for the education database

Explanation:

- Statement 1 merely assigns the name EDUCPDBD ("education physical DBD") to the DBD.

- Statement 2 defines the root segment as having the name COURSE and a length of 36 bytes.

- Statements 3–4 define the fields that go to make up COURSE. Each is given a name, a length in bytes, and a start position within the segment. Field COURSE# is defined (via the SEQ specification) to be the sequence field for COURSE segments, which means that (a) COURSE# values are unique within the database, and (b) COURSE segments (and therefore trees) will be sequenced within the database in ascending course number order.

    Note that IMS does not support any field data types, in the usual sense of that term; instead, all fields are considered simply as byte strings (all field comparisons are performed bit by bit from left to right). Note too that IMS also allows segments to have nonunique or omitted sequence fields. Details of these latter possibilities are beyond the scope of this chapter.

- Statement 5 defines PREREQ as a 3-byte segment that is a child of COURSE. Statement 6 defines the single field of PREREQ, namely field PREREQ#. That field is defined as the sequence field for PREREQ, which means that (a) PREREQ# values are unique within COURSE, and (b) for each occurrence of COURSE, PREREQ segments will be sequenced in ascending prerequisite number order (in other words, the SEQ specification defines "twin sequence" for PREREQ segments).

- Statements 7–10 are analogous to statements 5–6. The sequence field for OFFERINGs is OFF# (offering number).

- Statements 11–13 define TEACHER (a child of OFFERING) and its fields. Statements 14–17 define STUDENT similarly.

We turn now to "user views" and the PCB. Any particular user view is a subhierarchy of the underlying DBD hierarchy, derived from that underlying hierarchy in accordance with the following three rules:

1. Any field type can be omitted.

2. Any segment type can be omitted.

3. If a given segment type is omitted, then all of its children must be omitted too.

Rule 3 implies that the root of the PCB hierarchy must be the same as the root of the DBD hierarchy. Consider the education database of Fig. 1 once again. Ignoring Rule 1, there are basically ten user views that can be derived from that database. One is shown in Fig. 4. What are the others?

Those segments and fields included in the user view—segments COURSE,

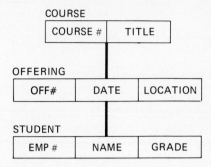

COURSE

| COURSE # | TITLE |

OFFERING

| OFF# | DATE | LOCATION |

STUDENT

| EMP # | NAME | GRADE |

Fig. 4 Sample user view of the education database

OFFERING, and STUDENT, with their constituent fields, in the case of Fig. 4—are said to be **sensitive**. A user of the view will not be aware of the existence of any other segments or fields. Thus the IMS "user view" mechanism, like the view mechanism in a relational system, protects the user from certain kinds of growth in the database. It also provides a degree of control over data security.

Fig. 5 shows a PCB for the user view of Fig. 4—except that, purely for the sake of the example, we have excluded the LOCATION field from the OFFERING segment. Sensitive segments and sensitive fields are specified by SENSEG and SENFLD statements, respectively; if no SENFLDs are specified for a given SENSEG, all fields of that segment are assumed to be sensitive by default. The PROCOPT entries in the SENSEG statements specify the types of operation the user will be permitted to perform on the corresponding segments; possible values include G ("get"), I ("insert"), R ("replace"), D ("delete"), or any combination. The PCB statement simply identifies the underlying DBD.

```
1    PCB        DBDNAME=EDUCPDBD
2    SENSEG     NAME=COURSE,PROCOPT=G
3    SENSEG     NAME=OFFERING,PARENT=COURSE,PROCOPT=G
4    SENFLD     NAME=OFF#,START=1
5    SENFLD     NAME=DATE,START=4
6    SENSEG     NAME=STUDENT,PARENT=OFFERING,PROCOPT=G
```

Fig. 5 PCB for the user view of Fig. 4 (excluding the LOCATION field)

5. DATA MANIPULATION

The IMS data manipulation language (DL/I) is invoked from the host language (PL/I, COBOL, or System/370 Assembler Language) by means of ordinary subroutine calls. Here is an example of such a call, in which the host is PL/I:

```
CALL PLITDLI ( SIX, GU, EDPCB, STUDENT_AREA, CSSA, OSSA, SSSA ) ;
```

This call is intended to retrieve a specific STUDENT segment from the education database. The operands are interpreted as follows:

- PLITDLI ("PL/I to DL/I") identifies the entry point into IMS from a PL/I program.

- SIX represents a PL/I numeric variable whose value (presumably six) represents a count of the number of arguments in the call, excluding the count argument itself.

- GU represents a PL/I character string variable whose value (presumably "GU") specifies the DL/I operation to be performed. ("GU" stands for "get unique"—see later.)

- EDPCB ("education PCB") represents a PL/I structure corresponding to the PCB for the user view against which the operation is to be performed. This argument is explained in more detail below.

- STUDENT_AREA represents a PL/I character string variable into which the desired STUDENT segment is to be retrieved. In other words, STUDENT_AREA represents the *I/O area* for the call.

- CSSA, OSSA, and SSSA represent PL/I character string variables whose values in turn are **segment search arguments** or *SSAs*. An SSA consists of a segment name, an optional set of "command codes" (see later), and an optional restriction condition. Typical SSAs might be:

```
CSSA:    COURSE    WHERE TITLE = 'Dynamics'
OSSA:    OFFERING  WHERE DATE  > '750101'
SSSA:    STUDENT   WHERE GRADE = 'A'
```

(not genuine IMS syntax). A "get unique" with these three SSAs will retrieve the first STUDENT in hierarchic sequence for which the grade is A and the offering date is greater than 750101 and the course title is Dynamics.

To explain the EDPCB argument, it is convenient to remind the reader of certain facilities of embedded SQL, namely *cursors* and the *SQL Communication Area* (SQLCA). Briefly, a cursor is a database position holder, and the SQLCA is a feedback area.* *EDPCB can be regarded as the IMS equivalent of a cursor and a corresponding feedback area in combination.*[†] In IMS, however, a program does not have just one feedback area as it does in SQL, but rather one feedback area for each "cursor" (i.e., each PCB—note that one IMS program can have any number of PCBs, just as one SQL program can have any number of cursors). And each

---

*The SQLCA is supported in certain SQL products, notably DB2, but is replaced by an encapsulated "diagnostics area" in the SQL/92 standard.

[†]It can also be regarded as the IMS equivalent of a *request area* in DATACOM/DB (see Chapter 12).

feedback area includes, not only a return code ("STATUS," analogous to SQLCODE or SQLSTATE in the SQLCA) and related information, but also the program's current position for the PCB in question—current position, that is, within the user view corresponding to that PCB. From the perspective of IMS, in fact, each "cursor"/feedback-area combination is considered to be simply an internalized form of the corresponding external PCB, and it is therefore actually referred to (somewhat confusingly) as a PCB. In this section we will follow normal IMS usage and take "PCB" to refer to the internalized form.

We now embark on a short explanation of the major DL/I operations. First we briefly summarize those operations:

- Get unique (GU):   Direct retrieval
- Get next (GN):   Sequential retrieval
- Get next within parent (GNP):   Sequential retrieval under current parent
- Get hold (GHU, GHN, GHNP):   As above but allow subsequent DLET/REPL
- Insert (ISRT):   Insert new segment
- Delete (DLET):   Delete existing segment
- Replace (REPL):   Update existing segment

To simplify our examples we choose not to use the genuine DL/I call syntax, but rather the hypothetical syntax illustrated by the following example:*

```
GU COURSE    WHERE TITLE = 'Dynamics' ,
   OFFERING WHERE DATE  > '750101' ,
   STUDENT  WHERE GRADE = 'A' ;
```

This example represents a "get unique" operation with a **path** of three SSAs. Simplifying the IMS rules considerably, we can say that (a) "get unique" and "insert" operations require SSAs specifying the entire hierarchic path from the root down; (b) "get next" and "get next within parent" operations might or might not involve SSAs, and if they do, then the SSAs must again specify a hierarchic path, but one that can start at any level, not necessarily at the root; and (c) "delete" and "replace" operations do not involve SSAs at all.

We now give examples of all of these possibilities in terms of the education database of Fig. 1. For simplicity, we assume that the "user view" consists of the entire database—i.e., all segments and fields are sensitive.

5.1 Direct Retrieval. Get the first offering for Stockholm.

```
GU COURSE ,
   OFFERING WHERE LOCATION = 'Stockholm' ;
```

This example illustrates (a) the use of an SSA without a condition and (b) a path of SSAs that stops short of the lowest level. If no condition is specified, any seg-

---

*Note that our simplified syntax omits all mention of both the PCB and the I/O area.

ment of the indicated type is considered to satisfy the SSA. Note that "first" in the problem statement means *first in hierarchic sequence;* in fact, "get unique" is really a misnomer—the operation is really "get *first.*"

Incidentally, this "get unique," like all other DL/I operations, should in practice be followed by an appropriate test on the STATUS field of the PCB (a blank STATUS value means the operation completed satisfactorily, a nonblank value means some exceptional condition occurred). We will generally ignore such testing in our examples.

5.2 Path Call. Get the first Stockholm offering and also its parent course.

```
GU COURSE * D ,
   OFFERING WHERE LOCATION = 'Stockholm' ;
```

Normally a DL/I retrieval operation such as GU retrieves only the segment at the lowest level of the path. In Example 5.1, for instance, only an OFFERING is retrieved. However, it is also possible to retrieve any *ancestor* of that lowest segment in addition,* by specifying the **command code** "D" in the applicable SSA(s). Command codes (there can be more than one) follow the segment name in the SSA and are separated from it by an asterisk.

5.3 Sequential Retrieval. Get all Stockholm offerings.

```
GU COURSE ;
do until no more OFFERINGs ;
   GN OFFERING WHERE LOCATION = 'Stockholm' ;
end ;
```

The operation of GN ("get next") is defined in terms of the **current database position** ("current position" for short). That position, in turn, is defined to be the segment last accessed by a "get" operation (of any type) or an "insert" operation.[†] In the example, therefore, the GU operation establishes an initial position, namely the first COURSE in the database. The first iteration of the loop then retrieves the first Stockholm OFFERING following that position, and establishes that OFFERING as the new current position; the second iteration then retrieves the second Stockholm OFFERING, and so on. The loop will be repeated until all OFFERINGs in the database have been scanned, at which point an appropriate nonblank STATUS value will be returned in the PCB.

Notice that the "path" of SSAs—actually a single SSA—in the GN in this example starts at a segment lower than the root. Note too that "next" in "get next" means (of course) "next in hierarchic sequence."

---

*An ancestor of a given segment is either the parent of that segment or an ancestor of that parent.

[†]More accurately, the program has several current positions, one for each PCB. Since our hypothetical syntax omits all reference to the PCB, we will usually assume for simplicity that there is in fact just one current position.

5.4 Sequential Retrieval Within a Parent. Get all Stockholm offerings for course M23.

```
GU COURSE WHERE COURSE# = 'M23' ;
do until no more OFFERINGs under current COURSE ;
   GNP OFFERING WHERE LOCATION = 'Stockholm' ;
end ;
```

The operation of GNP ("get next within parent") is defined in terms of both the current database position (as for GN) and also the **current parent position**. That current parent position, in turn, is defined to be the segment last accessed by "get unique" or "get next" (*not* "get next within parent") or "insert." In the example, therefore, the GU operation establishes the COURSE segment for course M23 as both the current database position and the current parent position. The first iteration of the loop then retrieves the first Stockholm OFFERING under that COURSE and establishes that OFFERING as the new current database position, but does not change the current parent position; the second iteration then retrieves the second Stockholm OFFERING under that COURSE, and so on. The loop will be repeated until all OFFERINGs under that COURSE have been scanned, at which point (again) an appropriate nonblank STATUS value will be returned in the PCB.

5.5 Sequential Retrieval Within a Parent. Get all grade A students for course M23.

```
GU COURSE WHERE COURSE# = 'M23' ;
do until no more STUDENTs under current COURSE ;
   GNP STUDENT WHERE GRADE = 'A' ;
end ;
```

"Get next within parent" is really a misnomer—the operation is really "get next within *ancestor*," as this example illustrates. The code will retrieve all grade A STUDENTs *for all OFFERINGs* for COURSE M23.

5.6 Sequential Retrieval Across Segment Types. Get any student taught by employee 421633 as a teacher.

```
GU COURSE ;
do until no more OFFERINGs ;
   GN OFFERING ;
   GNP TEACHER WHERE EMP# = '421633' ;
   if TEACHER found then
   do ;
      GNP STUDENT ;
      leave loop ;
   end ;
end ;
```

The GU is the by now familiar "initial position" call. In the loop, the GN establishes an OFFERING as the current parent position, and the GNP then searches to see whether the specified employee taught that offering; these two operations are repeated until an offering taught by the specified employee has been found. Then another GNP is executed to retrieve the first STUDENT under the current parent OFFERING (we assume for simplicity that such a STUDENT exists). Note, therefore, that we are explicitly taking advantage of the fact that STUDENTs follow TEACHERs in hierarchic sequence (for any given OFFERING, that is).

5.7 Use of Command Code F. Get the teacher (we assume there is only one) of the first offering of any course attended by employee 183009 as a student.

```
GU COURSE ;
do until no more OFFERINGs ;
   GN OFFERING ;
   GNP STUDENT WHERE EMP# = '183009' ;
   if STUDENT found then
   do ;
      GNP TEACHER * F ;
      leave loop ;
   end ;
end ;
```

This code is essentially similar to the code in the previous example, except for the presence of the F command code. Without that command code, the GNP for TEACHER would fail, because it would search *forward* from the current STUDENT, and (as explained in the previous example) TEACHERs precede STUDENTs with respect to the hierarchic sequence. What is needed is a means for stepping *backward* under the current parent, and that is what the F command code provides—it causes IMS to start its search at the *first occurrence* of the specified segment type under the current parent, regardless of the current database position. (Note that an F command code was unnecessary in Example 5.6 but would not have been wrong.)

5.8 Use of Command Code V. Get the teacher (we assume there is only one) of the first offering of any course attended by employee 183009 as a student (same as Example 5.7).

```
GU STUDENT WHERE EMP# = '183009' ;
GN OFFERING * V ,
   TEACHER * F ;
```

Before we can explain this example properly, it is first necessary to amplify the concept of "current database position" slightly. Basically, current database position is defined as the segment last accessed via a "get" or "insert" operation. In addition, however, each *ancestor* of the current position—that is, each segment in the path from the current position to the corresponding root—is also considered to be **the current segment of the applicable segment type**. In the example, therefore, the GU operation establishes a STUDENT—STUDENT *x*, say—as the current position (and therefore, of course, the current STUDENT); in addition, it also establishes the parent of *x*—OFFERING *y*, say—as the current OFFERING, and the parent of that OFFERING—COURSE *z*, say—as the current COURSE.

An SSA with a V command code directs IMS not to move away from the current segment of the type named in the SSA in attempting to satisfy the call. In the example, the GN will therefore not move away from OFFERING *y* in searching for the required TEACHER. In other words, the GN is equivalent to a "get next within parent" for TEACHERs under OFFERING *y*—except that OFFERING *y* is *not* the current parent.

This code is obviously much simpler than the code of the previous example. It is also more efficient. As a general rule, it is always preferable to use command code V rather than a GNP operation if possible. However, there are certain situations (details beyond the scope of this chapter) where it is not possible.

5.9 Segment Insertion. Insert a new student for offering 8 of course M23 (student employee number 275404, grade blank).

```
build new STUDENT segment in I/O area
    (EMP# = '275404', GRADE = ' ') ;
ISRT COURSE WHERE COURSE# = 'M23' ,
    OFFERING WHERE OFF# = '  8' ,
    STUDENT ;
```

5.10 Segment Deletion. Delete offering 8 of course M23.

```
GHU COURSE WHERE COURSE# = 'M23' ,
    OFFERING WHERE OFF# = '  8' ;
DLET ;
```

The segment to be deleted must first be retrieved via one of the "get hold" operations—"get hold unique" (GHU), "get hold next" (GHN), or "get hold next within parent" (GHNP). The DLET operation can then be executed (unless the user decides not to delete the segment after all, in which case processing simply continues as usual, e.g., with another "get hold" operation).

5.11 Segment Update. Change the location of offering 8 of course M23 to Helsinki.

```
GHU COURSE WHERE COURSE# = 'M23' ,
    OFFERING WHERE OFF# = '  8' ;
change OFFERING segment in I/O area
    (LOCATION = 'Helsinki') ;
REPL ;
```

As with "delete," the segment to be updated ("replaced") must first be retrieved via one of the "get hold" operations. It is then modified in the I/O area, and the REPL operation executed (again, unless the user decides not to update the segment after all). Note that sequence fields cannot be updated.

5.12 Use of More than One PCB. Get all offerings of all prerequisite courses of course M23.

```
GU COURSE WHERE COURSE# = 'M23' (using PCB-1) ;
do until "not found" on PCB-1 ;
   GN COURSE * V ,
      PREREQ (using PCB-1) ;
   GU COURSE WHERE COURSE# = PCB-1.PREREQ# (using PCB-2) ;
   do until "not found" on PCB-2 ;
      GN COURSE * V ,
         OFFERING (using PCB-2) ;
   end ;
end ;
```

This problem requires the ability to maintain two independent positions in the database simultaneously, and therefore needs two PCBs. One PCB, PCB-1, is used to scan the PREREQs of the given course; the other, PCB-2, is used to scan the OFFERINGs of the course corresponding to the PREREQ currently identified by PCB-1. The outer loop position (maintained by PCB-1) must not change while the inner loop (controlled by PCB-2) is executed. Note that our simplified syntax breaks down on this example, because of the need to be able to specify PCBs explicitly.

6. STORAGE STRUCTURE

IMS provides a very wide variety of physical storage structures, and it is certainly not our intention to cover them in detail here. However, some brief notes on the possibilities might prove useful, and in particular should serve to pave the way for an understanding of the next two sections.

1. First, each "physical database" is represented in storage by a *stored* database (note that physical databases are the only kind we have discussed so far in any detail). Each segment of a physical database is represented by a stored segment in the stored database. A stored segment consists of stored versions of the segment's data fields, together with a stored *prefix* (hidden from the user) containing pointers, flags, and other control information. Where the various storage structures differ is in the manner in which they represent the hierarchic sequence of the database—i.e., the manner in which stored segments are tied together to form trees and trees are tied together to form the complete database.

2. Next, IMS provides two principal storage structures, **hierarchic sequential** (HS) and **hierarchic direct** (HD). The difference between them (as indicated above) lies in the way they represent the database sequence—broadly speaking, HS uses physical contiguity and HD uses pointers. HS is intended for situations in which most access is sequential, HD is intended for situations in which most access is direct (though of course both structures can be used for both kinds of access, in general).

3. Each of the two principal structures has two principal variants—HS is supported by the **hierarchic sequential** and **hierarchic indexed sequential** access methods (HSAM and HISAM), HD is supported by the **hierarchic direct** and **hierarchic indexed direct** access methods (HDAM and HIDAM).

4. *HSAM:* In HSAM the hierarchic sequence of the database is represented entirely by physical contiguity, as on a magnetic tape (indeed, an HSAM database can actually be on tape). For an example, see Fig. 6 (where we assume that the next course after M23 in the education database is M27—M24, M25, and M26 do not exist). The only operations that can be used on an HSAM database are ISRT (allowed only when the database is first being built) and GU/GN/GNP (allowed only for an existing database). It follows that the most common use of HSAM involves the conventional old-master/new-master technique used in traditional sequential file processing; in other words, updating is done by reading an existing version of the database and writing a new one. HSAM is thus scarcely a *database* structure at all, in the usual sense of that term.

5. *HISAM:* HISAM provides indexed access to root segments, physical sequential access from roots to dependent segments. The index is on the root segment sequence field, and provides (of course) both sequential and direct access on the basis of values of that field. See Fig. 7.

6. The two HD structures both use pointers to tie segments together. For any given parent-child link, either **hierarchic** pointers or **child/twin** pointers can be used. With hierarchic pointers, each segment simply points to the next in hierarchic sequence; with child/twin pointers, each parent points to its first child of each type, and each child points to its next twin. Child/twin pointers give better direct access performance than hierarchic pointers but take up more space on the disk. Hierarchic pointers might give slightly better sequential performance than child/twin pointers. Figs. 8 and 9 show how the tree for course M23 would be stored (a) if hierarchic pointers were used exclusively (Fig. 8), (b) if child/twin pointers were used exclusively (Fig. 9).

7. *HDAM:* HDAM provides hash access to root segments, pointer access from

COURSE	PREREQ	PREREQ	OFFERING	TEACHER	STUDENT	STUDENT	
M23	M16	M19	730813	421633	102141	183009	...

STUDENT	OFFERING	OFFERING	COURSE	PREREQ	OFFERING	TEACHER	TEACHER	
761620	741104	750106	M27	L02	740602	421633	502417	...

Fig. 6 Part of the education database (HSAM)

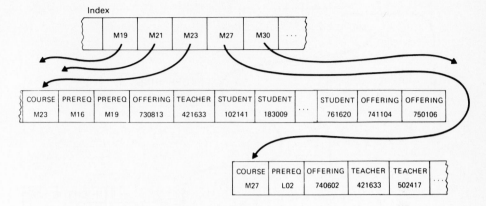

Fig. 7 Part of the education database (HISAM)

roots to dependent segments. The hash is on the root segment sequence field, and provides (of course) direct but not sequential access on the basis of values of that field. *Note:* Sequential access can be provided by means of a secondary index—see Section 8.

8. *HIDAM:* HIDAM provides indexed access to root segments, pointer access from roots to dependent segments. The index is on the root segment sequence

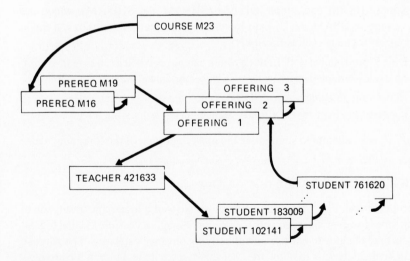

Fig. 8 Hierarchic pointers (example)

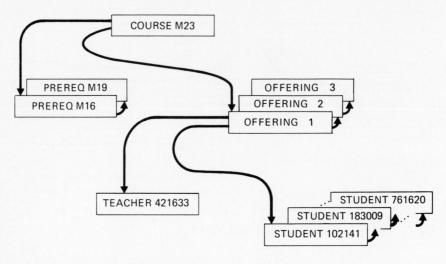

Fig. 9 Child/twin pointers (example)

field, and provides (of course) both sequential and direct access on the basis of values of that field.

9. For completeness we briefly mention the other IMS storage structures, which are as follows:

- Simple HSAM and simple HISAM (SHSAM and SHISAM), which are variants of HSAM and HISAM in which the database contains only a single type of segment (i.e., is *root-only*).

- Data Entry Databases (DEDBs), which can be regarded as an extended form of HDAM oriented specifically to high performance and high availability.

- Main Storage Databases (MSDBs), which are root-only databases that are kept entirely in primary (virtual) storage during processing.

Fig. 10 is an attempt to summarize the most important of the foregoing ideas.

7. LOGICAL DATABASES

A logical database, like a physical database, consists of a hierarchic arrangement of segments. However, the segments in question, though accessible via that logical database, really belong to one or more underlying physical databases. The purpose of the logical database is to allow the user to see the data in a hierarchic arrangement that differs—possibly quite drastically—from the arrangement in the underlying physical database(s).

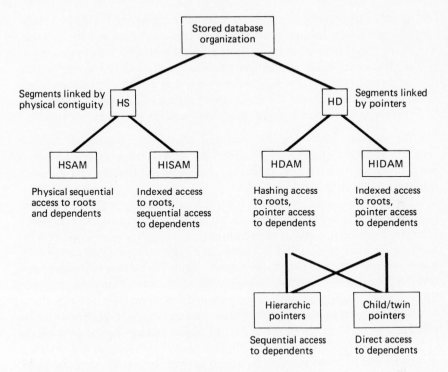

Fig. 10 The four basic storage structures

A logical database is defined by means of a **logical DBD**. And from the last sentence of the previous paragraph, it is clear that there must be some similarities between a logical DBD and a PCB. It is certainly true that both constructs define a (hierarchic) logical view of data that is different from the (hierarchic) physical structure of that data. But of course there are numerous differences as well. Some of the most important are as follows:

■   A logical DBD can be defined over several (physical) DBDs, whereas a PCB must be defined over a single (physical or logical) DBD.

■   A view defined by a logical DBD can differ much more considerably from the underlying physical structure than can a view defined by a PCB.*

■   Unlike the view defined by a PCB,† the view defined by a logical DBD is

---

*Except that a PCB can define a "secondary data structure"—see Section 8—which can in fact also be significantly different from the underlying physical structure.

†Again, we are ignoring here the possibility that the view defined by the PCB is in fact a secondary data structure.

directly supported by its own physical pointer chains (etc.). That is, a "logical" database in IMS is in fact a physical construct! Although the data segments "really belong" to one or more physical databases, the physical pointers (etc.) that define the logical database "really belong" to that logical database. Creating a new logical database is thus a nontrivial operation (certainly much more nontrivial than creating a view in a relational system), involving as it does a reorganization and restructuring of the physical data.

We illustrate these ideas by means of an IMS version of our familiar suppliers-and-parts example. A possible IMS representation of suppliers-and-parts, involving two physical databases (the suppliers database and the parts database), is shown in Fig. 11.

The parts database is root-only: It contains a single segment type (segment type P), which is effectively identical to the usual P relation. The suppliers database, by contrast, contains two segment types—segment type S, which is effectively identical to the usual S relation, and segment type SP (a child of S), which contains a QTY field and also a *pointer* field. The purpose of the pointer—which is not explicitly visible to the user, by the way—is to identify, for any given SP occurrence, the appropriate P occurrence in the parts database. See Fig. 12.

Now a logical database—the suppliers-and-parts logical database—can be defined, with the structure shown in Fig. 13.* Note that this logical database involves certain redundancies: Specifically, the name, color, weight, and city for a given part will be (conceptually) duplicated in every logical SP segment occurrence for that part. (In other words, the set of logical SP segments is not in third

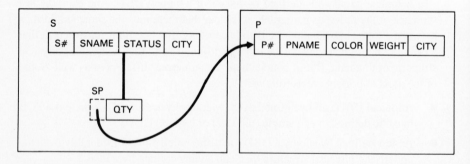

Fig. 11 Suppliers-and-parts as two physical databases

---

*For reasons beyond the scope of this book, the SP segment in the logical database will actually include *two copies* of the P# field.

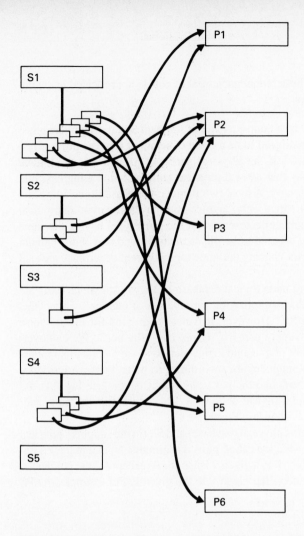

Fig. 12 Suppliers-and-parts physical databases: sample values

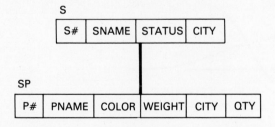

Fig. 13 The suppliers-and-parts logical database

normal form!) However, those redundancies are of course not reflected in the underlying physical databases.

Terminology: Segment SP is of course a child of segment S in the suppliers physical database. **It is also considered to be a child of segment P in the parts physical database.** We say that S is the **physical** parent of SP and P is the **logical** parent; equivalently, we say that SP is a **physical** child of S and a **logical** child of P. A given segment can have at most two parents; the possibilities are (a) no parents at all, (b) physical parent only, and (c) both physical parent and logical parent. Also, two child segment occurrences (of the same type) having the same physical parent occurrence are said to be **physical twins,** and two child segment occurrences (of the same type) having the same logical parent occurrence are said to be **logical** twins.

Now, the suppliers-and-parts logical database of Fig. 13, in which parts are subordinate to suppliers, does simplify the formulation of queries such as "Get parts supplied by supplier S1." However, it is not much good for the converse query "Get suppliers who supply part P1." (*Exercise:* Why not?). We can overcome this difficulty by means of a second logical database, the parts-and-suppliers logical database, in which suppliers are subordinate to parts. First we introduce another segment type, PS say, into the parts physical database (see Fig. 14). PS is a physical child of P and a logical child of S. Then we define the parts-and-suppliers logical database as shown in Fig. 15.

Segments PS (in the parts physical database) and SP (in the suppliers physical database) are examples of what are called **paired segments**. Note that the PS occurrence that connects a given P to a given S is identical (except for the pointer) to the SP occurrence that connects the given S to the given P. For example, the PS

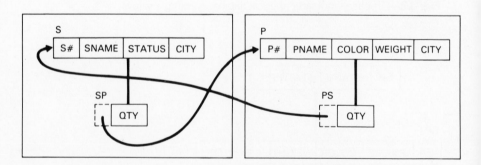

Fig. 14 Suppliers-and-parts as two physical databases (symmetric version)

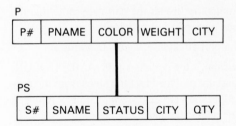

Fig. 15 The parts-and-suppliers logical database

occurrence connecting P1 to S1 is basically the same as the SP occurrence connecting S1 to P1. Thus the structure of Fig. 14 involves (once again) a certain amount of redundancy. However, (a) that redundancy will only be perceived, not real, if one of the paired segments is "virtual"; (b) even if both segments are "physical," the redundancy will at least be *controlled* (i.e., managed by IMS instead of by the user). For details, see the IMS manuals from IBM.

Referential integrity: For every segment that participates in a "logical relationship"—that is, for every segment that is a logical parent, or a logical child, or a physical parent that has a physical child that is also a logical child—the physical DBD for that segment must specify an *insert* rule, a *delete* rule, and a *replace* rule. Those rules govern the effect of ISRT, DLET, and REPL operations on the segment concerned—also, in many cases, on various related segments. Each rule can be any one of "physical," "logical," or "virtual".* Now, it is certainly not our intention here to describe these rules in detail, but we briefly discuss the possibilities for the suppliers-and-parts logical database of Fig. 13 specifically. For that particular database:

- Inserting a shipment for a nonexistent supplier (i.e., a supplier not already represented in the suppliers physical database) is impossible.

- Inserting a shipment for a nonexistent part (i.e., a part not already represented in the parts physical database):

    a. Fails if the insert rule for P is "physical";

---

*Or (in the case of the delete rule only) "bidirectional virtual." The "bidirectional virtual" rule is applicable only to databases that participate in a "bidirectional logical relationship" such as that illustrated in Fig. 14.

■ b. Succeeds otherwise, and automatically inserts the part also (note that the shipment includes all of the necessary part information).

■ Inserting a shipment for an existing part always succeeds. In addition:

a. If the insert rule for P is "virtual," the values of PNAME, COLOR, WEIGHT, and CITY for that part are replaced by the values from the new shipment, which in turn means that they are also simultaneously replaced (logically) in all existing shipments for that part;

b. Otherwise, the values of PNAME, COLOR, WEIGHT, and CITY for that shipment are replaced (logically) by the values from the existing part.

■ Deleting a supplier automatically deletes all shipments for that supplier.

■ Deleting a part (i.e., via the parts physical database—it is not directly accessible via the suppliers-and-parts logical database):

a. Fails if the delete rule for P is "physical" and the part has any corresponding shipments;

b. Succeeds otherwise, in the sense that the part is logically removed from the parts physical database. However, it remains accessible from the suppliers-and-parts logical database so long as there are any shipments that refer to it.

■ If the delete rule for P is "virtual," then deleting the last shipment referring to a given part causes that part to be physically removed from the parts physical database also.

■ Field S.S# cannot be updated.

■ Field P.P# cannot be updated (i.e., via the parts physical database—it is not directly accessible via the suppliers-and-parts logical database).

■ Field SP.P# cannot be updated. Note that there is of course no "SP.S#" field, so the question of updating such a field does not arise.

■ Updating fields SP.PNAME, SP.COLOR, SP.WEIGHT, and SP.CITY:

a. Fails if the replace rule for P is "physical";

b. Succeeds otherwise, in which case the updates are actually applied to the corresponding part, which in turn means that they are instantaneously applied (logically) to all other shipments for that part.

■ Updating fields P.PNAME, P.COLOR, P.WEIGHT, and P.CITY (i.e., via the parts physical database—they are not directly accessible via the suppliers-and-parts logical database):

a. Fails if the replace rule for P is "logical";

b. Succeeds otherwise, in which case the updates are instantaneously applied (logically) to all shipments for that part.

We remark that the rules as described above represent both less and more than the foreign key rules generally found in relational systems. Detailed comparisons are left as an exercise for the interested reader. Note too that the foregoing discussion treats the rules only in the context of the *simplest possible* kind of logical database. For details of what happens in more complex cases (such as the database of Fig. 14), the reader is referred to the IMS manuals.

8. SECONDARY INDEXES

The term *secondary index* is usually taken to mean an index on a field that is not the primary key. However, that usage tacitly assumes that the file to be indexed is a conventional "flat" sequential file. In IMS, of course, the file (i.e., database) is more complex—it is hierarchic, and the concept of secondary indexing needs to be extended accordingly. In IMS, in fact, a secondary index can index any segment, root or dependent, on the basis of any field of that segment or any field of any dependent (at any level) of that segment. In all cases, moreover, the "field" on which the index is based can actually be a combination of several fields (not necessarily contiguous) from the relevant segment.

To illustrate the possibilities, we return to the education database of Section 2. The following list outlines some of the many indexes that could be constructed for that database:

1. An index to COURSEs on field COURSE.TITLE
2. An index to COURSEs on field OFFERING.LOCATION
3. An index to OFFERINGs on field OFFERING.LOCATION
4. An index to OFFERINGs on field TEACHER.EMP#

We consider each of these four cases in some detail.

1. Indexing the root on a field not the sequence field

Secondary indexes are very definitely *not* "transparent to the user" in IMS. On the contrary, IMS will use a particular secondary index only if the DL/I call explicitly instructs it to do so. For example, suppose an index to COURSEs has been constructed on the basis of TITLE values. Then the definition of COURSE in the education database DBD must include an "XDFLD" statement, of the form

```
XDFLD   NAME=XTITLE,SRCH=TITLE
```

(say), to indicate that a reference in some DL/I call to the name XTITLE means that IMS is to use the TITLE index in responding to that call. For example, the DL/I call:

```
GU COURSE WHERE TITLE = 'Dynamics' ;
```

will *not* use the index, but the following DL/I call will:

```
GU COURSE WHERE XTITLE = 'Dynamics' ;
```

A secondary index also allows the database in question to be processed in a **secondary processing sequence**—namely, the sequence defined by that index. (The **primary** processing sequence is the sequence of trees in the underlying physical database—that is, it is the sequence defined by ascending values of the root segment sequence field, loosely speaking.) Requesting a secondary sequence is done by naming the appropriate secondary index in the PCB. "Get unique" and "get next" operations will then operate in terms of that secondary sequence. *Recommendation:* Whenever any given index is being used, the sequence requested in the PCB should be the sequence defined by that index; for otherwise the sequence that applies to GU and GN operations will not be the sequence represented by the index, and those operations will therefore be *extremely* inefficient.

2. Indexing the root on a field in a dependent

Suppose we wish to find all courses that have an offering in Stockholm. Assume we are not concerned with the problem of eliminating duplicate COURSEs. Then the following code will suffice:

```
position to start of primary sequence ;
do until no more OFFERINGs ;
   GN COURSE * D ,
      OFFERING WHERE LOCATION = 'Stockholm' ;
end ;
```

This code is not particularly efficient, however, since it consists essentially of a sequential scan of the entire database in primary sequence. A more efficient solution to the problem can be achieved by means of an index to COURSEs on the basis of OFFERING.LOCATION values. Suppose such an index is constructed, and the corresponding XDFLD statement (part of the definition of the COURSE segment in the education DBD) is

```
XDFLD    NAME=XLOC,SRCH=LOCATION,SEGMENT=OFFERING
```

(meaning that the user can instruct IMS to use the index on the LOCATION field of the OFFERING segment by specifying the name XLOC in the DL/I call). Suppose also that the secondary sequence defined by that index has been requested in the PCB. Then we can write

```
position to start of secondary (i.e., LOCATION) sequence ;
do until no more COURSEs ;
   GN COURSE WHERE XLOC = 'Stockholm' ;
end ;
```

And this code will probably be much more efficient, because it uses the index to go directly to just the OFFERINGs required.

Note, incidentally, that the index in this example contains as many index entries as there are OFFERINGs in the education database. Each index entry points to a COURSE segment. If there are m COURSEs altogether, and an average of n OFFERINGs per COURSE, then there will be $m * n$ entries in the index, of which (on average) n will point to any given COURSE. The secondary sequence defined by this index is (of course) ascending LOCATION sequence. If the database is processed in this sequence, then (on average) each COURSE, together with all of its dependents, will appear n times, once for each of its OFFERINGs. In other words, when seen via the index, the database appears n times larger than it really is! Furthermore, the n appearances of a given COURSE, with its dependents, will probably not all be grouped together.

3. Indexing a dependent on a field in that dependent

As indicated at the beginning of this section, the indexed segment does not have to be the root of the underlying database. If it is not, however, the effect is to restructure the hierarchy so that it *becomes* the root in the structure seen by the user. As an example, we consider the case of indexing OFFERINGs on the basis of LOCATION values. Fig. 16 shows the **secondary data structure** that results when the user specifies the secondary sequence corresponding to this index in the PCB.*

The rules for defining a secondary data structure are as follows:

- The indexed segment becomes the root.

- Ancestors of that segment become the leftmost dependents of the root, in reverse order (if COURSE had a parent CATEGORY in the education database, CATEGORY would be a *child* of COURSE in the secondary structure).

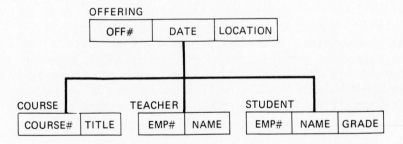

Fig. 16 Indexing OFFERINGs on LOCATION: secondary data structure

---

*We are assuming that the secondary processing sequence is being used (the normal case). If it is not, the restructuring described in this section does not occur.

- Dependents of the indexed segment appear exactly as in the underlying database, except that they are to the right of the dependents introduced by the rule of the previous paragraph.
- No other segments are included (in the example, PREREQs are omitted).

The SENSEG statements in the PCB must define the secondary structure in accordance with these rules. Note, therefore, that here we have a situation in which the view defined by the PCB is not just a simple subhierarchy of the hierarchy defined by the underlying DBD.*

As an illustration of a possible use for this facility, we extend our Stockholm courses example as follows. Suppose we wish to find, not only courses with an offering in Stockholm, but also the teachers of those Stockholm offerings. The index of the previous subsection (indexing COURSEs on OFFERING.LOCATION) is not particularly helpful here; it will enable us to find qualifying courses easily enough, but there is no immediate way of knowing which of the many subordinate teachers for those courses are in fact the teachers for the Stockholm offerings. But with the secondary structure of Fig. 16, we can write:

```
position to start of secondary (i.e., LOCATION) sequence ;
do until no more OFFERINGs ;
   GN OFFERING WHERE XLOC = 'Stockholm' ,
      COURSE ;
   do until no more TEACHERs ;
      GN OFFERING * V ,
         TEACHER ;
   end ;
end ;
```

Note that, in the hierarchy of Fig. 16, each OFFERING will have *exactly one* COURSE child.

4. Indexing a dependent on a field in a lower-level dependent

This, the last of the four possibilities, does not really illustrate any new points, but we include it for completeness. As our example, we consider the case of indexing OFFERINGs on the basis of TEACHER.EMP# values. The secondary data structure will be the same as that of Fig. 16; however, (a) OFFERINGs will now be accessible via the "XD field" XEMP# (say), corresponding to the real field TEACHER.EMP#, and (b) sequencing will be defined in terms of values of that XD field instead of LOCATION values. We present a single coding example. The problem is: "Find all Stockholm offerings taught by employee 876225."

---

*Secondary data structures are subject to severe update restrictions, as is probably only to be expected. For example, it is not possible to insert or delete COURSEs using the structure of Fig. 16. Full details of such restrictions are beyond the scope of this chapter.

```
position to start of secondary (i.e., TEACHER.EMP#) sequence ;
do until no more OFFERINGs ;
   GN OFFERING WHERE XEMP# = '876225'
               AND LOCATION = 'Stockholm' ;
end ;
```

9. CONCLUDING REMARKS

In this chapter, we have sketched a (hypothetical) hierarchic data model, and have described the major features of IMS (easily the most important example of the hierarchic approach). We stress the point once again that we have omitted a very great amount of detail from that description. By way of conclusion, we now offer the following critical comments on hierarchic systems in general.

First, refer back to the discussion of secondary indexing in Section 8. In that section we presented a particular problem—"Find courses with offerings in Stockholm"—and showed a solution to that problem involving a particular index. Then we modified the problem slightly—"Find corresponding teachers too"—and showed a solution to that modified problem involving a different index and a secondary data structure. Observe from this example how **a slight change in the problem can lead to a major change in the solution**. This *perturbation effect* can be attributed to the fact that secondary indexes represent an attempt to provide symmetry of access to a data structure that is fundamentally not symmetric. That is, access via an indexed field is made to look like access via the root segment sequence field, which implies that the indexed field has to *become* the root segment sequence field, which implies in turn that the hierarchy has to be logically restructured.

Let us abstract the foregoing argument a little. The essential point is that a hierarchic structure has a *builtin bias;* it is good for some applications but bad for others.* As a result, some kind of logical restructuring mechanism becomes desirable, so that the data can be logically rearranged into whatever hierarchic form is best suited for the application at hand. And of course that is exactly what the IMS secondary indexing facility is, a logical restructuring mechanism.[†] So too is the logical database facility, and so also is the PCB facility (to a lesser extent).

We have thus shown that a hierarchic system requires a restructuring mechanism, and that secondary indexes (etc.) provide such a mechanism in IMS. But the question is: Is such a restructuring facility sufficiently flexible to satisfy the range of demands that users are likely to make on it? There are several arguments that suggest that the answer to this question is probably *no:*

---

*The relational structure, by contrast, has no such bias—instead, it is rather neutral. For a given application, the necessary bias is provided by the relational operators, which effectively allow the user to *impose* a "hierarchic" structure (or any other kind of structure that might be desired) on the data dynamically, at run time.

[†]Of course it is a performance aid also, but performance is not the point at issue here.

- First, the number of possible hierarchies rises combinatorially with the number of records (segments). Two records can be arranged into two different hierarchies; three can be arranged into 12 different hierarchies; four, into 88; and so on (exercise for the reader). In any real environment, therefore, it is virtually certain that not all possible hierarchies will be directly supported, simply because there are so many of them. In IMS in particular, certain hierarchies *cannot* be directly supported, because of various IMS restrictions (for example, the root of a logical database must be the root of a physical database).

- Second, there are some applications for which no single hierarchy is directly suitable anyway. Example 5.12 is a case in point, and the suppliers-parts-projects database provides many others.

- Next, there is no good theory available (so far as this writer is aware) on which to base such a restructuring mechanism. In IMS in particular, the restructuring is quite *ad hoc,* with the result that users (not just the DBA, but also application programmers, and probably end users too) have to be aware of a large number of apparently arbitrary rules, restrictions, and interdependencies.

- In IMS also, the restructuring mechanism is cumbersome and not very dynamic. It is a nontrivial operation to define a new logical database or new secondary data structure over existing data. As a result, such operations must definitely be performed by an IMS specialist—certainly not by an end user.

Note carefully that all of the foregoing are arguments against hierarchies as a *logical* structure, not as a physical structure. There is no question that a hierarchic physical structure might be the best performer for certain applications (though of course not for all applications). But another criticism of hierarchic systems, or at least of IMS specifically, is precisely that there is no clear distinction between the logical and physical levels of the system. Secondary indexes, for example, are both a physical-level (performance-oriented) construct and a logical-level (data-structuring) construct in IMS. Similarly for logical databases, and similarly for numerous other IMS features.

Finally, some criticisms regarding IMS specifically:

- The choice as to whether or not to make use of a secondary index in a particular database request is in the hands of the user (i.e., the application programmer), instead of being under the control of the system. This is unfortunate, since not only do programs that use a secondary index thereby lose some measure of data independence, but also system performance can be critically dependent on a judicious choice of when and when not to use some particular index.

- Suppose we restrict our attention to two-level hierarchies only, for simplicity. Such a hierarchy, by definition, is best suited to representing a one-to-many relationship, such as the relationship of courses to offerings. A many-to-many relationship, such as that between suppliers and parts, can be considered as a combination of two one-to-many relationships (suppliers to shipments, parts to shipments), and can therefore be handled by two hierarchies that are inverses of one another (as we saw in Section 7)—though the details are hardly straightforward. But a many-to-many-to-many relationship, such as that involving suppliers, parts, and projects, cannot be represented in IMS in any reasonably direct manner at all, owing to the restriction that a given child segment can have at most two parents. (Suppliers-parts-projects can be regarded as a combination of *three* one-to-many relationships—suppliers to shipments, parts to shipments, and projects to shipments.)

■ The insert/delete/replace rules for segments that participate in a logical relationship are extremely complex, particularly with respect to the implications that a rule for one segment can have for operations on another. In some cases, in fact, defining a new logical database over one or more existing physical databases will invalidate programs that previously operated successfully on those existing databases. Furthermore, the rules are asymmetric, and do not provide all the function needed; yet they do provide some function for which the need is (to say the least) debatable.

EXERCISES

1. Fig. 17 represents an IMS database that contains information about published papers in a number of selected subject areas. The segments contain the following fields:
   - Subject: subject classification number (unique), name of subject
   - Paper: title, abstract, number of pages
   - Details: publishing house, journal name, volume number, issue number, date of publication (note that the same paper can be published several times in several different places)
   - Author: author name, address (note that a given paper can have several coauthors)
   Define an appropriate DBD for this information.

2. Define a PCB (all segments and fields sensitive) for the publications database. This PCB is to be used for both retrieval and update operations (all kinds).

3. Using the hypothetical syntax introduced in this chapter, write DL/I operations for the following:
   (a) Get all authors of papers on the subject of "Information Retrieval" (you can assume that this subject name is unique).
   (b) Get all papers for which Grace or Hobbs is (one of) the author(s).
   (c) Get all subjects on which Bradbury has published a paper.
   (d) Get the name of the paper and date of first publication for all papers published by Owen.
   (e) Get all authors who have had a paper published by the Cider Press since 1989.

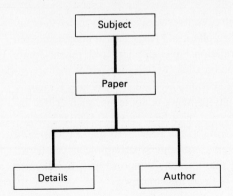

Fig. 17   The publications database

(f) Get all authors who have coauthored a paper with Bradman.

(g) A paper on the subject of science fiction, entitled "Computers in SF," was published on 1 January 1985 by the Galactic Publishing Corporation. The author's name is Hal. Add this information to the database. (You can assume that the subject "Science Fiction" is already represented.)

(h) For all papers currently available from more than one source, delete all details segments except the most recent.

4. Restructure the publications database as two physical databases, so that logical databases can be defined that are specifically suited to responding to both of the following queries:

 • Find the authors of a given paper;

 • Find all papers by a given author.

 What logical databases can the user see with your design?

5. A secondary index is to be built for the publications database. What structure does the user see:

 (a) If the subject segment is indexed on author name;

 (b) If the paper segment is indexed on author name;

 (c) If the author segment is indexed on author name?

6. Using the secondary structure of Exercise 5b, get all papers by Adams.

7. If the publications database contains:

 100 subject segments,
 average of 100 paper segments per subject,
 average of 1.5 details segments per paper,
 average of 1.2 author segments per paper,

 how many segments of each type are seen in the secondary structure of Exercise 5b?

REFERENCES AND BIBLIOGRAPHY

1. W. C. McGee, "The IMS/VS System," *IBM Sys. J. 16,* No. 2 (June 1977).

An extensive tutorial on both database and data communications aspects of IMS as it was in the 1970s (when it was known as "IMS/Virtual Storage," IMS/VS).

2. D. C. Tsichritzis and F. H. Lochovsky, "Hierarchical Data Base Management: A Survey," *ACM Comp. Surv. 8,* No. 1 (March 1976).

Includes a brief tutorial not only on IMS but also on System 2000 (another hierarchic system).

3. Dines Bjørner and Hans Henrik Løvengreen, "Formalization of Database Systems— And a Formal Definition of IMS," Proc. 8th International Conference on Very Large Data Bases, Mexico City (September 1982).

An attempt to define a formal data model for IMS. Note, however, that the following IMS features (among others) are not included:

- Command codes
- "Advanced features" such as multiple positioning
- Logical databases
- Access method dependent features
- Database positioning after an exception
- "Get hold" calls
- Inserted segment positioning other than FIRST

4. E. F. Codd, Interview in *Data Base Newsletter 10,* No. 2 (Boston, Mass.: Database Research Group Inc., March 1982).

5. C. J. Date, "Why Is It So Difficult to Provide a Relational Interface to IMS?", in *Relational Database: Selected Writings* (Reading, Mass.: Addison-Wesley, 1986).

To quote from the abstract: Several commercial DBMSs—but not however IMS—now claim to provide an interface by which users can obtain relational access to existing (i.e., nonrelational) data. This paper shows that there are certain inherent (and possibly insuperable) difficulties in trying to provide such an interface. It illustrates those difficulties by considering the specific case of attempting to provide an SQL interface to IMS.

ANSWERS TO SELECTED EXERCISES

```
1. DBD     NAME=PUBSDBD
   SEGM    NAME=SUBJECT,BYTES=45
   FIELD   NAME=(SUB#,SEQ),BYTES=7,START=1
   FIELD   NAME=SUBNAME,BYTES=38,START=8
   SEGM    NAME=PAPER,PARENT=SUBJECT,BYTES=762
   FIELD   NAME=(PAPER#,SEQ),BYTES=4,START=1
   FIELD   NAME=TITLE,BYTES=256,START=5
   FIELD   NAME=ABSTRACT,BYTES=500,START=261
   FIELD   NAME=PAGES,BYTES=2,START=761
   SEGM    NAME=DETAILS,PARENT=PAPER,BYTES=118
   FIELD   NAME=(DATE,SEQ),BYTES=6,START=1
   FIELD   NAME=HOUSE,BYTES=19,START=7
```

```
     FIELD   NAME=JOURNAL,BYTES=88,START=26
     FIELD   NAME=VOLUME,BYTES=3,START=114
     FIELD   NAME=ISSUE,BYTES=2,START=117
     SEGM    NAME=AUTHOR,PARENT=PAPER,BYTES=50
     FIELD   NAME=(AUTHNAME,SEQ),BYTES=16,START=1
     FIELD   NAME=AUTHADDR,BYTES=34,START=17

  2. PCB     DBDNAME=PUBSDBD
     SENSEG  NAME=SUBJECT,PROCOPT=GIRD
     SENSEG  NAME=PAPER,PARENT=SUBJECT,PROCOPT=GIRD
     SENSEG  NAME=DETAILS,PARENT=PAPER,PROCOPT=GIRD
     SENSEG  NAME=AUTHOR,PARENT=PAPER,PROCOPT=GIRD
```

3(a)
```
GU SUBJECT WHERE SUBNAME = 'Information Retrieval' ;
do until no more AUTHORs ;
   GNP AUTHOR ;
end ;
```

3(b)
```
position to start of database ;
do until no more AUTHORs ;
   GN PAPER * D ,
      AUTHOR WHERE AUTHNAME = 'Grace'
             OR AUTHNAME = 'Hobbs' ;
end ;
```

3(c)
```
position to start of database ;
do until no more AUTHORs ;
   GN SUBJECT * D ,
      PAPER ,
      AUTHOR WHERE AUTHNAME = 'Bradbury' ;
end ;
```

3(d)
```
position to start of database ;
do until no more AUTHORs ;
   GN AUTHOR WHERE AUTHNAME = 'Owen' ;
   GN PAPER * VD ,
      DETAILS * F ;
end ;
```

3(e)
```
position to start of database ;
do until no more DETAILS ;
   GN DETAILS WHERE DATE > '891231'
              AND HOUSE = 'Cider Press' ;
   do until no more AUTHORs ;
      GN PAPER * V ,
         AUTHOR ;
   end ;
end ;
```

3(f)
```
position to start of database ;
do until no more AUTHORs ;
   GN AUTHOR WHERE AUTHNAME = 'Bradman' ;
   GN PAPER * V ,
      AUTHOR * F ;
   do until no more AUTHORs ;
      GN PAPER * V ,
         AUTHOR ;
   end ;
end ;
```

3(g)
```
build PAPER segment in I/O area ;
ISRT SUBJECT WHERE SUBNAME = 'Science Fiction' ,
     PAPER ;
build DETAILS segment in I/O area ;
ISRT PAPER * V ,
```

```
            DETAILS ;
     build AUTHOR segment in I/O area ;
     ISRT PAPER * V ,
          AUTHOR ;
3(h) position to start of database ;
     do until no more PAPERs ;
        GN PAPER ;
        set count = 0 ;
        do until no more DETAILS ;
           GN PAPER * V ,
              DETAILS ;
           if not found leave inner loop ;
           set count = count + 1 ;
        end ;
        do while count > 1 :
           GHN PAPER * V ,
                DETAILS * F ;
           DLET ;
        end ;
     end ;
```

5. The user sees:

    (a)

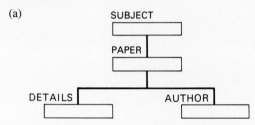

    In this case the hierarchic structure is unchanged.

    (b)

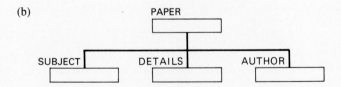

    (c)

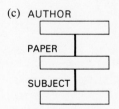

    In all three cases the structure is seen in AUTHNAME sequence, with as many trees as there are AUTHOR occurrences in the original database. See also the answer to Exercise 7.

6. position to start of secondary (i.e., AUTHNAME) sequence ;
   do until no more PAPERs ;
      GN PAPER WHERE XAUTH = 'Adams' ;
   end ;

We assume that XAUTH is the XD field for PAPER corresponding to the indexed field AUTHNAME.

7. PAPER   : 12000

   SUBJECT : 12000

   DETAILS : 18000

   AUTHOR : 14400

A Network System: IDMS

ABSTRACT

We present a tutorial overview of "the network model" and the leading example thereof, IDMS from Computer Associates.

COMMENTS ON REPUBLICATION

See the introduction to this part of the book.

1. BACKGROUND

IDMS—"Integrated Database Management System"—is a product of Computer Associates (previously Cullinet Software, Inc.). It runs on IBM mainframes under most of the standard IBM operating systems (VSE, MVS, etc.). It is probably the best known example of what is usually referred to as a "CODASYL system" (or

Originally published (in somewhat different form) in my book *An Introduction to Database Systems: Volume I,* 5th edition, pages 791–831 (Addison-Wesley, 1991). Reprinted by permission.

sometimes "DBTG system")—that is, a system based on the proposals of the Data Base Task Group (DBTG) of the Programming Language Committee (subsequently renamed the COBOL Committee) of the "Conference on Data Systems Languages" (CODASYL), the organization responsible for the definition of COBOL. The DBTG final report [1] was produced in 1971, and several systems based on it were built during the 1970s, among them IDMS.

The DBTG report contained proposals for three distinct database languages: a *schema data description language* (schema DDL), a *subschema data description language* (subschema DDL), and a *data manipulation language* (DML). The purpose of the three languages was as follows:

- The schema DDL was a language for describing a network-structured database. The DBTG term "schema" corresponds very approximately to the ANSI/SPARC term "conceptual schema"; however, the DBTG schema DDL is really much more "internal" than "conceptual" in nature—i.e., it includes many constructs that are quite storage-oriented, such as definitions of physical access paths.

- The subschema DDL was a language for defining an external view of the database (the DBTG "subschema" corresponds to the ANSI/SPARC external schema).

- The DML consisted of a set of (record-level) operators for manipulating a network database defined by means of the two data description languages. The user in DBTG is assumed to be an application programmer; thus, a given DML will have a syntax compatible with that of some programming language. The DML defined in [1] was intended for use with COBOL.

The dialects of these languages supported by IDMS are similar but not identical to those of reference [1]. In this chapter we base most of our examples and discussions on the IDMS dialects specifically.

One further preliminary remark: In 1983 Cullinet announced an extended version of IDMS called IDMS/R ("IDMS/Relational"). IDMS/R included all of the original CODASYL-style facilities of the base IDMS product, together with certain relational facilities; in fact, "IDMS/R" then became the official name for the entire product, replacing the old "IDMS" name. In this chapter, however, we are primarily concerned with the base CODASYL facilities, and it is convenient to continue to use the name "IDMS" to refer to those facilities specifically. Toward the end of the chapter we will briefly describe the relational features of IDMS/R. *Note:* In 1989, after the foregoing was first written, Computer Associates acquired Cullinet, renaming the product CA-IDMS/DB and announcing that it would be extended to support SQL. For obvious reasons, however, we concentrate in the present chapter on the original IDMS features *per se*.

As with DATACOM/DB and IMS, we precede our discussion of IDMS as such with a short discussion of the underlying data model. Once again that discussion is necessarily somewhat hypothetical, since IDMS and systems like it were not in fact designed in terms of any such predefined model; on the contrary (as in the case of hierarchic systems), the model was defined after the event by a process of abstraction—principally from the DBTG specifications, in the case of networks. In fact, this writer is not aware of the existence of any *formal* definition of such a model at all. Furthermore, the hypothetical model we do discuss is very much simplified in comparison with the "model" actually implemented in IDMS and systems like it, because we choose to stress only those features (such as links) that can be regarded as truly crucial to the network approach. Other features (such as areas, realms, and repeating groups) we simply ignore. The interested reader is referred to reference [1] for details of such features.

2. THE NETWORK MODEL

Network Data Structure

The network data structure can be regarded as an extended form of the hierarchic data structure as defined in Chapter 13. The principal distinction between the two is as follows: In a hierarchic structure, a child record has exactly one parent; in a network structure, a child record can have any number of parents* (including zero). We make these ideas a little more precise as follows.

A network database consists of a collection of **records** plus a collection of **links**—more accurately, a collection of any number of occurrences of each of several types of record, together with a collection of any number of occurrences of each of several types of link. Each link type involves two record types, a **parent**

---

*To jump ahead of ourselves a little: This distinction means that *every* relationship that is represented by a foreign key in a relational structure can in principle be represented by a link in a network structure. In a hierarchic structure, by contrast, some such relationships can be represented by links, but some must still be represented by foreign keys (as explained in Chapter 13). Even in a network structure, of course, there is no guarantee that *all* such relationships will in fact be represented by links—indeed, it is probable that they will not, because:

a. There are likely to be so many of them;

b. In any case, most systems do not support links having the same record type as both parent and child, implying that (e.g.) the foreign key MGR_EMP# in the relation EMP { EMP#, ENAME, MGR_EMP#, SALARY } cannot be replaced by a link;

and (perhaps most significant in practice)

c. It is a very nontrivial operation to add a new link to an existing database (see Exercise 6 at the end of the chapter). Hence, a field that was originally not a foreign key might very well become one as the database evolves over time.

record type and a **child** record type.* Each occurrence of a given link type consists of a single occurrence of the parent record type, together with an ordered collection of any number of occurrences of the child record type. Given a particular link type *L* with parent record type *P* and child record type *C:*

■   Each occurrence of *P* is the parent in *exactly* one occurrence of *L;*

■   Each occurrence of *C* is a child in *at most* one occurrence of *L.*

In addition, of course, record types are made up of field types in the usual way. *Note:* From now on we will (as usual) drop the "type" and "occurrence" qualifiers whenever it seems safe to do so.

As an example, we show in Fig. 1 how the suppliers-and-parts database could be represented in network form. The database contains three record types, namely S, P, and SP. S and P are essentially identical to their relational counterparts; SP, by contrast, contains only a QTY field. In place of the two foreign keys SP.S# and SP.P#, we have two link types, namely S-SP and P-SP:

■   Each occurrence of S-SP consists of a single occurrence of S, together with one occurrence of SP for each shipment by the supplier represented by that S occurrence;

■   Each occurrence of P-SP consists of a single occurrence of P, together with one occurrence of SP for each shipment of the part represented by that P occurrence.

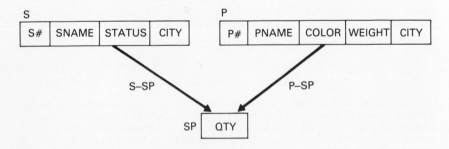

Fig. 1   The suppliers-and-parts database: network version (data structure)

---

*"Link," "parent," and "child" are not CODASYL terms. The CODASYL terminology is as follows: Links are called *sets* (a peculiarly unfortunate choice, since it is often necessary to use the same term "set" in its more usual mathematical sense, even in a CODASYL context); parents are called *owners;* and children are called *members.* In this section we choose to stay with the link/parent/child terminology, in order to stress the essential similarities and essential differences between hierarchies and networks. We will switch to the CODASYL terminology when we discuss IDMS specifically.

Some sample occurrences (corresponding to the usual set of sample data values) are shown in Fig. 2. Note that, for a given S occurrence, the SP occurrences appear in part number order; likewise, for a given P occurrence, the SP occurrences appear in supplier number order.

Each occurrence of a link represents a one-to-many relationship between the parent occurrence and the corresponding child occurrences. Now, there are many ways in which the connections between the parent and child occurrences in a given link occurrence might physically be made; one way (the one illustrated in Fig. 2) is via a chain of pointers that originates at the parent occurrence, runs through all the child occurrences, and finally returns to the parent occurrence. In practice, the connections might or might not be made by pointers *per se,* but the user can always think in terms of the pointer chain representation without any loss of generality (in other words, whatever method is chosen must be functionally equivalent to the pointer chain method). We will continue to assume the pointer representation, where it makes any difference.

A note on the figures: Drawing link occurrences as chains of pointers, as in Fig. 2, is a generally accepted convention. The technique for drawing link *types* illustrated in Fig. 1 is based on another widely accepted convention, due to Bachman [2], called **data structure diagrams** (or sometimes "Bachman diagrams"). The data structure diagram for a given link is very similar to the IMS diagram for such a link; the only differences are that (a) the link is labeled with its *name* (links are anonymous in IMS), and (b) the link is *directed* to indicate which is the parent and which the child* (in a network diagram, unlike an IMS diagram, it is not always possible to show the parent as being above the child).

There is no restriction on how record types can be combined into link types:

1. The child record type in one link type $L1$ can be the parent record type in another link type $L2$ (as in a hierarchy).

2. A given record type P can be the parent record type in any number of link types.

3. A given record type C can be the child record type in any number of link types.

4. There can be any number of link types with the same record type P as parent and the same record type C as child; and if $L1$ and $L2$ are two link types with the same parent type P and the same child type $C,$ then the arrangement of parents and children in the two links will in general be quite different. For example, Ci might be a child of Pj in $L1$ but a child of Pk in $L2$.

5. Record types X and Y might be parent and child types respectively in link type $L1,$ but child and parent types respectively in link type $L2$.

6. A given link type can have the same record type as both parent and child.

---

*We remark that data structure diagram arrows go the opposite way from the referential constraint or functional dependency arrows used in relational contexts.

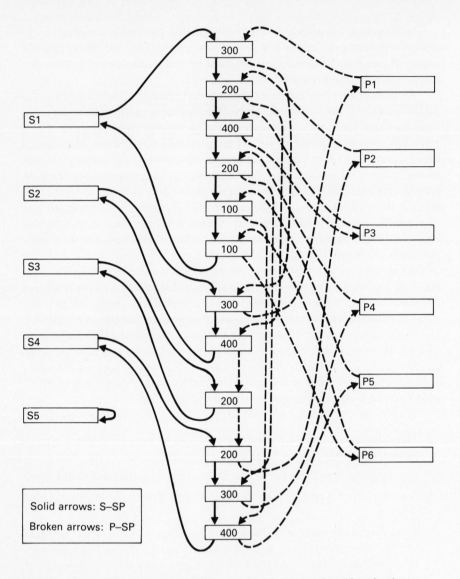

Fig. 2   The suppliers-and-parts database: network version (sample values)

Of the foregoing possibilities, only No. 3 is illustrated by the suppliers-and-parts example. For examples of Nos. 1, 2, and 4 (and 3 again), see Exercises 1–3 at the end of the chapter. Note that most commercial systems (including in particular IDMS) do not support No. 6.

One final point regarding data structure: Let us agree to call a record type that is not a child in any link a **root** record type. Then, just as in the hierarchic model it is convenient to regard all occurrences of the (single) root as being children of a hypothetical "system" record, so in the network model it might be convenient to regard all occurrences of a given root as children of a hypothetical "system" record in what we will call a "system link." In fact, it might be convenient to regard each root as the child in several distinct system links, each one imposing a different ordering over occurrences of that root. Note that each system link has *exactly one occurrence*. (In fact, a system link is basically nothing more than a conventional sequential file.) Fig. 3 shows an extended form of the suppliers-and-parts database, in which system links S-FILE and P-FILE have been introduced for the S and P record types, respectively. We might assume, purely for the sake of the example, that S-FILE is ordered on the basis of S.CITY values, and P-FILE is ordered on the basis of P.COLOR values.

It is sometimes desirable to introduce system links for nonroot record types also.

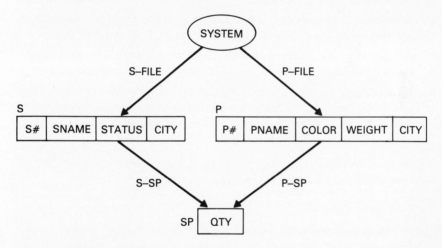

Fig. 3 The suppliers-and-parts database: network version (extended to include two system links)

Network Data Manipulation

A network data manipulation language consists of a set of operators for operating on data represented in the form of records and links. Examples of such operators include the following:

- An operator to locate a specific record, given a value for some field in that record—for example, an operator to locate the S record for supplier S1;

- An operator to move from a parent to its first child in some link—for example, an operator to step from the S record for supplier S1 to the SP record for supplier S1 and part P1 (via the S-SP link);

- An operator to move from one child to the next in some link—for example, an operator to step from the SP record for supplier S1 and part P1 to the SP record for supplier S1 and part P2 (via the S-SP link);

- An operator to move from a child to its parent within some link—for example, an operator to step from the SP record for supplier S1 and part P2 to the P record for part P2 (via the P-SP link);

- An operator to create a new record—for example, an operator to create an S record for a new supplier;

- An operator to destroy an existing record—for example, an operator to destroy the S record for an existing supplier;

- An operator to update an existing record—for example, an operator to change the status for an existing supplier;

- An operator to connect an existing (child) record into a link—for example, an operator to connect a particular SP record into the S-SP and P-SP links;

- An operator to disconnect an existing (child) record from a link—for example, an operator to disconnect a particular SP record from the S-SP and P-SP links;

- An operator to disconnect an existing (child) record from one occurrence of a given link (type) and reconnect it into another—for example, an operator to disconnect a particular SP record from the S-SP link with parent S1 and reconnect it into the S-SP link with parent S2;

and so on. Note that (as the examples suggest) such operators are typically all *record-level,* as in the inverted list and hierarchic models.

Network Data Integrity

Like the hierarchic model, the network model includes "builtin" support for certain forms of referential integrity, by virtue of its primary data structure, the link. For example, it is possible (but not required) to enforce the rule that a child cannot be inserted unless its parent already exists. We defer discussion of the details to Section 5; here we simply note that, for a given link, it is possible to achieve an effect that is approximately (but only approximately) equivalent to the following foreign key rules in a relational system:*

---

*In the case of IDMS specifically, not all of the possibilities shown are fully supported. See Example 5.10.

```
NULLS ALLOWED or NULLS NOT ALLOWED
DELETE ... CASCADES or RESTRICTED or NULLIFIES
UPDATE ... CASCADES
```

3. AN OVERVIEW OF IDMS

As explained in Section 1, the complete IDMS product now includes a base CODASYL (network) DBMS, together with certain relational extensions to that base. In this chapter, however, we are primarily concerned with the CODASYL aspects of the system; we therefore ignore the relational features entirely until we reach Sections 7 and 8. Please note too that, as with our discussions of IMS, we are forced to omit a very great amount of detail (on both CODASYL and relational aspects); some comparatively major topics will simply not be discussed at all.

An IDMS database is defined by a **schema,** written in the IDMS schema data description language (schema DDL). The schema for a given database defines the records in the database, the "elements" (fields) they contain, and the "sets" (links) in which they participate as either "owner" (parent) or "member" (child). Once written, the schema is compiled by the schema DDL compiler, and the output from the compilation is stored in the IDMS dictionary.

Users do not interact with the database *per se* but rather with a *user view* of that database, defined by a **subschema**. However, the view defined by a subschema is actually not all that different from the "view" defined by the underlying schema; the only really significant difference is that certain schema sets and/or records and/or fields can be excluded from the subschema. (Of course, "sets," "records," and "fields" here refer to types, not occurrences.) In other words, a subschema is *a simple subset of the schema,* loosely speaking.

Subschemas are written in the IDMS subschema DDL. Once written, they are compiled by the subschema DDL compiler, and again the output is stored in the IDMS dictionary.

As for data manipulation, IDMS (like IMS and DATACOM/DB) is basically invoked by means of a host language CALL interface. However, users do not have to code the calls directly; instead, IDMS provides a set of DML statements (FIND, GET, STORE, etc.), with a syntax that resembles the syntax of the host language, together with preprocessors to translate those DML statements into the appropriate host language calling sequences. Preprocessors are provided for the following host languages: COBOL, PL/I, FORTRAN, and System/370 Assembler Language.

The remainder of the chapter has the following structure. After this preliminary overview section, Section 4 explains IDMS data definition (i.e., the schema and subschema), and Section 5 describes the IDMS DML. Next, Section 6 presents a brief overview of the IDMS storage structure. Sections 7 and 8 then describe certain extensions to the base system; Section 7 discusses the *Logical Record Facility* (LRF) and Section 8 discusses the *Automatic System Facility* (ASF). Finally, Section 9 presents a few concluding remarks.

As in the case of IMS (Chapter 13), we do not have room in this book for a detailed discussion of such aspects of IDMS as recovery, concurrency, etc. We content ourselves instead with the following brief comments. First, IDMS does indeed provide full recovery and concurrency controls, very much along the lines of IMS (and DB2, for that matter). Second, it enforces security constraints through the subschema mechanism, which can be used not only to hide information but also to restrict the range of operations the user is allowed to perform. As for integrity, IDMS will optionally enforce certain field uniqueness constraints (see Section 4) and certain referential constraints (see Section 5).

IDMS also possesses an extensive and well-integrated family of auxiliary products, including a DC frontend (IDMS-DC), an integrated data dictionary (IDD, already mentioned a couple of times above), an online query interface (OLQ), a natural language interface (OnLine English*), an application generator (Application Development System/OnLine), a report writer (CULPRIT), and many others.

4. DATA DEFINITION

Fig. 4 shows a possible schema for the suppliers-and-parts database of Fig. 3. We remind the reader that we are ignoring numerous details in this chapter; in particular, Fig. 4 omits most of the details having to do with how the database is mapped to physical storage. However, some of those details will be discussed briefly in Section 6.

Explanation:

- Line 1 merely assigns the schema a name.
- Line 2 defines the existence of a record type S.
- Lines 3–4 define the **location mode** for record type S. In general, a record's location mode tells IDMS how to choose a storage location in the database for a new occurrence of the record type in question. The possibilities are CALC, VIA, and some other alternatives not discussed in this book:
  - a. CALC means hashing; the new record is stored at a location determined by hashing the specified **CALC key** (S# in the case at hand; we ignore the fact that "#" is not a legal character in an IDMS name). The CALC key can optionally be specified to be unique (DUPLICATES NOT ALLOWED, line 4).
  - b. VIA means "store the new record near its owner in the specified set" (see line 18 for an example).

---

*OnLine English is in fact the INTELLECT product (see Chapter 15), marketed under license from AICorp.

```
1     SCHEMA NAME IS SUPPLIERS-AND-PARTS.

2     RECORD NAME IS S.
3     LOCATION MODE IS CALC USING S#
4                             DUPLICATES NOT ALLOWED.
5         02 S#     PIC X(5).
6         02 SNAME  PIC X(20).
7         02 STATUS PIC 999 USAGE COMP-3.
8         02 CITY   PIC X(15).

9     RECORD NAME IS P.
10    LOCATION MODE IS CALC USING P#
11                            DUPLICATES NOT ALLOWED.
12        02 P#     PIC X(6).
13        02 PNAME  PIC X(20).
14        02 COLOR  PIC X(6).
15        02 WEIGHT PIC 999 USAGE COMP-3.
16        02 CITY   PIC X(15).

17    RECORD NAME IS SP.
18    LOCATION MODE IS VIA S-SP SET.
19        02 QTY    PIC 99999 USAGE COMP-3.

20    SET NAME IS S-SP.
21    ORDER IS NEXT.
22    OWNER IS S.
23    MEMBER IS SP OPTIONAL MANUAL.

24    SET NAME IS P-SP.
25    ORDER IS NEXT.
26    OWNER IS P.
27    MEMBER IS SP OPTIONAL MANUAL.

28    SET NAME IS S-FILE.
29    ORDER IS SORTED.
30    OWNER IS SYSTEM.
31    MEMBER IS S MANDATORY AUTOMATIC
32                ASCENDING KEY IS CITY.

33    SET NAME IS P-FILE.
34    ORDER IS SORTED.
35    OWNER IS SYSTEM.
36    MEMBER IS P MANDATORY AUTOMATIC
37                ASCENDING KEY IS COLOR.
```

Fig. 4 Schema (many details omitted) for suppliers-and-parts

- Lines 5–8 define the fields of record type S.

- Lines 9–16 define record type P similarly.

- Lines 17–19 define record type SP similarly, except that the location mode for SP is defined to be VIA S-SP SET, which means that each SP occurrence will be stored physically close to the corresponding S occurrence (e.g., on the same page, or one that is nearby).

- Line 20 defines the existence of a set type called S-SP.

■ Line 21 defines the sequence of member (SP) record occurrences within any given occurrence of the set S-SP. ORDER IS NEXT means that the sequence is program-controlled; that is, any program that creates a new member must procedurally specify the connection point for that new member. Other possibilities are FIRST (a new member appears in front of all existing members), LAST (a new member appears behind all existing members), PRIOR (another version of program-controlled ordering), and SORTED (ordering based on values of some field in the member record). In the case at hand, we want SP occurrences within a given S-SP occurrence to be kept in part number order; since P# is not a field of the record SP, that ordering cannot be specified as SORTED and so must be maintained by some application program, which is why we specified NEXT. See Example 5.8.

■ Line 22 specifies the owner record type for S-SP.

■ Line 23 specifies the member record type for S-SP. It also includes the **connect option** MANUAL (the alternative is AUTOMATIC) and the **disconnect option** OPTIONAL (the alternative is MANDATORY). We defer explanation of these options to Section 5. However, we note in passing that, in the case of S-SP (and P-SP) specifically, MANDATORY AUTOMATIC would be much more appropriate in practice than OPTIONAL MANUAL. We choose OPTIONAL MANUAL purely to serve as a basis for certain examples in Section 5.

■ Lines 24–27 define set type P-SP similarly.

■ Lines 28–32 define a **system-owned set** called S-FILE. System-owned sets correspond to the "system links" of Section 2. The set type S-FILE has exactly one occurrence, with a hypothetical SYSTEM record as owner and all S record occurrences as members, in ascending CITY order (by virtue of the specifications ORDER IS SORTED and ASCENDING KEY IS CITY; CITY is the "sort control key" for set S-FILE). The connect and disconnect options have been specified as AUTOMATIC and MANDATORY, respectively.

■ Lines 33–37 define the system-owned set P-FILE similarly.

We turn now to user views and the subschema. Any particular user view is a substructure of the underlying schema structure, derived from that underlying structure in accordance with the following rules:

1. Any field type can be omitted.
2. Any record type can be omitted.
3. Any set type can be omitted.
4. If a given record type is omitted, then all set types in which that record type participates (as either owner or member) must be omitted also.

Fig. 5 shows a possible subschema for the suppliers-and-parts database, in which only two record types are visible, some fields are omitted, and some sets are omitted.

```
1      ADD SUBSCHEMA NAME IS S-AND-P-ONLY
2          OF SCHEMA NAME IS SUPPLIERS-AND-PARTS.

3      ADD RECORD S.
4      ADD RECORD P
5          ELEMENTS ARE
6                   P#
7                   COLOR
8                   CITY.

9      ADD SET S-FILE.
10     ADD SET P-FILE.
```

Fig. 5 Possible subschema for the suppliers-and-parts schema (many details omitted)

5. DATA MANIPULATION

Preliminaries

For definiteness we base all our examples and discussions in this section on COBOL, since COBOL is the language most widely used with IDMS. We also assume for simplicity that the subschema is identical to the schema, in the sense that the program has unrestricted access to all sets, records, and fields defined in the schema. Our examples are of course based on the suppliers-and-parts database (schema of Fig. 4).

A program issuing IDMS DML operations must contain an IDMS *record description* for each subschema record type it intends to process. That description causes an area of storage to be reserved for records of the specified type; the name of that storage area and the names of its constituent fields are identical to those for the record type in question. Suppose, for example, that the program includes a record description for the supplier record type S. Then (e.g.) to create a new supplier record occurrence, the program could issue the following statements:

```
MOVE 'S13' TO S# IN S
MOVE 'Johnson' TO SNAME IN S
MOVE 45 TO STATUS IN S
MOVE 'Warsaw' TO CITY IN S
STORE S
```

The four MOVEs initialize the four fields in the record area in storage; the STORE then creates the new record in the database from the values in those four fields. *Note:* The original DBTG proposals [1] referred to the totality of all such record areas as the **User Work Area** (UWA), and we will occasionally make use of that term in this section.

An IDMS program must also include an *IDMS Communications Block* (ICB). The function of the ICB is similar to that of the SQLCA in SQL products such as DB2—that is, it provides feedback information to the program. In particular, it includes a field called ERROR-STATUS, which should be checked after each DML operation; a value of 0000 means that the operation completed satisfactorily, a nonzero value means that some exceptional condition occurred. As usual, we will not normally bother to show such checking in our examples.

Note: In practice, the IDMS preprocessors provide facilities to simplify (a) the process of constructing the ICB and UWA and (b) the process of testing for and dealing with ERROR-STATUS exceptions. Such facilities are beyond the scope of this chapter, however.

Currency

Before we can examine the statements of the DML in any detail, it is necessary to discuss the fundamental concept of *currency*. The concept of currency is analogous to the notion of "current position" in IMS or "current of cursor" in SQL—i.e., it is a generalization of the familiar notion of current position within a file. However, it is rather more complicated than the SQL or IMS concepts. The basic idea is as follows: For each program operating under its control—i.e., for each "run unit," to use the CODASYL term—IDMS maintains a table of **currency indicators**. A currency indicator is an object whose value at any given time is either *null* (meaning that it currently identifies no record) or the address of a record in the database (called a **database key** in IDMS; a database key is basically the same as what is more usually called a record ID or RID). In other words, a currency indicator is a *database pointer*. The currency indicators for a given run unit identify the record (occurrence) most recently accessed by that run unit for each of the following:*

- Each type of record

  For a record type *R,* the most recently accessed *R* occurrence is referred to as "the current record of type *R*" or "the current *R* occurrence."

- Each type of set

  For a set type *S,* the most recently accessed record occurrence that participates in an occurrence of *S* might be either an owner occurrence or a member occurrence. Whichever it is, it is referred to as "the current record of set type *S.*" Note that "the current record of set type *S*" also uniquely identifies a unique *set* occurrence—namely, the unique occurrence of set type *S* that con-

---

*"Most recently accessed" is not strictly accurate here. See Examples 5.5 and 5.6 later.

tains the current record of set type *S*. That uniquely identified set occurrence is referred to as "the current occurrence of set type *S*" or "the current *S* occurrence."

■ Any type of record

The most recently accessed record occurrence, no matter what its type and no matter what sets it participates in, is referred to as "the current record of the run unit" (usually abbreviated to just **current of run unit**). "Current of run unit" is the most important currency of all, as will shortly be made clear.

As an example, consider the following sequence of operations:

```
MOVE 'S4' TO S# IN S
FIND CALC S
FIND FIRST SP WITHIN S-SP
FIND OWNER WITHIN P-SP
```

The effect of these four statements is as follows. The MOVE initializes the UWA field S# IN S. The FIND CALC then locates the corresponding S record occurrence—namely, the S occurrence for supplier S4. The FIND FIRST . . . WITHIN then locates the first SP record occurrence within the S-SP set occurrence owned by supplier S4—namely, the SP occurrence for S4 and P2 (see Fig. 2). Last, the FIND OWNER then locates the owner record for that SP occurrence within the set P-SP—namely, the P occurrence for part P2. At the end of the sequence, therefore, that P occurrence is the current of run unit. As an exercise, try to complete the rest of the table:

```
Current of run unit                 P 'P2'
Current S occurrence
Current P occurrence
Current SP occurrence
Current record of set S-SP
Current record of set P-SP
Current S-SP occurrence
Current P-SP occurrence
```

The complete table is given in the Answers section at the end of the chapter.

Statements

We now embark on our explanation of the major DML statements. First a brief overview:

■	FIND	Locates an existing record occurrence and establishes it as current of run unit (updating other currency indicators as appropriate)
■	GET	Retrieves current of run unit
■	OBTAIN	Same as FIND followed by GET
■	MODIFY	Updates current of run unit

- CONNECT   Connects current of run unit into current occurrence of specified set
- DISCONNECT   Disconnects current of run unit from specified set
- ERASE   Deletes current of run unit
- STORE   Creates a new record occurrence and establishes it as current of run unit (updating other currency indicators as appropriate)

The importance of the notion "current of run unit" is apparent from this summary. So too is the importance of the FIND statement—it is logically required before each of the other statements, except for STORE (and OBTAIN, which we do not discuss any further in this section). The FIND statement has several variants, the most important of which we illustrate in Examples 5.1–5.6 below.

5.1 FIND CALC. Find the supplier record for supplier S4.

```
MOVE 'S4' TO S# IN S
FIND CALC S
```

FIND CALC can be used if and only if the record type in question has been defined with a location mode of CALC. IDMS finds the required record by taking the value supplied in the UWA field corresponding to the CALC key and hashing it. The record found becomes the current of run unit, the current of its record type, and the current of all sets in which it participates as either owner or member (this remark applies to all forms of FIND and will not be repeated every time in what follows).

5.2 FIND OWNER. Find the owner of the current occurrence of set P-SP.

```
FIND OWNER WITHIN P-SP
```

In general, FIND OWNER finds the owner in the specified set type of the current occurrence of that set type. *Note:* The FIND will fail if the specified set type does not include "owner linkage," except as explained in Section 6.

5.3 FIND member. Get part numbers for parts supplied by supplier S4.

```
MOVE 'S4' TO S# IN S
FIND CALC S
FIND FIRST SP WITHIN S-SP
while SP found
PERFORM
   FIND OWNER WITHIN P-SP
   GET P
   (add P# IN P to result list)
   FIND NEXT SP WITHIN S-SP
END-PERFORM
```

Two versions of "FIND member" are illustrated in this example. The FIND

FIRST locates the first SP occurrence within the current occurrence of set S-SP (namely, the S-SP occurrence owned by supplier S4). Then, on each iteration of the loop, the FIND OWNER and GET find and retrieve the corresponding part, and the FIND NEXT then locates the next SP occurrence for supplier S4. In general, FIND NEXT locates the next record within the current occurrence of the specified set, relative to the position defined by the current record of that set.

If and only if the specified set type has "prior linkage" (see Section 6), then the specification FIRST (or NEXT) in "FIND member" can be replaced by the specification LAST (or PRIOR). If and only if the specified set type has "mode chain" (again, see Section 6), then the specification FIRST (or NEXT, etc.) can be replaced by an integer n or the name of a program variable having an integer value n, representing a request for the nth member in the set.

5.4 FIND member USING. Get part numbers for red parts.

```
MOVE 'Red' TO COLOR IN P
FIND FIRST P WITHIN P-FILE USING COLOR IN P
while P found
PERFORM
   GET P
   (add P# IN P to result list)
   FIND NEXT P WITHIN P-FILE USING COLOR IN P
END-PERFORM
```

"FIND FIRST member USING" locates the first member of the current occurrence of the specified set having the same value for the specified field as the corresponding field in the UWA. Similarly, "FIND NEXT member USING" locates the next record within the current occurrence of the specified set, relative to the position defined by the current record of that set, having the same value for the specified field as the corresponding field in the UWA. In the example, the specified set happens to have owner SYSTEM, and therefore has only one occurrence; that single occurrence is considered to be the current occurrence at all times.

Note: "FIND member USING" can be used only if the specified set type is defined with ORDER IS SORTED, and the USING field is defined as the sort control key for that set type. Also, the comments under Example 5.3 regarding LAST, PRIOR, n, etc. in "FIND member" apply also to "FIND member USING."

5.5 FIND CURRENT. Establish the current record of type P as the current of run unit (note that this record is not necessarily the current of run unit already).

```
FIND CURRENT P
```

FIND CURRENT differs from the FIND formats so far described in that its *only* function is to update the table of currency indicators; it does not require any access to the database (since the record in question must already have been located by some previous operation, by definition). FIND CURRENT is frequently required to establish some record found earlier in the program as current of run unit, immediately prior to (say) a MODIFY operation. The possible FIND CURRENT formats are:

```
FIND CURRENT record
FIND CURRENT OF set
FIND CURRENT OF RUN UNIT
```

5.6 FIND DB-KEY. For each supplier who supplies part P4, find another part supplied by the same supplier, and print the supplier number and part number. For simplicity assume that each supplier that supplies P4 does in fact supply at least one other part.

First attempt /* **INCORRECT** */:

```
 1   MOVE 'P4' TO P# IN P
 2   FIND CALC P
 3   PERFORM "forever"
 4      FIND NEXT SP WITHIN P-SP
 5      IF SP not found
 6         leave outer loop
 7      IF SP found
 8         FIND OWNER WITHIN S-SP
 9         GET S
10         PERFORM "forever"
11            FIND NEXT SP WITHIN S-SP
12            FIND OWNER WITHIN P-SP
13            GET P
14            IF P# IN P NOT = 'P4'
15               leave inner loop
16            END-IF
17         END-PERFORM
18         (print S# IN S and P# IN P)
19      END-IF
20   END-PERFORM
```

As indicated, the code above is not correct—it contains a logical error (quite apart from the assumption mentioned in the problem statement, which of course would not be justified in practice). Try finding the error before reading the explanation below. It is probably a good idea to "play DBMS" and execute the procedure by hand on the sample data of Fig. 2.

The error is as follows. When the FIND OWNER in line 12 is executed, it establishes a P occurrence as the current of run-unit—also as the current record of all sets in which it participates (as either owner or member), including in particular set P-SP. This fact in turn means that the current occurrence of set P-SP becomes the one owned by that P occurrence. Thus, when the FIND NEXT in line 4 is executed on the next iteration of the outer loop (in an attempt to find the next supplier of P4), *the P-SP occurrence referenced in that statement will no longer be the one owned by P4.* To avoid this situation, we must do the following:

■   Following successful execution of the FIND NEXT in line 4, we must save the address (database key) of the SP record just found. This can be done by inserting the statement

```
ACCEPT SP-ADDR FROM SP CURRENCY
```

between lines 4 and 5 in the above code. The effect of this statement is to save the database key of the SP record just found in the program variable SP-ADDR.

■ Immediately before attempting to execute the FIND NEXT in line 4 again, we must manually restore the currency indicator for SP to the desired value (i.e., to the value that we saved in SP-ADDR). This can be done by inserting the statement

```
FIND SP DB-KEY IS SP-ADDR
```

between lines 19 and 20 in the above code. The effect of this statement is to find the SP record with database key as given by the program variable SP-ADDR (and thus of course to update all currency indicators accordingly). Like FIND CURRENT, FIND DB-KEY does not actually require any access to the database.

The technique illustrated by this example (saving and restoring currency indicators via ACCEPT and FIND DB-KEY) is needed very frequently in practice. Further examples of its use are given in Examples 5.8 and 5.9 below.

5.7 MODIFY. Add 10 to the status value for supplier S4.

```
MOVE 'S4' TO S# IN S
FIND CALC S
GET S
ADD 10 TO STATUS IN S
MODIFY S
```

5.8 STORE and CONNECT. Create an SP record relating supplier S4 to part P3 (shipment quantity 1000), and connect it into the S-SP occurrence for S4 and the P-SP occurrence for P3.

```
MOVE 'S4' TO S# IN S
FIND CALC S
ACCEPT S-SP-ADDR FROM S-SP CURRENCY
FIND LAST SP WITHIN S-SP
while SP found PERFORM
    ACCEPT S-SP-ADDR FROM S-SP CURRENCY
    FIND OWNER WITHIN P-SP
    GET P
    IF P# IN P < 'P3'
        leave loop
    END-IF
    FIND PRIOR SP WITHIN S-SP
END-PERFORM
MOVE 'P3' TO P# IN P
FIND CALC P
ACCEPT P-SP-ADDR FROM P-SP CURRENCY
FIND LAST SP WITHIN P-SP
while SP found PERFORM
    ACCEPT P-SP-ADDR FROM P-SP CURRENCY
```

```
    FIND OWNER WITHIN S-SP
    GET S
    IF S# IN S < 'S4'
        leave loop
    END-IF
    FIND PRIOR SP WITHIN P-SP
END-PERFORM
MOVE 1000 TO QTY IN SP
FIND DB-KEY IS S-SP-ADDR
FIND DB-KEY IS P-SP-ADDR
STORE SP
CONNECT SP TO S-SP
CONNECT SP TO P-SP
```

This code is not straightforward! Furthermore, it assumes that:

1. The connect options for S-SP and P-SP are specified as MANUAL. If instead they are AUTOMATIC, the two explicit CONNECT statements above will be unnecessary (and in fact illegal); the rest of the code, however, will remain unchanged. A connect option of AUTOMATIC means that, when a new occurrence of the member record type is first stored, it will automatically be connected into the current occurrence of the set (at the position dictated by the ORDER specification for that set—see paragraph 2 below). AUTOMATIC is probably more reasonable in the case of suppliers-and-parts specifically, since it is unlikely that we would want to allow an SP occurrence in the database *not* to be connected into some S-SP occurrence and some P-SP occurrence. The AUTOMATIC connect option thus corresponds very roughly to the "NULLS NOT ALLOWED" foreign key rule in relational systems (though there are several subtle differences, beyond the scope of this chapter).

2. The order options for S-SP and P-SP are specified as NEXT. ORDER IS NEXT means that, when the CONNECT is done, the new record is to be connected into the set at the point immediately following the position identified by the current record of the set.

3. Sets S-SP and P-SP have been specified with both "prior linkage" and "owner linkage" (as mentioned under Examples 5.2 and 5.3 above).

Note also the need for the various ACCEPT CURRENCY and corresponding FIND DB-KEY statements in this example. The STORE statement establishes the SP record just stored as the current of run-unit but *not* as the current of S-SP or the current of P-SP (because it is not automatically connected into those sets). The FIND DB-KEY statements are needed in order to establish the correct current positions within those sets, as required by paragraph 2 above; note that those statements do not specify a record type, because the record type identified by the specified database key can be either owner or member, in general. (For example, if supplier S4 currently supplies no parts, then the variable S-SP-ADDR will identify an S record, otherwise it will identify an SP record.) Finally, the CONNECT statements connect the SP record just stored into sets S-SP and P-SP appropriately.

Note, incidentally, that the FIND DB-KEY statements *must* precede the STORE statement (why?).

5.9 DISCONNECT. Disconnect the SP record relating supplier S4 and part P3 from the occurrences of sets S-SP and P-SP that contain it.

```
MOVE 'S4' TO S# IN S
FIND CALC S
PERFORM "forever"
   ACCEPT S-SP-ADDR FROM S-SP CURRENCY
   FIND NEXT SP WITHIN S-SP
   FIND OWNER WITHIN P-SP
   GET P
   IF P# IN P = 'P3'
      leave loop
   END-IF
   FIND DB-KEY IS S-SP-ADDR
END-PERFORM
FIND CURRENT SP
DISCONNECT SP FROM S-SP
DISCONNECT SP FROM P-SP
```

The foregoing code assumes that the disconnect options for S-SP and P-SP are specified as OPTIONAL. If instead they are MANDATORY, the DISCONNECT statements above will fail. A disconnect option of MANDATORY means that, once an occurrence of the member record type has been connected into some occurrence of the set, it can never be disconnected from the set again unless it is deleted from the database entirely (see the next example). In practice, of course, MANDATORY is more likely than OPTIONAL in the specific case of sets S-SP and P-SP.

5.10 ERASE. Delete the S occurrence for supplier S4.

The question here is, of course, what to do about the fact that there happen to be some SP occurrences for supplier S4. The answer to that question depends on the format of the ERASE statement. There are four possible formats, as the following code indicates:

```
MOVE 'S4' TO S# IN S
FIND CALC S
ERASE S [ PERMANENT | SELECTIVE | ALL ]
```

The four ERASE formats behave as follows:

- No qualification

  The current of run unit is deleted only if it is not the owner of any nonempty set occurrence. This option corresponds roughly to a foreign key rule of DELETE RESTRICTED; but note that the rule applies to *all* sets for which the record type is the owner—it cannot be varied on a set-by-set basis.

- PERMANENT

The current of run unit is deleted, together with MANDATORY member occurrences of any set occurrences of which it is the owner—OPTIONAL member occurrences being merely disconnected, not deleted. This option corresponds roughly to a foreign key rule of DELETE CASCADES in the MANDATORY case and DELETE NULLIFIES in the OPTIONAL case.

■ SELECTIVE

The effect is the same as for PERMANENT, except that OPTIONAL members not participating as members in any other set occurrence are deleted, not just disconnected. This option corresponds roughly to DELETE CASCADES, but note that SELECTIVE effectively allows the program to *override* the static schema specifications.

■ ALL

The current of run unit is deleted, together with all member occurrences of any set occurrence of which it is the owner, regardless of disconnect options. This option resembles DELETE CASCADES again, except that again the program is overriding the schema specifications.

In each case, if any deleted member occurrence is itself the owner of another set occurrence, then the effect is as if the original ERASE (with the specified qualification) had been applied directly to that member occurrence.

6. STORAGE STRUCTURE

As with our discussion of IMS in Chapter 13, it is certainly not our intention to cover all possible IDMS storage structures in detail in this chapter. However, there are a few general remarks that can usefully be made.

1. First, as in IMS, each stored record includes a hidden *prefix,* containing (principally) pointers to represent the record's participation as owner or member in various sets, as described in the next few paragraphs.

2. Next, IDMS provides two principal storage representations for the set construct, namely **chained sets** and **indexed sets**. The representation for a given set is defined in the schema, via the specification (not shown in Fig. 4) MODE IS CHAIN or MODE IS INDEX. See the next two paragraphs.

3. MODE IS CHAIN means that the set is stored essentially as described in Section 2—i.e., with a chain of pointers for each set occurrence, linking the owner to the first member, the first member to the second member, . . . , and the last member back to the owner. The chain can optionally be specified as two-way: **prior linkage**. Prior linkage means that the owner also points back to the last member, the last member also points back to the previous member, . . . , and the first member also points back to the owner. **Owner linkage**

can also optionally be specified, meaning that each member also includes a pointer to the owner (this option does not apply to system-owned sets; see paragraph 6 below). As noted in Section 5, prior linkage is required for FIND PRIOR and FIND LAST, and owner linkage is required for FIND OWNER.

4. MODE IS INDEX means that each occurrence of the set uses an index instead of a pointer chain to identify (and sequence) the members in that occurrence. Note, therefore, that there are as many occurrences of the index as there are occurrences of the set; see Fig. 6, which represents the occurrence of set S-SP for supplier S1 as it would appear in storage if MODE IS INDEX were specified. (For simplicity we have shown the index entries as if each required a separate index record, though in practice they would probably all be contained within just one such record.) Note that the owner and index records are chained by means of next, prior, and owner pointers. In addition, the index records point to the members (of course), and the members also point to the index records; in addition, the members can (optionally) point direct to the set owner. However, such owner linkage is *not* required to support FIND OWNER on an indexed set.

5. Note that MODE IS INDEX does not necessarily imply ORDER IS SORTED. Member sequence within the set is represented by entry sequence within the index, and that sequence in turn can be any of the usual IDMS possibilities—NEXT, PRIOR, FIRST, LAST, or SORTED. For ORDER IS SORTED, the index is multi-level (basically a form of B-tree). In the other cases it is single-level.

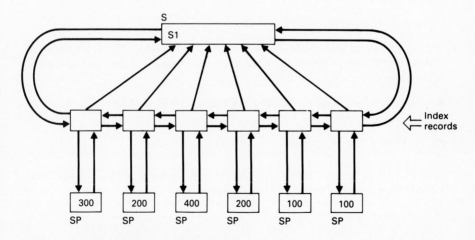

Fig. 6 Sample occurrence of an indexed set

6. MODE IS INDEX is used in particular to implement system-owned sets in IDMS. For such a set, of course, there is exactly one occurrence of the owner record (supplied by IDMS and not directly visible to the user), and hence exactly one occurrence of the index.

7. The location mode VIA SET has an extended interpretation if the set in question is defined with MODE IS INDEX and ORDER IS SORTED, as follows: In addition to causing each member record to be stored close to the corresponding owner, it also causes all member records for a particular owner to be stored in a physical order that approximates their logical order. *Note:* In the particular case where the set in question is system-owned, this facility is similar to the "clustering index" feature of DB2 (for readers who might be familiar with that feature).

8. Finally, we remind the reader of the location mode option CALC (hashing). A difference between IMS and IDMS is that hashing access can be provided to *any* record type in IDMS—it is not restricted to root records only, as it is in IMS.

7. THE LOGICAL RECORD FACILITY

The IDMS Logical Record Facility (LRF) provides a "flat record view" layer on top of an IDMS database. In other words, LRF is a mechanism that allows the application programmer to be unaware of the detailed structure of the underlying database and to operate in terms of "logical records" instead—where a logical record (type) is essentially just a *virtual table,* in relational terms. For example, LRF could be used on the suppliers-and-parts database of Fig. 1 to define the following logical record (or view)—

```
SCP ( S#, SCITY, PCITY, P# )
```

—representing supplier number and city plus part number and city for suppliers and parts that are colocated.* Then the programmer could perform operations against that view such as the following:

- OBTAIN the FIRST (or NEXT) SCP record WHERE SCITY = 'London'
- MODIFY or ERASE the SCP record most recently OBTAINed
- STORE a new SCP record

Note that the user in LRF is still an application programmer, not an end user. Note too that the user still operates in terms of one (virtual) record at a time.

---

*Actually the SCP logical record would appear in LRF to contain two *group items* called S and P, each of which in turn contained two elementary items—S# and CITY in S and P# and CITY in P. LRF does not actually provide field renaming as our example suggests.

In discussing LRF, it is important to distinguish carefully between two DMLs, the *application programming DML* and the *view definition DML* (not LRF terms). We refer to them below as U-DML and D-DML for short (U for user and D for DBA or definer):

- U-DML is the DML the application programmer uses to operate on the view. The statements OBTAIN, MODIFY, ERASE, and STORE mentioned above are statements of that DML (in fact, they are basically the *only* statements of that DML).

- D-DML is the DML the database administrator uses to define the view and to define the semantics of U-DML operations on the view. D-DML consists basically of a somewhat extended version of the regular IDMS DML (actually it looks rather like U-DML plus some additional statements).

In outline, then, LRF works as follows:

1. Views (i.e., logical records) are defined by the DBA as part of the relevant subschema.

2. Users can operate on such views by means of the U-DML operations, which (unlike the regular IDMS DML operations) can include a WHERE clause. Such WHERE clauses can involve arbitrary Boolean combinations of simple comparisons, with parentheses if necessary to force a desired order of evaluation. The simple comparisons in turn can involve the usual comparison operators and also certain string matching operators, and the comparands can consist of arbitrary arithmetic expressions in which the operands can be constants, program variables, or database fields. A comparison can also be a "keyword"—that is, a term defined by the DBA as a shorthand for a longer, more detailed condition. For example:

```
OBTAIN NEXT SCP WHERE FRENCH
```

Here FRENCH might be a DBA-defined keyword standing for the condition

```
    SCITY = 'Paris'
 OR SCITY = 'Nice'
 OR SCITY = 'Marseille'
 OR SCITY = 'Amiens'
```

3. Each view is derived from the records of the underlying database by means of a DBA-written procedure, or rather by means of several such procedures (see paragraphs 4 and 5 below), expressed in D-DML. D-DML effectively allows the (procedural) definition of views that are derivable via certain combinations of the relational restrict, "project," and Cartesian product operations ("project" in quotes because duplicates are not eliminated). It does not of course support the restrict, project, and product oper-

ations directly.* Note too that not all possible restrict/project/product views are derivable; for example, it is not possible to define a view that involves a join of a table with itself.

4. As indicated in paragraph 3, the DBA actually provides several procedures (or *paths,* to use the LRF terminology) for each view. The purpose of the procedures is basically to tell IDMS what it has to do to support U-DML operations on the view. In the case of the view SCP shown above, for example, the following procedure might be specified for the U-DML operation

```
OBTAIN ... SCP WHERE SCITY = x
```

(where ". . ." stands for FIRST or NEXT, and x is a parameter; the D-DML pseudocode shown below is intended to be similar but not identical to genuine D-DML code):

```
/* Entry point for FIRST invocation : */
OBTAIN FIRST S WITHIN S-FILE WHERE CITY = x
while S found PERFORM
    extract S.S#, S.CITY
    OBTAIN FIRST P WITHIN P-FILE WHERE CITY = x
    while P found PERFORM
        extract P.P#, P.CITY
        return S.S#, S.CITY, P.CITY, P.P# to user
        /* Entry point for NEXT invocation : */
        OBTAIN NEXT P WITHIN P-FILE WHERE CITY = x
    END-PERFORM
    OBTAIN NEXT S WITHIN S-FILE WHERE CITY = x
END-PERFORM
```

Each time the programmer issues the U-DML OBTAIN operation shown above, LRF will invoke this procedure to construct the required next record. Note that LRF is able to remember the point it left off execution of the procedure on the previous invocation, so it knows what "next" means in this context.

5. In general, the DBA must provide a "path" or procedure for each distinct operation that the user is to be allowed to perform on the view. In particular, the DBA will have to provide several distinct *retrieval* procedures for a given view. In the case of view SCP, for example, retrieval by supplier number might best be implemented by a procedure involving FIND CALC on the S record; retrieval by part number might best be implemented by a procedure involving FIND CALC on the P record; retrieval by an equality condition on

---

*Cartesian product is effectively implemented by simply concatenating the names of the records concerned in the definition of the logical record in the subschema. Likewise, "projection" is effectively implemented by simply omitting fields from the definitions of those records in the subschema. Only restriction is implemented purely by executable D-DML code.

SCITY might best be implemented by a procedure involving FIND USING on the S-FILE system-owned set; and so on. Thus the complete definition for the view SCP might look something like the following:

```
ADD SUBSCHEMA NAME IS ...

ADD RECORD S
    ELEMENTS ARE S# CITY.

ADD RECORD P
    ELEMENTS ARE P# CITY.

ADD SET S-SP etc.

ADD LOGICAL RECORD NAME IS SCP
    ELEMENTS ARE S P.

ADD PATH-GROUP OBTAIN SCP
    SELECT FOR FIELDNAME-EQ S#
        OBTAIN S WHERE CALCKEY EQ S# OF REQUEST
        ... etc ...
    SELECT FOR FIELDNAME-EQ P#
        OBTAIN P WHERE CALCKEY EQ P# OF REQUEST
        ... etc ...
    SELECT FOR FIELDNAME-EQ SCITY
        OBTAIN ...
        ... etc ...
    SELECT FOR FRENCH
        OBTAIN ...
        ... etc ...

ADD PATH-GROUP MODIFY SCP
    SELECT ...
    ... etc ...

ADD PATH-GROUP STORE SCP
    SELECT ...
    ... etc ...

ADD PATH-GROUP ERASE SCP
    SELECT ...
    ... etc ...
```

For a given user request, LRF will search through the D-DML procedures in sequence as written and will take the first it finds that matches the request. If it finds no match, it will reject the request. Thus, for example, if users are not to be allowed to access SCP records by SCITY value, it is sufficient for the DBA simply not to supply a retrieval procedure for that kind of access.

Having thus briefly sketched the way LRF works, we are now in a position to analyze it and compare it with the conventional relational view mechanism. We offer the following comments.

1. First, of course, LRF is not relational, because the U-DML does not support the relational operators (neither does the D-DML, come to that). In addition,

the views seen by the user can include duplicate records and can involve repeating groups and/or "redefined" fields and/or essential ordering.*

2. However, if the underlying IDMS database is sufficiently disciplined and does not (for example) rely on essential ordering, then LRF could—and indeed probably should—be used to provide a "true" relational view of that database (the previous point notwithstanding). For example, it could be used to define a relational view of the network version of suppliers-and-parts (Fig. 1) that consisted precisely of the familiar relations S, P, and SP. Of course, the U-DML operations would still be record-at-a-time, but at least the structure would be relational.

3. Note that each view definition requires the construction of a new subschema, a rather static kind of operation. Note too that it is not possible to construct "views on views"—i.e., to refer to existing views in D-DML procedures.

4. The views definable in D-DML are not arbitrary derived relations —they are basically just restrictions of Cartesian products, with certain fields optionally omitted. In particular, it is not possible to construct a view that involves a union or difference operation.

5. Of course, a view *can* be a join, since a join is just (a projection of) a restriction of a product. Furthermore, LRF allows the user to perform updates on a join view. However, LRF *per se* has no knowledge of what "update of join" means in any kind of general sense; instead, the meaning of such an operation (just like the meaning of every other U-DML operation) must be spelled out by the DBA in the form of a D-DML procedure. In other words, "update of join" and similar operations still require someone to write *ad hoc,* procedural application code—but that someone is the DBA, not the ordinary user.

6. It follows from the previous paragraph that it is not sufficient to tell the user what views are available and what U-DML operations can be performed on those views; it is of course also necessary to explain the *meaning* of those views and operations, which in some cases will amount to explaining the underlying structure of the database. For example, consider the following LRF view of suppliers-and-parts:

```
SQP ( S#, QTY, P# )
```

(with the conventional "shipment" interpretation). Depending on how the DBA chooses to write the D-DML procedures, a U-DML ERASE operation on a record of SQP might (a) be disallowed, or (b) delete the corresponding supplier, with or without that supplier's shipments, or (c) delete the corresponding part, with or without that part's shipments, or (d) just delete the

---

*See Chapter 11 for a discussion of essential ordering.

shipment, or (e) take any of an infinite number of other possible actions. Furthermore, each of these possibilities has interactions with the SCP view shown at the beginning of the section. And all of this needs to be explained to the user.*

Of course, remarks analogous to the foregoing apply to the relational view mechanism also, but with this significant difference: In the relational case, the underlying database and the view—and the mapping between them—are all based on the same (relational) model of data, which therefore provides a framework in which the explanations can make sense. In LRF the different levels are based on different models.

7. Note that the requirement that the DBA provide a procedure for each and every operation that the user is to be able to perform means that (a) the user able to issue *only* those predefined operations, and (more important) (b) *the DBA is hand-optimizing those predefined operations.* Note too that by "hand-optimizing predefined operations" we do not mean, for example, hand-optimizing a generic join operation—we mean hand-optimizing *each and every join operation separately.* Also, of course, if the physical structure of the database is changed, then reoptimization (i.e., reprogramming by the DBA) will be necessary.

8. Finally, we cannot resist pointing out that implementing a mechanism like LRF in terms of the implicit currency indicators of CODASYL must be significantly more complicated than implementing a similar mechanism in a system with explicit position holders (i.e., cursors). In fact, the IDMS manuals specifically advise LRF users not to mix LRF operations and regular CODASYL DML operations in the same program, because the regular operations will affect the currency indicators that control the LRF operations behind the scenes. For similar reasons, LRF users cannot dynamically switch from one path to another before the first is exhausted (i.e., before a "not found" condition has occurred). In the following sequence of U-DML operations, for example, the second OBTAIN NEXT will produce an unpredictable result:[†]

```
OBTAIN NEXT SCP WHERE S# = 'S1'
OBTAIN NEXT SCP WHERE SCITY = 'London'
```

These same currency difficulties are probably also the source of the limitation that views cannot be defined in terms of other views.

---

*It is the responsibility of the DBA to provide the necessary explanations by including extensive comments in the subschema along with the logical record definitions. An IDMS utility is provided to generate an explanatory report for the user from such comments.

[†]Unless the first happens to give "not found." In this special case the currency indicators will be set to null, with the result that the second OBTAIN NEXT will be interpreted as OBTAIN FIRST.

8. THE AUTOMATIC SYSTEM FACILITY

The Automatic System Facility (ASF) is the justification for the "R" in "IDMS/R." It is the component that provides (most of) the relational function of the system. It can be regarded as a frontend to the base IDMS product, supporting simple relational definitional and manipulative operations through a set of forms-based interfaces. Functionally, in fact, it somewhat resembles the forms-based QBF and definitional interfaces (only) of INGRES, as described in Chapter 15. It runs under the IDMS data communications component IDMS-DC.

Before we go any further, it might perhaps be helpful to point out what ASF is not. It is not a command-driven query language processor. Nor is it a report writer. Furthermore, it does not support the use of relational operators in application programs. On the contrary:

- The interactive query and report writer function is provided by the existing OnLine Query product OLQ. Relations created through ASF can be accessed through OLQ. However, OLQ does not support the full set of relational operators—in particular, it does not support join—and neither does it allow update. It does however allow the result of a query to be saved as a table in the database.

- The batch report writer function is provided through the existing report writer product CULPRIT.

- Since relations are implemented as LRF logical records (see below), application programs can access them using the operators of "U-DML." Applications can also be written to operate directly against the underlying database using conventional IDMS DML, as described in Section 5. Note, however, that all such access is basically one-record-at-a-time (in both cases).

In addition, the forms generated automatically by ASF can be customized if desired by means of the IDMS application generator ADS/OnLine, much as QBF forms can be customized via VIFRED in INGRES (see Chapter 15).

The primary purpose of ASF is to support the definition of, and subsequent access to, new (relational) databases. However, *it can also be used to provide a relational view of, and relational processing of, existing network databases.** We defer consideration of this latter possibility (relational access to networks) to the end of this section.

As indicated above, ASF is implemented on top of LRF, just as LRF is implemented on top of the base DBMS. In other words, ASF supports relations by treating them as LRF logical records, and LRF supports logical records by mapping them to (sub)schema records via access procedures expressed in "D-DML," as explained in Section 7. In the case of ASF, however, those access procedures are

---

*"Relational" should really be in quotes here, because the data structure shown to the user might not be a genuine relation—it might involve essential ordering, repeating groups, etc.

not written by the DBA but are generated automatically by ASF from specifications provided by the person defining the relation. See Fig. 7.

A given ASF table can be *stored* (the IDMS version of a base table) or it can be a *view*. We consider stored tables first.

Creating a Stored Table

Suppose the user wishes to create a new stored table. Through the appropriate ASF definitional forms, then, the user will specify:

1. The fact that this is a stored table, not a view;
2. The table name and field names;
3. The field data types (the possibilities are TEXT, NUMERIC, and CURRENCY—i.e., dollars and cents);
4. Optional integrity constraints on the table (basically simple restriction conditions);

and

5. Optional "keys" (i.e., fields or field combinations to be indexed; note that there is no way to specify a CALC key, and hence no way to obtain a hash structure). Each such "key" can optionally be specified to be UNIQUE.

When the definition is complete, the user issues the ASF "generate" command. ASF then does all of the following:

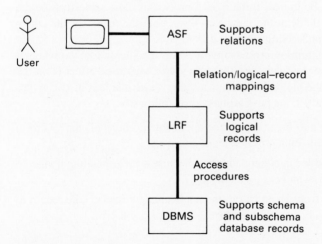

Fig. 7   ASF is implemented on top of LRF

1. Adds a definition of the new stored record type to the "relational schema." The relational schema is an internal-level description of the relational database ("internal" in the ANSI/SPARC sense); it contains definitions of all the records, CODASYL "indexed sets," etc., that appear in the stored form of the database. The initial relational schema is created when IDMS/R is first installed (it does not have to be defined by the DBA, unlike a network schema).

2. Adds a definition of an indexed set to the relational schema for each defined "key."

3. Creates a subschema defining the table as an LRF logical record, with corresponding OBTAIN, MODIFY, STORE, and ERASE access procedures. Those procedures make use of the defined "keys" (and hence indexes) as appropriate.

4. Compiles the subschema.

5. Generates code to support forms-based access (via the subschema) to the new table.

The user can now load data into the table, run simple restriction queries (only) on it, and update it, all very much as in QBF in INGRES (see Chapter 15). Note clearly however that all such operations are by definition *single-table* operations.

Creating a View

The operations available for defining a view are basically restrict, "project" (in quotes because as usual there is no question of eliminating duplicates), and join (but the join can involve a maximum of five ANDed join conditions, meaning that at most six tables can be joined; furthermore, no two of those tables can be the same). The names of fields in the view can differ from the names of the corresponding fields in the underlying table(s).

Part of the view definition process involves the specification of (a) whether updates are allowed on the view, and (b) if they are, what their effect is on the underlying tables. In the particular case of a view V that is a join of two tables (possibly views) $T1$ and $T2,$ the possibilities are as follows:*

- Inserting a record into V can cause (the applicable portions of) the record to be inserted into both, either, or neither of $T1$ and $T2$;

- Updating a field in V can either cause or not cause a corresponding update to a field in $T1$ or $T2$ (whichever is applicable);

- Deleting a record from V can cause (the applicable portions of) the record to be deleted from both, either, or neither of $T1$ and $T2$.

---

*This feature is not supported at the time of writing.

Updates to views are monitored to ensure that inserted or changed records satisfy the view-defining condition. Note in particular that the "update of join" mechanism just described could be used to enforce certain referential integrity constraints—*provided* all updates are made through appropriate views and not directly on the underlying stored tables. We shall have more to say regarding this possibility in the next section.

When the definition of the view is complete, the user issues the ASF "generate" command (as in the case of a stored table). ASF then does the following:

1. Creates a subschema defining the view as an LRF logical record, with corresponding access procedures as indicated by the view-defining expression and the update specifications.

2. Compiles the subschema.

3. Generates code to support forms-based access (via the subschema) to the new view.

The user can now operate on the view in all the usual ways, just as if it were a stored table, subject of course to any specified update constraints. Note once again that all such operations are by definition single-table operations—but here the "single table" can be a (predefined) join of up to six tables, any of which can in turn be a (predefined) join of up to six tables, etc., etc.

Further Definitional Operations

ASF supports several further data definition operations in addition to the table creation operations discussed above. First, of course, any existing table can be deleted ("dropped," to use the SQL term). Second, columns can be added to and removed from both stored tables and views. Third, "key" specifications (and therefore indexes) can also be added and removed. Finally, any of the following can be changed (again, for both stored tables and views, in general, except where the change would be meaningless):

- Field names, lengths, and data types
- "Key" specifications
- Integrity constraints
- View-defining expressions

Note: The full implications of some of these changes are very unclear at the time of writing. Some cases—for example, changing the data type of a field—will almost certainly require the table in question to be unloaded and reloaded.

Following any such definitional changes to a given table, the user is required to reissue the "generate" command. ASF will then modify the schema and subschema appropriately, restructure the database if necessary, and rebuild the forms-based application code. If the user makes changes to one table that affect other tables derived from it, ASF will flag those derived tables as "invalid." It *will* change the source-code definitions of those derived tables to bring them into line with the changes to the table(s) from which they are derived, but it will not automatically go through the "regenerate" procedure for them. The purpose of propagating the changes at the source-code level is to simplify the subsequent "regenerate" procedure, if the user does decide to request that procedure, but not to automate it. Any application programs that have been developed against the now changed tables will *not* automatically be invalidated; it is the user's responsibility to change such programs manually and then recompile them (if necessary).

Creating an ASF View of a Network Database

In order to construct an ASF view of an existing network database as a collection of relations, the DBA must go through the following steps:

1. Copy all the network definitions—for CODASYL records, CODASYL sets, etc.—over from the network schema into the relational schema. *Note:* It is the DBA's responsibility to ensure that the two schemas are kept in synch once the copying has been done.

2. Write a (CODASYL-style) subschema for each desired relation (i.e., view), specifying all the CODASYL records, CODASYL sets, etc., involved in the definition of that relation (view).

3. Construct an ASF view definition for each desired relation (view), specifying the derivation of that relation in terms of CODASYL records and CODASYL sets. The source records in a given derivation can be either network records or relational records, in general; in the case at hand, of course, they will be network records. For network records, an additional form of join condition can be specified in the derivation condition—"SET setname," meaning that each member record is to be joined to its owner record in the designated CODASYL set.

4. Issue "generate" for each such view.*

---

*Of course, the views defined by this procedure will only be as "relational" as the original network structure permits. For example, they can (as pointed out earlier) involve repeating groups, essential ordering, and similar nonrelational constructs. Also, given the limitations on updating views in ASF, they might not be updatable; and even if they are, there are likely to be certain difficulties. For example, foreign keys might not be updatable, because such updates correspond to a DISCONNECT plus a (re)CONNECT at the underlying database level, and membership is very likely to have been specified as MANDATORY. (Given the relation SP(S#,P#,QTY) as a relational view of the network database of Fig. 1, how could a shipment for part P1 be updated to become a shipment for part P2 instead, if membership were MANDATORY?) And another question: What are the semantics of a relational STORE operation if the "relation" involves essential ordering? Analogous questions arise for MODIFY and ERASE, of course.

Finally, the foregoing raises the possibility of tuning an existing IDMS/R *relational* database by adding CODASYL-style (chained) owner-member sets to link existing tables together. (Such sets would almost certainly be inessential, MANDATORY, and AUTOMATIC.) The DBA would then have to modify the source-level (ASF) view definitions to exploit those sets—i.e., by changing the derivation conditions to specify "SET setname"—and then reissue the "generate" command for those views. Such tuning might well be appropriate in certain situations.

9. CONCLUDING REMARKS

In this chapter, we have sketched a hypothetical network data model (abstracted from the CODASYL DBTG proposals), and we have described the major features of IDMS, a well known example of the CODASYL approach. We stress the point once again that we have omitted a very great amount of detail from that description. By way of conclusion, we now offer the following critical comments on network systems in general, and CODASYL systems and IDMS in particular.

Network Systems in General

Networks are complicated. The structure is complex; see Exercise 3 for an illustration of this point (if further illustration is needed). The operators are complex; and note that they would still be complex, even if they functioned at the set level instead of just on one record at a time (see reference [4] for evidence and further discussion of this claim). And, as reference [4] also shows, this increase in complexity (compared with relational systems) does not lead to any corresponding increase in functionality.

It is usually claimed, however, that network systems do at least provide good performance. However, good performance is by no means a foregone conclusion in such a system, for at least the following two reasons:

■ First, the network data structure tends to *fragment information*. For example, the supplier number for a particular shipment in the network structure of Fig. 1 is not part of the shipment record, but is instead part of the supplier record that is the owner of the shipment in a certain CODASYL set. As a result, it is possible that a given application can require significantly more I/O on a network database than it would on an equivalent relational database.

■ Second, as pointed out at several points in this chapter and elsewhere, much of the optimization in such a system is likely to be done manually, either by application programmers or by the DBA.

In fact, many of the criticisms of hierarchic systems made in Chapter 13 apply to network systems also.

CODASYL and IDMS

CODASYL in particular is considerably more complex than the hypothetical network model presented in Section 2 (though we omitted much of that additional complexity in our discussions in Sections 3–5). The concept of currency is an especially rich source of complexity (and error, we might add). Likewise, the complexity of the manual CONNECT process for essential sets—see Example 5.8—is sufficiently severe to suggest that sets should almost always be inessential in practice, which in turn raises the question of why the CODASYL set construct should be visible at all at the logical level.

In the case of IDMS specifically, application programs are not very data-independent: FIND CALC works if and only if the named record type has CALC location mode; FIND PRIOR and LAST work if and only if the named set type has prior linkage; FIND OWNER works only if the named set type has owner linkage (unless it is an indexed set); FIND USING works if and only if the named set type has SORTED order and the named field is the sort control key; DISCONNECT works if and only if the named set type has a disconnect option of MANUAL; and so on (this is not an exhaustive list).

LRF

A number of criticisms of LRF were made in Section 7, and there is no need to repeat the points here. Now that the ASF frontend is available, LRF should be regarded primarily as a stepping stone (i.e., implementation vehicle) to that frontend. However, LRF does also allow (record-level) application programs to be written against databases defined through ASF, and such programs will of course still be needed in many situations.

ASF

To repeat from the introduction to Section 8: ASF is basically a forms-based system for defining relations and performing simple manipulative operations on them. It is not intended to be a report-writing or command-driven query language system, nor does it support the use of relational operations in application programs. It might be regarded as a *minimally relational* system, in that it does support the restrict, project, and join operators (with the limitations noted in Section 8). It does not support:*

1. Duplicate elimination

2. Union or difference operations

3. Aggregate operations (SUM, AVG, etc.) and grouping

---

*Numbers 3 and 4 in this list are supported by OnLine Query, however.

4. Dynamic ordering (as in SQL "ORDER BY")

5. Set-level update operations (e.g., "UPDATE WHERE")

Nor does it support a truly dynamic, *ad hoc* join operation; instead, joins are specified definitionally, as part of the definition of a view (accessing the view then causes the predefined join to be executed).

We now turn our attention to the question of referential integrity. As we have seen, IDMS/R does not have the necessary knowledge of primary and foreign keys to approach this question in a systematic and "automatic" manner. Instead, the approach seems to be basically as follows. For a given pair of tables that are connected in a primary-key/foreign-key relationship, the DBA must:

1. Construct a view of the tables concerned, joining the tables together on the basis of that primary-to-foreign-key match;

2. Next, specify the set of updates the user is allowed to perform on that view;

3. Finally, specify the effects of those allowed updates on the underlying tables.*

In other words, referential integrity support appears to be bundled in with the view mechanism. In this writer's opinion such a bundling is an architectural mistake, for the following reasons among others:

- The "same" rules will have to be specified for several views. Consider suppliers and parts, for example. Suppose we want to specify (the equivalent of) DELETE CASCADES for shipments with respect to suppliers. Then we can certainly define a view SSP as the join of S and SP (over supplier numbers), and define the effect of DELETE—or rather ERASE—against that view appropriately. But suppose we also need a view SSPP, defined as the join of S and SP and P (over supplier numbers and part numbers). Presumably, then, we will have to define the effect of DELETE against this view analogously. (For why should SSP be updatable and SSPP not?)

- "Same" was in quotes in the previous paragraph for the obvious reason that the rules might in fact be defined differently for different views over the same data—though it is hard to imagine why that would be a good thing.

- What if the user updates the stored tables directly, without going through the view?

The fundamental point, of course, is that referential integrity constraints (like all integrity constraints) are more logically a property of the *base data,* not of some particular user's view of that base data. They should therefore be specified once and for all as part of the definition of that base data.

---

*We remind the reader that "update of join" is currently not supported, so that referential integrity is in fact currently not supported either.

Finally, what about performance? As in any relational system, the answer to this question must depend to a large extent on the quality of the system optimizer. Although we did not say so explicitly in Section 8, the ASF component that generates LRF access procedures is of course a relational optimizer. Note that optimization is therefore done at "generate" time, not at run time, which is definitely a point in IDMS/R's favor.

However, since it cascades through LRF, the sophistication of the ASF optimizer is automatically bounded by the sophistication of LRF. For example, LRF selects a strategy for responding to a particular request by means of a simple sequential search through the strategies available to it, which is obviously not as flexible as a scheme that evaluates many alternatives and chooses the cheapest. Suppose, for example, that table T has two indexed fields A and B; suppose also that the strategy "access via the A index" precedes the strategy "access via the B index" in the (ASF-generated) LRF list of strategies. Then a condition involving both A and B will always use the A index, never the B index (and never both). Furthermore, a condition that could be evaluated by access to the indexes alone, without any access to the data at all, can never be recognized as such by LRF.

Following on from the previous point: It is also not clear that the classification of strategies recognized by LRF is fine-grained enough to discriminate adequately between different kinds of query—for example:

- To distinguish between a condition of the form "condition AND condition" and one of the form "condition OR condition";

- To distinguish between a condition of the form "field $\geq$ value" (for which an index is probably a good choice) and one of the form "field $\neq$ value" (for which an index is probably a bad choice);

- To allow different queries involving the "same" relational operators to have those operators applied in different sequences;

and so on. Furthermore, note that the optimizer is definitely *not* intelligent enough to take automatic advantage of CODASYL links (if such links exist). For if such a link does exist, then the DBA must explicitly tell the optimizer to use it, via the join condition "SET setname" (see the subsection on creating an ASF view of a network database in Section 8). And if the DBA does specify link X (say) as such an access path, the optimizer will presumably *always* use that link, even though it might well not be optimal in all cases.

Note finally that at the time of writing the optimization process does not make any use of database statistics (table cardinalities, index selectivities, clustering information, etc.). Nor can it involve any dynamic sorting (which is unfortunate, since dynamically sorting one or both tables is frequently the best technique for implementing a join).

EXERCISES

1. Draw a data structure diagram for a network version of the education database of Chapter 13, in which the foreign keys TEACHER.EMP#, STUDENT.EMP#, and PREREQ.PREREQ# are each replaced by a link.

2. Write a schema for the education database of Exercise 1.

3. Suppose in the education database of Exercise 1 that courses have prerequisites as indicated in the following table:

COURSE#	PREREQ#
C1	C2
C1	C4
C2	C4
C3	C6
C5	C3
C5	C6
C6	C1

Draw an occurrence diagram for this data corresponding to the schema given in your answer to Exercise 2.

4. Write a schema for a network version of the suppliers-parts-projects database (see the exercises in Chapter 1).

5. Using your answer to Exercise 4 as a basis, write DML procedures for the following:
   (a) Get S# values for suppliers who supply project J1.
   (b) Get S# values for suppliers who supply project J1 with part P1.
   (c) Get P# values for parts supplied to all projects in London.
   (d) Get J# values for projects not supplied with any red part by any London supplier.
   (e) Get P# values for parts supplied by at least one supplier who supplies at least one part supplied by supplier S1.
   (f) Get all pairs of CITY values such that a supplier in the first city supplies a project in the second city.
   (g) Change the color of all red parts to orange.
   (h) The quantity of P1 supplied to J1 by S1 is now to be supplied by S2 instead (in addition to any quantity of P1 that S2 already supplies to J1). Make all the necessary changes.

6. Suppose that a new set type *OM* (owner *O*, member *M*) is added to the database. To what extent can existing programs remain unaffected by this addition? You should consider each of the following cases (and each combination of cases, where combinations make sense):
   (a) *O* and *M* both new record types (additions)
   (b) *O* and *M* both old (existing) record types
   (c) *O* old and *M* new
   (d) *O* new and *M* old
   (e) *M* AUTOMATIC with respect to *OM*

   (f) *M* MANUAL with respect to *OM*
   (g) *M* MANDATORY with respect to *OM*
   (h) *M* OPTIONAL with respect to *OM*
   (i) *OM* essential
   (j) *OM* inessential

REFERENCES AND BIBLIOGRAPHY

1. Data Base Task Group of CODASYL Programming Language Committee, *Report* (April 1971).

2. C. W. Bachman, "Data Structure Diagrams," *Data Base* (journal of ACM SIGBDP) *1*, No. 2 (Summer 1969).

3. C. W. Bachman, "The Programmer as Navigator," *CACM 16*, No. 1 (November 1973).

Contains the lecture Bachman gave on the occasion of his receiving the 1973 Turing Award. Bachman contrasts the earlier view of data processing, in which the computer was central and data was considered as flowing through the machine as it was processed, with the more modern view, in which the database is the major resource and the computer is merely a tool for accessing it. The term "navigation" (nowadays *manual* navigation, to distinguish it from the automatic navigation found in relational systems) is used to describe the process of traveling through the database, following explicit paths from one record to the next in the search for some required piece of data.

4. C. J. Date, "An Introduction to the Unified Database Language (UDL)," in *Relational Database: Selected Writings* (Reading, Mass.: Addison-Wesley, 1986).

UDL is a language that supports all three of relations, hierarchies, and networks in a consistent and uniform style. Its design is such as to stress both the essential similarities and the essential differences among the three approaches. It therefore serves to illustrate very clearly the point that the nonrelational approaches add complexity but not power.

ANSWERS TO SELECTED EXERCISES

The currency table in Section 5 should be completed as follows:

```
Current of run unit              P 'P2'
Current S occurrence             S 'S4'
Current P occurrence             P 'P2'
Current SP occurrence            SP linking S4 and P2
Current record of set S-SP       ditto (member)
Current record of set P-SP       P 'P2' (owner)
Current S-SP occurrence          owned by S 'S4'
Current P-SP occurrence          owned by P 'P2'
```

1. See Fig. 8.

2. SCHEMA NAME IS EDUCATION-DATABASE.

```
RECORD NAME IS COURSE.
LOCATION MODE IS CALC USING COURSE# DUPLICATES NOT ALLOWED.
    02 COURSE#  PIC X(3).
    02 TITLE    PIC X(33).
```

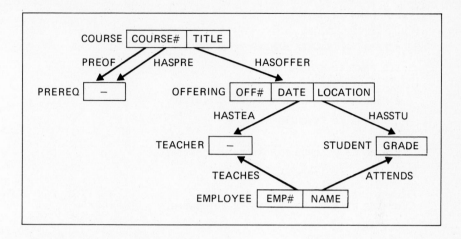

Fig. 8 Network version of the education database

```
RECORD NAME IS PREREQ.
LOCATION MODE IS VIA HASPRE SET.

RECORD NAME IS OFFERING.
LOCATION MODE IS VIA HASOFFER SET.
    02 OFF#    PIC X(3).
    02 DATE    PIC X(6).
    02 LOCATION PIC X(12).

RECORD NAME IS TEACHER.
LOCATION MODE IS VIA HASTEA SET.

RECORD NAME IS STUDENT.
LOCATION MODE IS VIA HASSTU SET.
    02 GRADE    PIC X.

RECORD NAME IS EMP.
LOCATION MODE IS CALC USING EMP# DUPLICATES NOT ALLOWED.
    02 EMP#    PIC X(6).
    02 NAME    PIC X(18).

SET NAME IS HASPRE.
ORDER IS NEXT.
OWNER IS COURSE.
MEMBER IS PREREQ MANDATORY AUTOMATIC.

SET NAME IS PREOF.
ORDER IS NEXT.
OWNER IS COURSE.
MEMBER IS PREREQ MANDATORY AUTOMATIC.

SET NAME IS HASOFFER.
ORDER IS SORTED.
OWNER IS COURSE.
MEMBER IS OFFERING MANDATORY AUTOMATIC
        ASCENDING KEY IS OFF# DUPLICATES NOT ALLOWED.
```

```
SET NAME IS HASTEA.
ORDER IS NEXT.
OWNER IS OFFERING.
MEMBER IS TEACHER MANDATORY AUTOMATIC.

SET NAME IS HASSTU.
ORDER IS NEXT.
OWNER IS OFFERING.
MEMBER IS STUDENT MANDATORY AUTOMATIC.

SET NAME IS TEACHES.
ORDER IS NEXT.
OWNER IS EMP.
MEMBER IS TEACHER MANDATORY AUTOMATIC.

SET NAME IS ATTENDS.
ORDER IS NEXT.
OWNER IS EMP.
MEMBER IS STUDENT MANDATORY AUTOMATIC.

SET NAME IS COURSE-FILE.
ORDER IS SORTED.
OWNER IS SYSTEM.
MEMBER IS COURSE MANDATORY AUTOMATIC
          ASCENDING KEY IS COURSE#.

SET NAME IS EMP-FILE.
ORDER IS SORTED.
OWNER IS SYSTEM.
MEMBER IS EMP MANDATORY AUTOMATIC
          ASCENDING KEY IS EMP#.
```

3. See Fig. 9.

4. SCHEMA NAME IS S-P-J.

```
RECORD NAME IS S.
LOCATION MODE IS CALC USING S# DUPLICATES NOT ALLOWED.
    02 S#     PIC X(5).
    02 SNAME  PIC X(20).
    02 STATUS PIC 999 USAGE COMP-3.
    02 CITY   PIC X(15).

RECORD NAME IS P.
LOCATION MODE IS CALC USING P# DUPLICATES NOT ALLOWED.
    02 P#     PIC X(6).
    02 PNAME  PIC X(20).
    02 COLOR  PIC X(6).
    02 WEIGHT PIC 999 USAGE COMP-3.
    02 CITY   PIC X(15).

RECORD NAME IS J.
LOCATION MODE IS CALC USING J# DUPLICATES NOT ALLOWED.
    02 J#     PIC X(4).
    02 JNAME  PIC X(20).
    02 CITY   PIC X(15).

RECORD NAME IS SPJ.
LOCATION MODE IS VIA S-SPJ SET.
    02 QTY     PIC 99999 USAGE COMP-3.

SET NAME IS S-SPJ.
ORDER IS NEXT.
OWNER IS S.
MEMBER IS SPJ MANDATORY AUTOMATIC.
```

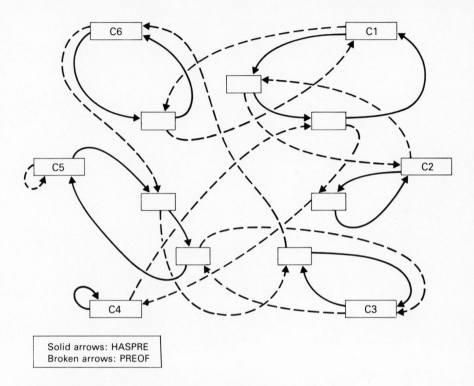

Solid arrows: HASPRE
Broken arrows: PREOF

Fig. 9 Sample occurrence diagram for COURSEs and PREREQs

```
SET NAME IS P-SPJ.
ORDER IS NEXT.
OWNER IS P.
MEMBER IS SPJ MANDATORY AUTOMATIC.

SET NAME IS J-SPJ.
ORDER IS NEXT.
OWNER IS J.
MEMBER IS SPJ MANDATORY AUTOMATIC.

SET NAME IS S-FILE.
ORDER IS SORTED.
OWNER IS SYSTEM.
MEMBER IS S MANDATORY AUTOMATIC ASCENDING KEY IS S#.

SET NAME IS P-FILE.
ORDER IS SORTED.
OWNER IS SYSTEM.
MEMBER IS P MANDATORY AUTOMATIC ASCENDING KEY IS P#.

SET NAME IS J-FILE.
ORDER IS SORTED.
OWNER IS SYSTEM.
MEMBER IS J MANDATORY AUTOMATIC ASCENDING KEY IS J#.
```

CHAPTER **15**

Frontend Subsystems

ABSTRACT

An introduction to the basic concepts and facilities of report writers, business graphics subsystems, application generators, and so forth.

COMMENTS ON REPUBLICATION

Any general-purpose database system will include a variety of vendor-provided applications or tools whose overall intent is to support the creation of applications without requiring the user to write COBOL (or similar) code. Examples of such tools include report writers, business graphics subsystems, application generators, and so forth. And a knowledge of such tools is prerequisite to a broad and comprehensive understanding of the field of database management in general, even though those tools are of course not part of the "database engine" *per se*.

Now, most such tools nowadays make use of *graphical user interfaces* (GUIs) and are highly interactive; conventional linear text thus might not be the best medium for describing or explaining them. Nevertheless, it is still my feeling that a conventional text explanation of the *basics* of such tools is the best way to

Originally published (in somewhat different form) in my book *An Introduction to Database Systems: Volume I,* 5th edition, pages 491–512 (Addison-Wesley, 1991). Reprinted by permission.

489

give the user the necessary conceptual foundation—a foundation on which to build during actual hands-on learning and experimentation with actual tools. Thus, the chapter that follows is not intended as a substitute for real hands-on experience; rather, it is intended to serve as an introduction merely, but an introduction that can help the user understand the purpose, functionality, terminology, and overall structure of what can sometimes seem to be a bewildering array of products.

Given all of the above, it seemed to me worthwhile to revise the paper that follows for inclusion in this book.

1. INTRODUCTION

The DBMS alone is not a "total solution" to the problems of the enterprise using it, nor was it ever intended to be. The problems in question are, of course, problems of *information management*—i.e., problems of storing, accessing, manipulating, controlling, presenting, and otherwise using information. To repeat, the DBMS does not solve all of these problems; but it does provide a basis for solving them, by providing an extensive repertoire of basic functions to support the various higher-level software components—report writers, business graphics subsystems, and the like—that do more directly address them.

We see, therefore, that the DBMS should be regarded, not as an end in itself, but rather as the foundation for a family of interrelated *frontend subsystems*. In this chapter we take a brief look at some of the components of that family. Our discussions are necessarily very superficial, for reasons of space; our primary purpose is simply to explain what the components are and the kinds of functions they provide, rather than to describe in great detail how they work (indeed, such a description could easily fill another book).

The components in question subdivide—not always in a very clearcut way—into a number of separate categories, as follows:

- Data access components
- Data presentation components
- Application generation components
- Other components

The "other" category includes such tools as statistical packages, word processors, spreadsheet programs, expert system shells, etc. For obvious reasons, all of these tools need to be integrated with the underlying DBMS to a greater or lesser extent. For example, it should be possible to incorporate database data into a business letter that is being prepared on a word processor; it should be possible to apply the functions of a statistical package to database data; and so on. Additional "other" components include application testing tools, copy management tools (e.g., micro-to-mainframe upload and download tools), database design tools, and many more (of course, this list is completely open-ended). These components are mostly beyond the scope of this chapter, however. Rather, we concentrate on the first three categories specifically: Section 2 discusses data access, Section 3 data presentation, and Section 4 application generation.

Note: In order to impose some semblance of unity on what is an essentially diverse collection of topics, we take most of our examples from a single system, namely Commercial INGRES (as of the late 1980s). However, we certainly do not mean to suggest that the facilities of INGRES are somehow superior to those to be found in other commercial systems; the reader should clearly understand that most currently available products provide analogous facilities in most of the areas we discuss (not always in so nicely integrated a manner, however). See also reference [13], which presents an overview of more recent research and development in this general area.

2. DATA ACCESS

The term **data access** refers to the process of locating and retrieving some requested set of data. By contrast, the term **data presentation** (the topic of the next section) refers to the process of displaying that data to the end user in some appropriate fashion. In a nutshell: Data access means the *query,* data presentation means the *result* (loosely speaking). Elsewhere in this book we have not bothered to distinguish very carefully between the two, but now it becomes necessary to do so. One reason (not the only one) for stressing the distinction is that it might be possible to issue a given query once and display the result of that query several times in several different ways. Such a facility is provided by the IBM product QMF, for example ("Query Management Facility"). We discuss data access in this section and data presentation in the next.*

Some common styles of data access are the following:

- Command-driven interfaces (query languages)
- Menu- and forms-driven interfaces
- Natural language interfaces

Of these, query languages will obviously be familiar to the reader already. Menu-

---

*Of course, any mechanism for data access must include *some* facility for presenting results to the user; however, that presentation facility need only be quite primitive. For example, compare the builtin query component of IBM's DB2 ("DB2 Interactive," DB2I) with the end user query product QMF. Both of those products support SQL queries against a DB2 database. However, the output from a query in DB2I is stored simply as a string of text in a conventional MVS file, and must subsequently be displayed by means of a conventional text editor; the output from a query in QMF, by contrast, is displayed directly by QMF as a customized and formatted report, with page numbers, explanatory headings, subtotals, and other additional material.

and forms-driven interfaces and natural language are discussed briefly later in this section. Other possibilities for the data access interface, not discussed in this chapter in any detail, include:

- *Icon-based interfaces:* An *icon* is a pictorial representation of some object (for example, a truck or car in a vehicles database, though of course the picture is likely to be much more abstract in most cases). Queries are formulated by "touching" icons in some sequence with the screen cursor. Icon-based systems are in common use today, of course, but they are not readily described by means of conventional text; we will therefore have little to say about them. Reference [8] describes an early forerunner of today's icon-based systems.

- *"Pointing" interfaces:* In a pointing interface, the screen cursor movement is achieved by means of a mouse or a touch-sensitive screen. Such interfaces are typically used in conjunction with the icon-based interfaces just briefly discussed.

- *Voice input systems:* Such systems are still primarily in the realms of research rather than a commercial reality at the time of writing. Note that natural language support is likely to be a prerequisite for voice input.

Windows, pulldown menus, prompts, and other similar techniques can be used in conjunction with most of the foregoing in order to make the interface still more appealing to users who are not necessarily IT professionals (IT = Information Technology).

Menu- and Forms-Driven Interfaces

We illustrate the ideas of menu- and forms-driven interfaces by discussing the INGRES facilities specifically. A **form** in INGRES is basically just a screen-display version of a familiar paper form. Such a form can be used for both input to the system and output to the user. In outline, the INGRES forms system works as follows.

- First, INGRES automatically creates a *default* form for every table (base table or view) described in the catalog. As an example, the default form for the parts table P might look as shown in Fig. 1. As you can see, the form consists essentially of a simple heading line, together with a set of display fields corresponding to the columns of the table, in the order in which those columns were defined when the table was created. Each display field is labeled with the name of the corresponding database column and has a width that is determined from the data type of that database column. *Note:* The line at the bottom of the figure is not part of the form but is the associated *menu* of operations that the user of the form can execute. The combination of form and menu is called a **frame** (see Section 4 for further discussion of frames).

```
TABLE IS p

pno:            pname:                    color:

weight:         city:




Help   Go    Query    End :
```

Fig. 1 Default form for table P

■   By calling up a copy of the default form on the screen and filling in some of the blank entries, the user can use that form to formulate simple queries concerning table P. Various control keys can be used during this process to step from field to field across the screen. As an example, Fig. 2 shows a formulation for the query "Get blue parts that weigh more than 10 pounds." After formulating a query, the user will choose the "Go" option from the menu, and INGRES will then retrieve the required rows and display them one at a time in the same format (i.e., by means of the default form, but with all values filled in). The user can thus examine the rows one at a time at leisure (this process is sometimes known as **database browsing**).

The INGRES component that supports the process just described is called **Query By Forms** (QBF). As the example shows, QBF allows the user to issue simple queries against an INGRES database without requiring any knowledge of

```
TABLE IS p

pno:            pname:                    color: Blue

weight: >10     city:




Help   Go    Query    End :
```

Fig. 2 Sample query using the default form for P

SQL or QUEL, the formal INGRES query languages. QBF queries can involve base tables or views; joins of several tables; certain combinations of AND and OR; and the usual comparison operators (equals, less than, etc.). The ability to query joins is particularly attractive, of course; for example, a query such as "Find suppliers who supply at least one part in a quantity greater than 200" is very easy to formulate through QBF. Note, however, that the join in question must be predefined to QBF by means of what is called a *JoinDef* (see later). The person defining the join need not (and very likely will not) be the person who performs the subsequent queries, however.

Note: For readers who might be familiar with Query-By-Example (QBE), we offer the following comment. At first glance QBF and QBE might look somewhat similar; however, they are in fact rather different, as can be seen from the way they handle update operations (see below). Query-By-Example is really nothing more than an ordinary command-driven query language that happens to be dressed up in an appealing syntactic style. (This remark is not meant disparagingly, of course; on the contrary, considered *as* a command-driven language, QBE is a very attractive proposition.) QBF, by contrast, is not just a command-driven language, as we will see in a moment—on the contrary, it represents an entirely different *style* of database access (though it is only fair to point out that in principle there is no reason why QBE should not follow that style also).

QBF also supports simple update and data entry operations. Suppose, for example, that the user wishes to browse through all parts in London and possibly update some of them. The relevant part rows can be retrieved and displayed one by one, using the mechanism already described; and, during that process, the user can at any time delete the row currently being displayed, or change it by simply overtyping values on the screen.* This process is sometimes called **database editing**.

As for data entry, that can be done by (again) filling in values on the form, and storing the rows so created one at a time. After storing each row, QBF will optionally redisplay the field values from that row on the next form, so that only values that are different from those in the previous row need be entered each time. In this way the data entry process can be made very fast (in fact, this is the normal way of doing data entry in INGRES).

As can be seen from the foregoing discussion, the QBF mechanism is very easy to use, and indeed quite powerful. However, the default forms are perhaps a little utilitarian (though no doubt adequate in simple cases). For that reason INGRES provides a number of facilities for the creation of forms that are more carefully tailored to the needs of specific applications:

---

*Incidentally, QBF even allows joins to be updated in this manner. However, the effect of such updates on the underlying base tables is not "automatically" understood by INGRES but has to be specified by the person who creates the JoinDef.

■ First (as already mentioned), it is possible to create a form that corresponds to a join instead of just to a single table. For such a form it is also possible to specify whether or not the join can be updated, and if so what the effect of such updates should be.

■ Second, it is also possible to have several rows displayed on a single form, instead of being limited to one row per form as described above. This facility is particularly useful in connection with one-to-many joins, where several rows from the "many" table can be shown together with a single row from the "one" table on the same form. For such a form INGRES provides automatic scrolling through the rows of the "many" table for each row of the "one" table.

■ Third, forms of considerable sophistication can be created by means of another INGRES component, the **Visual Forms Editor** (VIFRED). Using VIFRED, the user can create a brand new form from scratch or edit an existing form (default or user-created).

We briefly sketch the possibilities available with VIFRED. Suppose the user wishes to edit some form—say the default form for table P from Fig. 1. On request, VIFRED will display that form on the screen. The user can then use VIFRED editing commands to rearrange items on the screen, to add, change, or delete headings, footings, and similar explanatory text, and to add, change, or delete display fields. In the case of fields, the user can specify:

■ The label to be used on the display (which need not be the same as the name of the corresponding column in the database)

■ Whether the field is to be displayed in a box frame, and/or in reverse video, and/or blinking, and/or underlined, and/or in a different brightness from the rest of the form

■ What color the field is to be displayed in

■ Whether the field is for "display only" or the user of the form is to be allowed to enter a value into the field

■ Whether the value from the previous row should be displayed in this field (useful for data entry)

■ Whether a value is mandatory for this field on data entry

■ A validation check to be applied when the form user supplies new values for this field*

---

*Such checks can even include a limited form of referential constraint checking. Note, however, that specifying integrity checks as part of the form definition means that the corresponding checking is being done by the (generated) application code, *not* by the base DBMS *per se*. While the ability to specify such checks in the form definition is undoubtedly useful, the fact remains that integrity checking *ought* to be done by the DBMS, not by application code, for more reasons than we have room to discuss here.

- A message to display if that check is violated
- A default value to be supplied for the field if the user of the form omits to supply a value on data entry

All INGRES form definitions, for both default and user-defined forms, are of course stored in the INGRES catalog.

Natural Language Interfaces

Natural language interfaces have been the subject of research for some considerable time, and a few commercial products do exist in the marketplace. We briefly describe two natural language systems here—RENDEZVOUS [1–3], an experimental system developed by Codd at IBM Research in the early to mid 1970s, and INTELLECT [4], a system originally developed by Harris at approximately the same time at Dartmouth College (under the name ROBOT [5]) and now commercially available from Artificial Intelligence Corporation (AICorp). *Note:* Other companies, including IBM, also market INTELLECT under license from AICorp (not always under the INTELLECT name, however).

First RENDEZVOUS. In outline, RENDEZVOUS operates as follows. First, it transforms the original natural language query into an expression of the relational calculus. In doing this, it makes use of what is usually called a **knowledge base**.* Since some kind of knowledge base is found in all natural language systems, we digress for a moment to discuss its function very briefly.

The knowledge base is what enables the system to "understand" natural language queries. It includes (among several other things):

- Copies of certain of the tables from the database catalog;
- Tables of commonly occurring data values;
- A set of phrase transformation rules, which allow the system to perform certain substitutions, such as replacing "how many" by "count"; and
- A **lexicon,** which is a table defining certain natural language words (English words, in the case of RENDEZVOUS) that are likely to be used in queries. Such words fall into two broad classes—those that are specific to the database to be queried (such as *supplier, part, shipment*), and those that are more general (such as *find, have, with*).

Part of the process of installing a natural language system must be to construct the database-specific portion (at least) of the lexicon, and possibly other portions of the knowledge base also, such as database-specific phrase transformation rules. In some cases, the system might subsequently be capable of adding new

---

*The term "knowledge base" is used in *deductive DBMSs* with a somewhat wider meaning. See this book's predecessor *Relational Database Writings 1989–1991* (Addison-Wesley, 1992).

terms to the knowledge base on its own initiative (for example, after learning from some user that "London" is the name of a city—see the example below).

To return to RENDEZVOUS specifically: The process of transforming the original query into a calculus expression is actually done in a fragmentary fashion. In general, there will be pieces of the original query that RENDEZVOUS can understand immediately and pieces that it cannot. For those latter pieces, RENDEZVOUS will attempt to extract the meaning from the user by means of a *clarification dialog.* For example:

```
User:     How many London parts are there?

System:   The word "London" is unfamiliar. Is it one of the
          following:

                1  part number     4  part weight
                2  part name       5  part city
                3  part color      6  none of the above

          Select by number the closest catalog item.

User:     5
```

Once RENDEZVOUS has completed its internal formulation of a relational calculus expression, it then transforms that expression back into English for approval by the user:

```
System:   This is what the system understands your query to be:

          COUNT THE NUMBER OF PARTS STORED IN LONDON.

          Is the system's understanding

                1  correct and complete
                2  not yet complete
                3  incorrect

          Select exactly one item by number.

User:     1

System:   The answer to your query is:

          THERE ARE 3 PARTS STORED IN LONDON.
```

As Cuff remarks in reference [5], the dialogs in RENDEZVOUS (clarification dialogs and also other kinds, not discussed here) tend to have a rather plodding quality, with the result that the entire interaction can become somewhat cumbersome from the user's point of view. For example, the user might be asked to make choices where one of the alternatives is "obviously" (from a human point of view) much less likely than the other (is London a color?). On the other hand, straightforward queries do seem to be dealt with smoothly, and the system seems to be quite robust.

We turn now to the INTELLECT system. The internal structure of INTELLECT is significantly different from that of RENDEZVOUS in a number of respects. First, INTELLECT does not indulge in clarification dialog. Instead, it employs its builtin knowledge of English syntax to generate an initial set of feasible (at least syntactically feasible) interpretations of the original query. (By contrast, RENDEZVOUS does not have a deep understanding of English syntax. To quote reference [1], it cannot even "distinguish a noun from a verb!" Of course, this lack of emphasis on syntax was a deliberate design decision.)

Next, if it now has many possible interpretations for the query, INTELLECT *searches the database* in an attempt to discover the user's intended meaning. In this way it can (for example) learn that London is the name of a city, and thereby discover what the query "How many London parts are there?" means, without having to ask the user for that information. Note that in a sense, therefore, INTELLECT uses the database itself as a dynamic extension to the lexicon.

Like RENDEZVOUS, INTELLECT will—optionally—"echo back" a formal English statement of its interpretation of the original query to the user. Unlike RENDEZVOUS, however, it does not then offer the user the option of revising that interpretation; the purpose of the "echo" is simply to make clear to the user exactly what query it is that the system is responding to.

Comparing the two approaches (RENDEZVOUS and INTELLECT), we can observe that the INTELLECT idea of examining the database is preferable to the RENDEZVOUS scheme of interrogating the user, in that (obviously) it involves less effort on the part of the user. On the other hand, searching the database is likely to be expensive if the database is large (even if the searching is restricted to indexed columns). Moreover, the RENDEZVOUS approach is more suitable to implementation on an intelligent workstation or personal computer that is physically remote from the central system, because there is no need to access the database (except for the catalog, which can be locally cached) until the time comes to execute the final and completed version of the query. Indeed, suitability for such remote implementation was one of RENDEZVOUS's original objectives [2].

We conclude this brief discussion of natural language interfaces with a few miscellaneous observations:*

1. Note that RENDEZVOUS and INTELLECT (like all other natural language systems known to this writer) are both read-only. Update operations are not supported.

2. As mentioned earlier, part of the process of installing a natural language system must be to construct at least the database-specific portion of the lexicon. In practice, it seems that lexicon construction is likely to be quite difficult, requiring highly specialized skills, for all but rather simple databases.

3. Natural language systems tend to be expensive, in the sense that they typically require a lot of main memory.

4. Finally, icon-based and pointing interfaces (using a mouse or a touch-sensitive

---

*I am indebted to Larry Rowe for most of these comments.

screen) seem to be just as easy to use in practice as natural language systems, and they are much easier to build and are faster.

3. DATA PRESENTATION

Techniques of data presentation include the following:

- Simple tabular reports
- Tailored reports
- Business graphics
- Pictorial displays
- Voice output

Of this list, simple tabular reports will already be familiar to the reader, and pictorial and voice output still lie primarily in the province of specific applications (such as flight arrival time or real estate enquiry systems) instead of general-purpose database systems. The remaining two possibilities, tailored reports and business graphics, form the principal topic of the rest of this section.

Report Writers

The term "report" is used to mean a set of formatted output from the database, either on the screen or on paper ("hard copy"). A **report writer** (or report **generator**) is a software component that supports the production of such reports. In this subsection we use the INGRES report writer to illustrate the kind of facilities typically found in report writers in general.

The user invokes the INGRES report writer by issuing the command

```
REPORT   name
```

where *name* is either

1. The name of the table (possibly a view) from which the report is to be produced, or
2. The name of a **report specification** which in turn includes either
   - the name of that table, or
   - a query (i.e., QUEL RETRIEVE or SQL SELECT operation), possibly parameterized, in which case the report is produced from the *derived* table that is the result of that query. Values for the parameters (if the query is parameterized) are supplied in the REPORT command.

In Case 1, INGRES automatically generates a *default* report specification for the table in question, so in fact there is always a report specification (default or user-generated) to control the details of how the finished report will look. All report specifications are kept in the INGRES catalog.

Suppose it is desired to produce a report showing supplier cities, suppliers in those cities, the parts they supply, and the corresponding quantities. Suppose too—without loss of generality—that an appropriate table (actually a view) exists containing precisely the required information. In QUEL, that table could be defined as follows:

```
DEFINE VIEW CITYSHIPS
     ( CITY     = S.CITY,
       SUPPLIER = S.S#,
       PART     = SP.P#,
       QUANTITY = SP.QTY )
     WHERE S.S# = SP.S#
```

Then the command

```
REPORT CITYSHIPS
```

(using the INGRES default report specification) will produce the "default report" shown in Fig. 3.

Default reports are adequate in many cases, but sometimes it is desirable to produce a report that is more carefully tailored to some specific requirement. Tailored reports require a user-generated report specification. User-generated specifications can be created in two ways:

1. They can be created interactively through the forms-based system **Report By Forms** (RBF). This is the simpler method.

2. They can be written using the report writer's **report definition language,** which does provide certain additional facilities not supported under Method 1 but which also requires some degree of conventional programming expertise.

```
25-JUL-93                                               21:49:19
                    Report on Table: Cityships

    City              Supplier            Part          Quantity

    London            S1                  P1               300
                      S1                  P2               200
                      S1                  P3               400
                      S1                  P4               200
                      S1                  P5               100
                      S1                  P6               100
                      S4                  P2               200
                      S4                  P4               300
                      S4                  P5               400
    Paris             S2                  P1               300
                      S2                  P2               400
                      S3                  P2               200

                              - 1 -
```

Fig. 3 A default report

The interactive RBF interface is to the report writer what VIFRED is to QBF. In other words, RBF is an interactive editor for forms (like VIFRED); however, the forms it is designed to edit are, specifically, the forms that make up a report specification. In fact, the starting point for RBF is always one of INGRES's own default specifications—the user is not allowed to create a new report specification from scratch, but instead must work by editing one of the default specifications. A pictorial representation of the relationship between the INGRES report writer and RBF is shown in Fig. 4.

Using RBF, the user can specify display formats (etc.) for the data in the desired report. In particular, the user might designate CITY as a *break column*, and CITY, SUPPLIER, and PART (in that major-to-minor order) as *sort columns*, using an RBF **report structure form:**

Column name	Sorting Sequence (0 - 127)	Sorting Order ('a'/'d')	Break Column? ('y'/'n')
City	1	a	y
Supplier	2	a	
Part	3	a	
Quantity	0		

Next, the user can call up an RBF **column options form** for each of these four columns and make entries in those four forms as follows (we show the forms for the CITY and QUANTITY columns only, slightly simplified as usual). First CITY:

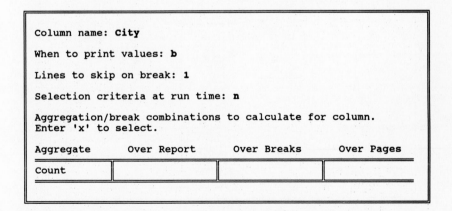

```
Column name: City

When to print values: b

Lines to skip on break: 1

Selection criteria at run time: n

Aggregation/break combinations to calculate for column.
Enter 'x' to select.

Aggregate      Over Report      Over Breaks      Over Pages

Count
```

The "b" ("When to print values") means "Print on control breaks". The "n" ("Selection criteria at run time") means "None". If the user had specified "v" (Value)

502

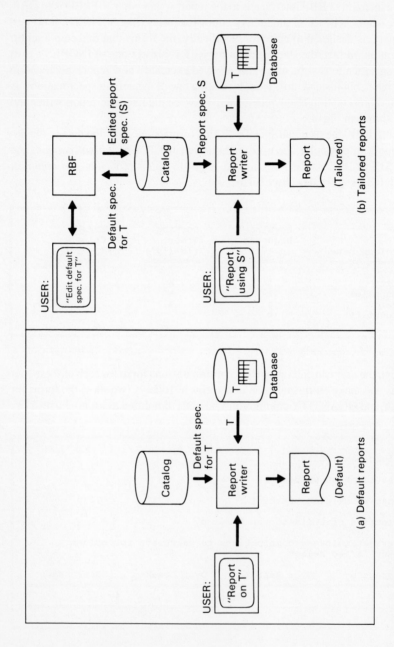

Fig. 4 Relationship between RBF and the INGRES report writer

or "r" (Range of values), the report writer would prompt for a (range of) CITY value(s) each time a report is produced using this specification; in this way, tailored reports for specific individual cities could be produced. Notice that the only aggregate option offered is "Count," because CITY is a character string column and counting is the only aggregation that makes sense. In fact we have chosen not to specify any aggregation for CITY at all.

Now the column options form for QUANTITY. Here we have requested totaling ("Sum") to be performed for each value of the break column (i.e., for each CITY value) and also for the report as a whole:

```
Column name: Quantity

Selection criteria at run time: n

Aggregation/break combinations to calculate for column.
Enter 'x' to select.

Aggregate        Over Report        Over Breaks        Over Pages

Count
Sum                    x                   x
Average
Minimum
Maximum
```

The resulting report is shown in Fig. 5.

Business Graphics

The graphics component of INGRES—**Visual Graphics Editor** or VIGRAPH— is somewhat analogous to the report writing component, except that the final "report" consists of a two-dimensional graph rather than simple tables and lines of text, etc. For many kinds of data, a graph is a much more effective means of communication than a conventional report. As a trivial illustration, compare the bar chart in Fig. 6 with the same data in conventional report form (Fig. 5).

VIGRAPH supports four basic graph types: bar charts, pie charts, scatter graphs, and line plots (with certain variations, in the case of bar charts). In all cases, the data to be graphed consists of a table, derived in some way from the tables of the underlying database; it might be an existing base table or view, or it might be defined by means of a QUEL or SQL query whose result is the desired table. That table must have either two or three columns (referred to generically as the X, Y, and Z columns). For example, here is a QUEL query corresponding to the bar chart shown above:

```
25-JUL-93                                             21:57:07
                    Report on Table: Cityships

    City              Supplier              Part        Quantity

    London            S1                    P1               300
                      S1                    P2               200
                      S1                    P3               400
                      S1                    P4               200
                      S1                    P5               100
                      S1                    P6               100
                      S4                    P2               200
                      S4                    P4               300
                      S4                    P5               400

    Totals: London
    Sum:                                                    2200


    Paris             S2                    P1               300
                      S2                    P2               400
                      S3                    P2               200

    Totals: Paris
    Sum:                                                     900

    Grand Totals: REPORT
    Sum:                                                    3100

                              - 1 -
```

Fig. 5 A tailored report

```
RANGE OF CS IS CITYSHIPS
RETRIEVE ( X = CS.PART,
           Y = SUM ( CS.QUANTITY BY CS.CITY, CS.PART ),
           Z = CS.CITY )
```

The meanings of the three columns X, Y, and Z depend on the type of graph, as follows:

- *Bar chart:* X represents the independent variable (the labels on the bars); Z (if present) represents labels of "sub-bars" within each bar (city names in the example of Fig. 6); Y represents the dependent variable (the bar or "sub-bar" heights).

- *Pie chart:* X represents the independent variable (the labels on the slices), Y represents the dependent variable (the slice areas, given as a percentage of the total). Z should not be present for this type of graph.

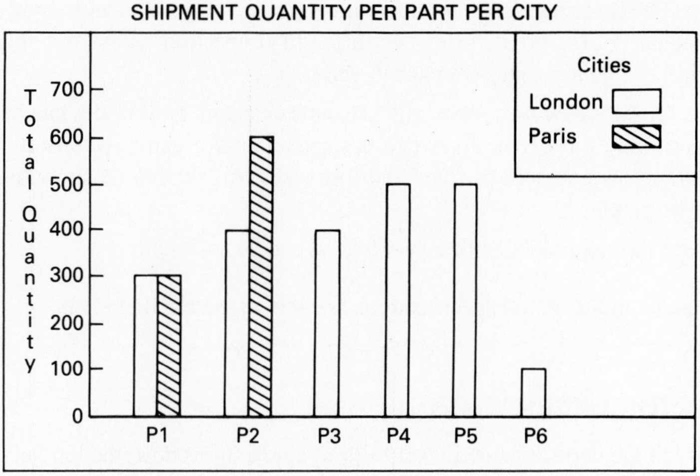
SHIPMENT QUANTITY PER PART PER CITY
Cities
London
Paris
Total Quantity
700
600
500
400
300
200
100
0
P1
P2
P3
P4
P5
P6

Fig. 6 Example of a bar chart

- *Scatter graph:* X and Y represent (X,Y)-coordinates, where (as usual) X represents the independent variable and Y the dependent variable. Different sets of points are plotted for each distinct value of Z.
- *Line plot:* X and Y again represent (X,Y)-coordinates. For each value of Z, VIGRAPH will assume that the set of (X,Y) points represent a continuous function, and will connect adjacent points together by straight line segments, step curves, or continuous curved arcs. Alternatively, it will approximate the function by drawing the straight line that most closely fits the set of points ("linear regression").

After specifying the table to be graphed, the user can get VIGRAPH to create a default **graph specification** to control the display of the resulting graph. Subsequently, the user can modify that default graph specification, much as the user can modify a default report specification under RBF. Following are some of the changes the user can apply to the default graph specification:

- *Bar charts:* The fill patterns or colors for the bars can be changed. The chart can be switched from vertical to horizontal or vice versa.
- *Pie charts:* Different fill patterns or colors can be specified for each slice. Slices can be "exploded." The pie can be rotated.
- *Scatter graphs:* The displayed character representing individual (X,Y)-points can be changed (on an individual Z-value basis).

- *Line plots:* The character used for data points can be changed (on an individual Z-value basis). Different colors and different connection types (straight, curved, etc.) can be requested for each Z-value.

- *All graphs except pie charts:* Axis origins can be changed. Axis scales can be set to logarithmic (base 10). Axes can be labeled and/or can have specific values marked, in a variety of fonts and font sizes. A grid can be superimposed on the graph.

- *All graphs:* Placement details, title, and legend can be adjusted.

Like report specifications, graph specifications are kept in the INGRES catalog.

4. APPLICATION GENERATION

The availability of the various generalized (builtin) applications described in Sections 2 and 3 certainly reduces the need for special-purpose, user-written application programs. Indeed, it might even be possible to avoid having to write any such programs at all in some installations. Usually, however, it will still be necessary to develop at least a few applications that are specialized to the installation's own particular needs. Even then, it might still be possible to avoid programming in the traditional sense (i.e., programming in a conventional language such as C or COBOL), if the system includes a suitable **application generator**.

Application generators are *rapid application development tools*. They can be regarded as an advance over the conventional high-level languages (COBOL, etc.), just as those languages were an advance over assembler language and assembler language in turn was an advance over machine code. For this reason, application generators are sometimes referred to as **fourth generation** tools—machine code, assembler language, and high-level languages constituting the first three generations—and the user interface to an application generator is accordingly sometimes known as a **fourth generation language** (4GL). We prefer not to use the "4GL" terminology, however, since it does not seem to have any very precise definition.

The user of an application generator—i.e., the application designer—is thus presented with a very high-level application development language, in which the primitive operations include not only the usual arithmetic and control flow facilities of conventional languages, but also facilities for database definition and access, terminal screen layout definition, screen input/output, screen data manipulation, and so on. Furthermore, the process of actually developing an application is typically done—at least in part—not by writing code in any conventional manner, but rather by conducting some kind of interactive dialog with the system. We illustrate these general ideas by (once again) using the facilities of INGRES as a concrete example; however, the reader is warned that different application generators differ very considerably from one another at the detail level, and hence that the facilities of INGRES should not necessarily be regarded as typical.

The INGRES application generator is called **Applications By Forms** (ABF). ABF is specifically designed to support the development of **forms-based** applications—that is, applications that communicate with the end user by means of forms displayed on the screen. QBF, RBF, VIGRAPH, and VIFRED are all special cases of forms-based applications. (So is ABF itself, for that matter.) Any such application can be regarded as consisting of a hierarchical arrangement of **frames,** where each frame in turn consists of a **form** and an associated **menu**. See Fig. 7.

The hierarchy of Fig. 7 is meant to be interpreted as follows. Frame 1 represents the entry point to the application—i.e., it is the frame displayed when the user first invokes the application. Frames 1.1–1.3 represent three possible successor frames (corresponding to three possible menu choices on frame 1—for example, "Produce sales report," "Enter new order," or "Update customer information," in a SALES application). Likewise, frames 1.2.1–1.2.2 represent two possible successor frames to frame 1.2, and so on. Note, incidentally, that several frames can share the same form, thus presenting a consistent set of interfaces to the application user at run time.

As an aside, we note that the entire INGRES system is in fact presented to the user as one large forms-based application in the foregoing sense. The user initially invokes INGRES by entering the command:

```
INGMENU database
```

INGRES responds by displaying the "INGRES main menu" frame. Options on that frame then allow the user to do any of the following:

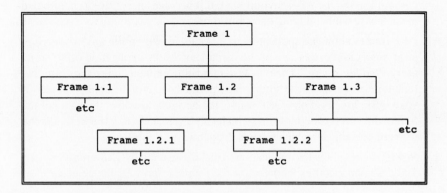

Fig. 7 Structure of a forms-based application

- Invoke QBF or RBF or ABF or VIFRED or VIGRAPH
- Perform data definition operations such as creating tables
- Issue interactive SQL or QUEL operations
- Run saved queries or reports or graphs

and so on. And each of these options in turn leads to further, more detailed frames for the operation(s) in question.

To return to the main thread of our discussion: In order to create a forms-based application, therefore, the application designer needs to be able to specify:

1. The frames involved in the application;
2. For each such frame, the form and menu items to be displayed;
3. For each such menu item, the sequence of operations to be performed if the application user selects that item. Note that, for a given menu item, the sequence of operations will include (but will not usually be limited to) the operation of invoking the frame to be displayed next.

There are four possible types of frame: user-specified frames, QBF frames, report frames, and VIGRAPH frames. The purposes of the four types are as follows:

- *User-specified* frames* are frames that are completely specific to the application in question (such as Frame 1, the entry frame, in the SALES application sketched above). For each such frame, the designer specifies the name of the frame, the name of the associated form, the menu, and the set of operations corresponding to each menu item (see the discussion of "OSL" below). If the associated form does not yet exist, the designer can create it using VIFRED, without leaving the ABF environment. The designer can also use QBF, again without leaving the ABF environment, if it becomes necessary to interrogate the database while building the application.

- *QBF* frames allow the application to make use of the builtin QBF code. Suppose, for example, that one of the menu choices the application offers to its user is "*ad hoc* query." Then, instead of writing explicit code to perform that function, the designer can simply incorporate code into the application to invoke QBF directly. For a QBF frame, the designer specifies the name of the frame, the corresponding form (which can be created via VIFRED), and the name of the table on which QBF is to operate.

- *Report* frames allow the application to make use of the INGRES report writer. The designer specifies the name of the frame, a form for the acquisition of

---

*"User" here refers to the application designer, not to the application end user.

run-time parameters for the report (if any), and the corresponding report specification (which can be built via RBF).

■ Finally, *VIGRAPH* frames allow the application to invoke the builtin VIGRAPH code. These frames are analogous to the report frames just discussed.

In the case of a user-specified frame, the application designer must also (as already stated) define the *operations* corresponding to each menu item in the frame. This function is performed by means of the ABF **Operation Specification Language,** OSL.* OSL can be regarded as a very high-level programming language. Some idea of its power can be obtained from the following brief outline of some of its most important statements.

■ *Database statements:*

OSL basically includes the entire set of QUEL (or SQL) data manipulation functions as an integrated data sublanguage. In particular, it allows values to be retrieved from the database directly into a form for display; it also allows values entered into a form by the application user to be used to update the database or to condition further database retrievals.

■ *Form control statements:*

Form control statements control what appears on the screen. For example, the *clear* statement clears one or more fields on the screen, the *message* statement displays a single-line message at the foot of the screen, the *assignment* statement assigns the value of some expression to a field on the screen, and so on. Mention should also be made of the "validate" statement, which is used to cause the validation checks specified for the form (via VIFRED—see Section 2) to be applied.

■ *Control flow statements:*

Examples of control flow statements include various forms of *if* statement, statements to *call* another (user-specified) frame, statements to *call* one of the INGRES-supplied frames (such as a QBF frame), statements to *return* to the previous frame, and statements to *call* a user-specified procedure. (User-specified procedures can be written in any of the INGRES programming languages—Ada, BASIC, C, COBOL, FORTRAN, Pascal, and PL/I—and can include embedded QUEL or SQL statements. Note, however, that such procedures should not be needed very often in practice, because most of the relevant functions are directly available from within OSL itself.)

---

*Subsequently renamed "INGRES/4GL." We stay with the original "OSL" name for the purposes of our explanations.

The application designer creates OSL text by means of a standard operating system editor, which can be invoked directly from ABF. User-specified procedures (if necessary) are created in the same fashion.

At any point during construction of the application, the designer can ask ABF to *run* the current version, even though it might still be incomplete. ABF will then invoke all the necessary compilers, loaders, etc., to convert the application to (temporarily) executable form, and will then try to execute it. Syntax errors will be diagnosed. If a call is encountered to a frame or procedure that does not yet exist, ABF will display a message, together with a trace of the control flow to that point. The application designer can then request execution to continue from a different point or can stop the run. When errors are discovered, the designer can use ABF to make corrections to frames and procedures, and can then try to execute the application again.

Finally, when the application is executing successfully, the designer can *install* it on the host system. Installation involves creating an **executable image** of the application (which is done via an appropriate ABF form) and defining a host system command by which that "image" can be invoked. Thereafter the application can be invoked directly from the host system level, instead of having to access it through ABF.

We conclude this section with a brief mention of **application packages**. Application packages exploit the fact that many applications tend to fall into a small number of rather stereotyped patterns. For example, the account maintenance procedures for bank *A* are unlikely to differ very significantly from those for bank *B*. As a consequence, it is feasible to provide prewritten, generalized programs or "packages" to perform commonly required functions, such as account maintenance. Such packages can be tailored to some installation's specific requirements by simply providing values for some small number of parameters. When available (and suitable), such packages probably represent the most cost-effective form of "application generator" of all. Of course, the distinction between a package and a generator might not be all that clearcut in practice.

EXERCISES

1. Distinguish among the following:

   command-driven interfaces
   menu- and forms-driven interfaces
   natural language interfaces
   icon-based interfaces
   "pointing" interfaces

2. Define the following terms:

   database browsing
   database editing

report writer
application generator
fourth generation language

3. State the principal functions of the INGRES components QBF, RBF, ABF, VIGRAPH, and VIFRED.

4. What are the relative advantages and disadvantages of natural language interfaces?

5. What do you understand by the terms *knowledge base* and *lexicon*?

REFERENCES AND BIBLIOGRAPHY

1. E. F. Codd, "Seven Steps to Rendezvous with the Casual User," in J. W. Klimbie and K. L. Koffeman (eds.), *Data Base Management,* Proc. IFIP TC-2 Working Conference on Data Base Management (New York, N.Y.: North-Holland, 1974).

2. E. F. Codd *et al.*, "RENDEZVOUS Version 1: An Experimental English Language Query Formulation System for Casual Users of Relational Data Bases," IBM Research Report RJ 2144 (January 1978).

3. E. F. Codd, "How About Recently? (English Dialog with Relational Data Bases Using RENDEZVOUS Version 1)," in Ben Shneiderman (ed.), *Databases: Improving Usability and Responsiveness* (Orlando, Fla.: Academic Press, 1978).

4. Larry R. Harris, "The ROBOT System: Natural Language Processing Applied to Data Base Query," Proc. ACM Annual Conf. (December 1978).

5. Rodney N. Cuff, "Database Query Using Menus and Natural Language Fragments," Man-Machine Systems Laboratory, Department of Electrical Engineering Science, University of Essex, UK (April 1982).

6. I. D. Hill, "Wouldn't It Be Nice If We Could Write Computer Programs in Ordinary English—Or Would It?", *BCS Comp. Bulletin* (June 1972).

Discusses, in an entertaining and nontechnical manner, some of the problems involved in attempting to understand natural language.

7. James Martin, *Application Development Without Programmers* (Englewood Cliffs, N.J.: Prentice-Hall, 1982).

Argues that the application development process needs to be made dramatically more efficient (i.e., by becoming more automated), and presents a survey of currently available tools and techniques (as of 1982) for achieving such an improvement.

8. Christopher F. Herot, "Spatial Management of Data," *ACM TODS 5,* No. 4 (December 1980).

Describes the implementation of an experimental system—the Spatial Data Management System (SDMS)—with an icon-based interface.

9. M. M. Zloof, "Office-By-Example: A Business Language that Unifies Data and Word Processing and Electronic Mail," *IBM Sys. J. 21,* No. 3 (1982).

Describes a very elegant extension of Query-By-Example to handle, not only database query and update, but also database browsing and editing, document processing and text editing, electronic mail, application development, etc., etc., all in a highly integrated and "user-friendly" fashion.

10. L. A. Rowe and K. Shoens, "A Forms Application Development System," Proc. 1982 ACM SIGMOD International Conference on Management of Data, Orlando, Fla. (June 1982).

11. K. Shoens, "A Forms Application Development System," Ph.D. Dissertation, EECS Dept., University of California at Berkeley (November 1982).

References [10] and [11] describe the prototype forerunner of the Commercial INGRES forms-based systems.

12. Lawrence A. Rowe, "Fill-in-the-Form Programming," Proc. 11th International Conference on Very Large Data Bases, Stockholm, Sweden (August 1985).

Extends the discussions of references [10] and [11], arguing strongly that the "fill-in-the-form" approach is more satisfactory than more conventional "fourth generation languages" as a basis for developing interactive database applications.

13. Various authors, *ACM SIGMOD Record 21,* No. 1 (March 1992).

Marrying Objects and Relational

COMMENTS ON REPUBLICATION

The first book in this series, *Relational Database: Selected Writings* (Addison-Wesley, 1986), included the transcript (slightly edited) of an interview I gave to *Data Base Newsletter* in 1983. As I wrote in my "Comments on Republication" at that time:

> I have included [this interview] here because it touches on so many of the topics that are treated at greater length in the body of the book . . . As so often in such cases, the style of the original interview (published version) ranged all the way from the excessively chatty to the extremely stilted. I have made some slight revisions in the version printed here in order to remove the worst stylistic offenses, but I fear that the style of the revised version is still somewhat uneven.

Originally published in two parts. Part I appeared in *Data Base Newsletter,* Vol. 22, No. 3 (May/June 1994), Part II in *Data Base Newsletter,* Vol. 22, No. 4 (July/August 1994). Reprinted by permission of Database Research Group, Inc.

The afterword that follows consists of the transcript (again slightly edited) of a second interview that was conducted by *Data Base Newsletter* in 1994, and exactly the same remarks apply. However, I need to make a few additional editorial comments here:

■   I have edited the transcript to use the abbreviation "OO" throughout. I use this abbreviation generically as an abbreviation for "object-oriented" or "object orientation," as the context demands; sometimes it even stands for "object-oriented database(s)" or "object-oriented database [management] system(s)." In all cases, the context should make it clear which interpretation is intended.

■   I use "table" and "relation" interchangeably, sometimes even using both terms in the same sentence.

■   The footnotes did not appear in the interview as originally published but were added for the purposes of the present book.

1. RELATIONAL *vs.* OO SYSTEMS

Newsletter: How do the backgrounds of OO and relational database management differ and what effects do those differences have on their usefulness for business-oriented applications?

Date: OO and relational database systems have arisen from two very different perceptions of the problem to be solved. OO database systems originated in the OO programming world as a means of providing persistent storage for objects created by applications written in OO languages like C++ and Smalltalk. The OO database systems that have resulted tend to focus on application-specific support. Although OO vendors have recently begun to extend their products to include traditional database functions like recovery and concurrency controls, the application-specific origins of those products are still evident.

Relational systems, by contrast, were designed to support both data sharing across applications and *ad hoc* uses of data that (by definition) cannot be predicted at the time the database is first implemented. The relational model has also been concerned, from its inception, with the need to provide an application-independent means of ensuring data integrity.

Newsletter: Which OO features would be worthwhile additions to a relational system?

Date: OO has precisely two good ideas, **user-defined data types** and **inheritance**—where (a) the concept "user-defined data types" includes the concept of user-defined operators or functions that act on instances or values of the type in question, and (b) the term "inheritance" means operator inheritance in type hierarchies.

Hugh Darwen and I have been working on something we call "The Third

Manifesto," which is a prescription for the future of data management.* It deals specifically with how the good ideas of relational and OO could be married. The manifesto is currently under review within the database community and we hope to publish it more formally later this year.

Newsletter: Why have you called it the **third** manifesto?

Date: Because there have been two prior ones—the *Object-Oriented Database Management System Manifesto* developed by Malcolm Atkinson and his colleagues, and the *Third Generation Database Systems Manifesto* developed by Michael Stonebraker and his colleagues. We feel that the first of these effectively ignores the relational model, which is a terrible thing to do. The second, while it does pay attention to the relational model, basically gives up and says that relational means SQL, which it refers to as "intergalactic dataspeak."

Newsletter: Why do you believe that another manifesto is needed?

Date: We want to reinstate the relational model as the most appropriate foundation for data management, clarify the fact that the relational model and SQL are **not** equivalent, and show how relational systems can incorporate the good ideas of OO. We would like to see database management systems built on these ideas—systems that are categorically still relational, but incorporate user-defined data types, user-defined functions, and inheritance.

Newsletter: Is a user-defined data type the same thing as an object class in an OO system?

Date: I would say yes. But it's often difficult to say exactly what a given OO concept means because there is no commonly accepted object model. To get formal about it, one would first have to pin down precisely what is meant by "the object model" before dealing with the central business of comparing it to the relational model. What Hugh Darwen and I are doing is assuming what seems to be a sensible and charitable "object model" and then trying to figure out how to incorporate the good ideas of that model into relational systems.

Newsletter: If the relational model is to be a complete and robust specification for data management, isn't it essential that it be extended to support user-defined data types?

Date: User-defined data types are essential, but they're not an extension! The relational model needs **no** extensions, corrections, or perversions in order to get the good features of the object world. Moreover, nothing in the relational model has to be thrown away either in order to incorporate the good ideas of OO. The proper way of moving forward must be firmly rooted in the relational model.

Newsletter: What is it that the OO community overlooks about relations?

---

*See Chapter 8 of this book.

Date: Relations are just one way of manifesting **predicates**. Predicates and the logic of predicates are what the relational model is all about. And predicate logic is absolutely fundamental. With relational theory, we are effectively reducing the database problem to a particular application of a highly respectable branch of science, already well understood, with an impeccable pedigree. With such a solid foundation, it would be insane to throw the relational model away.

Newsletter: What does it mean to say that relations are a way of manifesting predicates?

Date: Consider an employee relation with columns EMP#, ENAME, DEPT#, and SALARY. That relation represents a predicate that states that EMP# identifies an employee in the real world, ENAME is the name of that employee, DEPT# is the number of the department to which that employee is actually assigned, and SALARY is that employee's salary. You can think of this predicate as a truth-valued function with four parameters.

   If values are provided for each of those parameters—for example, EMP# "E1," ENAME "Smith," DEPT# "D1," and SALARY $40,000—you get what is called a **proposition**. A proposition is a statement that is either *true* or *false*. And the original relation contains precisely those rows that represent true propositions. The predicate is thus the criterion for the acceptability of an update to the relation—a row can be inserted only if the proposition it represents corresponds to a *true* instantiation of the predicate.

2. MAPPING OBJECT CLASSES TO THE RELATIONAL MODEL

Newsletter: The key issue in successfully marrying OO with the relational model is in determining how to map the notion of object class onto the components of the relational model. To what is an object class analogous in the relational model?

Date: The mapping choices are either to equate domains and object classes or to equate relations and object classes. I believe very strongly that the first equation is correct and the second is wrong. Domains and object classes are the same thing. A domain is a data type (often user-defined) of arbitrary complexity which has operators that apply to its values. It is precisely the same notion as "object class" in OO.

   Object classes are **not** the same thing as relations. Unfortunately, many, if not most, of the OO proponents and implementers are running with the wrong equation. They are trying to equate object class and relation.

Newsletter: Why isn't an object class a relation?

Date: The consequences of equating relation and object class are contradictory and more than a little strange. Let's see what happens if we do assume that relation and object class are the same thing. If I have an employee relation with (say) EMP#, ENAME, DEPT#, and SALARY columns, I can project that relation over

DEPT# and SALARY. The result is another relation. Is it also an object class? Object classes have methods. What methods apply to the result of the projection? The answer is probably none. We therefore have a relation that is apparently not an object class because it has no methods.

If I accept the consequence that once I do a projection I get something that is not an object class, then my system has lost the property of closure. If I now take the employee relation and project it over **all** columns, the result is a projection, too. In most relational languages, projection across all columns is done by writing just the relation name. Apparently, therefore, if I look at the employee relation from the left-hand side (as it were), it is an object class and has methods; if I look at it from the right-hand side, it is a projection and doesn't have methods. In other words, the semantics of "R" and "R" are different!

The problem isn't limited to projections. For instance, it also applies to joins. Suppose I have an employee object class or relation and a department object class or relation and I join them together. What methods apply to the result of the join? The typical response I get from OO proponents and from relational DBMS designers trying to incorporate object ideas is that they haven't really thought that question through yet . . .

This is not an exhaustive list of the problems.

Newsletter: Why have OO database vendors and proponents equated object classes and relations?

Date: If an application issues an SQL statement that creates a table (relation) called EMPLOYEE with columns EMP#, ENAME, DEPT#, and SALARY, that looks very much like an OO programming statement that creates an object class called EMPLOYEE with public instance variables EMP#, ENAME, DEPT#, and SALARY. Object classes and tables are equated because of this superficial similarity.

If you think about it, however, the analogy simply doesn't work. An object class is a type. A table is not a type. A table is a set of rows. Furthermore, the rows in a table change over time, but a type doesn't change over time. Domains (that is, types) are static and relations are dynamic. The values in a relation change as applications do inserts, updates, and deletes, but the values in the domain don't change. They're fixed; they are the set of **all possible** values for a particular type. So there's something wrong right away with the "object class = relation" equation.

Newsletter: Isn't a type code like "Type of Account" an example of a domain whose values can change over time as the organization adds and deletes valid types?

Date: Well, of course, it's not completely true that domains never change. The domain of zip codes, for example, might change from five digits to nine. Domain changes, however, are "metalevel," definitional changes, not everyday data value changes like those expected in relations. Domain changes are often so fundamental that they require a database reorganization in order to be implemented.

Newsletter: If an object class is the same thing as a domain, could the term "domain" be discarded without doing harm to the relational model?

Date: The term we use is not really very important. What matters is ensuring that the concept itself is well-defined and understood.

Newsletter: If object class maps to domain, what would a relation be in a relational system incorporating OO concepts?

Date: A relation would still be just what it always has been—a set of rows. But let me point out here that there has always been some confusion about the concept of a relation. If, in a programming language, I say "DECLARE N INTEGER," N is a variable whose values are integers—different integers at different times. If, in SQL, I say "CREATE TABLE T," T is a variable whose values are tables—different tables at different times. We say loosely that T is a table, but it isn't really. It is a table-valued variable.

In mathematics, if the value 4 is inserted into the set {1,2,3}, the result is the new set {1,2,3,4}. It's not an "updated version" of the old set, it's a **new set**. Similarly, if I insert a row into T, the original table is replaced by a new table that includes the additional row. The value of the table-valued variable T has been replaced in total. We have always had a confusion between tables *per se,* which are values, and table-valued variables.

A relation, which is a set of rows, is a value, not a variable. A relation-valued variable is a variable whose values are different relations at different times.

Having said all that, I must also say that it is very difficult to get out of the habit of saying "relation" when we really mean "relation-valued variable." The distinction is perhaps not too important if we're not trying to be absolutely correct.

Newsletter: If a relation is a set of rows, then what is a row?

Date: A row is a collection of column-name/column-value pairs. Those column values are values from domains and they can be as complex as you like—numbers, strings, maps, books, arrays, or anything else you can think of.

Newsletter: What effect does incorporating OO concepts into relational systems have on the concept of a relation?

Date: RELATION becomes a type constructor that **must** be supported. We already know that the relational model has powerful capabilities. We also know that every other data model that has been proposed is mappable to the relational model. To be useful, a data management facility must be able to construct types whose values are relations. This is one of the prescriptions we are including in our manifesto.

Newsletter: Why is a relation-valued variable not just another object class?

Date: A variable is not a type. A variable **has** a type.

Newsletter: Could a completely encapsulated object class—containing no public attributes—be thought of as a relation?

Date: No. Something that is encapsulated can be operated upon solely by the operators defined for the class. The object class DEPARTMENT, for example, might have operators for adding an employee to a department and for removing an employee from a department. If those were the only operators defined for the class, then those would be the only things that could be done with departments. By contrast, a DEPARTMENT **relation** could be operated upon in unforeseen ways using such operations as join, union, or project—even if the need to perform such operations was not considered when the DEPARTMENT relation was first created.

Newsletter: Are the join, union, and project (etc.) operators generally available for every relation?

Date: Yes, and they would not be available to a DEPARTMENT object class unless they had specifically been included in the definition of that class. Pure object classes have operators (or methods) and no public attributes. Relations have columns, which are analogous to public attributes, and no methods. One has methods and no visible attributes and the other has visible attributes and no methods. To repeat, therefore, object classes and relations are very different things.

Newsletter: Is it true then that an object class that has no public attributes cannot be treated as a relation?

Date: Yes. Since domain values or objects can only be manipulated by domain or class operators, the domain or class designer must think very carefully about what operators will be necessary. Orthodox OO proponents would say they know what operations the class needs to perform because they know the applications. Traditional database designers would say they don't know all of the applications because there are always new requirements coming along.

The solution is to define a set of operators for the domain that permits unforeseen things to be done with the domain values. What that translates into is defining a set of operators for each domain that have the effect of exposing **one candidate representation** for the domain values.

Many people have criticized OO systems for not supporting *ad hoc* query. OO proponents have answered that they don't need to do *ad hoc* queries because they know what the applications are. *Ad hoc* query is not possible if the system supports only predefined methods and the predefined methods do not expose at least one candidate representation of the object. Incidentally, exposing a candidate representation also permits declarative enforcement of integrity constraints.

Newsletter: Is the candidate representation equivalent to a set of public attributes?

Date: Well, it might be. There is no necessary correlation, however, between public attributes and the private representation. A domain of POINTs, for example, could expose a candidate representation that permits the user to see and change Cartesian coordinates (X and Y) while being privately represented using polar coordinates. Whether the candidate representation is exposed as attributes or by operators is merely a matter of syntax.

Newsletter: Exposure of a candidate representation of the object would therefore be a necessary condition for supporting a query language?

Date: That's the only way I can see to do it.

Newsletter: Where does that leave encapsulation?

Date: The orthodox emphasis on encapsulation seems to me to miss the point. Attention should be focused instead on what functionality is provided and how much data independence is achieved. If a user were to define a relation (not a domain) called POINT, with columns X and Y, nothing in the relational model says that the X and Y coordinates have to be physically stored. We could, for example, store the polar coordinates instead. In principle, therefore, relations can give us exactly the same functionality and the same degree of data independence as "encapsulated objects."

Newsletter: Malcolm Atkinson has stated that persistence should be orthogonal to type. Do you agree?

Date: Well, I agree with the sentiment behind the statement. Of course, my model of a database contains only relations; however, those relations can, in turn, contain objects or values of any type you like. Relations, and therefore the values they contain, "persist" from the time they are created until they are destroyed.

The kinds of data types or domains to be supported is a question that is completely orthogonal to the question of what constitutes the relational model. The relational model has nothing to say about the kinds of data types or domains a particular implementation should support. It is true that implementations have traditionally supported rather simple data types like INTEGER, FLOAT, and CHAR—but I would argue that this is because it is usual to try to deal with simple things first, and also because the products were originally designed to support commercial applications that used only those simple types. However, it is nowhere written that the relational model has to be limited to such simple domains. Domains could, for example, be as complex as photographs, maps, or books.

3. TABLES WITHIN TABLES

Newsletter: Given a relational system with support for user-defined types and their operators, would that mean that any object class could be formed as a composite of object classes?

Date: Yes. It is quite possible to have composite types that are made up of other types. It would be reasonable, for example, to define a type "array of sets of numbers." One value of that type would be a single array. Each element of such an array would be a set and each element in each of those sets would be a number.

Newsletter: Would such a capability allow the definition of tables within tables?

Date: Yes. We must, however, be very careful and clear on what such a capability would mean. Remember that a row is basically a set of column name and value pairs. Those values are, by definition, atomic values—which means the table is in first normal form. Suppose the row has just two values: a number and a character string. We would say that those are atomic values, but we also know that (for example) the string contains individual characters and substrings. Thus, the string is atomic at one level of abstraction, but not at a lower level.

If it is legal for a table to contain a string in one of its cells, it must be legal for a table to contain a **set** (or table) in one of its cells. At a certain level of abstraction, a set, too, is a single thing. Sometimes you want to talk about the set of employees in a department as a single thing. Other times you want to know about the individual employees—going down to the next level of abstraction. Thus, a row could have a department number and a set of employees—two atomic values.

Newsletter: In your interview in the September/October 1983 issue of *Data Base Newsletter,* you stated: "The relational model does not permit repeating groups. It does that very deliberately because there is nothing you can do with them that you can't also do without them. You simply eliminate unnecessary choices." Now it appears, however, that even though values in tables are still defined to be atomic, suddenly those "atomic" values are permitted to have internal structure and the table could end up containing repeating groups. How should the practitioner view this new development?

Date: This is an area that I have come to understand better over the years. The repeating group notion violates encapsulation. In the example of a row with department number and a set of employees, if the set of employees is seen as a repeating group, then the application is looking **inside** the set of employees at the same time that it is looking **outside** at the department number. The application is operating at two levels at once. Repeating groups in this sense are still illegal because they violate first normal form. If the set is treated as a single thing, however, that is not a violation of first normal form.

I am categorically **not** advocating what some people call NF^2 relations. NF^2 stands for NFNF or non first normal form. It means you not only permit tables within tables but you also permit the user to look inside the inner table while looking outside it at the same time. Such mixing of levels greatly complicates the relational algebra and calculus. Some people even claim that it leads to paradoxes.

The point is this. As soon as people understand that domains, and therefore tables, can contain absolutely anything, they start thinking about arrays in tables, lists in tables, and so on. But I want to examine what benefits we might get from having **tables** in tables. You see, tables are familiar structures with a powerful set of operators that have already been defined. Consequently, support for tables within tables would require definition of very few new operators. And it turns out that tables within tables do lead to some significant benefits. So we get a good bang for the buck.

Newsletter: Would you recommend the use of tables within tables in a business application's database design?

Date: No, most likely not.

Newsletter: Why is such a design good in theory and not in practice?

Date: I didn't mean to imply that. To consider the usefulness and implications of tables within tables, let me first distinguish between base tables on the one hand, and tables that are produced or derived from base tables by means of relational operators like join or union on the other.

The ability to have tables within **derived** tables produces a number of beneficial results. In particular, outer join becomes completely unnecessary! Outer join, which produces a derived table containing nulls in rows that have no counterpart in one of the two input tables, has always been an uncomfortable compromise in relational systems.

Suppose, for example, that a database includes department and employee relations and some departments have no employees. If it is permissible to derive a relation with rows containing a department number and the set of all employees in that department, then a department with no employees produces a row with a department number and an empty set of employees. An empty set is a value, not a null. An empty set in the real world is thus being represented by an empty set within the system, which seems like a much better idea than representing an empty set by one of these mysterious "nulls" (as the outer join would do).

Newsletter: Given that the ability to nest tables within tables is good in the case of derived tables, should base tables also be permitted to contain tables as values?

Date: From a theoretical standpoint, we certainly don't want any artificial distinctions between base and derived tables, so base tables must be **allowed** to include tables as values. The question then is whether or not such a design is desirable. The answer is that it is usually not. A base table that contains departments and sets of employees looks very much like a hierarchy, and so all the old problems with hierarchies rear their ugly heads—bringing such difficulties as update anomalies and unnecessarily complex operators. The rule of thumb should be not to design base tables that way.

In some cases, however, it is categorically correct to violate this rule of thumb. Suppose, for example, that you were developing a database design tool that would record information about the candidate keys for any given relation. A candidate key is a set of columns that can be used to uniquely identify a row in the relation. Your design tool's database might therefore include a relation with one column representing the candidate keys for the given relation. That column would contain **sets** of column names. In other words, it would contain tables!—tables that in turn contain one column each. This design is not only the logically obvious and correct one, it also makes it much easier to specify the necessary integrity constraints (for example, to ensure that no candidate key is a superset of any other) than a traditional design without nested tables.

Newsletter: Couldn't the difficulty associated with defining such constraints in traditional systems be more a function of shortcomings in rule expression than in the types of data permitted in table columns?

Date: You might adopt that position, but I don't think it stands up. The kinds of problems that are helped by permitting tables within base tables tend to be much more complex than the rather simple candidate key example.

Newsletter: Does that mean that the incorporation of user-defined data types is not being driven solely by new kinds of applications with new data needs but might instead also be applied to solving traditional data problems in new ways?

Date: Yes.

Newsletter: What guidance can you give to a practitioner faced with the opportunity of defining tables within tables?

Date: Don't do it unless you have a really good reason!

Newsletter: SQL is predicated on the fact that tables have no multivalued fields. Doesn't the inclusion of tables as values in a column lead to the forfeiture of simplicity in queries?

Date: No. **Every** new data type permitted in tables requires new language features to handle operations on values of that type. Numbers require numeric operations, strings require string operations, and so on. Thus, if tables are permitted to contain tables, the system needs table operations for handling values of that type, but relational systems already have table operations, so the extension is much simpler than the addition of just about any other new type. The OO proponents want to allow things like arrays, sequences, and bags in their databases. That's fine, but every one of those things requires additional operators for handling the associated values.

Newsletter: Have you worked the nested table extensions out yet?

Date: I wouldn't claim to have worked them out in full detail yet, but I'm working on it.

4. VIEWS AND OBJECT CLASSES

Newsletter: Is it proper to treat a relational view as simply another type of object class?

Date: No. A view is a relation and object classes are not relations. Let me remark here that it's very unfortunate that SQL so often refers to "tables and views," which encourages people to think of tables and views as different things. *Au contraire,* the whole point about a view is that it **is** a table! A failure to appreciate this point has led to numerous mistakes, not least in the design of SQL itself.

Newsletter: Isn't it necessary within the data manipulation language to distinguish between tables that are stored and those that are produced as the result of table operations?

Date: I think you mean rather, doesn't there need to be a distinction between **base** tables (not stored tables) and tables that are derived by means of table operations? A base table and a stored table are **not** necessarily the same thing. That is, there is no necessity for a one-to-one correspondence between the base tables and what is physically stored on the disk. The only requirement is that the base tables be derivable from what is stored on the disk. A system could, for example, have a base table of employees that was actually stored with the London employees on a disk in London and the New York employees on a disk in New York. In that case, the one base table would be derived from two stored tables.

Let me now try to answer the question I think you were asking! In fact, making a distinction between base tables and derived tables (views in particular) is both unnecessary and very undesirable from the end user or programmer perspective.

You can think of a relational database as a **logical system**. Any logical system, whether it is arithmetic, a relational database, or whatever, has both **axioms** and **theorems;** the theorems are derived from the axioms according to certain rules. Looking at a database as a logical system, the base tables correspond to axioms and the derived tables correspond to theorems. Now, in a logical system, the choice of axioms is typically somewhat arbitrary. Similarly, the choice of base tables in a database is typically arbitrary too.

Consider again the situation in which a company's employees are in either London or New York. The database designer could choose to have a single base table representing all employees and have two views representing London employees and New York employees, respectively; alternatively, the designer could choose to have two base tables, one for London employees and one for New York employees, and then have a view representing all employees. From a logical point of view, the choice is arbitrary.

Incidentally, normalization can be thought of as guidelines for helping to choose the database's axioms (or base tables): It helps us decide which one out of a set of information-equivalent designs is "best" in a certain sense.

Newsletter: Some critics of relational systems say that views are not particularly useful because they cannot be used for updating. Is that a fair criticism?

Date: It certainly is a fair criticism of relational products today.* The fact that the

---

*I didn't mean to suggest here that today's relational products don't support view updating at all, only that they don't support view updating in anything like as general a manner as they should.

choice as to which tables are to be base tables and which views is somewhat arbitrary implies that it must be permissible to update views. For example, in the London and New York employees example, it must be possible to update the database no matter which design the designer has chosen. The rule about whether or not a table is updatable should have nothing to do with whether you chose to make it a base table or you chose to make it a view. What is needed is a set of update rules or protocols that work for all tables regardless of whether they are base tables or views.

Newsletter: Given that updating views is theoretically desirable, wouldn't the fact that views can be derived from other views make actual implementation of view update rather difficult?

Date: The possibility of multiple levels of view derivation merely implies that the update rules must be capable of recursive application. David McGoveran and I are currently working on such a set of rules.* That work is due to be published very soon (possibly before this interview appears in print).

5. ENCAPSULATION

Newsletter: You have been quoted as saying that domains encapsulate and relations do not. What do you mean by this?

Date: Values from domains, which is to say values in row-and-column cells in tables, can be operated upon solely by means of the operators defined for the relevant data type. Every time a data type is defined, the operators that act upon that type must be defined as well. The "innards" of the values are not exposed (except to the code that implements the operators). So domains are encapsulated.

Relations, by contrast, expose their innards to the user, which makes it possible to perform operations that get at those innards—doing joins and other operations that depend on the structure of the table. The structure of the table is not hidden, whereas the structure of values inside the table **is** hidden.

Newsletter: Certain aspects of relations are therefore unencapsulated because of the need to perform *ad hoc* query operations?

Date: Yes. The operations that can be performed on relations—join, union, and the others—categorically depend on being able to see the "inside" or structure of tables. The operations that can be performed on values within tables categorically do not depend on being able to see the internal structure of those values.

Let me stress, however, that exposing the structure of a table only means exposing the **logical** structure. What the table looks like physically is both undefined and irrelevant.

---

*See Chapters 5 and 6 of this book.

Newsletter: One of the basic tenets of OO is the encapsulation of functionality within objects. Although that might be a very good idea with respect to programming, are there dangers in applying that same notion of encapsulated functionality to databases?

Date: The more appropriate concern should be to what extent data independence is achieved and how much functionality is provided. Encapsulation provides a high degree of data independence. But *ad hoc* query and declarative enforcement of integrity constraints are incompatible with complete encapsulation, unless that encapsulation is done in accordance with a strict discipline, which in practice it doesn't seem to be. Thus, encapsulation in database systems must be applied very judiciously.

Newsletter: Does excessive use of encapsulation lower the flexibility of database applications?

Date: If it's done without regard to the discipline I mentioned, yes. That's the other side of the coin. If the designer doesn't expose a candidate representation of the objects, the database will not be able to support requirements that arise after its initial implementation.

Newsletter: Is it your view that every operation or method must be encapsulated with only one data type or object class?

Date: This is an area where I part company with the orthodox OO community. I don't think methods should **ever** be bundled with a particular object class. As a very trivial example, a designer could define object classes Time, Velocity, and Distance. The method that produces a Distance object by calculating the product of a Time object and a Velocity object doesn't really belong with either Time or Velocity. Bundling the method with Distance doesn't work well either because the Distance object doesn't exist until after the method is executed; you can't pretend you're sending a message to the Distance object saying "Create yourself"!

Newsletter: How does that differ from operators like constructors that OO systems define as belonging to the class as a whole rather than to objects?

Date: Well, let me change the question slightly. What is the argument for bundling operators with classes? It is surely that if an operator is bundled with class C, then it is privy to the internal representation of objects of class C. The trouble is, most operators need to know about the internal representation of multiple objects, not just one. That's how OO systems got into their need for "friends" and other *ad hoc* tricks.

The underlying issue is surely one of **authorization**—which objects' internal representation should be visible to which operations. It seems to me that a much better way of dealing with this requirement is to extend the DBMS authorization mechanism appropriately, rather than trying to bundle each operator with exactly one object class and then playing games with "friends" and the like. Remember that this whole OO database idea came out of OO programming; since OO programming languages typically didn't have security concerns, they never developed authorization schemes.

Newsletter: Proponents of OO claim that the insistence that each function be encapsulated in only one object class provides a superior means of partitioning or "normalizing" a system's functionality. Do you accept their claim that this approach produces smaller procedures and therefore more maintainable systems?

Date: No. Their need to introduce *ad hoc* workarounds like "protected" attributes and "friends" demonstrates the awkwardness of the approach.

6. INHERITANCE AND TYPE HIERARCHIES

Newsletter: OO proponents seem to use the notion of inheritance in more than one way. Have you noted variations in the meaning given to inheritance and, if so, which of them seems to be the most valid?

Date: OO proponents talk about both structural and behavioral inheritance. Structural inheritance involves properties or attributes that are inherited from the supertype whereas behavioral inheritance involves the inheritance of operators. In the object model I'm moving toward, there would be no such thing as structural inheritance. There would be behavioral inheritance only. OO purists claim that objects should have no visible attributes, they should have operators only. So, in a pure object system, there would be no structure to inherit. Only behavioral inheritance would exist.

Newsletter: Doesn't inheritance of attributes make sense from the standpoint of database design—permitting the designer, for example, to model the fact that people have names and employees, as people, would therefore also have names?

Date: Inheritance would not apply to employees because employees would (probably) be implemented as a relation and not a domain. Object classes are domains. Questions about inheritance therefore apply to domains, not to relations.

Newsletter: Doesn't common sense suggest, however, that properties like person name ought to be able to be inherited in a data model?

Date: It is true that a concept of inheritance could be designed for relations, but that is entirely different from what the OO proponents mean by structural inheritance. We could define a kind of type hierarchy where the nodes were tables rather than objects, but, to my knowledge, this idea has not been fully worked out.

Newsletter: What is the appropriate definition of type hierarchy?

Date: That's a very good question. Cleaveland, in his book *An Introduction to Data Types,* says that there is no commonly accepted standard definition and gives eight different possible interpretations. While I think that inheritance is a good idea in principle, the definition must be clarified before it can be incorporated into a formal model. The problem is that there are several possible definitions, and it's not at all clear at this time which if any is most useful.

Newsletter: Do you credit proponents of OO with having invented type hierarchies or is it a more general concept that the OO community has seized upon more effectively than have other implementers?

Date: I don't know what the origins of type hierarchies were. I do know that we were talking about them in the relational world as early as 1975 or 1976, which is when John and Diane Smith were publishing papers on the topic. I would have to go back and reread those papers to determine whether their ideas were brand new or had originated in OO programming. I suspect in fact that the notion predates computers entirely.

7. DATABASE DESIGN

Newsletter: Is normalization still relevant even in those applications where the designers intend to take an OO approach?

Date: Yes!

Newsletter: Do you think that someone developing an OO database would be well advised to ignore the prescriptions of normalization?

Date: Absolutely not. The problems that normalization is intended to solve do not go away simply because the basis of data representation has changed. Being able to define a hierarchic structure doesn't mean such structures are a good idea.

OO, in opening up so many different ways of doing the same thing, is making the database design task much more complex. The OO world originally addressed application-specific databases in which the design issues were not so difficult. If the OO proponents genuinely want to use OO techniques for general-purpose databases, they are going to have to address some horrendous design questions. So far I don't see anyone addressing them.

Newsletter: What is the proper role for normalization in database design today?

Date: I have always viewed normalization as a sort of final step in database design. Database design should use a top-down methodology like entity-relationship modeling to produce a set of tables that are then examined to ensure that they conform to the principles of normalization.

Newsletter: Do you anticipate that the evolution toward support of more complex data structures will lead to the development of important new ideas for database design?

Date: It's hard to say. I've always characterized normalization as the one tiny piece of science in an otherwise artistic endeavor. It would be nice to have more science in database design. I don't see any immediate reason to be optimistic about major breakthroughs, though.

David McGoveran and I have recently come up with another tiny piece of science that is somewhat like a normalization principle.* It's related to our work on view updating, and it too is due for publication very soon.

Newsletter: Suppose we did have structural inheritance for relations, as discussed previously. Should database design principles address the problem of update anomalies that arise when inheritable attributes in a relation are stored redundantly—for example, storing both person name and employee name?

Date: Yes. The new principle that David McGoveran and I have developed does address that problem as a special case. Normalization is about reducing redundancy within relations. Our new principle is about reducing redundancy across relations.

8. BUSINESS RULES

Newsletter: One of the current weaknesses of the object model is its lack of appreciation for the importance of declarative constraints or business rules. Vendors of relational systems haven't demonstrated much understanding or support for business rules either. In your opinion, is the relational model better positioned than the object model to provide support for declarative constraints?

Date: Yes. In the abstract, an integrity constraint and a query are the same kind of thing. If you have a particular integrity constraint X, then there is an associated query—"retrieve all pieces of information where X is not *true*"—that should return an empty set. If you have a way of formulating queries, you automatically have a way of formulating integrity constraints. Now, the relational model has always been very strong on query support, since the ability to do *ad hoc* queries was one of the primary motivators for its original formulation. Likewise, the potential for supporting declarative integrity constraints has always been there. All that is necessary are some minor syntactic adjustments.[†]

Newsletter: In what area would the syntax of the relational query language need to evolve in order to provide full support of declarative integrity constraints?

Date: One practical area that would need to be addressed would be enabling the designer to tell the system what to do if an integrity constraint is violated. We would also have to determine how general the procedure that handles the violation can be. Should it be permitted to do updates? If so, what should happen if those

---

*See Chapter 4 of this book.

[†]All that is necessary from a language definition point of view, that is! Implementation is another matter.

updates violate another constraint? What if the procedure violates its **own** constraints? These problems have not been solved generically, so far as I know.

Newsletter: Even though the extension of relational query capabilities provides a consistent method of supporting declarative constraints, wouldn't the complex business rules typical in database applications be difficult for a user or analyst to write?

Date: Yes, but only if the business rule itself is complex. The alternative, which is to express the rule in procedural code, is much worse.

Newsletter: Might it not be possible to define a higher-level language that permitted more direct expression of business rules?

Date: Technically, an integrity constraint—the formal expression of a business rule—is what is called a **closed formula** of predicate logic. And I have already said that predicate logic has a very long and respectable history of its own. Thus, anyone who proposes something other than predicate logic for expressing integrity constraints (or queries) is going to be hard-pressed to show that what they propose is, in any sense, an improvement. (Is this a criticism of SQL? Yes, it is.)

Newsletter: Can you really expect analysts to write predicate logic expressions to describe what is a very simple rule in the mind of the user?

Date: Absolutely. If a person is describing an absolutely crucial part of the database design or a query requirement, and that person doesn't have a good understanding of predicate logic, then I wouldn't trust that design or that query. Predicate logic is not difficult to learn. SQL is much more complex than predicate logic. Part of the training for a database analyst ought to be a short course in predicate logic. It would only take a couple of days.

Now, there might be ways to get at integrity constraints in an *ad hoc,* intuitive way, just like entity-relationship modeling is an intuitive way of getting at which tables are needed. Eventually, however, the database designer must get formal in order to define the database. I am proposing that the necessary formal language be predicate logic.

Newsletter: How important is support for declarative constraints to database management systems in the 1990s?

Date: I think it is, in some ways, the biggest issue in database management. Integrity is crucial. All results are suspect when produced from a database that is not in a state of integrity. Since a database is a logical system, a database without integrity is like a logical system that contains a contradiction. It can be used to prove absolutely anything, like $1 = 0$.

Expressing integrity constraints declaratively makes it possible for the data management system to do the work of enforcement rather than leaving enforcement to the application. In turn, that means better optimization, better performance, the possibility of checking constraint correctness, and greater system independence. More generally, everything that is done declaratively makes the system more intelligent, which is, by definition, a good thing.

Newsletter: Is achieving that high degree of integrity unlikely in an orthodox OO system that depends on message communication to achieve the same result?

Date: Yes. If certain disciplines are applied in the use of an OO system, then the database can **approach** the functionality of a (good) relational system.* I strongly suspect that in most implementations that discipline has not been applied.

Newsletter: Why has the OO community been slow to recognize the importance of declarative integrity constraints?

Date: It comes back to the issue of origins. OO database systems were originally application-specific and integrity was taken care of by the application.

Newsletter: What is different about the database world that causes greater emphasis to be placed on declarative integrity constraints?

Date: The database is shared by many applications. If integrity is handled procedurally—that is, by one or more applications—then one applications's bugs can infect other applications.

Newsletter: Is there any relationship between declarative constraints and database performance?

Date: If the database management system is aware of declarative constraints, then in principle it could make use of that information for what is called semantic optimization. Constraints are a form of knowledge about the database's semantics. If the optimizer can rely on those constraints being satisfied, then it can optimize queries in ways that would generally not be valid, but in fact are valid because of the constraints. Imagine for a moment a company with offices in London and New York and a parts database that is physically distributed across those two locations. If a user issues a query to find all red parts and a constraint states that all red parts are in London, the query can be optimized to look only in London.

Newsletter: Dr. E. F. Codd has always emphasized that the relational model is perfectly free of semantics. Do you agree with him?

Date: Well, I'm not sure he said exactly that. When he wrote his paper on RM/T, he said that capturing the semantics of any given situation is a never-ending task and that we can only claim to capture some tiny piece of the semantics in the database. In deemphasizing semantics, Dr. Codd was trying to avoid basing his relational model on fuzzy or debatable constructs like entities and relationships. The formal model that he did define, however, does include constructs that can be used to **represent** informal semantic things like entities and relationships. Fur-

---

*By a "good" relational system here, I mean one that supports declarative integrity constraints properly. By this definition, most current systems are not good.

thermore, the original model also contains domains, primary keys, and foreign keys, all of which are semantic constructs.

9. OO SYSTEMS

Newsletter: In your interview in the September/October 1983 issue of *Data Base Newsletter,* you explained that the relational model "precludes users or programmers from seeing explicit connections or links between tables or having to traverse between tables on the basis of such links." OO proponents claim that is precisely what is needed for the new kinds of applications they support. Do you still believe that such navigational support is inappropriate?

Date: Yes. We already know the pitfalls of navigational access. It is up to the OO proponents to prove that they cannot do what they need to do in a nonnavigational manner.

Newsletter: High performance is a crucial requirement in database support for many current operational systems and newer applications like computer-aided design (CAD) and multimedia. Relational products, which do not support manual navigational access, have never proven that they can meet the high performance requirement in a completely satisfactory way. Doesn't this fact tip the balance toward an OO future?

Date: Of course I agree with the need for high performance; however, I totally reject the idea that manual navigation of the database is ever required. I repeat: Advocates of the need for navigational access must justify their claim. In the *Third Generation Database System Manifesto,* Mike Stonebraker and his colleagues say something like "Manual navigation only as a last resort." I would say "Manual navigation **never**."

The reason relational products have never proven they can meet the requirements of high performance is partly historical. Even Rick Cattell, in his book on object data management, says that the superior performance achieved by OO databases in benchmarks against relational systems was **not** due to the different data models but to differences in engineering. I see no reason why the performance-enhancing techniques used in OO systems—caching, pointer swizzling, etc.—couldn't be used in the implementation of relational systems. Doesn't this whole discussion remind you of the relations *vs.* hierarchies arguments of 20 years ago? Or high-level languages *vs.* assembler language? Or 4GLs *vs.* COBOL?

Newsletter: Are you suggesting that the relational database vendors have yet to step up to the challenge of higher performance?

Date: I wouldn't criticize the vendors in that way. I prefer to believe they haven't addressed the high performance requirements of these new application areas because they've been addressing other requirements that were more pressing.

Newsletter: In your 1983 *Data Base Newsletter* interview, you observed that in benchmarking new database technologies, "they typically take a problem defined in the old way and see how it will perform under the new." You maintained that was unfair to relational because it ignores the new types of problems that it allows designers to solve. Aren't you guilty of doing the same thing with OO systems as they currently exist?

Date: That's a fair comment. In a way, yes, I am. I justify it by noting that the OO vendors themselves are claiming that OO systems can be used as general-purpose database management systems. If you took a CAD/CAM application and compared one of today's OO systems with one of today's relational systems, the OO system would probably run rings around the relational system. That difference in performance is not inherent, however.

Newsletter: OO proponents claim that support for recursive structures is essential to emerging applications. Is it true that the relational model doesn't support recursion well?

Date: I agree that recursion support is essential. The problem of supporting recursion in the relational model has already been solved in research, but it has yet to be properly implemented in product form. What is needed is a good, generalized transitive closure operation in the relational algebra. Again, it is my belief that vendors haven't implemented such an operation yet because they have been working on other, higher-priority items.

Newsletter: OO proponents put a lot of emphasis on the notion of object identity. From the standpoint of database management, how useful is object identity?

Date: The difficulty with object identity is not with the idea *per se* but rather with putting object identifiers or pointers inside other objects. In relational terms, such a use of object identifiers translates into putting object pointers inside table cells. That practice leads to manual navigation of the database, which is completely unnecessary. If a column of a table is defined to contain objects of type X, it should contain objects of type X and not pointers to such objects.

Newsletter: Does that mean that object identity is not only unnecessary but undesirable?

Date: As used by OO proponents, object identity is undesirable. I am not opposed to the use of meaningless identifiers or keys, but if such things are used they must still be values, not pointers to values.

Newsletter: Does OO's notion of "message" add anything new to our understanding of information systems or is it simply new jargon for a function call?

Date: The term "message" seems to me to be just jargon. In OO systems, a message is a function call where one of the parameters (the object that is to receive the message) is given special treatment. Distinguishing one parameter from the others is not only not useful, it is misleading.

Some people would argue that the distinction between messages and function calls is that messages are asynchronous and function calls are synchronous. But some programming languages—PL/I, for example—have the ability to make asynchronous calls, so that distinction doesn't stand up.

Newsletter: With respect to its suitability for database management, what important concepts are missing from the object model today?

Date: This question is a little difficult to answer because there is still no consensus on exactly what constitutes "the object model." However, there are certainly a number of important database concepts that seem to be getting little or no attention in the OO literature. For example, *ad hoc* query and declarative integrity constraints are typically missing. In addition, there is a lack of closure and a lack of symmetric exploitation. (Closure means that the output of an operation is the same kind of thing as the inputs to the operation; symmetric exploitation means that a user can access an object on the basis of any set of properties as input and obtain all of the other properties as output.) The object model is also missing such concepts as primary keys, foreign keys, views, cascade deletes, and a common catalog.

10. FUTURE DEVELOPMENTS IN DATA MANAGEMENT

Newsletter: What are the most difficult challenges you see facing data management for the remainder of the 1990s?

Date: I am really concerned about this whole discussion regarding the relationship between relational and OO systems. The question people are asking is whether OO systems are going to replace relational systems.

The question itself is based on a fundamental mistake. The fault lies with the early relational advocates (myself included!). Back in the early days, you see, in trying to prove that relations were a viable technology, we necessarily got into comparisons of relational systems and products like IMS and IDMS. We had to show that the problems that IMS and IDMS could solve could, at least in principle, be solved by relational systems too. In the process, we unwittingly reinforced the notion that relations were the same kind of thing as hierarchies and networks; hence, just as relational technology has replaced hierarchies and networks, relational might eventually be replaced by something else.

That view is fundamentally mistaken. The relational model is different from hierarchic and network systems. The relational model embodies the fundamental principles of database management. All database systems, whether or not they look relational on the outside, should at least be relational on the inside. A database management system that can't do a join is like a computer that can't add.

Operations like join are fundamental things that database management systems really must be able to do. That's why I believe that even if you have a system that looks object-oriented on the outside, it should still be relational inside.

Newsletter: Is it your view that a single data management facility, relational or not, can ever solve all of the problems of data management?

Date: I have no idea. You never know what kind of problem might be lurking round the next corner. But we mustn't confuse model and implementation. It probably is true that different implementations of the same model would be more appropriate for different applications. On the other hand, we currently know of no applications for which a well-implemented relational system would not be appropriate.

My overall philosophy is that life in general is so difficult that anything we can to make it a bit easier, we should do. If we can do everything with one data management facility instead of two, then Occam's Razor would suggest that we use only one.

Newsletter: Michael Stonebraker has emphasized three major areas that future database management systems must address—data management, object/type management, and knowledge management. Do you agree that those are the important areas for future database development?

Date: Yes.

Newsletter: Is it your understanding that support of knowledge management, which would include declarative integrity constraints, is not as far along as database support for objects or data types?

Date: Again, yes.

Newsletter: With respect to database system support for declarative constraints, aren't we a long way from understanding all of the conflicts that the system might have to recognize and deal with?

Date: Probably.

Newsletter: In the confrontation between OO and the relational model, do you see a clear winner emerging or will there be some sort of synthesis that incorporates the best ideas of both?

Date: I have tried to show that I would like to see a synthesis. Although current attempts to marry the concepts have not been done correctly, a synthesis is technically feasible. Actual availability of such a product, of course, depends on market forces, and I don't know enough about them to make a prediction.

Newsletter: Which would be simpler—evolving an OO database system to handle traditional database management functions or adding OO capabilities to a relational system?

Date: Since I am not an implementer, I can't say which would be simpler. My concern is with the end product, which should be the same in either case.

Newsletter: Do you think that existing, large-scale DBMS products like DB2 can incorporate complex data types?

Date: I don't know. I haven't had an opportunity to give it much thought. But I have a horrible suspicion that the answer is *no.*

Newsletter: Why should the confrontation between OO and the relational model be of interest to database professionals?

Date: Both sides have something to offer, and it would be nice to get the good ideas from each. Unfortunately, we tend to rush in and implement things before we really understand them. We rushed into a very inelegant realization of the relational model and then compounded the problem by turning further development over to a committee . . . As a result, users of relational systems face problems that never should have existed. For example, not only are queries often difficult to express in SQL, but, in some cases, it is impossible to determine ahead of time whether they are even expressible or not. Having numerous ways of doing the same thing in SQL should never have happened. Lack of support for declarative constraints should not have happened either.

   The whole reason we are hearing so much hype about OO systems today is that relational vendors failed to step up to the challenge of implementing the relational model correctly. If relational had been implemented correctly, we would have had the functionality we need.

Newsletter: Did relational vendors really understand user-defined data types twenty years ago when the relational products were first being developed?

Date: No. But, you see, the vendors never implemented the notion of domains at all. If we had domains, we would at least have a hook to hang user-defined data types onto. The failure to correctly implement the relational model is the basis for my skepticism about the possibility of extending existing relational products to support user-defined types.

Newsletter: Do you think your new manifesto will help to move database technology forward?

Date: I hope so. John Lennon once said that war is over—if we want it. I am certain that we can build a system that would be properly relational and would incorporate objects. The question is whether we want it.

Index